D0165158

BUSINESS ETHICS

CONCEPTS & CASES

Seventh Edition

Manuel G. Velasquez
Santa Clara University

PEARSON

Boston Columbus Indianapolis New York San Francisco Upper Saddle River
Amsterdam Cape Town Dubai London Madrid Milan Munich Paris Montreal Toronto
Delhi Mexico City São Paulo Sydney Hong Kong Seoul Singapore Taipei Tokyo

For my family

Editorial Director: *Craig Campanella*
Editor in Chief: *Dickson Musslewhite*
Executive Editor: *Ashley Dodge*
Editorial/Project Manager: *Kate Fernandes*
Director of Marketing: *Brandy Dawson*
Senior Marketing Manager: *Laura Lee Manley*
Marketing Assistant: *Lisa Kirlick*
Senior Managing Editor: *Maureen Richardson*
Production/Senior Project Manager: *Harriet Tellem*
Operations Supervisor: *Mary Fischer*
Operations Specialist: *Sherry Lewis*
Cover, Creative Director: *Jayne Conte*
Cover Designer: *Suzanne Behnke*
Cover Images: *John Kellerman/Alamy*
Digital Imaging Specialist: *Corin Skidds*
Media Project Manager: *Rachel Comerford*
Full-Service Project Management: *Chitra Ganesan/PreMediaGlobal*
Composition: *PreMediaGlobal*
Printer/Binder: *Edwards Brothers*
Cover Printer: *Lehigh-Phoenix Color*
Text Font: 10/12 Janson Text

Credits and acknowledgments borrowed from other sources and reproduced, with permission, in this textbook appear on page 485.

Copyright © 2012, 2006, 1998, 1992, by Pearson Education, Inc.
All rights reserved. Printed in the United States of America. This publication is protected by Copyright and permission should be obtained from the publisher prior to any prohibited reproduction, storage in a retrieval system, or transmission in any form or by any means, electronic, mechanical, photocopying, recording, or likewise. To obtain permission(s) to use material from this work, please submit a written request to Pearson Education, Inc., Permissions Department, One Lake Street, Upper Saddle River, New Jersey 07458 or you may fax your request to 201-236-3290.

Library of Congress Cataloging-in-Publication Data
Velasquez, Manuel G.
Business ethics : concepts and cases / Manuel G. Velasquez.—7th ed.
p. cm.
Includes bibliographical references.
ISBN-13: 978-0-205-01766-9
ISBN-10: 0-205-01766-5
1. Business ethics. 2. Business ethics—Case studies. I. Title. HF5387.V44 2011
174'.4—dc23

2011018696

10 9 8 7 6 5 4 3 2 1

Student Edition:
ISBN-13: 978-0-205-01766-9
ISBN-10: 0-205-01766-5

á la carte edition:
ISBN 13: 978-0-205-01809-3
ISBN 10: 0-205-01809-2

Contents

Preface

Business Ethics: Concepts and Cases continues to be one of the most widely used textbooks on business ethics, and remains popular among students because of its accessible style and lucid explanations of complex theories and concepts. Providing clear explanations of ideas without oversimplifying them into caricatures of themselves is a major challenge for texts in this field (as any instructor knows who has examined several texts on business ethics). Instructors who have used previous editions of this textbook have said that it does an outstanding job of meeting this challenge, while also providing an excellent balance of ethical theory and managerial practice. But the world does not stand still. Not only have our technologies, organizational forms, and managerial practices changed over the last few years, but our understanding of ethical reasoning has developed and new moral issues have continued to challenge business. So it was necessary to revise the text and to provide fresh and updated treatments of these and other enduring ethical issues in business. To facilitate the study of these issues, this edition incorporates a number of valuable and exciting pedagogical devices including:

- Six new and seven updated end-of-chapter cases
- Twelve completely new "On the Edge" short cases and six updated short cases in the body of the chapters
- Eight newly illustrated short cases
- Eight ABC News video clips posted online on the book's companion website, www.mythinkinglab.com to accompany eight of the end-of-chapter cases.
- New graphs and charts, new pictures, and other visual materials
- Study questions at the beginning of each chapter
- Definitions of key terms in the margins and in the glossary
- Summaries in the margins of all the basic ideas discussed in the text
- New discussions of: moral reasoning, corporate social responsibility, impediments to moral behavior, the influence of unconscious processes on moral behavior, globalization, technology, predatory pricing, the fraud triangle, sustainability, the value of work, recent business scandals, and much more.
- Up-to-date statistics and data in all chapters.
- End-of-chapter web resources

Although this new edition updates the contents of its predecessor, it retains both the basic organization and the conceptual framework of previous versions.

The primary aims of the text remain the same as in earlier editions. They are: (1) to introduce the reader to the ethical concepts that are relevant to resolving moral issues in business; (2) to impart the reasoning and analytical skills needed to apply ethical concepts to business decisions; (3) to identify the moral issues involved in the management of specific problem areas in business; (4) to provide an understanding of the social, technological, and natural environments within which moral issues in business arise; and (5) to supply case studies of actual moral dilemmas faced by businesses and business people.

The text is organized into four parts each containing two chapters. Part One provides an introduction to basic ethical theory. A fundamental perspective developed here is the view that ethical behavior is the best long-term business strategy for a company. By this I do not mean that ethical behavior is never costly. Nor do I mean that ethical behavior is always rewarded or that unethical behavior is always punished. It is obvious, in fact, that unethical behavior sometimes pays off, and that ethical behavior can impose serious losses on a company. When I argue that ethical behavior is the best long-range business strategy, I mean merely that over the long run, and for the most part, ethical behavior can give a company important competitive advantages over companies that are not ethical. I present this idea and argue for it in Chapter 1, where I also indicate how we come to accept ethical standards and how such standards can be incorporated into our moral reasoning processes. Chapter 2 critically discusses four kinds of moral principles: utilitarian principles, principles based on moral rights, principles of justice, and the principles of an ethic of care. These four kinds of moral principles, it is argued, provide a framework for resolving most of the kinds of ethical dilemmas and issues that arise in business. In addition, Chapter 2 discusses virtue theory as an alternative to a principles-based approach and discusses automatic moral decision-making and casuistry.

Having defined the nature and significance of ethical standards and having identified four basic criteria for resolving moral issues in business, I then bring the resulting theory to bear on specific moral issues. Thus, Part Two examines the ethics of markets and prices; Part Three discusses environmental and consumer issues; and Part Four looks at employee issues. I assume in each part that in order to apply a moral theory to the real world we must have some information (and theory) about what that world is really like. Consequently, each chapter in these last three parts devotes several pages to laying out the empirical information and theory that the decision-maker must have if he or she is to apply morality to reality. The chapter on market ethics, for example, provides a neoclassical analysis of market structure; the chapter on discrimination presents several statistical and institutional indicators of discrimination; the chapter on the individual in the organization relies on three models of organizations.

Each chapter of the text contains two kinds of materials. The main text of the chapter sets out the conceptual materials needed to understand and address some particular type of moral issue. In addition, each chapter includes short cases in the main body of the chapter, and longer cases at the end of the chapter, that describe real business situations in which these moral issues are raised. I have provided these discussion cases on the pedagogical assumption that a person's ability to reason about moral matters will improve if the person attempts to think through some concrete moral problems and allows himself or herself to be challenged by others who resolve the issue on the basis of different moral standards. These kinds of challenges, when they arise in dialogue and discussion with others, force us to confront the adequacy of our moral norms and motivate us to search for more adequate principles when our own are shown to be inadequate. Some of the rationale for these pedagogical assumptions is discussed in Chapter 1 in the section on moral development and moral reasoning. I hope that I have provided sufficient materials to allow the reader to develop, in discussion and dialogue with others, a set of ethical norms that they can accept as adequate.

New to this Edition

Although dozens of large and small revisions have been made in all the chapters of this edition, the following changes from the previous edition's text should be noted by previous users of this text.

Chapter 1 includes new discussions of corporate social responsibility, integrative social contracts theory, the link between emotions and moral reasoning, and impediments to moral behavior. A new "On the Edge" short case has been added entitled "A Traditional Business," and an older one entitled "Was National Semiconductor Morally Responsible?" has been removed and, like all other deleted cases, was archived on the Companion Website. The end-of-chapter case "Aaron Beam and the HealthSouth Fraud" is added, and "Enron's Fall" was removed and archived.

Chapter 2 has an expanded discussion of the mistakes people can make when approaching utilitarian theory for the first time; a new discussion of the claim that context, not character, determines moral behavior; a new section on the influence of unconscious mental processes on moral behavior; and a new discussion of the relation between conscious moral reasoning on the one hand, and unconscious moral decision-making, moral intuition, and cultural influences on the other hand. The "On the Edge" short case, "Conflict Diamonds" was dropped and a new one added titled "Should Companies Dump Their Wastes in Poor Countries?" The end-of-chapter case "Publius" was removed and archived, and a new case added named "Traidos Bank and Roche's Drug Trials in China."

Chapter 3 has a revised introduction and an expanded discussion of "alienation" in Marx. New "On the Edge" short cases include: "Commodification or How Free should Free Markets Be?" and "Marx's Children," while "Brian's Franchise" was removed and archived. The older end-of-chapter case "Glaxo-SmithKline, Bristol-Myers Squibb, and AIDS in Africa" was replaced with the new case "The GM Bailout."

Chapter 4 has a revised introduction, a new discussion of predatory pricing, and a new section on "Incentives, Opportunities, and Rationalization." The new end-of-chapter case "Intel's 'Rebates' and Other Ways It 'Helped' Customers" replaces the older "Playing Monopoly: Microsoft."

The introduction to Chapter 5 has been revised, and its discussions of pollution and resource depletion have been revised and completely updated with new charts and graphs. A new section on sustainability was added. The new "On the Edge" short case, "Ford's Toxic Wastes" replaced "The Aroma of Tacoma," and the short case, "The Auto Companies in China" was extensively revised and updated. Both of the two end-of-chapter cases were revised and updated.

The introduction to Chapter 6 has been revised. The new short case "Selling Personalized Genetics" was added, and the other two cases on the tobacco industry were revised. At the end of the chapter, the case "Reducing Debts at Credit Solutions of America" was added and "The Ford/Firestone Debacle" was removed.

In Chapter 7 all the statistical materials were brought up to date and several new graphs were added, while the section on comparable worth programs was removed. Two new "On the Edge" short cases in this chapter are "Helping Patients at Plainfield Healthcare Center" and "Driving for Old Dominion." The older short case "Wall Street: It's a Man's World" was removed and archived. Both of the end-of-chapter cases have been updated.

In Chapter 8 all the statistics have been updated and the discussion of conflicts of interest was revised; the older section, "Working Conditions: Job Satisfaction" was removed and a new discussion on the value of work was added. All of the older "On the Edge" short cases were removed, and three completely new short cases were added entitled "HP's Secrets and Oracle's New Hire," "Insider Trading or What Are Friends For?" and "Sergeant Quon's Text Messages." The new end-of-chapter case "Death at Massey Energy Company" replaces "Gap's Labor Problems."

Support for Instructors and Students

The moment you know. Educators know it. Students know it. It's that inspired moment when something that was difficult to understand suddenly makes perfect sense. Our MyLab products have been designed and refined with a single purpose in mind—to help educators create that moment of understanding with their students. The new MyThinkingLab delivers **proven results** in helping individual students succeed. It provides **engaging experiences** that personalize, stimulate, and measure learning for each student. And, it comes from a **trusted partner** with educational expertise and an eye on the future. MyThinkingLab can be used by itself or linked to any learning management system (LMS). MyThinkingLab—the moment you know.

Instructor's Manual with Tests

(0-205-01767-3):

For each chapter in the text, this valuable resource provides a detailed outline, list of objectives, and discussion questions. In addition, test questions in multiple-choice, true/false, fill-in-the-blank, and short answer formats are available for each chapter; the answers are page referenced to the text. For easy access, this manual is available at Preface vii **www.pearsonhighered.com/irc**.

PowerPoint Presentation Slides for Ethics: Theory and Practice

(0-205-01769-X):

These PowerPoint Slides help instructors convey ethical principles in a clear and engaging way. For easy access, they are available at **www.pearsonhighered.com/irc**.

MyTest Test Generator

(0-205-01768-1):

This computerized software allows instructors to create their own personalized exams, edit any or all of the existing test questions, and add new questions. Other special features of the program include random generation of test questions, creation of alternate versions of the same test, scrambling question sequence, and test preview before printing. For easy access, this software is available at **www.pearsonhighered.com/irc**.

Acknowledgments

Like every textbook author, I owe a very large debt of gratitude to the numerous colleagues and other scholars around the world from whom I have shamelessly borrowed ideas and materials. They all, I hope, have been duly recognized in the notes. Thank you to Marc Orlitzky, The University of Redlands; Barbara Fechner, South East Community College; and Rodney Stevenson, University of Wisconsin—Madison for their feedback. I owe a special debt to my colleagues in the Management Department where I teach, especially to Dennis Moberg. But my largest debt is owed to my wife and family who have patiently (and sometimes not so patiently) had to put up with me while I remained obsessively preoccupied with writing and revising the present edition of this book. To Maryann, Brian, Kevin, and Daniel: Thank You.

Manuel G. Velasquez
Aptos, California

PART **ONE**

Basic Principles

BUSINESS ETHICS IS APPLIED ETHICS. IT IS THE APPLICATION OF OUR UNDERSTANDING OF WHAT IS GOOD AND RIGHT TO THAT ASSORTMENT OF INSTITUTIONS, TECHNOLOGIES, TRANSACTIONS, ACTIVITIES, AND PURSUITS THAT WE CALL *BUSINESS.* A DISCUSSION OF BUSINESS ETHICS MUST BEGIN BY PROVIDING A FRAMEWORK OF BASIC PRINCIPLES FOR UNDERSTANDING WHAT IS MEANT BY THE TERMS *GOOD* AND *RIGHT*; ONLY THEN CAN ONE PROCEED TO PROFITABLY DISCUSS THE IMPLICATIONS THESE HAVE FOR OUR BUSINESS WORLD. THESE FIRST TWO CHAPTERS PROVIDE SUCH A FRAMEWORK. CHAPTER 1 DESCRIBES WHAT BUSINESS ETHICS IS IN GENERAL AND EXPLAINS THE GENERAL ORIENTATION OF THE BOOK. CHAPTER 2 DESCRIBES SEVERAL SPECIFIC APPROACHES TO BUSINESS ETHICS, WHICH TOGETHER FURNISH A BASIS FOR ANALYZING ETHICAL ISSUES IN BUSINESS.

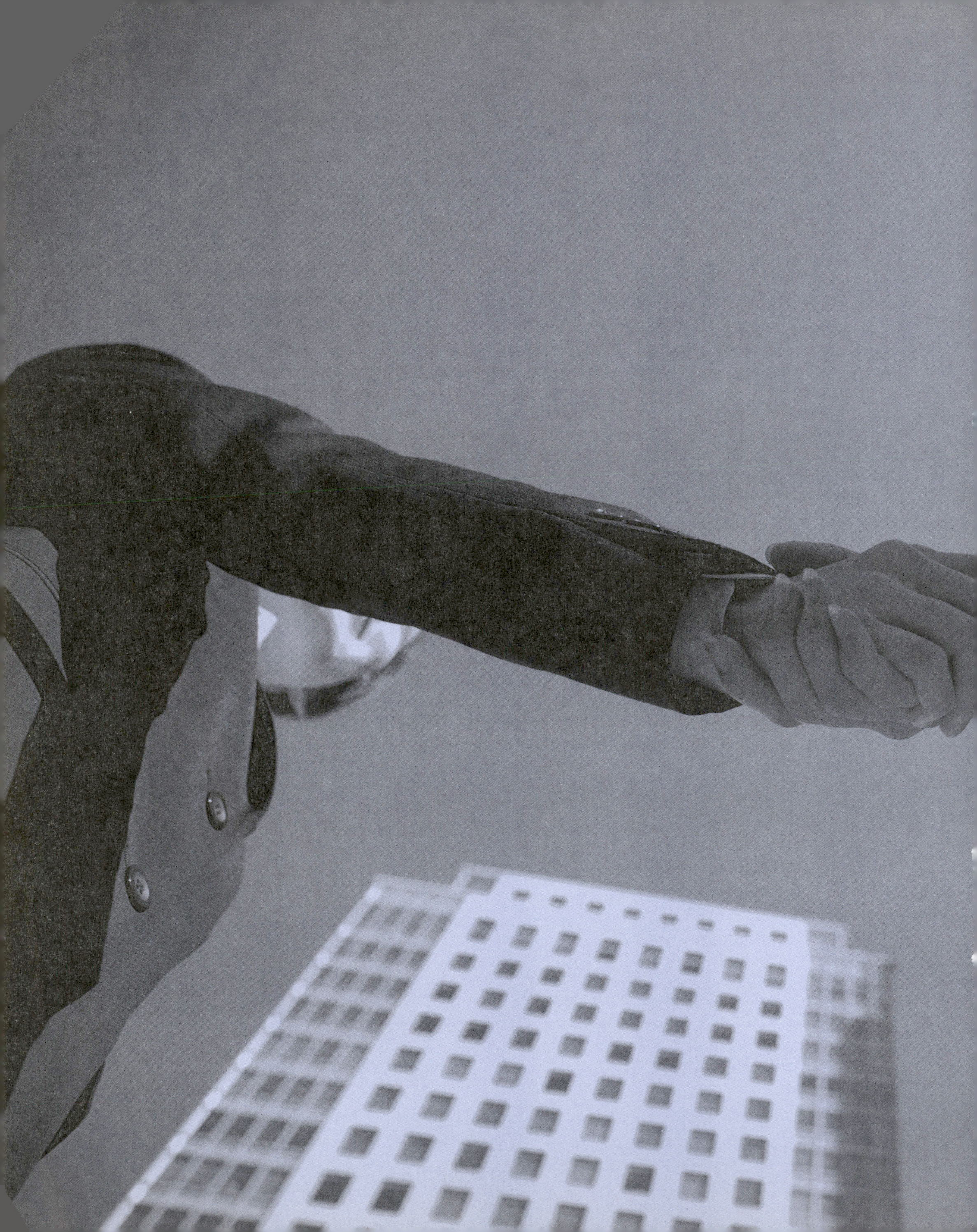

1

Ethics and Business

What is "business ethics"?

What is corporate social responsibility?

Is ethical relativism right?

How does moral development happen?

What role do emotions have in ethical reasoning?

What are the impediments to moral behavior?

When is a person morally responsible for doing wrong?

In business the handshake is an expression of trust, and ethical behavior is the foundation of trust.

INTRODUCTION

Listen to the Chapter Audio on mythinkinglab.com

Maybe the best way to introduce a discussion of business ethics is by looking at how a real company has incorporated ethics into its operations. Consider then how Merck & Co., Inc., a U.S. drug company, dealt with the issue of river blindness.

River blindness is a debilitating disease that has afflicted about 18 million impoverished people living in remote villages along the banks of rivers in tropical regions of Africa and Latin America. The disease is caused by a tiny parasitic worm that is passed from person to person by the bite of the black fly, which breeds in fast-flowing river waters. The tiny worms burrow under a person's skin, where they grow as long as 2 feet curled up inside ugly round nodules half an inch to an inch in diameter. Inside the nodules, the female worms reproduce by releasing millions of microscopic offspring called *microfilariae* that wriggle their way throughout the body moving beneath the skin, discoloring it as they migrate, and causing lesions and such intense itching that victims sometimes commit suicide. Eventually, the *microfilariae* invade the eyes and blind the victim. In some West African villages, the parasite had already blinded more than 60 percent of villagers over fifty-five. The World Health Organization estimated that the disease had blinded 270,000 people and left another 500,000 with impaired vision.

Pesticides no longer stop the black fly because it has developed immunity to them. Moreover, until the events described below, the only drugs available to treat the parasite in humans were so expensive, had such severe side effects, and required such lengthy hospital stays that the treatments were impractical for the destitute victims who lived in isolated rural villages. In many countries, young people fled the areas along the rivers, abandoning large tracts of rich fertile land. Villagers who stayed to live along the rivers accepted the nodules, the torturous itching, and eventual blindness as an inescapable part of life.

In 1980, Dr. Bill Campbell and Dr. Mohammed Aziz, research scientists working for Merck, discovered evidence that one of the company's best-selling animal drugs, Ivermectin, might kill the parasite that causes river blindness. Dr. Aziz, who had once worked in Africa and was familiar with river blindness, traveled to Dakar, Senegal, where he tested the drug on villagers who had active infections. Astonishingly, he discovered that a single dose of the drug not only killed all the microfilariae, it also made the female worms sterile and made the person immune to new infections for months. When Aziz returned to the United States, he and Dr. Campbell went to see Merck's head of research and development, Dr. P. Roy Vagelos, a former physician. They showed him their results and recommended that Merck develop a human version of the drug.

At the time, it cost well over $100 million to develop a new drug and test it in the large-scale clinical studies the U.S. government required. Roy Vagelos realized that even if they succeeded in developing a human version of the drug for the victims of river blindness, "It was clear that we would not be able to sell the medicine to these people, who would not be able to afford it even at a price of pennies per year."[1] And even if the drug was affordable, it would be almost impossible to get it to most of the people who had the disease since they lived in remote areas without access to doctors, hospitals, clinics, or drug stores. Moreover, if the drug had bad side effects for humans, these could threaten sales of the animal version of the drug, which were about $300 million a year. Finally, if a cheap version of the human drug was made available, it could be smuggled through black markets and resold for use on animals, thereby undermining the company's sales of Ivermectin to veterinarians.

Although Merck had worldwide sales of $2 billion a year, its net income as a percent of sales had been in decline due to the rapidly rising costs of developing new drugs, the increasingly restrictive and costly regulations being imposed by government agencies, a lull in basic scientific breakthroughs, and a decline in the productivity of company research programs. The U.S. Congress was getting ready to pass the Drug Regulation Act, which would intensify competition in the drug industry by allowing competitors to more quickly copy and market drugs originally developed by other companies. Medicare had recently put caps on reimbursements for drugs and required cheaper generic drugs in place of the branded-name drugs that were Merck's major source of income. In the face of these worsening conditions in the drug industry, was it a good idea for Merck to undertake an expensive project that showed little economic promise? On top of all this, Vagelos later wrote:

> There was a potential downside for me personally. I hadn't been on the job very long and I was still learning how to promote new drug development in a corporate setting. While we had some big innovations in our pipeline, I was still an unproven rookie in the business world. I would be spending a considerable amount of company money in a field, tropical medicine, that few of us other than Mohammed Aziz knew very well ... CEO Henry Gadsden had become worried—with good cause—about Merck's pipeline of new products, and he had hired me to solve that problem. It was as obvious to me as it was to Mohammed and Bill that even if Ivermectin was successful against river blindness, the drug wasn't going to pump up the firm's revenue and make the stockholders happy. So I was being asked to take on some risk for myself and for the laboratories.[2]

Vagelos knew he was faced with a decision that, as he said, "had an important ethical component." Whatever the risk to the company and his career, it was clear that without the drug, millions would be condemned to lives of intense suffering and partial or total blindness. After talking it over with Campbell, Aziz, and other managers, Vagelos came to the conclusion that the potential human benefits of a drug for river blindness were too significant to ignore. In late 1980, he approved a budget that provided the money needed to develop a human version of Ivermectin.

It took seven years for Merck to develop a human version of Ivermectin. The company named the human version Mectizan. A single pill of Mectizan taken once a year could eradicate from the human body all traces of the parasite that caused river blindness and prevented new infections. Unfortunately, exactly as Vagelos had earlier suspected, no one stepped forward to buy the miraculous new pill. Over the next several years, Merck officials—especially Vagelos who by then was Merck's chief executive officer (CEO)—pleaded with the World Health Organization (WHO), the U.S. government, and the governments of nations afflicted with the disease, asking that someone—anyone—come forward to buy the drug to protect the 100 million people who were at risk for the disease. None responded to the company's pleas.

When it finally became clear no one would buy the drug, the company decided to give Mectizan away for free to victims of the disease.[3] Yet, even this plan proved difficult to implement because, as the company had earlier suspected, there were no established distribution channels to get the drug to the people who needed it. Working with the WHO, therefore, the company financed an international committee to provide the infrastructure to distribute the drug safely to people in the Third World and to ensure that it would not be diverted into the black market to be sold for use on animals. Paying for these activities raised the amount it invested in developing, testing, and now distributing Mectizan to well over $200 million, without counting the cost of manufacturing the drug itself. By 2010, Merck had given away more than 2.5 billion tablets of Mectizan worth approximately $3.5 billion and was providing the drug for free to 80 million people a year in Africa, Latin America, and the Middle East. Besides using the drug to relieve the intense sufferings of river blindness, the company had expanded the program to include the treatment of elephantiasis, a parasitic disease that often coexists with river blindness which Merck researchers discovered could also be treated with Mectizan. By 2010, over 300 million people had received Mectizan to treat elephantiasis and 70 million more received it the following year.

When asked why the company invested so much money and effort into researching, developing, manufacturing, and distributing a drug that makes no money, Dr. Roy Vagelos, CEO of the company, replied that once the company suspected that one of its animal drugs might cure a severe human disease that was ravaging people, the only ethical choice was to develop it. Moreover, people in the Third World "will remember" that Merck helped them, he commented, and will respond favorably to the company in the future.[4] Over the years, the company had learned that such actions have strategically important long-term advantages. "When I first went to Japan 15 years ago, I was told by Japanese business people that it was Merck that brought streptomycin to Japan after World War II to eliminate tuberculosis which was eating up their society. We did that. We didn't make any money. But it's no accident that Merck is the largest American pharmaceutical company in Japan today."[5]

Having looked at how Merck dealt with its discovery of a cure for river blindness, let us now turn to the relationship between ethics and business. Pundits sometimes quip that *business ethics* is a contradiction in terms—an "oxymoron"—because there is an inherent conflict between ethics and the self-interested pursuit of profit. When ethics conflicts with profits, they imply, businesses always choose profits over ethics. Yet, the case of Merck suggests a different perspective—a perspective that many companies are increasingly taking. The managers of this company spent $200 million developing a product that they knew had little chance of ever being profitable because they felt they had an ethical obligation to make its potentially great benefits available to people. In this case, at least, a large and very successful business seems to have chosen ethics over profits. Moreover, the comments of Vagelos at the end of the case suggest that, in the long run, there may be no inherent conflict between ethical behavior and the pursuit of profit. On the contrary, the comments of Vagelos suggest that ethical behavior creates the kind of goodwill and reputation that expand a company's opportunities for profit.

Not all companies operate like Merck, and Merck itself has not always operated ethically. Many—perhaps most—companies will not invest in a research and development project that will probably be unprofitable even if it promises to benefit humanity. Every day newspapers announce the names of companies that choose profits over ethics or that, at least for a time, profited through unethical behavior—Enron, Worldcom, Global Crossing, Rite-Aid, Oracle, ParMor, Adelphia, Arthur Andersen, Louisiana-Pacific, and Qwest—are but a few of these. In 2004, even Merck was accused of failing to disclose heart problems associated with its drug Vioxx, and in 2010 the company put $4.85 billion into a fund to compensate patients who said they had suffered heart attacks or strokes because they had used Vioxx. (In spite of its significant lapse in regard to Vioxx, Merck has remained committed to operate ethically and has continued to win dozens of awards for its openness and ethically responsible operations.)[6]

Although there are many companies that at one time or another have engaged in unethical behavior, habitually unethical behavior is not necessarily a good long-term business strategy for a company. For example, ask yourself whether, as a customer, you are more likely to buy from a business that you know is honest and trustworthy or one that has earned a reputation for being dishonest and crooked. Ask yourself whether, as an employee, you are more likely to loyally serve a company whose actions toward you are fair and respectful or one that habitually treats you and other workers unjustly and disrespectfully. Clearly, when companies are competing against each other for customers and for the best workers, the company with a reputation for ethical behavior has an advantage over one with a reputation for being unethical.

This book takes the view that ethical behavior is the best long-term business strategy for a company—a view that has become increasingly accepted during the last few years.[7] This does not mean that occasions never arise when doing what is ethical will prove costly to a company. Such occasions are common in the life of a company, and we will see many examples in this book. Nor does it mean that ethical behavior is always rewarded or that unethical behavior is always punished. On the contrary, unethical behavior sometimes pays off, and the good guy sometimes loses. To say that ethical behavior is the best long-range business strategy just means that, over the long run and for the most part, ethical behavior can give a company significant competitive advantages over companies that are not ethical. The example of Merck suggests being ethical is good business strategy, and a bit of reflection on how we, as consumers and employees, respond to companies that behave unethically supports the view that unethical behavior leads to a loss of customer and employee support. Later, we will see what more can be said for or against the view that ethical behavior is the best long-term business strategy for a company.

The more basic problem is, of course, that the ethical course of action is not always clear to a company's managers. In the Merck case, Roy Vagelos decided that the company had an ethical obligation to proceed with the development of the drug. Yet to someone else the issue may not have been so clear. Vagelos notes he would be "spending a considerable amount of company money" in a way that would not "make stockholders happy" and that would put his own career at "some risk." Don't the managers of a company have a duty toward investors and shareholders to invest their funds in a profitable manner? Indeed, if a company spent all of its funds on charitable projects that lost money, wouldn't it soon be out of business? Then, wouldn't its shareholders be justified in claiming that the company's managers had spent their money unethically? And should Vagelos have risked his career, with the implications this had for his family? Is it so clear, then, that Vagelos had an ethical obligation to invest in an unprofitable drug? What reasons can be given for his belief that Merck had an obligation to develop the drug? Can any good reasons be given for the claim that Merck had no such obligation? Which view do you think is supported by the strongest reasons?

Although ethics may be the best policy, then, the ethical course of action is not always clear. The purpose of this book is to help you, the reader, deal with this lack of clarity. Although many ethical issues remain difficult and obscure even after a lot of study, gaining a better understanding of ethics will help you deal with ethical uncertainties in a more adequate and informed manner.

This text aims to clarify the ethical issues that you may face when you work in a business and perhaps, become part of a company's management team. This does not mean that it is designed to give you moral advice nor that it is aimed at persuading you to act in certain "moral" ways. The main purpose of the text is to provide you with a deeper knowledge of the nature of ethical principles and concepts along with an understanding of how you can use this knowledge to deal with the ethical choices you will encounter in the business world. This type of knowledge and skill should help you steer your way through ethical decisions like the one Vagelos had to make. Everyone in business is confronted with decisions like these, although usually not as significant as deciding whether to pursue a potential cure for river blindness. Before you even start working for a company, for example, you will be faced with ethical decisions about how "creative" your resume should be. Later, you may have to decide whether to cut corners just a little in your job, or whether to give your relative or friend a company contract, or whether to put a little extra into the expenses you report for a company trip you made. Or maybe you will catch a friend stealing from the company and have to decide whether to turn him in, or you will find out your company is doing something illegal and have to decide what you are going to do about it, or maybe your boss will ask you to do something you think is wrong. Ethical choices confront everyone in business, and this text hopes to give you some ways of thinking through these choices.

The first two chapters will introduce you to some methods of moral reasoning and some fundamental moral principles that can be used to analyze moral issues in business, as well as some of the obstacles that can get in the way of thinking clearly about ethical issues. The following chapters apply these principles and methods to the kinds of moral dilemmas that confront people in business. We begin in this chapter by discussing three preliminary topics: (1) the nature of business ethics and some of the issues it raises, (2) moral reasoning and moral decision-making, and (3) moral responsibility. Once these notions have been clarified, we devote the next chapter to a discussion of some basic theories of ethics and how they relate to business.

1.1 The Nature of Business Ethics

According to the dictionary, the term *ethics* has several meanings. One of the meanings given to it is: "the principles of conduct governing an individual or a group."[8] We sometimes use the term *personal ethics*, for example, when referring to the rules by which an individual lives his or her personal life. We use the term *accounting ethics* when referring to the code that guides the professional conduct of accountants.

A second—and for us more important—meaning of *ethics* according to the dictionary is this: Ethics is "the study of morality." Just as chemists use the term *chemistry* to refer to a study of the properties of chemical substances, ethicists use the term *ethics* to refer primarily to the study of morality. Although ethics deals with morality, it is not quite the same as morality. Ethics is a kind of investigation—and includes both the activity of investigating as well as the results of that investigation—whereas morality is the subject matter that ethics investigates.

Morality

morality The standards that an individual or a group has about what is right and wrong or good and evil.

So what, then, is morality? We can define **morality** as the standards that an individual or a group has about what is right and wrong, or good and evil. To clarify what this means, let's consider another case, one that is a bit different from the Merck case.

Several years ago, B. F. Goodrich, a manufacturer of vehicle parts, won a military contract to design, test, and manufacture aircraft brakes for the A7-D, a new light airplane the U.S. Air Force was designing. To conserve weight, Goodrich managers guaranteed that their compact brake would weigh no more than 106 pounds, contain no more than four small braking disks or "rotors," and be able to repeatedly stop the aircraft within a specified distance. The contract was potentially very lucrative for the company and so its managers were anxious to deliver a brake hat "qualified," that is, that passed all the tests the U.S. Air Force required for the A7-D.

An older Goodrich engineer, John Warren, designed the brake. A young engineer named Searle Lawson was given the job of determining the best material to use as the brake lining and testing the brake to make sure it "qualified." Searle Lawson was in his twenties. He had just graduated from school with an engineering degree and Goodrich had only recently hired him.

Lawson built a "prototype"—a working model—of the small brake to test lining materials. He found that when the brake was applied, the linings on the four rotors heated up to 1500 degrees and began disintegrating. When he tried other linings and got the same results, Lawson went over Warren's design and decided it was based on a mistake. By his own calculations, there was not enough surface area on the rotors to stop an airplane in the required distance without generating so much heat the linings failed. Lawson went to Warren, showed him his calculations and suggested Warren's design should be replaced with a new design for a larger brake with five rotors. Warren rejected the suggestion that his design was based on a mistake that a "green kid" just out of engineering school had discovered. He told Lawson to keep trying different materials for brake linings until he found one that worked.

But Lawson was not ready to give up. He went to talk with the manager in charge of the project and showed him his calculations. The project manager had repeatedly promised his own superiors that development of the brake was on schedule and knew he would probably be blamed if the brake was not delivered as he had promised. Moreover, he probably felt he should trust Warren who was one of his best engineers, rather than someone just out of engineering school. The project manager told Lawson that if Warren said the brake would work, then it would work. He should just keep trying different materials like Warren told him to do. Lawson left the project manager feeling frustrated. If he did not have the support of his superiors, he thought, he would just keep working with the brake Warren designed.

Several weeks later Lawson still had not found a lining that would not disintegrate on the brake. He spoke with his project manager again. This time his project manager told him to just put the brake through the tests required to "qualify" it for use on the A7-D airplane. Then, the manager told him in no uncertain terms that no matter what, he was to make the brake pass all its qualifying tests. His manager's orders shook Lawson and he later shared his thoughts with Kermit Vandivier, a technical writer who had been assigned to write a report on the brake:

> I just can't believe this is really happening. This isn't engineering, at least not what I thought it would be. Back in school I thought that when you were an engineer you tried to do your best, no matter what it cost. But this is something else. I've already had the word that we're going to make one more attempt to qualify the brake and that's it. Win or lose, we're going to issue a qualification report. I was told that regardless of what the brake does on tests, it's going to be qualified.[9]

Lawson put together a production model of the brake and ran it through the tests a dozen times. It failed every time. On the thirteenth attempt, Lawson "nursed" the brake through the tests by using special fans to cool the brake and by taking it apart at each step, cleaning it carefully, and fixing any distortions caused by the high heat. At one point, a measuring instrument was apparently deliberately miscalibrated so it indicated that the pressure applied on the brake was 1000 pounds per square inch (the maximum available to the pilot in the A7-D aircraft) when the pressure was actually 1100 pounds per square inch.

Kermit Vandivier, who was to write the final report on the tests, was also troubled. He talked the testing over with Lawson who said that he was just doing what the project manager had ordered him to do. Vandiver decided to talk with the senior executive in charge of his section. The executive listened, but then said, "It's none of my business and it's none of yours." Vandivier asked him whether his conscience would bother him if during flight tests on the brake something should happen resulting in death or injury to the test pilot. The Goodrich executive answered, "Why should my conscience bother me? ... I just do as I'm told, and I'd advise you to do the same."[10]

When Kermit Vandivier was told to write up a report that concluded the brake had passed all qualifying tests, he refused. Such a report, he felt, would amount to "deliberate falsifications and misrepresentations" of the truth.[11] But a short time later, he changed his mind. He later said:

> My job paid well, it was pleasant and challenging, and the future looked reasonably bright. My wife and I had bought a home . . . If I refused to take part in the A7-D fraud, I would have to either resign or be fired. The report would be written by someone anyway, but I would have the satisfaction of knowing I had had no part in the matter. But bills aren't paid with personal satisfaction, nor house payments with ethical principles. I made my decision. The next morning I telephoned [my superior] and told him I was ready to begin the qualification report.[12]

Lawson and Vandivier wrote the final report together. "Brake pressure, torque values, distances, times—everything of consequence was tailored to fit" the conclusion that the brake passed the qualifying tests.[13] A few weeks after Goodrich published their report, the U.S. Air Force put the brakes on A7-D test planes and pilots began flying them.

Below, we will talk about what happened when test pilots flew the planes equipped with the Goodrich brakes. At this point, note that Lawson believed that as an engineer he had an obligation "to do your best, no matter what it cost," and that Vandivier believed it was wrong to lie and to endanger the lives of others, and believed also that integrity is good and dishonesty is bad. These beliefs are all examples of moral standards. **Moral standards** include the *norms* we have about the kinds of actions we believe are morally right and wrong, as well as the *values* we place on what we believe is morally good or morally bad. Moral norms can usually be expressed as general rules about our actions, such as "Always tell the truth," "It's wrong to kill innocent people," or "Actions are right to the extent that they produce happiness." Moral values can usually be expressed with statements about objects or features of objects that have worth, such as "Honesty is good," and "Injustice is bad."

moral standards The norms about the kinds of actions believed to be morally right and wrong as well as the values placed on what we believe to be morally good and morally bad.

Where do moral standards come from? Typically, moral standards are first learned as a child from family, friends, and various societal influences such as church, school, television, magazines, music, and associations. Later, as we mature, our experience, learning, and intellectual development will lead us to think about, evaluate, and revise these standards according to whether we judge them to be reasonable or unreasonable. You may discard some standards that you decide are unreasonable, and may adopt new standards because you come to believe they are more reasonable than the ones you previously accepted. Through this maturing process, you develop standards that are more rational and so more suited for dealing with the moral issues of adult life. As Lawson and Vandivier's example shows, however, we do not always live up to the moral standards we hold; that is, we do not always do what we believe is morally right nor do we always pursue what we believe is morally good. Later in the chapter, we will look at how our actions can become disconnected from our moral beliefs.

Moral standards can be contrasted with norms or standards we hold about things that are not moral. Examples of **nonmoral standards and norms** (sometimes also called "conventional" standards and norms) include the standards of etiquette by which we judge people's manners as good or bad, the rules of behavior set by parents, teachers, or other authorities, the norms we call *the law* by which we determine what is legally right and wrong, the standards of language by which we judge what is grammatically right and wrong, the standards of art by which we judge whether a painting or a song is good or bad, and the sports standards by which we judge how well a game of football or basketball is being played. In fact, whenever we make judgments about

nonmoral standards The standards by which we judge what is good or bad and right or wrong in a nonmoral way.

the right or wrong way to do things, or judgments about what things are good and bad, or better and worse, our judgments are based on standards or norms of some kind. In Vandivier's case, we can surmise that he probably believed that reports should be written with good grammar; that having a well-paid, pleasant, and challenging job was a good thing; and that it's right to follow the law. The conventional norms of good grammar; the value of a well-paid, pleasant, and challenging job; and the laws of government are also standards, but these standards are not moral standards. As Vandivier's decision demonstrates, we sometimes choose nonmoral standards over our moral standards.

How do we distinguish between moral and nonmoral or conventional standards? Before reading any further, look at the two lists of norms below and see if you can tell which is the list of moral norms and which is the list of nonmoral norms:

Group One	**Group Two**
"Do not harm other people,"	"Do not eat with your mouth open,"
"Do not lie to other people,"	"Do not chew gum in class,"
"Do not steal what belongs to others."	"Do not wear sox that do not match."

During the last two decades, numerous studies have shown that the human ability to distinguish between moral norms and conventional or nonmoral norms emerges at a very early age and remains with us throughout life.[14] The psychologist Elliot Turiel and several others have found that by the age of three, a normal child has acquired the ability to tell the difference between moral norms and conventional norms. By age three, the child sees violations of moral norms as more serious and wrong everywhere, while violations of conventional norms are less serious and wrong only where authorities set such norms.[15] For example, three year olds will say that while it is not wrong to chew gum at schools where teachers do not have a rule against it, it is still wrong to hit someone even at schools where teachers do not have a rule against hitting. Because this ability to distinguish between moral and conventional norms develops in childhood, it was not just easy, but trivially easy for you to see that the norms in group one are moral norms, and those in group two are conventional. This innate ability to distinguish moral norms from conventional norms is not unique to Americans or Europeans or Westerners; it is an ability that every normal human being in every culture develops.[16] People in all cultures may not completely agree on which norms are moral norms (although there is a surprising amount of agreement) and which are conventional, but they all agree that the two are different and that the difference is extremely important.

Quick Review 1.1

Moral Norms and Nonmoral Norms

- From the age of three we can distinguish moral from nonmoral norms.
- From the age of three we tend to think that moral norms are more serious than nonmoral norms and apply everywhere independent of what authorities say.
- The ability to distinguish moral from nonmoral norms is innate and universal.

So what is the difference between moral norms and nonmoral or conventional norms? This is not an easy question to answer even if three year olds seem to know the difference. However, philosophers have suggested six characteristics that help pin down the nature of moral standards (and psychologists like Elliot Turiel and others have drawn on the work of philosophers to help them distinguish moral from nonmoral norms in their studies).

First, moral standards deal with matters that are serious, i.e., matters that we think can seriously wrong or significantly benefit human beings.[17] For example, most people in American society hold moral standards against theft, rape, enslavement, murder, child abuse, assault, slander, fraud, lawbreaking, and so on. All of these plainly deal with matters that people feel are serious forms of injury. Because they are about serious matters, violating moral standards is seen as seriously wrong and we feel that the obligation to obey moral standards has greater claim on us than conventional norms do. In

Quick Review 1.2

Six Characteristics of Moral Standards

- Involve serious wrongs or significant benefits
- Should be preferred to other values including self-interest
- Not established by authority figures
- Felt to be universal
- Based on impartial considerations
- Associated with special emotions and vocabulary

the Goodrich case, it was clear that both Lawson and Vandivier felt that lying in their report and endangering the lives of pilots were both serious harms and so both were moral matters, whereas adhering to grammatical standards was not. And because the benefits of developing a cure for river blindness were so significant, Dr. Vaglos felt that Merck had an obligation to develop the medicine Mectizan.

Second, and strikingly, we feel that moral standards should be preferred to other values including (and perhaps especially) self-interest.[18] That is, if a person has a moral obligation to do something, then he or she is supposed to do it even if this conflicts with other, conventional norms or with self-interest. In the Goodyear case, for example, we feel that Lawson should have chosen the moral values of honesty and respect for life over the self-interested value of keeping his job. This does not mean, of course, that it is always wrong to act on self-interest; it only means that when we believe a certain standard or norm is a moral norm, then we also feel that it would be wrong to choose self-interest over the moral norm. This second characteristic of moral standards is related to the first since part of the reason why we feel that moral standards should be preferred to other considerations is because moral standards deal with serious matters.

Third, unlike conventional norms, moral standards are not established or changed by the decisions of authority figures or authoritative bodies. Laws and legal standards are established by the authority of a legislature or the decisions of voters while family norms and classroom norms are set by parents and teachers. Authorities do not establish moral standards, however, nor does their validity rest on voters' preferences, and so they cannot be changed by the decision of any person or group. Instead, the validity of moral standards rests on whether the reasons that support and justify them are good or bad; when moral standards are based on good reasons, the standards are valid.

Fourth, moral standards are felt to be universal.[19] That is, if we genuinely hold that certain standards—such as "Do not lie" or "Do not steal"—are *moral* standards, then we will also feel that everyone should try to live up to those standards, and we will get upset when we see others transgressing them. When we learned that Bernard ("Bernie") Madoff, and the managers of Enron and Lehman Brothers had all been lying to us and to their investors, and that Pfizer managers stole at least $1 billion from taxpayers, while Tenet Healthcare and HCA managers stole almost as much, we did not feel that it was okay. for them to have violated our moral standards against lying and theft. We did not think: "It was okay for them to lie and steal, so long as *they* felt it was okay." Nor did we think: "Although *I* feel lying and stealing is wrong, *they* do not have to abide by *my* moral standards." On the contrary, the public got angry precisely because they felt that the standards against lying and stealing are *moral* standards, and so *everyone* has to abide by them, whether they want to or not. Conventional norms, on the other hand, are not seen as universal. Laws, for example, apply only within a specific jurisdiction; family rules are authoritative only within the family; game rules apply only to those playing the game, and so on.

Fifth, and generally, moral standards are based on impartial considerations.[20] The fact that you will benefit from a lie while others will be harmed is irrelevant to whether lying is morally wrong. Some philosophers have expressed this point by saying that moral standards are based on "the moral point of view"—that is, a point of view that does not evaluate standards according to whether they advance the interests of a particular individual or group, but one that goes beyond personal interests to a "universal" standpoint in which everyone's interests are impartially counted as equal.[21] Other philosophers have made the same point by saying that moral standards are based on the kinds of impartial reasons that an "ideal observer" or an "impartial spectator" would accept, or that in deciding moral matters "each counts for one and none for more than one."[22] As we are going to see in the next chapter, however, although impartiality is a characteristic of moral standards, it must be balanced with certain kinds of partiality, in particular, with the partiality that arises from legitimate caring for those individuals with whom you have a special relationship, such as family members and friends. Morality says that we should be impartial in those contexts where justice is called for, such as when we are setting salaries in a public company. But morality also identifies certain contexts, such as taking care of family members, where preferential caring for individuals can be morally legitimate and perhaps, even morally required.

Last, moral standards are associated with special emotions and a special vocabulary.[23] For example, if I act contrary to a moral standard, I will normally feel guilty, ashamed, or remorseful; I will describe my behavior as "immoral" or "wrong," and I will feel bad about myself and experience a loss of self-esteem. A careful reading of Lawson's and Vandivier's statements, for example, suggests that they felt ashamed and guilty about what they were doing. And when we see others acting contrary to a moral standard we accept, we normally feel indignation, resentment, or even disgust toward those persons; we say that they are not "living up" to their "moral obligations" or their "moral responsibilities" and we may esteem them less. This is perhaps what you felt when reading about what Lawson and Vandivier did.

Moral standards, then, are standards that deal with matters that we think are of serious consequence, are based on good reasons and not on authority, override self-interest, are based on impartial considerations, and are associated with special feelings such as guilt and shame, and with a special moral vocabulary such as "obligation," or "responsibility." We learn these standards as children from a variety of influences and revise them as we go through our lives.

Ethics

What, then, is ethics? **Ethics** is the discipline that examines your moral standards or the moral standards of a society. It asks how these standards apply to your life and whether these standards are reasonable or unreasonable—that is, whether they are supported by good reasons or poor ones. So you start to do ethics when you take the moral standards you have absorbed from family, church, and friends and ask yourself: What do these standards imply for the situations in which I find myself? Do these standards really make sense? What are the reasons for or against these standards? Why should I continue to believe in them? What can be said in their favor and what can be said against them? Are they really reasonable for me to hold? Are their implications in this or that particular situation reasonable?

Ethics The discipline that examines one's moral standards or the moral standards of a society to evaluate their reasonableness and their implications for one's life.

Take Vandivier and the B. F. Goodrich case as an example. Vandivier had apparently been raised to accept the moral standard that one has an obligation to tell the truth, and so he felt that in his particular situation, it would be wrong to write a false report on the brake. But we might ask whether writing what he felt was a false report was really wrong in his particular circumstances. Vandivier had several important financial obligations both toward himself and other people. He states, for example, that he had just married and bought a house, so he had mortgage payments to make each month and had to provide support for his family. If he did not write the report as he was ordered to do, then he would be fired and not be able to live up to these obligations. Do these moral obligations toward himself and his family outweigh his obligation not to write a false report? What is the basis of his obligation to tell the truth, and why is the obligation to tell the truth greater or lesser than a person's obligations toward oneself and one's family? Consider, next, Lawson's obligations toward his employer, B. F. Goodrich. Doesn't an employee have a moral obligation to obey his employer? Does the obligation to obey one's employer outweigh the obligation to "try to do your best" as an engineer? What is the source of both of these obligations, and what makes one greater or lesser than another? Consider, also, that the company and all its older and more experienced managers insisted that the best course of action was to write the report qualifying the brake. If something went wrong with the brake or the contract, B. F. Goodrich would be held accountable, not Lawson, who was a young and relatively low-level employee. Because the company, not Lawson, would be held accountable, did the company have the moral right to make the final decision about the report, instead of Lawson, who had just finished college? Does the moral right to make a decision belong to the party that will be held accountable for the decision? What is the basis of such a right, and why should we accept it? Consider, finally, that Vandivier states that, in the end, his personal refusal to participate in writing the report would have given him some "satisfaction," but would have made no difference to what happened because someone else would have been hired to write the report. Because the consequences would be the same whether he agreed or refused, did he really have a moral obligation to refuse? Can one have a moral obligation to do something that will make no difference? Why?

Notice the sort of questions to which we are led by the choices Vandivier and Lawson faced. They are questions about whether it is reasonable to apply various moral standards to their situation, whether it is reasonable to say that one moral standard is more or less important than another, and what reasons we might have to hold these standards. When you ask these kinds of questions about your own moral standards or about the moral standards of your society, you have started to do ethics. Ethics is the study of moral standards—the process of examining the moral standards you or your society (or other societies) hold in order to determine whether these standards are reasonable or unreasonable and how, if at all, they apply to the concrete situations and issues you face. The ultimate aim of ethics is to develop a body of moral standards that you feel are reasonable for you to hold—standards that you have thought about carefully and have decided are justified for you to accept and to apply to the choices that fill our lives.

Ethics is not the only way to study morality. The social sciences—such as anthropology, sociology, and psychology—also study morality, but do so in a way that is different from the approach to morality that ethics takes. While ethics is a *normative* study of morality, the social sciences engage in a *descriptive* study of morality. A **normative study** is an investigation that tries to reach normative conclusions—that is, conclusions about what things are good or bad or about what actions are right or wrong. In short, a normative study aims to discover what *ought* to be. As we have seen, ethics is the study of moral standards whose explicit purpose is to determine as far as possible which standards are correct or supported by the best reasons, and so it tries to reach conclusions about moral right and wrong and moral good and evil.

normative study An investigation that attempts to reach conclusions about what things are good or bad or about what actions are right or wrong.

descriptive study An investigation that attempts to describe or explain the world without reaching any conclusions about whether the world is as it should be.

A **descriptive study** is one that does not try to reach any conclusions about what things are truly good or bad or right or wrong. Instead, a descriptive study tries to describe or explain the world without reaching any conclusions about whether the world is as it *ought* to be. Anthropologists and sociologists, for example, may study the moral standards that a particular village or culture holds. In doing so, they try to develop accurate descriptions of the moral standards of that culture and perhaps, develop a theory that explains how they came to hold those standards. However, it is not the aim of anthropologists or sociologists to determine whether these moral standards are correct or incorrect.

Ethics, in contrast, is a study of moral standards whose explicit purpose is to determine as far as possible whether a given moral standard (or moral judgment based on that standard) is more or less correct. The sociologist asks, "Do Americans believe that bribery is wrong?" whereas the ethicist asks, "Is bribery wrong?" The ethicist, then, is concerned with developing reasonable normative claims and theories, whereas an anthropological or sociological study of morality aims at providing descriptive characterizations of people's beliefs.

Business Ethics

What we have said about ethics so far has been meant to convey an idea of what ethics is. Here, however, we are not concerned with ethics in general, but with a particular field of ethics: *business* ethics. **Business ethics** is a specialized study of moral right and wrong that focuses on business institutions, organizations, and activities. Business ethics is a study of moral standards and how these apply to the social systems and organizations through which modern societies produce and distribute goods and services, and to the activities of the people who work within these organizations. Business ethics, in other words, is a form of applied ethics. It not only includes the analysis of moral norms and moral values, but also tries to apply the conclusions of this analysis to that assortment of institutions, organizations, and activities that we call *business*.

business ethics A specialized study of moral right and wrong that concentrates on moral standards as they apply to business institutions, organizations, and behavior.

As this description of business ethics suggests, the issues that business ethics covers encompass a wide variety of topics. To introduce some order into this variety, it will help if we keep separate three different kinds of issues that business ethics investigates: systemic, corporate, and individual issues. *Systemic* issues in business ethics are ethical questions raised about the economic, political, legal, and other institutions within which businesses operate. These include questions about the morality of capitalism or of the laws, regulations, industrial structures, and social practices within which U.S. businesses operate. One example would be questions about the morality of the government contracting system through which B. F. Goodrich was allowed to test the adequacy of its own brake design for the A7-D. Another example would be questions about the morality of the international institutions with which Merck was forced to deal when it was looking for a way to get its cure for river blindness to the people who needed it most.

Quick Review 1.3

Business Ethics Is a Study of

- Our moral standards insofar as these apply to business
- How reasonable or unreasonable these moral standards we have absorbed from society are
- The implications our moral standards have for business activities.

Corporate issues in business ethics are ethical questions raised about a particular organization. These include questions about the morality of the activities, policies, practices, or organizational structure of an individual company taken as a whole. One set of examples of this kind of issue would be questions about the morality of B. F. Goodrich's corporate culture or questions about the company's corporate decision to "qualify" the A7-D brake. For example, did the Goodrich Company violate anyone's rights when it qualified the brake? What impact did the company's actions have on the welfare of the parties with whom it interacted? Were the company's actions just or unjust to other parties? Another set of examples would be questions about the morality of Merck's corporate decision to invest so many millions of dollars in a project that would probably not generate any profits. In doing this, did the company violate the rights of its stockholders? Was Merck's action fair and just to the various parties it affected? Yet other questions might be directed at B. F. Goodrich's corporate policies: Were ethics concerns part of its ongoing decision-making process? Did the company encourage or discourage employee discussions of how their decisions might impact the moral rights of other people?

Finally, *individual* issues in business ethics are ethical questions raised about a particular individual or particular individuals within a company and their behaviors and decisions. These include questions about the morality of the decisions, actions, or character of an individual. An example would be the question of whether Vandivier's decision to participate in writing a report on the A7-D brake, which he believed was false, was morally justified. A second example would be the question of whether it was moral for Merck's chair, Dr. P. Roy Vagelos, to allow his researchers to develop a drug that would probably not generate any profits.

Quick Review 1.4

Kinds of Ethical Issues

- Systemic—ethical questions about the social, political, legal, or economic systems within which companies operate
- Corporate—ethical questions about a particular corporation and its policies, culture, climate, impact, or actions
- Individual—ethical questions about a particular individual's decisions, behavior, or character

It is helpful when analyzing the ethical issues raised by a concrete situation or case to sort out the issues in terms of whether they are *systemic*, *corporate*, or *individual* issues. Often, the world presents us with decisions that involve a large number of extremely complicated interrelated kinds of issues that can cause confusion, unless the different kinds of issues are first carefully sorted out and distinguished from each other. Moreover, the kinds of solutions that are appropriate for dealing with systemic or corporate issues are not the same as the kinds of solutions that are appropriate for dealing with individual issues. If a company is trying to deal with a systemic issue—such as a government culture that permits bribery—then the issue must be dealt with on a systemic level; that is, it must be dealt with through the coordinated actions of many different social groups. On the other hand, corporate ethical issues can be solved only through corporate or company solutions. If a company has a culture that encourages moral wrongdoing, for example, then changing that culture requires the cooperation of the many different people that make up the company. Finally, individual ethical issues need to be solved through individual decisions and actions, and, perhaps, individual reform.

So what happened after Searle Lawson and Kermit Vandivier turned in their report and the U.S. Air Force put the Goodrich brakes on planes flown by their test pilots? Lawson was sent as Goodrich's representative to Edwards Air Force Base in California where the test flights took place. There, he watched as the brakes caused several near crashes when the pilots tried to land the planes. In one case, he saw an airplane go skidding down the runway when the pilot's braking produced such intense heat inside the brake that its parts fused together and the wheels locked up. Surprisingly, none of the pilots were killed. When Lawson returned home, both he and Vandivier quit and notified the F.B.I. of what had been going on; this was their way of dealing with the *individual* issues their actions had raised. A few days later, Goodrich announced that it was replacing the small brake with a larger five-disk brake at no extra charge to the U.S. government, and in this way they tried to deal with the *corporate* issues the brake incident had created. About a year later, Lawson and Vandivier came before the U.S. Congress and testified about their experiences at Goodrich. Shortly thereafter, the U.S. Department of Defense changed the way it let companies test equipment so that it became harder for companies to submit fraudulent reports. These changes were responses to a key *systemic* issue that became obvious once the truth came out.

Applying Ethical Concepts to Corporations

The statement that business ethics applies ethical or moral concepts to corporate organizations raises a puzzling issue. Can we really say that the acts of *organizations* are moral or immoral in the same way that the actions of *human individuals* are? Can we say that corporations are morally responsible for their acts in the same sense that individuals are morally responsible for what they do? Or must we say that it makes no sense to apply moral terms to organizations as a whole, but only to the individuals who make up the organization? A few years ago, for example, employees of Arthur Andersen, an accounting firm, were caught shredding documents potentially proving that Arthur Anderson accountants had helped Enron hide its debt through the use of several accounting tricks. The U.S. Justice Department then charged the now-defunct *firm* of Arthur Andersen with obstruction of justice, instead of charging the *employees* who shredded the documents. Critics afterward claimed that the U.S. Justice Department should have charged the individual employees of Arthur Andersen, not the company, because "Companies don't commit crimes, people do."[24] Can moral notions like *responsibility*, *wrongdoing*, and *obligation* be applied to groups such as corporations, or are individuals the only real moral agents?

Two views have emerged in response to this question.[25] At one extreme, is the view of those who argue that if we can say that something *acted* and that it acted *intentionally*, then we can say that thing is a "moral agent"; that is, it is an agent capable of having moral rights and obligations and being morally responsible for its actions, just like humans. The argument for this view goes like this: We can clearly say that corporations engage in *actions* and that they carry out those actions *intentionally*. Companies, for example, can "merge" together, make contracts, compete against other companies, and make products. And these things do not just happen: companies seem to do these things "intentionally." But if an agent can act intentionally, then it can be morally responsible for its actions and it can be blamed when it does what is morally wrong. It follows, therefore, that corporations are "morally responsible" for their actions, and that their actions are "moral" or "immoral" in exactly the same sense as those of an individual. The major problem with this argument, however, is that organizations do not seem to "act" or "intend" in the same sense that people do. Unlike individuals, organizations have no minds to form "intentions" and are conscious of neither pain nor pleasure nor anything else; and unlike individuals organizations do not act on their own but instead humans must act for them.

At the other extreme, is the view of those who hold that it makes no sense to hold companies "morally responsible" or to say that they have "moral" duties. These people argue that business organizations are the same as machines whose members must blindly conform to formal rules that have nothing to do with morality. Consequently, it makes no more sense to hold organizations "morally responsible" for failing to follow moral standards than it makes to criticize a machine for failing to act morally. But the major problem with this second view is that, unlike machines, at least some of the members of organizations usually know what they are doing and are free to choose whether to follow the organization's rules or even to change these rules. When an organization's members collectively, but freely and knowingly pursue immoral objectives, it ordinarily makes good sense to say that the actions they performed on behalf of the corporation are "immoral" and that the organization is "morally responsible" for these immoral actions.

Quick Review 1.5

Should Ethical Qualities be Attributed Only to People or Also to Corporations?

- One view says corporations, like people, act intentionally and have moral rights, and obligations, and are morally responsible.
- Another view says it makes no sense to attribute ethical qualities to corporations since they are not like people but more like machines; only humans can have ethical qualities.
- A middle view says that humans carry out the corporation's actions so they are morally responsible for what they do and ethical qualities apply in a primary sense to them; corporations have ethical qualities only in a derivative sense.

Which of these two views is correct? Perhaps neither is correct. The underlying difficulty with which both views are trying to struggle is this: Although we say that corporate organizations "exist" and "act" like individuals, they obviously are not human individuals. Yet, our moral categories are designed to deal primarily with human individuals who feel, reason, and deliberate, and who act on the basis of their own feelings, reasons, and deliberations. So, how can we apply these moral categories to corporate organizations and their "acts"? We can see our way through these difficulties if we first note that corporate organizations and their acts depend on human individuals. Because corporate acts originate in the choices and actions of human individuals, it is these individuals who are the *primary* bearers of moral duties and responsibility. Human individuals are responsible for what the corporation does because corporate actions flow wholly out of their decisions and behaviors. If a corporation acts wrongly, it is because of what some individual or individuals in that corporation chose to do; if a corporation acts morally, it is because some individual or individuals in that corporation chose to have the corporation act morally. As several law courts have held, the idea that the actions of a corporation are the actions of some "person" who is separate from the humans who carry out those actions, is a "legal fiction."[26] This fiction is set aside (by "piercing the corporate veil") when justice requires that those humans who really carried out the actions of the corporation should be held responsible for injuries "the corporation" caused.[27]

Nonetheless, it makes perfectly good sense to say that a corporate organization has moral duties and that it is morally responsible for its acts. However, organizations have moral duties and are morally responsible in a *secondary* or *derivative* sense. A corporation has a moral duty to do something only if some of its members have a moral duty to make sure it is done. And a corporation is morally responsible for something only if some of its members are morally responsible for what happened (i.e., they acted with knowledge and of their own free will—topics we will discuss later).

The central point is that when we apply the standards of ethics to business, we must not let the fiction of "the corporation" obscure the fact that human individuals control what the corporation does. Consequently, these human individuals are the *primary* carriers of the moral duties and moral responsibilities that we attribute in a *secondary* sense to the corporation. This is not to say, of course, that the human beings who make up a corporation are not influenced by each other and by their corporate environment. Corporate policies, corporate culture, and corporate norms all have an enormous influence on the behavior of corporate employees. However, a corporation's policies, culture, and norms do not make the employee's choices for him (or her) and so they are not responsible for the actions of that employee. We will return to this issue when we discuss moral responsibility toward the end of this chapter.

Objections to Business Ethics

We have described business ethics as the process of rationally evaluating our moral standards and applying them to business situations. However, many people raise objections to the very idea of applying moral standards to business activities. In this section, we address some of these objections and also look at what can be said in favor of bringing ethics into business.

Occasionally people object to the view that ethical standards should be applied to the behavior of people in business organizations. Persons involved in business, they claim, should single-mindedly pursue the financial interests of their firm and not sidetrack their energies or their firm's resources into "doing good works." Three different kinds of arguments are advanced in support of this view.

First, some have argued that in perfectly competitive free markets, the pursuit of profit will by itself ensure that the members of society are served in the most socially beneficial ways.[28] To be profitable, each firm has to produce only what the members of society want and has to do this by the most efficient means available. The members of society will benefit most, then, if managers do not impose their own values on a business, but instead devote themselves to the single-minded pursuit of profit and thereby to producing efficiently what the members of society value.

Arguments of this sort conceal a number of assumptions that require a much lengthier discussion than we can provide at this stage. Because we examine many of these claims in greater detail in the chapters that follow, here we only note some of the more questionable assumptions on which the argument rests.[29] First, most industrial markets are not "perfectly competitive" as the argument assumes. To the extent that firms do not have to compete, they can maximize profits despite inefficient production. Second, the argument assumes that any steps taken to increase profits will necessarily be socially beneficial. In fact, however, several ways of increasing profits actually injure society such as: allowing harmful pollution to go uncontrolled, deceptive advertising, concealing product hazards, fraud, bribery, tax evasion, price fixing, and so on. Third, the argument assumes that, by producing whatever the buying public wants (or values), firms are producing what all the members of society want. But the wants of large segments of society (the poor and disadvantaged) are not necessarily met when companies produce what buyers want, because these segments of society cannot participate fully in the marketplace. Fourth, the argument is essentially making a normative judgment ("managers *should* devote themselves to the single-minded pursuit of profits") on the basis of some unspoken and unproved moral standard ("people should do whatever will benefit those who participate in markets"). Thus, although the argument tries to show that ethics does not matter, it assumes an unproved ethical standard to show this. And the standard does not look very reasonable.

A second kind of argument sometimes advanced to show that business managers should single-mindedly pursue the interests of their firms and should ignore ethical considerations is embodied in what Alex C. Michales called the "loyal agent's argument."[30] The argument can be paraphrased as follows:

(1) As a loyal agent of his or her employer, the manager has a duty to serve the employer as the employer would want to be served (if the employer had the agent's expertise).
(2) An employer would want to be served in whatever ways will advance his or her interests.
(3) Therefore, as a loyal agent of the employer, the manager has a duty to serve the employer in whatever ways will advance the employer's interests.

Unethical managers have often used this argument to justify unethical conduct. For example, in 2005, Scott Sullivan, former finance executive for WorldCom, was accused of running an $11 billion accounting fraud that destroyed the retirement money thousands of employees had saved. Sullivan's defense was that his boss, Bernie Ebbers, had ordered him to "hit the numbers." Sullivan obeyed although, he says, he raised an objection: "I told Bernie, 'This isn't right.' "[31] Betty Vinson, a former WorldCom accounting executive, defended her part in the fraud by pleading that Sullivan had ordered her to "adjust" the books to hide the company's poor financial state from investors.[32] Both Sullivan and Venison thought that loyal obedience to their employer justified ignoring the fact, which both admitted they knew, that what they were doing was wrong. Notice that if in the Loyal Agent Argument, we replace *employer* with *government*, and *manager* with *officer*, we get the kind of argument that Nazi officers used after World War II to defend their murder of about 16 million Jews and others that Hitler's government labeled "undesirables." When they were captured and brought to trial, the Nazi officers repeatedly defended their actions by claiming: "I had to do it because I had a duty to serve my government by following its orders."

It takes only a little reflection to realize that the loyal agent's argument rests on questionable assumptions. First, the argument tries to show (again) that ethics does not matter by assuming an unproved moral standard ("the manager *should* serve the employer in whatever way the employer wants to be served"). But there is no reason to assume that this moral standard is acceptable as it stands and some reason to think that it would be acceptable only if it were suitably qualified (e.g., "the manager should serve the employer in whatever *moral* and *legal* way the employer wants to be served"). Second, the loyal agent's argument assumes that there are no limits to the manager's duties to serve the employer, when in fact such limits are an express part of the legal and social institutions from which these duties arise. An agent's duties are defined by what is called **the law of agency** (i.e., the law that specifies the duties of persons—"agents"—who agree to act on behalf of another party—the "principle"). Lawyers, managers, engineers, stockbrokers, and so on all act as agents for their employers in this sense. By freely entering an agreement to act as someone's agent, then, a person accepts a legal (and moral) duty to serve the client loyally, obediently, and in a confidential manner as specified in the law of agency.[33] Yet, the law of agency states that "in determining whether or not the orders of the [client] to the agent are reasonable . . . business or professional ethics are to be considered," and "in no

law of agency A law that specifies the duties of persons who agree to act on behalf of another party and who are authorized by an agreement so to act.

Quick Review 1.6

Arguments Against Ethics in Business

- In a free market economy, the pursuit of profit will ensure maximum social benefit so business ethics is not needed.
- A manager's most important obligation is loyalty to the company regardless of ethics.
- So long as companies obey the law they will do all that ethics requires.

event would it be implied that an agent has a duty to perform acts which are illegal or unethical."[34] The manager's duties to serve the employer, then, are limited by the constraints of morality, because it is with this understanding that the duties of a loyal agent are defined. Third, the loyal agent's argument assumes that if a manager agrees to serve an employer, then this agreement somehow justifies whatever the manager does on behalf of his employer. However, this assumption is false: An agreement to serve an employer does not automatically justify doing wrong on his or her behalf. If it is wrong for me knowingly to put people's lives at risk by selling them defective products, then it is still wrong when I am doing it for my employer. Agreements do not change the moral character of wrongful acts nor does the argument "I was following orders" justify them.

A third kind of objection is sometimes made against bringing ethics into business. This is the objection that to be ethical it is enough for businesspeople to follow the law: If it is legal, then it is ethical. For example, the managers at the financial company Goldman Sachs recently were accused of helping Greece hide loans larger than European Union rules allowed by disguising the loans as currency exchanges that legally did not have to be disclosed as debt. Greece's debt eventually got so huge that in 2010, it threw Greece and then the entire European Union into a financial crisis. Goldman Sachs' managers were accused of behaving unethically because they helped Greece hide debt that was more than it could handle. But the managers excused themselves with the statement that "these transactions were consistent with European principles [laws] governing their use and application at the time."[35] Since it was legal, they were saying, it was ethical.

It is wrong, however, to see ethics as no more than what the law requires. It is true that some laws require behavior that is the same as the behavior required by our moral standards. Examples of these are laws that prohibit murder, rape, theft, fraud, and so on. In such cases, law and morality coincide, and the obligation to obey such laws is the same as the obligation to be moral. However, law and morality do not completely overlap. Some laws have nothing to do with morality because they do not involve serious matters. These include parking laws, dress codes, and other laws covering similar matters. Other laws may even violate our moral standards so that they are actually contrary to morality. Our own pre-Civil War slavery laws, for example, required us to treat slaves like property, and the laws of Nazi Germany required anti-Semitic behavior. The laws of some Arab countries today require that businesses discriminate against women and Jews in ways that most people would say are clearly immoral. So it is clear that ethics is not simply following the law.

This does not mean, of course, that ethics has nothing to do with following the law.[36] Many of our moral standards have been incorporated into the law because enough of us feel that these moral standards should be enforced by the penalties of a legal system. On the other hand, laws are sometimes removed from our law books when it becomes clear that they violate our moral standards. Our moral standards against bribery, for example, were incorporated into the Foreign Corrupt Practices Act, and only a few decades ago it became clear that laws permitting job discrimination—like earlier laws permitting slavery—were blatantly unjust and had to be changed. Morality, therefore, has shaped and influenced many of the laws we have.

Moreover, most ethicists agree that all citizens have a moral obligation to obey the law so long as the law does not require clearly unjust behavior. This means that, in most cases, it is immoral to break the law. Tragically, the obligation to obey the law can create terrible conflicts when the law requires something that the businessperson knows or believes is immoral. In such cases, a person will be faced with a conflict between the obligation to obey the law and the obligation to obey his or her conscience. Such conflicts are not unusual. In fact you, the reader, likely will have to deal with such a conflict at some point in your business life.

The Case for Ethics in Business

We have looked at some arguments that try to show that ethics should not be brought into business. Is there anything to be said for the other side—that ethics should be brought into business? Offhand, it would appear that ethics should be brought into business simply because ethics should govern all voluntary human activities and business is a voluntary human activity. There does not seem to be anything special about business that would prevent us from applying the same standards of ethics to business activities that should be applied to all voluntary human activities.

It has been pointed out, in fact, that a business cannot exist unless the people involved in the business and its surrounding society adhere to some minimal standards of ethics. First, any individual business will collapse if all of its managers, employees, and customers come to think that it is morally permissible to steal from, lie to, or break their agreements with the company. Because no business can exist entirely without ethics, every business requires at least a minimal adherence to ethics on the part of those involved in the business. Second, all businesses require a stable society in which to carry on their business dealings. Yet, the stability of any society requires that its members adhere to some minimal standards of ethics. In a society without ethics, as the philosopher Hobbes once wrote, distrust and unrestrained self-interest would create "a war of every man against every man," and in such a situation, life would become "nasty, brutish, and short." The impossibility of conducting business in such a society—one in which lying, theft, cheating, distrust, and unrestrained self-interested conflict became the norm—is shown by the way in which business activities break down in societies torn by strife, conflict, distrust, and civil war. Because businesses cannot survive without ethics, then it is in the best interests of business to promote ethical behavior both among its own members as well as within its larger society.[37]

Quick Review 1.7

Arguments Supporting Ethics in Business

- Ethics applies to all human activities.
- Business cannot survive without ethics.
- Ethics is consistent with profit seeking.
- Customers, employees, and people in general care about ethics.
- Studies suggest ethics does not detract from profits and seems to contribute to profits.

Is there any evidence that ethics is consistent with what most people see as the core of business: the pursuit of profit? To begin with, there are many examples of companies in which good ethics has existed side-by-side with a history of profitability. Companies that have combined a good history of profit with consistently ethical behavior include Intel, Timberland, Hewlett-Packard, Cisco Systems, Levi Strauss, General Mills, Patagonia, Kimberly-Clark, Interface International, and Starbucks Coffee.[38] But many chance factors affect profitability (overcapacity in a particular industry, recessions, weather patterns, interest rates, changing consumer tastes, etc.). Consequently, these companies may be nothing more than the few companies in which ethics by chance happened to coincide with profits for a period of time. Is there any evidence that ethics in business is helpful to business? That is, what can be said for the proposition that good ethics is also good business?

Consider that when two people have to deal with each other repeatedly, it makes little sense for one person to inflict wrongs upon the other, especially when the person who is wronged can later retaliate against the person who wronged him or her. Now business interactions with employees, customers, suppliers, and creditors are repetitive and ongoing. If a business tries to take advantage of employees, customers, suppliers, or creditors through unethical behavior today, then they will likely find a way to retaliate against the business when the business has to work with them again tomorrow. The retaliation may take a simple form, such as refusing to buy from, refusing to work for, or refusing to do business with the unethical party. Or retaliation may be more complex, such as sabotage, getting others to boycott the unethical business, or getting even by inflicting other kinds of costs on the business. A business can sometimes, even often, get away with unethical behavior. In the long run, however, if interactions with others are repeated, and retaliation is possible, unethical behavior can impose heavy costs on the business. Ethical behavior, on the other hand, can set the stage for mutually beneficial interactions with others. Unethical behavior in business tends to be a losing proposition because it undermines the long-term cooperative relationships with customers, employees, and community members on which business success ultimately depends.

There is, in fact, a lot of research that shows that unethical behavior tends to generate harmful reprisals, while ethical treatment of people tends to produce cooperative behavior. Several studies have shown that most people so value ethical behavior that they will punish people when they see them behaving unethically and reward those who are perceived as ethical, even at some cost to themselves.[39] In one set of psychology experiments, for example, the experimenter paired up people and gave the first member of each pair $100 to divide between himself and the second member in any way the first member wanted to divide it. The second member of the pair, however, got to decide whether they would both keep the money or would both just return it all back to the experimenter. Perhaps, you can already guess what happened. Whenever the first member divided the money unequally by taking a lot more for himself and giving the second member just a little—five dollars or ten dollars, for example—the second member would usually say they both had to return all the money to the experimenter, even though this meant losing the amount he would have received. But when the first member divided the money up more or less equally, the second member decided they should both keep the money. When they were interviewed afterwards, the second member of each pair almost always said that a very unequal division of the money was morally wrong, and so he had punished the wrongdoer by forcing the wrongdoer to return his money, although this meant they would also lose the money they would have received. But when the money was divided up equally, this seemed morally right to the second member and so he decided they could keep the money.

There is a lot more research in social psychology showing that people in all kinds of social situations respond to perceived injustices with moral anger—whether the injustice is directed against themselves or others—and this anger motivates them to attempt to restore justice by punishing the party that inflicted the injustice.[40] Employees who feel their company's decision-making processes are unjust will exhibit higher absenteeism, higher turnover, lower productivity, and demand higher wages.[41] Customers will turn against a company if they perceive a gross injustice in the way it conducts its business and will be less willing to buy its products.[42] Customers and employees who feel a company has behaved unethically, for example, now sometimes start critical web sites such as *complaintsboard.com*, *ripoffreport.com*, *pissedconsumer.com*, and *screwedcentral.com*. On the other hand, when people feel that an organization is treating people fairly, they will reward it with loyalty and commitment. For example, when employees feel that an organization's decision-making processes are just, they exhibit lower levels of turnover and absenteeism, show higher levels of trust and commitment to the company and its managers, and demand lower wages.[43] When employees believe an organization is just, they are more willing to follow the organization's managers, do what managers say, and tend to see managers' leadership as legitimate.[44] In short, unethical behavior breeds reprisals while ethical behavior breeds cooperation.

What about the proposition that companies that are ethical are more profitable than those that are not? Is there any evidence that supports the view that ethical companies are more profitable than unethical ones? There are many difficulties involved in trying to study whether ethical companies are more profitable than unethical ones. There are many different ways of defining *ethical*, many different ways of measuring profit, many different ways of deciding which actions count as the actions of the company, many different factors that can affect a company's profits, and many different "ethical" dimensions along which companies can be compared. Despite these difficulties, several studies have tried to discover whether profitability is correlated with ethical behavior. The results have been mixed. Although the majority of studies have found a positive relationship between socially responsible behavior and profitability,[45] some have found no such relationship.[46] No studies, however, have found a negative correlation, which would have indicated that ethics is a drag on profits. Other studies have looked at how socially responsible firms perform on the stock market and have concluded that ethical companies provide higher returns than other companies.[47] Together, all these studies suggest that, by and large, ethics does not detract from profit and seems to contribute to profits.

There are, then, good reasons to think that ethics should be brought into business. Taken together, the arguments above—some philosophical and some more empirical—suggest that businesses are shortsighted when they fail to take the ethical aspects of their activities into consideration.

Business Ethics and Corporate Social Responsibility

Business ethics is sometimes confused with "corporate social responsibility" or "CSR." Although the two are related, they are not quite the same. It is important to understand how they are different as well as how they are related to each other. We will begin by clarifying what corporate social responsibility is because this will help us understand how business ethics and corporate social responsibility are related. Moreover, theories of corporate social responsibility provide answers to the important question: What is the purpose of business?

The phrase "corporate social responsibility" refers to a corporation's responsibilities or obligations toward society. There is some disagreement about what those obligations include. Do companies have a responsibility to donate to charities or to give their employees higher wages and customers safer products? Or are they obligated to maximize profits for their shareholders or stockholders?

At one extreme is the view of the late economist Milton Friedman. Friedman argues that in a "free enterprise, private-property system," corporate executives work for the "owners" of the company, and today these "owners" are the company's shareholders. As their employee, the executive has a "direct responsibility" to run the company "in accordance with their desires, which generally will be to make as much money as possible while conforming to the basic rules of the society, both those embodied in law and those embodied in ethical custom."[48]

On Friedman's view a company's *only* responsibility is to legally and ethically "make as much money as possible" for its owners, i.e., to maximize shareholder returns. We can call his view the "shareholder view" of corporate social responsibility. The main reason why Friedman holds this theory is that, in his view, shareholders own the company. Since the company is their, and only their, property, only they have the moral right to decide what it should be used for. These "owners" hire executives to run the business for them, so the executives have a moral obligation to do what the stockholders want, which, he claims, is to make them as much money as possible. Friedman does not say, however, that there are no limits to what executives can do to make stockholders as much money as possible. Executives, he explicitly says, must operate within the "rules of society" including both the rules of the "law" and the rules of "ethical custom."

According to Friedman's shareholder view of corporate social responsibility, a manager has no right to give company money to social causes when doing so will reduce shareholder's profits, because that money does not belong to the manager but to shareholders. Of course, managers can, and should, pay higher wages to employees, or provide better products for customers, or give money to local community groups or other causes, if doing so will make more profits for shareholders. For example, higher wages might make employees work harder, better products may increase customer sales, and giving to the local community may lead to lower taxes or better city services. But if using company resources to benefit employees, customers, or the community reduces the profits that would have gone to shareholders, then doing so is wrong because those resources belong to stockholders and should be used as they want them to be used, i.e., to make them more money. It is always wrong for managers to use company resources to help others at the expense of shareholders.

Although Friedman does not think managers should use company resources to benefit others at the expense of shareholders, he does think that companies ultimately provide great benefits for society. He argues that when a company tries to maximize stockholders' profits in a "free-enterprise" economy, competition will force it to use resources more efficiently than competitors, to pay employees a competitive wage, and to provide customers with products that are better, cheaper, and safer than those of competitors. So when managers aim at maximizing profits for stockholders in competitive markets, the companies they run will end up benefiting society.

Friedman has had many critics. Some object to his claim that the manager or executive is the employee of shareholders. Legally, these critics point out, the executive is the employee of the corporation and so the executive is legally required to serve the interests of the corporation—his true employer—not of its shareholders. Others have criticized Friedman's claim that stockholders are the "owners" of the corporation and that the corporation is their "property." Critics point out that shareholders only own stock and this gives them a few limited rights, such as the right to elect the board of directors, the right to vote on major company decisions, and the right to whatever remains after the corporation goes bankrupt and pays off its creditors. But shareholders do not have all the other rights that true owners would have and so they are not really owners of the corporation. A third objection criticizes his claim that the executive's core responsibility is to run the corporation as stockholders want it to be run. In reality the executive probably has no idea how stockholders want the company to be run, and legally, anyway, he is required to run the company in ways that serve many other interests (including employee interests and consumer interests) besides those of stockholders. Finally, some have argued against Friedman's view that by seeking to maximize shareholder returns, the corporation will best serve society. Sometimes competitive forces fail to steer companies in a socially beneficial way and, instead, lead them to act in a socially harmful manner. For example, a company might knowingly pollute a neighborhood with substance that is not yet illegal, in order to save the costs of reducing its pollution and thereby be more competitive.

A very different view of corporate social responsibility is what is now called "stakeholder theory." According to Edward Freeman and David Reed, the two scholars who pioneered this view, a **stakeholder** is "any identifiable group or individual who can affect the achievement of an organization's objectives or who is affected by the achievement of an organization's objectives."[49] In other words, a stakeholder is anyone the corporation can harm, benefit, or influence, as well as anyone that can harm, benefit, or influence the corporation. A stakeholder, in short, is anyone who has a "stake" in what the company does.

For example, General Motors impacts the lives of its customers when it decides how much safety it will build into its cars, it impacts employees when it sets salaries, it impacts the local community when it shuts down a plant, and it impacts its stockholders when it increases their dividends. On the other hand, government can impact General Motors through the laws and regulations it passes, creditors can impact it by raising their interest rates or calling back a loan, and suppliers can impact it by raising their prices or lowering the quality of the car parts they provide. General Motors' stakeholders, then, include customers, employees, local communities, stockholders, government, creditors, and suppliers. Of course, the influences between the company and its stakeholders can go both ways. For example, although General Motors influences its customers and employees, customers can also influence General Motors by refusing to buy its cars and employees can impact General Motors by going on strike. Other groups also are sometimes able to influence General Motors. For example, environmental activists or the media can impact General Motors by organizing demonstrations or by reporting on a safety defect of General Motors' cars. Thus, activist organizations, the media, and other interest groups can also become stakeholders of General Motors.

Quick Review 1.8

Corporate Social Responsibility Is a Business's Societal Obligations

- The shareholder view of Friedman says a manager's only responsibility is to legally and ethically make as much money as possible for shareholders.
- Stakeholder theory says managers should give all stakeholders a fair share of the benefits a business produces.
- Business ethics is both a part of corporate social responsibility and part of the justification for corporate social responsibility.

Unlike Friedman's shareholder view, which says the corporation should be run for the benefit *only of its shareholders*, "stakeholder theory" says it should be run for the benefit of *all stakeholders*. According to stakeholder theory, a manager should take all stakeholder interests into account when making decisions. Managers should try to "balance" the interests of stakeholders so each stakeholder gets a fair share of the benefits the corporation produces. The manager, then, has the responsibility of running the company in a way that will best serve the interests of all stakeholders.

Notice that stakeholder theory does not claim that managers should not try to make a profit; it does not even claim that managers should not try to maximize profits. The claims of stakeholder theory are about *who should get* the profits. Friedman's shareholder view says that the manager should try to maximize what goes to the stockholder, which means it should try to minimize what goes to other stakeholders (except, of course, when giving some stakeholders more would make even more profits for stockholders). Stakeholder theory, on the other hand, says that the manager should give stockholders a fair share of profits, but in a way that allows all other stakeholders to also get their fair share. This may mean, for example, investing in better working conditions for employees or in safer products for consumers, or in reducing pollution for the local community, even if this reduces the share of profits stockholders would get. Stakeholder theory, then, rejects Friedman's view that resources should not be used to benefit other stakeholders at the expense of shareholders.

Two main kinds of arguments support the "stakeholder" view of corporate social responsibility: "instrumental" arguments and "normative" arguments. Instrumental arguments claim that being responsive to all of its stakeholders is in the best interests of the corporation even though it may not be in the best interests of shareholders. The idea here is that if a company takes the interests of all its stakeholders into account, those stakeholders will be favorably disposed to do their part to support the company and its interests. Treating employees decently while paying them good salaries, for example, will make employees more loyal to the company, while treating them poorly may lead to shirking or even destructive behavior. Similarly, when a company is responsive to environmentalists or other activists, these groups are less likely to engage in activities that can damage the company's image or its reputation. Yet paying employees higher wages and investing in meeting environmentalists' demands may force a company to reduce shareholder dividends. In short, instrumental arguments for stakeholder theory claim that being responsive to all stakeholders is good for the business even though it may reduce the profits shareholders end up with.

Normative arguments for stakeholder theory claim that the company has a moral or ethical obligation to be responsive to all its stakeholders. One such argument, developed by Robert Phillips, is based on the "principle of fairness."[50] The principle of fairness says that if a group of people works together to provide some benefits at some cost to themselves, then anyone who takes advantage of those benefits has an obligation to contribute his or her share to the group. How does the principle of fairness support stakeholder theory? Stakeholder theory claims that a company's stakeholders work together to secure the conditions the company needs to operate successfully, and they do this at some cost to themselves. Communities contribute roads, a water system, a legal system, security, etc.; employees provide labor and expertise; investors provide capital, and so on. A company takes advantage of the benefits stakeholders provide at some cost to themselves, and so the company in turn has an obligation to contribute its part to the group. It does this by being responsive to the needs and interests of these various stakeholders, just as they each in their own way have been responsive to the company's needs.

Which of these two views is correct: stakeholder theory or shareholder theory? Today, many businesses accept stakeholder theory, and most of the fifty U.S. states have passed laws that recognize business' obligations to its many stakeholders even at the expense of stockholder interests. But readers will have to decide for themselves which theory makes the most sense and seems most reasonable. The two theories are critical to one's view of the important question: What is the purpose of business? Shareholder theory says the ultimate purpose of business is to serve the interests of stockholders and by doing so businesses in competitive markets will generally end up providing significant benefits to society. The stakeholder view says that the ultimate purpose of business is to serve the interests of all stakeholders and thereby the interests of all stakeholders are explicitly addressed even when competitive markets fail to secure their interests. We cannot discuss these important questions any farther. Our aim here is only to explain corporate social responsibility so that we can explain how corporate social responsibility is related to business ethics.

So how are business ethics and corporate social responsibility related? Being ethical, according to most scholars, is one of the obligations companies owe to society. In this respect, business ethics is a *part* of corporate social responsibility. In what has become a widely accepted description of the kinds of social responsibilities companies can have, for example, Archie Carroll writes: "The social responsibility of business encompasses the economic, legal, ethical, and discretionary expectations that society has of organizations ... "[51]Corporate social responsibility, then, is the larger more inclusive notion and business ethics is just one part of this larger notion. In addition to its ethical obligations, a company's corporate social responsibility includes those legal obligations, economic contributions, and those "discretionary" or philanthropic contributions society expects from companies. Notice that both the shareholder view and the stakeholder view can accept this way of defining what corporate social responsibility includes. For example, Friedman explicitly says that a company should live up to the ethical and legal expectations of society, that by pursuing shareholder profits it will make the greatest economic contribution to society, and that it should make whatever other discretionary contributions it needs to make so that society will enable it to operate profitably. Stakeholder theory says that companies should be responsive to all its stakeholders and that would include making the economic and discretionary contributions society expects, as well as behaving ethically and legally toward its stakeholders.

But the relation between ethics and corporate social responsibility is more complicated than we have so far suggested. As we have seen, the arguments underlying the various views of business's obligations to society—both the arguments that say businesses are *obligated* only to stockholders, and those that say they have *obligations* to all stakeholders—are ethical arguments. Friedman, for example, holds that owners have the *right* to say how the corporation should be run because they own the corporation and so managers have the *obligation* to do what stockholders want. And the normative argument for stakeholder theory, as we saw, says that *fairness* implies that business has *obligations* to all stakeholders. All of these concepts—rights, obligations, and fairness—are ethical concepts so ethics is not only part of a company's social responsibilities. Ethics also provides the basic normative reasons for corporate social responsibility. Paradoxically, then, ethics is one of business' social responsibilities, but business has these responsibilities to society because it is what ethics demands.

1.2 Ethical Issues in Business

Technology and Business Ethics

Technology consists of all those methods, processes, and tools that humans invent to manipulate and control their environment. To an extent never before realized in history, contemporary businesses and societies are being continuously and radically transformed by the rapid evolution of new technologies that raise new ethical issues for business.

This is not the first time that new technologies have had a revolutionary impact on business and society. Several thousand years ago, during what is sometimes called the *Agricultural Revolution*, humans developed the farming technologies that enabled them to stop relying on foraging and on the luck of the hunt and to develop instead, farming methods that provided a reasonably constant and consistent supply of food. The invention of irrigation, the harnessing of water and wind power, and the development of levers, wedges, hoists, and gears during this period eventually allowed humans to accumulate more goods than they could consume, and out of this surplus grew trade, commerce, and the first businesses. And with commerce came the first issues related to business ethics such as being fair in trading, setting a just price, and using true weights and measures.

In the eighteenth century, the technology of the Industrial Revolution again transformed Western society and business, primarily through the introduction of electromechanical machines powered by fossil fuels such as the steam engine, automobile, railroad, and cotton gin. Prior to the Industrial Revolution, most businesses were small organizations that operated in local markets and were managed by owners overseeing relatively few workers who assembled goods by hand. The Industrial Revolution brought with it new forms of machine production that enabled businesses to make massive quantities of goods to ship and sell in national markets. These changes, in turn, required large organizations to manage the enormous armies of people that had to be mobilized to process the output of these machines on long assembly lines in huge factories. The result was the large corporation that came to dominate our economies and that brought with it a host of new ethical issues, including the possibilities of exploiting the workers who labored at the new machines, manipulating the new financial markets that financed these large enterprises, and producing massive damage to the environment.

New technologies developed in the closing decades of the twentieth century and the opening years of the twenty-first century are again transforming society and business and creating the potential for new ethical problems. Foremost among these developments are the revolutions in biotechnology and in what is sometimes called **information technology**, including not only the use of powerful and compact computers, but also the development of the Internet, wireless communications, digitalization, and numerous other technologies that have enabled us to capture, manipulate, and move information in new and innovative ways. These technologies have spurred a number of changes, such as increasingly rapid globalization and the decreasing importance of distance; the rise of new ways to communicate and transfer any kind of media—movies, newspapers, music, books, mail—instantaneously from one place to

information technology The use of extremely powerful and compact computers, the Internet, wireless communications, digitalization, and numerous other technologies that have enabled us to capture, manipulate, and move information in new and creative ways.

another; the acceleration of change as product life cycles get shorter and revolutionary new products are invented and marketed ever more quickly; and the ability to create new life forms and new mechanisms whose benefits and risks are unpredictable. To cope with these rapid changes, business organizations have had to become smaller, flatter, and more nimble. Some have completely refashioned themselves as they have entered the world of e-commerce (buying and selling goods and services over the Internet) and left their brick-and-mortar operations behind by transforming themselves into Web-based entities that exist largely in **cyberspace**, a term used to denote the existence of information on an electronic network of linked computer systems. These developments have forced companies to deal with a host of intriguing new ethical issues.

cyberspace A term used to denote the existence of information on an electronic network of linked computer systems.

Almost all ethical issues raised by new technologies are related in one way or another to questions of risk: Are the risks of a new technology predictable? How large are the risks and are they reversible? Are the benefits worth the potential risks, and who should decide? Do those persons on whom the risks will fall know about the risk, and have they consented to bear these risks? Will they be justly compensated for their losses? Are the risks fairly distributed among the various parts of society, including poor and rich, young and old, future generations and present ones?

Quick Review 1.9

New Technologies Raise New Ethical Issues for Business

- The agricultural and industrial revolutions introduced new ethical issues.
- Information technology raises new ethical issues related to risk, privacy, and property rights.
- Nanotechnology and biotechnology raise new ethical issues related to risk and to the spread of dangerous products.

Many of the ethical issues new technologies have created—especially information technologies like the computer—are related to privacy. Computers enable us to collect detailed information on individuals on a scale that was never possible before (by tracking users on the Internet; gathering information on customers at cash registers; collecting information on credit card purchases; retrieving information from applications for licenses, bank accounts, credit cards, e-mail, monitoring employees working at computers, etc.). They have the power to quickly link this information to other databases (containing financial information, purchase histories, addresses, telephone numbers, driving records, arrest records, credit history, medical and academic records, memberships), and they can quickly sift, sort, or retrieve any part of this information for anyone who has access to the computer. Because these technologies enable others to gather such detailed and potentially injurious information about ourselves, many people have argued that they violate our right to privacy: the right to prohibit others from knowing things about us that are private.

Information technologies have also raised difficult ethical issues about the nature of the right to property when the property in question is information (such as computer software, computer code, or any other kind of data—text, numbers, pictures, sounds—that have been encoded into a computer file) or computer services (access to a computer or a computer system). Computerized information (such as a software program or digitized picture) can be copied perfectly countless times without in any way changing the original. What kind of property rights does one have when one owns one of these copies? What kind of property rights does the original creator of the information have and how does it differ from the property rights of someone who buys a copy? Is it wrong for me to make a copy without the permission of the original creator when doing so in no way changes the original? What, if any, harms will society or individuals suffer if people are allowed to copy any kind of computerized information at will? Will people stop creating information? For example, will they stop writing software and stop producing music? What kind of property rights does one have over computer systems? Is it wrong to use my company's computer system for personal business, such as to send personal e-mail or to log onto web sites that have nothing to do with my work? Is it wrong for me to electronically break into another organization's computer system if I do not change anything on the system but merely "look around"?

nanotechnology A new field that encompasses the development of tiny artificial structures only nanometers (billionths of a meter) in size.

Computers have also aided in the development of **nanotechnology**, a new field that encompasses the development of tiny artificial structures only nanometers (billionths of a meter) in size. Futurists have predicted that nanotechnology will enable us to build tiny structures that can assemble themselves into tiny computers or serve as diagnostic sensors capable of traveling through the bloodstream. But critics have raised questions about the potential harms posed by the release of nanoparticles into the environment. Greenpeace International, an environmental group, has suggested that nanoparticles could be harmful if accidentally inhaled by humans (carbon nanotubes, for example, have caused cancer in rats when inhaled) or if they carried toxic ingredients. In light of the potential risks, should businesses refrain from commercializing nanotechnology products?

Biotechnology has created yet another host of difficult ethical issues. **Genetic engineering** refers to a large variety of new techniques that let us change the genes in the cells of humans, animals, and plants. Genes, which are composed of deoxyribonucleic acid (DNA), contain the blueprints that determine what characteristics an organism will have. Through recombinant DNA technology, for example, the genes from one species can be removed and inserted into the genes of another species to create a new kind of organism with the combined characteristics of both species. Businesses have used genetic engineering to create and market new varieties of vegetables, grains, sheep, cows, rabbits, bacteria, viruses, and numerous other organisms. Bacteria have been engineered to consume oil spills and detoxify waste, wheat has been engineered to be resistant to disease, grass has been engineered to be immune to herbicides, and a French laboratory is said to have inserted the fluorescent genes from a jellyfish into a rabbit embryo that was born glowing in the dark just like the jellyfish. Is this kind of technology ethical? Is it wrong for a business to change and manipulate life in this way? When a company creates a new organism through genetic engineering, should it be able to patent the new organism so that it in effect *owns* this new form of life? Often the consequences of releasing genetically modified organisms into the world cannot be predicted. Engineered animals may drive out natural species, and engineered plants may poison wild organisms. The pollen of a species of corn that had been engineered to kill certain pests, for example, was later found to also be killing off certain butterflies. Is it ethical for businesses to market and distribute such engineered organisms throughout the world when the consequences are so unpredictable?

genetic engineering A large variety of new techniques that allows change in the genes of the cells of humans, animals, and plants.

International Issues in Business Ethics We have so far discussed some of the main issues with which business ethics has had to deal during human history. But the issues we have talked about are the kinds of issues that for the most part, arise within the national borders of a single country. We will turn now to look at some of the business ethics issues that emerge in the international arena.

Globalization and Business Ethics Many of the most pressing issues in business ethics today are related to the phenomenon of globalization. **Globalization** refers to the way nations are becoming more connected so that goods, services, capital, knowledge, and cultural artifacts move across national borders at an increasing rate. Of course, for centuries people have moved and traded goods across national boundaries. Merchants have been carrying goods over the trading routes of Europe, Asia, and the Americas since our recorded history began. But the sheer volume of goods that are being moved and traded across national boundaries has grown almost exponentially since World War II, and it has transformed the face of our world. Globalization has resulted in a phenomenon that is familiar to anyone who travels outside their country: The same products, music, foods, clothes, inventions, books, magazines, movies, brand names, stores, cars, and companies that we are familiar with at home are available and enjoyed everywhere in the world. McDonald's hamburgers and Kentucky Fried Chicken can be eaten on the sidewalks of Moscow, London, Beijing, Paris,

globalization The worldwide process by which the economic and social systems of nations have become connected facilitating between them the flow of goods, money, culture, and people.

Tokyo, Jerusalem, or Bangkok. Great Britain's *Harry Potter* novels are read by children and adults in India, Japan, China, Italy, and Germany. People of every nation know the same bands, the same songs, the same singers, the same actors, and the same movies that entertain Americans.

Multinational corporations are at the heart of this process of globalization and are responsible for much of the enormous volume of international transactions that take place today. A **multinational corporation** is a company that has manufacturing, marketing, service, or administrative operations in many different nations. Multinationals make and market their products in whatever nations offer manufacturing advantages and attractive markets. They draw capital, raw materials, and human labor from wherever in the world they are cheap and available. Virtually all of the 500 largest U.S. industrial corporations today are multinationals. General Electric, for example, which was founded by Thomas Edison and is headquartered in New York, has operations in more than 100 countries around the world and gets almost half of its revenues from outside the United States. It has metallurgy plants in Prague; software operations in India; product design offices in Budapest, Tokyo, and Paris; and assembly operations in Mexico.

multinational corporation A company that maintains manufacturing, marketing, service, or administrative operations in several "host" countries.

Globalization has brought the world tremendous benefits. As multinationals like Nike, Motorola, General Electric, and Ford build factories and establish assembly operations in countries with low labor costs, they bring jobs, skills, income, and technology to regions of the world that were formerly underdeveloped, raising the standard of living in these areas and providing consumers everywhere with lower-priced goods. According to the World Bank, between 1981 and 2005—years during which globalization has been operating at top speed—the percentage of poor people in the developing world was cut in half, from 52 percent to 25 percent.[52] Thus, globalization has helped millions of people emerge from poverty in countries such as China, India, Bangladesh, Brazil, Mexico, and Viet Nam. Between 1981 and 2005 (the most recent year for which figures are available) the number of people living on less than $1.25 per day in developing nations declined by 500 million. As a group, in fact, the economies of developing nations grew at about 5 percent per capita while developed nations such as the United States grew by only 2 percent.

Globalization has also enabled nations to specialize in producing and exporting those goods and services that they can produce most efficiently, and then trade for what they do not make. India has specialized in software production; France and Italy in fashion and footwear design; Germany in chemical production; the United States in computer hardware design; Mexico in television assembly; and many developing regions such as Central America and Southeast Asia have specialized in apparel, shoe, and other low-skill assembly operations. Such specialization has increased the world's overall productivity, which in turn has made all participating nations better off than they would be if each nation tried to produce everything on its own.

Quick Review 1.10

Globalization Is

- To a large extent driven by multinationals
- Beneficial in that it has brought great benefits to developing countries including jobs, skills, income, technology, a decrease in poverty, specialization
- Blamed for many ills including rising inequality, cultural losses, a "race to the bottom," introduction of inappropriate technologies into developing countries.

But globalization has been blamed for inflicting significant harms on the world. Critics of globalization argue that while it has benefited developed nations that have high-value products to sell (such as high-tech products), many poorer nations that have only cheap agricultural products to trade have been left behind. Moreover, the World Bank reports, as globalization has spread, inequality has increased both between nations and within nations.[53] And globalizing multinationals have brought Western culture everywhere through movies, books, songs, games, toys, television shows, electronic gadgets, dances, fast foods, brands, art, magazines, and clothes, driving out distinctive local cultures and traditions that are in danger of diminishing or disappearing altogether. Instead of eating their own traditional foods, for example, people everywhere eat McDonalds' hamburgers and fries. Instead of enjoying traditional forms of ethnic dancing, people everywhere go to movie theaters to watch *Avatar*, *Harry Potter*, and *Batman*.

Globalization is also charged with paving the way for multinationals to have a kind of mobility that critics say has had adverse effects. Multinationals can now pull their operations out of one country and insert them into another that offers cheaper labor, less stringent laws, or lower taxes. This ability to move operations from nation to nation, critics claim, enables the multinational to play one country off against another. If a multinational does not like one nation's environmental, wage, or labor standards, for example, it can move or threaten to move to a country with lower standards. Critics claim this has created a "race to the bottom." As countries lower their standards to attract foreign companies, the result is a global decline in labor, environmental, and wage standards. Some companies that have established assembly operations in developing nations, for example, have introduced sweatshop working conditions and exploitive wages. Moreover, when companies move their operations from one country to another in search of cheaper labor, they close down factories in their home countries, leaving thousands of workers there without jobs.

Critics also claim that multinationals sometimes import technologies or products into developing nations that cannot yet deal with their risks. Some chemical companies—for example, Amvac Chemical Corporation, Bayer, and BASF—have been accused of marketing toxic pesticides in developing nations whose farm workers do not know about, and cannot protect themselves against, the problems those chemicals can inflict on their health. The advertising campaigns of certain food companies—such as Nestle, Mead Johnson, and Danone—persuade new mothers in poor nations to spend their meager food budgets on infant formula powder. Yet in developing nations that do not have sanitary water supplies, new mothers will mix the powdered infant formulas with unsanitary water which, according to the World Health Organization, leads annually to diarrhea and death for more than 1.5 million newborns. Tobacco companies—such as Philip Morris, British American Tobacco, and Imperial Tobacco—have heavily marketed their cigarettes in developing nations whose populations do not have a good understanding of the long-range health costs of smoking.

Globalization, then, is a "mixed bag." While it has brought tremendous economic benefits to many poor nations, it has done so at a price. And both the benefits and the costs of globalization are, to a large extent, due to the activities of multinationals.

Differences Among Nations Globalization has also forced companies to operate in nations whose laws, governments, practices, levels of development, and cultural understandings are sometimes much different from those with which the multinational's managers are familiar.[54] This creates significant dilemmas for their managers. For example, the laws that the managers of Dow Chemical Company are used to in the United States, are very different from the laws they find in Mexico and other host countries. Laws regulating workers' exposure to workplace toxins and other safety hazards are stringent in the United States, whereas they are vague, lax, or altogether lacking in Mexico. Consumer product safety and labeling laws, which require careful quality controls, rigorous product tests, and warnings of risk in the United States, are very different in Mexico, which allows lower levels of quality control, much less testing of products, and fewer warnings directed at consumers. The environmental pollution laws of the U.S. government are strict and set at very high levels, whereas those of Mexico are virtually nonexistent or unenforced.

Quick Review 1.11

Differences Among Nations

- Include differences in laws, governments, practices, levels of development, cultural understandings
- Raise the question whether managers in foreign countries should follow local standards or their home standards.

Even entire governments can be completely different from the kind of government managers are accustomed to in industrialized nations. Although the U.S. government has its shortcomings, it is responsive to the needs of its citizens for instance. The same cannot be said for the governments of many other nations. Some governments are so corrupt that their legitimacy is questionable. The former government of

Haiti, for example, was notoriously corrupt and consistently promoted the interests and wealth of a small group of government elites at the expense of the needs of the general population.

Managers also often find themselves in countries that are very undeveloped compared to their home country.[55] Industrialized countries have relatively high levels of technological, social, and economic resources available, whereas the resources of poorer countries can be quite undeveloped. Technological sophistication, unions, financial markets, unemployment insurance, social security, and public education are widespread in more developed nations, but are lacking in some undeveloped countries. The lack of these things mean that managerial actions can affect people in undeveloped countries very differently from the way those same actions affect people in developed countries. Worker lay-offs in developing nations that do not provide unemployment insurance, for example, inflict greater pains on workers there than in the United States, which provides unemployment insurance (at least for a period of time). A warning fixed on a product label may be suitable when it is sold to educated consumers in Japan, but it may be inadequate when the same product is sold to illiterate consumers in a developing nation.

Moreover, the cultural views of some nations that managers of multinationals enter can be so different from their own that they misinterpret or misunderstand many of the behaviors they encounter there. In the United States, for example, it is considered to be a lie for a company to provide the government with income statements that materially understate the company's actual earnings. In some periods of Italy's history, however, it was accepted as a matter of course that all businesses would understate their annual earnings by one-third when they reported their taxes to the government. Knowing this, the government would automatically inflate each company's income statements by one-third and levy taxes on this more accurate estimate, which companies willingly paid. Thus, because of a cultural practice that was understood both by the business community and the government, Italian companies did not actually lie to their government when they understated their income: What looked like a lie to an outsider was, in the cultural context, a clearly understood signal of a company's true income.

When in a foreign country whose laws, government, level of development, and culture are significantly different from what the manager is used to, what should the manager of a multinational do? Some scholars have suggested that when operating in less developed countries, managers from developed nations should try to stick to the higher standards that are typical in their home countries.[56] But this suggestion ignores the real possibility that introducing practices that have evolved in a developed country may do more harm than good in a less developed nation. For example, if an American company operating in Mexico pays local workers U.S. wages, it may draw all the skilled workers away from local Mexican companies that cannot afford to pay the same high salaries. Other scholars have gone to the opposite extreme and argued that multinationals should always follow local practices and laws. But going along with a local practice or law may be worse than trying to operate by the higher standards of a developed country. The lower environmental standards of Mexico, for example, may permit pollution levels that seriously harm the health of local residents. Moreover, the governments of many countries, as we have noted, are corrupt and their laws serve the interests of ruling elites and not the public interest.

It is clear, then, that both a blanket rule to always go along with local practices, as well as one that always tries to adhere to the higher standards of developed nations, are both inadequate. Instead, managers who want to operate ethically in foreign countries must judge each case as it comes along. When judging the ethics of a particular policy, practice, or action in a foreign country, they must take into account the nature of the country's laws, how corrupt and how representative its government is, what the country's level of technological, social and economic development is, and what cultural understandings affect the meaning of the policy, practice, or action that is being judged. In some cases, going along with local practices may be what is right, while in other cases it may be better to adopt the standards found in more developed nations. And in some cases, managers may have to choose between staying in a country and going along with a local practice that is clearly and seriously evil, or doing what is right and leaving the country.

Business and Ethical Relativism There are certain cultural differences that create a special problem for managers. Managers of multinationals often find it hard to know what to do when they encounter *moral* standards that are different from the ones they personally hold and that are accepted in their home country. Nepotism and sexism, although condemned as morally wrong in the United States, for example, are accepted as a matter of course in some foreign business environments. The people of certain Arab societies hold that business bribery is morally acceptable, although Americans believe that it is immoral. What should a manager do when a government official in such a society asks for a bribe to perform some routine duty the official is supposed to provide for nothing? Or when the hiring department of a U.S. factory in Thailand seems to hire only relatives of those already working for the factory? Or when a group of South American managers refuse to accept a woman as a manager because they feel that women cannot be good managers?

The fact that different cultures have different moral standards, leads many people to adopt the theory of ethical relativism. **Ethical relativism** is the theory that there are no ethical standards that are true absolutely, i.e., that the truth of all ethical standards depends on (is relative to) what a particular culture accepts. Consequently, there are no moral standards that should be used to evaluate the ethics of everyone's actions no matter what culture they belong to. Instead, the ethical relativist holds that a person's action is morally right if it accords with the ethical standards accepted in that person's culture, and is wrong if it violates the ethical standards accepted in that person's culture. To put it another way: Ethical relativism is the view that, because different societies have different moral beliefs, there is no rational way of determining whether a person's action is morally right (or wrong) other than by asking whether the members of the person's own society believe it is morally right (or wrong).

ethical or moral relativism The theory that there are no ethical standards that are absolutely true and that apply or should be applied to the companies and people of all societies.

The ethical relativist will say, for example, that it is wrong for a U.S. manager to engage in nepotism in the United States because everyone there believes that it is wrong, but it is not wrong for a person in Thailand, for example, to engage in nepotism there because people there do not see it as wrong. The ethical relativist would advise the manager of a multinational who works in a society whose moral standards are different from her own, that she should follow the moral standards prevalent in the society in which she works. Since moral standards differ and since there are no absolute standards of right and wrong, the best a manager can do is follow the old adage, "When in Rome, do as the Romans do." But is ethical relativism a reasonable view to hold?

The ethical relativist is clearly right to claim that there are numerous practices that are judged immoral by people in one society that people of other societies believe are morally acceptable. Some examples of practices societies disagree about include polygamy, abortion, infanticide, slavery, bribery, homosexuality, racial and sexual discrimination, genocide, patricide, and the torture of animals. Yet critics of ethical relativism have pointed out that it does not follow that there are *no* moral standards which are binding on people everywhere. Although societies disagree about some moral standards, they agree on others. Critics of ethical relativism have argued, in fact, that there are certain basic moral standards that the members of any society must accept if that society is to survive and if its members are to interact with each other effectively.[57] Thus, all societies have norms against injuring or killing their own members, norms about using language truthfully among themselves, and norms against taking the goods that belong to other members of society. Moreover, anthropologists have found numerous moral values and norms that are universal, i.e., that all known human groups recognize. Among these universals are: the appropriateness of reciprocity, the appropriateness of cooperation, the prohibition of incest, the prohibition of rape, empathy, friendship, the difference between right and wrong, fairness, the requirement to compensate injuries, the goodness of courage, the requirement that parents care for their children, restrictions on some forms of violence, the prohibition of murder, the prohibition against breaking promises, the appropriateness of feeling guilt and shame for wrongdoing, the appropriateness of having pride for one's achievements, and the requirement that actions one could control should be treated differently from those one could not control.

In addition, many apparent moral differences among societies turn out on closer examination to mask deeper underlying similarities. For example, anthropologists tell us that in some Alaskan Inuit societies it was morally acceptable for families to abandon their aged to die outdoors during times of hardship, whereas other Indian societies have felt that abandoning someone to freeze to death outdoors is akin to murder. Yet on closer examination, it can turn out that underlying this difference between Inuit society and other Indian societies is the same moral standard: the moral duty of ensuring the long-term survival of one's family. In their harsh environment, Inuit people may have had no way of ensuring the family's survival when food supplies ran short other than by abandoning their aged. Other Indian societies have believed that family survival required protecting the elders who carried within them the knowledge and experience the family needed. The differences between Inuits and other Indians is not due to a real difference in values, but is due, rather, to the fact that one and the same value can lead to two different moral judgments when the value is applied in two very different situations.

Quick Review 1.12

Objections to Ethical Relativism

- Some moral standards are found in all societies.
- Moral differences do not logically imply relativism.
- Relativism has incoherent consequences.
- Relativism privileges whatever moral standards are widely accepted in a society.

Other critics of ethical relativism have pointed out that when people have different moral beliefs about some issue, it does not follow that there is no absolute truth about that issue nor that all beliefs about it are equally acceptable. All that follows when two people or two groups have different beliefs is that at least one of them is wrong. For example, the late philosopher James Rachels points out:

> The fact that different societies have different moral codes proves nothing. There is also disagreement from society to society about scientific matters: in some cultures it is believed that the earth is flat, and that disease is caused by evil spirits. We do not on that account conclude that there is no truth in geography or in medicine. Instead, we conclude that in some cultures people are better informed than in others. Similarly, disagreement in ethics might signal nothing more than that some people are less enlightened than others. At the very least, the fact of disagreement does not, by itself, entail that truth does not exist. Why should we assume that, if ethical truth exists, everyone must know it?[58]

Perhaps the most important criticism of ethical relativism is that it has incoherent consequences. If ethical relativism were true, opponents claim, then it would not make sense to criticize the practices of other societies so long as their practices conformed to their own standards. For example, we could not say that child slavery, as practiced in many societies around the world, is wrong, nor that the discrimination

A Traditional Business

In over 28 countries, mostly North African nations, female circumcision—or "female genital mutilation" as its critics call it—is generally accepted. Female circumcision is normally performed when a girl is between 7 and 12 years old. It involves cutting away most of the girl's external genitalia including the clitoris and labia. In most countries, the procedure is done by a female "practitioner" who uses a small knife or razor blade but no anesthesia. A young girl will often resist so several women must hold her down while the practitioner works. The women who perform circumcisions charge for their services and see their work as a business. It is estimated that in countries where the practice is widely accepted, the annual fees collected by all the businesses that provide circumcision services total tens of millions of dollars.

Mothers in these countries feel they must have their daughters circumcised because otherwise no "good" man will marry them. Many believe that circumcision controls a woman's sexual desires, and cleanses her spiritually so that others can eat what she cooks. Although the practice is not mentioned in the Koran, many North African Muslims believe that female circumcision is required by certain sayings they attribute to Mohammad, the founder of Islam. However, Muslim scholars dispute both the authenticity and the interpretation of these sayings.

Many Americans and Europeans feel strongly that female genital mutilation is an immoral assault on a helpless and unwilling girl, an assault that provides her no medical benefit, risks serious infection, and permanently deprives her of the ability to feel sexual pleasure. They have pressured foreign governments to outlaw the practice and to crack down on the women who make a business of it because they are violating the human rights of thousands of girls.

Practitioners claim that Westerners who want to prohibit female circumcision are trying to impose their own morality on others. A Somali practitioner said: "This is a great offence and a great interference with our lives and our lifestyle. For too long Europeans have come into our countries and told us how to live our lives and how to behave and we believe that is totally unacceptable. We will not allow foreigners to tell us how to behave or put our businesses at risk any longer. In order for our daughters to be free they must have this procedure. It is their right as women and our obligation as adults to make them into the best young women we can. Circumcision is a fundamental part of becoming a young woman and we will not deny them that because of some misplaced sense of morality from foreigners."

Phillip Waites, a doctor and medical analyst for a news service noted, "The core issue here is whether or not Europeans have the right to step into another country and demand that they change their traditions and culture." Remarking on the many practitioners for whom female circumcision is a business, he said: "There aren't a whole lot of jobs in Somalia. There really isn't a whole lot of anything in Somalia frankly, and these women have a specialty that not only garners them a good living but also gives them a certain status in the country that they might not otherwise have."

1. Is the business of providing female circumcision services morally wrong? Why? If a practitioner asks for a small business loan from a Western "micro-finance lender" like *www.Kiva.org* would it be wrong for the lender to refuse? Would it be wrong for the lender to agree? Explain.
2. Is it wrong for Westerners to pressure North African governments to prevent practitioners from doing female circumcisions?
3. Does this case support ethical relativism or does it suggest that there are certain things that are wrong no matter what, or neither of these positions?

Sources: William Ashford, "Genital Mutilators Protest Scandinavian Efforts to Crack Down on Trade," September 27, 2009 accessed August 9, 2010 at *http://scrapetv.com/News/News%20Pages/Business/pages-3/Genital-mutilators-protest-Scandanavian-efforts-to-crack-down-on-trade-Scrape-TV-The-World-on-your-side.html;* Amit R. Paley, "For Kurdish Girls, A Painful Ancient Ritual," *The Washington Post,* December 29, 2008.

practiced in the society of apartheid South Africa in the twentieth century was unjust, nor that it was immoral for the Germans to kill Jews in the Nazi society of the 1930s. For, in each of these societies, people were just doing what the standards of their society said they should do.[59]

Critics of ethical relativism also argue that if ethical relativism were correct, then it would make no sense—in fact it would be morally wrong—to criticize any of the moral standards or practices accepted by our own society. If our society accepts that a certain practice—such as slavery—is morally right, then as members of this society, we too must accept that practice as morally right, at least according to ethical relativism. For example, ethical relativism implies that it was wrong for Southern abolitionists to object to slavery since slavery was accepted in Southern society before the Civil War. According to critics, then, the theory of ethical relativism implies that whatever the majority in one's society believes about morality is automatically correct and so their beliefs cannot be criticized.

The fundamental problem with ethical relativism, critics allege, is that it holds that the moral standards of a society are the only standards by which actions in that society can be judged. The theory gives the moral standards of each society a privileged place that is above all criticism by members of that society or by anyone else: For the relativist, a society's moral standards cannot be mistaken. Clearly, opponents say, this implication of ethical relativism indicates that the theory is wrong.; we all know that at least some of the moral standards of our own society as well as those of other societies may be mistaken.

The theory of ethical relativism, then, does not seem to be correct. But even if the theory of ethical relativism is ultimately rejected, this does not mean that it has nothing to teach us. The ethical relativist correctly reminds us that different societies have different moral beliefs and that we should not simply dismiss the moral beliefs of other cultures when they do not match our own. However, ethical relativism seems to be mistaken in its basic claim that all moral beliefs are equally acceptable and that the only criteria of right and wrong are the moral standards prevalent in a given society. And if ethical relativism is wrong, then there are some moral standards that should be applied to the behaviors of everyone, regardless of what society they live in. In the next chapter, we will explore what kind of standards these might be.

The upshot of our discussion is that there are two kinds of moral standards: those that differ from one society to another, and those that should be applied in all societies. One way of thinking about these two kinds of moral standards is to adopt a framework called "Integrative Social Contracts Theory" or ISCT for short.[60] According to the ISCT framework, there are two kinds of moral standards: (1) Hypernorms, which consist of those moral standards that should be applied to people in all societies, and (2) Microsocial norms, which are those norms that differ from one community to another and that should be applied to people only if their community accepts those particular norms.

Quick Review 1.13

Integrative Social Contracts Theory Indicates that

- Hypernorms should apply to people in all societies
- Microsocial norms apply only in specific societies and differ from one society to another.

ISCT holds that it is useful to think of hypernorms as part of a social contract that all people have accepted, and to think of microsocial norms as part of a social contract that the members of a specific community have accepted. Examples of some hypernorms might be human rights principles and principles of justice that apply to all people in all communities. On the other hand, one example of a microsocial norm is the norm that allows a father and a son to take on a common wife, a moral norm that is accepted in Tibet but rejected in all other communities. Another microsocial norm is the norm that when traveling a married woman must be accompanied by her husband or a male relative, a norm that is accepted in Saudi Arabia and several other Arab countries but not in the United States nor in Europe.

ISCT claims that hypernorms take priority over microsocial norms. That is, microsocial norms must not contradict hypernorms. If a microsocial norm violates a hypernorm, then it is unethical and should be rejected. Nevertheless, ISCT assumes that hypernorms must allow every community to have some "moral free space." Moral free space consists of the range of norms that a community is free to accept because they do not violate any hypernorms.

The people of a community, according to ISCT, ought to follow the microsocial norms that are accepted in their community. However, the members of a community must be free to leave their community if they strongly disagree with their community's microsocial norms. Moreover, according to ISCT, when a manager is operating in a foreign community, the manager should follow the microsocial norms of that community, so long as they do not violate any hypernorms. If the microsocial norms of a community violate a hypernorm, then the manager should not follow that microsocial norm.

Many critics reject the ISCT view that hypernorms should be thought of as part of a social contract that all reasonable people have accepted, while relativists reject the very idea that there are any absolute universal hypernorms. Nevertheless, the distinction between hypernorms and microsocial norms is a useful one. Assuming that there are hypernorms, the distinction provides a useful way to think about the interplay between absolute moral norms that should apply to all people everywhere, and local norms that differ from one society to another. It provides a useful framework for understanding how to deal with moral differences. We have argued that there are absolute moral norms that should apply everywhere; what these might be is a question that we will discuss in the next chapter.

1.3 Moral Reasoning

We have said that ethics is the study of morality and that a person begins to do ethics when he or she turns to look at the moral standards learned from family, church, friends, and society and begins asking whether these standards are reasonable or unreasonable and what these standards imply for the situations and issues we face. In this section, we examine more closely this process of examining one's moral standards and the reasoning process by which we apply our standards to the situations and issues we face. We begin by describing how a person's ability to use and critically evaluate moral standards develops in the course of a person's life, and then we describe some of the reasoning processes through which these moral standards are evaluated and used, and some of the ways they can go wrong.

Moral Development

Many people assume that our values are formed during childhood and do not change after that. In fact, a great deal of psychological research, as well as our own personal experience, demonstrates that as we mature, we change our values in deep ways. Just as people's physical, emotional, and cognitive abilities develop as they age, so also their ability to deal with moral issues develops as they move through their lives. In fact, just as there are identifiable stages of growth in physical development, so the ability to make reasoned moral judgments also develops in identifiable stages. As children, we are simply told what is right and what is wrong, and we obey so as to avoid punishment. As we mature into adolescence, these conventional moral standards are gradually internalized, and we start trying to live up to the expectations of family, friends, and surrounding society. Finally, as adults we learn to be critical about the conventional moral standards bequeathed to us by our families, peers, culture, or religion. We start to evaluate these moral standards and to revise them where we think they are inadequate, inconsistent, or unreasonable. We begin, in short, to do ethics and to develop moral principles that we feel are better and more reasonable than what we accepted earlier.

There is a good deal of psychological research that shows people's moral views develop more or less in this manner. The psychologist Lawrence Kohlberg, for example, who pioneered research in this field, concluded on the basis of over 20 years of research that there is a sequence of six identifiable stages in the development of a person's ability to deal with moral issues.[61] Kohlberg grouped these stages of moral development into three levels, each containing two stages. At each level, the second stage is the more advanced and organized form of the general perspective of that level. The sequence of the six stages can be summarized as follows.

Level One: Preconventional Stages[62]

At these first two stages, the child can apply the labels good, bad, right, and wrong. But good and bad, and right and wrong are seen in terms of the pleasant or painful consequences of actions or what authority figures demand. If you were to ask a 4- or 5-year-old child, for example, whether stealing is wrong, he will say it is. But when you ask the child *why* it's wrong, his answer will be something like, "Because Mommy puts me in time-out if I steal." The child at this level can see situations mainly from his own point of view and so his primary motivations are self-centered.

Stage One: Punishment and Obedience Orientation At this stage, the demands of authority figures or the pleasant or painful consequences of an act define right and wrong. The child's reason for doing the right thing is to avoid punishment or defer to the power of authorities. There's little awareness that others have needs and desires like one's own.

Stage Two: Instrumental and Relative Orientation At this stage, right actions become those through which the child satisfies his own needs. The child is now aware that others have needs and desires like he does and uses this knowledge to get what he wants. The child behaves in the right way toward others, so others later will do the same toward him.

Level Two: Conventional Stages

At these next two stages, the older child or younger adolescent sees moral right and wrong in terms of living up to the conventional norms of his or her family, peer group, or society. The young person at these stages is loyal to these groups and their norms. He sees right or wrong in terms of "what my friends think," "what my family taught me," "what we Americans believe," or even "what the law says." The person has the ability to take the point of view of other similar people in his groups.

Stage Three: Interpersonal Concordance Orientation Good behavior at this early conventional stage is living up to the expectations of those for whom the person feels loyalty, affection, and trust, such as family and friends. Right action is conforming to what's expected in one's role as a good son, good daughter, good friend, and so on. At this stage, the young person wants to be liked and thought well of.

Stage Four: Law and Order Orientation Right and wrong at this more mature conventional stage are based on loyalty to one's nation or society. The laws and norms of society should be followed so society will continue to function well. The person can see other people as parts of a larger social system that defines individual roles and obligations, and he can distinguish these obligations from what his personal relationships require.

Quick Review 1.14

Kohlberg's Three Levels of Moral Development

- Preconventional (punishment and obedience; instrumental and relative)
- Conventional (interpersonal concordance; law and order)
- Postconventional (social contract; universal principles).

Level Three: Postconventional Stages

At these next two stages, the person no longer simply accepts the values and norms of her group. Instead, the person tries to see right and wrong from an impartial point of view that takes everyone's interests into account. The person can question the laws and values of her society and judge them in terms of moral principles that she believes can be justified to any reasonable person. When an adult at this stage is asked why something is right or wrong, the person can respond in terms of what's "fair for everyone" or in terms of "justice," or "human rights," or "society's wellbeing."

Stage Five: Social Contract Orientation At this first postconventional stage, the person becomes aware that people have conflicting moral views, but believes there are fair ways of reaching consensus about them. The person believes that all moral values and moral norms are relative and that, apart from a democratic consensus, all moral views should be tolerated.

Stage Six: Universal Moral Principles Orientation At this second postconventional stage, right action comes to be defined in terms of moral principles chosen because of their reasonableness, universality, and consistency. These are general moral principles that deal, for example, with justice, social welfare, human rights, respect for human dignity, or treating people as ends in themselves. The person sees these principles as the criteria for evaluating all socially accepted norms and values.

Kohlberg's theory is useful because it helps us understand how our moral capacities develop and reveals how we may mature in our understanding of our own moral standards. Research by Kohlberg and others has shown that, although people generally progress through the stages in the same sequence, not everyone progresses through all the stages. Kohlberg found that many people remain stuck at one of the early stages throughout their lives. Those who stay at the preconventional level continue to see right and wrong in the egocentric terms of avoiding punishment and doing what powerful authority figures say. Those who reach the conventional level, but never get past it continue defining right and wrong in terms of the conventional norms and expectations of their social groups or of their nation and its laws. And those who reach the postconventional level and take a rational and critical look at the conventional moral standards they have been raised to hold will come to define right and wrong in terms of moral principles they have chosen because they are reasonable.

It is important to see that Kohlberg believes that the moral reasoning of people at the later stages of moral development is better than the reasoning of those at earlier stages. First, he claims, people at the later stages have the ability to see things from a wider and fuller perspective than those at earlier stages. The person at the preconventional level can see situations only from the person's own egocentric point of view; the person at the conventional level can see situations only from the familiar viewpoints of people in the person's own social groups; and the person at the postconventional point of view has the ability to look at situations from a universal perspective that tries to take everyone into account. Second, people at the later stages have better ways of justifying their decisions to others than those at earlier stages. The person at the preconventional level can justify decisions only in terms of how the person's own interests will be affected, and therefore justifications are ultimately persuasive only to the person. The person at the conventional level can justify decisions in terms of the norms of the group to which the person belongs, and so justifications are ultimately persuasive only to members of the person's group. Finally, the person at the postconventional level can justify her choices on the basis of moral principles that are impartial and reasonable and that therefore any reasonable person can accept.

Kohlberg's theory has, however, been subjected to a number of criticisms.[63] First, Kohlberg has been criticized for claiming that the higher stages are morally preferable to the lower stages. This criticism is surely right. Although the higher Kohlberg levels incorporate broader perspectives and more widely acceptable justifications, it does not follow that these perspectives are *morally* better than the lower ones. To establish that the higher stages are *morally* better will require more argument than Kohlberg provides. In later chapters, we will see what kind of reasons can be given for the view that the moral principles that define the later Kohlberg stages are morally preferable to the criteria used in the preconventional and conventional stages.

A second significant criticism of Kohlberg is one that arises from the work of Carol Gilligan, a psychologist. She argues that, although Kohlberg's theory correctly identifies the stages through which men pass as they develop, it fails to adequately trace out how women's morality develops.[64] Because most of Kohlberg's subjects were male, Gilligan has argued, his theory failed to take into account how women think about morality.

Gilligan claimed that there are , "male" and "female" approaches to morality. Males, she argued, tend to deal with moral issues in terms of impersonal, impartial, and abstract moral principles—exactly the kind of approach that Kohlberg says is characteristic of postconventional thinking. However, Gilligan claimed, there is a second, "female," approach to moral issues that Kohlberg's theory does not take into account. Females, Gilligan claimed, tend to see themselves as part of a "web" of relationships with family and friends. When females encounter moral issues, they are concerned with nurturing these relationships, avoiding hurt to others in these relationships, and caring for their well-being. For women, morality is primarily a matter of "caring" and "being responsible" for those with whom we have personal relationships. Morality is not a matter of following impartial principles. Gilligan claimed that the female approach to morality develops through stages that are different from those Kohlberg described. Moral development for women is marked by progress toward better ways of caring and being responsible for oneself and others with whom we are in relationship. In her theory, the earliest or preconventional level of moral development for women is one marked by caring only for oneself. Women move to a second or conventional level when they internalize conventional norms about caring for others and in doing so come to neglect themselves. As women move to the postconventional or most mature level, they become critical of the conventional norms they had earlier accepted, and they come to achieve a balance between caring for others and caring for oneself.

Quick Review 1.15

Gilligan's Theory of "Female" Moral Development

- For women morality is primarily a matter of caring and responsibility.
- Moral development for women is progress toward better ways of caring and being responsible.
- Women move from a conventional stage of caring only for oneself, to a conventional stage of caring for others to the neglect of oneself, to a postconventional stage of achieving a balance between caring for others and caring for oneself.

Is Gilligan right? Although additional research has shown that male and female moral development does not differ in the ways that Gilligan originally suggested, that same research has confirmed the claim that Gilligan has identified a way of thinking about moral issues that is different from the way that Kohlberg emphasizes.[65] Moral issues can be dealt with from a perspective of impartial moral principles or from a perspective of caring for persons and relationships, and these two perspectives are distinct. However, women as well as men sometimes approach moral issues from the perspective of impartial moral principles, and men as well as women sometimes approach moral issues from the perspective of caring for persons and relationships.[66] Although research on the "care perspective" that Gilligan described is still ongoing, it is clearly an important moral perspective that both men and women should take into account. We look more carefully at this care perspective in the next chapter, where we will assess its relevance to business ethics.

For our purposes, it is important to notice that both Kohlberg and Gilligan agree that there are stages of growth in our moral development. Both also agree that moral development moves from a preconventional stage focused on the self, through a conventional stage in which we uncritically accept the conventional moral standards of society around us, and on to a mature stage in which we learn to critically and reflectively examine how reasonable the conventional moral standards we earlier accepted are, and to develop more adequate standards of our own, both standards of caring as well as standards of impartiality.

We said earlier that you begin to do ethics when you begin to examine critically the moral standards you have accepted from family, friends, and society and ask whether these standards are reasonable or unreasonable. In terms of the stages of moral development that Kohlberg and Gilligan proposed, ethics begins when you move from a simple acceptance of the conventional moral standards that we absorb from society and try to critically and reflectively develop standards based on more adequate reasons and capable of dealing with a wider range of moral issues in a more adequate manner. The study of ethics is the process of developing our ability to deal with moral issues—a process that should enable you to acquire the more reflective understanding of "right" and "wrong" that characterizes the later postconventional stages of moral development. One of the central aims of the study of ethics is the stimulation of this moral development.

This is an important point—one that should not be lost on the reader. The text and cases that follow are designed to be read and discussed with others—students, teachers, friends—to stimulate in ourselves the kind of moral development that we have been discussing. Engaged interaction and discussion of moral issues with the people around us develops our ability to move beyond a simple acceptance of the moral standards we absorb from family, peers, nation, or culture. By discussing, criticizing, and reasoning about the moral judgments that you and others make, you acquire habits of thinking and reasoning that you can use to decide for yourself the moral principles that you feel are reasonable because you have tested them in the heat of discussions with others.

The moral principles that are produced by the kind of analysis and reflection that are characteristic of the latter stages of moral development in both Kohlberg and Gilligan, then, are "better" but not because they come at a later stage. One set of moral principles is "better" than another only when it has been carefully examined and found to be supported by better and stronger reasons—a process that is enhanced through discussions with, and challenges from, other people. The moral principles that appear in the later stages of moral development, then, are better because and to the extent, that they are the product of the kind of reasoned examination and discussion with others that tends to emerge as people improve their moral reasoning skills, grow in their understanding and knowledge of human life, and interact with others to develop a firmer and more mature moral perspective.

Kohlberg's (and Gilligan's) theory of moral development has been extended by psychologists who have looked at how moral development is related to self-identity and to the motivation to be moral. William Damon, for example, found that "morality does not become a dominant characteristic of the self until ... middle adolescence."[67] This means that until middle adolescence, we tend not to see morality as an important part of who we really are. This is significant because he also found that the more morality becomes part of who we are, the stronger our motivation to do what is morally right. In fact, there are "exemplary people" who have so united "self and morality" that when they do what is morally right, "rather than denying the self, they define it with a moral center ... [and so do not see] their moral choices as an exercise in self-sacrifice."[68] The psychologist Augusto Blasi has argued that part of the process of making morality part of who we feel we really are, is asking ourselves not just "What kind of person do I want to be?" but also "What kind of person should one ... be?"[69] Blasi points out that people have "reflexive desires, namely desires about their own desires," so another way of asking what kind of person we want to be

Quick Review 1.16

Research on Moral Identity Suggests

- Morality is not an important part of the self until middle adolescence
- The more morality becomes part of the self, the stronger the motivation to be moral
- Judgments of right and wrong depend in part on the kind of person we think the self is, i.e., on the virtues we think are part of our self.

ON THE EDGE

WorldCom's Whistleblower

In March 2002, when WorldCom was struggling to coordinate and integrate the complex mess created by the 65 companies it had acquired, WorldCom's then highly respected chief financial officer, Scott Sullivan, moved $400 million from a reserve account and recorded it as "income" in the company's public financial reports. Alerted to this, Cynthia Cooper, the perfectionist head of WorldCom's internal audit department, began to secretly examine the company's books at night. She soon discovered that Scott Sullivan (named a "best CFO" by *CFO Magazine* in 1998) and David Myers, WorldCom's controller, for years had publicly reported billions of dollars as "capital expenditures" when they were really operating costs, ignored uncollectible receivables, and reported as "income" what were really reserve funds, and did all this with the help of Arthur Andersen, the company's auditor and accounting firm. Though angrily threatened by Sullivan, and risking her job and career, on June 20, 2002, an apprehensive Cooper courageously met with the audit committee of WorldCom's board of directors and told them what had been going on. On June 25, WorldCom's directors announced the company had inflated its profits by over $3.8 billion—an amount later raised to $9 billion—in the greatest accounting fraud in history. Sullivan and Myers were arrested; WorldCom shareholders lost $3 billion; 17,000 WorldCom workers lost their jobs; Arthur Andersen was shut down for shredding evidence of other accounting frauds at other firms. Even today, many WorldCom managers and employees do not speak to her and she sometimes cries. Says Cooper: "There is a price to be paid. [But] it comes back to the values and ethics that you learn .... The fear of losing my job was secondary to the obligation I felt."

1. Which of Kohlberg's six stages of moral development would you say that Cynthia Cooper had reached? Explain.
2. Do her actions and motives support or undermine Carol Gilligan's views? What would you say is unique about her or what she did?
3. How does William Damon's theory of moral identity apply to Cynthia Cooper?

Protesters outside Federal Hall in New York's financial district protest against a possible settlement between WorldCom and securities regulators in June, 2003.

DECEMBER 30, 2002 / JANUARY 6, 2003 SPECIAL DOUBLE ISSUE

PERSONS OF THE YEAR

TIME

The Whistleblowers

CYNTHIA COOPER OF WORLDCOM | COLEEN ROWLEY OF THE FBI | SHERRON WATK OF ENRON

Former WorldCom chairman Bernard J. Ebbers and chief financial officer Scott Sullivan are sworn in before testifying before Congress on July 8, 2002.

I am Arthur Andersen

Arthur Andersen employees rally in support of their embattled accounting firm, which was implicated in the WorldCom scandal.

is to ask, "What kind of desires do I want (or desire) to have?"[70] A major finding of research in moral identity is that it has an important influence on our moral reasoning. That is, in many situations what we judge we should do depends on the kind of person we think we are. For example, if I see myself as an honest person, then I will generally decide I should be honest when tempted to lie. Ethicists have called this approach to ethics the "virtue" approach. Virtues are moral aspects of our character like honesty or courage. This kind of reasoning is somewhat different from reasoning about moral principles. Exactly how it differs we will see in the next chapter when we discuss virtue ethics.

It is important to note also that ethics is not just a matter of logic, reasoning, and cognition. This would leave out the central role that our emotions and feelings play in our moral decisions.[71] We noted earlier that one of the defining features of moral standards is that they are connected to special emotions and feelings, like guilt, shame, compassion, and empathy. But, in addition, moral thinking is, and has to be, aided by our emotions. Of course, emotions can sometimes get in the way of clear thinking. But we cannot engage in moral reasoning without the presence of our emotions.[72] People who have suffered damage to those parts of the brain that are responsible for producing emotions, and so who no longer experience emotions, become incapable of engaging in moral reasoning. They are still able to reason logically and can think abstractly, but they can no longer apply moral standards to their interactions with other people.

Quick Review 1.17

Psychological Research on Moral Reasoning

- Suggests that emotions are necessary for moral reasoning.

Phineas Gage, for example, was a well-liked and respected young man who one day at work happened to lean over an explosive charge while holding an iron rod. The charge exploded with such force that it instantly drove the rod upward through his cheek, behind his left eye, through the front part of his brain, and out at high speed through the top of his skull. Miraculously he survived and recovered without any loss of his ability to walk, move, perceive, speak, think, remember, and reason. But the front part of the brain plays a critical role in the production of emotions so Gage lost most of his ability to experience emotions. And with that loss, he also lost something else. According to witnesses, he was now "fitful, irreverent, indulging at times in the grossest profanity which was not previously his custom, manifesting but little deference for his fellows, impatient of restraint or advice when it conflicts with his desires, at times pertinaciously obstinate, yet capricious and vacillating, devising many plans of future operations, which are no sooner arranged than they are abandoned."[73] With the loss of his emotions, the young Gage lost the ability to engage in the kind of foresight and moral thinking that previously enabled him to deal ethically with his friends and other fellow human beings. Many other people who, like Gage have lost the ability to have emotions, have also lost the ability to engage in moral reasoning. The link between moral reasoning and emotions has also been supported by studies that show that when we engage in moral reasoning, one of the parts of our brain that becomes active is the part that is active when we experience emotions, the part of the brain that Gage lost.

How do our emotions and reasoning work together? Consider a simple example: our emotional reaction—e.g., empathy—to seeing a woman in front of us being treated badly will suddenly focus our attention on her and how she feels and what is happening to her, driving other concerns out of our mind. The information we get from this focused perception might then make us feel sympathy and this may move us to ask ourselves, and reason about, whether she deserves to be treated as she is being treated. If we judge that she does not deserve it and is being treated unjustly, we may then feel anger, which drives us to think about what we can do to end the injustice. This is just one small example of how our feelings and reasoning can work together.

Moreover, it should be enough to suggest how some of our feelings can even give us information about what is going on around us. Empathy, for example, allows us to know what the victim is feeling and to even experience what she is experiencing. Emotions like sympathy can make us recognize that we are faced with a situation that raises ethical issues and motivate us to try to understand and reason about what is happening. And anger can drive us to think about what we can and ought to do, and then push us into action.

A lot of the discussion that follows focuses on the reasoning processes upon which moral decisions are based. However, it is important to keep in mind that these reasoning processes are driven by, and suffused with, emotions and feelings. Reasoning about ethics is important, but without emotions we would be like Gage: unable to become focused on and concerned about ethics and no longer moved to engage in moral reasoning about ourselves and those around us.

Moral Reasoning

We have used the term *moral reasoning* repeatedly. What does it mean? **Moral reasoning** refers to the reasoning process by which human behaviors, institutions, or policies are judged to be in accordance with or in violation of moral standards. Moral reasoning always involves three components: (1) an understanding of our moral standards and what they require, prohibit, value, or condemn; (2) evidence or information about whether a particular person, policy, institution, or behavior has the features that these moral standards require, prohibit, value, or condemn; and (3) a conclusion or moral judgment that the person, policy, institution, or behavior is prohibited or required, right or wrong, just or unjust, valuable or condemnable, and so on. Here is an example of moral reasoning whose author is offering us his reasons for the moral judgment that some U.S. social institutions are unjust:

moral reasoning The reasoning process by which human behaviors, institutions, or policies are judged to be in accordance with or in violation of moral standards.

> Blacks and other minorities live in our society and a disproportionate number fight the wars that keep our society safe: 20 percent of the military is black yet only 11 percent of the U.S. is black. Minorities take the dirty jobs (30 percent of cleaners are Hispanics, who are 7 percent of the workforce) and contribute cheap labor (44 percent of farm workers are Hispanic) that lets us live and eat disproportionately well. Yet minorities do not get society's benefits. Twenty-six percent of blacks and 25 percent of Hispanics fall below the poverty line compared to 12 percent of whites. Black and Hispanic infant mortality is double that of whites. Blacks are 11 percent of the U.S. work force but hold only 7 percent of all management positions and 6 percent of all engineering jobs. Discrimination that prevents minorities from getting out of their society what they contribute is unjust.[74]

In this example, the author has in mind a moral standard that he sets out at the end of the paragraph: "Discrimination that prevents minorities from getting out of their society what they contribute is unjust." The earlier part of the paragraph is devoted to citing factual evidence showing that U.S. society exhibits the kind of discrimination this moral principle condemns. The author's moral judgment about U.S. society is not explicitly stated, but it is obvious enough: U.S. society is unjust. So this example of moral reasoning has the usual components: (1) a moral standard on which the moral judgment is based, (2) evidence or factual information about the institution that is being judged, and (3) a moral judgment or conclusion that is supposed to be drawn

Figure 1.1
View the Image on mythinkinglab.com

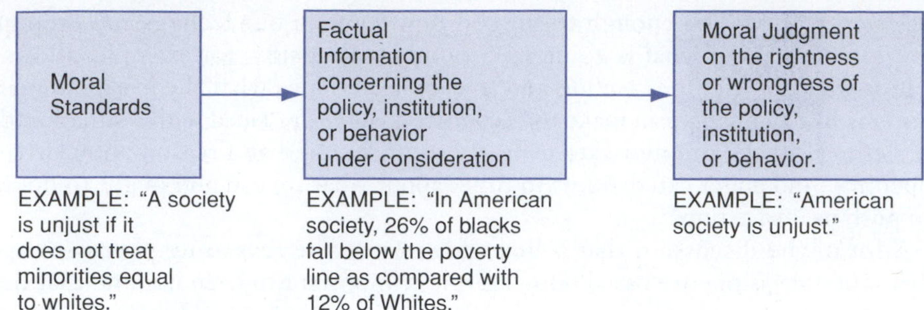
Moral Standards
Factual Information concerning the policy, institution, or behavior under consideration
Moral Judgment on the rightness or wrongness of the policy, institution, or behavior.
EXAMPLE: "A society is unjust if it does not treat minorities equal to whites."
EXAMPLE: "In American society, 26% of blacks fall below the poverty line as compared with 12% of Whites."
EXAMPLE: "American society is unjust."

from (1) and (2). Schematically, then, moral or ethical reasoning generally has the kind of structure indicated in Figure 1.1.[75]

Sometimes one of the three parts of moral reasoning is not expressed. In the example of moral reasoning above, the conclusion was not explicitly stated because it was so obvious. More often, however, people do not explicitly state the moral standards on which their moral judgments are based and we may have to search for them. For example, a person might say, "U.S. society is unjust because it allows 26 percent of Negroes to fall below the poverty line while only 12 percent of whites are below the poverty line." Here the moral judgment is "U.S. society is unjust" and the evidence is "it allows 26 percent of Negroes to fall below the poverty line while only 12 percent of whites are below the poverty line." But what is the moral standard on which this judgment is based? The unspoken moral standard has to be something like: "A society is unjust if it allows a higher percentage of people of one race to be poor than those of another race." How do we know? Because the **factual information** that *26 percent of Negroes fall below the poverty line while 12 percent of whites are below the poverty line* can serve as evidence for the **moral judgment** that *U.S. society is unjust* only if we accept the **moral standard** that *a society is unjust if it allows a higher percentage of people of one race to be poor than those of another race*. Without this moral standard, the factual information would have no logical relation to the conclusion and so could not be evidence for the conclusion. So to uncover the unspoken moral standards someone is using when he or she makes a moral judgment, we have to trace his or her reasoning back to its moral assumptions. This involves asking (a) what factual information does the person think is evidence for his moral judgment, and (b) what moral standards are needed to logically relate this factual information to his moral judgment.[76]

> *Quick Review 1.18*
>
> **Moral Reasoning Involves**
> - The moral standards by which we evaluate things
> - Information about what is being evaluated
> - A moral judgment about what is being evaluated.

One reason we do not make our moral standards explicit in our moral reasoning is that we generally assume these moral standards are obvious. So we put most of our efforts into looking at whether there is evidence that a given situation does or does not violate our (unspoken) moral standards. But we put little or no effort into examining the (unspoken) moral standards on which our judgments rely. Yet if we do not make our moral standards explicit, we can end up basing our judgments on moral standards we do not even realize we hold. Or, worse, we may rely on standards that we would reject if we explicitly thought about them. Our unspoken moral standards might be inconsistent, they might be unreasonable, or they might have implications we do not accept. In the example of moral reasoning, we have been discussing the unspoken moral standard: A society is unjust if it allows a higher percentage of people of one race to be poor than those of another race. But now that we have made this standard explicit, we might not be so sure it is right. For example, some people have suggested that the inequalities in the percentages of each race that are poor are the result of different natural characteristics the two races possess. And if they are the result of natural differences, then do such inequalities show a society is unjust? We may reject the suggestion that inequalities are the result of natural racial differences, but the suggestion should at least lead us to look more carefully at whether the moral standards we are using are justified. Making explicit the moral standards upon which our moral judgments are based, then, is crucial to understanding whether the moral standards that underlie our reasoning are really justified.

The moral standards upon which adults base their moral judgments are usually a lot more complex than these simple examples suggest. A person's moral standards usually include qualifications, exceptions, and restrictions that limit their scope. Also, they may be combined in various ways with other important moral standards. Still, the general method of uncovering people's unspoken moral standards remains roughly the same however complex their standards are. We need to ask: What general moral standards are needed to relate this person's factual evidence to the moral judgment he or she is making?

Hopefully, this explanation of moral reasoning has not suggested that it is always easy to separate factual information from moral standards in a piece of moral reasoning—nothing could be farther from the truth. In practice, the two are sometimes intertwined in ways that are hard to disentangle. Also, there are several theoretical difficulties in trying to draw a precise line separating the two.[77] Although the difference between the two is usually clear enough for practical purposes, the reader should be aware that sometimes they cannot be clearly distinguished.

Analyzing Moral Reasoning

There are various criteria that ethicists use to evaluate how good a piece of moral reasoning is. First, moral reasoning must be logical. This means that when we evaluate a person's moral reasoning, we should first make the person's unspoken moral standards explicit. We should also understand what evidence the person offers to support his or her conclusion, and know exactly what the person's conclusion is. Then, we can determine whether the person's moral standards together with the evidence he or she offers logically support his or her conclusion.

Second, the factual evidence the person cites in support of his or her moral judgment must be *accurate*, *relevant*, and *complete*.[78] For example, the illustration of moral reasoning quoted earlier cites several statistics ("Although blacks are 11 percent of the U.S. work force, they hold only 7 percent of all management positions and only 6 percent of all engineering jobs.") and relationships ("minorities contribute cheap labor that lets the rest of us live and eat disproportionately well") that are said to exist in the United States. If the moral reasoning is to be adequate, these statistics and relationships must be *accurate*: They must rest on reliable statistical methods and well-supported scientific theory. In addition, evidence must be *relevant*: It must show that the behavior, policy, or institution being judged has precisely those characteristics that are condemned by the moral standards involved. For instance, the statistics and relationships in the illustration of moral reasoning given above must show that some people are "prevented from getting out of [U.S.] society what they contribute," the precise characteristic that is condemned by the moral standard cited in the illustration. Finally, evidence must be *complete* in this sense: It should take into account all relevant information and must not selectively consider only evidence that tends to support a single point of view.

Third, the moral standards involved in a person's moral reasoning must be *consistent*. They must be consistent with each other and with the other standards and beliefs

> *Quick Review 1.19*
>
> **Moral Reasoning Should**
> - Be logical
> - Rely on evidence or information that is accurate, relevant, and complete
> - Be consistent.

the person holds. Inconsistency between our moral standards can be uncovered and corrected by examining situations in which these moral standards require incompatible things. Suppose I believe that (1) it is wrong to disobey an employer whom one has contractually agreed to obey, and I also believe that (2) it is wrong to help a person who is putting people's lives at risk. Then, suppose that one day my employer tells me to sell a product that may be dangerous, perhaps fatal, to people who use it. The situation now reveals an inconsistency between these two moral standards: I can either obey my employer and avoid disloyalty, or I can disobey my employer and avoid helping him or her do something that endangers people's lives, but I cannot do both.

When inconsistencies between one's moral standards are uncovered in this way, one (or both) of the standards has to be changed. In this example, I might decide that orders of employers have to be obeyed except when they threaten human life. Notice that, to determine what kinds of modifications are called for, one has to examine the reasons one has for accepting the inconsistent standards and weigh these reasons to see what is more important and worth retaining and what is less important and subject to modification. In this example, for instance, I may have decided that the reason that employee loyalty is important is that it safeguards property, but the reason that the refusal to endanger people is important is that it safeguards human life. Human life, I then decide, is more important than property. This sort of criticism and adjustment of one's moral standards is an important part of the process through which moral development takes place.

There is another kind of consistency that is perhaps even more important in ethical reasoning. Consistency also refers to the requirement that one must be willing to accept the consequences of applying one's moral standards consistently to all persons in similar circumstances.[79] This consistency requirement can be phrased as follows. Suppose "doing A" refers to some type of action, and "circumstances C" refers to the circumstances in which someone carried out that action. Then, we can say:

> If you judge that one person is morally justified (or unjustified) in doing A in circumstances C, then you must accept that it is morally justified (or unjustified) for any other person to perform any act relevantly similar to A, in any circumstances relevantly similar to C.

That is, you must apply the same moral standards to the action of one person in one situation that you applied to another that was relevantly similar. (Two actions or two circumstances are "relevantly similar" when all those factors that have a bearing on the judgment that an action is right or wrong in one case are also present in the other.) For example, suppose that I judge that it is morally permissible for me to fix prices because I want the high profits. If I am going to be consistent, I have to hold that it is morally permissible for my *suppliers* to fix prices when they want high profits. If I am not willing to consistently accept the consequences of applying to other, similar persons the standard that price fixing is morally justified for those who want high prices, I cannot rationally hold that the standard is true in my own case.

The consistency requirement is the basis of an important method of discovering that we need to change or modify our moral standards: the use of counterexamples or hypotheticals. If we are wondering whether a moral standard is acceptable, we can often test it by seeing whether we are willing to accept the consequences of applying that standard to other similar hypothetical cases. For instance, suppose I claim that it was morally justified for me to lie to protect my own interests because "It is always morally justified for a person to do whatever will benefit himself or herself." We can evaluate whether this principle is really acceptable by considering the hypothetical example of an individual who knowingly injures me or someone I love, and who claims he or she was morally justified because the injury was to his or her own benefit. If, as is likely, I do not think another person would be morally justified in injuring me or someone I love simply because it benefits him or her, then I need to qualify or reject the principle that "It's always morally justified for a person to do whatever will benefit himself or herself." I have to qualify or reject it because consistency requires that if I really accept the idea that I am justified in injuring someone when it benefits me, then I would have to accept that anyone else would be justified in injuring me whenever it benefits him or her. The point is that hypothetical examples can be used effectively to show that a moral standard is not really acceptable and so must be rejected or at least modified.

Moral Behavior and Its Impediments

We have spent some time discussing what moral reasoning is. But moral reasoning is only one of the processes that lead up to ethical or unethical behavior. Studies of the main steps that lead up to ethical or unethical action have converged on the view, first proposed by the moral psychologist James Rest, that four main processes precede ethical action: (1) recognizing or becoming aware that we are faced with an ethical issue or situation, i.e., an issue or situation to which we can respond ethically or unethically, (2) making a judgment about what the ethical course of action is, (3) forming an intention or decision to do or not do what we judge is right, and (4) carrying out or acting on the intention or decision we have made.[80] These four processes do not have to occur in sequence; in fact, one or all of them may occur simultaneously. Moreover, it is not always easy to distinguish them from each other, especially when they are simultaneous.

Quick Review 1.20

Four Steps Leading to Ethical Behavior

- Recognizing a situation is an ethical situation
- Judging what the ethical course of action is
- Deciding to do the ethical course of action
- Carrying out the decision.

Notice that moral reasoning is concerned only with the second of these processes, i.e., making a judgment about what the ethical response to an issue or situation should be. Moreover, moral reasoning, as we will see, is not the only way to make a decision about what the right thing to do is. We will discuss those other ways in the next chapter. In this chapter, we are going to look at the four main processes that lead up to ethical (or unethical) action. In particular, we are going to look closely at several impediments that can hamper these processes. Understanding these impediments will perhaps help you deal with them more effectively when you encounter them in your own life.

The First Step toward Ethical Behavior: Recognizing an Ethical Situation

Every day we encounter situations that raise ethical issues. But before we will even start thinking about those issues, we first have to recognize that the situation we have encountered is one that calls for ethical reasoning. There are many different ways we can see or categorize a situation. To deal with each type of situation, we use ways of thinking that are appropriate for that type of situation. For example, we can see a situation as being a "business" situation that calls for using business rules and business reasoning, or we can see it as a "legal" situation, or a "family" situation. When a situation is recognized as a *business* situation we may start thinking about what we can do to save money, or about the impact our actions will have on revenues or sales or profits. When a situation is seen as a *legal* situation, we may start thinking about the laws or regulations that apply to the situation and ask whether this or that course of action would be legal and what we need to do to comply with the law. And when we see a situation as a *family* situation, we may start thinking of what a parent or son or daughter or husband should do in this kind of situation. We can use the word "frame" to refer to the way we see a situation—i.e., the type of situation we think we have encountered—*and* the kind of thinking that should be used to deal with that type of situation. Most situations, of course, will fall within several frames. A business situation can also be a personal one, and a legal situation can also involve family.

Quick Review 1.21

Recognizing a Situation as Ethical

- Requires framing it as one that requires ethical reasoning
- Situation is likely to be seen as ethical when it involves serious harm that is concentrated, likely, proximate, imminent, and potentially violates our moral standards
- Obstacles to recognizing a situation is ethical include: euphemistic labeling, justifying our actions, advantageous comparisons, displacement of responsibility, diffusion of responsibility, distorting the harm, and dehumanization, and attribution of blame.

Besides business, legal, and personal frames, we also apply moral or ethical frames to situations. When we "frame" a situation as a moral or ethical situation, we recognize it as one that raises ethical questions or issues and we start thinking about it in moral ways, i.e., we start using moral reasoning and moral standards to deal with it. Situations that we correctly frame as "ethical" will ordinarily also fall within some other frame, such as a legal or business frame; that is, a legal or business situation can also be an ethical one. What are the features of situations that lead us to frame them as ethical situations? Some psychologists have argued that there are six criteria that we can and do use to decide whether to frame a situation as an ethical situation calling for ethical reasoning.[81] Simplified somewhat, the six criteria are:

(1) Does the situation involve the infliction of serious harm on one or more people?
(2) Is the harm concentrated on its victims so that each victim will, or already has, sustained a significant amount of harm?
(3) Is it likely that the harm will occur (or has actually occurred)?
(4) Are the victims proximate, i.e., close or accessible to us?
(5) Will the harm occur fairly soon (or has it already occurred)?
(6) Is there a possibility the infliction of harm violates the moral standards we or most people accept?

The more of these questions that we answer affirmatively, the more "important" the situation will be for us, and the more likely we will frame it as an ethical situation calling for ethical reasoning. Notice that we can use these criteria to determine whether or not we *should* frame a situation as an ethical one. That is, we can deliberately use these six questions to determine whether the situation before us is one we should be treating as an ethical situation. The more of these questions that we answer affirmatively the more likely that we *should* frame the situation as ethical. We can sharpen our ability to recognize ethical situations, then, by training ourselves to pay moral attention when we see situations that involve harm that is concentrated, likely, proximate, imminent, and that possibly violates our moral standards.

While there are ways of improving our ability to recognize whether a situation requires ethical thinking, there are also a number of impediments that can get in the way—or that we can put in the way—of recognizing an ethical situation. Albert Bandura identified six forms of "moral disengagement," for example, that can prevent us (or that we can deliberately use to prevent ourselves) from recognizing or becoming aware that a situation is an ethical one.[82] The main forms of moral disengagement that function as impediments to framing a situation as an ethical one are:

Euphemistic Labeling We can use euphemisms to change or veil the way we see a situation we have encountered. Instead of thinking about the fact that we are firing people, for example, we try to think of what we are doing as "downsizing," "rightsizing," or "outsourcing." The U.S. military refers to the killing of civilians as "collateral damage." Politicians have referred to torture as "enhanced interrogation techniques," and to lies as "misstatements," "technically inaccurate statements," or "less than precise words." By using such euphemisms, we change how we see the situation and instead of framing it as an ethical situation, we frame it to ourselves as only a business, a military, or a political one.

Rationalizing Our Actions We can tell ourselves that the harm we intend is justified because we are pursuing a worthy and moral cause, so we do not need to look at our actions through an ethical frame. When a terrorist is planning to plant a bomb that will kill innocent civilians, for example, he or she might see himself or herself as a courageous fighter against a brutal oppressor. Therefore, the terrorist feels that what he or she plans to do is justified and does not have to frame his or her actions as needing ethical evaluation. Rationalization can also take place after we have inflicted an injury on others. When rationalization is used after an injury has been inflicted, it is usually part of an attempt to escape responsibility for the injury. We will look at such uses of rationalization below when we discuss the nature of moral responsibility.

Diminishing Comparisons By seeing a situation in the context of other larger evils, we can diminish the magnitude of our own wrongdoing and make the harms that we inflict appear minor or inconsequential. For example, when we see the losses our company inflicted on customers, we may think "Well, it's not as bad as what that other company did." Or we may steal office supplies while thinking, "This is minor in comparison to what the company has done to me." Such comparisons allow us to see the harms we inflict as so small they do not need to be seen through an ethical frame.

Displacement of Responsibility When we do our jobs in a way that harms others, we can see the harm as inflicted by whoever told us to do it and thereby, we mentally remove ourselves from the chain of actors responsible for the harm. For example, if I learn that customers are being badly injured by a product I help manufacture, I can tell myself that my bosses are the ones who are responsible for the injuries because they ordered me to do what I did, and so I am not involved in these harms. I then do not have to put a moral frame on my own actions since "I wasn't really involved in injuring our customers."

Diffusion of Responsibility I can obscure my involvement in activities that harm someone by seeing myself as playing only a small role in a large group that is responsible for the harm. For instance, if I am a member of an engineering team that designed a product that harmed buyers, then I may tell myself it was really the team that produced the injury and I had only a minor or negligible role in what happened. Again, I do not have to apply an ethical frame to my own actions since "I was just one person out of a lot of people, so I wasn't very involved in the situation."

Disregarding or Distorting the Harm We can deny, disregard, or distort the harm that our actions produced. I can choose to believe, for example, that "There's really no good evidence that anyone was hurt." Or I can discredit the evidence by thinking, "You can't believe the victims since they probably exaggerated their injuries so they could sue us for a lot of money." If we convince ourselves that there is no real harm involved, then we do not have to frame our actions as needing ethical scrutiny.

Dehumanizing the Victim We can think of the victims we injure as not real or not full human beings with human feelings and concerns so that we can avoid seeing we are harming real people. During wars countries often dehumanize their "enemies," by putting nonhuman labels on them so they do not have to think about their actions through an ethical frame. Before Hitler and the German Nazis murdered six million Jews, they labeled them "parasites," "an infestation," and "a disease." When a bank in Berkeley, California wanted to construct a building on an empty lot that was occupied by homeless people living in tents, it began calling them "squatters," and "vagrants." Instead of thinking of the employees we are firing as human beings, we may think of them as "human resources."

Redirecting Blame We can blame what we have done on our adversary or on the circumstances so that we see ourselves as innocent victims provoked by others or by the circumstances. When a worker complains to the human resources department that his manager is harassing other workers, the manager may get angry and retaliate against the worker by firing him while thinking that the worker "deserved it" for being disloyal, or that the worker "started it" and as a manager he was "forced" to fire him to establish his authority.

These six forms of moral disengagement are obstacles that, without our knowledge, can prevent us from framing the situation we are in as an ethical situation and thereby, keep us from thinking about it in moral or ethical terms. But we can also deliberately use these forms of moral disengagement to avoid framing a situation as an ethical situation when we more or less unconsciously suspect that seeing it in ethical terms will force us to admit that we are doing something wrong. As I am sure you have already realized, all of these forms of disengagement are common occurrences in our ordinary daily human life, and they are just as common in business where they are invoked by employees, especially when their company is discovered to be engaged in unethical behavior. Hopefully, being aware of these obstacles will help you avoid them in your own future work life.

The Second Step toward Ethical Behavior: Making a Judgment about the Ethical Course of Action As we saw earlier, before we judge a situation we should try to gather information about it that is accurate, relevant, and complete. Our attempts to gather such information, however, can be affected by biases that prevent us from getting the information we need. A bias is an assumption that distorts our beliefs, perceptions, and understanding of a situation. Several forms of bias have been studied, and these are usually put into three groups: biased theories about the world, biased theories about other people, and biased theories about ourselves.[83]

Biased Theories about the World Theories about the world refer to the beliefs we have about how the world works, the causes that make things happen, and how our actions affect the world. The world presents us with such a flood of complicated information that we cannot think about it unless we somehow simplify it. One way we simplify is by limiting the amount of information we allow ourselves to think about. When we are thinking about the consequences of our actions, however, these limits can create biases. In particular: we tend to ignore low-probability consequences; we discount the role of chance and err in assessing the risks attached to our actions; we do not consider all of the stakeholders our actions will impact; we ignore the possibility that the public will find out what we did; we discount consequences relatively far in the future; and we do not take into account the indirect effects of our actions. These biases can lead us to ignore critically important information about the ethical situations we face. For example, on April 20, 2010 a British Petroleum (BP) oil-well platform in the Gulf of Mexico blew up, killing 11 workers and releasing millions of gallons of oil into the Gulf where it created an environmental disaster. British Petroleum had installed a "blowout preventer" but by chance the preventer failed, a low probability consequence that BP did not prepare for.[84] BP had a history of ignoring how its actions might affect the natural environment and had not seen that it would be subjected to intense public scrutiny as a result of a blowout since most blowouts are relatively minor and ignored by the press.[85] A government report on an earlier BP oil rig explosion in Texas stated that although "warning signs of a possible disaster were present," the company had not tried to prevent the possibility of such a future event. And because of a single-minded focus on cost-cutting and "a false sense of confidence," the company had not made needed investments on safety processes. Because

Quick Review 1.22

A Judgment About the Ethical Course of Action

- Requires moral reasoning that applies our moral standards to the information we have about a situation
- Requires realizing that information about a situation may be distorted by biased theories about the world, about others, and about oneself.

of its many indirect effects, the 2010 Gulf oil spill ended up having a devastating and long-lasting impact on the economy of all Gulf states and on the Gulf environment. Thus, the 2010 Gulf oil spill illustrates all of the biases above. BP failed to prepare for the low probability event of a major blowout; it did not take chance into account, consider all the potential stakeholders, consider how the press might publicize its history of unethical behavior, discounted what might happen in the future so it could invest more in its present activities, and didn't think about all the indirect effects its actions might have. If the company had taken these pieces of information into account when deciding what kind of safety precautions it should invest in, the blowout might never have happened.

Biased Theories about Others Biased theories about others include the beliefs we have about how "we" differ from "them" or what the members of certain groups are like. *Ethnocentrism* refers to one important class of such beliefs. Ethnocentrism refers to the belief that what *our* nation, group, or culture ("we") does, seems normal, ordinary, and good, while what *others* ("they") do, seems foreign, strange, and less good. "Our" way is superior while "their" way is inferior. Such beliefs lead to unintentional discrimination. Banks with mostly white mortgage lending agents, for example, tend to reject a larger proportion of non-white loan applicants than white loan applicants. Even after taking into account differences in income, employment, and credit history, etc., the difference in rejection rates remains. When this is pointed out, lending agents vigorously deny that they are intentionally discriminating. Their denial is probably an honest one because the differences are likely due to an unconscious bias that leads them to unintentionally favor white people like themselves over non-whites who are "different."

Stereotypes are beliefs that work like ethnocentric beliefs but they are beliefs we can have about the members of any group, not just groups that are culturally or ethnically different from ours. Stereotypes are fixed beliefs we have about what "all" or "most" members of various groups are like, such as people of a certain nationality, or a certain gender, or race, or religion, or occupation. Stereotypes can also lead to unfair, false, and possibly illegal decisions about people. Stereotypes, for example, can lead us to unconsciously and wrongly think that men are more effective leaders than women, that blacks are all good at sports, that Asians always study hard, that Mexicans are lazy, that gays are effeminate, that all Muslims support terrorism, that women are better nurses than men, etc. Stereotypes can result in unethical decisions regarding promotions, hiring, firing, salaries, job placement, and other decisions that depend on our judgments of people.

Biased Theories about Oneself Perhaps not surprisingly, research has shown that our own views of ourselves tend to be flawed. We generally—and unrealistically—believe we are more capable, insightful, courteous, honest, ethical, and fair than others, and are overconfident about our ability to control random events. We tend to believe that we deserve any rewards, bonuses, or pay-increases that we receive for the work we do, in part because we believe that we contribute more to the organization's successes than others who hold similar positions. We tend to be overly optimistic about our future because we overestimate the likelihood that we will experience good events, while underestimating the likelihood that we will be the ones who experience bad events. For example, people believe that they are less likely than others to experience divorce, alcoholism, or a serious auto injury. Because they believe they are immune to risks, managers sometimes commit their organization to risky courses of action. British Petroleum's managers, for example, decided to take the risk of not investing in safety measures, thereby committing the company to a course that led to the disastrous 2010 Gulf oil spill. They had, perhaps, a false confidence that matters could not go wrong when they were in charge.

We tend to be overly confident also about what we think we know. For example, in a series of psychology experiments in which people were asked to answer simple factual questions (like "Which city is farther north, Rome or New York?"), people regularly overestimated the probability that their answers were correct. We also tend to overestimate our ability to be objective when making judgments about a transaction between our employer and ourselves (or someone close to us). Suppose that I am the purchasing agent for my company and I am supposed to choose the supplier that can sell us the highest quality materials, but one of the suppliers is a company my spouse owns. Most of us would say that we can be objective although one of the suppliers we are evaluating is owned by one's spouse. Yet studies show that no matter how confident people are about their ability to remain objective, in reality their judgments are almost always biased toward their own interests or the interests of people close to them.[86]

There are, then, a number of biases about ourselves, about others, and about the world around us that lead us to mistaken beliefs about the situations we encounter. If we are not aware of, and alert to, the influence of such biases, we may think that we are basing our decisions on solid information when, in fact, we are basing our judgments on distortions or falsehoods. And, perhaps even worse, these biases may make us confident that we are right when in fact we are completely wrong.

The Third Step toward Ethical Behavior: Deciding to Do What Is Right Even after I determine what the morally right and morally wrong course of action should be in a given situation, there is no guarantee that I will decide to do what is right. People often decide on unethical behavior even though they realize it is unethical, or they fail to commit to what is ethical although they know it is the ethical course of action. That is, in fact, the essential nature of evil: knowing something is wrong but deciding to do it anyway. There are a number of factors that influence whether we decide to do what we know is right, or decide instead to do what we know is wrong.

People's decisions to do what is ethical are greatly influenced by their surroundings, particularly by their organizational surroundings such as the "ethical climate" and the "ethical culture" of the organization.[87] Ethical climate refers to the beliefs an organization's members have about how they are *expected* to behave. In organizations with "egoistic" climates, employees feel they are expected to be self-seeking and so they are; while in organizations with "benevolent" climates, employees feel they are expected to do what is best for various stakeholders such as employees, customers, suppliers, and the community. Not surprisingly, members of organizations with "egoistic" climates find it harder to make ethical decisions about what they know is right, than do members in organizations with benevolent climates.

Ethical culture refers to the kind of behavior an organization *encourages or discourages* by repeated use of examples of appropriate behavior, incentives for ethical behavior, clear rules and ethics policies, rewards for exemplary conduct, stories of notable ethical actions, etc. While ethical climate refers to employee beliefs about an organization, ethical culture refers to the ways an organization encourages some behaviors and discourages others. The culture of some organizations encourage and reward only business objectives with no attention to ethics while the cultures of other organizations encourage and reward ethical behavior and not just bottom-line results. Organizations with a strong ethical culture make it easier for us to decide to do what is right, while those with strong business cultures can make it harder to decide to do what is right.

Quick Review 1.23

Deciding to do What is Ethical can be Influenced by

- The culture of an organization
- Moral seduction

Organizations can also generate a form of "moral seduction" that can exert subtle pressures that can gradually lead an ethical person into decisions to do what he or she knows is wrong. A team of psychologists found, for example, that:

> Moral seduction occurs one step at a time. For example, in one year, an auditor might decline to demand that the client change an accounting practice that is at the edge of permissibility. The next year, the auditor may feel the need to justify the previous year's decision and may turn a blind eye when the client pushes just past the edge of permissibility. The following year, the auditor might endorse accounting that clearly violates GAAP rules in order to avoid admitting the errors of the past two years and in the hope that the client will fix the problem before the next year's audit. By the fourth year, the auditor and client will both be actively engaged in a cover-up to hide their past practices.[88]

An organization that accepts unethical practices, then, can draw a new, young, and perhaps idealistic person into gradually accepting unethical practices that earlier the person might have rejected out-of-hand because the person knew that they were clearly unethical. The person first may be asked to do something that is only slightly questionable, perhaps as a favor or to be a "team player." Then the person may be asked to go along with something just slightly more serious, until step by step the person finally finds himself deeply involved in the unethical practices of the organization, and so compromised by his past actions that the person feels that he has to continue his involvement. Ethical seduction can lead a person to decide to do what in his heart the person knows is unethical and should not be done.

The Fourth Step toward Ethical Behavior: Carrying Out One's Decision Good intentions do not always result in good behavior because we often fail to do what we intended to do. I may be genuinely committed to doing what is right, but when the time comes to act, I may lack the determination to do what I intended. What factors influence whether a person acts on the moral decisions he or she has made?

First, there is the personal or individual factor that the Greek philosopher Aristotle called "weakness of will" and its opposite, "strength of will."[89] Strength of will refers to our ability to regulate our actions so that we resolutely do what we know is right even when powerful emotions, desires, or social pressures urge us not to. Weakness of will refers to the inability (or low ability) to regulate our actions so that we fail to do what we know is right when emotions, desires, or external pressures tempt us. Some psychologists refer to this ability as "ego strength": the ability to be resistant to impulses and to follow one's own convictions. Some people have a high level of ego strength, while others have low levels. Aristotle argued that a person develops weakness of will by repeatedly giving in to the temptation to overindulge one's appetites and emotions; while by repeatedly resisting the temptation to overindulge one's appetites and emotions a person develops strength of will.[90]

A second important factor that affects whether a person will decide to do what the person judges is wrong is their belief about their *locus of control*. Locus of control refers to whether a person believes that what happens to him or her is primarily within his or her control, or instead believes that what happens to him or her is primarily the result of external forces such as other powerful people, or luck, or circumstances. People who believe they are in control of their own lives tend to have better control of their behavior and are more likely to do what they believe is right, whereas those who believe that what happens to them is not in their control, but is determined by external forces, are more often swayed by external forces to do what they do not think is right. In short, if you believe you are in control of your life, you will acquire greater

Quick Review 1.24

Carrying Out One's Decision Can Be Influenced by

- One's strength or weakness of will
- One's belief about the locus of control of one's actions.

control of your life and increase your ability to do what you think is right. But if you believe you are not in control of your life, the belief itself can lead you to relinquish the control you do have.

A third important factor that can keep a person from doing what he or she knows is right is the person's willingness to obey authority figures. Studies in social psychology have demonstrated that many people willingly obey authority figures even when they believe or suspect they are doing something wrong. For example, several years ago the psychologist Stanley Milgram tested subjects to see how far they would go when an authority figure ordered them to give another person increasingly severe electric shocks from an electric "shock machine."[91] He found that if the authority figure—in this case the experimenter—said things like: "It is absolutely essential that you continue," or "You have no choice, you must go on," or "The responsibility is mine, please go on," about two-thirds of his subjects obeyed and continued increasing the voltage of the shocks they were giving the other person, up to and beyond the level they felt could seriously harm or even kill the person. Unknown to the subjects, the electric "shock machine" was not real and the person they were "shocking" was an actor. When questioned afterwards, his subjects almost all admitted that they felt or suspected that what they were being asked to do was wrong, but they nevertheless felt they had to obey the experimenter since he was the person in charge. The experiment showed, Milgram said, that most ordinary people would follow orders even when asked to do what they believed was wrong—even kill a person. In light of the Milgram experiments, it is easy to see that in business organizations, many people are likely to feel they "have to" go along with what managers ask them to do, even when they believe it is morally wrong.

There are several impediments, then, that can trip up a person even at the fourth and final stage of the road to ethical behavior: i.e., the stage of actually carrying out a decision to do what is right. Three such impediments are people's weakness of will, their views about whether they are in control of what happens to them, and their willingness to obey authority figures. There are other impediments to doing what we have decided is right but that we can here only mention: pressures our peers put on us to do what we know is wrong, fears of the personal costs of doing what we know is right, and limited self-control or limited impulse-control.

Impediments, then, can hamper any of the four processes that should lead up to ethical behavior: recognizing an ethical issue, making a judgment about the right thing to do, deciding to do what we judge to be right, and carrying out our decision. We have described these impediments so that armed with the knowledge of what they are and how they can impede you, you will be better equipped to overcome them.

1.4 Moral Responsibility and Blame

So far our discussion has focused on judgments about right and wrong, and good and evil. Moral reasoning, however, is sometimes directed at a different kind of judgment: determining whether a person is *morally responsible* for an injury or for a wrong.[92] A judgment about a person's moral responsibility for wrongdoing is a judgment that the person acted intentionally and so should be blamed or punished, or should pay restitution.

The kind of moral responsibility we are discussing here should not be confused with a second but distinct form of "moral responsibility." The term *moral responsibility* is sometimes used to mean "moral duty" or "moral obligation." For example, when we say, "Vandiver had a moral responsibility not to lie," we are using the words "moral responsibility" to mean "moral obligation." This is *not* the kind of moral responsibility that we are talking about here. The kind of moral responsibility we are discussing is when we say a person is *to blame* for something. For example, if we say, "Vandiver is morally responsible for the deaths of any pilots who crashed when trying to land the A7-D plane," then we are using the words "is morally responsible" to mean "is to blame." It is this second meaning of moral responsibility that we are talking about here.

Getting clear about what moral responsibility (i.e., being to blame) involves is important for several reasons. First, and most importantly, determining who is morally responsible for a wrong allows us to identify who should fix the wrong. If, for example, you are morally responsible for harming your neighbor, then you are the one who should compensate your neighbor for his or her losses, at least to the extent that those losses can be compensated. Second, determining whether or not someone is really morally responsible for, say, breaking a law or a rule, allows us to ensure that we do not mistakenly punish, penalize, or blame an innocent person. Most businesses, for example, have rules against "conflicts of interest" and employees sometimes break these rules without realizing what they were doing. It would be a mistake to punish such employees if they really were not morally responsible for what they did. Third, determining whether you are or are not morally responsible for someone's injury helps to ensure that you do not end up feeling shame or guilt when you should not be feeling these emotions. For example, if you inflict a bad injury on a fellow worker while operating a machine, you will probably feel pretty bad about what happened. But whether you should feel guilty or ashamed depends on whether you are morally responsible for what happened for if, say, the injury was an accident then you are not morally responsible and so are not guilty. And fourth, knowing exactly what moral responsibility is may help keep us from wrongly trying to rationalize our conduct. When a person realizes that her actions resulted in serious injuries to others, she may not want to accept her responsibility for what she did. In such situations, we sometimes try to escape responsibility for our actions by coming up with rationalizations that we use to deceive ourselves, as well as others. Hopefully, being clear about what moral responsibility involves will help us see our own responsibility more clearly and help us avoid rationalizations and self-deception.

People are not always morally responsible for the injuries they inflict on others. A person, for example, who injures someone by accident is "excused" from any blame. So when is a person morally responsible—or to blame—for an injury? We can summarize the traditional view in this way: A person is morally responsible for an injury when the person *caused* the injury and did so *knowingly* and *of his or her own free will.* But this characterization ignores the fact that people are sometimes responsible for injuries which they did not cause, but which they could and should have prevented. That is, they are morally responsible for their omissions when they had a duty to act. So a more accurate—but more complicated—way of characterizing moral responsibility is the following:

A person is morally responsible for an injury or a wrong if:

(1) the person caused or helped cause it, or failed to prevent it when he or she could have and should have; and
(2) the person did so knowing what he or she was doing; and
(3) the person did so of his or her own free will.

For shorthand purposes, we will refer to the three elements of moral responsibility as the requirements of: (1) causality, (2) knowledge, and (3) freedom. This means the absence of any of these three elements will completely eliminate a person's responsibility for an injury and so will fully "excuse" a person from any blame for the injury.[93] Several manufacturers of asbestos, for example, were recently judged responsible for the lung diseases suffered by some of their workers.[94] The judgment was based in part on the finding that the manufacturers should have warned their workers of the known dangers of working with asbestos, yet they knowingly failed to perform this duty, and the lung diseases were a foreseen result of their failure to warn. In their defense, some asbestos manufacturers denied the *causality* requirement when they claimed that the lung injuries suffered by their workers were not caused by working with asbestos, but by smoking. Other manufacturers denied the *knowledge* requirement by claiming that they did not know that conditions in their plants would cause lung cancer in their workers. And yet others denied the *freedom* requirement by saying that they were not free to prevent the injuries because they had tried to get their workers to wear protective masks, but the workers refused. Thus, the workers were injured because of circumstances that the manufacturers could not change. Most courts did not accept these claims. But the point here is that if any of these claims were true, then the manufacturers could not be morally responsible for the lung diseases of their workers.

It is important to understand these three conditions well enough to be able to judge on your own whether a party (you or someone else) was morally responsible for something. Let us begin by examining the first requirement for moral responsibility: The person must either cause the injury or wrong or else must fail to prevent it when he or she could and should have done so. In many cases, it is easy to determine whether a person's actions "caused" an injury or a wrong (such actions are "commissions"). But this is not so easy when a party does not cause an injury but merely fails to prevent it (such failures are "omissions"). For example, Nike, the athletic shoe company, was, for a long time, at the center of a controversy over its responsibility for the mistreatment of the workers who make its shoes. Nike does not actually manufacture any of the athletic shoes it sells. Instead, Nike designs its shoes in Seattle, Washington, and then pays other companies in developing countries to make the shoes according to its designs. It was these foreign supplier companies (in China, Indonesia, India, etc.) that directly mistreated and exploited their workers. Nike claimed that it was not morally responsible for this mistreatment because the suppliers caused the injuries, not Nike. Critics have responded that although it is true that Nike did not directly cause the injuries, nevertheless the company could have prevented those injuries by forcing its suppliers to treat their workers humanely. If it is true that Nike had the power to prevent the injuries, and should have done so, then the company met the first condition for moral responsibility. But if Nike was truly powerless to prevent these injuries—if Nike truly had no control over the actions of its suppliers—then it did not meet the first condition and so was not morally responsible for the way the workers were being treated.

Quick Review 1.25

A Person is Morally Responsible for an Injury Only If:

- Person caused or helped cause the injury, or failed to prevent it when he or she could and should have.
- Person did so knowing what he or she was doing
- Person did so of his or her own free will

Notice that the first condition says that people are morally responsible for an injury when they failed to prevent it, *only if* they "should have" prevented it. This qualification is necessary because people cannot be held morally responsible for all the injuries they know about and fail to prevent. Each of us is not morally responsible, for example, for failing to save all the members of all the starving groups in the world that we learn about by reading the newspapers, even if we could have saved some of them. If we were morally responsible for all these deaths, then we would all be murderers many times over and this seems wrong. Instead, we must say that a person is responsible for failing to prevent an injury only when, for some reason, the person had an obligation to prevent that particular injury. Such an obligation generally requires some sort of special relationship to the injury or the injured party. For example, if I know that I am the only person near enough to save a drowning child, and I can do so easily, then my special physical relationship to the child creates an obligation for me to save the child. Therefore, I'm morally responsible for the child's death if I fail to prevent it. Or if I am a police officer on duty and see a crime that I can prevent, then, because it is specifically my job to prevent such crimes, I have an obligation to prevent this crime and am morally responsible if I fail to do so. Employers, likewise, have a special obligation to prevent work injuries from being inflicted on their employees and so are morally responsible for any foreseen work injuries they could have prevented.

The second requirement for moral responsibility is this: The person must know what he or she is doing. This means that if a person is ignorant of the fact that his or her actions will injure someone else, then he or she cannot be morally responsible for that injury. Ignorance, however, does not always excuse a person. One exception is when a person deliberately stays ignorant of a certain matter to escape responsibility. For example, if Nike managers told their suppliers that they did not want to know what was going on in their factories, they would still be morally responsible for whatever mistreatment went on that they could have prevented. A second exception is when a person negligently fails to take the necessary steps to find out about something he or she knows is important. A manager in an asbestos company, for example, who has reason to suspect that asbestos may be dangerous, but who fails to become informed on the matter out of laziness, cannot later plead ignorance as an excuse.

There are two kinds of ignorance. A person can be ignorant of either the relevant *facts* or the relevant *moral standards*. For example, I may be sure that bribery is wrong (a moral standard) but do not realize that by tipping a customs official I am actually bribing him or her into canceling the import fees I owe (a fact). Or I might be genuinely ignorant that bribing government officials is wrong (a moral standard), but know that by tipping the customs official, I am bribing him or her into reducing the fees I owe (a fact).

Ignorance of *fact* eliminates moral responsibility because a person cannot be responsible for something which he or she cannot control.[95] Because people cannot control matters of which they are ignorant, they are not moral responsible for such matters. Negligently or deliberately created ignorance is an exception to this principle because such ignorance can be controlled. Insofar as we can control the extent of our ignorance, we become morally responsible for it and, therefore, also for its injurious consequences. Ignorance of the relevant *moral standards* generally also removes responsibility because a person is not responsible for failing to meet obligations of whose existence he or she is genuinely ignorant. However, to the extent that our ignorance of moral standards is the result of freely choosing not to figure out what these standards are, we are responsible for our ignorance and for its wrongful or injurious consequences.

The third requirement for moral responsibility is that the person must act of his or her own free will. A person acts of his or her own free will when the person acts deliberately or purposefully and is not forced to act by some uncontrollable mental impulse or external force. In other words, a person acts of his or her own free will when he or she chooses to do something for a reason or a purpose and is not forced to do it by some internal or external force over which he or she has no control. A person is not morally responsible, for example, if he or she causes an injury because he or she lacked the power, skill, opportunity, or resources to prevent the injury. Nor is a person morally responsible when he or she is physically forced to do something that injures another person or when a person's mind is psychologically impaired in a way that prevents him or her from controlling his or her actions. An employee, for example, may injure a fellow worker when a machine he thought he knew how to operate, suddenly swings out of his control. A manager working under extremely stressful circumstances may be so tense that one day she is overcome by rage at a subordinate and genuinely is unable to control her actions toward that subordinate. An engineer who is part of a larger operating committee may be unable to prevent the other committee members from making a decision that the engineer feels will result in injury to other parties. In all these cases, the person is not morally responsible for the wrong or the injury because the person either did not choose the action deliberately or purposefully or was forced to act as he or she did. Mental impairments or external forces eliminate a person's responsibility because, again, a person cannot have any moral responsibility for something over which the person had no control.

Although the absence of any of the three requirements (causality, knowledge, and freedom) will completely remove a person's moral responsibility for a wrong, there are also several "mitigating factors" that can lessen a person's moral responsibility depending on the severity of the wrong. Mitigating factors include: (a) circumstances that minimize but do not completely remove a person's involvement in an act (these affect the degree to which the person *caused* the wrongful injury), (b) circumstances that leave a person somewhat uncertain about what he or she is doing (these affect the person's *knowledge*), and (c) circumstances that make it difficult but not impossible for the person to avoid doing what he or she did (these affect the extent to which the person acted freely). The extent to which these three factors lessen a person's responsibility for an injury depends on a fourth factor: (d) the seriousness of the wrong. To clarify these, we will next discuss each of them in turn.

First, a person's responsibility can be mitigated by circumstances that diminish the person's *contribution* to the act that caused or brought about an injury. An engineer may contribute to an unsafe product, for example, by knowingly drawing up an unsafe design and so fully contributes to the act that causes future injuries. In contrast, the engineer may know about the unsafe features in somebody else's design, but he or she passively stands by without doing anything about it because "that's not my job." In such a case, the engineer makes less of a contribution to causing any future injuries. In general, the less one's actual actions contribute to the outcome of an act, the less one is morally responsible for that outcome (depending, however, on how serious the wrong is). However, if a person is specifically assigned the duty to report or prevent certain wrongdoings, then that person is morally responsible for acts he or she does not try to prevent, even if the person makes no other contribution to the act. An accountant, for example, who was hired to report fraudulent activity cannot plead diminished responsibility for a fraud he or she discovers but does not report, even if the accountant pleads that he or she did not carry out the fraudulent act. In such cases where a person has a special (specifically assigned) duty to prevent an injury, freely and knowingly failing to try to prevent it is wrong. One is responsible for the act (along with the other guilty party or parties) if one should and could have prevented it but did not.

Second, circumstances can produce *uncertainty* about a variety of matters. A person may be fairly convinced that doing something is wrong yet may still be doubtful about some important facts, or may have doubts about the moral standards involved, or doubts about how seriously wrong the action is. For example, an office worker who is asked to carry proprietary information to a competitor might feel fairly sure that doing so is wrong, yet may also have some genuine uncertainty about how serious the matter is. Such uncertainties can lessen a person's moral responsibility for a wrongful act.

Quick Review 1.26

Depending on How Serious a Wrong is, Moral Responsibility for it Can be Mitigated by

- Minimal contribution
- Uncertainty
- Difficulty.

Third, a person may find it *difficult to avoid* a certain course of action because he or she is subjected to threats or duress of some sort or because avoiding that course of action will impose heavy costs on the person. A middle manager, for example, might be pressured or even threatened by his or her superior who orders the manager to keep workplace hazards secret from workers, although it is clearly unethical to do so.[96] If the pressures on a manager are so great that it is extremely difficult for him or her to disobey, then the manager's responsibility is correspondingly diminished. Although the manager is to blame for the wrong, his or her blame is mitigated.

Fourth, the extent to which these three mitigating circumstances can diminish a person's responsibility for a wrongful injury depends on *how serious* the wrong was. For example, if doing something is very seriously wrong, then even heavy pressures and minimal contribution may not substantially reduce a person's responsibility for the act. If my employer, for example, threatens to fire me unless I sell a defective product that I know will kill someone, it would be wrong for me to obey him or her even though loss of a job will impose a heavy cost on me. However, if only a relatively minor matter is involved, then the threat of being fired can mitigate my responsibility. When determining your moral responsibility for a wrongful act, therefore, you have to judge your uncertainties, the difficulty of avoiding or preventing the act, and your level of contribution, and then weigh these three against how serious the wrong is. Judgments like these are often extremely difficult to make.

It may be helpful to summarize here the essential points of this somewhat long and complicated discussion of moral responsibility. First, an individual is morally responsible for an injury when (1) the person caused the injury or failed to prevent it when he or she could and should have done so, (2) the person knew what he or she was doing, and (3) the person acted of his or her own free will. Second, moral responsibility is completely eliminated (excused) by the absence of any of these three elements. Third, moral responsibility for a wrong or an injury is mitigated by (a) minimal contribution (although minimal contribution does not mitigate if you have a specific duty to prevent the wrong), (b) uncertainty, and (c) difficulty. But the extent to which these three factors lessen your responsibility depends on (d) how serious the wrong is: the more serious the wrong, the less these three factors mitigate.

Critics have contested whether all of the mitigating factors we have discussed above really affect a person's responsibility. Some have claimed that evil may never be done no matter what personal pressures are exerted on a person.[97] Other critics have claimed that I am as responsible when I refrain from stopping a wrong as I am when I perform the wrong myself because *passively allowing* something to happen is morally no different from *actively causing* it to happen.[98] If these critics are correct, then mere passive involvement in something does not mitigate moral responsibility. Although neither of these criticisms seems correct, you should make up your own mind on the matter.

When we are accused of being responsible for some wrongdoing, either by others or by ourselves, we often resort to rationalization. Our hope is that the rationalization somehow excuses what we have done, i.e., that it eliminates or diminishes our responsibility. But unlike the factors we have discussed above (causality, knowledge, and freedom), many rationalizations do not affect responsibility for wrongdoing. Here, for example, are some popular rationalizations that we ourselves may use: "Everybody does it!" "There's no rule against it!" "If I didn't do it, somebody else would." "The company owed it to me!" "There are worse things!" "I was just following orders." "My boss made me do it!" "That's not my job!" "They had it coming to them!" "People like that deserve what they get." Some of these rationalizations, in special circumstances, may justify an injury we inflicted. But for the most part, they are inadequate attempts to escape responsibility that, in reality, is ours.

Responsibility for Cooperating with Evil

Within the modern corporation, responsibility for a corporate act is often distributed among many cooperating parties. Corporate acts normally are brought about by the actions or omissions of many different people all cooperating together so that their linked actions and omissions jointly produce the corporate act. For example, each member of an executive committee may knowingly vote to do something fraudulent and their resulting vote may license a corporate activity that defrauds stockholders; one team of managers designs a car, another team tests it, and a third team builds it; a manager orders something illegal and employees carry out those orders; one group knowingly defrauds buyers and another group silently enjoys the resulting profits; one person supplies the means and another person carries out the act; one group does the wrong and another group conceals it. The possible variations on cooperation in evil are endless.

Who is morally responsible for such jointly produced acts when the acts themselves are evil? The traditional view is that each person who knowingly and freely cooperates to produce a corporate act is morally responsible for the act.[99] In this view, situations in which a person needs the help of others to bring about a wrongful corporate act are no different in principle from situations in which a person needs some tool or instrument to commit a wrong. For example, if I want to shoot a person I have to rely on my gun to go off, just as if I want to defraud my company, I may have to rely on others to do their part. In both cases, if I knowingly and freely bring about the wrong, even though I rely on other things or people, I am fully morally responsible for the wrongs I inflict, even though this responsibility is shared with others.

Critics of this traditional view of the individual's responsibility for corporate acts have claimed that when the members of an organized group such as a corporation act together, their corporate act should be attributed to the group and, consequently, the corporate group and not the individuals who make up the group, must be held responsible for the act.[100] For example, we normally credit the manufacture of a defective car to the corporation that made it and not to the individual engineers involved in its manufacture. The law typically attributes the acts of a corporation's managers to the corporation (so long as the managers act within their authority) and not to the managers as individuals. Traditionalists, however, can reply that, although we sometimes attribute acts to corporate groups, this linguistic and legal fact does not change the moral reality behind all corporate acts: Individuals had to carry out the particular actions that brought about the corporate act. Because individuals are morally responsible for the known and intended consequences of their free actions, any individual who knowingly and freely joins his or her actions together with those of others, intending thereby to bring about a certain corporate act, will be morally responsible for that act.[101]

People sometimes claim, however, that when a subordinate acts on the orders of a legitimate superior, the subordinate is absolved of responsibility for that act. Only the superior is morally responsible for the wrongful act although the subordinate was the one who carried it out. The loyal agent's argument which we discussed above was based on this very same claim: the argument says that if an employee loyally does what the company ordered him or her to do, then it is the company, not the employee, who should be held responsible. Several years ago, for example, the managers of a company that made computer parts ordered their employees to write a government report that falsely stated that the computer parts the company sold to the government had been tested for defects when in fact they had not.[102] Some employees objected to falsifying the government reports, but when the managers insisted it was an order and the company wanted it, the employees complied with their orders. When the falsified reports were discovered, the managers argued that employees should not be held morally responsible because they were following orders.

Quick Review 1.27

Moral Responsibility is not Removed nor Mitigated by

- The cooperation of others
- Following orders

ON THE EDGE

Gun Manufacturers and Responsibility

John Allen Muhammad and John Lee Malvo shot and killed 13 people in Alabama, Georgia, Louisiana, Maryland, Virginia, and Washington, D.C. They used a semiautomatic assault rifle manufactured by Bushmaster Firearms, Inc. The two killers bought the rifle from Bull's Eye Shooter Supply, a gunshop in Tacoma, Washington, although federal law prohibited the shop from selling the gun to either Muhammad, who had a record of domestic battery, or to Malvo, who was a minor. Survivors of the victims have claimed that although Muhammad and Malvo were directly responsible for the deaths of the victims, both Bushmaster Firearms, Inc., and Bull's Eye Shooter Supply (and their owners) also "should be held responsible." Audits by the Bureau of Alcohol, Tobacco, and Firearms showed that Bull's Eye Shooter Supply had "lost" guns (238 in a 3-year period) or "lost" documentation—including its records of the Muhammad–Malvo sale—yet Bushmaster Firearms continued to sell its guns to the shop. Survivors of the victims claimed that Bushmaster Firearms had an obligation not to create an unreasonable risk of foreseeable harm from the distribution of its guns. The company, they claimed, failed to adequately investigate or screen this dealer's record of weapons handling, failed to adequately monitor and supervise how its dealer was selling its guns, and failed to provide training or incentives for its dealer to comply with gun laws. If Bull's Eye and Bushmaster had acted as they had an obligation to act, Muhammad and Malvo would have been prevented from obtaining the assault rifle they needed to kill their victims since federal laws prohibited both from buying guns. Bull's Eye and Bushmaster helped cause the deaths, the wife of a victim claimed, and so "they share the responsibility for my husband's death and many others."

1. Are Bull's Eye and Bushmaster morally responsible for the Washington, D.C. victims' deaths? Why or why not?
2. Are gun manufacturers or gun dealers ever morally responsible for deaths caused by the use of their guns? Explain.
3. Are manufacturers ever morally responsible for deaths caused by the use of their products? Why or why not?

Source: Chris Mcgann, "Families of 2 Sniper Victims Sue Arms Dealer, Manufacturer," *Seattle Post-Intelligencer*, January 17, 2003, p. 1A.

But the idea that following orders somehow absolves me of any blame for what I do is mistaken. As we have seen, I am responsible for whatever injuries I cause so long as I knew what I was doing and did it of my own free will. Therefore, when I knowingly and of my own free will cause an injury, the fact that I was following orders at the time does not change the reality that I fulfilled the three conditions that qualify me as morally responsible for my actions—causality, knowledge, and freedom—and so I am necessarily morally responsible for the injury. This is not to say that it is always easy to refuse to follow orders. In fact, it is often extremely difficult and can carry great personal costs. And as the Milgram experiment showed, most people are willing to obey the orders of an authority even when they know they are being ordered to do something wrong. Nevertheless, when I know that if I follow an order, I will be cooperating with evil, I must do everything I can to summon the strength and courage to refuse.

Study and Review on mythinkinglab.com

Questions for Review and Discussion

1. Define the following concepts: moral standards, non-moral standards, ethics, business ethics, normative study, descriptive study, systemic ethical issue, corporate ethical issue, individual ethical issue, corporate social responsibility, stakeholder, stakeholder theory, shareholder theory, globalization, ethical relativism, Integrative Social Contracts Theory, preconventional morality, conventional morality, post-conventional morality, moral reasoning, consistency requirement, framing a situation, euphemistic labeling, rationalizing our actions, diminishing comparisons, displacement of responsibility, diffusion of responsibility, distorting the harm, dehumanizing the victim, biased theory, moral seduction, weakness of will, strength of will, locus of control, moral responsibility, mitigated responsibility.
2. "Ethics has no place in business." Discuss this statement.
3. In your judgment, did the managers of Merck have a moral obligation to spend the money needed to develop the drug for river blindness? Can you state the general moral standard or standards on which you base your judgment? Are you willing to apply the "consistency requirement" to your moral standard or standards?
4. Read again the account of B. F. Goodrich, Lawson, and Vandivier. Which, if any, of the "obstacles to moral behavior" do you see operating in this B. F. Goodrich situation?
5. "Kohlberg's views on moral development show that the more morally mature a person becomes, the more likely it is that the person will obey the moral norms of his or her society." Discuss this statement.

Web Resources

Readers who would like to research the general topic of business ethics on the Internet might want to begin by accessing the following web sites. The web site of Santa Clara University's Markkula Center for Applied Ethics has outstanding articles and other content plus hundreds of annotated links to other Web resources on ethics at *www.scu.edu/ethics*. Larry Hinman's Ethics Updates at the University of San Diego also has a large collection of articles and links to numerous topics in ethics at *ethics.sandiego.edu*. Still a useful resource for business ethics research on the Web is Sharon Stoeger's web site which provides links to numerous online business ethics resources at *www.web-miner.com/busethics.htm*. The Essential Organization provides links to numerous organizations and data resources that deal with corporate social responsibility at *www.essential.org*. Corporate Watch has information on various companies and issues related to business ethics at *www.corpwatch.org* as does Resources for Activists at *www.betterworldlinks.org/book100.htm*, World Watch at *www.worldwatch.org*; and Mallenbaker's web site on corporate social responsibility at *www.mallenbaker.net/csr*.

CASES

Explore the Concept on mythinkinglab.com

Slavery in the Chocolate Industry[1]

Forty-five percent of the chocolate we consume in the United States and in the rest of the world is made from cocoa beans grown and harvested on farms in the Ivory Coast, a small nation on the western coast of Africa. Few realize that a portion of the Ivory Coast cocoa beans that goes into the chocolate we eat was grown and harvested by slave children. The slaves are boys between 12 and 16—but sometimes as young as 9—who are kidnapped from villages in surrounding nations and sold to the cocoa farmers by traffickers. The farmers whip, beat, and starve the boys to force them to do the hot, difficult work of clearing the fields, harvesting the beans, and drying them in the sun. The boys work from sunrise to sunset. Some are locked in at night in windowless rooms where they sleep on bare wooden planks. Far from home, unsure of their location, unable to speak the language, isolated in rural areas, and threatened with harsh beatings if they try to get away, the boys rarely attempt to escape their nightmare situation. Those who do try are usually caught, severely beaten as an example to others, and then locked in solitary confinement. Every year unknown numbers of these boys die or are killed on the cocoa farms that supply our chocolate.

The plight of the enslaved children was first widely publicized at the turn of the twenty-first century when True Vision, a British television company, took videos of slave boys working on Ivory Coast farms and made a documentary depicting the sufferings of the boys. In September 2000, the documentary was broadcast in Great Britain, the United States, and other parts of the world. The U.S. State Department, in its *Year 2001 Human Rights Report*, estimated that about 15,000 children from the neighboring nations of Benin, Burkina Faso, Mali, and Togo had been sold into slavery to labor on Ivory Coast farms. The International Labor Organization reported on June 11, 2001 that child slavery was indeed "widespread" in Ivory Coast and a Knight-Ridder newspaper investigation published on June 24, 2001 corroborated the use of slave boys on Ivory Coast cocoa farms. In 2006, *The New York Times* reported that child slavery continued to be a problem in West Africa. In 2007, *BBC News* published several stories on the "thousands" of children who were still working as slaves on cocoa farms in Ivory Coast. *Fortune Magazine* in 2008 reported that slavery in the Ivory Coast was still a continuing problem, and a *BBC* documentary entitled *Chocolate: The Bitter Truth*, broadcast on March 24, 2010, a decade after the use of slave boys in the chocolate industry was first revealed, showed young boys were still being used as slaves on the cocoa farms of the Ivory Coast.

Although slavery is illegal in the Ivory Coast, the law is poorly enforced. Open borders, a shortage of enforcement officers, and the willingness of local officials to accept bribes from people trafficking in slaves, all contribute to the problem. In addition, prices for cocoa beans in global markets have been depressed most years since 1996. As prices declined, the already impoverished cocoa farmers turned to slavery to cut their labor costs. Although prices began to improve during the early years of the twenty-first century, cocoa prices fell again in 2004 and remained low until the summer of 2010 when they again began to rise.

The poverty that motivated many Ivory Coast cocoa farmers to buy children trafficked as slaves was aggravated by other factors besides low cocoa prices. Working on isolated farms, cocoa farmers cannot communicate among themselves nor with the outside world to learn what cocoa is selling for. Consequently they are at the mercy of local middlemen who drive out to the farms, buy the farmers' cocoa for half of its current market price, and haul it away in their trucks. Unable to afford trucks themselves, the farmers must rely on the middlemen to get their cocoa to market.

Chocolate is a $13 billion industry in the United States which consumes 3.1 billion pounds each year. The names of the four largest U.S. chocolate manufacturers—all of whom use the morally "tainted" cocoa beans from the Ivory Coast in their products—are well known: Hershey Foods Corp. (maker of Hershey's milk chocolate, Reeses, and Almond Joy), M&M Mars, Inc. (maker of M&Ms, Mars, Twix, Dove, and Milky Ways), Nestlé USA, (maker of Nestlé Crunch, Kit Kat, Baby Ruth, and Butterfingers), and Kraft Foods (which also uses chocolate in its baking and breakfast products). Less well known, but a key part of the industry, are the names of Archer Daniels Midland Co., Barry Callebaut, and Cargill Inc., all of whom serve as middlemen who buy the beans from the Ivory Coast, grind and process them, and then sell the processed cocoa to the chocolate manufacturers.

While all the major chocolate companies used beans from Ivory Coast farms, a portion of which relied on the labor of enslaved children, many smaller companies avoided using chocolate made from Ivory Coast beans and instead turned to using chocolate processed from "untainted" beans grown in other parts of the world. These companies include: Clif Bar, Cloud Nine, Dagoba Organic Chocolate, Denman Island Chocolate, Gardners Candies, Green and Black's, Kailua Candy Company, Koppers Chocolate, L.A. Burdick Chocolates, Montezuma's Chocolates, Newman's Own Organics, Omanhene Cocoa Bean Company, Rapunzel Pure Organics, and The Endangered Species Chocolate Company. Other small companies turned to using fair trade chocolate and organic chocolate because these are made from beans grown on farms that are regularly monitored and so they, too, are made from untainted beans.

That many farmers in the Ivory Coast use slave boys to farm their cocoa beans was already known to American chocolate-makers when media reports first began publicizing the issue. In 2001, the Chocolate Manufacturers Association, a trade group of U.S. chocolate manufacturers (whose members include Hershey, Mars, Nestlé, and others), admitted to newspapers that they had been aware of the use of slave boys on Ivory Coast cocoa farms for some time. Pressured by various antislavery groups, the Chocolate Manufacturers Association stated on June 22, 2001 that it "condemned" "these practices" and agreed to fund a "study" of the situation.

On June 28, 2001, U.S. Representative Eliot Engel sponsored a bill aimed at setting up a labeling system that would inform consumers whether the chocolate they were buying was "slavefree," i.e., guaranteed not to have been produced by slave children. The measure passed the House of Representatives by a vote of 291 to115. Before a measure can become law, however, both the House of Representatives and the Senate must approve it. U.S. Senator Tom Harkin therefore prepared to introduce the same bill in the Senate. Before the Senate could consider the bill, the U.S. chocolate industry—led by Mars, Hershey, Kraft Foods and Archer Daniels Midland and with the help of lobbyists Bob Dole and George Mitchell—mounted a major lobbying effort to fight the "slave-free" labeling system. The companies argued that a labeling system would not only hurt their own sales, but in the long run could hurt poor African cocoa farmers by reducing their sales and lowering the price of cocoa which would add to the very pressures that led them to use slave labor in the first place. As a result of the industry's lobbying, the "slave-free" labeling bill was never approved by the Senate. Nevertheless, Representative Engel and Senator Harkin threatened to introduce a new bill that would prohibit the import of cocoa produced by slave labor, unless the chocolate companies voluntarily eliminated slave labor from their production chains.

On October 1, 2001, the members of the Chocolate Manufacturers Association and the World Cocoa Foundation, caught in the spotlight of media attention, announced that they intended to put in place a system that would eliminate "the worse forms of child labor" including slavery. In spring of 2002, the Chocolate Manufacturers Association and the World Cocoa Foundation as well as the major chocolate producers—Hershey's, M&M Mars, Nestle, and World's Finest Chocolate—and the major cocoa processors—Blommer Chocolate, Guittard Chocolate, Barry Callebaut, and Archer Daniels Midland—all signed an agreement to establish a system of certification that would verify and certify that the cocoa beans they used were not produced by the use of child slaves. Known as the "Harkin-Engel Protocol," the agreement also said the chocolate companies would fund training programs for cocoa bean farmers to educate them about growing techniques while explaining the importance of avoiding the use of slave labor. The members of the Chocolate Manufacturers Association also agreed to "investigate" conditions on the cocoa farms and establish an "international foundation" that could "oversee and sustain efforts" to eliminate child slavery on cocoa farms. In July, 2002, the first survey sponsored by the Chocolate Manufacturers Association concluded that some 200,000 children—not all of them slaves—were working in hazardous conditions on cocoa farms and that most of them did not attend school.

Unfortunately, in 2002, Ivory Coast became embroiled in a civil war that continued until an uneasy peace was established in 2005 and finalized in 2007; rebel forces, however, continued to control the northern half of the country. Reports claimed that much of the money funding the violence of both the government and rebel groups during these years came from sales of cocoa, and that buyers of "blood chocolate" from Ivory Coast were supporting this violence.

The 2005 deadline the major chocolate companies and their associations had set, came, and passed without the promised establishment of a certification system to ensure beans were not being produced by slave children. At this point, the chocolate companies amended the protocol to give themselves more time by extending their own deadline to July, 2008, saying that the certification process had turned out to be more difficult than they thought it would, particularly with the outbreak of a civil war. Although the companies did not establish a certification system while the civil war raged, however, they did manage to secure enough cocoa beans to keep their chocolate factories going at full speed throughout the war.

By early 2008, the companies had still not started work on establishing a certification system or any other method of ensuring that slave labor was not used to produce the cocoa beans they used. The companies issued a new statement in which they extended to 2010 the deadline for complying with their promise to establish a certification system. According to the companies, they had been investing several million dollars a year into a foundation that was working on the problem of child labor. However, an investigative reporter, in an article published in *Fortune Magazine* on February 15, 2008, found the foundation had only one staff member working in Ivory Coast. The activities of the staff member were limited to giving "sensitization" workshops to local people during which he would explain that child labor is a bad thing. The foundation was also helping a shelter that provided housing and education to homeless street children. The reporter found no signs of work being done on a certification system. By now the monitoring systems used in the fair trade and organic parts of the industry had been functioning for several years, yet the larger companies operating in Ivory Coast seemed unable or uninterested in learning from their example.

The existence of a large and well-organized system for trafficking children from surrounding countries onto Ivory Coast farms was once against demonstrated on June 18, 2009. On that date INTERPOL, the international police organization, carried out a series of raids of several farms believed to harbor slave children and managed to rescue 54 children. Aged between 11 and 16, the children had been working 12 hours a day for no salary; many were regularly beaten and none had received any schooling. In a public statement, INTERPOL estimated that "hundreds of thousands of children are working illegally in the plantations."

On September 30, 2010, the Payson Center at Tulane University issued a report on the progress that had been made on the certification system the chocolate industry in 2002 had promised to establish, as well as on the progress the industry had made regarding its promise to eliminate "the worse forms of child labor," including child slavery, on the farms from which the industry sourced its cocoa. The report was commissioned by the United States Department of Labor who had been asked by Congress to assess progress on the "Harkin-Engel Protocol," and who gave Tulane University an initial grant of $4.3 million in 2006, and an additional $1.2 million in 2009 to compile the report. According to the report, "Industry is still far from achieving its target to have a sector-wide independently verified certification process fully in place ... by the end of 2010." The report found that between 2002—the date of the original agreement—and September 2010, the Industry had managed to contact only about 95 (2.3 percent) of Ivory Coast's cocoa farming communities, and that to complete its "remediation efforts" it would have to contact an additional 3,655 farm communities. While the Tulane group "confirmed" that forced labor was being used on the cocoa farms, it also found that no industry efforts to "remediate" the use of forced labor "are in place."

Not surprisingly, the problem of certification still remained unresolved in 2011. After the media attention had died down, the manufacturers and distributors buying Ivory Coast cocoa beans seemed incapable of finding a way to "certify" that slavery was not used to harvest the beans they purchased. Representatives of the chocolate companies argued that the problem of certification was difficult because there are more than 600,000 cocoa farms in Ivory Coast; most of them small family farms located in remote rural regions that are difficult to reach and that lack good roads and other infrastructure. Critics, however, pointed out that these difficulties did not seem to pose any obstacles to obtaining beans from these many scattered cocoa farms. Cocoa bean farmers, poor and buffeted by the low price of cocoa beans, continued to use enslaved children although they were secretive about it. To make matters worse, on February 2011, fighting between the rebels in the north and the Ivory Coast government in the south again broke out for a brief period in a dispute over who was the legitimate winner of the 2010 presidential election. The fighting ended in April 2011 when one of the candidates finally conceded the election, allowing Allassane Ouattara to be declared the legitimate president.

In 2010 another film, this one entitled *The Dark Side of Chocolate*, once more documented the continuing use of enslaved children on Ivory Coast farms, although representatives of the chocolate companies interviewed in the film denied the problem or claimed they did not know anything about it. The beans tainted by the labor of slave boys are therefore still being quietly mixed together in bins and warehouses with beans harvested by free paid workers, so that the two are indistinguishable. From there they still make their way into the now tainted chocolate candies that Hershey's, M&M Mars, Nestle and Kraft Foods make and that we buy here and in Europe. Without an effective system of certification, in fact, virtually all the chocolate we eat that is made from West African (Ivory Coast and Ghana) cocoa contains a portion of tainted chocolate made from beans harvested by enslaved children.

Questions

1. What are the systemic, corporate, and individual ethical issues raised by this case?
2. In your view, is the kind of child slavery discussed in this case absolutely wrong no matter what, or is it only relatively wrong, i.e., if one happens to live in a society (like ours) that disapproves of child slavery? Explain your view and why you hold it.
3. Who shares in the moral responsibility for the slavery occurring in the chocolate industry?
4. Consider the bill that Representive Engle and Senator Harkin attempted to enact into a law, but which never became a law because of the lobbying efforts of the chocolate companies. What does this incident show about the view that "to be ethical it is enough for businesspeople to follow the law"?

Note

1. Sudarsan Raghavan and Sumana Chatterjee, "Child Slavery and the Chocolate Trade," *San Jose Mercury News*, June 24, 2001, p. 1A; Stop Child Labor, "There's Nothing Sweet About Child Slave Labor in the Cocoa Fields," accessed on April 26, 2004 at *http://www.stopchildlabor.org/internationalchildlabor/chocolate.htm*; Sharon LaFraniere, "Africa's World of Forced Labor in a 6 Year-Old's Eyes," *The New York Times*, October 29, 2006; Rageh Omaar, "The World of Modern Child Slavery," *BBC News* [Online], March 27, 2007, accessed April 29, 2010 at *http://news.bbc.co.uk/2/hi/programmes/this_world/6458377.stm*; Christian Parenti, "Chocolate's Bittersweet Economy," *Fortune Magazine*, February 15, 2008; Payson Center for International Development and Technology Transfer Tulane University, *Fourth Annual Report: Oversight of Public and Private Initiatives to Eliminate the Worse Forms of Child Labor in the Cocoa Sector in Cote d'Ivoire and Ghana*, September 30, 2010, accessed March 10, 2011 at *http://www.childlabor-payson.org/Final%20Fourth%20Annual%20Report.pdf*.

CASES

Aaron Beam and the HealthSouth Fraud

Explore the Concept on mythinkinglab.com

After graduating from Ourso College of Business, Aaron Beam went on to become a Certified Public Accountant in 1978 and two years later met Richard Scrushy whom he described as a "charismatic" leader, an engagingly "charming" person, and a "brilliant" businessman. At the time Scrushy was working for Lifemark Corporation, a health care company where he had worked his way up to the position of Chief Operating Officer after having taught briefly in the respiratory therapy program of the University of Alabama and at Wallace State Community College. In 1983 Scrushy invited Beam to join him in starting HealthSouth, a new company that would provide medical rehabilitation services to hospitals and their outpatients in Birmingham, Alabama. Scrushy believed that they would be able to provide rehabilitation therapy to patients at lower costs than regular hospitals and so hospitals would be glad to send their patients to them for rehabilitation. He would turn out to be right.[1]

They founded the company in 1984 with Scrushy as Chief Executive Officer and Beam as Chief Financial Officer. Beam later said that Scrushy ran the company like a "dictator," and with a self-assurance that intimidated people and sometimes made Aaron and others fearful of contradicting him. Scrushy, he said, was "almost a cult-like figure," who inspired intense loyalty and whom people eagerly followed, willingly carrying out his confident orders.[2] Another employee said Scrushy "had boundless energy" and "was a great motivator" who worked "so hard himself, it was almost like you couldn't let him down."[3]

From the beginning Scrushy and Beam both knew the company had to appear profitable to satisfy investors and lenders and to later succeed in issuing and selling company stock to the public. Although the company was doing reasonably well, Scrushy told Beam that he should do whatever he could to make their financial reports look even better. Although Beam was reluctant at first, he felt both pressured and awed by Scrushy and so eventually moved some of the company's startup costs from the "expenses" column to the "capital investments" column, which made their net profits look larger.[4] While he realized this might be "a little" misleading, Beam felt it was technically within the bounds of accounting rules and that investors would be sophisticated enough to understand what was happening. He described the move to himself as "aggressive accounting" but definitely "not fraudulent."

In 1986, the company successfully went public and both Scrushy and Beam, as well as their investors, made a great deal of money. Moreover, the company continued to expand rapidly and revenues continued to climb upward just as quickly. With his new riches, Beam was able to buy a beach house, a condo in the French Quarter of New Orleans, a private plane, fancy cars, and $30,000 worth of Hermes ties. Everywhere he went he was known and respected:

> I was a rock star. I could go into any restaurant and see people pointing out that they wanted to talk to me, meet me and tell me what a great job I was doing. It was pretty heavy stuff.[5]

Scrushy also celebrated his new wealth. He had divorced his first wife and married his second, a woman named Karen with whom he had four children and a passionate but stormy relationship. He bought two Cessna jets, Lamborghini and Rolls Royce cars, ten yachts, expensive art works, several multimillion-dollar houses, and built himself an estate with a 20-room 14,000 square foot mansion and a helicopter pad. He made lavish donations to charities, gave money to schools that gratefully named buildings after him, and made such a large gift to a local community college that it named a whole campus the "Richard M. Scrushy Campus." In high school Scrushy had taught himself to play the guitar and had played in garage bands; now he recruited several professional musicians, formed a country music group named Dallas County Line, and with himself as lead singer, cut a CD and financed a world tour for the group.

Over the next ten years the HealthSouth company grew into a $3 billion Fortune 500 company. With 22,000 employees, it was the nation's largest provider of rehabilitation, surgery, and therapy outpatient services. Beam continued using "aggressive accounting" practices in the company's financial reports. When the company expanded to other locations, he had some of the costs capitalized instead of being expensed, and sometimes the added revenues from the new locations were listed as revenue growth from the company's previous locations. And instead of writing off unpaid receivables, Beam just kept them on the books as company "assets." He continued to reassure himself with the thought that "astute investors knew what we were doing and saw it as financial gamemanship and not outright fraud."[6]

But part way through the second quarter of 1996, Scrushy and Beam realized that the company, for the first time, would fall short of meeting Wall Street analysts' expectations of quarterly revenue by about $50 million. The two men were sure this was a one-time event and that the company would return to meeting analysts' targets the following financial quarter like it had for the past 40 quarters. But at the time, the company was negotiating a new credit agreement with a syndicate of 32 lenders from around the world, and while the banks had agreed to extend HealthSouth a line of credit totaling $1.25 billion, they had also made clear that the company had to provide them with favorable quarterly financial statements.[7] Scrushy assured Beam that if the banks got wind of the shortfall it would cripple the company they had worked so hard to build, so Beam had to do everything he could to keep as much information about the shortfall as possible from leaking out of the company. If they could just get through the quarter, Scrushy felt, then everything would be okay.[8]

Agreeing with Scrushy's assessment of the situation, Beam decided to fix the company books "this one time." "I knew if we did report bad earnings, it would be disastrous," Beam said later, so "I let myself slip into agreeing to commit fraud." Beam convinced two of the people working for him in the Finance Department to come in on the plan: Bill Owens, the company controller, and Mike Martin, the company treasurer. With the help of a few other employees, they went through the earnings reports that each of the dozens of HealthSouth clinics scattered around the country turned in to company headquarters each financial quarter. They carefully inflated the numbers by inserting many small additional revenue entries throughout each report. Then they consolidated the reports into a single corporate report.[9] The numerous fictitious additions they made on the reports were all small because they knew the external auditors would only check the validity of large revenue entries, and were highly unlikely to check the many small fictitious entries they were making.[10] Moreover, Scrushy had earlier told Beam that he did not allow the company's own internal auditors access to the corporate general ledgers, which is where the fraud was being carried out.

Although he realized these actions violated generally accepted accounting principles, Beam felt that what he was doing was for the good of everyone in the company. If the company failed, a lot of people would be hurt. And anyway, he was only going to do it just this one time.

Unfortunately, the following quarter company earnings again fell short of Wall Street expectations. This time Scrushy did not have to persuade Beam. After the first time, Beam later said, it had become "a little easier going down that road."[11] The fraud proceeded much like it had the previous quarter, except that more people were brought into the scheme. Ken Livesay, the assistant controller, helped by downloading all of the clinic reports from around the country to his computer and figuring out the gap between the company's true earnings and what Wall Street expected—about $70 million this time.[12] He reported these figures to Bill Owens and Mike Martin. Then Beam, Owens, Martin, Livesay, and a few others worked their way through the clinics' reports inserting enough fictitious revenue entries to fill in the gap. Because earnings kept falling short of expectations, the process had to be repeated each quarter. Eventually more finance personnel were added to the group until it grew to about 15 people who started referring to themselves as "the family."

By 1997 HealthSouth was the largest rehabilitation services company in the industry and, with a total of $106 million in compensation, Scrushy was the third-highest-paid CEO in America. A year earlier his second wife had divorced him and now he married his third, Leslie, with whom he had two more children. He became an active member of the Guiding Light Church to which he made sizable donations, and he and his wife eventually began hosting a daily evangelical television show that was broadcast from the church.

Although he was now hardly hesitating to tamper with the company reports, Beam still felt anguished and guilty:

> I just didn't have the courage or the ethical bearing to stand up to Richard. I didn't say 'No, this is wrong.' My life changed. I couldn't sleep. I had crossed the line and had done something I couldn't deal with and it was just terrible.[13]

Ashamed of what he was now so willingly doing, Beam decided to retire from the company in 1997. He bought several acres of land in the country and there he and his wife built their 5,000 square-foot "dream house." Beam assumed the company's earnings would eventually improve and that it would once again do well enough to stop having to falsify its financial reports. He was wrong.

The fraudulent accounting at HealthSouth continued for six more years, until 2003 when the F.B.I. began investigating whether Scrushy might be part of an insider trading scheme. As part of its investigation, the F.B.I. interviewed Weston Smith who had replaced Beam as Chief Financial Officer. Smith had little to say about the insider trading scheme; instead he informed the surprised investigators about the fraud that had been going on at HealthSouth.

By the time the government stepped in and prosecuted HealthSouth's executives in 2003, HealthSouth's earnings had been overstated by $2.7 billion. In 2005, saying he did not know that fraudulent entries were being inserted into the books, and in spite of being accused by Beam, Smith, Martin, Owens, Livesay, and others of having known about the scheme, Scrushy was declared innocent of any criminal wrongdoing by a jury. Beam and the other members of "the family" were not so lucky. He and 15 other HealthSouth employees who had helped carry out the fraud were fined and jailed or placed on probation.

Although Scrushy was not convicted of any wrongdoing in the HealthSouth fraud, in 2006 he was found guilty of paying $500,000 in bribes to Alabama Governor Don Siegelman in exchange for a seat on a state hospital regulatory board. Scrushy was sentenced to seven years in prison for the bribe, a sentence he began serving in 2007. Scrushy believed that government prosecutors had filed the bribery charges against him in retaliation for their inability to secure his conviction in the HealthSouth trial, but his lawyers failed to win the appeals they filed on Scrushy's behalf. In 2009, while serving his jail sentence, Scrushy lost a $2.8 billion civil lawsuit brought against him by the company's shareholders; at the end of that trial, the judge said that it was clear to him that "Scrushy knew of and actively participated in the fraud." Scrushy's bank accounts were seized and his houses, boats, cars, and other remaining property were auctioned off to pay the $2.8 billion judgment against him. Distraught by the outcome of the lawsuit which left his wife and children penniless, Scrushy continued to maintain his innocence in both the HealthSouth fraud and in the Siegelman bribe case. His wife remained loyal to him and brought their children to visit him every week while he served his prison sentence. Both his wife and his former pastor at the Guiding Light Church continued to believe in Scrushy's innocence.

Although he could have received up to 30 years in jail and fined up to $1 million, Aaron Beam spent only 3 months in a federal prison and paid $285,000 in fines and another $250,000 in lawyer's fees. After he was released from prison in 2006, Beam said his experience had taught him some hard lessons, but he still blamed Scrushy for much of what had happened:

> There are a lot of sociopaths heading major corporations. They have huge egos, they intimidate people, they totally believe that they are right in everything they do or say, and they have no empathy for other people. If you're in the workplace and you have a boss like that, be aware. Realize that one day, you could be asked to do something you shouldn't do. Don't be overly influenced by others to the point that you do wrong. You have to have some moral character about how you conduct yourself in the business world. The pressure to make earnings, to make money, can lead you down a path that you shouldn't go.[14]

Aaron Beam now runs a lawn service called "Green Beam Lawn Service" in Alabama using a lawnmower he bought by bartering 50 of his last remaining Hermes ties. He has this to say about his present life:

> I have no employees, it's just me. But I'm living my life honestly now, and there is a lot of peace of mind in that. When I mow somebody's grass, and they pay me $50 in the heat in south Alabama, I know I've earned that money, and I sleep well at night.[15]

Questions

1. Which of the "obstacles" to moral behavior do you see at work in Aaron Beam's behavior and thinking? In Scrushy's?
2. Explain how Aaron Beam might have used the "loyal agent's argument" to defend his actions. Do you think that in Aaron Beam's situation the "loyal agent's argument" might have been valid? Explain.
3. In terms of Kohlberg's views on moral development, at what stage of moral development would you place Aaron Beam? Explain. At what stage would you place Richard Scrushy?
4. Was Aaron Beam *morally responsible* for engaging in the "aggressive accounting" methods he used? Explain. Was his responsibility *mitigated* in any way? Explain. Was he *morally responsible* for changing the clinic reports to increase the company's earnings? Was his responsibility for this *mitigated*? Explain. Were those who *cooperated* in his actions morally responsible for those actions? Was their responsibility mitigated? Do you think Richard Scrushy was morally responsible for the accounting fraud? Explain.

Notes

1. Seth Fox, "A World Unraveled," *Business Report*, August 1, 2006, accessed September 3, 2010 at *http://www.bus.lsu.edu/accounting/faculty/lcrumbley/unraveled.htm*; John Helyar, "The Insatiable King Richard. He started as a nobody. He became a hotshot CEO. He tried to be a country star. Then it all came crashing down. The bizarre rise and fall of HealthSouth's Richard Scrushy," *Fortune*, July 7, 2003.
2. Jeanine Ibrahim, "American Greed," *CNBC*, [Producer's Notes], accessed September 3, 2010 at *http://www.cnbc.com/id/27087295*; Jimmy DeButts, "Crossing the Line: HealthSouth CFO Aaron Beam Speaks Out," *Birmingham Business Journal*, October 2, 2009
3. Helyar, "The Insatiable King Richard."
4. *Fox*, "A World Unraveled."
5. *University of Texas News*, "Auditors Get an Insider's View of Corporate Fraud," April 12, 2010, accessed September

3, 2010 at *http://www.utdallas.edu/news/2010/4/12-2391_Auditors-Get-an-Insiders-View-of-Corporate-Fraud_article.html*

6. Aaron Beam, *HealthSouth: The* Wagon *to Disaster*, (Fairhope, Alabama: Wagon Publishing [self-published book], 2009)
7. *U.S. Department of Justice*, "Former HealthSouth Chief Financial Officer Aaron Beam Charged with Ban Fraud," April 24, 2003, [news release], accessed September 3, 2010 at *http://www.justice.gov/opa/pr/2003/April/03_crm_255.htm*
8. Steve Chiotakis, "How HealthSouth Started a Fraud," *American Public Media Marketplace*, January 6, 2010, accessed September 3, 2010 at *http://marketplace.publicradio.org/display/web/2010/01/06/am-scrushy/*
9. "Accountant Describes How HealthSouth Fraud Happened," *USA Today*, January 28, 2005.
10. John A. MacDonald, "Video Depositions Fill Much of Afternoon in First Day of Richard Scrushy Civil Trial," *The Birmingham News*, May 11, 2009.
11. Aaron Beam, *HealthSouth: The Wagon to Disaster*.
12. Jay Reeves, "Ex-HealthSouth Exec Details Fraud," *The SeattleTimes*, February 24, 2005.
13. *University of Texas News*, "Auditors Get an Insider's View of Corporate Fraud."
14. Aaron Beam, "Aaron Beam, Former Chief Financial Officer of HealthSouth," posted on the Aaron Beam web site and accessed on September 3, 2010 at *http://www.aaronbeam.net/bio.html*
15. Chiotakis, "How HealthSouth Started a Fraud."

2

Ethical Principles in Business

What is the utilitarian approach to moral decision-making?

How do human rights apply to business situations?

What is "justice"?

Why are personal relationships essential to an "ethic of care"?

How can we integrate the various approaches to moral evaluation?

What role does character play in morality?

Why do many of our moral decisions seem to be automatic and unconscious?

Even when buying vegetables at a farmer's market, customers expect to be treated with honesty, fairness, and respect.

INTRODUCTION

Listen to the Chapter Audio on mythinkinglab.com

It was the middle of the last century, 1948, when the whites-only National Party first won control of the government of South Africa. Earlier racial laws had decreed that only whites, who were 10 percent of the population, had the right to vote, and denied political participation to blacks, who were about 80 percent of the population, as well as to "mixed-race coloreds" and Indians who together made up the remaining 10 percent. The whites-only National Party passed stringent apartheid legislation as soon as they gained power. Apartheid laws were designed to preserve the racial purity and supremacy of whites by keeping other races socially and physically separated from them, restricting nonwhites to inferior jobs, housing and farmlands, and strengthening earlier laws that made whites the effective rulers of South Africa's diverse population. The apartheid system deprived the entire black population of all civil rights. They had no right to freedom of speech, no right to unionize, and no right to freedom of assembly. Blacks, coloreds, and Indians had to live in racially segregated areas, received grossly discriminatory wages, could not intermarry with whites, could not supervise whites, had to attend separate and inferior schools, use separate bathrooms, enter public buildings by separate entrances, eat in separate dining rooms, and avoid socializing with whites.

These oppressive racial laws incited black resistance that the white government met with force. Over the years, as blacks repeatedly demonstrated against the increasingly brutal regime, the government responded with ever more violent killings, arrests, and repression. Beginning with the leadership of Prime Minister Strijdom, known as an honest but inflexible and belligerent hardline racist, the government ruthlessly killed hundreds of young black activists and jailed thousands more. Among those imprisoned was the energetic (some said "hotheaded") activist, Nelson Mandela, an inspiring, charismatic, resilient, and brave son of a black tribal chief. Opposition political parties were outlawed and their leaders were imprisoned. These white supremacy policies of the apartheid government remained in place until the 1990s.

While the apartheid regime was in power, Caltex, an American oil company located in South Africa, operated a chain of gas stations and several oil refineries that it supplied with oil it imported from other countries. Jointly owned by Texaco and Standard Oil, Caltex had repeatedly expanded its operations in South Africa, giving the South African government greater access to the oil it needed. The South African economy relied on oil for 25 percent of its energy needs, and South African law required refineries to set aside some of their oil for the government. In addition, stiff corporate taxes channeled a high percentage of Caltex annual revenues into the hands of the apartheid government.

Many stockholders of Texaco and Standard Oil bitterly opposed Caltex's operations in South Africa. In 1983, 1984, and 1985, they introduced shareholder resolutions requiring Caltex to either break off relations with the South African government or leave South Africa altogether.[1] A leader of the dissident stockholders had earlier stated why Caltex and other U.S. companies should leave South Africa:

> Nonwhites in South Africa are rightless persons in the land of their birth … [The black South African] has no rights in "white areas." He cannot vote, cannot own land, and may not have his family with him unless he has government permission.… The two major political parties have been banned and hundreds of persons detained for political offenses … strikes by Africans are illegal and meaningful collective bargaining is outlawed.… By investing in South Africa, American companies inevitably strengthen the status quo of white supremacy.… The leasing of a computer, the establishment of a new plant, the selling of supplies to the military all have political overtones.… And among the country's white community, the overriding goal of politics is maintenance of white control. In the words of Prime Minister John Vorster …"We are building a nation for whites only."[2]

The management of Caltex, however, did not feel that it should stop selling petroleum products to the South African government or leave South Africa. The company acknowledged that its operations provided a strategic resource for South Africa's government and that the government was racist. Nevertheless, the company claimed that its operations ultimately helped black South Africans, particularly the company's black workers toward whom the company had special responsibilities. In a statement opposing one of the many stockholders' resolutions, Caltex managers made their position clear:

> Texaco believes that continuation of Caltex's operations in South Africa is in the best interests of Caltex's employees of all races in South Africa. . . . In management's opinion, if Caltex were to withdraw from South Africa in an attempt to achieve political changes in that country, as the proposal directs, . . . such withdrawal would endanger prospects for the future of all Caltex employees in South Africa regardless of race. We are convinced that the resulting dislocation and hardship would fall most heavily on the nonwhite communities. In this regard, and contrary to the implications of the stockholders' statement, Caltex employment policies include equal pay for equal work and the same level of benefit plans for all employees as well as a continuing and successful program to advance employees to positions of responsibility on the basis of ability, not race.[3]

Caltex managers argued that foreign corporations in South Africa had helped black incomes rise by more than 150 percent during the 1970s. Moreover, they claimed that U.S. corporations with internal policies of "equal pay for equal work," had narrowed the gap between black and white incomes by a significant amount.

Among those who vigorously supported the resolutions asking U.S. companies to leave the country was Desmond Tutu, an outspoken black South African bishop of the Anglican Church who won the Nobel Peace Prize in 1984. Described as a "modest, cheerful man of faith, with a great passion for justice," Tutu advocated nonviolent opposition to apartheid. Tutu led numerous peaceful protests, marches, and boycotts against the racist regime and against what he would later call its "human rights abuses." Although in constant danger for his life, Tutu was described as "courageously" calling on the world's multinationals to exert economic pressure on South Africa's white government by leaving and staying away until apartheid was ended. To suggest that U.S. companies should stay in South Africa because they paid higher wages and provided other economic benefits, Tutu said, was to "attempt to polish my chains and make them more comfortable. I want to cut my chains and cast them away."

The debate over whether Caltex should have continued to operate in South Africa during the apartheid regime was a moral debate. The debate was not about what the laws of South Africa required. The requirements of the law were clear. Instead, the debate centered on whether apartheid laws were morally acceptable and whether companies should help support the government responsible for those laws. The arguments on both sides of these issues appealed to moral considerations. They appealed, in fact, to four basic kinds of moral standards: utilitarianism, rights, justice, and caring. At several points, moreover, the debate referred to the virtues and vices of various people involved in the struggle over apartheid.

Those who argued that Caltex should leave South Africa, for example, argued that the company was actively supporting policies of inequality that were unjust because they discriminated against blacks and laid burdens on blacks that whites did not have to bear. They also argued that these government policies violated black people's human rights, including their right to participate in the political life of their nation, to speak freely, to come and go as they wanted, to unionize, and to be free of the humiliations of racial segregation. And they claimed that the apartheid regime divided families and communities thereby destroying morally significant human relationships. These arguments were appeals to two distinct kinds of moral principles. Judgments about *justice* are based on moral principles that identify fair ways of distributing benefits and burdens among the members of a society. Judgments about human *rights* are based on moral principles that advocate respect for people's freedom and well-being. And judgments about the importance of human relationships can be based on what is called an *ethic of care*.

The arguments of Caltex managers also appealed to moral considerations. They argued that if the company stayed in South Africa, then black as well as white Caltex employees, would be better off because the company would provide them with economic and social benefits that would allow them to have richer and more satisfying lives. On the other hand, they argued, if the company left, blacks would suffer greatly and be burdened with "dislocations and hardship" because they would be deprived of the many economic benefits the company provided. In these arguments, Caltex's managers were appealing to what is called a *utilitarian* standard of morality. Utilitarianism is the moral view that in any situation the right course of action is the one that will provide people with the greatest amount of benefits while minimizing harms. In addition, Caltex managers also argued that they took special care of their black workers and that the company's special responsibility for the well-being of its workers implied that it should not abandon them. These additional considerations are closely linked to an *ethic of care* that emphasizes the value of human relationships and of caring for the well-being of those who are dependent upon us.

ethic of care An ethic that emphasizes caring for the concrete well being of those near to us.

Finally, embedded in the debate were references to the moral virtues and vices of various persons involved in the struggle around apartheid. Archbishop Tutu, for example, was described as modest, courageous, nonviolent, cheerful, and passionate for justice. Prime Minister Strijdom, who used violent force to protect apartheid, was known as an honest, but inflexible and belligerent racist who could also be ruthless. Nelson Mandela was characterized as energetic, hotheaded, inspiring, courageous, resilient, and charismatic. The character traits attributed to these people are examples of the kind of virtues that are encouraged and the vices that are discouraged by an *ethic of virtue*.

ethic of virtue An ethic based on evaluations of the moral character of persons or groups.

These kinds of approaches to moral judgments are the most important types of ethical standards studied by moral philosophers—although, as we will see, there are other approaches. As the case of Caltex in South Africa demonstrates, these approaches are the common and natural ways we discuss and debate the morality of what we were doing. Each approach to moral evaluation employs distinct moral concepts, and each emphasizes aspects of moral behavior that are neglected or at least not emphasized by the others. The purpose of this chapter is to explain each of these approaches to moral judgments. We will describe each approach, explain the kinds of concepts and information that each employs, identify their strengths and weaknesses, and explain how these approaches can be used to clarify the moral issues that confront us in business.

2.1 Utilitarianism: Weighing Social Costs and Benefits

We begin by looking at an approach to moral decision-making the Caltex managers took. They claimed that one of the reasons that Caltex should remain in South Africa was because that course of action would have the most beneficial consequences and the fewest harms, at least in comparison to the results of abandoning South Africa. This approach is sometimes referred to as a *consequentialist* approach to ethics and, more specifically, as a *utilitarian* approach. To see more clearly what the approach involves, let's look at a situation where this approach was a basic consideration in a business decision that had a dramatic impact on the lives of many people.

During the last decades of the twentieth century, Ford Motor Company began losing market share to Japanese companies who were making compact, fuel-efficient cars. Lee Iaccoca, Ford's president at the time, determined to regain its share of the market by quickly developing a small car called the Pinto.[4] The Pinto would weigh less than 2,000 pounds, cost less than $2,000, and be on market within 2 years instead of the normal 4 years. Because the Pinto was a rush project, styling considerations dictated engineering design to a greater degree than usual. In particular, Pinto's styling required that the gas tank be placed behind the rear axle that had protruding bolts. In that position, the tank could be punctured by the rear-axle bolts if a rear-end collision pushed it against the axle. When an early model of the Pinto was crash-tested, it was found that, when struck from behind at 20 miles per hour or more, the gas tank would sometimes break open. Gas would then spray out and enter the passenger compartment as well as under and around the car. In a real accident, stray sparks could explosively ignite the spraying gasoline and fire might engulf and burn the occupants, particularly if, as often happened in accidents, the doors jammed, trapping the victims.

Ford managers decided, nonetheless, to go ahead and manufacture the Pinto without changing the gas-tank design. There had several reasons for their decision. First, the design met all the legal and government standards then in effect. At the time, government regulations required that a gas tank only remain intact in a rear-end collision of less than 20 miles per hour. Second, Ford managers felt that the car was comparable in safety to several of the cars other companies were making and putting on the market. Third, according to an internal cost–benefit study by Ford, modifying the Pinto would be more costly than leaving its design unchanged. The study stated that approximately 12.5 million of the autos would eventually be built. Modifying the gas tank of each Pinto would cost about $11 a unit. The total costs of modifying all the Pintos the company planned to build, then, were simple to calculate:

Costs:

$11 × 12.5 million autos = $137 million

What benefits would customers derive from the $137 million they would have to pay if the Pinto's gas tank was modified? Statistical data showed that modifying the gas tank could prevent the future loss of about 180 burn deaths, 180 serious burn injuries, and 2,100 burned vehicles. At the time (1970), the government valued a human life at $200,000, a figure it needed to use to decide whether to spend money on a project that might save several lives or spend it on some other project that might save several million tax dollars.; Insurance companies valued a serious burn injury at $67,000 when they paid for losses due to burns (including the losses of pain and suffering); and the average residual value on subcompacts was estimated at $700. Therefore, in monetary terms, modifying the gas tank would have the benefit of preventing losses that added up to a total value of only $49.15 million.:

Benefits:

(180 deaths × $200,000) + (180 injuries × $67,000) + (2,100 vehicles × $700) = $49.15 million

Thus, if the car's gas tank was modified, customers would have to pay $137 million for a benefit worth $49.15 million, for a net loss of $87.85 million. It was not right, the Ford study argued, to have society invest in a "fix" of the Pinto's gas tank that would result in a greater loss than leaving things as they were. That is, although making no changes to the Pinto's design would result in losses of about $49.15 million, this was less than the net loss of $87.85 million that would be the consequence of changing the design.

Ford managers went ahead and produced the Pinto without modifying its gas tank. It is estimated that in the decade that followed about 60 persons died in fiery accidents involving Pintos and that at least twice that many suffered severe burns over large areas of their bodies, many requiring years of painful skin grafts. Ford, however, kept the Pinto on the market until 1980.

utilitarianism A general term for any view that holds that actions and policies should be evaluated on the basis of the benefits and costs they will impose on society.

The kind of analysis that Ford managers used in their cost-benefit study is a version of what has traditionally been called *utilitarianism*. **Utilitarianism** is a general term for the view that actions and policies should be evaluated on the basis of the benefits and costs they produce for everyone in society. Specifically, utilitarianism holds that the morally right course of action in any situation is the one that, when compared to all other possible actions, will produce the greatest balance of benefits over costs for everyone affected.

Ford managers reduced costs and benefits primarily to economic costs and benefits (such as medical costs, loss of income, and damage to buildings) and these were measured in monetary terms. But the benefits of an action may include any desirable goods (pleasures, health, lives, satisfactions, knowledge, happiness) produced by the action, and costs may include any of its undesirable evils or harms (such as pain, which the Ford study took into account, as well as sickness, death, dissatisfaction, ignorance, unhappiness). The inclusive term used to refer to the net benefits of any sort produced by an action is **utility**. Hence, the term *utilitarianism* is used for any theory that advocates selection of that action or policy that maximizes utility.

utility The inclusive term used to refer to any net benefits produced by an action.

It is important to understand that Ford's managers were not saying that making no changes to the Pinto's gas tank would save them money. That is, their claim was not that leaving the design unchanged was in Ford's best interests (recall that the buyers of the Pinto would ultimately pay all costs). If that had been their claim, then it would have been based on self-interest and not on utilitarian ethics. Their claim, instead, was that leaving the car's design unchanged was best for *society as a whole*. From society's point of view, and considering everyone's best interests, it was better to keep the design. Utilitarianism is not a theory of calculated selfishness: it is a theory that says that we should strive to do what is best for everyone in society, and that we do what is best for everyone when we take into account all the benefits and harms that everyone will bear as the result of our actions.

Many business analysts hold that the best way to evaluate the ethical propriety of a business decision—or any other decision—is by relying on utilitarian cost-benefit analysis.[5] The socially responsible course for a business to take is the one that will produce the greatest net benefits for society or impose the lowest net costs. Several government agencies, many legal theorists, numerous moralists, and a variety of business analysts advocate utilitarianism.[6] We begin our discussion of ethical principles by examining this popular approach.

Traditional Utilitarianism

Jeremy Bentham (1748–1832) and John Stuart Mill (1806–1873) are generally considered the founders of traditional utilitarianism.[7] Bentham and Mill sought an objective basis for making value judgments that would provide a common and publicly acceptable norm for determining the best social policy and social legislation, as well as the morally best course of action. The most promising way to reach such an objective basis of moral and social decision-making, they believed, is by looking at the various policies or courses of action that could be chosen, and comparing their beneficial and harmful consequences. The right course of action from an ethical point of view would be to choose the policy or action that would produce the greatest amount of utility. The utilitarian principle holds that:

> An action is right from an ethical point of view, if and only if, the sum total of utilities produced by that act is greater than the sum total of utilities produced by any other act the agent could have performed in its place.

The utilitarian principle assumes that we can somehow measure and add together the quantities of benefits produced by an action and then measure and subtract from those benefits the quantities of harm the action will produce. Once we do this for every action we could take, we then chose the action that produces the greatest net benefits or the lowest net costs. That is, utilitarianism assumes that any benefits or costs an action can produce can be measured on a common quantitative scale and then added or subtracted from each other.[8] The satisfactions that an improved work environment imparts to workers, for example, might be equivalent to 500 positive units of utility, whereas the resulting bills that arrive the next month might be equivalent to 700 negative units of utility. Therefore, the total combined utility of this act (improving the work environment) would be 200 units of *negative* utility.

There are three important mistakes to watch out for when using utilitarianism. Almost everyone makes these mistakes when they first start thinking about utilitarianism, so it is important to be aware of them at the start. First, when the utilitarian principle says that the right action for a particular occasion is the one that produces more utility than any other possible action, it does not mean that the right action is the one that produces the most utility for *the person performing* the action. Rather, an action is right if it produces the most utility for *all persons* affected by the action, including of course, the person who performed the action. As John Stuart Mill wrote:

> The happiness which forms the utilitarian standard of what is right in conduct, is not the agent's own happiness, but that of all concerned. As between his own happiness and that of others, utilitarianism requires him to be as strictly impartial as a disinterested and benevolent spectator. In the golden rule of Jesus of Nazareth, we read the complete spirit of the ethics of utility: "To do as you would be done by," and "to love your neighbor as yourself," constitute the ideal perfection of utilitarian morality.[9]

A second misunderstanding is to think that the utilitarian principle requires us to consider only the direct and immediate consequences of our actions. Instead, both the immediate and *all foreseeable future* costs and benefits that each alternative will provide for each individual must be taken into account, as well as any significant indirect effects.

However, the most important mistake to watch out for is a third common misunderstanding: the utilitarian principle does not say that an action is right so long as its *own* benefits outweigh its *own* costs. Instead, utilitarianism says that the right action is the one whose combined benefits and costs outweigh the combined benefits and costs of *every other action* the agent could carry out. In other words, utilitarianism holds that to determine the morally right action in any given situation, we *must compare* the utility of all of the actions that one could carry out in that situation; only then can we determine which action will produce more utility than any of the others. Notice that if utilitarianism said that any action is right so long as its benefits outweigh its costs, then in any situation, several actions could be right because several actions could have benefits that outweigh their costs. However, utilitarianism claims that in any situation only one action is morally right: that one action whose utility is *greatest by comparison to the utility of all the other alternatives*.

To determine, then, how I should behave in a particular situation according to utilitarianism, I must do four things. First, I must determine what alternative actions or policies are available to me in that situation. The Ford managers, for example, were implicitly considering two alternatives: to redesign the Pinto by putting a rubber bladder around the gas tank or to leave it as originally designed. Second, for each alternative action, I must estimate the direct and indirect benefits and costs that the action will probably produce for each and every person affected by the action in the near future. Ford's calculations of the costs and benefits that all affected parties would have to bear if the Pinto design were changed, and those that all parties would have

Should Companies Dump Their Wastes In Poor Countries?

Lawrence Summers, Director of the White House National Economic Council for President Barack Obama, once wrote a memo claiming that the world's welfare would improve if the wastes of rich countries were sent to poor countries. He gave four arguments for this claim which we can summarize as follows:

1. Clearly, it will be best for everyone if pollution is shipped to the country where its health effects will have the lowest costs. The costs of "health impairing pollution" depend on the wages lost when pollution makes people sick or kills them. So the country with the lowest wages will be the country where the health effects of pollution will be lowest. So with "impeccable" "economic logic" we can infer that it will be best for everyone if we dump our toxic wastes in the lowest wage countries.
2. Adding more pollution to an environment that is already highly polluted has worse health effects, than putting that same pollution into a clean environment where it can disperse. So we can reduce the harm pollution causes by transferring it out of highly polluted cities like Los Angeles, and dumping it into countries in Africa that "are vastly under-polluted." This will make better use of those countries' clean air quality which we now are using "vastly inefficiently," and it will improve "world welfare."
3. The same pollution will cause more harm in a country where people have "long life-spans," than in a country where people die young. When people have "long life-spans," they survive long enough to get diseases, like prostate cancer, that people who die young do not get. So pollution will cause more diseases like prostate cancer in countries where people have long lives than countries where people die young. It follows that we can reduce the diseases pollution causes by moving it out of rich countries where people have long lives, and dumping it into poor countries where people die young.
4. Pollution can cause "aesthetic" damage, such as dirty-looking air, that "may have very little direct health impact." Since the wealthy are willing to pay more for clean-looking air than the poor, clean-looking air is worth more to the wealthy than to the poor. So it should be possible for people in wealthy countries to find people in poor countries who are willing to trade their clean air for the money the wealthy are willing to offer. This kind of trade will be "welfare enhancing" for both parties.

Source: "Let Them Eat Pollution," *The Economist*, February 8, 1992.

Director of President Obama's National Economic Council until 2010, controversial American economist Lawrence Summers testifies before Congress.

Women in New Delhi, India, picking through western economic wastes.

River polluted with waste in Guiyu, China, a notorious dump site for western countries.

1. Explain which parts of the reasoning in this memo a utilitarian would have to accept and which parts a utilitarian could reject.
2. Assuming the four arguments are correct, do you agree or disagree with the conclusion that those in rich countries should ship their wastes to poor countries (perhaps by paying poor countries to take them)? Explain why or why not.

Economic wastes from western countries dumped in Nigeria (above) and in Ghana (right).

to bear if it were not changed, are examples of such estimates. Third, for each action I must subtract the costs from the benefits to determine the net utility of each action. This is what the Ford managers did when they calculated the net social costs of leaving the Pinto's design unchanged ($49.15 million), and the net social costs of modifying it ($87.85 million). Fourth, the action that produces the greatest sum total of utility must be chosen as the ethically appropriate course of action. The Ford managers, for example, decided that the course of action that would impose the lowest costs and the greatest benefits would be to leave the Pinto design unchanged.

Although it can easily be misunderstood and misused, utilitarianism is an attractive ethical theory in many ways. For one thing, it matches fairly nicely the views that we tend to advocate when discussing the choice of government policies and public goods. Most people agree, for example, that when the government is trying to determine on which public projects it should spend tax monies, the proper course of action would be for it to adopt those projects that objective studies show will provide the greatest benefits for the members of society at the least cost. Of course, this is just another way of saying that the proper government policies are those that would have the greatest measurable utility for people—or, in the words of a famous slogan coined by Bentham, those that will produce "the greatest good for the greatest number."

Utilitarianism also seems consistent with the intuitive criteria that people use when discussing moral conduct.[10] For example, when people explain why they have a moral obligation to perform some action, they often proceed by pointing out how the action will benefit or harm people. Moreover, morality requires that one impartially take everyone's interests equally into account. Utilitarianism meets this requirement insofar as it takes into account the effects actions have on everyone and insofar as it requires us to be impartial when we choose the action with the greatest net utility regardless of who gets the benefits or who gets the costs.

Utilitarianism also has the advantage of being able to explain why we hold that certain types of activities are generally morally wrong (lying, adultery, killing) while others are generally morally right (telling the truth, fidelity, keeping one's promises). The utilitarian can say that lying is generally wrong because of the costly effects lying has on people. When people lie to each other, they are less apt to trust each other or to cooperate with each other. The less trust and cooperation, the more our welfare declines. Telling the truth is generally right because it strengthens cooperation and trust and thereby improves everyone's well-being. In general, then, it is a good rule of thumb to tell the truth and to refrain from lying. Traditional utilitarians would deny, however, that any kinds of actions are always right or always wrong. They would deny, for example, that dishonesty or theft is necessarily always wrong. If, in a certain situation more good consequences would flow from being dishonest than from any other act a person could perform in that situation, then, according to traditional utilitarian theory, dishonesty would be morally right in that particular situation.

Quick Review 2.1

Utilitarianism

- Advocates maximizing utility
- Matches well with moral evaluations of public policies
- Appears intuitive to many people
- Helps explain why some actions are generally wrong and others are generally right
- Influenced economics.

Utilitarian views have also been highly influential in economics.[11] A long line of economists, beginning in the nineteenth century, argued that economic behavior could be explained by assuming that human beings always attempt to maximize their utility and that the utilities of commodities can be measured by the prices people are willing to pay for them. With these and other simplifying assumptions (such as the use of indifference curves), economists were able to derive the familiar supply and demand curves of sellers and buyers in markets and explain why prices in a perfectly competitive market gravitate toward an equilibrium. More important, economists were also able to demonstrate that a system of perfectly competitive markets would lead to a use of resources and price variations that would enable consumers to maximize their utility (defined in terms of Pareto optimality) through their purchases.[12] On utilitarian grounds, therefore, these economists concluded that such a system of markets is better than any other alternative.

Utilitarianism is also the basis of the techniques of economic **cost-benefit analysis.**[13] This type of analysis is used to determine the desirability of investing money in a project (such as a dam, factory, or public park) by figuring out whether its present and future economic benefits outweigh its costs and comparing this to the costs and benefits of other ways of investing our money. To calculate these costs and benefits, discounted monetary prices are estimated for all the effects the project will have on the present and future environment and on present and future populations. Carrying out these sorts of calculations is not always an easy matter, but various methods have been devised for determining the monetary prices of even such intangible benefits as the beauty of a forest (e.g., we might ask how much people pay to see the beauty of a similar privately owned park). If the monetary benefits of a certain public project exceed the monetary costs and if the excess is greater than the excess produced by any other feasible project, then the project should be undertaken. In this form of utilitarianism, the concept of utility is restricted to monetarily measurable costs and benefits.

cost-benefit analysis A type of analysis used to determine the desirability of investing in a project by calculating whether its present and future economic benefits outweigh its present and future economic costs.

Finally, we can note that utilitarianism fits nicely with a value that many people prize: efficiency. **Efficiency** can mean different things to different people, but for many it means operating in the manner that produces the most from a given amount of resources, or that produces a desired output with the lowest resource input. Such efficiency is precisely what utilitarianism advocates because it holds that one should always adopt the course of action that will produce the greatest benefits at the lowest cost. If we read "desired output" in the place of "benefits" and "resource input" in place of "cost," utilitarianism implies that the right course of action is always the most efficient one.

efficiency Operating in such a way that one produces a desired output with the lowest resource input.

Measurement Problems

One major set of problems with utilitarianism is centered on the difficulties of trying to measure utility.[14] One problem is this: How can the utilities different actions have for different people be measured and compared as utilitarianism requires? Suppose you and I would both enjoy getting a certain job: How can we figure out whether the utility you would get out of having the job is more or less than the utility I would get out of having it? Each of us may be sure that he or she would benefit most from the job, but because we cannot get "into each other's skin," we have no objective way of making this judgment. Comparative measures of the values things have for different people cannot be made, the critics argue, so there is no way of knowing whether utility would be maximized by giving me the job or by giving you the job. If we cannot know which actions will produce the greatest amounts of utility, then we cannot apply the utilitarian principle.

A second problem is that there are certain kinds of benefits and costs that seem impossible to measure. For example, critics say, how can you measure the value of health or life?[15] Suppose that installing an expensive exhaust system in a workshop will eliminate a large portion of certain carcinogenic particles that workers might otherwise inhale. Suppose that as a result some of the workers will live 10 years longer than they would have. How can we calculate the value of those years of added life, and how can we compare this value to the costs of installing the exhaust system? Moreoever, because we cannot predict all of the future benefits and costs of an action, there is no way we can measure them.[16]

Yet another problem is that it is unclear exactly what should count as a benefit and what should count as a cost.[17] This lack of clarity is especially a problem when we are dealing with controversial things on which different people place very different values. Suppose a bank must decide, for example, whether to extend a loan to the manager of a local pornographic theater or to the manager of a bar that caters to homosexuals. One group of people may see the increased enjoyment of pornography connoisseurs or the increased enjoyment of homosexuals as beneficial for society. A conservative religious group, however, may see these enjoyments as harmful and hence, as costs.

Finally, the utilitarian assumption that all benefits are measurable implies that all benefits can be traded for equivalents of each other: For a given quantity of one good, there is some quantity of any other good that you should be willing to trade for the first good. For example, suppose that for you the enjoyment of eating two slices of pizza right now has the same value as the enjoyment of a half hour of listening to your favorite music right now. Then, you should be willing to trade one for the other (at least right now) since they are for you at the present moment equal in value. Now utilitarianism says that what is true of pizza and music is true of everything else. Since the value of each good can be measured, we should be able to measure the value of given amounts of our enjoyment of X, and the value of given amounts of our enjoyment of Y, no matter what goods X and Y are. Therefore, once we measure the value of a certain amount of enjoyment of X, we should be able to measure how much enjoyment of Y will have the same value as that amount of enjoyment of X. And once we know how much enjoyment of X is equal to a given amount of enjoyment of Y, we should be willing to trade one for the other, no matter what X and Y are. Utilitarianism implies, then, that we should be willing to trade any one good for some quantity of any other good.

Critics say this shows utilitarianism is mistaken. For example, utilitarianism implies that if you enjoy spending time with your son (or your mother or your lover), and you also enjoy drinking beer, then you should be willing to trade all the time you will ever spend enjoying your son (or your mother or your lover) for some quantity of the enjoyment you get from drinking beer. But on this point, critics have argued, utilitarianism has led us to a mistaken and ridiculous conclusion: who would ever agree to trade all the time they will ever have enjoying their son (or mother or lover) for the enjoyment of beer? There are some **noneconomic goods**—such as the enjoyment of love, freedom, health, and fatherhood—that we would not be willing to trade for any amount of the enjoyment of economic goods because noneconomic goods cannot be measured in economic terms.[18] For example, no matter how much money you would offer me, I would never be willing to trade away all the hours of enjoyment my son will give me, for the enjoyment of that amount of money. Critics of utilitarianism claim that the enjoyment of some things just cannot be traded for our enjoyment of other things; there are values that are "incommensurable."

noneconomic goods Goods, such as life, love, freedom, equality, health, beauty, whose value is such that it cannot be measured in economic terms.

The critics of utilitarianism contend that all these measurement problems undercut whatever claims utilitarian theory makes to provide an objective basis for determining moral questions. In too many cases, they say, there are no objective quantitative measures of the values we prize, and too many differences of opinion even over what should be valued.[19] One way of resolving these problems is to arbitrarily accept the valuations of one social group or another; but this in effect bases utilitarian cost–benefit analysis on the subjective biases and tastes of that group.

Utilitarian Replies to Measurement Objections

The defender of utilitarianism has an array of replies ready to counter the measurement objections we outlined above.

First, the utilitarian may argue that, although utilitarianism ideally requires accurate quantifiable measurements of all costs and benefits, this requirement can be relaxed when such measurements are not possible.[20] Utilitarianism merely insists that the consequences of any projected act be expressly stated with as much clarity and accuracy as is humanly possible, and that all relevant information concerning these consequences be presented in a form that will allow them to be systematically compared and impartially weighed against each other. Expressing this information in quantitative terms would make such comparisons and weightings easier. However, where quantitative data are unavailable, one may legitimately rely on shared and commonsense judgments of the comparative values things have for most people. For example, we know that, by and large, cancer is a greater injury than a cold no matter who has the cancer and who has the cold. Similarly, a steak has a greater value as food than a peanut no matter whose hunger is involved.

The utilitarian can also point to several commonsense criteria that can be used to determine the relative values that should be given to various categories of goods. One criterion, for example, depends on the distinction between *intrinsic* and *instrumental* goods.[21] **Instrumental goods** are things that are considered valuable only because they lead to other good things. A painful visit to the dentist, for example, is only an instrumental good (unless I happen to be a masochist!) since it is desired only as a means to health. **Intrinsic goods**, however, are things that are desirable independent of any other benefits they may produce. For example, health is an intrinsic good: It is desired for its own sake. (Many things, of course, have both intrinsic and instrumental value. I may use a skateboard, for example, not only because skateboarding is a means to health and rapid transportation but also because I simply enjoy skateboarding.) Now, it is clear that intrinsic goods take priority over instrumental goods. Under most circumstances, for example, money, which is an instrumental good, must not take priority over life and health, which have intrinsic values. Consequently, when we are comparing an instrumental good that is a means to some intrinsic good, we know that the intrinsic good has more value than the instrumental good.

instrumental goods Things that are considered valuable because they lead to other good things.

intrinsic goods Things that are desirable independent of any other benefits they may produce.

A second common-sense criterion that can be used to weigh goods turns on the distinction between needs and wants.[22] To say that someone needs something is to say that without it that person will be harmed in some way. People's "basic" needs consist of their needs for things without which they will suffer some fundamental harm such as injury, illness, or death. Among a person's basic needs are the food, clothing, and housing required to stay alive; the medical care and hygienic environment needed to stay healthy; and the security and safety required to remain free from injury and harm. On the other hand, to say that a person wants something is to say that the person desires it: The person believes it will advance his or her interests in some way. A need, of course, may also be a want: If I know I need something, then I may also want it. Many wants, however, are not needs but simply desires for things without which the individual would not suffer any fundamental harm. I may want something because I enjoy it, even though it is a luxury I could do without. Desires of this sort that are not also needs are called *mere* wants. In general, satisfying a person's basic needs is more valuable than satisfying his or her mere wants. If people do not get something for which they have a basic need, they may be injured in a way that makes it impossible for them to enjoy the satisfaction of any number of mere wants. Because the satisfaction of a person's basic needs makes possible not only the intrinsic values of life and health but also the enjoyment of most other intrinsic values, satisfaction of the basic needs has a value that is greater than that of satisfying mere wants.

However, these commonsense methods of weighing goods are only intended to aid us in situations where quantitative methods fail. In actual fact, the consequences of many decisions are relatively amenable to quantification, the convinced utilitarian will claim. This constitutes the utilitarian's second major reply to the measurement objections we previously outlined.

The best way to provide a common quantitative measure for the benefits and costs associated with a decision, the utilitarian may hold, is in terms of their monetary equivalents.[23] Basically, this means that the value a thing has for a person can be measured by the price the person is willing to pay for it. If a person will pay twice as much for one thing as for another, then for that person the first thing has exactly twice the value of the second. To determine the average values items have for a group of people, then, one needs to look at the average prices given to those items when everyone is allowed to bid for them on open markets. In short, market prices can serve to provide a common quantitative measure of the various benefits and costs associated with a decision. To determine the value of a thing to people in general, then, one need merely ask what it sells for on an open market. If the item does not sell on an open market, then one can ask what is the selling price for similar items. To determine the value of a thing to a specific person, we need to ask what that person would be willing to pay for it.

The use of monetary values also has the advantage of allowing one to take into account the effects of the passage of time and the impact of uncertainty. If the known monetary costs or benefits lie in the future, then their present values can be determined by discounting them at the appropriate rate of interest. If the monetary costs or benefits are only probable and not certain, then their expected values can be computed by multiplying the monetary costs or benefits by the appropriate probability factor.

A standard objection against using monetary values to measure all costs and benefits is that some goods, such as health and life, cannot be priced. The utilitarian may argue, however, that not only is it possible to put a price on health and life but that we do so almost daily. Anytime people place a limit on the amount of money they are willing to pay to reduce the risk that some event poses to their lives, they have set an implicit price on their own lives. For example, suppose that you are willing to pay $25 for a piece of safety equipment that will reduce the probability of your being killed in an auto accident from .00005 to .00004, but you are not willing to pay more. Then, in effect, you have implicitly decided that .00001 of your life is worth $25—or, in other words that a life is worth $2,500,000. Such pricing is inevitable and necessary, the utilitarian may hold, so long as we live in an environment in which risks to health and life can be lowered only by giving up (trading off) other things that we may want and on which we set a clear price. Using money to measure the value of things we greatly prize is not bad in itself. What is bad is to fail to place any quantitative value on things and, as a result, end by unthinkingly trading a greater value for a lesser one because we refused to figure out *how much* each was worth.

Finally, the utilitarian may say, where market prices are incapable of providing quantitative data for comparing the costs and benefits of various decisions, other sorts of quantitative measures are available.[24] Should people disagree, for example, as they often do, over the harmful or beneficial aspects of various sexual activities, then sociological surveys or political votes can be used to measure the intensity and extensiveness of people's attitudes. Economic experts can also provide informed judgments of the relative quantitative values of various costs and benefits. Thus, the utilitarian will grant that the problems of measurement utilitarianism has to deal with are real enough. Yet, we can at least partially solve them by the various methods just described. There are, however, other criticisms of utilitarianism.

Problems with Rights and Justice

The major difficulty with utilitarianism, according to some critics, is that it is unable to deal with two kinds of moral issues: those relating to rights and those relating to justice.[25] That is, the utilitarian principle implies that certain actions are morally right when in fact, they are unjust or they violate people's rights. Some of the following examples may serve to indicate the sort of difficult counterexamples critics pose for utilitarianism.

First, suppose that your uncle has an incurable and painful disease, so that he is quite unhappy but does not choose to die. Although he is hospitalized and will die within a year, he continues to run his chemical plant. Because of his misery, he deliberately makes life miserable for his workers and has insisted on not installing safety devices in his chemical plant, although he knows that as a result, one life will certainly be lost over the next year. You, his only living relative, know that upon your uncle's death you will inherit his business and not only will you be wealthy and immensely happy, but you also intend to prevent any future loss of life by installing the needed safety devices. You are cold-blooded and correctly judge that you could secretly murder your uncle without being caught and without your happiness being at all affected by it afterward. If it is possible for you to murder your uncle without in any way diminishing anyone else's happiness, then according to utilitarianism, you have a moral obligation to do so. By murdering your uncle, you are trading his life for the life of the worker, and you are gaining your happiness while doing away with his unhappiness and pain—the gain is obviously on the side of utility. However, the critics of utilitarianism claim, it seems quite clear that the murder of your uncle would be a gross violation of his right to life. Utilitarianism has led us to approve an act of murder that is an obvious violation of an individual's most important right.

Second, utilitarianism can also go wrong, according to the critics, when it is applied to situations that involve justice. For example, suppose that subsistence wages force a small group of migrant workers to continue doing the most undesirable agricultural jobs in an economy, but produce immense amounts of satisfaction for the vast majority of society's members, because they enjoy cheap vegetables and savings that allow them to indulge other wants. Suppose also that the amounts of satisfaction thereby produced, when balanced against the unhappiness and pain imposed on the small group of farm workers, results in a greater net utility than would exist if everyone had to share the burdens of farm work. Then, according to the utilitarian criterion, it would be morally right to continue this system of subsistence wages for farm workers. However, to the critics of utilitarianism, a social system that imposes such unequal sharing of burdens is clearly immoral and offends against justice. The great benefits the system may have for the majority does not justify the extreme burdens that it imposes on a small group. The shortcoming this counterexample reveals is that utilitarianism allows benefits and burdens to be distributed among the members of society in any way whatsoever, so long as the total amount of benefits is maximized. In fact, some ways of distributing benefits and burdens (like the extremely unequal distributions involved in the counterexample) are unjust regardless of how great the store of benefits such distributions produce. Utilitarianism looks only at how much utility is produced in a society and fails to take into account how that utility is distributed among the members of society.

To see more clearly how utilitarianism ignores considerations of justice and rights, consider how Ford's managers dealt with the Pinto design. Had they decided to change the Pinto design and add $11 to the cost of each Pinto, they would have forced all the buyers of the Pinto to share in paying the $137 million that the design change would cost. Each buyer would pay an equal share of the total costs of changing this aspect of the Pinto design. However, by not changing the Pinto design, the Ford managers were in effect forcing the 180 people who would die to absorb all the costs of this aspect of the Pinto design. So we should ask: Is it more just to have 180 buyers bear all the costs of the Pinto design by themselves, or is it more just to distribute the costs equally among all buyers? Which is the fairest way of distributing these costs?

Consider, next, that when Ford's managers decided to make no change to the Pinto design, they were not only making the Pinto cheaper, they were also building a car with a certain amount of risk (to life). Those who drove the Pinto would be driving a car that posed a slightly greater risk to life than they might have reasonably assumed it posed. It is possible that drivers of the Pinto would have gladly accepted this slightly added risk to life in exchange for the lower price of the car. But they had no choice in the matter because they did not know the car carried this added risk. So we should ask:

Do people have the right to know what they are buying when they choose to purchase a product? Do people have a right to choose whether to have greater risk added to their lives? Did the makers of the Pinto violate the basic right of customers to freely choose for themselves whether to accept a riskier car in return for a lower price?

justice Distributing benefits and burdens fairly among people.

rights Individual entitlements to freedom of choice and well-being.

Thus, the Pinto case makes clear that utilitarianism seems to ignore certain important aspects of ethics. Considerations of **justice** (which look at how benefits and burdens are distributed among people) and **rights** (which look at individual entitlements to freedom of choice and well-being) seem to be ignored by an analysis that looks only at the costs and benefits of decisions.

Utilitarian Replies to Objections on Rights and Justice

rule-utilitarianism A form of utilitarianism that limits utilitarian analysis to evaluations of moral rules.

To deal with the sorts of counterexamples that critics of traditional utilitarianism have offered, utilitarians have proposed an important and influential alternative version of utilitarianism called **rule-utilitarianism**.[26] The basic strategy of the rule-utilitarian is to limit utilitarian analysis to the evaluations of moral rules. According to the rule-utilitarian, when trying to determine whether a particular action is ethical, one is never supposed to ask whether that particular action will produce the greatest amount of utility. Instead, one is supposed to ask whether the action is required by the correct moral rules that everyone should follow. If the action is required by such rules, then one should carry out the action. But what are the "correct" moral rules? It is only this second question, according to the rule-utilitarian, that is supposed to be answered by reference to maximizing utility. The correct moral rules are those that would produce the greatest amount of utility if everyone were to follow them. The following example may make this clear.

Suppose I am trying to decide whether it is ethical for me to fix prices with a competitor. Then, according to the rule-utilitarian, I should not ask whether this particular instance of price-fixing will produce more utility than anything else I can do. Instead, I should first ask myself: What are the correct moral rules with respect to price-fixing? Perhaps I might conclude, after some thought, that the following list of rules includes all the candidates:

1. Managers are never to meet with competitors for the purpose of fixing prices.
2. Managers may always meet with competitors for the purpose of fixing prices.
3. Managers may meet with competitors for the purpose of fixing prices when they are losing money.

Which of these three is the correct moral rule? According to the rule-utilitarian, the correct moral rule is the one that would produce the greatest amount of utility for everyone affected. Let us suppose that after analyzing the economic effects of price-fixing, I conclude that within our economic and social circumstances people would benefit much more if everyone followed Rule 1 than if everyone followed Rule 2 or 3. If this is so, then Rule 1 is the correct moral rule concerning price-fixing. Now that I know what the correct moral rule on price-fixing is, I can go on to ask a second question: Should I engage in this particular act of fixing prices? To answer this second question, I only have to ask: What is required by the correct moral rules? As we have already noted, the correct rule is never to fix prices. Consequently, even if on this particular occasion, fixing prices actually would produce more utility than not doing so I am, nonetheless, ethically obligated to refrain from fixing prices because this is required by the rules from which everyone in my society would most benefit.

The theory of the rule-utilitarian, then has two parts, which we can summarize in the following two principles:

I. An action is right from an ethical point of view if and only if the action would be required by those moral rules that are correct.

II. A moral rule is correct if and only if the sum total of utilities produced if everyone were to follow that rule is greater than the sum total of utilities produced if everyone were to follow some alternative rule.

Thus, according to the rule-utilitarian, the fact that a certain action would maximize utility on one particular occasion does not show that it is right from a rule-utilitarian point of view.

For the rule-utilitarian, the flaw in the counterexamples that the critics of traditional utilitarianism offer is that in each case, the utilitarian criterion is applied to particular actions and not to rules. Instead, the rule-utilitarian would urge that we must use the utilitarian criterion to find out what the correct moral rule is for each counterexample and then, evaluate the particular actions involved in the counterexample only in terms of this rule. Doing this allows utilitarianism to escape the counterexamples undamaged.

The counterexample involving the rich uncle and the murderous heir, for example, is a situation that deals with killing a sick person. In such situations, the rule-utilitarian might argue, it is clear that a moral rule that forbids killing without the due process of law will, in the long run, produce greater utility for society than other kinds of rules. Therefore, such a rule is the correct one to apply to the case. It would be wrong for the heir to kill his uncle because doing so would violate a correct moral rule, and the fact that murder would, on this particular occasion, maximize utility is irrelevant.

The case dealing with subsistence wages, the rule-utilitarian would argue, should be treated similarly. It is clear that a rule that forbade unnecessary subsistence wages in societies would in the long run result in more utility than a rule that allowed them. Such a rule would be the correct rule to invoke when asking whether paying subsistence wages is morally permissible. In terms of this rule, the practice of paying subsistence wages would be ethically wrong even if the practice would maximize utility on a particular occasion.

The ploy of the rule-utilitarian, however, has not satisfied the critics of utilitarianism, who have pointed out an important difficulty in the rule-utilitarian position: According to its critics, rule-utilitarianism is traditional utilitarianism in disguise.[27] These critics argue that rules that allow (beneficial) exceptions will produce more utility than rules that do not allow any exceptions. However, once a rule allows these exceptions, the critics claim, it will allow the same injustices and violations of rights that traditional utilitarianism allows. Some examples may help us see more clearly what these critics mean. The critics claim that if a rule allows people to make an exception whenever an exception will maximize utility, then it will produce more utility than a rule that allowed no exceptions. For example, more utility would be produced by a rule that says, "People are not to be killed without due process *except when doing so will produce more utility than not doing so*," than would be produced by a rule that simply says, "People are not to be killed without due process." The first rule will *always* maximize utility, whereas the second rule will maximize utility only *most of the time* (because the second rule would require due process even when dispensing with due process would produce more utility). Because the rule-utilitarian holds that the correct moral rule is the one that produces more utility, he or she must hold that the correct moral rule is the one that allows exceptions when exceptions will maximize utility. Once the exception clause is made part of the rule, the critics point out, then applying the rule to an action will have exactly the same consequences as applying the traditional utilitarian criterion directly to the action because the utilitarian criterion is now part of the rule.

> *Quick Review 2.2*
>
> **Criticisms of Utilitarianism**
>
> - Critics say not all values can be measured.
> - Utilitarians respond that monetary or other commonsense measures can measure everything.
> - Critics say utilitarianism fails with rights and justice.
> - Utilitarians respond that rule-utilitarianism can deal with rights and justice.

In the case of the sick uncle and murderous heir, for example, the rule that "people are not to be killed without due process *except when doing so will produce more utility than not doing so*" will now allow the heir to murder his uncle exactly as traditional utilitarianism did before. Similarly, more utility would be produced by a rule that says, "Subsistence wages are prohibited *except in those situations where they will maximize utility*" than would be produced by a rule that simply says, "Subsistence wages are prohibited." Therefore, the rule that allows exceptions will be the "correct" one.

But this "correct" rule will now allow the society we described earlier to institute wage slavery exactly as traditional utilitarianism did. Rule-utilitarianism, then, is a disguised form of traditional utilitarianism, and the counterexamples that set difficulties for one seem to set similar difficulties for the other.

Many rule-utilitarians do not admit that rules produce more utility when they allow exceptions. Because human nature is weak and self-interested, they claim, humans would take advantage of any allowable exceptions, and this would leave everyone worse off. Other utilitarians refuse to admit that the counterexamples of the critics are correct. They claim that if killing a person without due process really would produce more utility than all other feasible alternatives, then all other alternatives must have greater evils attached to them. If this is so, then killing the person without due process really would be morally right. Similarly, if in certain circumstances subsistence wages really are the least (socially) injurious means to use to get a job done, then in those circumstances, subsistence wages are morally right exactly as utilitarianism says.

So utilitarianism faces two main difficulties. First, it asks us to measure values that are difficult—perhaps impossible—to quantify. Second, it seems unable to deal adequately with questions of rights and justice. A third issue we have hardly discussed but which we should mention is that utilitarianism assumes decision makers—like the Ford managers designing the Pinto—need not consult the people their decisions touch: if a manager's decision will maximize utility, it is morally right even if those affected are not consulted. Critics object that it is unjust and a violation of people's rights when they are given no say in decisions that affect their lives.

2.2 Rights and Duties

On May 17, 2009 a 17-year-old boy, Yiu Wah, who had been hired at the age of 15, was crushed and killed while trying to clear a jammed machine in the factory of a Chinese supplier that was making products for the Walt Disney Company, the world's second-largest media conglomerate.[28] Witnesses claimed that the use of child labor was a human rights violation that was common at the factory of Disney's supplier.

This was not the first time that Walt Disney Company had been accused of having human rights violations in its supply chain. On March 3, 2004, executives of Walt Disney were confronted by a group of stockholders concerned about the company's human rights record in China. In addition to owning several theme parks, television and radio networks (ABC, the Disney Channel, ESPN), and film studios, Walt Disney markets merchandise based on its characters and films, including toys, apparel, watches, consumer electronics, and accessories. Much of this merchandise is manufactured in China in factories that contract with Disney to produce the merchandise according to Disney's specifications. The Congressional-Executive Commission on China, a group established by the U.S. Congress in 2001, reported in 2003, however, that:

> China's poor record of protecting the internationally recognized rights of its workers hasn't changed significantly in the past year. Chinese workers can't form or join independent trade unions, and workers who seek redress for wrongs committed by their employers often face harassment and criminal charges. Moreover, child labor continues to be a problem in some sectors of the economy, and forced labor by prisoners is common.

In its March, 2003 *Country Reports on Human Rights Practices*, the U.S. State Department said China's economy also made massive use of forced prison labor.[29] China's prisons contained large numbers of political dissidents who were forced to engage in unpaid, exhausting, and dangerous labor to "reform" or "reeducate" them. Factories often purchased materials made in these prisons and then incorporated them into their own products.

Even earlier, in 2001, the Hong Kong Christian Industrial Committee had made on-site undercover visits to a dozen of Walt Disney's Chinese factories and reported that it found "excessively long hours of work, poverty wages, unreasonable fines, workplace hazards, poor food and dangerously overcrowded dormitories." Another report issued in 2002 by the National Labor Committee, entitled, "Toys of Misery," noted horrific working conditions in the nineteen Disney factories the committee investigated. According to the report, not only were workers paid substandard wages, but they "face long hours of forced overtime that leave them with two or three hours of sleep a night," and "they are exposed constantly to chemicals that make them sick." In 2004, the National Labor Committee reissued its report, now entitled "Toys of Misery, 2004," in which they found that Disney factories were still engaged in the kind of practices they had found two years earlier.

Concerned by these reports on conditions in Chinese factories and that the factories might be using materials made by forced labor, a group of stockholders urged all Disney stockholders to vote in favor of having the company adopt 11 "principles." These principles "were designed to commit a company to a widely accepted and thorough set of human and labor rights standards for China." The six most important principles were:

(1) No goods or products produced within our company's facilities or those of suppliers shall be manufactured by bonded labor, forced labor, within prison camps or as part of reform-through-labor or reeducation-through-labor programs.
(2) Our facilities and suppliers shall adhere to wages that meet workers' basic needs, fair and decent working hours, and at a minimum, to the wage and hour guidelines provided by China's national labor laws.
(3) Our facilities and suppliers shall prohibit the use of corporal punishment, any physical, sexual or verbal abuse or harassment of workers.
(4) Our facilities and suppliers shall use production methods that do not negatively affect the worker's occupational safety and health.
(5) Our facilities and suppliers shall not call on police or military to enter their premises to prevent workers from exercising their rights.
(6) We shall undertake to promote the following freedoms among our employees and the employees of our suppliers: freedom of association and assembly, including the rights to form unions and bargain collectively; freedom of expression, and freedom from arbitrary arrest or detention. . . .[30]

Disney's managers did not want to endorse these human rights principles because the company already had a code of ethics and already inspected factories to ensure compliance with its code. Critics, however, replied that Disney's code was too narrow, that it was not enforced, that its inspection system was flawed, and that if the company did not adopt human rights principles, it would likely continue to have problems. Subsequent events seemed to support the critics. In 2005, 2006, and 2007, Students and Scholars against Corporate Misbehavior, published reports on the human rights violations and sweatshop conditions their investigations had discovered in a large number of Chinese factories making toys for Disney.[31] China Labor Watch, a workers' rights group, released a report in 2007 detailing "brutal" conditions in several Chinese factories making toys for Disney.[32] In 2008, the National Labor Committee reported on a Chinese factory that was making Disney toys, but that was actually a sweatshop noted for abusing the rights of its workers.[33] And in 2009, came the announcement of the terrible death of the 17-year-old boy, Yiu Wah.

The concept of a *right* plays a crucial role in many of the moral arguments and moral claims invoked in controversies involving business ethics. Employees, for example, argue that they have a "right to equal pay for equal work"; managers assert that unions violate their "right to manage"; investors complain that taxation violates their "property rights"; and consumers claim that they have a "right to know." Moreover, many historic documents employ the notion of a right. The U.S. Constitution enshrines a long Bill of Rights, defined largely in terms of the duties the federal government has to not interfere in certain areas of its citizens' lives. The Declaration of Independence was based on the idea that "all men ... are endowed by their Creator with certain unalienable rights ... among these are life, liberty, and the pursuit of happiness." In 1948, the United Nations adopted a "Universal Declaration of Human Rights" which claimed that "all human beings" are entitled, among other things, to:

> the right to own property alone as well as in association with others ...
> the right to work, to free choice of employment, to just and favorable conditions of work, and to protection against unemployment ...
>
> the right to just and favorable remuneration ensuring for [the worker] and his family an existence worthy of human dignity ...
>
> the right to form and to join trade unions ...
>
> the right to rest and leisure, including reasonable limitation of working hours and periodic holidays with pay ...

ON THE EDGE

Working for Eli Lilly & Company

Before a newly discovered drug is approved for sale, the U.S. Food and Drug Administration (FDA) requires that it be tested on healthy humans to determine whether it has dangerous side effects. Unfortunately, most healthy people will not take an untested substance that is not intended to cure them of anything and that may have crippling or deadly effects. Test subjects can die; suffer paralysis, organ damage, and other chronically debilitating injuries. Eli Lilly, a large pharmaceutical company, however, discovered a group of "volunteers" willing to take untested drugs for only $85 a day plus free room and board: homeless alcoholics desperate for money recruited in soup kitchens, shelters, and jails. Since tests run for months, the men can make as much as $4,500—a hefty sum to someone surviving on handouts. The tests provide enormous benefits for society and many tests might not be performed at all but for the pool of homeless alcoholics. Moreover, providing the men with a warm bed, food, and good medical care before sending them out drug- and alcohol-free and with money in their pockets seems beneficial. The FDA requires that participants in such medical tests must give their "informed consent" and make a "truly voluntary and uncoerced decision." Some question whether the desperate circumstances of hungry, homeless, and penniless alcoholics allow them to make a truly voluntary and uncoerced decision. When asked, one homeless drinker hired to participate in a test said he had no idea what kind of drug was being tested on him even though he had signed an informed-consent form.

1. Discuss Eli Lilly's practice from the perspectives of utilitarianism and rights.
2. In your judgment, is the policy of using homeless alcoholics for test subjects morally appropriate?

Source: Laurie P. Cohen, "Stuck for Money," *Wall Street Journal*, November 14, 1996, p. 1.

The concept of a right and the correlative notion of duty, then, lie at the heart of much of our moral discourse. This section is intended to provide an understanding of these concepts and of some of the major kinds of ethical principles and methods of analysis that underlie their use.

The Concept of a Right

In general, a ***right*** is an individual's entitlement to something.[34] A person has a right when that person is entitled to act in a certain way or is entitled to have others act in a certain way toward him or her. The entitlement may derive from a legal system that permits or empowers the person to act in a specified way or that requires others to act in certain ways toward that person; the entitlement is then called a **legal right**. The U.S. Constitution, for example, guarantees all citizens the right to freedom of speech, and commercial statutes specify that each party in a valid contract has a right to whatever performance the contract requires from the other person. Legal rights are limited, of course, to the particular jurisdiction within which the legal system is in force.

right An individual's entitlement to something.

legal right An entitlement that derives from a legal system that permits or empowers a person to act in a specified way or that requires others to act in certain ways toward that person.

Entitlements can also derive from a system of moral standards independently of any particular legal system. The right to work, for example, is not guaranteed by the U.S. Constitution, but many argue that it is a right that all human beings possess. Such rights, which are called ***moral rights*** or ***human rights***, are based on moral norms and principles that specify that all human beings are permitted or empowered to do something or are entitled to have something done for them. **Moral rights**, unlike legal rights, are usually thought of as being universal insofar as they are rights that all human beings of every nationality possess to an equal extent, simply by virtue of being human beings. Unlike legal rights, moral rights are not limited to a particular jurisdiction. If humans have a moral right not to be tortured, for example, then this is a moral right that human beings of every nationality have regardless of the legal system under which they live.

moral rights or **human rights** Rights that all human beings everywhere possess to an equal extent simply by virtue of being human beings.

Rights are powerful devices whose main purpose is to enable the individual to choose freely whether to pursue certain interests or activities and to protect those choices. In our ordinary discourse, we use the term *right* to cover a variety of situations in which individuals are enabled to make such choices in very different ways. First, we sometimes use the term *right* to indicate the mere absence of prohibitions against pursuing some interest or activity. For example, I have a right to do whatever the law or morality does not positively forbid me to do. In this weak sense of a right, the enabling and protective aspects are minimal. Second, we sometimes use the term *right* to indicate that a person is authorized or empowered to do something to secure the interests of others or to secure one's interests. An army or police officer, for example, acquires legal rights of command over subordinates that enable the officer to pursue the security of others, whereas a property owner acquires legal property rights that enable doing as the owner wishes with the property. Third, the term *right* is sometimes used to indicate the existence of prohibitions or requirements on others that enable the individual to pursue certain interests or activities. For example, the U.S. Constitution is said to give citizens the right to free speech because it contains a prohibition against government limits on speech, and federal law is said to give citizens the right to an education because it contains a requirement that each state must provide free public education for all its citizens.[35]

Notice that although violations of people's rights often involve the infliction of injuries on those people, still a person's rights can be violated without the person being injured or hurt in any obvious way. This aspect of rights is one of the ways in which rights considerations differ from utilitarian considerations since wrongdoing in utilitarianism always involves the infliction of injuries. To see how rights can be

Quick Review 2.3

Characteristics of Rights

- A right is an individual's entitlement to something.
- Rights derived from a legal system confer entitlements only on individuals who live where that legal system is in force.
- Moral or human rights are entitlements that moral norms confer on all people regardless of their legal system.

violated without injury, let's take the example of the right to privacy, which, for the sake of the example, we will assume is a right everyone has. Suppose, then, that one day a couple was involved in activities that they (and we) considered private and that they would feel ashamed about if they thought that anyone else knew they engaged in those activities. They do these things only when they feel certain that no one can see them because they are behind locked doors and drawn window shades. But one day, you manage to climb a tree and with powerful binoculars trained on a tiny tear in their window shades, you manage to look inside their house and see what they are doing. Although what you see disgusts you, you continue to look at them inside their house for some time, and then climb down from your tree and go home. Afterwards you never tell anyone, and you never have any kind of contact with the couple again nor have any impact on their lives of any kind, and the couple never find out you saw them. They blissfully continue to feel for the rest of their lives that no one else knew what they did that day and they never experience the slightest discomfort or pain or injury of any kind from what transpired on that day. It is clear that you violated the rights of the couple—their right to privacy—yet the couple apparently experienced no injury of any sort from you.

Let's take another example: your friend, Joe, owns a large diamond worth hundreds of thousands of dollars that he keeps in his house in a safe with a combination lock. You discover the combination to the safe and take the diamond without Joe's knowledge. You use the diamond as collateral to borrow ten thousand dollars which you invest in the stock market and which you manage to turn into one hundred thousand dollars. With this money you redeem the diamond and replace it in Joe's safe completely unchanged in any way. You never tell Joe and he never finds out; moreover, what you did never affects him in any way whatsoever, nor does it ever affect your interactions or friendship with him. It is clear again, that here you have violated your friend's rights yet he has suffered no injury. A person's rights can be violated, then, even when the person is not injured or hurt in any obvious way. From a rights' perspective, a person can be wronged without being hurt. Notice, also, that this implies that when rights violations are concerned, it is a mistake for a person to say that he or she did nothing wrong because "no one was hurt." The absence of "hurt" does not by itself show that no one's rights were violated.

The most important moral rights—and those that will concern us in this chapter—are rights that impose prohibitions or requirements on others and allow or empower individuals to pursue certain interests or activities. These moral rights (we mean these kinds of rights when we use the term *moral rights*) identify activities or interests that the individual is empowered to pursue, or must be left free to pursue, or must be helped to pursue, as the individual chooses. They protect the individual's pursuit of those interests and activities within the boundaries specified by the rights. The right to freedom of religion, for example, identifies religious activities as protected activities that individuals must be left free to pursue as they choose. These kinds of moral rights have three important features that define these enabling and protective functions.

First, moral rights are tightly correlated with duties.[36] This is because one person's moral right generally can be defined—at least partially—in terms of the moral duties other people have toward that person. To have a moral right necessarily implies that others have certain duties toward the bearer of that right. The moral right freedom of religion, for example, can be defined in terms of the moral duties other people have to not interfere in my chosen form of religious worship. The moral right to a suitable standard of living (assuming this is a moral right) can be defined in terms of the duty that governments (or some other agents of society) have to ensure a suitable standard of living for their citizens. Duties, then, are generally the other side of moral rights: If I have a moral right to do something, then other people have a moral duty not to interfere with me when I do it. If I have a moral right to have someone do something for me, then that other person (or group of persons) has a moral duty to do it for me. Thus, moral rights impose correlative duties on others—either duties of noninterference or duties of positive performance.

In some cases, the correlative duties imposed by a right may fall not on any specific individual, but on all the members of a group. For example, if a person has the "right to work" (a right mentioned in the UN Universal Declaration of Human Rights), this does not necessarily mean that any specific employer has a duty to provide that person with a job. Rather, it means that all the members of society, through their public agencies, have the duty of ensuring that jobs are available to workers.

Second, moral rights provide individuals with autonomy and equality in the free pursuit of their interests.[37] That is, a right identifies activities or interests that people must be free to pursue or not pursue as they choose (or must be helped to pursue as they freely choose). This pursuit must not be subordinated to the interests of others except for special and exceptionally weighty reasons. If I have a right to worship as I choose, for example, then this implies that I am free to worship, if and as I personally choose, and that I am not dependent on anyone's permission to worship. It also implies that I cannot generally be forced to stop worshipping on the basis that society will gain more benefits if I am kept from worshipping. The gains of others do not generally justify interference with a person's pursuit of an interest or an activity when that pursuit is protected by a moral right. To acknowledge a person's moral right, is to acknowledge that there is an area in which the person is not subject to my wishes and in which the person's interests are not subordinate to mine. There is an area, in short, within which we stand as autonomous equals.

Third, moral rights provide a basis for justifying one's actions and for invoking the protection or aid of others.[38] If I have a moral right to do something, then I have a moral justification for doing it. Moreover, if I have a right to do something, then others have no justification for interfering with me. On the contrary, others are justified in restraining any persons who try to prevent me from exercising my right, or others may have a duty to aid me in exercising my right. When a stronger person helps a weaker one defend his or her rights, for example, we generally acknowledge that the act of the stronger person was justified.

Because moral rights have these three features, they provide bases for making moral judgments that differ substantially from utilitarian standards. First, moral rights express the requirements of morality from the point of view of the *individual*, whereas utilitarianism expresses the requirements of morality from the point of view of *society as a whole*. Moral standards concerned with rights indicate what is due to the individual from others, promote the individual's welfare, and protect the individual's choices against encroachment by society. Utilitarian standards promote society's aggregate utility, and they are indifferent to the individual's welfare except insofar as it affects this social aggregate. Second, rights limit the validity of appeals to social benefits and to numbers. That is, if a person has a right to do something, then it is wrong for anyone to interfere, even if a large number of people might gain much more utility from such interference. If I have a right to life, for example, then it is morally wrong for someone to kill me even though many others might gain much more from my death than I will ever gain from living. If the members of a minority group have a right to free speech, then the majority must leave the minority free to speak, even if the majority is much more numerous and intensely opposed to what the minority will say.

Although rights generally override utilitarian standards, they are not immune from all utilitarian considerations: If the utilitarian benefits or losses imposed on society become great enough, they might be sufficient to breach the protective walls

Quick Review 2.4

Moral Rights

- Can be violated even when "no one is hurt"
- Are correlated with duties others have toward the person with the right
- Provide individuals with autonomy and equality in the free pursuit of their interests
- Provide a basis for justifying one's actions and for invoking the protection or aid of others
- Focus on securing the interests of the individual unlike utilitarian standards which focus on securing the aggregate utility of everyone in society.

the right sets up around a person's freedom to pursue individual interests. In times of war or major public emergencies, for example, it is generally acknowledged that civil rights may legitimately be restricted for the sake of "the public welfare." The property rights of factory owners may be restricted to prevent pollution that is imposing major damages on the health of others. The more important the interest protected by a right, the larger the utilitarian trade-offs must be. Rights erect higher walls around more important interests, and so the level of social benefits or costs needed to breach the walls must be greater.

negative rights Duties others have to not interfere in certain activities of the person who holds the right.

Negative and Positive Rights A large group of rights called **negative rights** are rights that can be defined wholly in terms of the duties others have to not interfere in certain activities of the person who holds a given right.[39] For example, if I have a right to privacy, this means that every other person, including my employer, has the duty not to invade my private affairs. If I have a right to use, sell, or destroy my personal business assets, this means that every other person has the duty not to prevent me from using, selling, or destroying my business property as I choose.

positive rights Duties of other agents (it is not always clear who) to provide the holder of the right with whatever he or she needs to freely pursue his or her interests.

In contrast, **positive rights** do more than impose negative duties. They also imply that some other agents (perhaps society in general) have the positive duty of providing the holders of the right with whatever they need to pursue what the right guarantees.[40] For example, if I have a right to an adequate standard of living, this does not mean merely that others must not interfere; it also means that if I am unable to provide myself with an adequate income, then I must be provided with such an income (perhaps by the government). Similarly, the right to work, the right to an education, the right to adequate health care, and the right to social security are all rights that go beyond noninterference to also impose a positive duty of providing people with something when they are unable to provide it for themselves.

Seventeenth and eighteenth century writers of manifestos (such as the U.S. Declaration of Independence and the Bill of Rights) often appealed to negative rights, particularly when they wanted to protect individuals against the power of kings, queens, and emperors. On the other hand, until the twentieth century, people only occasionally invoked positive rights (the right to be protected from violence by the state, for example, is one positive right that was widely accepted long before the twentieth century). Positive rights became more important in the twentieth century when society increasingly provided the necessities of life for its members who were unable to provide for themselves. These included the right to an education and the right to social security. The UN Universal Declaration of Human Rights is influenced by this trend when it provides for the rights "to food, clothing, housing, and medical care." The change in the meaning of the phrase "the right to life" is another indication of the rising importance of positive rights. The eighteenth century interpreted the "right to life" as the negative right not to be killed (this is the meaning the phrase has in the Declaration of Independence). The twentieth century, however, has reinterpreted the phrase to refer to the positive right to be provided with the minimum necessities of life.

Quick Review 2.5

Three Kinds of Moral Rights

- Negative rights require others leave us alone.
- Positive rights require others help us.
- Contractual or special rights require people keep their agreements.

Much of the debate over moral rights has concentrated on whether negative or positive rights should be given priority. This is the crux of the debate over whether government efforts should be restricted to protecting property and securing law and order (i.e., protecting people's negative rights) or whether government should also provide the needy with jobs, job training, housing, medical care, and other welfare benefits (i.e., provide for people's positive rights). So-called "conservative" thinkers have claimed that government efforts should be limited to enforcing negative rights and not expended on providing positive rights.[41] So-called "liberals," in contrast, hold that positive rights have as strong a claim to being honored as negative rights and, consequently, government has a duty to provide for both.[42] Liberal thinkers have also pointed out that the right to have the government provide citizens with protection of their property, and the right to have government provide law and order are both positive rights. Therefore, the idea that government should only enforce negative rights and not provide for people's positive rights is incoherent because the government can enforce negative rights only if it provides protective services.

Contractual Rights and Duties Contractual rights and duties (sometimes called *special rights and duties* or *special obligations*) are the limited rights and correlative duties that arise when one person enters an agreement with another person.[43] For example, if I contract to do something for you, then you are entitled to my performance. You acquire a contractual *right* to whatever I promised, and I have a contractual *duty* to perform as I promised.

Contractual rights and duties are distinguished, first, by the fact that they attach to *specific* individuals and the correlative duties are imposed only on other *specific* individuals. If I agree to do something for you, everyone else does not acquire new rights over me, nor do I acquire any new duties toward them. Second, contractual rights arise out of a specific transaction between particular individuals. Unless I actually make a promise or enter some other, similar arrangement with you, you do not acquire any contractual rights over me.

Third, contractual rights and duties depend on a publicly accepted system of rules that define the transactions that give rise to those rights and duties.[44] Contracts, for example, create special rights and duties between people only if these people recognize and accept a system of conventions that specifies that, by doing certain things (such as signing a paper), a person undertakes an obligation to do what the person agrees to do. When a person goes through the appropriate actions, other people know that person is taking on an obligation because the publicly recognized system of rules specifies that such actions count as a contractual agreement. Because the publicly recognized system obligates or requires the person to do what is agreed to, or suffer the appropriate penalties, everyone understands that the person can be relied on to keep the contract and that others can act in accordance with this understanding.

Without the institution of contract and the rights and duties it can create, modern business societies could not operate. Virtually every business transaction at some point requires one of the parties to rely on the word of the other party to the effect that the other party will pay later, will deliver certain services later, or will transfer goods of a certain quality and quantity. Without the social institution of contract, individuals in such situations would be unwilling to rely on the word of the other party, and the transactions would never take place. The institution of contracts provides a way of ensuring that individuals keep their word, and this, in turn, makes it possible for business society to operate. Employers, for example, acquire contractual rights to the services of their employees in virtue of the work contract that employees enter, and sellers acquire contractual rights to the future cash that credit buyers agree to give them.

Contractual rights and duties also provide a basis for the special duties or obligations that people acquire when they accept a position or role within a legitimate social institution or an organization. For example, married parents have a special duty to care for the upbringing of their children, doctors have a special duty to care for the health of their patients, and managers have a special duty to care for the organization they administer. In each of these cases, there is a publicly accepted institution (such as a familial, medical, or corporate institution) that defines a certain position or role (such as parent, doctor, or manager) on which the welfare of certain vulnerable persons (such as the parents' children, the doctor's patients, or the

Quick Review 2.6

Contractual Rights and Duties

- Are created by specific agreements and conferred only on the parties involved
- Require publicly accepted rules on what constitutes agreements and what obligations agreements impose
- Underlie the special rights and duties imposed by accepting a position or role in an institution or organization
- Require (1) the parties know what they are agreeing to, (2) no misrepresentation, (3) no duress or coercion, (4) no agreement to an immoral act.

manager's corporate stakeholders) depends. Society attaches to these institutional roles special duties of caring for these vulnerable dependents and protecting them from injury—duties that the people who enter the role know they are expected to fulfill. When a person freely enters the role knowing what duties society attaches to the acceptance of the role, that person in effect enters an agreement to fulfill those duties. The existence of a system of contractual obligations ensures that individuals fulfill these agreements by laying on them the public obligations that all agreements carry. As a result, these familial, medical, and corporate institutions can continue to exist, and their vulnerable members are protected against harm. We should recall here that a person's institutional duties are not unlimited. In the first chapter, we noted that as a "loyal agent," the manager's duties to care for the corporation are limited by the ethical principles that govern any person. Similarly, a doctor cannot kill some patients to obtain vital organs for other patients whom he or she has a duty to care for.

What kind of ethical rules govern contracts? The system of rules that underlies contractual rights and duties has been traditionally interpreted as including several moral constraints:[45]

1. Both of the parties to a contract must have full knowledge of the nature of the agreement they are entering into.
2. Neither party to a contract must intentionally misrepresent the facts of the contractual situation to the other party.
3. Neither party to the contract must be forced to enter the contract under duress or coercion.
4. The contract must not bind the parties to an immoral act.

Contracts that violate one or more of these four conditions have traditionally been considered void.[46] The basis of these sorts of conditions is discussed next.

A Basis for Moral Rights: Kant

How do we know that people have rights? This question can be answered in a fairly straightforward way when it is asked about legal rights: A person has legal rights because the person lives within a legal system that guarantees those rights. However, what is the basis of moral rights?

Utilitarians have suggested that utilitarian principles can provide a basis for moral rights. They have argued that people have moral rights because having moral rights maximizes utility. It is doubtful, however, that utilitarianism provides an adequate basis for moral rights. To say that someone has a moral right to do something is to say that person is entitled to do it regardless of the utilitarian benefits it provides for others. Utilitarianism cannot easily support such a nonutilitarian concept.

A more satisfactory foundation for moral rights is provided by the ethical theory developed by Immanuel Kant (1724–1804).[47] Kant, in fact, attempts to show that there are certain moral rights and duties that all human beings possess regardless of any utilitarian benefits that the exercise of those rights and duties may provide for others.

categorical imperative
In Kant a moral principle that obligates everyone regardless of their desires and that is based on the idea that everyone should be treated as a free person equal to everyone else.

Kant's theory is based on a moral principle that he called the **categorical imperative** and that requires that everyone should be treated as a free person equal to everyone else. That is, everyone has a moral right to such treatment, and everyone has the correlative duty to treat others in this way. Kant provides more than one way of formulating this basic moral principle; each formulation serves as an explanation of the meaning of this basic moral right and correlative duty.

The First Formulation of Kant's Categorical Imperative

Kant's first formulation of the categorical imperative is as follows: "I ought never to act except in such a way that I can also will that my maxim should become a universal law."[48] A **maxim** for Kant is the reason a person in a certain situation has for doing what he or she plans to do. A maxim would "become a universal law" if every person in a similar situation chose to do the same thing for the same reason. Kant's first version of the categorical imperative, then, comes down to the following principle:

maxim The reason a person in a certain situation has for doing something he or she plans to do.

> An action is morally right for a person in a certain situation if, and only if, the person's reason for carrying out the action is a reason that he or she would be willing to have every person act on, in any similar situation.

Quick Review 2.7

Kant's First Version of the Categorical Imperative

- We must act only on reasons we would be willing to have anyone in a similar situation act on.
- Requires universalizability and reversibility.
- Similar to questions: "What if everyone did that?" and "How would you like it if someone did that to you?"

An example may help clarify what Kant's principle of the categorical imperative means. Suppose that I am trying to decide whether to fire an employee because I do not like the employee's race. According to Kant's principle, I must ask myself whether I would be willing to have an employer fire any employee whenever the employer does not like the race of the employee. In particular, I must ask myself whether I would be willing to be fired myself should my employer not like my race. If I am not willing to have everyone act in this way, even toward me, then it is morally wrong for me to act in this way toward others. A person's reasons for acting, then, must be "reversible"; one must be willing to have all others use those reasons even against oneself. There is an obvious similarity, then, between Kant's categorical imperative and the so-called *golden rule*: "Do unto others as you would have them do unto you."

Kant points out that sometimes it is not even possible to *conceive* of having everyone act on a certain reason, much less be *willing* to have everyone act on that reason.[49] To understand this, consider a second example. Suppose that I am thinking of breaking a contract because it is committed me to do something I do not want to do. Then, I must ask whether I would be willing to allow everyone to break any contract that they did not want to keep. But it is impossible to even conceive of everyone making contracts they do not have to keep. Why? Because if everyone knew that they were allowed to break any contract they did not want to keep, then people would not bother to make contracts. Why would anyone make a contract that no one had to keep?. Consequently, because it is impossible to conceive of a world in which people make contracts they do not have to keep, it is also impossible for me to be willing to have everyone make contracts they do not have to keep. How can I will something I cannot even conceive? It would be wrong, therefore, for me to break a contract simply because I do not want to keep it. A person's reasons for acting, then, must also be *universalizable*: It must be possible, at least in principle, for everyone to act on those reasons.

The first formulation of the categorical imperative, then, incorporates two criteria for determining moral right and wrong—universalizability and reversibility:

> UNIVERSALIZABILITY: The person's reasons for acting must be reasons that everyone could act on at least in principle.
>
> REVERSIBILITY: The person's reasons for acting must be reasons that that person would be willing to have all others use, even as a basis of how they treat him or her.

This formulation of Kant's categorical imperative is attractive for a number of reasons. One important reason is that it captures some of the ways we ordinarily determine moral right and wrong. Frequently, for example, we say to a person who has wrongly injured someone or who is about to wrongly injure someone: "How would you like it if he did that to you?" or "How would you like it if you were in his (or her) place?" When we say this, we are appealing to something like reversibility. We are saying that an action cannot be right if it does not pass the test of reversibility, which is the basis of Kant's categorical imperative. On the other hand, we may say to the person who is considering doing something wrong: "What if everybody did that?" When we ask this question, we are appealing to universalizability. We are, in effect, saying that it is wrong to do something if it does not pass the test of universalizability, which again, is what Kant's categorical imperative requires.

How does Kant argue for the categorical imperative? To begin with, consider that Kant's categorical imperative focuses on a person's interior motivations and not on the external consequences of his or her actions. Moral right and wrong, according to Kant, are distinguished not by what a person accomplishes, but by the reasons or motives the person has for doing what he or she does. Kant argues that an action "has no moral worth," if a person does the action *only* out of self-interest or *only* because it gives him or her pleasure. In other words, morality is not about pursuing self-interest nor about doing what gives us pleasure; morality is about doing what is right whether or not it is in our self-interest and whether or not it makes us feel good. A person's action has "moral worth" then, only to the degree that it is *also* motivated by a sense of "duty," that is, a belief that it is the right way for all people to behave in similar circumstances. Therefore, Kant claims, to be motivated by a sense of "duty" is to be motivated by reasons that I believe everyone should act on when they are in similar circumstances. Consequently, Kant concludes, my action has "moral worth" (i.e., it is morally right) only to the extent that it is motivated by reasons that I would be willing to have every person act on when they are in similar circumstances. This consequence or conclusion is Kant's categorical imperative.

The Second Formulation of Kant's Categorical Imperative

The second formulation Kant gives of the categorical imperative is this: "Act in such a way that you always treat humanity, whether in your own person or in the person of any other, never simply as a means, but always at the same time as an end."[50] Or never treat people *only* as means, but always *also* as ends. What Kant means by "treating humanity as an end" is that we should treat each human being as a free and rational person. This means two things: (1) Respect each person's freedom by treating that person only as she has freely and rationally consented to be treated, and (b) contribute to each person's ability to pursue those ends she has freely and rationally chosen to pursue.[51] The phrase "freely and rationally" here refers to the kind of choices a person makes when her choices are not forced and she both knows and chooses what is in her best interests. On the other hand, to treat a person *only* as a means is to use the person as an instrument for advancing one's own while disregarding the person's choices and interests. This *neither* respects her freedom to choose for herself what she will do, *nor* contributes to her ability to pursue what she has freely and rationally chosen to pursue. Kant's second version of the categorical imperative, then, can be expressed in the following principle:

> An action is morally right for a person if, and only if, in performing the action, the person does not use others *only* as a means for advancing his or her own interests, but always (1) treats them as they have freely and rationally consented to be treated, and (2) contributes to their ability to pursue what they have freely and rationally chosen to pursue.

Quick Review 2.8

Kant's Second Version of the Categorical Imperative

- Never use people only as a means to your ends, but always treat them as they freely and rationally consent to be treated and help them pursue their freely and rationally chosen ends.
- Based on the idea that humans have a dignity that makes them different from mere objects.
- It is, according to Kant, equivalent to the first formulation.

This version of the categorical imperative implies that human beings have a dignity that sets them apart from things such as tools or machines and that is incompatible with being manipulated, deceived, or otherwise unwillingly exploited to satisfy the self-interests of another. The principle in effect says that people should not be treated as objects incapable of free and rational choice. By this principle, an employee may legitimately be asked to perform the unpleasant (or even dangerous) tasks involved in a job if the employee freely and rationally consented to take the job knowing that it would involve these tasks. However, it would be wrong to subject an employee to health risks without the employee's knowledge. In general, deception, force, and manipulation fail to respect people's freedom to choose for themselves and are therefore unethical (unless, perhaps, a person first freely consented to have force used against him or herself).

Kant argues that making fraudulent contracts by deceiving others is wrong and that deliberately refraining from giving others help when they need it is also wrong. By deceiving a person into making a contract that the person would not knowingly choose to make, I am deliberately treating her in a way that she has not freely and rationally consented to be treated, and so I am only using her to advance my own interests. By intentionally refraining from helping another person when I see that person needs the help that I can provide, I fail to contribute to the person's ability to pursue the ends she has chosen to pursue.

The second formulation of the categorical imperative, according to Kant, is really equivalent to the first.[52] The first version says that what is morally right for me must be morally right for others: Everyone is of equal value. If this is so, then no person's freedom should be subordinated to that of others so that the person is used merely to advance the interests of others. Because everyone is of equal value, no one's freedom to choose can be sacrificed for the sake of the interests of others. This, of course, is what the second version of the categorical imperative requires. Both formulations come down to the same thing: People are to treat each other as beings who are equally free to pursue what they themselves choose to pursue.

Kantian Rights

A large number of authors have held that the categorical imperative (in one or the other of its formulations) explains why people have moral rights.[53] As we have seen, moral rights identify interests that all humans must be left free to pursue as they choose (or must be helped to pursue as they choose) and whose free pursuit must not be subordinated to the interests of others. That is precisely what both formulations of Kant's categorical imperative require in holding that people must be respected as free and rational in the pursuit of their interests. In short, *moral rights* identify the specific major areas in which we must deal with each other as free and rational persons, and Kant's *categorical imperative* implies that persons generally should deal with each other in precisely this way.

The categorical imperative, however, cannot by itself tell us what particular moral rights we have. To know what particular moral rights we have, two things are necessary. First, we must determine what specific interests human beings have simply in virtue of being human beings. Second, we must determine which particular interests are so important that they merit being given the status of a right. In light of Kant's two versions of the categorical imperative, an interest would have such importance if (1) we would not be willing to have everyone (including ourselves) deprived of the freedom to pursue that interest, and (2) the freedom to pursue that interest is necessary if we are to live as free and rational beings. For example, to establish that we have a right to free speech, we have to show that we have an interest in freedom of speech

Quick Review 2.9

Kant and Moral Rights

- Kant's theory implies that individuals generally must be left equally free (or helped) to pursue their interests while moral rights identify the specific interests individuals should be entitled to freely pursue (or be helped to pursue).
- An interest is important enough to become a right if (1) we would not be willing to have everyone deprived of the freedom to pursue that interest, and (2) the freedom to pursue that interest is needed to live as free and rational beings.

and that it is so important to us that we are not willing for everyone to be deprived of it and, moreover, it is needed if we are to live as free rational persons. Many people have argued that freedom of speech is indeed critically important for several reasons: it protects us against government and other powerful parties; it lets wrongdoing and injustice be known; it enables us to govern ourselves; it allows us to determine the truth through discussion; and it lets us express our true feelings and convictions.[54] For these reasons, free speech seems to be so important that we would not be willing to have everyone (including ourselves) deprived of freedom of speech, and freedom of speech seems necessary if we are to live as free and rational beings. If this is true, then our interest in free speech is one that should be elevated to the status of a right and we can, therefore, conclude that humans have a moral right to freedom of speech. However, insofar as free speech conflicts with other human interests that are of equal or greater importance (such as our interest in not being harmed or libeled), the right to freedom of speech must be limited.

Although later chapters of this book present various arguments in support of several particular rights, it might be helpful here to give a rough sketch of how some rights have been plausibly defended on the basis of Kant's two formulations of the categorical imperative. First, human beings have a clear interest in by being provided with the work, food, clothing, housing, and medical care they need to live on when they cannot provide for themselves. Suppose we agree that we would not be willing to have everyone (especially ourselves) deprived of such help when it is needed and that such help is necessary if a person's capacity to choose freely and rationally is to develop and even survive.[55] (We can hardly choose freely and rationally when we are starving, homeless, and sick.) If so, then no individual should be deprived of such help. That is, human beings have *positive* moral or human rights to the work, food, clothing, housing, and medical care they need to survive when they cannot provide for themselves and these goods are available.

Second, human beings also have a clear interest in being free from injury or fraud and in being free to think, have privacy, and associate with whomever they choose. Suppose we agree that we are unwilling to have everyone be deprived of these freedoms and that interference in these freedoms limits a person's capacity to freely and rationally choose for themselves what they will do.[56] If so, then Kant's moral principles imply that everyone should be free of the interference of others in these areas. That is, human beings have these negative rights: the right to freedom from injury or fraud, freedom of thought, freedom of association, freedom of speech, and the right to privacy.

Third, as we have seen, human beings have a clear interest in preserving the institution of contracts. Suppose we agree that we would lose the institution of contracts (which we are unwilling to do) if everyone stopped honoring their contracts, or if everyone had to honor contracts that were made under duress or without full information. Suppose we also agree that we show respect for people's freedom and rationality by honoring the contracts they freely make with us and by leaving them free and fully informed about any contracts they make with us.[57] If so, then everyone should honor their contracts and everyone should be fully informed and free when making contracts. That is, human beings have a contractual right to what they have been promised in contracts, and everyone also has a right to be left free and fully informed when contracts are made.

We have only sketched in barest outline some of the rights that Kant' moral principles can support. A full justification of each of these rights requires a lot more in the way of qualifications, adjustments with other (conflicting) interests, and full supporting arguments. Crude as it is, however, the brief sketch above provides some idea of how Kant's categorical imperative can explain and justify positive, negative, and contractual rights.

Problems with Kant

Despite the attractiveness of Kant's theory, critics have argued that, like utilitarianism, it has limitations and inadequacies. A first problem that critics have traditionally pointed out is that Kant's theory is not clear enough to always be useful. One difficulty lies in trying to determine whether one would (as the first formulation requires) "be willing to have everyone follow" a certain policy. Although the general thrust of this requirement is more or less clear, it sometimes leads to problems. For example, suppose I am a murderer: Would I then be willing to have everyone follow the policy that all murderers should be punished? In a sense, I would be willing to because I would want to be protected from other murderers. Yet, in another sense, I would not be willing because I do not want to be punished myself. Which sense is correct?[58] It is also sometimes difficult to determine whether one person is using another "merely as a means" (as the second formulation states we should never do). Suppose, for example, that Ms. Jones, an employer, only pays minimum wages to her employees and refuses to install the safety equipment they want, yet she says she is "respecting their capacity to freely choose for themselves" because she is willing to let them work elsewhere if they choose. Is she then treating them merely as means or also as ends? Critics complain that Kant's theory is too vague to answer such questions.[59] There are cases, then, where the requirements of Kant's theory are unclear.

A second problem is that some critics claim that, although we might be able to agree on the kinds of interests that have the status of moral rights, there is substantial disagreement concerning what the limits of each of these rights are and concerning how each of these rights should be balanced against other conflicting rights.[60] Kant's theory does not help us resolve these disagreements. For example, we all agree that everyone should have a right to associate with whomever they want, as well as a right not to be injured by others. However, how should these rights be balanced against each other when a certain association of people begins to injure others? For example, suppose the loud music of a group of trombone players disturbs others, or suppose a corporation (or just any association of people) pollutes the air and water on which the health of others depends. Kant's categorical imperative does not tell us how the conflicting rights of these persons should be adjusted to each other. Which right should be limited in favor of the other?

Quick Review 2.10

Criticisms of Kant

- Both versions of the categorical imperative are unclear.
- Rights can conflict and Kant's theory cannot resolve such conflicts.
- Kant's theory implies moral judgments that are mistaken.

A defender of Kant, however, can counter this second criticism by holding that Kant's categorical imperative is not intended to tell us how conflicting rights should be limited and adjusted to each other. To decide whether one right should be curtailed in favor of a second right, one has to examine the relative importance of the interests that each right protects. What arguments can be given to show, for example, that a corporation's interest in financial gains is more or less important than the health of its neighbors? The answer to this question determines whether a corporation's right to use its property for financial gains should be limited in favor of its neighbors' right not to have their health injured. All that Kant's categorical imperative is meant to tell us is that everyone must have equal moral rights and everyone must show as much respect for the protected interests of others as they want others to show for their own. It does not tell us what interests people have nor what their relative importance is.

A third group of criticisms that have been made of Kant's theory is that there are counterexamples that show the theory sometimes goes wrong. Most counterexamples to Kant's theory focus on the criteria of universalizability and reversibility.[61] Suppose that an employer can get away with discriminating against black employees by paying them lower wages than white employees for the same work. Suppose also that he is so fanatical in his dislike of blacks that he is willing to accept the proposition that if his or her own skin were black, employers should also discriminate against him.

Then, according to Kant's theory, the employer would be acting morally when he discriminates against blacks. Kant's theory here has clearly led us to a false conclusion because discrimination is obviously immoral.

Defenders of a Kantian approach to ethics, of course, would reply that it is the critics, not Kant, who are mistaken. If the employer genuinely and conscientiously would be willing to universalize the principles on which he is acting, then the action is, in fact, morally right for him.[62] For us, who would be unwilling to universalize the same principle, the action would be immoral. We may also find that it would be morally right for us to impose sanctions on the employer to stop him from discriminating. Insofar as the employer is trying to remain true to his own universal principles, he is acting conscientiously and, therefore, in a moral manner.

The Libertarian Objection: Nozick

libertarian philosophers Believe that freedom from human constraint is necessarily good and that all constraints imposed by others are necessarily evil except when needed to prevent the imposition of greater human constraints.

Several **libertarian philosophers** have proposed important views on rights that are different from the ones we have previously discussed. Libertarian philosophers go beyond the general presumption that freedom from human constraint is usually good; they claim that such freedom is necessarily good and that all constraints imposed by others are necessarily evil except when needed to prevent the imposition of greater human constraints. The late philosopher Robert Nozick, for example, claimed that the only basic right that every individual possesses is the negative right to be free from the coercion of other human beings.[63] This negative right to freedom from coercion, according to Nozick, must be recognized if individuals are to be treated as distinct persons with separate lives, each of whom has an equal moral weight that may not be sacrificed for the sake of others. The only circumstances under which coercion may be exerted on a person is when it is necessary to keep that person from coercing others.

According to Nozick, prohibiting people from coercing others constitutes a legitimate moral constraint that rests on "the underlying Kantian principle that individuals are ends and not merely means; they may not be sacrificed or used for the achieving of other ends without their consent."[64] Thus, Nozick seems to hold that Kant's theory supports his own views on freedom.

Quick Review 2.11

Robert Nozick

- Claimed the only moral right is the negative right to freedom which implies that restrictions on freedom are unjustified except to prevent greater restrictions on freedom
- Claimed the right to freedom requires private property, freedom of contract, free markets, and the elimination of taxes to pay for social welfare programs
- Since the freedom of one person always restricts the freedom of others, Nozick's claim that restrictions on freedom are unjustified implies that freedom itself is unjustified.

Nozick goes on to argue that the negative right to freedom from the coercion of others implies that people must be left free to do what they want with their own labor and with whatever products they manufacture by their labor.[65] This, in turn, implies that people must be left free to acquire property, to use it in whatever way they wish, and to exchange it with others in free markets (so long as the situation of others is not thereby harmed or "worsened"). Thus, the libertarian view that coercive restrictions on freedom are immoral (except when needed to restrain coercion) is also supposed to justify the free use of property, freedom of contract, a free market system, and the elimination of taxes to pay for social welfare programs. However, there is no basis for any positive rights nor for the social programs they might require.

Nozick and other libertarians, however, pass over the fact that the freedom of one person necessarily imposes constraints on others. Such constraints are inevitable because when one person is granted freedom, other persons must be constrained from interfering with that person. If I am to be free to do what I want with my property, for example, other people must be constrained from trespassing on it and from taking it from me. Even the "free market system" advocated by Nozick depends on an underlying system of coercion: I can sell something only if I first own it, and ownership depends essentially on an enforced (coercive) system of property laws. Consequently, because granting a freedom to one person necessarily imposes constraints on others, it follows that if constraints require justification, freedom will also always require justification.

The same point can be made in a different way. Because there are many different kinds of freedoms, the freedom one group of agents is given to pursue some of its interests will usually restrict the freedom other agents have to pursue other, conflicting interests. For example, the freedom of corporations to use their property to pollute the environment as they want can restrict the freedom of individuals to breathe clean air whenever they want. The freedom of employees to unionize as they want can conflict with the freedom of employers to hire whatever nonunion workers they want. Consequently, allowing one kind of freedom to one group requires restricting some other kind of freedom for some other group: A decision in favor of the freedom to pursue one interest implies a decision against the freedom to pursue another kind of interest. This means that we cannot argue in favor of a certain kind of freedom by simply claiming that constraints are always evil and must always be replaced by freedom. Instead, an argument for a specific freedom must show that the interests that can be satisfied by that kind of freedom are somehow better or more worth satisfying than the interests that other, opposing kinds of freedoms could satisfy. Libertarians generally fail to supply such arguments.

Moreover, it is not obvious that Kant's principles can support the libertarian views of Nozick. Kant holds, as we saw, that we should respect the dignity of every person and contribute to each person's ability to pursue the ends they have freely and rationally chosen to pursue. Because we have these duties to each other, government coercion is legitimate when it is needed to ensure that the dignity of citizens is being respected or when it is needed to help people pursue ends they freely and rationally choose to pursue. This, as Kant argues, means that government may legitimately place limits on the use of property and on contracts and impose market restrictions and compulsory taxes when these are needed to, as he wrote, help persons "who are not able to support themselves."[66] Kant gives us no reason to think that only negative rights exist. People can also have positive rights, and Kant's theory supports these as much as it supports negative rights.

2.3 Justice and Fairness

Several years ago, a Senate subcommittee heard the testimony of several workers who had contracted "brown lung" disease by breathing cotton dust while working in cotton mills in the South.[67] Brown lung is a chronic disabling respiratory disease with symptoms similar to asthma and emphysema and is a cause of premature death. The disabled workers were seeking a federal law that would facilitate the process of getting disability compensation from the cotton mills, similar to federal laws covering "black lung" disease contracted in coal mines.

Senator Strom Thurmond:

A number of people have talked to me about this and they feel that if the federal government enters the field of black lung, it should enter the field of brown lung; and if those who have suffered from black lung are to receive federal consideration, then it seems fair that those who have suffered from brown lung receive federal consideration.... If our [state's cotton mill] workers have been injured and haven't been properly compensated, then steps should be taken to see that it is done. We want to see them treated fairly and squarely and properly, and so we look forward to ... the testimony here today.

Mrs. Beatrice Norton:

> I started in the mill when I was fourteen years old and I had to get out in 1968.... I worked in the dust year after year, just like my mother. I got sicker and sicker ... I suddenly had no job, no money, and I was sick, too sick to ever work in my life again.... State legislators have proven in two successive sessions that they are not going to do anything to help the brown lung victims, so now we come to you in Washington and ask for help. We've waited a long time, and many of us have died waiting. I don't want to die of injustice.

Mrs. Vinnie Ellison:

> My husband worked for twenty-one years [in the mill] in Spartanburg, and he worked in the dustiest parts of the mill, the opening room, the cardroom, and cleaning the air-conditioning ducts.... In the early sixties he started having trouble keeping up his job because of his breathing. His bossman told him that he had been a good worker, but wasn't worth a damn anymore, and fired him.... He had no pension and nothing to live on and we had to go on welfare to live.... My husband worked long and hard and lost his health and many years of pay because of the dust. It isn't fair that [the mill] threw him away like so much human garbage after he couldn't keep up his job because he was sick from the dust. We are not asking for handouts; we want what is owed to my husband for twenty-five years of hard work.

Disputes among individuals in business often refer to *justice* or *fairness*. This is the case, for example, when one person accuses another of *unjustly* discriminating against him or her, showing *unjust* favoritism toward someone else, or not shouldering a *fair* share of the burdens involved in some cooperative venture. Resolving disputes like these requires that we compare and weigh the conflicting claims of each of the parties and strike a balance between them. Justice and fairness are essentially comparative. They are concerned with how one group's treatment compares to the way another group is treated, particularly when benefits and burdens are distributed, when rules and laws are administered, when members of a group cooperate or compete with each other, and when people are punished for the wrongs they have done or compensated for the injuries they have suffered. Although the terms *justice* and *fairness* are used almost interchangeably, we tend to reserve the word *justice* for matters that are especially serious, although some authors have held that the concept of fairness is more fundamental.[68]

Standards of justice are generally taken to have more weight than utilitarian considerations.[69] If a society is unjust to many of its members, then we normally condemn that society, even if the injustices secure more utilitarian benefits for everyone. If we think that slavery is unjust, for example, then we condemn a society that uses slavery even if slavery makes that society more productive. Greater benefits for some cannot justify injustices against others. Nonetheless, we also seem to hold that if the social gains are sufficiently large, a certain level of injustice may legitimately be tolerated.[70] In countries with extreme deprivation and poverty, for example, we seem to hold that some degree of equality may be traded for major economic gains that leave everyone better off.

Quick Review 2.12

Types of Justice

- Distributive Justice: just distribution of benefits and burdens
- Retributive Justice: just imposition of punishments and penalties
- Compensatory Justice: just compensation for wrongs or injuries

Standards of justice do not generally override the moral rights of individuals. Part of the reason for this is that, to some extent, justice is based on individual moral rights. The moral right to be treated as a free and equal person, for example, is part of what lies behind the idea that benefits and burdens should be distributed equally.[71]

More important is the fact that, as we saw, a moral right identifies interests people have, the free pursuit of which may not be subordinated to the interests of others except where there are special and exceptionally weighty reasons. For the most part, the moral rights of some individuals cannot be sacrificed merely in order to secure a somewhat better distribution of benefits for others. However, correcting extreme injustices may justify restricting the rights of some individuals. Property rights, for example, might be legitimately redistributed for the sake of justice. We will discuss these kinds of trade-offs more fully in this chapter after we have determined what *justice* means.

Issues involving questions of justice and fairness are usually divided into three categories. **Distributive justice**, the first and basic category, is concerned with the fair distribution of society's benefits and burdens. In the brown lung hearings, for example, Senator Thurmond pointed out that if federal law helped workers afflicted by black lung, then it was only "fair" that it also help workers afflicted by brown lung. **Retributive justice**, the second category, refers to the just imposition of punishments and penalties on those who do wrong. A just penalty is one that in some sense is deserved by the person who does wrong. Retributive justice would be at issue, for example, if we were to ask whether it would be fair to penalize cotton mills for causing brown lung disease among their workers. **Compensatory justice**, the third category, concerns the just way of compensating people for what they lost when others wronged them. A just compensation is one that, in some sense, is proportional to the loss suffered by the person being compensated (such as loss of livelihood). During the brown lung hearings, both Mrs. Norton and Mrs. Ellison claimed that, in justice, they were owed compensation from the cotton mills because of injuries inflicted by the mills.

distributive justice Requires distributing society's benefits and burdens fairly.

retributive justice Requires fairness when blaming or punishing persons for doing wrong.

compensatory justice Requires restoring to a person what the person lost when he or she was wronged by someone.

This section examines each of these three kinds of justice separately. The section begins with a discussion of a basic principle of distributive justice (equals should be treated as equals) and then examines several views on the criteria relevant to determining whether two persons are equal. The section then turns to much briefer discussions of retributive and compensatory justice.

Distributive Justice

Questions of distributive justice arise when different people make claims on society's benefits and burdens and all the claims cannot be satisfied.[72] The central cases are those where there is a scarcity of benefits—such as jobs, food, housing, medical care, income, and wealth—as compared with the numbers and desires of the people who want these goods. The other side of the coin is that there may be too many burdens—unpleasant work, drudgery, substandard housing, health injuries of various sorts—and not enough people willing to shoulder them. If there were enough goods to satisfy everyone's desires and enough people willing to share society's burdens, then conflicts between people would not arise and distributive justice would not be needed.

When people's desires and aversions exceed the adequacy of their resources, they are forced to develop principles for allocating scarce benefits and undesirable burdens in ways that are just and that resolve the conflicts in a fair way. The development of such principles is the concern of distributive justice.

The fundamental principle of distributive justice is that equals should be treated equally and unequals treated unequally.[73] More precisely, the fundamental principle of distributive justice may be expressed as follows:

> Individuals who are similar in all respects relevant to the kind of treatment in question should be given similar benefits and burdens, even if they are

> dissimilar in other irrelevant respects; and individuals who are dissimilar in a relevant respect ought to be treated dissimilarly, in proportion to their dissimilarity.

For example, if Susan and Bill are both doing the same work for me and there are no relevant differences between them or the work they are doing, then, in justice, I should pay them equal wages. However, if Susan is working twice as long as Bill and if length of working time is the relevant basis for determining wages on the sort of work they are doing, then, to be just, I should pay Susan twice as much as Bill. To return to our earlier example, if the federal government rightly helps workers who have suffered from black lung and there are no relevant differences between such workers and workers who have suffered from brown lung, then, as Senator Thurmond said, it is "fair that those who have suffered from brown lung [also] receive federal consideration."

This fundamental principle of distributive justice, however, is purely formal.[74] It is based on the purely logical idea that we must be consistent in the way we treat similar situations. The principle does not indicate the "relevant respects" that can provide the basis for similarity or dissimilarity of treatment. For example, is race relevant when determining who should get what jobs? Most of us would say "no," but then what characteristics are relevant when determining what benefits and burdens people should receive? We turn now to examine different views on the kinds of characteristics that may be relevant. Each of these views provides a material principle of justice (i.e., a principle that gives specific content to the fundamental principle of distributive justice). For example, one simple principle that people often use to decide who should receive a limited or scarce good is the "first-come, first-served" principle that operates when waiting in line to receive something, as well as in the seniority systems used by businesses. The "first-come, first-served" principle assumes that being first is a relevant characteristic for determining who should be the first party served when not all can be served at once. The reader can undoubtedly think of many other such simple principles that we use. However, here we will concentrate on several principles that are often thought to be more fundamental than principles such as "first-come, first-served."

Justice as Equality: Egalitarianism

Egalitarians hold that there are no relevant differences among people that can justify unequal treatment.[75] According to the egalitarian, all benefits and burdens should be distributed according to the following formula:

> Every person should be given exactly equal shares of a society's or a group's benefits and burdens.

Egalitarians base their view on the proposition that all human beings are equal in some fundamental respect and that, in virtue of this equality, each person has an equal claim to society's goods.[76] According to the egalitarian, this implies that goods should be allocated to people in equal portions.

Equality has been proposed as a principle of justice not only for entire societies, but also within smaller groups or organizations. Within a family, for example, it is often assumed that children should over the course of their lives receive equal shares of the goods parents make available to them. In some companies and in some workgroups, particularly when the group has strong feelings of solidarity and is working at tasks that require cooperation, workers feel that all should receive equal compensation for their work. Interestingly, when workers in a group receive equal compensation, they tend to become more cooperative with each other and to feel greater solidarity with each other.[77] Also interestingly, workers in countries such as Japan, which is characterized as having a more collectivist culture, prefer the principle of equality more than workers in countries such as the United States, which is characterized as having a more individualistic culture.[78]

Equality has appeared to many to be as an attractive social ideal, and inequality as a defect. "All men are created equal," states the U.S. Declaration of Independence, and the ideal of equality has been the driving force behind the emancipation of slaves; the prohibition of indentured servitude; the elimination of racial, sexual, and property requirements on voting and holding public office; and the institution of free public education. People in the United States have long prided themselves on the lack of overt status consciousness in their social relations.

Despite their popularity, however, egalitarian views have been subjected to heavy criticisms. One line of attack has focused on the egalitarian claim that all human beings are equal in some fundamental respect.[79] Critics claim that there is no quality that all human beings possess in precisely the same degree: Human beings differ in their abilities, intelligence, virtues, needs, desires, and all other physical and mental characteristics. If this is so, then human beings are unequal in all respects.

A second set of criticisms argues that the egalitarian ignores some characteristics that should be taken into account in distributing goods both in society and in smaller groups: need, ability, and effort.[80] If everyone is given exactly the same things, critics point out, then the lazy person will get as much as the industrious one, although the lazy one does not deserve as much. If everyone is given exactly the same, then the sick person will get only as much as a healthy one, although the sick person needs more. If everyone is given exactly the same, the handicapped person will have to do as much as a more able person, although the handicapped person has less ability. If everyone is given exactly the same, then individuals will have no incentives to exert greater efforts in their work. As a result, society's productivity and efficiency may decline.[81] Critics allege that egalitarianism must be mistaken because the egalitarian formula ignores all these facts, and because it is clear that they should be taken into account.

Some egalitarians have tried to strengthen their position by distinguishing two different kinds of equality: political equality and economic equality.[82] **Political equality** refers to an equal participation in, and treatment by, the means of controlling and directing the political system. This includes equal rights to participate in the legislative process, equal civil liberties, and equal rights to due process. **Economic equality** refers to equality of income and wealth and equality of opportunity. The criticisms leveled against equality, according to some egalitarians, only apply to economic equality and not to political equality. Although everyone will concede that differences of need, ability, and effort may justify some inequalities in the distribution of income and wealth, everyone will also agree that political rights and liberties should not be unequally distributed. Thus, the egalitarian position may be correct with respect to political equality even if it is mistaken with respect to economic equality.

political equality Equal participation in, and treatment by, the political system.

economic equality Equality of income, wealth, and opportunity.

Other egalitarians have claimed that even economic equality is defensible if it is suitably limited. Thus, they have argued that every person has a right to a minimum standard of living and that income and wealth should be distributed equally until this standard is achieved for everyone.[83] The economic surplus that remains after everyone has achieved the minimum standard of living can then be distributed unequally according to need, effort, and so on. A major difficulty that this limited type of economic egalitarianism must face, however, is specifying what it means by *minimum standard of living*. Different societies and cultures have different views as to what constitutes the necessary minimum standard. A relatively primitive economy will place the minimum at a lower point than a relatively affluent one. Nonetheless, most people would agree that justice requires that affluent societies satisfy at least the basic needs of their members and not let them die of starvation, exposure, or disease.

Justice Based on Contribution: Capitalist Justice

Some writers have argued that a society's benefits should be distributed in proportion to what each individual contributes to a society and/or to a group. The more a person contributes to a society's pool of economic goods, for example, the more that person is entitled to take from that pool; the less an individual contributes, the less that individual should get. The more a worker contributes to a project, the more that worker should be paid. According to this capitalist view of justice, when people engage in economic exchanges with each other, what a person gets out of the exchange should be at least equal in value to what the person contributed. Justice requires, then, that the benefits people receive should be proportional to the value of their contribution. In a more simple statement:

> Benefits should be distributed according to the value of the contribution the individual makes to a society, a task, a group, or an exchange.

The principle of contribution is perhaps the principle of fairness most widely used to establish salaries and wages in U.S. companies. In workgroups, particularly when relationships among the members of the group are impersonal and the product of each worker is independent of the efforts of the others, workers tend to feel that they should be paid in proportion to the work they have contributed.[84] Salespeople out on the road, for example, or workers at individual sewing machines sewing individual garments or doing other piecework tend to feel that they should be paid in proportion to the quantity of goods they have individually sold or made. Interestingly, when workers are paid in accordance with the principle of contribution, this tends to promote among them an uncooperative and even competitive atmosphere in which resources and information are less willingly shared and in which status differences emerge.[85] Workers in countries that are characterized as having a more individualistic culture, such as the United States, like the principle of contribution more than workers in countries that are characterized as having a more collectivist culture, such as Japan.[86]

The main question raised by the contributive principle of distributive justice is how the "value of the contribution" of each individual is to be measured. One long-lived tradition has held that contributions should be measured in terms of *work effort*. The more effort people put forth in their work, the greater the share of benefits to which they are entitled. The harder one works, the more one deserves. This is the assumption behind the **Puritan ethic**, which held that individuals had a religious obligation to work hard at their *calling* (the vocation to which God summons each individual) and that God justly rewards hard work with wealth and success, while He justly punishes laziness with poverty and failure.[87] In the United States, this Puritan ethic has evolved into a secularized **work ethic**, which places a high value on individual effort and which assumes that, whereas hard work does and should lead to success, loafing is and should be punished.[88]

puritan ethic The view that every individual has a religious obligation to work hard at his or her *calling* (the career to which god summons each individual).

work ethic The view that values individual effort and believes that hard work does and should lead to success.

However, there are many problems with using effort as the basis of distribution.[89] First, to reward a person's efforts without any reference to whether the person produces anything worthwhile through these efforts is to reward incompetence and inefficiency. Second, if we reward people solely for their efforts and ignore their abilities and relative productivity, then talented and highly productive people will be given little incentive to invest their talent and productivity in producing goods for society. As a result, the welfare of society will decline.

A second important tradition has held that contributions should be measured in terms of **productivity**: The greater the quantity of a person's contributed product, the more that person should receive. (*Product* here should be interpreted broadly to include services rendered, capital invested, commodities manufactured, and any type of literary, scientific, or aesthetic works produced.[90]) A major problem with this second proposal is that it ignores people's needs. Handicapped, ill, untrained, and immature persons may be unable to produce anything worthwhile; if people are rewarded on the basis of their productivity, the needs of these disadvantaged groups will not be met. The main problem with this second proposal is that it is difficult to place any objective measure on the value of a person's product, especially in fields such as science, the arts, entertainment, athletics, education, theology, and health care. Who would want to have their products priced on the basis of someone else's subjective estimates?

productivity The amount an individual produces or that a group produces per person.

To deal with the last difficulty mentioned, some authors have suggested a third and highly influential version of the principle of contribution. They have argued that the value of a person's product should be determined by the market forces of supply and demand.[91] The value of a product would then depend not on its intrinsic value, but on the extent to which it is both relatively scarce and is viewed by buyers as desirable. In other words, the value of a person's contribution is equal to whatever that contribution would sell for in a competitive market. People then deserve to receive whatever the market value of their product is worth in exchange with others. Unfortunately, this method of measuring the value of a person's product still ignores people's needs. Moreover, to many people, market prices are an unjust method of evaluating the value of a person's product precisely because markets ignore the intrinsic values of things. Markets, for example, reward entertainers more than doctors. Also, markets often reward a person who, through pure chance, has ended with something (e.g., an inheritance) that is scarce and that people happen to want. To many, this seems the height of injustice.

Justice Based on Needs and Abilities: Socialism

Because there are probably as many kinds of socialism as there are socialists, it is somewhat inaccurate to speak of "the" socialist position on distributive justice. Nonetheless, the dictum proposed first by Louis Blanc (1811–1882) and then by Karl Marx (1818–1883) and Nikolai Lenin (1870–1924) is traditionally taken to represent the socialist view on distribution: "From each according to his ability, to each according to his needs."[92] The socialist principle, then, can be paraphrased as follows:

> Work burdens should be distributed according to people's abilities, and benefits should be distributed according to people's needs.

This socialist principle is based first on the idea that people realize their human potential by exercising their abilities in productive work.[93] Because the realization of one's full potentiality is a value, work should be distributed in such a way that a person can be as productive as possible, and this implies distributing work according to ability. Second, the benefits produced through work should be used to promote human happiness and well-being. This means distributing them so that people's basic biological and health needs are met and then using what is left to meet people's other non-basic needs. Perhaps, most fundamental to the socialist view is the notion that societies should be communities in which benefits and burdens are distributed on the model of a family. Just as able family members willingly support the family, and just as needy family members are willingly supported by the family, so also the able members of a society should contribute their abilities to society by taking up its burdens while the needy should be allowed to share in its benefits.

As the example of the family suggests, the principle of distribution according to need and ability is used within small groups as well as within larger society. The principle of need and ability, however, is the principle that tends to be least acknowledged in business. Managers sometimes invoke the principle when they pass out the more difficult jobs among the members of a workgroup to those who are stronger and more able, but they often retreat when these workers complain that they are being given larger burdens without higher compensation. Managers also sometimes invoke the principle when they make special allowances for workers who seem to have special needs. (This was, in fact, a key consideration when Congress passed the Americans with Disabilities Act.) However, managers rarely do so and are often criticized for showing favoritism when they do.

Nevertheless, there is something to be said for the socialist principle: Needs and abilities certainly should be taken into account when determining how benefits and burdens should be distributed among the members of a group or society. Most people would agree, for example, that we should make a greater contribution to the lives of cotton mill workers with brown lung disease who have greater needs than to the lives of healthy persons who have all they need. Most people would also agree that individuals should be employed in occupations for which they are fitted, and that this means matching each person's abilities to a job as far as possible. Vocational tests in high school and college, for example, are supposed to help students find careers that match their abilities.

However, the socialist principle has also had its critics. First, opponents have pointed out that, under the socialist principle, there would be no relation between the amount of effort a worker puts forth and the amount of remuneration the worker receives (because remuneration would depend on need, not on effort). Consequently, opponents conclude, workers would have no incentive to put forth any work efforts at all knowing that they will receive the same regardless of whether they work hard. The result, it is claimed, will be a stagnating economy with a declining productivity (a claim, however, that does not seem to be borne out by the facts).[94] Underlying this criticism is a deeper objection—namely, that it is unrealistic to think that entire societies could be modeled on familial relationships. Human nature is essentially self-interested and competitive, the critics of socialism hold, and so outside the family people cannot be motivated by the fraternal willingness to share and help that is characteristic of families. Socialists have usually replied to this charge by arguing that human beings are trained to acquire the vices of selfishness and competitiveness by modern social and economic institutions that inculcate and encourage competitive, self-interested behavior, but that people do not have these vices by nature. By nature, humans are born into families where they instinctively value helping each other. If these instinctive and "natural" attitudes continued to be nurtured, instead of being eradicated, humans would continue to value helping others even outside the family and would acquire the virtues of being cooperative, helpful, and selfless. The debate on what kinds of motivations human nature is subject to is still largely unsettled.

A second objection that opponents of the socialist principle have argued is that, if the socialist principle were enforced, it would obliterate individual freedom.[95] Under the socialist principle, the occupation each person entered would be determined by the person's abilities and not by free choice. If a person has the ability to be a university teacher but wants to be a ditchdigger, the person will have to become a teacher. Similarly, under the socialist principle, the goods a person gets will be determined by the person's needs and not by free choice. If a person needs a loaf of bread but wants a bottle of beer, the person will have to take the loaf of bread. The sacrifice of freedom is even greater, the critics claim, when one considers that in a socialist society, some central government agency has to decide what tasks should be matched to each person's abilities and what goods should be allotted to each person's needs. The decisions of this central agency will then have to be imposed on other persons at the expense of their freedom to choose for themselves. The socialist principle substitutes paternalism for freedom.

Justice as Freedom: Libertarianism

The last section of this chapter discussed libertarian views on moral rights; libertarians also have some clear and related views on the nature of justice. The libertarian holds that no particular way of distributing goods can be said to be just or unjust apart from the free choices individuals make. Any distribution of benefits and burdens is just if it is the result of individuals freely choosing to exchange with each other the goods each person already owns. Robert Nozick, a leading libertarian, suggested this principle as the basic principle of distributive justice:

> From each according to what he chooses to do, to each according to what he makes for himself (perhaps with the contracted aid of others) and what others choose to do for him and choose to give him of what they've been given previously (under this maxim) and haven't yet expended or transferred.[96]

ON THE EDGE

ExxonMobil, Amerada Hess, and Marathon Oil in Equatorial Guinea

People in West African countries, among the poorest in the world, survive on $1 a day and have a life expectancy of 46 years. But in 2004, Equatorial Guinea had a GDP (Gross Domestic Product) of $4,472 per person, the highest in West Africa. In 1995, Equatorial Guinea found oil off its coast, and by 2004, ExxonMobil, Amerada Hess, and Marathon Oil—all U.S. oil companies—were helping that West African country produce $4 billion of oil revenues a year. Equatorial Guinea's inexperienced government agreed to give 80 percent of these revenues to the oil companies that drilled the oil for them, although oil companies in developing nations usually take about 50 percent of revenues from oil projects. The oil companies channel—through Riggs Bank, a 2004 Senate report revealed—hundreds of millions of dollars to Equatorial Guinea's president, T. Nguema, and his family for "land purchases," "security services," and "office leases." A Department of Energy report says that because Nguema and his family run the government, the 20 percent of oil revenues that go to the government are spent on "lavish personal expenditures," and so most oil money is "concentrated in the hands of top government officials while the majority of the population remains poor." If Nguema had not been paid, of course, the Equatorial Guinea government would never have approved the oil project. ExxonMobil says it has spent "$4 million" and Marathon Oil and Amerado Hess claim to have "invested millions of dollars" on schools, libraries; programs for the eradication of malaria, polio, and AIDS; health clinics, bridges, waterways, and electricity. A U.S. human rights report says Equatorial Guinea's government violates its citizens' rights of free speech, of the press, of assembly, of due process, of association, of religion, and of movement and uses torture, beatings, and other physical abuse against political opponents.

1. What would utilitarianism, rights theory, and justice say about these activities of ExxonMobil, Amerada Hess, and Marathon Oil in Equatorial Guinea?

Quite simply, "From each as they choose, to each as they are chosen." For example, if I choose to write a novel or carve a statue out of a piece of driftwood, then I should be allowed to keep the novel or statue if I choose to keep it. If I choose, I should be allowed to give it away to someone else or exchange it for another object with whomever I choose. In general, people should be allowed to keep everything they make and everything they are freely given. Obviously, this means it would be wrong to tax one person (i.e., take the person's money) to provide welfare benefits for the needs of someone else.

Nozick's principle is based on the claim (which we have already discussed) that every person has a right to freedom from coercion that takes priority over all other rights and values. The only distribution that is just, according to Nozick, is one that results from free individual choices. Any distribution that results from an attempt to impose a certain pattern on society (e.g., imposing equality on everyone or taking from the "haves" and giving to the "have-nots") will therefore be unjust.

We have already noted some of the problems associated with the libertarian position. The major difficulty is that the libertarian enshrines a certain value—freedom from the coercion of others—and sacrifices all other rights and values to it without giving any persuasive reasons why this should be done. Opponents of the libertarian view argue that other forms of freedom must also be secured, such as freedom from ignorance and freedom from hunger. In many cases, these other forms of freedom override freedom from coercion. If a man is starving, for example, his right to be free from the constraints imposed by hunger is more important than the right of a satisfied man to be free of the constraint of being forced to share his surplus food. To secure these more important rights, society may impose a certain pattern of distribution even if this means that, in some cases, some people will have to be coerced into conforming to the distribution. Those with surplus money, for example, may have to be taxed to provide for those who are starving.

A second related criticism of libertarianism claims that the libertarian principle of distributive justice will generate unjust treatment of the disadvantaged.[97] Under the libertarian principle, a person's share of goods will depend wholly on what can be produced through personal efforts or what others choose to give the person out of charity (or some other motive). Both of these sources may be unavailable to a person through no fault of the person. A person may be ill, handicapped, unable to obtain the tools or land needed to produce goods, too old or too young to work, or otherwise incapable of producing anything through personal efforts. Other people (perhaps out of greed) may refuse to provide that person with what is needed. According to the libertarian principle, such a person should get nothing. But this, say the critics of libertarianism, is surely mistaken. If people, through no fault of their own, happen to be unable to care for themselves, their survival should not depend on the outside chance that others will provide them with what they need. Each person's life is of value, and consequently each person should be cared for, even if this means coercing others into distributing some of their surplus to the person.

Justice as Fairness: John Rawls

These discussions have suggested several different considerations that should be taken into account in the distribution of society's benefits and burdens: political and economic equality, a minimum standard of living, needs, ability, effort, and freedom. What is needed, however, is a comprehensive theory capable of drawing these considerations together and fitting them into a logical whole. John Rawls provides one approach to distributive justice that at least approximates this ideal of a comprehensive theory.[98]

Rawls's theory is based on the assumption that conflicts involving justice should be settled by first devising a fair method for choosing the principles by which the conflicts are resolved. Once a fair method of choosing principles is devised, the principles we choose by using that method should serve us as our own principles of distributive justice. Rawls proposes two basic principles that, he argues, we would select if we were to use a fair method of choosing principles to resolve our social conflicts.[99] The principles of distributive justice that Rawls proposes can be paraphrased by saying that the distribution of benefits and burdens in a society is just, if and only if,:

1. each person has an equal right to the most extensive basic liberties compatible with similar liberties for all, and
2. social and economic inequalities are arranged so that they are both
   a. to the greatest benefit of the least advantaged persons, and
   b. attached to offices and positions open to all under conditions of fair equality of opportunity.

Rawls tells us that Principle 1 is supposed to take priority over Principle 2 if the two of them ever come into conflict, and within Principle 2, Part *b* is supposed to take priority over Part *a*.

Principle 1 is called the **principle of equal liberty**. Essentially it says that each citizen's liberties must be protected from invasion by others and must be equal to those of others. These basic liberties include the right to vote, freedom of speech and conscience and the other civil liberties, freedom to hold personal property, and freedom from arbitrary arrest.[100] If the principle of equal liberty is correct, then it implies that it is unjust for business institutions to invade the privacy of employees, pressure managers to vote in certain ways, exert undue influence on political processes by the use of bribes, or otherwise violate the equal political liberties of society's members. According to Rawls, moreover, because our freedom to make contracts would diminish if we were afraid of being defrauded or were afraid that contracts would not be honored, the principle of equal liberty also prohibits the use of force, fraud, or deception in contractual transactions and requires that just contracts should be honored.[101] If this is true, then contractual transactions with customers (including advertising) should morally be free of fraud and employees have a moral obligation to render the services they have justly contracted to their employer.

principle of equal liberty The claim that each citizen's liberties must be protected from invasion by others and must be equal to those of others.

Principle 2a is called the **difference principle**. It assumes that a productive society will incorporate inequalities, but it then asserts that steps must be taken to improve the position of the most needy members of society, such as the sick and the disabled, unless such improvements would so burden society that they make everyone, including the needy, worse off than before.[102] Rawls claims that the more productive a society is, the more benefits it will be able to provide for its least-advantaged members. Because the difference principle obliges us to maximize benefits for the least advantaged, this means that business institutions should be as efficient in their use of resources as possible. If we assume that a market system such as ours is most efficient when it is most competitive, then the difference principle will in effect imply that markets should be competitive and that anticompetitive practices such as price-fixing and monopolies are unjust. In addition, because pollution and other environmentally damaging external effects consume resources inefficiently, the difference principle also implies that it is wrong for firms to pollute.

difference principle The claim that a productive society will incorporate inequalities, but takes steps to improve the position of the neediest members of society.

Principle 2b is called the **principle of fair equality of opportunity**. It says that everyone should be given an equal opportunity to qualify for the more privileged positions in society's institutions.[103] This means that not only job qualifications should be related to the requirements of the job (thereby prohibiting racial and sexual discrimination), but that each person must have access to the training and education needed to qualify for the desirable jobs. A person's efforts, abilities, and contribution would then determine remuneration.

principle of fair equality of opportunity The claim that everyone should be given an equal opportunity to qualify for the more privileged positions in society's institutions.

The principles that Rawls proposes are quite comprehensive and bring together the main considerations stressed by the other approaches to justice that we have examined. However, Rawls not only provides us with a set of principles of justice, he also proposes a general method for evaluating the adequacy of any moral principles in a fair way. The method consists of determining what principles a group of rational self-interested persons would choose to live by if they knew they would live in a society governed by those principles, but they did not yet know what each of them would turn out to be like in that society.[104] We might ask, for example, whether such a group of rational self-interested persons would choose to live in a society governed by a principle that discriminates against blacks when none of them knows whether he or she will turn out to be a black person in that society. The answer, clearly, is that such a racist principle would be rejected and consequently, according to Rawls, the racist principle would be unjust. Thus, Rawls claims that a principle is a morally justified principle of justice if, and only if, the principle would be acceptable to a group of rational self-interested persons who know they will live in a society governed by the principles they accept, but who do not know what sex, race, abilities, religion, interests, social position, income, or other particular characteristics each of them will possess in that future society.

original position An imaginary meeting of rational self-interested persons who must choose the principles of justice by which their society will be governed.

veil of ignorance The requirement that persons in the original position must not know particulars about themselves which might bias their choices such as their sex, race, religion, income, social status, etc.

Rawls refers to the situation of such an imaginary group of rational persons as the ***original position***, and he refers to their ignorance of any particulars about themselves as the ***veil of ignorance***.[105] The purpose and effect of saying that the parties to the original position do not know what particular characteristics each of them will possess is to ensure that none of them can protect his or her own special interests. Because they are ignorant of their particular qualities, the parties to the original position are forced to be fair and impartial and to show no favoritism toward any special group. They must look after the good of all.

According to Rawls, the principles that the imaginary parties to the original position accept will *ipso facto* turn out to be morally justified.[106] They will be morally justified because the original position incorporates three moral ideas of Kant that we saw earlier: (1) reversibility (the parties choose principles that they will apply to themselves), (2) universalizability (the principles must apply equally to everyone), and (3) treating people as ends (each party has an equal say in the choice of principles). The principles are further justified, according to Rawls, because they are consistent with our deepest considered intuitions about justice. The principles chosen by the parties to the original position match most of the moral convictions we already have; where they do not, according to Rawls, we would be willing to change them to fit Rawls's principles once we reflect on his arguments.

Quick Review 2.13

Summary of Principles of Distributive Justice

- Fundamental: distribute benefits and burdens equally to equals and unequally to unequals
- Egalitarian: distribute equally to everyone
- Capitalist: distribute according to contribution
- Socialist: distribute according to need and ability
- Libertarian: distribute by free choices
- Rawls: distribute by equal liberty, equal opportunity, and needs of disadvantaged.

Rawls goes on to claim that the parties to the original position would in fact choose his (Rawls's) principles of justice—that is, the principle of equal liberty, the difference principle, and the principle of fair equality of opportunity.[107] The principle of equal liberty would be chosen because the parties will want to be free to pursue their major special interests whatever these might be. In the original position, each person is ignorant of what special interests he or she will have, thus everyone will want to secure a maximum amount of freedom so that they can pursue whatever interests they have on entering society. The difference principle will be chosen because all parties will want to protect themselves against the possibility of ending in the worst position in society. By adopting the difference principle, the parties will ensure that even the position of the neediest is cared for. The principle of fair equality of opportunity will be chosen, according to Rawls, because all parties to the original position will want to protect their interests should they turn out to be among the talented. The principle of fair equality of opportunity ensures that all have an equal opportunity to advance through the use of their own abilities, efforts, and contributions.

If Rawls is correct in claiming that the principles chosen by the parties to the original position are morally justified, and if he is correct in arguing that the parties to the original position would choose his principles, then it follows that his principles are in fact morally justified to serve as our own principles of justice. These principles would then constitute the proper principles of distributive justice.

Critics, however, have objected to various parts of Rawls's theory.[108] Some have argued that the original position is not an adequate method for choosing moral principles. According to these critics, the mere fact that a set of principles is chosen by the hypothetical parties to the original position tells us nothing about whether the principles are morally justified. Other critics have argued that the parties to the original position would not choose Rawls's principles at all. Utilitarians, for example, have argued that the hypothetical parties to the original position would choose utilitarianism and not Rawls's principles. Still other critics have claimed that Rawls's principles are mistaken because they are opposed to some of our basic convictions concerning what justice is.

Despite the many objections that have been raised against Rawls's theory, his defenders still claim that the advantages of the theory outweigh its defects. For one thing, they claim, the theory preserves the basic values that have become embedded in our moral beliefs: freedom, equality of opportunity, and concern for the disadvantaged. Second, the theory fits easily into the basic economic institutions of Western societies; it does not reject the market system, work incentives, or the inequalities consequent on a division of labor. Instead, by requiring that inequalities work for the benefit of the least-advantaged and by requiring equality of opportunity, the theory shows how the inequalities that attend the division of labor and free markets can be compensated for and thereby, made just. Third, the theory incorporates both the communitarian and individualistic strains that are intertwined in Western culture. The difference principle encourages the more talented to use their skills in ways that will rebound to the benefit of fellow citizens who are less well off, thereby encouraging a type of communitarian or fraternal concern.[109] The principle of equal liberty leaves the individual free to pursue whatever special interests the individual may have. Fourth, Rawls's theory takes into account the criteria of need, ability, effort, and contribution. The difference principle distributes benefits in accordance with need, whereas the principle of fair equality of opportunity in effect distributes benefits and burdens according to ability and contribution.[110] Fifth, the defenders of Rawls argue that there is the moral justification that the original position provides. The original position is defined so that its parties choose impartial principles that take into account the equal interests of everyone, and this, they claim, is the essence of morality.

Retributive Justice

Retributive justice concerns the justice of blaming or punishing persons for doing wrong. Philosophers have long debated the justification of blame and punishment, but we need not enter these debates here. More relevant to our purposes is the question of the conditions under which it is just to punish a person for doing wrong.

retributive justice
Fairness when blaming or punishing persons for doing wrong.

The first chapter of this book discussed some major conditions under which people could not be held morally responsible for what they did: ignorance and inability. These conditions are also relevant to determining the justice of punishing or blaming someone for doing wrong. If people do not know or do not freely choose what they are doing, they cannot justly be punished or blamed for it. For example, if the cotton mill owners mentioned at the beginning of this section did not know that the conditions in their mills would cause brown lung disease, then it would be unjust to punish them when it turns out that their mills caused this disease.

A second kind of condition of just punishments is certitude that the person being punished actually did wrong. For example, many firms use more or less complex systems of due process that are intended to ascertain whether the conduct of employees was really such as to merit dismissal or some other penalty.[111] Penalizing an employee on the basis of flimsy or incomplete evidence is rightly considered an injustice.

A third kind of condition of just punishments is that they must be consistent and proportioned to the wrong. Punishment is consistent only when everyone is given the same penalty for the same infraction; punishment is proportioned to the wrong when the penalty is no greater in magnitude than the harm that the wrongdoer inflicted.[112] It is unjust, for example, for a manager to impose harsh penalties for minor infractions of rules or to be lenient toward favorite employees but harsh toward all others. If the purpose of a punishment is to deter others from committing the same wrong or to prevent the wrongdoer from repeating the wrong, then punishment should not be greater than what is consistently necessary to achieve these aims.

Compensatory Justice

compensatory justice Fairness when restoring to a person what the person lost when he or she was wronged by someone else.

Compensatory justice concerns the justice of restoring to a person what the person lost when someone wronged him or her. We generally hold that when one person wrongfully inflicts losses on another person, the wrongdoer has a moral duty to compensate his or her victim for those losses. For example, if I maliciously destroy someone's property or steal it from him or her, I have an obligation to pay him or her whatever the property I destroyed or stole was worth.

There are no hard and fast rules for determining how much compensation a wrongdoer owes the victim. Compensatory justice requires that compensation should leave the victim as well off as he or she would have been if the wrongdoer had not injured him or her. This would usually mean that the amount of compensation should equal the losses the wrongdoer inflicted on the victim. However, some losses are very hard to measure. If I maliciously injure someone's reputation, for example, how much compensation equals the loss of reputation? Some losses, moreover, cannot be restored at all: How can the loss of life or the loss of sight be compensated? In situations such as the Ford Pinto case, where the injury is such that it is not possible to adequately compensate for the loss, we seem to hold that the wrongdoer should at least pay for all economically measurable past, present, and future monetary losses the victim suffered, plus a reasonable estimate of the value of intangible or non-quantifiable losses. These losses could arise from temporary or chronic pain, mental stress and suffering, disfigurement, impaired mental or physical abilities, loss of the enjoyment of life, loss of companionship, damaged reputation, etc.

Not all injuries deserve compensation. Suppose, for example, that while on a crowded street doing nothing wrong, I am shoved against you and in spite of my best efforts to catch myself, my shove causes you to fall and injure yourself. Although I am the one who directly caused your injury, since I am not morally responsible for what happened, I am not obligated to compensate you. Under what conditions is a person bound to compensate a party he or she injures? Traditional moralists have argued that a person has a moral obligation to compensate an injured party only if three conditions are present:[113]

1. The action that inflicted the injury was wrong or negligent. For example, if by efficiently managing my firm I undersell my competitor and run him or her out of business, I am not morally bound to compensate him or her since such competition is neither wrongful nor negligent. But if I steal from my employer, then I owe him or her compensation, or if I fail to exercise due care in my driving, then I owe compensation to those whom I injure.

2. The person's action was the real cause of the injury. For example, if a banker loans a person money and the borrower then uses it to cheat others, the banker is not morally obligated to compensate the victims; but if the banker defrauds a customer, the customer must be compensated.
3. The person inflicted the injury voluntarily. For example, if I injure someone's property accidentally and without negligence, I am not morally obligated to compensate the person. (I may, however, be legally bound to do so depending on how the law chooses to distribute the social costs of injury.) But if I deliberately burn down the house of a person I dislike, then I am bound to compensate the person for the losses I inflicted.

2.4 The Ethics of Care

At 8:00 P.M. on the night of December 11, 1995, an explosion near a boiler room rocked the Malden Mills factory in Lawrence, Massachusetts.[114] Fires broke out in the century-old brick textile factory. Fanned by winds, the fires quickly gutted three factory buildings, injuring 25 workers, destroying nearly all of the plant, and putting nearly 1,400 people out of work two weeks before Christmas.

Founded in 1906, Malden Mills, a family-owned company, was one of the few makers of textiles still operating in New England. Most other textile manufacturers had relocated to the South and then to Asia in their search for cheap, nonunion labor. The president and major owner of the company, Aaron Feuerstein, however, had refused to abandon the community and its workers, who he said were "the most valuable asset that Malden Mills has, … not an expense that can be cut." Emerging from a brush with bankruptcy in 1982, Feuerstein had refocused the company on the pricier end of the textile market, where state-of-the-art technology and high-quality goods are more important than low costs. Shunning low-margin commodity fabrics such as plain polyester sheets, the company focused on a new synthetic material labeled *Polartec* that company workers had discovered how to make through trial and error during the early 1980s. The new material was a fleecy, lightweight, warm material that could wick away perspiration and that required precise combinations of artificial yarns, raising and shaving the pile, and weaving at specially invented (and patented) machines operated at exactly the right temperature, humidity, and speed. Workers had to develop special skills to achieve the correct weave and quality. Several apparel companies soon recognized Polartec as the highest quality and most technically advanced fabric available for performance outdoor clothing. Patagonia, L.L Bean, Eddie Bauer, Lands' End, North Face, Ralph Lauren, and other upscale outfitters adopted the high-priced material. Polartec sales climbed from $5 million in 1982 to over $200 million by 1995. With additional revenues from high-quality upholstery fabrics, Malden Mills' revenues in 1995 had totaled $403 million, and its employees, who now numbered nearly 3,200, were the highest paid textile workers in the country. Feuerstein, who frequently provided special help to workers with special needs, kept an open-door policy with workers whom he tried to treat as members of a large family.

> *Quick Review 2.14*
>
> **An Ethic of Care**
> - Claims ethics need not be impartial, unlike traditional ethical theories which assume ethics has to be impartial
> - Emphasizes preserving and nurturing concrete valuable relationships
> - Says we should care for those dependent on and related to us
> - Argues that since the self requires caring relationships with others, those relationships are valuable and should be nurtured.

The morning after the December fire, however, with the factory in smoldering ruins, newspapers predicted that owner Aaron Feuerstein would do the smart thing and collect over $100 million that insurers would owe him, sell off the remaining assets, and either shut down the company or rebuild in a Third World country where labor was cheaper. Instead, Feuerstein announced that the company would rebuild in Lawrence. In a move that confounded the industry, he promised that every employee forced out of work by the fire would continue to be paid full wages, receive full

> *Quick Review 2.15*
>
> **In an Ethic of Care**
>
> - Caring is not detached but an engrossed "caring for" a person
> - Relationships are not valuable when characterized by domination, oppression, harm, hatred, violence, disrespect, viciousness; injustice, or exploitation
> - The demands of caring and of justice can conflict and such conflicts should be resolved in ways that do not betray our voluntary commitments to others and relationships with them.

medical benefits, and be guaranteed a job when operations restarted in a few months. Rebuilding in Lawrence would cost over $300 million and keeping 1,400 laid-off workers on full salaries for a period of up to 3 months would cost an additional $20 million. "I have a responsibility to the worker, both blue-collar and white-collar," Feuerstein later said. "I have an equal responsibility to the community. It would have been unconscionable to put 3,000 people on the streets and deliver a death blow to the cities of Lawrence and Methuen. Maybe on paper our company is [now] worth less to Wall Street, but I can tell you it's [really] worth more."

The Malden Mills incident suggests a perspective on ethics that is not adequately captured by the moral views we have so far examined. Consider that from a utilitarian perspective Feuerstein had no obligation to rebuild the factory in Lawrence or to continue to pay his workers while they were not working. Moreover, relocating the operations of Malden Mills to a Third World country where labor is cheaper would not only have benefited the company, it would also have provided jobs for Third World workers who arguably are more needy than U.S. workers. From an impartial utilitarian perspective, then, more utility would have been produced by bringing jobs to Third World workers than by spending the money to preserve the jobs of current Malden Mills employees in Lawrence, Massachusetts. It is true that the Malden Mills workers were close to Feuerstein and that over the years they had remained loyal to him and had built a close relationship to him. However, from an impartial standpoint, the utilitarian would say such personal relationships are irrelevant and should be set aside in favor of whatever maximizes utility.

A rights perspective would also not provide any support for the decision to remain in Lawrence nor to continue to pay workers full wages while the company rebuilt. Workers certainly could not claim to have a moral right to be paid while they were not working. Nor could workers claim to have a moral right to have a factory rebuilt for them. The impartial perspective of a rights theory, then, does not suggest that Feuerstein had any special rights-based obligations to his employees after the fire.

Nor, finally, could one argue that justice demanded that Feuerstein rebuild the factory and continue to pay workers while they were not working. Although workers were pivotal to the success of the company, the company had rewarded them by paying them very generous salaries over many years. Impartial justice does not seem to require that the company support people while they are not working nor does it seem to require that Feuerstein rebuild a factory for them at considerable cost to himself. In fact, if one is impartial, then it seems more just to move the factory to a Third World country where people are needier than to keep the jobs in the United States where people are relatively well-off.

Partiality and Care

The approaches to ethics that we have seen, then, all assume that ethics should be impartial and that, consequently, any special relationships that one may have with particular individuals such as relatives, friends, or one's employees, should be set aside when determining what one should do.[115] Some utilitarians have claimed, in fact, that if a stranger and your parent were both drowning and you could save only one of them, and if saving the stranger would produce more utility than saving your parent (perhaps the stranger is a brilliant surgeon who would save many lives), then you would have a moral obligation to save the stranger and let your parent drown.[116] Such a conclusion, many people have argued, is perverse and mistaken.[117] In such a situation, the special relationship of love and caring that you have with your parents gives you a special obligation to care for them in a way that overrides obligations you may have toward strangers. Similarly, in the Malden Mills incident, Feuerstein felt he had a special obligation to take care of his workers precisely because they were dependent on him and had built concrete relationships with him, helping him build his business and create the revolutionary new fabrics that gave Malden Mills its amazing competitive advantage in the textile industry. This obligation toward these particular workers, who had a special relationship with Feuerstein and who were dependent on him, it could be argued, overrode any obligations he may have had toward strangers in the Third World.

This view—that we have an obligation to exercise special care toward those particular persons with whom we have valuable close relationships, particularly relations of dependency—is a key concept in an **"ethic of care,"** an approach to ethics that many feminist ethicists have recently advanced. We briefly discussed this approach to ethics in the first chapter when we noted the new approach to moral development worked out by psychologist Carol Gilligan. A morality of care "rests on an understanding of relationships as a response to another in their terms."[118] According to this "care" view of ethics, the moral task is not to follow universal and impartial moral principles, but instead to attend and respond to the good of particular concrete persons with whom we are in a valuable and close relationship.[119] Compassion, concern, love, friendship, and kindness are all sentiments or virtues that normally manifest this dimension of morality. Thus, an ethic of care emphasizes two moral demands:

ethic of care An ethic that requires caring for the concrete well being of those particular persons with whom we have valuable close relationships, particularly those dependent on us.

1. We each exist in a web of relationships and should preserve and nurture those concrete and valuable relationships we have with specific persons.
2. We each should exercise special care for those to whom we are concretely related by attending to their particular needs, values, desires, and concrete well-being as seen from their own personal perspective, and by responding positively to these needs, values, desires, and concrete well-being, particularly of those who are vulnerable and dependent on our care.

For example, Feuerstein's decision to remain in the community of Lawrence and care for his workers by continuing to pay them after the fire was a response to the imperative of preserving the concrete relationships he had formed with his employees. It was also a response to the imperative of exercising special care for the specific needs of these individuals who were economically dependent on him. This requirement to take care of this specific group of individuals is more significant than any moral requirement to care for strangers in Third World countries.

It is important not to restrict the notion of a concrete relationship to relationships between two individuals or to relationships between an individual and a specific group. The examples of relationships that we have given so far have been of this kind. Many advocates of an ethic of care have argued that it should also encompass the larger systems of relationships that make up concrete communities.[120] An ethic of care, therefore, can be seen as encompassing the kinds of obligations that a so-called *communitarian ethic* advocates. A **communitarian ethic** is an ethic that sees concrete communities and communal relationships as having a fundamental value that should be preserved and maintained.[121] What is important in a communitarian ethic is not the isolated individual, but the community within which individuals discover who they are by seeing themselves as integral parts of a larger community with its traditions, culture, practices, and history.[122] The broad web of concrete relationships that make up a particular community, then, should be preserved and nurtured just as much as the more limited interpersonal relationships that spring up between individual people.

communitarian ethic An ethic that sees concrete communities and communal relationships as having a fundamental value that should be preserved and maintained.

What kind of argument can be given in support of an ethic of care? An ethic of care can be based on the claim that the identity of the self—who I am—is based on the relationships the self has with other selves: The individual cannot exist, cannot even be who he or she is, in isolation from caring relationships with others.[123] I need others to feed and care for me when I am born; I need others to educate me and care for me as I grow; I need others as friends and lovers to care for me when I mature; and I must always live in a community on whose language, traditions, culture, and other benefits I depend and that come to define me. It is in these concrete relationships with others that I form my understanding of *who* and *what* I am. Therefore, to whatever extent the self has value, to that same extent the relationships that are necessary for the self to exist and be what it is, must also have value and so should be maintained and nurtured. The value of the self, then, is ultimately derivative from the value of the community.

It is also important in this context to distinguish three different forms of caring: caring *about* something, caring *after* someone, and caring *for* someone.[124] The kind of caring demanded by an ethic of care is the kind expressed by the phrase "caring for someone." The paradigm example of caring for someone is the kind of caring that a mother extends toward her child.[125] Such caring is focused on persons and their well-being, not on things; it does not seek to foster dependence, but nurtures the person's development so that he or she becomes capable of making his or her own choices and living his or her own life. It is not detached, but is "engrossed" in the person and attempts to see the world through the eyes and values of the person. In contrast, caring about something is the kind of concern and interest that one can have for things or ideas, and not the concern one has for a person in whose subjective reality one becomes engrossed. Such caring for objects or ideas is not the kind of caring demanded by an ethics of care. One can also become busy taking care of people in a manner that looks after their needs but remains objective and distant from them as, for example, often happens in bureaucratic service institutions such as the post office or a social welfare office. Caring after people in this way, although often necessary, is not the kind of caring demanded by an ethic of care.

Two additional issues are important to note. First, not all relationships have value, and so not all would generate the demands of care. Relationships in which one person attempts to dominate, oppress, or harm another; relationships that are characterized by hatred, violence, disrespect, and viciousness; and relationships that are characterized by injustice, exploitation, and harm to others lack the value that an ethic of care requires. An ethic of care does not obligate us to maintain, remain in, or nurture such relationships. However, relationships that exhibit the virtues of compassion, concern, love, friendship, and loyalty do have the kind of value that an ethic of care requires, and an ethic of care implies that such relationships should be maintained and nurtured.

Second, it is important to recognize that the demands of caring are sometimes in conflict with the demands of justice. Consider two examples. First, suppose that one of the employees whom a female manager supervises is a friend of hers. Suppose that one day she catches her friend stealing from the company. Should she turn in her friend, as company policy requires, or should she say nothing, to protect her friend? Second, suppose that a female manager is supervising several people, one of whom is a close friend of hers. Suppose that she must recommend one of these subordinates for promotion to a particularly desirable position. Should she recommend her friend simply because she is her friend, or should she be impartial and follow company policy by recommending the subordinate who is most qualified even if this means passing over her friend? Clearly, in each of these cases, justice would require that the manager not favor her friend. However, the demands of an ethic of care would seem to require that the manager favor her friend for the sake of their friendship. How should conflicts of this sort be resolved?

First, notice that there is no fixed rule that can resolve all such conflicts. One can imagine situations in which the manager's obligations of justice toward her company would clearly override the obligations she has toward her friend. (Imagine that her friend stole several million dollars and was prepared to steal several million more.) One can imagine situations in which the manager's obligations toward her friend override her obligations toward the company. (Imagine, for example, that what her friend stole was insignificant, that her friend desperately needed what she stole, and that the company would react by imposing an excessively harsh punishment on the friend.)

Although no fixed rule can resolve all conflicts between the demands of caring and the requirements of justice, some guidelines can be helpful in resolving such conflicts. Consider that when the manager was hired, she voluntarily promised those who hired her that she would accept the position of manager along with the duties and privileges that would define her role as a manager. Among the duties to which she committed herself is the duty to protect the resources of the company and abide by company policy. Therefore, the manager betrays her commitments to those who hired her and harms her relationships with the people to whom she made these commitments, if she now shows favoritism toward her friend in violation of the company policies she voluntarily agreed to uphold. The institutional obligations we voluntarily accept and to which we voluntarily commit ourselves, then, can require that we are impartial toward our friends and that we pay more attention to the demands of impartial justice than to the demands of an ethic of care. What about situations in which there is a conflict between our institutional obligations and the demands of a relationship, and the latter is so important to us that we feel we must favor the relationship over our institutional obligations? Then morality would seem to require that we relinquish the institutional role that we have voluntarily accepted. Thus, the manager who feels that she must favor her friend because she cannot be impartial, as she voluntarily agreed to be when she accepted her job, must resign. Otherwise, the manager is in effect living a lie: By keeping her job while favoring her friend, she would imply that she was living up to her voluntary agreement of impartiality when, in fact, she was being partial toward her friend.

We noted that primarily feminist ethicists have been responsible for the development of the care approach to ethics. The care approach, in fact, originated in the claim of psychologist Carol Gilligan that women and men approach moral issues from two different perspectives: Men approach moral issues from an individualistic focus on rights and justice, whereas women approach moral issues from a nonindividualistic focus on relationships and caring. Empirical research, however, has shown that this claim is mistaken for the most part, although there are some differences in the way that men and women respond to moral dilemmas.[126] Most ethicists have abandoned the view that an ethic of care is for women only and have argued, instead, that just as women must recognize the demands of justice and impartiality, so men must recognize the demands of caring and partiality.[127] Caring is not the task of only women, but a moral imperative for both men and women.

Quick Review 2.16

Objections to Care Approach to Ethics

- Objection: an ethic of care can degenerate into favoritism
- Response: conflicting moral demands are an inherent characteristic of moral choices
- Objection: an ethic of care can lead to "burnout"
- Response: adequate understanding of ethic of care will acknowledge the need of the caregiver to care for him or herself.

Objections to Care

The care approach to ethics has been criticized on several grounds. First, it has been claimed that an ethic of care can degenerate into unjust favoritism.[128] Being partial, for example, to members of one's own ethnic group, to a sexist *old-boy* network, to members of one's own race, or to members of one's own nation can all be unjust forms of partiality. Proponents of an ethic of care, however, can respond that, although the demands of partiality can conflict with other demands of morality, this is true of all approaches to ethics. Morality consists of a wide spectrum of moral considerations that can conflict with each other. Utilitarian considerations can conflict with considerations of justice, and these can conflict with moral rights. In the same way, the demands of partiality and caring can also conflict with the demands of utility, justice, and rights. What morality requires is not that we get rid of all moral conflicts, but that we learn to weigh moral considerations and balance their different demands in specific situations. The fact that caring can sometimes conflict with justice, then, does not make an ethic of caring less adequate than any other approach to ethics, but points out the need to weigh and balance the relative importance of caring versus justice in specific situations.

A second important criticism of an ethic of care is that its demands can lead to "burnout." In demanding that people exercise caring for children, parents, siblings, spouses, lovers, friends, and other members of the community, an ethic of care seems to demand that people sacrifice their own needs and desires to care for the well-being of others. However, proponents of caring can respond that an adequate view of caring will balance caring for the caregiver with caring for others.[129]

2.5 Integrating Utility, Rights, Justice, and Caring

Quick Review 2.17

Moral Judgments Should be Based on
- Maximizing the net utility of our actions
- Respecting the moral rights of individuals
- Ensuring a just distribution of benefits and burdens
- Caring for those in concrete relationships.

The last three sections have described the four main kinds of moral standards that today lie at the basis of most of our moral reasoning and that force us to bring distinctive kinds of considerations into our moral thinking. Utilitarian standards are appropriate when decisions involve limited but valuable resources that can be used in many different ways. In such cases, it is important to avoid wasting the resources we have and so we are forced to consider the benefits and costs of deciding to use them in one way rather than another, and to identify the decision that will use them in the most beneficial way. When we try to make these kinds of utilitarian decisions we have to rely on measurements, estimates, and comparisons of the relevant benefits and costs involved. Such measurements, estimates, and comparisons constitute the information on which the utilitarian moral judgment is based.

Our moral judgments are also partially based on standards that specify how individuals must be treated or respected. These sorts of standards must be employed when the actions we choose are likely to affect people's positive or negative rights. When choosing whether to carry out such actions, our moral reasoning must identify the rights of the people our actions will affect, the agreements or expectations that are in place and that impose special obligations on us, and whether our actions treat everyone affected as free and rational persons. This, in turn, requires that we have adequate information concerning how our actions will impact the people involved; how informed they are about what will happen to them; whether any force, coercion, manipulation, or deception will be used on them; and what agreements we have made with them or what legitimate expectations they may have of us.

Third, our moral judgments are also in part based on standards of justice that indicate how benefits and burdens should be distributed among the members of a group. These sorts of standards must be employed when evaluating various actions that could have very different distributive effects. The moral reasoning on which such judgments are based will incorporate considerations concerning whether the behavior distributes benefits and burdens equally or in accordance with the needs, abilities, contributions, and free choices of people as well as the extent of their wrongdoing. In turn, these sorts of considerations rely on comparisons of the benefits and burdens going to different groups (or individuals) and comparisons of their relative needs, efforts, and contributions.

Fourth, our moral judgments are also based on standards of caring that indicate the kind of care that is owed to those with whom we have special concrete and valued relationships. Standards of caring are essential when our moral decisions involve persons with whom we have personal relationships, particularly relationships of dependency. Moral reasoning that invokes standards of caring will incorporate information about the particular characteristics and needs of those persons with whom one has a concrete relationship, the nature of one's relationships with those persons, the forms of caring and partiality that are called for by those relationships, and the kind of actions that are needed to sustain those relationships.

Our morality, then, contains these four kinds of basic moral considerations, each of which emphasizes certain morally important aspects of our behavior, but no one of which captures all the factors that must be taken into account in making moral judgments. Utilitarian standards consider only the aggregate social welfare, but ignore the way that welfare is distributed as well as the moral claims of individuals. Moral rights consider the individual but discount both aggregate well-being and distributive considerations. Standards of justice consider distributive issues, but they ignore aggregate social welfare and the individual as such. Although standards of caring consider the partiality that must be shown to those close to us, they ignore the demands of impartiality. These four kinds of moral considerations do not seem to be reducible to each other, yet all seem to be necessary parts of our morality. That is, there are some moral problems for which utilitarian considerations are appropriate. For other problems, the decisive considerations are the rights of individuals or the justice of the distributions involved or how those close to us should be cared for. This suggests that moral reasoning should incorporate all four kinds of moral considerations, although only one or the other may turn out to be relevant or decisive in a particular situation. One simple strategy for ensuring that all four kinds of considerations are incorporated into our moral reasoning is to inquire systematically into the utility, rights, justice, and caring issues that are raised by the situation about which we are making a moral judgment, as in Figure 2.1. We might, for example, ask a series of questions about an action that we are considering: (a) Does the action, as far as possible, maximize benefits and minimize harms? (b) Is the action consistent with the moral rights of those whom it will affect? (c) Will the action lead to a just distribution of benefits and burdens? (d) Does the action exhibit appropriate care for the well-being of those who are closely related to or dependent on us?

Bringing together different moral standards in this way, however, requires that we keep in mind how they relate to each other. As we have seen, moral rights identify areas in which other people generally may not interfere even if they can show that they would derive greater benefits from such interference. Generally speaking, therefore, standards concerned with moral rights have greater weight than either utilitarian standards or standards of justice. Similarly, standards of justice are generally accorded greater weight than utilitarian considerations. And standards of caring seem to be given greater weight than principles of impartiality in those situations that involve close relationships (such as family and friends) and privately owned resources.

But these relationships hold only in general. If a certain action (or policy or institution) promises to generate sufficiently large social benefits or prevent sufficiently large social harms, the enormity of these utilitarian consequences may

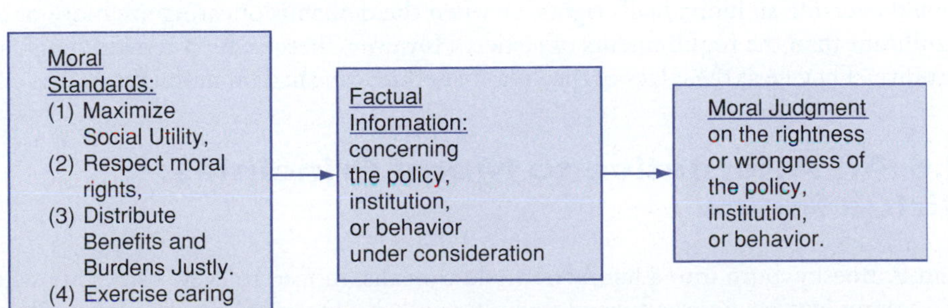

Figure 2.1
View the **Image** on **mythinkinglab.com**

justify limited infringements on the rights of some individuals. Sufficiently large social costs and benefits may also be significant enough to justify limited departures from standards of justice. The correction of large and widespread injustices may be important enough to justify limited infringements on some individual rights. When a large injustice or large violation of rights, or even large social harms, are at stake, the demands of caring may have to give way to the demands of impartiality.

At this time, we have no comprehensive moral theory capable of determining precisely when utilitarian considerations become "sufficiently large" enough to outweigh limited infringements on a conflicting right, a standard of justice, or the demands of caring. Nor can we provide a universal rule that will tell us when considerations of justice become "important enough" to outweigh infringements on conflicting rights or on the demands of caring. Moral philosophers have been unable to agree on any absolute rules for making such judgments. However, there are some rough criteria that can guide us in these matters. Suppose, for example, that only by invading my employees' right to privacy (with hidden cameras and legal on-the-job phone taps), will I be able to stop the continuing theft of several life-saving drugs that some of them are clearly stealing. How can I determine whether the utilitarian benefits here are sufficiently large to justify infringing on their right to privacy? First, I might ask whether the *kinds* of utilitarian values involved are clearly more important than the *kinds* of values protected by the right (or distributed by the standard of justice). The utilitarian benefits in the present example include the saving of human life, whereas the right to privacy protects (let us suppose) the values of freedom from shame and blackmail and freedom to live one's life as one chooses. Considering this, I might decide that human life is clearly the more important kind of value because without life, freedom has little value. Second, I might then ask whether securing the more important kind of value will, in this situation, affect the interests of more (or fewer) people than would be affected by securing the less important kind of value. For example, because the recovered drugs will (we assume) save several hundred lives, whereas the invasion of privacy will affect only a dozen people, securing the utilitarian values will affect the interests of substantially more people. Third, I can ask whether the actual injuries sustained by the persons whose rights are violated (or to whom an injustice is done) will be large or small. For example, suppose that I can ensure that my employees suffer no shame, blackmail, or restriction on their freedom as a result of my uncovering information about their private lives (I intend to destroy all such information), then their injuries will be relatively small. Fourth, I can ask whether the potential breakdown in trusting relationships that surveillance risks is more or less important than the theft of life-saving resources. Let us suppose, for example, that the potential harm that surveillance will inflict on employee relationships of trust is not large. Then, it would appear that my invasion of the privacy of employees is justified.

Hence, there are rough and intuitive criteria that can guide our thinking when it appears that, in a certain situation, utilitarian considerations might be sufficiently important to override conflicting rights, standards of justice, or the demands of caring. Similar criteria can be used to determine whether, in a certain situation, considerations of justice should override an individual's rights, or when the demands of caring are more or less significant than the requirements of justice. However, these criteria remain rough and intuitive. They lie at the edges of the light that ethics can shed on moral reasoning.

2.6 An Alternative to Moral Principles: Virtue Ethics

Ivan F. Boesky, born into a family of modest means, moved to New York City when, as a young lawyer, he was turned down for jobs by Detroit's top law firms. By the mid-1980s, the hard-working Boesky had accumulated a personal fortune estimated at over $400 million and was CEO of a large financial services company. He was famous in financial circles for his extraordinary skills in arbitrage, the art of spotting differences in the prices at which financial securities are selling on different world markets and profiting by buying the securities where they are priced low and selling them where they are priced high. As a prominent member of New York society, Boesky enjoyed a reputation as a generous philanthropist.[130]

However, on December 18, 1987, Boesky was sentenced to 3 years in prison and paid a penalty of $100 million for illegally profiting from *insider information.* According to court records, Boesky paid David Levine, a friend who worked inside a firm that arranged mergers and acquisitions, to provide him with information about companies that were about to be purchased by another party (usually a corporation) for much more than the current price of their stock on the stock market. Relying on this insider's information and before it became public, Boesky would buy up the stock of the companies on the stock market—in effect buying the stock from stockholders who did not realize that their companies were about to be purchased for much more than the current stock market price. When the purchase of the company was announced, the stock price rose and Boesky would sell his stock at a handsome profit. Buying and selling stock on the basis of insider information at the time was legal in many countries (e.g., Italy, Switzerland, Hong Kong). Many economists argue that the economic benefits of the practice (it tends to make the price of a company's stock reflect the true value of the company) outweigh its harms (it tends to discourage noninsiders from participating in the stock market). Nevertheless, the practice is illegal in the United States due to its perceived unfairness and its potential to harm the stock market.

What drove a man who already had hundreds of millions of dollars and everything else most people could ever want or need, to become so obsessed with making money that he deliberately broke the law? Much of the answer, it was claimed, lay in his character. A former friend is quoted as saying, "Maybe he's greedy beyond the wildest imaginings of mere mortals like you and me."[131] Boesky once described his obsession to accumulate ever more money as "a sickness I have in the face of which I'm helpless."[132] In a speech at the University of California, Berkeley, he told students, "Greed is alright, by the way. I think greed is healthy. I want you to know that I think greed is healthy. You can be greedy and still feel good about yourself."[133] Others said of him that:

> He was driven by work, overzealous, and subject to severe mood swings. Intimates of Mr. Boesky say he vacillated between "being loud, and harsh and aggressive, to mellifluously soft-spoken, charming and courtly." He was also fiendish about his pursuit of information. "When somebody got an edge on something, he would go bananas." When it came to money and business dealings, he was quite ruthless and pursued his goal with a single-minded purpose.... Although his first love was money, he hankered for the genteel respectability and status that are generally denied the nouveau riche.[134]

The story of the fall of Ivan Boesky is the story of a man brought down by greed. What stands out in this story are the descriptions of his moral character—the character of a man driven by an obsessive "love" of money. Boesky is described as being "greedy," "sick," "aggressive," "fiendish," and "ruthless." Because what he said of himself did not match his secret dealings, some said he "lacked integrity" and others that he was "hypocritical" and "dishonest." All of these descriptions are judgments about the moral character of the man, not judgments about the morality of his actions. In fact, although it is clear that trading on insider information is illegal, the fact that the practice is legal in many countries and that many economists support it suggests that the practice is not in itself immoral. What was immoral was that greed led Boesky to knowingly break the law he had an obligation to follow.

As the story of Boesky makes clear, we evaluate the morality of people's character as well as their actions. The approaches to ethics that we have examined so far all focus on action as the key subject matter of ethics and ignore the character of the agent who carries out the action. Utilitarianism, for example, tells us that "*actions* are right in proportion as they tend to promote happiness," and Kantian ethics tells us that "I ought never to *act* except in such a way that I can also will that my maxim should become a universal law." However, the central issue that emerges in the case of Boesky, and in many similar stories of unethical behavior by men and women in business, is not the wrongness of their actions, but the flawed nature of their character.

Many ethicists have criticized the assumption that actions are the fundamental subject matter of ethics. Ethics, they have argued, should look not only at the kinds of actions an agent ought to perform, but should pay attention to the kind of person an agent ought to be. An "agent-based" focus on what one ought to be, in contrast to an "action-based" focus on how one ought to act, would look carefully at a person's moral character including whether a person's moral character exhibits virtue or vice. A more adequate approach to ethics, according to these ethicists, would take the virtues (such as honesty, courage, temperance, integrity, compassion, self-control) and the vices (such as dishonesty, ruthlessness, greed, lack of integrity, cowardliness) as the basic starting points for ethical reasoning.

Although virtue ethics looks at moral issues from a very different perspective than action-based ethics, it does not follow that the conclusions of virtue ethics will differ radically from the conclusions of an action-based ethic. As we will see, there are virtues that are correlated with utilitarianism (e.g., the virtue of benevolence), virtues that are correlated with rights (e.g., the virtue of respect), and virtues that are correlated with justice and caring. The virtues, then, should not be seen as providing a fifth alternative to utility, rights, justice, and caring. Instead, the virtues can be seen as providing a perspective that surveys the same ground as the four approaches, but from an entirely different perspective. What the principles of utility, rights, justice, and caring do from the perspective of action evaluations, an ethic of virtue does from the perspective of character evaluations.

The Nature of Virtue

moral virtue An acquired disposition that is valued as part of the character of a morally good human being and that is exhibited in the person's habitual behavior.

What exactly is a moral virtue? A **moral virtue** is an acquired disposition to behave in certain ways that is valued as part of the character of a morally good human being and that is exhibited in the person's habitual behavior. A person has a moral virtue when he is disposed to behave habitually as a morally good person would behave, and with the reasons, feelings, and desires that are characteristic of a morally good person. Honesty, for example, is a virtue of morally good people. A person possesses the virtue of honesty when he is disposed to habitually tell the truth and does so because he believes telling the truth is right. The honest person feels good when he tells the truth and uncomfortable when he lies, and always wants to tell the truth out of respect for the truth and its importance in human communication. If a person told the truth on occasion, or did so for the wrong reasons or with the wrong desires, we would not say that the person is honest. We would not say a person is honest, for example, if the person frequently lies, tells the truth only because he thinks it is the way to get people to like him, or told the truth out of fear and with reluctance. Moreover, a moral virtue must be acquired, and is not just a natural characteristic such as intelligence, or beauty, or natural strength. A moral virtue is praiseworthy, in part, because it is an achievement—its development requires effort.

The Moral Virtues

The basic issues, from the perspective of virtue ethics, are the questions: What are the traits of character that make a person a morally good human being? Which traits of character are moral virtues? On this issue, there have been numerous views. The Greek philosopher Aristotle proposed what is still the most influential theory of virtue.

Aristotle argued that a moral virtue is a habit that enables a human being to live according to reason. He argued that a person lives according to reason when the person knows and habitually chooses the reasonable middle ground between going too far and not going far enough in his feelings and actions. "Moral virtue is … a mean between two vices, one of excess and the other of deficiency, and … it aims at hitting the mean in emotions and actions." With respect to fear, for example, *courage* is the virtue of feeling a level of fear that is appropriate to a situation and facing what is fearful when it is worth doing so. *Cowardliness* is the vice of feeling more fear than situations merit and fleeing anything fearful even when one should stand firm, and *recklessness* is the vice of feeling less fear than one should and of rushing into fearful situations even when one should not. With respect to pleasure, *temperance* is the virtue of enjoying reasonable amounts of pleasure, whereas self-indulgence is the vice of indulging in pleasure to excess, and self-deprivation is the vice of indulging too little. With respect to the action of giving people what they deserve, justice is the virtue of giving people exactly what they deserve, whereas injustice is the vice of giving them more than they deserve or giving them less than they deserve. In addition to these three key virtues—courage, temperance, and justice—Aristotle describes a number of other virtues and their corresponding vices of excess and deficiency as indicated in Figure 2.2. In Aristotle's classic account, then, virtues are habits of dealing with one's emotions and actions in ways that strike the reasonable mean between the extremes of excess and deficiency, whereas vices are habits of going to the unreasonable extreme of either excess or deficiency.

Aristotle suggests that virtues, like other habits, are acquired through repetition. By repeatedly standing firm when I am fearful, I become courageous; by repeatedly

The emotion or action involved	The Vice of excess in the emotion or action	The Virtue of the mean in the emotion or action	The Vice of deficiency in the emotion or action
Fear	Recklessness	Courage	Cowardliness
Pleasure	Self-indulgence	Temperance	Self-deprivation
Taking one's due	Injustice: taking more	Justice	Injustice: taking less
Donating money	Prodigality	Generosity	Stinginess
Spending money	Ostentatiousness	Refinement	Cheapness
Feeling admired	Vanity	Confidence	Self-abasement
Seeking honor	Over-ambition	Ambition	Unambitiousness
Anger	Irascibility	Good temper	Apathy
Shame	Self-consciousness	Self-esteem	Arrogance
Talking about oneself	Boastfulness	Honesty	False modesty
Entertaining people	Buffoonery	Wittiness	Boorishness
Socializing	Obsequiousness	Friendliness	Quarrelsomeness

Figure 2.2

View the **Image** on **mythinkinglab.com**

exercising control over my appetites, I become temperate; and by repeatedly giving people what they deserve, I become just. But this suggestion of how virtues are acquired leads to a puzzle: how can I engage in virtuous acts before I am virtuous? For example, how can I behave courageously before I am courageous? Aristotle points out that when a person does not yet have a virtue, the person can be trained or forced to do what a virtuous person would do. A child, for example, can be forced to behave courageously although he does not yet have the virtue of courage. The person who does not yet have the virtue will gradually come to acquire it by repeatedly being made to do what the virtue requires.

Aristotle held that the virtuous person chooses the "reasonable" middle path between the extremes of excess and deficiency. How does one know what is reasonable? Aristotle believed that prudence is the virtue of our intellect that enables us to determine what is reasonable in a given situation. The aim of human life is happiness, he argues, and so the reasonable choice in a situation is the one that contributes toward a happy human life. A person with prudence has the ability to figure out which choices these are, an ability a person acquires through learning and experience. The moral virtues—like courage, temperance, and justice—enable a person to control his desires, emotions, and actions. The person can thus carry out the choices that prudence determines are right for the situation, and can restrain himself from making the wrong "excessive" choices that his desires and emotions may tempt him to make. Prudence and the other moral virtues work together, then. Prudence determines the choices that are likely to make a person's life a happy one, while the other virtues give a person the self-control needed to carry out those choices.

St. Thomas Aquinas, a Christian philosopher of the Middle Ages, followed Aristotle in holding that the moral virtues enable people to follow reason in dealing with their desires, emotions, and actions and also accepted that the four pivotal or cardinal moral virtues are courage, temperance, justice, and prudence. But as a Christian, and so, unlike Aristotle, Aquinas held that the purpose of a person is not merely a happiness in this life that is achieved through the exercise of reason, but a happiness in the next life that is achieved through union with God. Aquinas added the "theological" or Christian virtues of faith, hope, and charity—the virtues that enable a person to achieve union with God to Aristotle's list of the moral virtues. Moreover, Aquinas expanded Aristotle's list of the moral virtues to include others that make sense within the life of a Christian, but would have been foreign to the life of the Greek aristocratic citizen on whom Aristotle had focused. For example, Aquinas held that for the Christian humility is a virtue and pride is a vice, whereas Aristotle had argued that for the Greek aristocrat pride is a virtue and humility is a vice.

Quick Review 2.18

Theories of Moral Virtue

- Aristotle: virtues are habits that enable a person to live according to reason by habitually choosing the mean between extremes in actions and emotions
- Aquinas: virtues are habits that enable a person to live reasonably in this world and be united with God in the next
- MacIntyre: virtues are dispositions that enable a person to achieve the good at which human "practices" aim
- Pincoffs: virtues are dispositions we use when choosing between persons or potential future selves.

More recently, the American philosopher Alasdair MacIntyre has claimed that a virtue is any human disposition that is praised because it enables a person to achieve the good at which human "practices" aim:

> The virtues ... are to be understood as those dispositions which will not only sustain practices and enable us to achieve the goods internal to practices, but which will also sustain us in the relevant kind of quest for the good, by enabling us to overcome the harms, dangers, temptations and situations which we encounter, and which will furnish us with increasing self-knowledge and increasing knowledge of the good.[135]

Critics have argued, however, that MacIntyre's approach does not seem to get things quite right. When Ivan Boesky, for example, was criticized as "greedy," "dishonest," "ruthless," and so on, people were not faulting him for failing to have the virtues proper to the practices within which he was pursuing his vision of the good. The moral defects for which Boesky was criticized were his alleged failings as a human being, regardless of how well or poorly he did in the various human practices in which he was engaged. The moral virtues seem to be those dispositions that enable one to live a morally good human life in general and not merely those that enable one to engage successfully in some set of human practices.

Edmund L. Pincoffs, in particular, criticizes MacIntyre for claiming that virtues include only those traits required by our social practices. Instead, Pincoffs suggests that virtues include all those dispositions to act, feel, and think in certain ways that we use as the basis for choosing between persons or between potential future selves.[136] When deciding, for example, whom to choose as a friend, spouse, employee, or manager, we look to people's dispositions: Are they honest or dishonest, sincere or insincere, greedy or selfish, reliable or unreliable, trustworthy or untrustworthy, dependable or undependable? Similarly, when thinking about a moral decision, we often think not so much of what we are obligated to do, but instead of the kind of person we would be if we were to do it. In carrying out the action, would I be honest or dishonest, sincere or insincere, selfish or unselfish?

However, what makes one disposition a moral virtue and another a moral vice? There is no simple answer to this question, Pincoffs claims. He rejects Aristotle's view that every virtue can be understood as "a mean between extremes." Instead, Pincoffs argues, virtues should be understood in terms of the roll they play in human life. Some dispositions, he points out, provide specific grounds for preferring a person because they make a person good or bad at specific tasks such as painting houses. Specific dispositions that aim at specific tasks are *not* virtues. However, other dispositions are generally desirable because they make a person good at dealing with the kinds of situations that frequently and typically arise in human life. The virtues consist of such "generally desirable dispositions" that it is desirable to have in view of the "human situation, of conditions, that is, under which human beings must (given the nature of the physical world and of human nature and human association) live." Because the human situation often requires concerted effort, for example, it is desirable that we have persistence and courage. Because tempers often flare, we need tolerance and tact. Because goods must often be distributed by consistent criteria, we need fairness and nondiscrimination. However, selfishness, deceptiveness, cruelty, and unfairness are vices: They are generally undesirable because they are destructive to human relationships. The moral virtues, then, are those dispositions generally desirable for people to have in the kinds of situations they typically encounter in living together. They are desirable because they are useful either "for everyone in general or for the possessor of the quality."

Pincoff's theory of virtue seems more adequate than a theory like MacIntyre's which confines virtue to traits connected with practices. The virtues seem to be dispositions that enable us to deal well with all of the exigencies of human life and not merely the exigencies of practices. For example, both Aristotle and Aquinas felt that, in articulating the moral virtues, they were articulating those habits that enable a person to live a human life well and not merely to do well in social practices.

As we have seen, however, Aristotle and Aquinas had different views on exactly what human life required. This suggests that to some extent what counts as a moral virtue will depend on one's beliefs about the kinds of situations that humans will face. Nevertheless, as Pincoffs suggests, "we share a good deal of well-grounded agreement on the question of who is the right sort of person in general," because people in all societies have to face similar problems in living together. Catholics, for example, can recognize when a Buddhist is not just a good Buddhist, but also a person of good moral character: "Courage is not more a Catholic than it is a Buddhist virtue; honesty commends itself to Presbyterian and Coptic Christian alike." The moral virtues include that wide variety of dispositions that people in all societies recognize as desirable because they "serve as reasons for preference in the ordinary and not-so-ordinary exigencies of life." The four classical virtues on which Aristotle and Aquinas both agreed—courage, temperance, justice, and prudence—fall into this class. However, the three theological virtues—faith, hope, and charity—that Aquinas added because of their special importance for a Christian life would not count as moral virtues because they are desirable only within a special kind of life devoted to the pursuit of special religious objectives. Similarly, pride, which was a quality admired in Greek society, would, not count as a moral virtue because it, too, is desirable only within a specific kind of society.

Virtues, Actions, and Institutions

Thus far we have ignored a key aspect of virtue theory: How does it help us decide what we are to do? Can an ethic of virtue do more than tell us the kind of people we should be? Is an ethic of virtue able to provide us with any guidance about how we should live our lives, how we should behave? One of the major criticisms made against virtue theory, in fact, is that it fails to provide us with guidance on how we are to act. When a woman is trying to decide whether to have an abortion, for example, she may ask a friend, "What should I do?" In such situations, it does not help to be told what kind of character one should have. In such situations, one needs advice about what kinds of actions are appropriate in one's situation, and virtue theory seems incapable of providing such advice. This criticism—that virtue theory provides no guidance for action—is not surprising because virtue theory deliberately turns away from action and focuses on moral character as the fundamental moral category. Nevertheless, although virtue is the foundation of virtue theory, this does not mean that virtue theory cannot provide any guidance for action.

virtue theory The theory that the aim of the moral life is to develop those general dispositions called *moral virtues*, and to exercise and exhibit them in the many situations that human life sets before us.

Virtue theory argues that the aim of the moral life is to develop those general dispositions we call the *moral virtues* and to exercise and exhibit them in the many situations that human life sets before us. Insofar as we exercise the virtues in our actions, insofar as our actions exhibit the virtues, or insofar as our actions make us virtuous, those actions are morally right actions. Yet, insofar as our actions are the exercise of vice or insofar as our actions develop a vicious character, to that extent the actions are morally wrong. The key action-guiding implication of virtue theory, then, can be summed up in this claim:

> An action is morally right if in carrying out the action the agent exercises, exhibits, or develops a morally virtuous character, and it is morally wrong to the extent that by carrying out the action the agent exercises, exhibits, or develops a morally vicious character.

Quick Review 2.19

Virtue Theory Claims

- We should exercise, exhibit, and develop the virtues
- We should avoid exercising, exhibiting, and developing vices
- Institutions should instill virtues not vices.

From this perspective, then, the wrongfulness of an action can be determined by examining the kind of person the action tends to produce or the kind of person that tends to produce the action. In either case, the ethics of the action depends on its relationship to the virtues and vices of the agent. For example, it has been argued that the morality of abortion, adultery, or any other action should be evaluated by attending to the kind of character evidenced by people who engage in such actions. If the decision to engage in such actions tends to make a person more responsible, caring, principled, honest, open, and self-sacrificing, then such actions are morally right. However, if the decision to engage in such actions tends to make people more self-centered, irresponsible, dishonest, careless, and selfish, then such actions are morally wrong. Actions are not only evaluated by the kind of character they develop; we also condemn certain actions precisely because they are the outcome of a morally vicious character. For example, we condemn cruel actions because they exhibit a vicious character, and we condemn lies because they are products of a dishonest character.

Virtue theory is not only able to provide a criterion for evaluating actions, it also provides a useful criterion for evaluating our social institutions and practices. For example, it has been argued that some economic institutions make people greedy, that large bureaucratic organizations make people less responsible, and that the practice of providing government "handouts" to people makes them lazy and dependent. All such arguments evaluate institutions and practices based on a theory of virtue. Although such arguments may be false, they all appeal to the idea that institutions are morally defective when they tend to form morally defective characters.

We noted that according to Pincoffs, moral virtues are dispositions that are generally desirable because they are required by the human situations with which all people everywhere must cope. Some dispositions are moral virtues, for example, because people everywhere are tempted by their emotions and desires to not do what they know they should do. Courage, temperance, and, in general, the virtues of self-control are of this sort. Some virtues are dispositions to engage willingly in specific kinds of moral action that are valued in all societies, such as honesty. Pincoffs suggests that some dispositions can be classified as "instrumental virtues" because they enable people everywhere to pursue their goals effectively as individuals (persistence, carefulness, determination) or as part of a group (cooperativeness), whereas some are "non-instrumental virtues" because they are desirable for their own sake (serenity, nobility, wittiness, gracefulness, tolerance, reasonableness, gentleness, warmth, modesty, and civility). Some virtues are cognitive and consist of understanding the requirements of morality toward ourselves and others, such as wisdom and prudence. Other virtues are dispositions that incline one to act according to general moral principles. The virtue of benevolence, for example, inclines one to maximize the happiness of others, the virtue of respect for others inclines one to exercise consideration for the rights of individuals, the virtue of justice inclines one to behave according to the principles of justice, and the virtue of caring inclines one to live up to the tenets of care.

Challenges to Virtue Theory Some philosophers have argued that virtue theory is not consistent with the findings of modern psychology.[137] In a study involving theology students at Princeton University Divinity School, students were asked to read a Bible story about a good Samaritan who helps a wounded man lying next to the road, and then each was told he had to rush to another building for an extremely important appointment he was almost late for.[138] As each student hurried to the other building, he had to go past a man lying on the ground who looked sick or injured. Ninety percent of the theology students glanced at the man, stepped over him or went around him, and hurried on without helping. Yet, the students had not only just read about and, presumably, thought about the importance of helping (particularly helping an injured person lying by one's path), they were also largely good people with a virtuous character aspiring to be ministers. The authors of the study concluded that a person's behavior is determined by his external situation, not by his moral character.

In a different study involving students at Stanford University, 21 male students were randomly assigned to be either a "prisoner" or a "guard" in a "prison" in the basement of the Psychology Department.[139] The students were selected from 75 volunteers and given psychological tests to establish that among the volunteers, they were the most emotionally stable, most mature, least anti-social, normal, and psychologically healthy young men. The guards had uniforms, wore mirrored sunglasses to prevent eye contact, and had wooden batons to establish their authority but not to be used

Quick Review 2.20

Objections to Virtue Theory

- It is inconsistent with psychology which showed in the Milgram and Princeton studies that behavior is determined by the external situation, not moral character.
- Defenders of virtue say moral character determines behavior in a person's familiar environment and recent psychology shows behavior is determined by one's moral identity which includes one's virtues and vices.

to punish the prisoners. The prisoners wore poorly fitting dress-like white smocks that reached only to their knees and that had a number on the back. Each prisoner wore a chain around his ankles and was referred to by his number and not by name. The experiment was to go on for two weeks but was stopped after six days because it had spun out of control. As the experiment progressed, the guards became increasingly domineering and abusive, harassed the prisoners, punished them by forcing them to do "push-ups" or to sleep on the concrete floor without a mattress, made some go nude to degrade them, and humiliated all of them in numerous petty ways. About a third of the guards became "sadistic" and "cruel." The "prisoners" became increasingly passive, servile, dehumanized, erratic, and hateful of the "guards." They exhibited extreme depression, crying, rage, and acute anxiety. Philip Zimbardo, author of the experiment, concluded that the experiment showed that a person's behavior is not determined by personal psychological or moral traits, but by the external environment. If placed in an environment that approves of, legitimizes, and supports domineering and cruel behavior, people will exhibit those behaviors regardless of what virtues they happen to have. Zimbardo later claimed that the torture and sadistic behavior that U.S. soldiers inflicted on their prisoners in the Abu Ghraib military prison in 2004 was a result of the same kind of environment that his experiment had studied.[140]

More recent work in psychology, however, has tended to be more supportive of virtue theory.[141] Some psychologists have argued that people may learn to act on their virtues within certain familiar types of situations, but not beyond. If those psychologists are correct, then the subjects tested in the Princeton and Stanford studies may have failed to act on their virtues only because the situations in which the studies placed them were unusual and not familiar situations. People's behavior may be governed by their virtues, but only within certain more or less familiar kinds of situations. The Princeton and Stanford studies should not lead us to give up on the virtues, but should spur us to figure out how to widen the range of situations in which they come into play.

Moreover, more direct studies on the relationship between character and behavior has suggested that the virtues influence our moral decisions more or less as predicted by virtue theory. One set of studies argues that moral decisions that harmonize with those character traits a person feels are part of who he or she is—part of his or her identity—are more stable and enduring characteristics of a person than decisions that conflict with those traits.[142] Other studies show that a person's understanding of his or her own moral character or identity influences his or her behavior because failing to live up to one's moral identity creates emotional discomfort and a feeling of having betrayed oneself.[143] Although strange or unusual environmental factors can reduce the influence of virtue on behavior (as the Princeton and Stanford studies indicated), an understanding of one's own character will ordinarily influence one's behavior. As virtue theory suggests, when making a moral decision, people with a strong sense of themselves as caring, compassionate, fair, friendly, generous, helpful, hardworking, honest, and kind will consider how a person like themselves should behave. Ordinarily their decision will be consistent with their sense of the kind of person they are.[144]

Virtues and Principles

What is the relationship between a theory of virtue and the theories of ethics that we considered earlier (utilitarian theories, rights theories, justice theories, and care theories)? As a glance at the many kinds of dispositions that count as virtues suggests, the moral virtues support or facilitate adherence to moral principles, but they do this in a variety of different ways. There is, then, no single, simple relationship between the virtues and our moral principles. Some virtues enable people to do what moral principles require. Courage, for example, enables us to stick to our moral principles even when fear of the consequences tempts us to do otherwise. Some virtues consist of a readiness to act on moral principles. Justice, for example, is the virtue of being disposed to follow principles of justice. Some virtues are dispositions that our moral principles require us to develop. Utilitarianism, for example, requires us to develop dispositions such as kindness and generosity that will lead us to increase the happiness of people.

Hence, there is no conflict between theories of ethics that are based on principles and theories of ethics based on virtues. However, a theory of virtue differs from an ethic of principles in the perspective from which it approaches moral evaluations. A theory of virtue judges actions in terms of the dispositions that are associated with those actions, whereas an ethic of principles judges dispositions in terms of the actions associated with those dispositions. For an ethic of principles actions are primary, whereas for an ethic of virtue dispositions are primary. We may say, then, that both an ethic of principles and an ethic of virtue identify what the moral life is about. However, principles look at the moral life in terms of the actions that morality obligates us to perform, whereas the virtues look at the moral life in terms of the kind of person morality obligates us to be. An ethic of virtue, then, covers much of the same ground as an ethic of principles, but from a very different standpoint.

An ethic of virtue, then, is not a fifth kind of moral principle that should take its place alongside the principles of utilitarianism, rights, justice, and caring. Instead, an ethic of virtue fills out and adds to these principles by looking not at the actions people are required to perform, but at the character they are required to have. An adequate ethic of virtue, then, will look at the virtues that are associated with utilitarianism, with rights, with justice, and those associated with caring. In addition, it will (and in this respect an ethic of virtue goes beyond an ethic of principles) look at the virtues people need to adhere to their moral principles when their feelings, desires, and passions tempt them to do otherwise. It will look at the many other virtues that the principles of utilitarianism, rights, justice, and caring require a person to cultivate. An ethic of virtue, then, addresses the same landscape of issues that an ethic of principles does, but it also addresses issues related to motivation and feelings that are largely ignored by an ethic of principles.

2.7 Unconscious Moral Decisions

We saw in this chapter and in chapter one that moral reasoning is the process of applying our moral principles to the knowledge or understanding we have about a situation, and making a judgment about what ought to be done in that situation. The managers of Ford Motor Company, for example, were faced with a car design that could injure passengers in a rear collision. They searched for more information and found a fix for the problem and calculated the costs and benefits of making the fix. They applied their utilitarian principles to the knowledge they had gathered and judged they should not change the design of the car.

Now, think for a moment about the many times today that you decided to do what was morally right. For example, you probably had several conversations during which you told the truth instead of lying, or you walked past other people's property and did not steal it, or you kept your promise when you told someone that you would meet her after class or that you would return a pen she loaned you.

Notice that as you made these ethical decisions throughout your day, you did not go through the conscious and deliberate process of moral reasoning we have been discussing. When you talk you usually tell the truth without a second thought, you respect people's property without reasoning about what your moral principles say, and you keep your promises without thinking about it. It seems that we make many of our ethical decisions without the kind of conscious moral reasoning about utility, rights, justice, caring, and virtue that we have been discussing. Instead, we seem to be making many of our moral decisions automatically and without any conscious reasoning. What is going on here?

A large number of psychological studies of the brain and its processes have suggested that we have two ways of making moral decisions: through conscious reasoning and through unconscious mental processes. Our brain is capable of taking in information and then making decisions automatically and unconsciously, and it is also able to engage in conscious and deliberate reasoning processes. The kinds of moral reasoning that we have been discussing in this chapter are part of our conscious reasoning abilities, but many of our daily ethical decisions seem to arise from unconscious mental processes. We will look briefly now at what we know about these unconscious processes. It is important for us to do this for two reasons. First, the unconscious processes seem to be the processes by which we make the vast majority of our moral decisions. Yet, we have said almost nothing about these unconscious processes. If we want to understand moral reasoning, then, it is important for us to understand these unconscious processes that play such a significant role in our moral decision-making. Second, because these processes are unconscious and automatic, it is easy to conclude that they are unrelated to the conscious and logical reasoning processes we have been studying. However, if they are unrelated to our conscious and logical reasoning processes, then aren't we in effect saying that they are non-logical and non-rational? Could these processes even be completely irrational? And if most of our moral decisions are made through these non-logical and non-rational—possibly irrational—processes, then does it follow that, in the end, most of our moral life is based on a possibly irrational foundation that we are not even aware of? What is the point of studying all the stuff we have been studying about moral reasoning, moral standards, and so on? It is important, then, that we look at these processes and try to answer these pressing questions.

Unconscious Moral Decision-Making

Scott Reynolds, a psychologist, calls the unconscious processes by which we automatically make many of our moral decisions the "X-System" and the conscious reasoning through which we also make moral decisions the "C-system."[145] The X system, Reynolds and others have argued, is based on the use of "schemas" or "prototypes."[146] Prototypes are general memories of the kinds of situations we have experienced in the past, together with the kinds of sounds, words, objects, or people those situations involved, the kind of emotions we felt, the way we behaved in those situations, the type of moral norms or rules that we followed, etc. The brain uses these stored "prototypes" to analyze the new situations we encounter each day and to determine how to behave in those situations. Our brain does this by trying to match each new situation we experience with its store of prototypes. If the new situation matches a stored prototype, then the brain recognizes that the new situation is the kind of situation represented by the prototype. The brain then uses the information stored in the prototype to identify what kind of behavior is appropriate for that kind of situation, what kind of moral norms apply in such a situation, what emotions are usual for such situations, etc.

> *Quick Review 2.21*
>
> **Unconscious Moral Decisions**
> - Comprise most of our moral decisions
> - Made, according to psychologists, by the brain's "X-system" using stored prototypes to automatically and unconsciously identify what it perceives and what it should do.

Although these matching processes go on unconsciously, once a match is made, the conscious brain becomes aware of the match. That is, when the brain matches a situation with a stored prototype, we become conscious of recognizing the kind of situation we are in, and what behavior is appropriate in this kind of situation. When we are having a conversation, we consciously recognize that we are in a conversation and know what to do, for example, although we are not conscious of everything our brain had to do to come up with that recognition and that knowledge. In this way, we do not have to use up our limited conscious reasoning resources to figure out what is happening and what we should do each time we experience something. Without expending any conscious reasoning efforts, we immediately know what kind of situation we are in and how we should act because all the work of coming up with that conscious knowledge was done by the unconscious matching processes of the brain.

Prototypes are not fixed and unchanging. As we go through life and experience the same types of situation again and again, we add to their prototypes whatever new information we get from each experience. A prototype, for example, may be one that stores information about conversations we have had. As time goes on and we experience more conversations, we may learn that in such situations truthful behavior is appropriate. The prototype will store that information, and the next time we are in a conversation, the brain will match this new situation with that prototype and know it is involved in a conversation and automatically decide to be truthful in that situation. Because of the thousands of prototypes we eventually store in our brains, we not only recognize a great many kinds of situations, but we also know how to behave in those situations without having to think about it consciously.

Once we are conscious of the kind of situation we are in, however, we can begin to use our conscious reasoning processes—our C-system processes—to deal with it. We may be conscious, for example, that we are having a conversation with a friend and that in this kind of situation, we tell the truth. But suppose this time we know that if we tell the truth, we will hurt our friend's feelings, so we consider lying. Our conscious reasoning processes then have to swing into action to deliberately figure out what to do: do we lie or do we tell the truth? These conscious reasoning processes are part of our C-system.

The C-system or conscious reasoning system uses processes that, as we have learned in this chapter, are more complicated than the simple matching of prototypes the X-system uses. As we saw in chapter one, conscious moral reasoning can deliberately gather information about a situation we are considering. It can draw upon our store of moral principles to see which ones might apply to this kind of situation, and it can then figure out what those moral principles require for the situation we face.

We also rely on conscious reasoning when we find ourselves in a new or unusual situation that our unconscious X-system cannot match up with any of its stored prototypes. For example, we may come upon some kind of object we have never seen before. Then the C-system takes over and begins trying to reason out what it is that we have encountered. We may consciously try to gather more information about the strange object, we may call upon the rules and principles we know to see if any of them tell us what to do with such objects. Should we touch it? Should we throw water on it? Should we eat it? Should we run? Eventually we figure out what to do and we then store up a new prototype that contains the information about this new kind of object. Our conscious reasoning processes, then, are one basic source of the prototypes our X-system uses and the information contained in those prototypes.

The countless automatic and unthinking moral decisions we make throughout an ordinary day, then, can be understood as the outcomes of our unconscious reliance on prototypes of past situations that include information about the actions that are morally appropriate for the situation we are in. Although these moral decisions are made without much thought, this is possible in part because we have previously experienced similar situations and so we earlier consciously figured out what to do. Those past experiences allowed us to build a store of prototypes—a kind of wisdom—which we can now use without having to consciously figure everything out again from the beginning. Prototypes thus serve an important and liberating purpose: they free us from having to engage in the labors of moral reasoning repeatedly throughout the day. Think of how impossible life would be if we had to constantly be stopping to engage in the kind of conscious, logical, and slow moral reasoning we have been discussing in this and the previous chapter! The prototype system of the brain saves us—liberates us—from being continuously bogged down in the laborious processes of conscious moral reasoning.

The Legitimacy of Unconscious Moral Decision-Making

Although our use of prototypes is an unconscious process, this does not mean that it is a disreputable or irrational kind of process. To see that it is not an irrational process, we can compare it to some conscious forms of reasoning that are very similar to the use of prototypes, but that are clearly legitimate and rational. One form of conscious moral reasoning that is very similar to the unconscious use of prototypes is casuistry. Casuistry is a kind of moral reasoning that was widely used until the seventeenth century, and that began to be used again toward the end of the twentieth century, especially in medical ethics where it continues to be an influential form of moral reasoning that is widely accepted as legitimate and rational.

Casuistry is a way of making moral decisions by relying on previous "paradigm" cases.[147] A paradigm case is a past situation where it was clear what the ethical response should be and the reasons why that was the ethical response. Casuist reasoning uses those previous clear cases to decide what is ethical in a new situation. When a new situation presents itself, casuist reasoning first tries to identify a previous paradigm case that seems similar to this new situation. Casuist reasoning then tries to determine whether the new situation is similar enough to the paradigm, that we are justified in making the same decision now that we made in that previous paradigm case. If we find, however, that our new situation differs from the previous paradigm in a morally relevant way, then we are not justified in relying on the old paradigm to resolve our current situation but must fall back on regular moral reasoning to figure out what to do. Some examples may clarify how "casuist" reasoning works.

Suppose that a salesperson is wondering whether she should tell a customer about the dangers of using a product he wants to buy even though telling him may lose the sale. If the saleperson were to use casuist reasoning to make her decision, she would try to recall situations like the one she is in now, but in which she knew the right thing to do. Perhaps, the salesperson recalls a situation in which she considered lying to a customer, but realized it was wrong because she would be misleading the customer instead of allowing him to make an informed decision. Her current situation does not quite match that previous experience because the issue then was whether to actively lie, while now the issue is whether to passively withhold information. The salesperson realizes, however, that the two situations are similar insofar as both cases involve misleading the customer and both cases involve not allowing the customer the opportunity to make an informed decision. Since her present situation matches the previous one in these important moral respects, and since the salesperson knows misleading the customer would have been wrong in the previous case, she decides it would be just as wrong to withhold information in the current situation.

Casuist reasoning might also conclude that a new situation is *not* similar to a paradigm case. Suppose, for example, that you borrowed a gun from a friend who now

Quick Review 2.22

Prototypes and Rationality

- The brain's use of prototypes is similar to using paradigms in casuistry or precedents in common law which are both rational processes.
- This similarity implies the use of prototypes is also a rational process.
- Conscious reasoning can also correct and shape our prototypes.

says he wants it back and you suspect he will use it to harm himself or someone else. What should you do? You remember several cases when you borrowed something and believed you had a moral obligation to return it. However, there is an important moral difference between your current situation and those previous ones: in your present situation a person may be killed if you return what you borrowed. Because the obligation to preserve human life outweighs the obligation to return what you borrow, you decide that the difference between your situation now and then is morally significant and justifies *not* following those earlier cases. Instead, you consider other cases that involved potential harm to others. Perhaps, in some of those cases you were sure that it would be wrong to cooperate in harming another person. The similarity between your present situation and cases that involved cooperating in harming someone are significant enough that you decide it would be wrong to return the gun because that would be contributing to a potential harm.

Notice that "casuist" moral reasoning uses paradigms that function much like the prototypes the brain uses in its unconscious decision-making processes. Casuist reasoning is virtually a conscious version of the brain's unconscious use of prototypes. Casuistry is not the only kind of reasoning that is similar to our unconscious reliance on prototypes. Judges in common law legal systems, like the system we have in the United States, rely on past "precedents" to decide what to do in a current case.[148] A precedent is a legal case that was decided previously by a higher court or by the court that is deciding the current case. If the current case involves issues or facts that are the same as the issues or facts that were involved in a precedent, then a judge will normally make the same decision in the current case that was made in the precedent. Yet another form of reasoning that is similar to the brain's use of prototypes is "case-based reasoning" which is widely used in artificial intelligence computer systems.[149] Here, again, the process involves relying on matching previous cases to decide what to do in a current case.

Our unconscious use of prototypes, then, which is how we make many of our moral decisions, is not an irrational process nor is it illegitimate. It is, in fact, an unconscious version of the decision-making processes that are legitimately used in many fields, including in an important form of conscious moral reasoning, i.e., casuistry. The similarity between our unconscious use of prototypes and the conscious and legitimate reasoning processes we have been discussing provides good reason to think that our unconscious prototype-based decision-making processes are neither illegitimate nor irrational.

Cultural Influences and Intuition

We mentioned earlier that some of the prototypes on which we base our actions are the products of conscious moral reasoning. But not all prototypes originate in conscious moral reasoning. There are at least two other ways in which we acquire our convictions about what morality requires of us. We mentioned in Chapter 1 that many of our moral beliefs are derived from the cultural influences that surrounded us as we grew up, i.e., from family, peer groups, stories, songs, magazines, television, radio, church, novels, newspapers, and so on. These cultural influences no doubt are incorporated into our prototypes and thereby, shape our actions. Of course, just because we acquire a moral belief from the culture around us, does not mean that it is necessarily correct, or incorrect. In fact, one of the roles of traditional moral reasoning is to critically evaluate the beliefs we have picked up from family, peers, etc. and that have become part of the prototypes we use, in order to determine whether these beliefs are reasonable or unreasonable.

Conscious moral reasoning and cultural influences are not the only sources of the prototypes that guide our ordinary actions. Some of our strongest, most tenaciously held moral beliefs seem to be based on sheer intuition, i.e., we do not acquire them from our environment, nor are they based on any moral or non-moral reasons or reasoning.[150] The psychologist Jonathan Haidt suggests we consider the following story, which he made up and which, he says, will reveal a moral belief that we all share, but that does not seem to be based on conscious moral reasoning:

> Julie and Mark are brother and sister. They're traveling together in France on summer vacation from college. One night they're staying alone in a cabin near the beach. They decide that it would be interesting and fun if they tried making love. At the very least, it would be a new experience for each of them. Julie was already taking birth control pills, but Mark uses a condom too, just to be safe. They both enjoy making love, but they decide never to do it again. They keep that night as a special secret, which makes them feel even closer to each other. What do you think about that? Was it ok for them to make love?[151]

Probably your answer to the last question Haidt asks is that what Julie and Mark did was morally wrong. (That would certainly be my own answer!) But what reasoning led us to this conclusion? What reasons do we have for our conviction that their incest was immoral? No one else was harmed by what they did, and, let us suppose, they suffered no bad consequences, did not feel guilt, their relationship was not affected, etc. In addition, what they did was not unjust, violated no one's moral rights, nor was it uncaring. There is a biological reason why close relatives should not have children together (namely because inbreeding increases the likelihood of defective offspring), but this reason does not apply to the situation of Julie and Mark. What reasons do you and I have for our conviction that what they did was wrong? Most of us will not be able to find a clear reason, yet this will not change our minds. We might end up saying something like this: "Although I don't know why it's wrong, I still know that it's wrong!" Haidt argues that the fact that we cannot find a justification for our conviction that incest is wrong implies that we did not acquire this conviction by reasoning, i.e., it is not based on reasons. Moreover, the fact that this conviction is one that almost everyone in every culture in every age has accepted, suggests that this conviction is just built into the human brain. It is based on intuition that seems to be "hardwired" into our brains. This, of course, does not mean the conviction is wrong or right; it only means that it is not originally based on a reasoning process. (Whether the conviction is right or wrong would require examining it at much greater length with the use of conscious moral reasoning.)

Quick Review 2.23

Moral Intuitions

- Prototypes can be shaped by "hardwired" moral intuitions, as well as by conscious moral reasoning and cultural influences.
- Hardwired intuitions seem to include: incest is wrong; harming by action is worse than harming by omission; harming as a means to a goal is worse than harming as a foreseen side effect; harming by physical contact is worse than harming without physical contact.

There are other moral beliefs that, like our conviction that incest is wrong, seem to be based on intuition; we have the beliefs but cannot provide the reasons why we believe them. Here are three principles that the social psychologist Marc Hauser has found that most people accept when they make judgments about the morality of harming people:

> *The Action Principle:* Harm caused by action is morally worse than equivalent harm caused by an omission. (For example, it is worse to kill a person than it is to allow a person to die without doing anything to prevent his death.)
>
> *The Intention Principle:* Harm intended as the means to a goal is morally worse than equivalent harm foreseen as the side effect of a goal. (For example, it is worse to jump out of a boat deliberately intending to kill myself by drowning than it is to jump out of a lifeboat so that there will be room for other survivors of a sinking ship even if I ultimately drown.)

The Contact Principle: Using physical contact to cause harm to a victim is morally worse than causing equivalent harm to a victim without using physical contact. (For example, it is worse for a soldier to stab and kill an innocent villager, than it is for a pilot to drop a bomb that he knows will kill an unseen innocent villager.) [152]

By analyzing the responses people give to several scenarios (like the examples within parentheses above), Hauser has shown that almost all people accept these principles when deciding whether it is morally worse to cause harm in one way rather than another. But when pressed for the reasons why we accept these principles, most of us cannot provide any. We seem to accept these principles not because we have reasoned them out but because they seem to be based on intuition.

The prototypes that we unconsciously use to make most of our everyday moral decisions, then, can also draw from these moral principles that we know by intuition, as well as from the cultural influences around us and from our conscious moral reasoning. It is worth repeating that merely because we accept a principle based on intuition, it does not follow that the principle is correct or incorrect. Moral reasoning may ultimately show us, for example, that the action principle, the intention principle, and the contact principle are correct; or future reasoning may show that they are mistaken. In fact, some philosophers have argued that the action, intention, and contact principles are mistaken, while others have argued that these three principles are correct.[153] The reasoning that we use to prove or disprove these three moral principles, of course, is conscious moral reasoning, i.e., the kind of reasoning that deliberately gathers evidence, appeals to moral principles like utilitarianism, and reaches a considered judgment. While conscious moral reasoning is probably not "in the driver's seat" all of the time, it plays a crucial role when we want to determine whether our intuitions are right or wrong, as well as when we want to see whether the beliefs we learned from our culture are reasonable or unreasonable.

> *Quick Review 2.24*
>
> **Conscious Moral Reasoning**
> - Is used in new, strange, or unusual situations for which the brain has no matching prototypes
> - Consists of the conscious, logical but slow processes of the brain's "C-system"
> - Evaluates how reasonable or unreasonable are our intuitions, our cultural beliefs, and the norms stored in our prototypes.

Our moral decisions, then, are based on two different processes: the unconscious and automatic use of prototypes that we gradually accumulate as we go through life, and the conscious use of moral reasoning that appeals to evidence and to moral standards like utility, rights, justice, and caring. Our unconscious prototype processes are responsible for many—perhaps even most—of our automatic everyday moral decisions, and these prototypes are shaped by our cultural surroundings, our moral intuitions, and past conscious moral reasoning. On the other hand, we rely on conscious moral reasoning when we need to decide what to do in a new or unusual situation (one that does not match any of our prototypes), as well as when we want to figure out whether the beliefs we get from intuition or from our culture are reasonable or unreasonable. Although during much of our lives we depend on the kind of automatic and almost unthinking behavior that prototypes enable us to engage in, we also often find that we need to fall back on moral reasoning to correct or extend our prototypes, when they fall short of providing the kind of guidance we need.

The processes on which we base our moral decisions, then, can be rational even though they are unconscious. The unconscious use of prototypes is much like casuistry and other forms of conscious reasoning that we accept as rationally justified. Moreover, the rules and norms that become part of our brain's prototypes often originate in previous episodes of conscious moral reasoning. And, most important of all, it is possible for us to stand back and consciously think about the norms and rules that our brain seems to have incorporated into its prototypes and ask whether these norms and rules can be given any rational support. By doing this, we can correct these previously accepted norms and rules. We can do this not only to the norms and rules that we have accumulated from our culture—from parents, friends, movies, books, and other cultural influences—but also to the norms and rules that we know by intuition and that seem to be hardwired into the brain. However, thinking about and weighing all the norms we have accumulated as we have grown older is a long and difficult process. It is the work of ethics, a work that can take a lifetime.

✓ Study and Review on mythinkinglab.com

Questions for Review and Discussion

1. Define the following concepts: utilitarianism, utility, intrinsic good, instrumental good, basic need, mere wants, rule-utilitarianism, rights, legal rights, moral rights, negative rights, positive rights, contractual rights, categorical imperative (both versions), the libertarian view on rights, distributive justice, the fundamental (or formal) principle of distributive justice, material principle of justice, egalitarian justice, capitalist justice, socialist justice, libertarian justice, justice as fairness, principle of equal liberty, difference principle, principle of fair equality of opportunity, the "original position," retributive justice, compensatory justice, caring, ethic of caring, concrete relationship, virtue, ethics of virtue, prototype, casuist reasoning.
2. A student incorrectly defined *utilitarianism* this way: "Utilitarianism is the view that so long as an action provides me with more measurable economic benefits than costs, the action is morally right." Identify all of the mistakes contained in this definition of utilitarianism.
3. In your view, does utilitarianism provide a more objective standard for determining right and wrong than moral rights do? Explain your answer fully. Does utilitarianism provide a more objective standard than principles of justice? Explain.
4. "Every principle of distributive justice, whether that of the egalitarian, or the capitalist, or the socialist, or the libertarian, or of Rawls, in the end is illegitimately advocating some type of equality." Do you agree or disagree? Explain.
5. "An ethic of caring conflicts with morality because morality requires impartiality." Discuss this criticism of an ethic of caring.
6. "An ethic of virtue implies that moral relativism is correct, while an action-centered ethic does not." Do you agree or disagree? Explain.

Web Resources

Readers who would like to conduct research on ethics through the Internet may want to begin with the web site of the Council for Ethical Leadership (*http://www.businessethics.org*); the Business Social Responsibility Organization (*http://www.bsr.org*); the Guide to Philosophy on the Internet (*http://www.earlham.edu/~peters/gpi/index.htm*); The Stanford Encyclopedia of Philosophy (*http://plato.stanford.edu/*); The Internet Encyclopedia of Philosophy (*http://www.iep.utm.edu*); Utilitarianism Resources (*http://www.utilitarianism.com*); Kant on the Web (*http://www.hkbu.edu.hk/~ppp/Kant.html*); John Rawls (http://people.wku.edu/jan.garrett/ethics/johnrawl.htm); Julia Annas' Page on Virtue Ethics (*http://www.u.arizona.edu/~jannas/forth/coppvirtue.htm*).

CASES

Explore the Concept on mythinkinglab.com

Traidos Bank and Roche's Drug Trials in China

On September 23, 2010, Traidos Bank, a small British financial institution with a 2009 income of $127.3 million and a net profit of $13.6 million, publicly announced that they had removed the Swiss pharmaceutical giant, Roche, from its investment portfolio because "Roche's clinical trials with transplanted organs in China do not meet Traidos criteria for selection."[1]

Traidos Bank noted on its web site that it was an "ethical bank which offers savings accounts and investments" and it prided itself on being "the world's leading ethical and sustainable bank." Traidos declared that its day-to-day decision-making was guided by six principles:

We will

- **promote sustainable development**–considering the social, environmental and financial impacts of everything we do
- **respect and obey the law**–in every country where we do business
- **respect human rights**–of individuals, and within different societies and cultures; supporting the aims of the United Nation's Universal Declaration of Human Rights
- **respect the environment**–doing all we can to create and encourage positive environmental effects
- **be accountable**–to anyone for anything we do
- **improve continuously**–always looking for better ways of doing things in every area of our business.[2]

Besides offering savings accounts and providing loans to "organizations that bring real social, cultural or environmental benefits," Traidos Bank offered 13 funds in which individuals could invest their money. The funds, in turn, invested this money in "sustainable" businesses or purchased shares of stock of companies that met its "stringent ethical criteria" and "that provide sustainable products or services, or achieve above average social and environmental performance, and actively contribute to sustainable development."

In 2009, Traidos Bank had reviewed the operations of Roche and had determined that the pharmaceutical company met the bank's ethical criteria and so qualified for including its stock in the bank's portfolio of investments. In fact, Roche looked like an outstanding addition to its investment fund portfolio:

> Our results placed the company in the best performing 50% of pharmaceutical companies in Europe. We considered Roche to be transparent about sustainability issues, with a comprehensive position regarding genetic engineering and clear ethical guidelines for clinical trials. It has systems in place to monitor and enforce social standards in its supply chains, and it favors suppliers with certified environmental management systems. Also, Roche has ambitious targets to reduce energy consumption and greenhouse gas emissions.[3]

But several months later the bank learned about Roche's research programs in China, and after further investigations, the bank decided Roche no longer met its ethical criteria. What the Bank discovered was that in January, 2010:

> Roche received the Public Eye Award that is sponsored by the Berne Declaration and Greenpeace. The award names and shames corporations with unethical social or ecological behaviour.... Roche received the award because of its clinical trials in China for the drug CellCept, which prevents the rejection of transplanted organs. Since a large part of transplanted organs in China originate from executed prisoners and Roche does not verify the origins of the organs in its China-based trials, its position is questionable.[4]

Roche was testing the drug CellCept on Chinese transplant patients because Chinese law requires that any drug sold in China must first be tested on Chinese patients. CellCept is a drug that prevents a patient's immune system from rejecting an organ that has been transplanted into the patient. Transplanted organs are taken from people who have recently died or been declared "brain dead," or from living donors who donate an organ or part of an organ when their remaining organs can regenerate or can take over the work of the donated organ (such as a kidney or part of a liver). In most countries, there are strict rules governing the removal of organs from donors. In particular, most countries do not allow organs to be taken from donors, living or dead, unless they earlier give their free and informed consent and many countries do not allow donors to trade their organs for money. Such requirements were problematic in China, according to the bank, because most transplant organs came from prisoners and the conditions under which the organ had been removed were often not known:

> Up to 90 percent of all transplanted organs in China come from executed prisoners. Regulation

> surrounding transplantation in China has improved in the last couple of years and includes better safeguards for prisoners' rights. But even when a prisoner supposedly consents to an organ donation, such consent while imprisoned cannot be considered of free will.... In our final assessment we balanced the gathered information and concluded that Roche's approach to clinical trials in China is not acceptable. The company's size and influence warrant a much clearer position on the origin of transplanted organs. Since the company no longer meets our human rights minimum standard, it has been excluded from the Traidos sustainable investment universe and will be removed from all Traidos investments within the short term.[5]

Roche was concerned by the growing controversy over its participation in transplant operations that in many cases, the company knew, had to use organs taken from prisoners without their consent or with "consent" that had been forced out of them. According to the company, while it was true that a certain percentage of the organs of its test patients had to have been harvested from prisoners, it was not possible for the company to find out what was the source of any of its Chinese patients' organs. However, the company pointed out, if it did not test its drug on transplant patients in China, whatever the source of their organs, then it could not market its drug there. The company felt that the greater good would be served by going ahead with its drug tests even though many of the transplanted organs in its test patients were harvested from prisoners. Otherwise, thousands of future Chinese transplant patients would not only be deprived of the benefits of the drug, but would in many cases suffer harmful and costly outcomes because they needed the drug but it would not be available. In a report on the company's annual shareholders' meeting on March 2, 2010, Roche provided a summary of the statement of Dr. Schwan, a company spokesperson who outlined the company's position:

> Dr Schwan stated that CellCept was a medicine which had saved and continued to save thousands of patients' lives by preventing post-transplant organ rejection. Withdrawing the medicine from the market in any country would be morally unthinkable, he said, as this would jeopardize human lives. He noted that, in all countries, independent institutions handled organ procurement and donor information was confidential. Roche had no way of directly influencing this process, he said .... Roche was studying the optimal CellCept dosage for Chinese patients, whose responses to CellCept may differ from those of Western patients owing to ethnic factors or differences in constitution, Dr Schwan said. The focus of the trials was on [CellCept's] safety and efficacy in Chinese patients.[6]

In May, 2007, the Chinese government banned the sale of human organs and required that living donors could donate their organs only to spouses, blood relatives, or step and adopted family members. Nevertheless, the organ trade continued to flourish in China.[7] Not only were the organs of deceased people (including executed prisoners whose organs it was still legal to "harvest") sold covertly to doctors, hospitals, or organ "brokers," but living donors also secretly sold their organs by using easily forged documents testifying that they were related to the recipient of their organs.[8]

A large number of China's prisoners were political dissidents or those who had been jailed because of their religious or political beliefs and not because they had violated the law or inflicted harm on others. Since 2006, the Falun Gong, a Chinese quasi-Buddhist spiritual group banned in 1999 and now actively persecuted by the government, had been providing credible evidence that many of the hundreds of thousands of their members imprisoned by the Chinese government and who had subsequently "disappeared," had been killed for their organs which were then sold or given to transplant candidates.[9] In the summer of 2010, human rights groups announced that their investigations had uncovered evidence that more than 9,000 members of Falun Gong had been executed in Chinese prisons for their corneas, lungs, livers, kidneys, and skin. Imprisoned members of other religious groups including Christians, Muslims, and Tibetan Buddhists had also been imprisoned and executed for their organs.[10] Critics of Roche feared that many of the transplanted organs of Roche's test patients had been harvested from such prisoners of conscience against their will.

Questions

1. Explain how utilitarianism might provide a defense for Roche and how a rights-based ethic might instead condemn Roche's drug trials in China. Which of these two approaches is stronger or more reasonable? Explain the reasons for your answer.
2. Is it ethical for Roche to continue testing CellCept on its Chinese transplant patients?
3. Is Traidos Bank ethically justified in excluding Roche's stock from the funds it offers its customers? Consider your answer in light of the bank's duty to invest money wisely and in light of its own conclusion that Roche was among "the best performing 50% of pharmaceutical companies in Europe," was "transparent about sustainability issues," had "a comprehensive position regarding

genetic engineering and clear ethical guidelines for clinical trials," enforced high "standards" for its suppliers, and strove to "reduce energy consumption and greenhouse gas emissions."

4. Are Traidos Bank's ethical standards set too high?

Notes

1. Traidos Bank web site, accessed January 14, 2010 at *www.triodos.com/en/about-triodos-bank/news/newsletters/newsletter-sustainability-research/pharmaceutical-company*
2. Traidos Bank web site, accessed January 14, 2010 at *www.triodos.co.uk/en/about-triodos/who-we-are/mission-principles/business-principles/*
3. Traidos Bank web site, accessed January 14, 2010 at *www.triodos.com/en/about-triodos-bank/news/newsletters/newsletter-sustainability-research/pharmaceutical-company*
4. Ibid.
5. Ibid.
6. Minutes of the 92nd Annual General Meeting of the Shareholders of Roche Holding Ltd, Basel, held at 10.30 A.M. on March 2, 2010 at the Convention Centre, Basel Trade Fair Complex, Basel; accessed January 12, 2010 at *www.roche.com/annual_general_meeting_2010_en.pdf*
7. Liu Zhen and Emma Graham-Harrison, "Organ Trafficking Trial Exposes Grisly Trade," *Reuters*, May 19, 2010.
8. Shan Juan, "Organ Trafficking Ring to Go on Trial," China Daily, March 17, 2010; accessed January 15, 2011 at *http://www.chinadaily.com.cn/china/2010-03/17/content_9599832.htm*
9. David Matas and David Kilgour, *Bloody Harvest: Organ Harvesting of Falun Gong Practitioners in China*, (Woodstock, ON, Canada: Seraphim Editions, 2009).
10. "Chinese Accused of Vast Trade in Organs," *The Washington Times*, April 27, 2010.

CASES

Explore the **Concept** on **mythinkinglab.com**

Unocal in Burma[1]

Union Oil Company of California, or Unocal, was founded in 1890 to develop oil fields around Los Angeles and other parts of California. By 1990, Unocal had operations in all aspects of the oil business, including extraction, refining, distribution, marketing, and even retail (the company owned a chain of Union 76 gas stations). With most oil fields in the United States nearing depletion, the company had turned to investing in energy projects outside the country. Unocal's strategy was to market itself to governments as a company that had expertise in all aspects of oil and gas production. According to Roger C. Beach, CEO of the company, "What every government likes about Unocal is one-stop shopping—one group able to take the whole project from development to the marketing end."[2]

One of the international projects that attracted the company's attention was a natural gas field called the "Yadana Field" that belonged to Burma. The Yadana Field is located in the Andaman Sea beneath 150 feet (46 meters) of water off Burma's shore. Estimates indicated the field contained more than 5 trillion cubic feet of natural gas, enough to produce natural gas continuously for approximately 30 years.[3] In 1992, the government of Burma had formed a state-owned company named the Myanmar Oil and Gas Enterprise (MOGE) to find private companies to help it develop the Yadana Field. In 1992, it signed a contract with Total S.A, a French company that gave Total the right to develop the field and build a pipeline to transport the gas from Yadana to Thailand, where the government of Thailand would buy the gas. The government of Burma stood to net an estimated $200–$400 million per year for the life of the project. A portion of these revenues would be paid to the companies that partnered with Burma.

MOGE, the government-owned company, signed a contract with Total agreeing to "assist by providing security protection and rights of way and easements as may be requested by" the companies with which it partnered.[4] While its partner companies would actually construct the project, Burma would provide security through its army, which would also ensure that land was cleared and rights of way secured for the passage of the pipeline through Burma.

The Burmese project appealed to Unocal. Burma was attractive for several reasons. First, labor was cheap and relatively educated. Second, Burma was rich in natural gas resources, and its many other untapped resources presented major opportunities. Third, Burma was an entry point into other potentially lucrative international markets. Burma not only offered a potentially large market itself, it also occupied a strategic location that could serve as a link to markets in China, India, and other countries in Southeast Asia. Finally, the Burmese government maintained a stable political climate. With the military to maintain law and order, the political environment was extremely dependable.

Before committing itself to the project, Unocal evaluated its risk position by conducting research on the social-political environment of the country. Burma is a Southeast Asian country with a population of 42 million and land mass about the size of Texas. Burma is bounded by India to the northwest, China to the north and northeast, Laos to the east, Thailand to the east and southeast, and the Andaman Sea to the south. The majority of the population, some 69 percent, is Burmese, while Karens, Kachins, Shans, Chins, Rakhines, Indians, and Chinese are minorities in the nation. The Karens, clustered in rural parts of Southern Burma, had periodically fielded rebel groups against the government. Burma as a country is poor. Economically, Burma's per capita gross domestic product is approximately $200–$300, and inflation is above 20 percent. Socially, Burma suffers a high infant mortality rate (95 deaths for every 1,000 live births) and a low life expectancy (53 years for males and 56 for females). The natural gas project could provide much-needed revenues and significant benefits to the people of the impoverished nation.

The only real problem the company saw with its involvement in the project was that the government of Burma, with which it would be a partner, was a military dictatorship accused of continually violating the human rights of the Burmese people. In 1988, after crushing major countrywide prodemocracy demonstrations, Burma's military seized power and made the 19-member State Law and Order Restoration Council (SLORC) head of the government. The SLORC, which was made up of senior military officers, imposed martial law on the entire country. The U.S. State Department, in its annual "Country Reports on Human Rights Practices, 1991," wrote that the army of the SLORC maintained law and order through "arrests, harassment, and torture of political activists.... Torture, arbitrary detentions, and compulsory labor persisted.... Freedom of speech, the press, assembly, and association remain practically nonexistent."[5]

Many groups, including the U.S. State Department, accused the SLORC of numerous human rights abuses, particularly against Burmese minority groups. In its "Country Reports on Human Rights Practices, 1995," the Department wrote:

> The [Burmese] Government's unacceptable record on human rights changed little in 1994.... The Burmese military forced hundreds of thousands, if not millions, of ordinary Burmese (including women and children) to "contribute" their labor, often under harsh working conditions, to construction projects throughout the country. The forced resettlement of civilians also continued.... The SLORC continued to restrict severely basic rights to free speech, association and assembly.[6]

Amnesty International, in an August, 1991 report on Burma, wrote that the ruling Burmese army "continues to seize arbitrarily, ill-treat and extrajudicially execute members of ethnic and religious minorities in rural areas of the country. The victims ... include people seized by the [army] and compelled to perform porterage—carrying food, ammunition and other supplies—or mine-clearing work."[7] Responding to these reports, the U.S. Congress on April 30, 1994 voted to place Burma on a list of international "outlaw" states, and in 1996, President Bill Clinton barred Burmese government officials from entering the United States.

To check the situation for themselves, Unocal managers hired a consulting firm, the Control Risk Group. The report of the consulting firm warned: "Throughout Burma the government habitually makes use of forced labor to construct roads.... In such circumstances Unocal and its partners will have little freedom of maneuver."[8]

Despite the risks, Unocal decided to invest in the project. S. Lipman, a Unocal vice president, later stated that Unocal managers had discussed with Total the "hazards" that were involved in having the Burmese army provide "security" for the project: "we said that ... having the military provide protection for the pipeline construction ... might proceed ... not in the manner that we'd like to see them proceed, I mean, going to the excess."[9] Nevertheless, the company felt that the benefits, both to itself and to the people of Burma and Thailand, outweighed the risks. Moreover, the company would later assert, "engagement" rather than "isolation" was "the proper course to achieve social and political change in developing countries with repressive governments."[10] The company stated that "based on nearly four decades of experience in Asia, [Unocal] believes that engagement is by far the more effective way to strengthen emerging economies and promote more open societies."[11]

In December, 1992, Unocal, through a wholly owned subsidiary, paid $8.6 million to Total, S.A. for part of Total's stake in the project. Unocal became one of four investors in the Yadana Field project, each of whom would contribute financially in proportion to their stakes in the project. Unocal held a 28.26 percent stake in the project as a whole; Total had a 31.24 percent stake; Thailand's PTT Exploration & Production Public Co. had a 25.5 percent stake; and the Burmese government (MOGE) had a 15 percent stake.[12]

It was agreed that Total would be responsible for overall coordination of the project, would develop the wells at the Yadana field, and extract the gas. Unocal would construct the 256-mile pipeline that would carry the gas from Yadana to Thailand. Most of the pipe would lie under the ocean, but the final 40 miles would cross over southern Burma through the region inhabited by the Karen, the minority ethnic group most hostile to the Burmese government. The military, it appeared, might have to use force to secure the area before construction could begin. It would also have to build roads and other facilities such as base camps, buildings, barracks, fences, airplane landing strips, river docks, and helipads.

The period between 1993 and 1996 was devoted to preparing the way for construction of the pipeline, including clearing land and building roads, camps, housing, and other facilities. Actual construction of the pipeline began in

1996 and was completed in 1998. Throughout the time of preparation and construction of the pipeline, human rights groups—including Human Rights Watch and Amnesty International—issued numerous reports claiming that the Burmese army was using forced labor and brutalizing the Karen population as it provided "security" for Unocal workers and equipment. Roads, buildings, and other structures, these critics claimed, were being built with the use of forced labor recruited from local Karen groups by the Burmese military, and hundreds of Karen were being forced to clear the way for the pipeline and to provide slave labor for the project. Moreover, they claimed, Unocal was aware of this and aware of the brutal methods the army used to provide "security" for Unocal workers and equipment.[13] Several human rights groups, including Greenpeace, Amnesty International, and Human Rights Watch, met with Unocal executives in Los Angeles and informed them that forced labor and other violations of human rights were taking place in the pipeline region.

In May, 1995, Joel Robinson, a Unocal official who monitored the Yadana project for Unocal, spoke with U.S. Embassy officials stationed in Burma. The Embassy reported that:

> On the general issue of the close working relationship between Total/Unocal and the Burmese Military, Robinson [of Unocal] had no apologies to make. He stated forthrightly that the companies have hired the Burmese military to provide security for the Project and pay for this through the Myanmar Oil and Gas Enterprise (MOGE). He said Total's security officials meet with their military counterparts to inform them of the next day's activities so that soldiers can ensure the area is secure and guard the work perimeter while the survey team goes about its business.... Total/Unocal uses [aerial photos, precision surveys, and topography maps] to show the [Burmese] military where they need helipads built and facilities secured."[14]

Unocal hired another consultant in 1995 to investigate conditions on the Yadana project. The consultant reported in a letter to Unocal officials:

> My conclusion is that egregious human rights violations have occurred, and are occurring now, in southern Burma ... the most common [of which] are forced relocation without compensation of families from land near/along the pipeline route; forced labor to work on infrastructure projects supporting the pipeline (SLORC calls this government service in lieu of payment of taxes); and imprisonment and/or execution by the army of those opposing such actions.[15]

Work on the project continued and commercial natural gas production in the Yadana project began in 2000. The companies by then had instituted a number of social-economic programs to benefit the people around the pipeline. Unocal claimed that it provided 7,551 paid jobs to Burmese workers during construction and that while production continued it would continue to employ 587 Burmese workers. By 2004, the project was delivering 500–600 million cubic feet of gas per day to Thailand, benefitting that nation's rapidly expanding economy, providing an efficient and reliable source of energy, and enabling Thailand to use cleaner-burning natural gas to fuel its electrical plants instead of fuel oil. Revenues from sales to Thailand yielded several hundred million dollars a year to the Burmese military government. Unocal reported that besides its initial investment of $8.6 million, it spent a total of $230 million constructing the pipeline. It is estimated that it costs Unocal $10 million a year to operate the project. In return, Unocal's share of gas revenues was $75 million a year, which would continue for the course of the 30-year contract. Unocal's total gain is expected to reach approximately $2.2 billion dollars.

The benefits that the people in the region around the pipeline were deriving from the programs that Unocal and the other companies had initiated in that area were summarized by Unocal:

> An extensive, multimillion-dollar socioeconomic development program associated with the project has brought real and immediate benefits to thousands of families who live in the pipeline region. These benefits include significantly improved health care, improvements in education, new transportation infrastructure and small business opportunities. The impact of these programs has been enormous. Infant mortality in the pipeline region, for example, had dropped to 31 deaths per 1,000 live births by the year 2000, compared to 78 deaths per 1,000 live births for Myanmar overall. In 2002, the infant mortality rate in the pipeline region declined again to just 13 deaths per 1,000 live births (national figures not yet available).[16]

These claims were corroborated by the Collaborative for Development Action, Inc. (CDA), an independent group headquartered in Massachusetts and funded by the governments of the Netherlands, Denmark, Canada, and Germany and by the World Bank. After three visits to the pipeline region, the CDA reported in February, 2004 that "the number of people benefitting from the Socio-Econ Program is steadily increasing."[17] Although "the program has mainly benefitted the middle class," this "middle class has grown, relatively, wealthy" and the program was refocusing on "programs for the poorer people in the corridor." The CDA noted, however, that "the educated middle-class" still wanted "freedom" and a government "based on a constitution."[18] Moreover, it appeared that benefits from the Yadana project were not benefiting the people of Burma outside the pipeline region, with the exception of the military government, whose stake in the project gave it a steady stream of income.

Not all Burmese citizens were pleased with the development of the Yadana Field. In October, 1996, 15 members of the Burmese Karen minority group, who alleged that they or their family members had been subjected to relocation, forced labor, torture, murder, and rape on the Yadana pipeline project, filed class action suits in U.S. courts against Unocal: one suit in U.S. federal court (*Doe vs. Unocal*) and a second in California state court. Both suits argued that Unocal should be held responsible for the injuries inflicted on hundreds of Karen by the Burmese military because the activities of the military were conducted on behalf of the pipeline project in which Unocal held a major stake and from which Unocal benefitted. The suit in federal court was based on the federal 1789 Alien Tort Statute, which has been interpreted to authorize civil suits in U.S. courts for violations of internationally recognized human rights. On June 29, 2004, the U.S. Supreme Court upheld the right of foreigners to use the statute to seek compensation in U.S. courts for violations abroad. On December 20, 2004, Unocal announced it would settle the federal lawsuit, compensate the Karen villagers, and provide funds for social programs for people from the pipeline region. The terms of the settlement were not revealed.

Four months after the settlement, Chevron Corporation, announced it would purchase Unocal for $16.2 billion and so assume Unocal's stake in the Yadana project. Chevron now was accused of complicity in continuing human rights abuses in the pipeline area. EarthRights International (ERI), an NGO that had helped the villagers win their lawsuit, claimed in a series of reports that the Burmese army still provided security for the oil companies and while doing so engaged in human rights abuses "including torture, rape, murder, and forced labor." In 2007 the military regime brutally suppressed nationwide demonstrations against its rule, shooting and killing dozens of Buddhist monks who led the peaceful protests, and imprisoning thousands of others. ERI claimed that revenues from the Yadana project financed these and other brutalities of the military regime. In a 2009 report, *Total Impact*, ERI calculated that the regime's share of the Yadana revenues was $1.02 billion in 2008. Since 2000, according to a 2010 ERI report, *Energy Insecurity*, the project gave the regime $9 billion. ERI claimed much of that money went into offshore bank accounts owned by Burmese generals, while public expenditures on health and education remained the lowest in the region and poverty was widespread.

Questions

1. Assess whether from a utilitarian, rights, justice, and caring perspective, Unocal did the right thing in deciding to invest in the pipeline and then in conducting the project as it did. Assuming there was no way to change the outcome of this case and that the outcome was foreseen, was Unocal then justified in deciding to invest in the pipeline?
2. In your view, is Unocal morally responsible for the injuries inflicted on some of the Karen people? Explain. Is Chevron?
3. Do you agree or disagree with Unocal's view that "engagement" rather than "isolation" is "the proper course to achieve social and political change in developing countries with repressive governments." Explain.

Notes

1. This case was coauthored with Matthew Brown, former law student at Santa Clara University.
2. A. Pasztor and S. Kravetz, "Unocal is Shifting Strategy to International Operations," *The Wall Street Journal*, November 20, 1996, p. B4.
3. Unocal, "Background: The Yadana Project & The Activist Lawsuits," December 2, 2003, accessed May 26, 2003 at *http://www.unocal.com/myanmar/suit.htm*
4. *Doe vs. Unocal*, 110 F. Supp. 2d 1294 (2000); accessed February 22, 2003 at *http://www.earthrights.org/unocal/index.shtml*; also available as 2000 U.S. Dist. Lexis 13327.
5. Accessed on April 2003 at *http://www.state.gov/www/global/human_rights/hrp_reports_mainhp.html*
6. Ibid.
7. Amnesty International, "Myanmar (Burma): Continuing Killings and Ill-treatment of Minority Peoples," August 1991, accessed May 20, 2004 at *www.web.amnesty.org/library/index/engasa160051991*
8. *Doe vs. Unocal*
9. Ibid.
10. Unocal statement accessed June 20, 2004 at *http://www.unocal.com/myanmar/index.htm*
11. Ibid.
12. Unocal, "Background: The Yadana Project & The Activists Lawsuits," December 2, 2003, accessed June 5, 2004 at *http://www.unocal.com/myanmar/suit.htm*
13. U.S. Department of Labor, Bureau of International Labor Affairs, "Report on Labor Practices in Burma," accessed April 20, 2004 at *http://purl.access.gpo.gov/GPO/LPS5259*
14. *Doe vs. Unocal.*
15. Ibid.
16. Unocal, "Background: The Yadana Project," *loc. cit.*
17. Luc Zandvliet and Doug Fraser, "Corporate Engagement Project, Field Visit Report, Third Visit, Yadana Gas Transportation Project," (Cambridge, MA: Collaborative for Development Action, February 2004), p. 5; accessed June 20, 2004 at *http://www.cdainc.com/cep/publications.php*
18. Ibid, p. 13.

PART **TWO**

The Market and Business

Business happens in markets. A business buys supplies, raw materials, and machinery in industrial markets; it finds workers in labor markets; it sells its finished products to retailers in wholesale markets; and the final sale to consumers happens in retail markets. The next two chapters look at the ethics of markets. Chapter 3 discusses the ethics of the market system as a whole: its moral justifications, strengths and weaknesses. Chapter 4 looks at the ethics of particular practices within the market system, like price-fixing, predatory pricing, bribery, and market concentration.

412
410
TT 213 PSA
PSA
PSA
TT 191 PSA
TT80
PSA
TT 095
MGM
PSA
PSA
TT166

The Business System: Government, Markets, and International Trade

Why did John Locke say government has no right to take anyone's private property?

Why did Adam Smith claim that government should not interfere with the free market?

What benefits did David Ricardo attribute to free trade?

What injustices did Karl Marx say were inherent in free market capitalism?

Shipping containers at one of the terminals of the Port of Singapore. As the world's busiest hub for containerized cargo, the Port of Singapore is at the center of international trade. Singapore's government has embraced globalization and supports free trade

INTRODUCTION

Listen to the Chapter Audio on mythinkinglab.com

globalization The process by which the economic and social systems of nations are connected together so that goods, services, capital, and knowledge move freely between nations.

Since about 1980, **globalization** has surged forward to a degree that is unprecedented in our world's history.[1] Globalization has connected nations together so that goods, services, capital, and knowledge increasingly flow freely between them. These are carried by ever faster and cheaper transportation and communication systems, and these flows are facilitated by free trade agreements and international institutions like the World Trade Organization and the World Bank. As nations have opened their borders to free trade with other nations, businesses have had to face numerous challenges. In every country, individual companies and entire industries have been wiped out as globalization has forced them to compete with companies in other parts of the world. Workers have found themselves jobless when companies have relocated factories to other nations with cheaper wages. And companies have been accused of manipulating the institutions that regulate trade between nations to enrich themselves at the expense of the poor. To understand these accusations consider how two companies, Swingline—a manufacturer of staplers—and Abbott Labs—a pharmaceutical company—each in different ways took advantage of the business opportunities globalization has provided.

Jack Linsky, a Ukrainian immigrant, invented the modern easy-to-use "Swingline" stapler. In 1925 he built a stapler factory in New York where he hired immigrants from everywhere. Linsky's workers liked him and with their hard work the company prospered until 1987 when he sold it for $210 million.[2] But globalization and WTO agreements in 1995 began allowing foreign companies to freely import and sell their copycat staplers in the U.S. By 1997 the company was struggling to compete against these companies whose labor costs were much lower than its own. In 2000 the company fired all of its workers at its New York plant, closed the factory and moved its operations to Nogales, Mexico.[3] There the new North American Free Trade Agreement (NAFTA) allowed the company to make Swingline staplers using Mexico's cheap labor and then import them into the U.S. without paying import tariffs.[4] Cheap labor was plentiful in Nogales because NAFTA had also allowed U.S. farmers to sell their corn in Mexico. Since the U.S. government gives its corn farmers $5 to $10 billion a year in subsidies, U.S. corn growers could sell their corn in Mexico for less than Mexican farmers could.[5] Between 1994 and 2004, 1.5 million Mexican corn farmers lost their only source of income and migrated to Nogales and other border cities to work for U.S. companies like Swingline. But by 2003 jobs in Mexico had began leaving the country and heading for China.[6] China's workers were paid even less than Mexican workers, and often worked in appalling "sweatshop" conditions. In 2010 the Swingline factory again fired all its workers, closed its Nogales factory, and contracted to have a Chinese factory make its staplers.

The example of Swingline raises a number of moral questions. Is it right for a company to abandon workers who have given decades of their lives to making it succeed? What obligations, if any, does a company have to the workers left behind when it moves to another country? Should government allow companies to move their operations to other countries in this way? What kind of obligations do companies have toward their foreign workers? As companies search for ever cheaper labor, will this produce a "race to the bottom" that will reduce workers' standard of living throughout the world? Is it good or bad for countries to enter "free trade" agreements that threaten the livelihoods of their workers? Is global free trade itself good or bad?

Global free trade has been criticized not only for the impact it has had on workers like Swingline's employees, but because of the impact it has had on all people, particularly those who live in poor nations. Many critics of free trade have argued that the international agreements and institutions that make free trade possible benefit global businesses, but harm the world's poor and powerless. To understand these criticisms, consider, how Abbott Laboratories responded when Thailand's government announced a new policy designed to provide its poorest people with a life-saving drug.

On March 21, 2007, Abbott Laboratories, a U.S. drug manufacturer with annual revenues of $26 billion and profits of $4.5 billion, angrily announced it would not allow seven of its unique new drugs to be sold in Thailand, including the HIV/AIDS drug Aluviathat, that, unlike similar drugs, did not have to be refrigerated in Thailand's hot climate. Abbott was punishing Thailand who had decided to make a cheap version of Kaletra, a drug that Abbott had developed and to which it held the patent. The head of the AIDS Healthcare Foundation said: "I am horrified that Abbott would deprive poor people in need of lifesaving medications, particularly for those living with HIV/AIDS, in a country as hard-hit by the epidemic as Thailand."[7]

With about 600,000 of its people sick with HIV/AIDS and an average annual income of only $2,190 per person, Thailand was struggling to provide its HIV/AIDS patients with medications called "antiretrovirals." Although HIV/AIDS is incurable, in 1996 scientists discovered that if HIV patients regularly took a combination of three "antiretroviral" drugs, the amount of the HIV virus in their bodies declined to where they could live healthy normal lives. But drug companies charged so much for the combination antiretroviral drugs—$10,000 to $15,000 per year in year 2000—that AIDS victims in poor developing countries could not afford them.[8]

In 2001, however, Cipla, an Indian drug company, began to make "generic" versions of the antiretroviral drug combinations for as little as $350 for a year's supply and by 2007 its price was below $100.[9] A "generic" drug is a chemically equivalent copy of a brand-name drug, but the company that makes it does not own the patent to the drug. Large drug companies discover, develop, and test new brand name drugs at an estimated cost of about $800 million per drug.[10] A company with a new drug can ask its government for a "patent" for the drug, and if granted, the patent recognizes that the drug formula is the property of the company and that it alone has a right to make that drug for a set number of years. The large U.S. and European drug companies held that without patents and respect for their property rights, they could not recover, and would have little incentive to pay, the huge costs needed to develop and test new drugs, and drug research would come to an end. The drug companies therefore objected to Cipla's action, especially when Cipla started to sell the low-priced generic versions of their drugs to other poor countries.

Until 1994, U.S. patent laws gave a new drug only 17 years of protection and only inside the United States. But in the early 1990s, U.S. drug companies began lobbying hard to get the U.S. government to pressure all countries to make patent laws part of the rules for the new World Trade Organization (WTO) that was then being formed.[11] The WTO was to be a group of countries that agreed to abide by rules that would establish free and open markets among themselves. Pushed by the U.S. drug companies who made lavish donations to politicians, officials of the U.S. government insisted that WTO rules should require all member nations to adopt strict patent and copyright laws like those of the United States. Although the poor nations strongly objected to this, when the WTO was finalized in 1995, its rules included an article entitled "Trade Related Aspects of Intellectual Property Rights" (TRIPS) which required all WTO countries to adopt patent and copyright laws modeled on U.S. laws.[12] Since it is difficult for a country to sell its goods to WTO nations unless it too belongs to the WTO, most nations joined the WTO in spite of their objections to TRIPS.

Under TRIPS, a patent given to a drug company by one WTO nation had to be respected by all other WTO nations for 20 years. The least developed or poorest countries, like India and Brazil, however, did not have to comply with TRIPS until 2006, and this deadline was later extended to 2016. TRIPS also included Article 31, which allowed an exception to its strict patent rules. Article 31 said that in case of "national emergencies," or "other circumstances of extreme urgency" a poor country could make a patented drug without the authorization of the company that held the patent. In 2001, the WTO issued a ruling affirming that Article 31 of TRIPS allowed a poor country to protect the health of its citizens by giving its own drug companies a "compulsory license" to make a patented drug (a compulsory license is one that a government forces a patent-holder to grant). The WTO ruling also stated that a poor country that could not manufacture drugs could instead import a patented drug that another poor country was making with a "compulsory license." Moreover, the WTO stated, each nation had the right "to determine the grounds upon which such licenses are granted." U.S. and European pharmaceutical companies had lobbied hard to defeat Article 31, but in the end enough WTO countries supported it and it had became an official WTO rule. The U.S. and European drug companies, however, vowed they would continue to oppose the rule and its use, especially by a company like Cipla that claimed TRIP rules allowed it to make and sell cheap copies of their patented drugs.

On January 25, 2007, Thailand announced that it was issuing a "compulsory license" to one of its own government-owned drug companies so it could make a generic version of Abbott's Kaletra. Kaletra was one of a new group of expensive "second-line" antiretroviral drugs Abbot had developed and patented. When an AIDS victim began treatment, the antiretroviral drugs he or she received was called a "first-line" treatment and it was relatively cheap since companies like Cipla could provide cheap generic versions. Often, however, the patient's HIV became resistant to the first-line drugs, and they stopped working. The patient then had to be given the newer antiretroviral drug combinations that were called a "second line" of treatment and that were expensive since only the large drug companies were making those. Thailand's government estimated that about 80,000 of its AIDS victims now needed a "second-line" drug like Abbott's Kaletra. However, it said, it could not afford even the "discounted" price of $2,200 Abbott insisted poor countries had to pay for a year's supply of Kaletra.

Abbott Laboratories said that if Thailand started making a version of Kaletra, it would be taking Abbott's property since the company held the patent and it had discovered, developed, and tested the drug using several hundred million dollars of its own money. Moreover, Abbott said, under its interpretation of TRIPS, Thailand had no right to ignore Abbott's patent simply because it did not want to pay for the drug; reluctance to pay did not constitute an "emergency."[13] The head of Doctors Without Borders in Thailand said of Abbott's position: "For me, it's just evil. It's appalling ... It reflects so badly on the multinational companies."[14]

The conflict between Thailand and Abbott Laboratories raises issues that have made globalization and free trade controversial, issues quite different from the labor issues raised by Swingline's move to Mexico and later to China. Many poor countries argue that the new free trade rules benefit multinational companies at the same time that they place poor countries at a disadvantage. Poor countries say that multinational companies—like the large drug companies—have been able to influence the rules that govern international trade and bend them to serve their own corporate interests. In the name of free trade, the rich nations have forced the poor nations to accept rules that benefit the companies of the rich nations, while ignoring the welfare of the people of poor nations. Moreover, critics argue, new forms of property—such as patents on drugs—have been developed that seem to actually conflict with free trade, since they restrict the free flow of the formulas and knowledge that constitute these new forms of "intellectual property."

These controversies over globalization and free trade are but the latest episodes in a great and centuries-long moral debate: Should governments impose restrictions on business activities and economic exchanges, or should they leave business firms free to pursue their own interests within free markets, and allow them also to trade freely with members of other nations? Do governments align themselves with the interests of wealthy corporations, and if so, is it right for them to do so? One side argues that free markets and free trade are defective because they cannot deal with many of the problems business activities create, such as unfair competition, global pollution, unfair labor practices, sweatshops, discrimination, and disregard for the wellbeing of the poor. The other side argues that government restrictions on business are bad because they violate their property rights and right to freedom, lead to unfairness, and leave us all worse off. This chapter examines these moral arguments for and against allowing businesses to operate in free markets and free trade systems.

Economic Systems

Arguments about free markets and free trade are arguments about economic systems. An **economic system** is the system a society (or group of societies) uses to provide the goods and services it needs to survive and flourish.[15] This system must accomplish two basic economic tasks. First, is the task of actually producing goods and services, which requires determining what will be produced, how it will be produced, and who will produce it. The second is the task of distributing these goods and services among its members, which requires determining who will get what and how much each will get. To accomplish these two tasks, economic systems rely on three kinds of social devices: traditions, commands, and markets. Each of these three provides a way to organize people's activities, a way to motivate people, and a way to decide who owns or controls society's productive resources.

economic system The system a society uses to provide the goods and services it needs to survive and flourish.

So-called primitive societies used economic systems based primarily on tradition. **Tradition-based societies** are small and rely on traditional communal roles and customs to carry out the two basic economic tasks. Individuals are motivated by the community's expressions of approval or disapproval, and the community's productive resources—such as its herds—are often owned in common. A small nomadic tribe, for example, that survives by hunting and herding might rely on the traditional roles of husband, wife, mother, father, son, and daughter to decide both who does what and who gets what and may hold its herd in common. Societies that are almost completely tradition-based exist even today among Bushmen, the Inuit, Kalahari hunters, and Bedouin tribes.

tradition-based societies Societies that rely on traditional communal roles and customs to carry out basic economic tasks.

Large modern societies carry out the two main economic tasks primarily through two very distinctive ways of organizing themselves: commands and markets.[16] In an economic system based primarily on **commands**, a government authority (a person or a group) makes the economic decisions about what enterprises must produce, which enterprises will produce it, and who will get it.[17] Productive resources such as land and factories are mostly owned or controlled by government and are considered to belong to the public or to "the people." Individuals are motivated to put forth the required effort by the rewards and punishments government doles out and by its exhortations to serve society. China, Viet Nam, North Korea, Cuba, the former Soviet Union, and several other nations, at different times, have run their economies primarily on the basis of commands.

command economy An economic system based primarily on a government authority (a person or a group) making the economic decisions about what is to be produced, who will produce it, and who will get it.

By contrast, in a system based primarily on **markets**, private companies make the main decisions about what they will produce and who will get it.[18] Productive resources like land and factories are owned and managed by private individuals, not by government, and are considered the individual's "private property." People are motivated to work primarily by the desire to get paid for voluntarily supplying the things others are willing to pay for. England in the nineteenth century is often cited as a prime example of an economy that was based primarily on a market system.

market economy An economic system based primarily on private individuals making the main decisions about what they will produce and who will get it.

Economies today contain elements of all three of these: traditions, commands, and markets.[19] The United States, for example, is highly "market-oriented," yet some citizens still consider some jobs (such as primary school teachers and nurses) to be "women's work," while others (like police officers and truck drivers) are "men's work," so for them "tradition" determines who does those jobs. Moreover, the U.S. government not only issues "commands" that regulate business, labor, and international trade, but also owns or has owned several important businesses, including the Export-Import Bank, the U.S. Postal Service, the Federal Prison Industries, Ginnie Mae, the Tennessee Valley Authority, Amtrak, the Corporation for Public Broadcasting, and several others. In 2010, the U.S. government acquired full or partial ownership of dozens of failing businesses including car companies (General Motors), banks (Citigroup), and insurance companies (AIG).

It would be undesirable to run an economy completely on the basis of traditions, or commands, or markets. If an economy was a pure market system, for example, with no economic interventions by government, there would be no constraints whatsoever on the property one could own or what one could do with it. Slavery would be entirely legal, as would prostitution and all drugs including hard drugs. Today, the governments of even the most market-oriented economies decree that there are some things that may not be owned (such as slaves), some things that may not be done with one's own property (such as pollution), some exchanges that are illegal (children's labor), and some exchanges that are imposed (through taxation). Such limitations on markets are intrusions of a command system: Government concern for the public welfare leads it to issue commands concerning which goods may or may not be produced or exchanged. Similarly, even under the almost all-encompassing command system of the former Soviet Union's harsh Stalinist regime, local markets—many of them so-called "black markets"—existed where workers could trade their wages for the goods they wanted.

Since the eighteenth century, debates have raged over whether economies should be based more on commands or on markets.[20] Should we have more government commands in the form of more economic regulations and more government control of business enterprises, or should government stand back and trust the economy more to the workings of the "market" and the decisions of private owners of companies? Sometimes these debates have been expressed in terms of whether economic activities should be more or less "free" of government "intrusions" and then the discussion is about "**free markets**" ("free," that is, of government limits) and "free trade."[21] Sometimes the debate is about "laissez-faire" policies, which, literally, is the French phrase for policies that "let us act" free of government controls.

free markets Markets in which each individual is able to voluntarily exchange goods with others and to decide what will be done with what he or she owns without interference from government.

Today, these debates continue on two levels: (1) whether a nation's own internal economy should be organized as a "free market" economy, and (2) whether exchanges between nations should be based on "free trade" principles. The reader should not confuse the two different levels of these debates, although the two levels are related. The debate at the first level asks whether a nation's government should regulate business exchanges between its citizens or, instead, allow its citizens to freely exchange goods with each other. The debate at the second level asks whether a nation's government should allow its citizens to freely trade goods with the citizens of other nations or, instead, impose tariffs, quotas, or other limits on the goods citizens may want to buy from foreign citizens. We can call the first the debate over free markets, and the second the debate over free trade. In this chapter, we will examine the arguments on both sides of these debates, which are, in the end, about the proper role of governments and of markets both nationally and internationally.

In analyzing these arguments on free markets and free trade, on government commands and markets, we in effect analyze what sociologists refer to as *ideologies*.[22] An **ideology** is a system of normative beliefs shared by members of some social group. The ideology expresses the group's answers to questions about human nature (e.g., Are human beings only motivated by economic incentives?), the basic purpose of our social institutions (e.g., What is the purpose of government?

ideology A system of normative beliefs shared by members of some social group.

Of business? Of property?), how societies actually function (e.g., Are markets really free? Does big business control government?), and the values society should try to protect (e.g., freedom, productivity, equality).

The ideologies that we here in the United States hold today incorporate ideas drawn from Adam Smith, John Locke, David Ricardo, and other influential thinkers whose normative views we will examine and evaluate in this chapter. We discuss these ideas not only because of the significant influence they have on our ideologies, but because many people today argue that these ideologies must be adjusted if they are to meet the contemporary needs of business and society.[23] It would be a valuable exercise for the reader to identify the ideology he or she holds and to examine and criticize its elements while reading this chapter.

We will begin this chapter by looking at two important arguments for free markets in Sections 3.1 and 3.2. The first argument, which we examine in Section 3.1, originated with John Locke and is based on a theory of moral rights that uses many of the concepts we discussed in the second section of Chapter 2. The second argument in favor of free markets, which we examine in Section 3.2, was first clearly proposed by Adam Smith and is based on the utilitarian principles we discussed in the first section of Chapter 2. In Section 3.3, we turn from free-market arguments to focus on international free-trade arguments. Here we will discuss the ideas of David Ricardo, whose life overlapped that of Adam Smith and who, like Smith, based his views about free trade on utilitarian principles. Finally, in Section 3.4, we will discuss the important but opposing arguments of Karl Mark, who held that without government controls, free market systems promote injustice both nationally and internationally.

3.1 Free Markets and Rights: John Locke

One of the most popular cases for allowing government to play only a very limited role in markets derives from the idea that human beings have certain "natural rights" that only a free market system can protect. The two natural rights that free markets are supposed to protect are the right to freedom and the right to private property. Free markets are supposed to preserve the right to freedom insofar as they enable each individual to voluntarily exchange goods with others free from the coercive power of government. They are supposed to preserve the right to private property insofar as each individual is free to decide what will be done with what he or she owns without interference from government.

John Locke (1632–1704), an English political philosopher, is generally credited with developing the idea that human beings have a "natural right" to liberty and a "natural right" to private property.[24] Locke argued that if there were no governments, human beings would find themselves in a *state of nature*. In this state of nature, each individual would be the political equal of all others and would be perfectly free of any constraints other than the *law of nature*—that is, the moral principles that God gave to humanity and that each individual can discover by the use of God-given reason. As he puts it, in a state of nature, everyone would be in:

> a *state of perfect freedom* to order their actions and dispose of their possessions and persons as they think fit, within the bounds of the law of nature, without asking leave, or depending upon the will of any other man. A state also of equality, wherein all the power and jurisdiction is reciprocal, no one having more than another... without subordination or subjection [to another].... But ... the state of nature has a law of nature to govern it, which obliges everyone: and reason, which

> is that law, teaches all mankind, who will but consult it, that being all equal and independent, no one ought to harm another in his life, health, liberty, or possessions.[25]

According to Locke, the law of nature "teaches" that each has a right to liberty and that, consequently, "no one can be put out of this [natural] estate and subjected to the political power of another without his own consent."[26] The law of nature also informs us that all have rights of ownership over their bodies, their labor, and the products of their labor, and that these ownership rights are "natural"—that is, they are not invented or created by government nor are they the result of a government grant:

> Every man has a property in his own person: This nobody has a right to but himself. The labor of his body, and the work of his hands, we may say, are properly his. Whatsoever then he removes out of the state that nature has provided and left it in, he has mixed his labor with, and joined to it something that is his own, and thereby makes it his property.... [For] this labor being the unquestionable property of the laborer, no man but he can have a right to what that [labor] is once joined to, at least where there is enough, and as good, left in common for others.[27]

Quick Review 3.1

In Locke's State of Nature

- All persons are free and equal.
- Each person owns his body and labor, and whatever he mixes his own labor into.
- People's enjoyment of life, liberty, and property are unsafe and insecure.
- People agree to form a government to protect and preserve their right to life, liberty, and property.

The state of nature, however, is a perilous state in which individuals are in constant danger of being harmed by others, "for all being kings as much as he, every man his equal, and the greater part no strict observers of equity and justice, the enjoyment of the property he has in this state is very unsafe, very insecure."[28] Consequently, individuals inevitably organize themselves into a political body and create a government whose primary purpose is to provide the protection of their natural rights that is lacking in the state of nature. Because the citizen consents to government "only with an intention... to preserve himself, his liberty and property... the power of the society or legislature constituted by them can never be supposed to extend farther" than what is needed to preserve these rights.[29] Government cannot interfere with any citizen's natural right to liberty and natural right to property except insofar as such interference is needed to protect one person's liberty or property from being invaded by others.

Although Locke never explicitly used his theory of natural rights to argue for free markets, several twentieth-century authors have employed his theory for this purpose.[30] Friedrich A. Hayek, Murray Rothbard, Gottfried Dietze, Eric Mack, and many others have claimed that each person has the right to liberty and property that Locke credited to every human being and that, consequently, government must leave individuals free to exchange their labor and their property as they voluntarily choose.[31] Only a free private enterprise exchange economy, in which government stays out of the market and in which government protects the property rights of private individuals, allows for such voluntary exchanges. The existence of the **Lockean rights** to liberty and property, then, implies that societies should incorporate private property institutions and free markets.

Lockean rights
The right to life, liberty, and property.

Locke's views on the right to private property have had a significant influence on American institutions of property, an influence that has continued to be felt in today's computer society. First, and most important, throughout most of its early history, U.S. law held to the theory that individuals have an almost absolute right to do whatever they want with their property and that government has only a limited right to interfere with or confiscate an individual's private property even for the good of society. The Fifth Amendment to the U.S. Constitution states that "No person shall be... deprived of life, liberty, or property without due process of law; nor shall private property be taken for public use, without just compensation." This amendment (which quotes Locke's phrase, "life, liberty, and property") ultimately derives from Locke's view that private property rights are established "by nature" (when an individual "mixes" labor into a thing) and so are prior to government. Government does not grant or create private property rights. Instead, it must respect and protect the property rights that are naturally generated through labor and trade.

It is only relatively recently, in the late nineteenth and twentieth centuries, that this Lockean view began to give way in the United States to the more "socialist" view that government may limit an individual's private property rights for the good of society. Even today in the United States, there is a strong presumption that government does not create property rights, but must respect and enforce the property rights that individuals create through their own efforts. U.S. law explicitly recognizes, for example, that if a person produces a literary text, the text is his property even without a government-issued copyright. It is important to see that this Lockean view of property is not universal. In some countries, such as Japan, resources are not seen as things over which individuals have an absolute private property right. Instead, in Japan, as in many other Asian societies, resources are seen as functioning primarily to serve the needs of society as a whole, and so the property rights of individuals should give way to the needs of society when there is a conflict between the two.

Second, underlying many U.S. laws regarding property and ownership is Locke's view that, when a person expends labor and effort to create or improve a thing, that person "by nature" acquires property rights over that thing. If a person writes a book or software program, for example, then that book or software program automatically becomes the property of the person who "mixed" his labor into it. A person may, of course, agree to "sell" labor to an employer, and thereby agree that the employer will gain ownership of whatever the person creates. However, even such employee agreements assume that the employee has the right to "sell" labor, and this means that the employee must have been the original owner of the labor used to create the object. Software developers, for example, are declared the rightful owners of the software programs they develop not only because they have invested a great deal of time and energy into developing these programs, but also because they have paid the software engineers who "sold" them their labor to produce these programs. These views on property, of course, all assume that "private property" is really a bundle of rights. To say that X is my private property is to say that I have a right to use it, consume it, sell it, give it away, loan it, rent it, keep anything of value it produces, change it, destroy it, and, most important, exclude others from doing any of these things without my consent.

Let's consider the actions of Abbott Laboratories in light of Locke's views. Recall that Abbot Laboratories withheld several lifesaving drugs from Thailand's people when their government announced its intention to manufacture a drug that Abbott had patented. Abbott claimed that Thailand was "stealing" the company's "intellectual property."[32] Regardless of what any government or other ruling body might say, Abbott insisted, it had created the formula for the drug and invested the money needed to develop it, and so it was Abbott's property and no one else had a right to use it without Abbott's authorization. Abbott's position was based on the Lockean view that private property is created by one's labor and not by government. The right to property, like the right to liberty, are prior to, or more basic than, government's authority and, as Locke insisted, government is created to protect these fundamental rights. The head of a pharmaceutical association that represented Abbot and other multinational drug companies said: "After the company does 10 years of research, and then suddenly the Thai government would like to impose a compulsory license, taking away their property, their assets—this is not right."[33]

Thailand's government, on the other hand, issued a report in which it stated that it had "fully complied with [all] the national and international legal frameworks," including TRIPS.[34] It pointed out that the World Trade Organization (WTO) had explicitly declared that to protect its citizens' health, a country could issue a compulsory license and manufacture a drug without the authorization of the company that held the patent. Consequently, Thailand said, it was not wrong to manufacture the drug even though Abbott held the patent since the legal framework that created the patent and turned the drug formula into a form of "property," explicitly allowed them to use the formula. Thailand's view, then, was that property rights are created by government and its laws, a view that is decidedly unLockean.[35] Also unlike Locke, Thailand held that property rights are not absolute. Thailand said in its report that its decision was based on its "commitment to put the right to life above trade interests." Property rights, then, are limited by "the right to life" because human life is more important than the international rules that protect "trade interests" by protecting property rights.

The views of both Abbot Laboratories and Thailand, then, were shaped by their ideologies, i.e., by their views about which rights are most basic, about the purpose of government, and about the nature of private property.

Criticisms of Lockean Rights

Criticisms of the Lockean defense of the right to liberty both within and outside of markets, have focused on four of its major weaknesses: (1) the assumption that individuals have the "natural rights" Locke claimed they have, (2) the conflict between these negative rights and positive rights, (3) the conflict between these Lockean rights and the principles of justice, and (4) the individualistic assumptions Locke makes and their conflict with the demands of caring.

First, the Lockean defense of free markets rests on the assumption that people have rights to liberty and property that take precedence over all other rights. If humans do not have the overriding rights to liberty and property, then the fact that free markets would preserve the rights does not mean a great deal. Neither Locke nor his twentieth-century followers, however, have provided the arguments needed to establish that human beings have such "natural" rights. Locke merely asserted that, "reason . . . teaches all mankind, who will but consult it" that these rights exist.[36] Instead of arguing for these rights, therefore, Locke fell back on the bare assertion that the existence of these rights is "self-evident": All rational human beings are supposed to be able to intuit that the alleged rights to liberty and to property exist. Many reasonable people, however, say they have tried but failed to have this intuition.[37]

Locke's failure to provide arguments for his view will be clearer if we look more closely at what he says about the natural right to property. Locke says that when a person "mixes" labor into some object that is unclaimed, the object automatically (naturally) becomes that person's property. For example, if I find a piece of driftwood on a seashore and whittle it into a pretty statue, the statue becomes my property because I have taken something of mine—my labor—and "mixed" it into the wood so as to make it more valuable. Investing effort and work into making something more valuable makes that thing mine. But why should this be? As the philosopher Robert Nozick has asked, if I "mix" my labor into something that is not yet mine, then why isn't this just a way of losing my labor?[38] Suppose that I own a cup of water and I throw my cup of water into the ocean so that I mix my water with the *unowned* water of the ocean. Does the ocean become "mine"? Clearly, in this case at least, mixing something of mine into something that is not mine is merely a way of losing what was mine, not a way of acquiring something that was not mine. Why is it that when I invest my work in improving or changing some object so as to make it more valuable, that object becomes my "property"? Locke provides no answer to this question, apparently thinking that it is "self-evident."

Second, even if human beings have a natural right to liberty and to property, it does not follow that these rights must override all other rights. The right to liberty and to property are "negative" rights in the sense defined in Chapter 2. As we saw there, negative rights can conflict with people's positive rights. For example, the negative right to liberty may conflict with someone else's positive right to food, medical care, housing, or clean air. Why must we believe that in such cases the negative right has greater priority than the positive right? Critics argue that we have no reason to believe that the rights to liberty and property are overriding. Consequently, we also have no reason to be persuaded by the argument that free markets must be preserved because they protect this right.[39]

The third major criticism of the Lockean defense of free markets is based on the idea that free markets create unjust inequalities.[40] In a free market economy, a person's productive power is proportioned to the amount of labor or property already possessed. Those individuals who have accumulated a great deal of wealth and who have access to education and training will be able to accumulate even more wealth by purchasing more productive assets. Individuals who own no property, who are unable to work, or who are unskilled (such as the handicapped, infirm, poor, aged) will be unable to buy any goods at all without help from the government. As a result, without government intervention, the gap between the richest and poorest widens until large disparities of wealth emerge. Unless government intervenes to adjust the distribution of property that results from free markets, large groups of citizens will remain poor while others grow ever richer.

To prove their point, critics cite the high poverty levels and large inequalities evident in "free market" nations such as the United States. In 2008, for example, 39.8 million Americans, or 13.2 percent of the population, were living in poverty; the same year the richest 20 percent of U.S. households had an average income of $171,057.[41] In 2008, the poorest 20 percent of U.S. households had an average income of $11,984 while the average income of the richest 5 percent of U.S. households was $322,881 or 27 times the average of the poorest 20 percent.[42] Some 17 million U.S. households—about 51 million people—suffered from hunger during 2008 because they did not have enough food to meet the basic needs of all household members.[43] About 46.3 million people had no health insurance during 2008.[44] Between 2.3 million and 3.5 million people (1.35 million of them children) are homeless in a given year.[45] In contrast, the top 1 percent of the population held almost half of America's net financial wealth, owned more than a third of the nation's total net worth, received one-fifth of the country's income, and lived in households worth an average of $18,529,000.[46] Critics point to the highly unequal distribution of income and wealth found in the United States, as Table 3.1 indicates. By standard measures of inequality, such as the so-called "Gini Index," U.S. inequality has been rising steadily (see Figures 3.1 and 3.2). Figure 3.3 shows how the richest 20 percent of U.S. households now take in as much income as all the rest combined.

Table 3.1 *Distribution of Income and Wealth Among Americans, 2007*

Group	Percent of Total U.S. Income	Percent of Total U.S. Financial Wealth	Percent of Total U.S. Net Worth	Average Household Net Worth	Percent of Total U.S. Stock
Top 1%	21.3	42.7	34.6	$18,529,000	38.3
Top 20%	61.4	93.0	85.0	$2,278,000	91.1
Second 20%	17.8	6.8	10.9	$291,000	6.4
Third 20%	11.1	1.3	4.0	$71,200	1.9
Bottom 40%	9.6	–1.0	0.2	$2,200	0.6

("Top 20%" includes "Top 1%"; the negative sign under Financial Wealth indicates debt.)

Source: Edward N. Wolff "Recent Trends in Household Wealth In the United States: Rising Debt and the Middle-Class Squeeze—An Update to 2007," working paper 589 in the Levy Economics Institute Working Paper Collection, March 2010, accessed June 2, 2010 at *www.levyinstitute.org/pubs/wp_589.pdf.*

Figure 3.1
View the Image on mythinkinglab.com

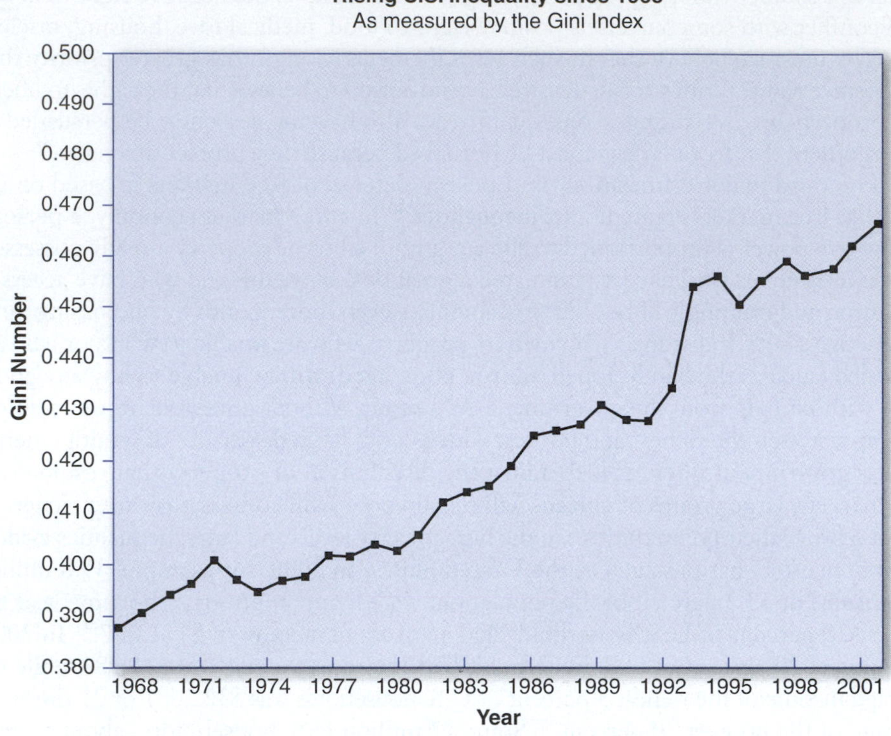

Figure 3.2
View the Image on mythinkinglab.com

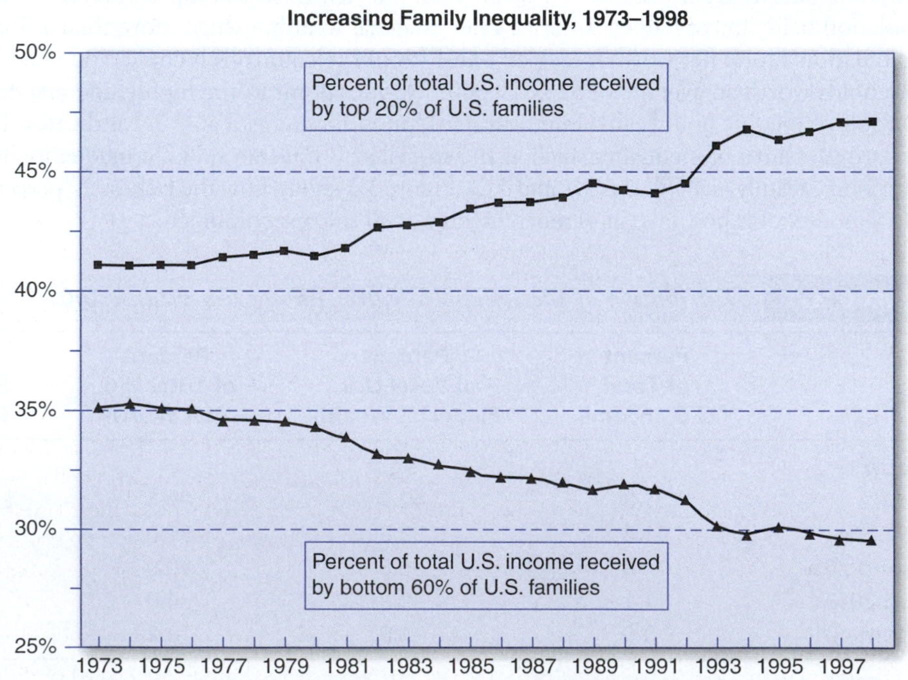

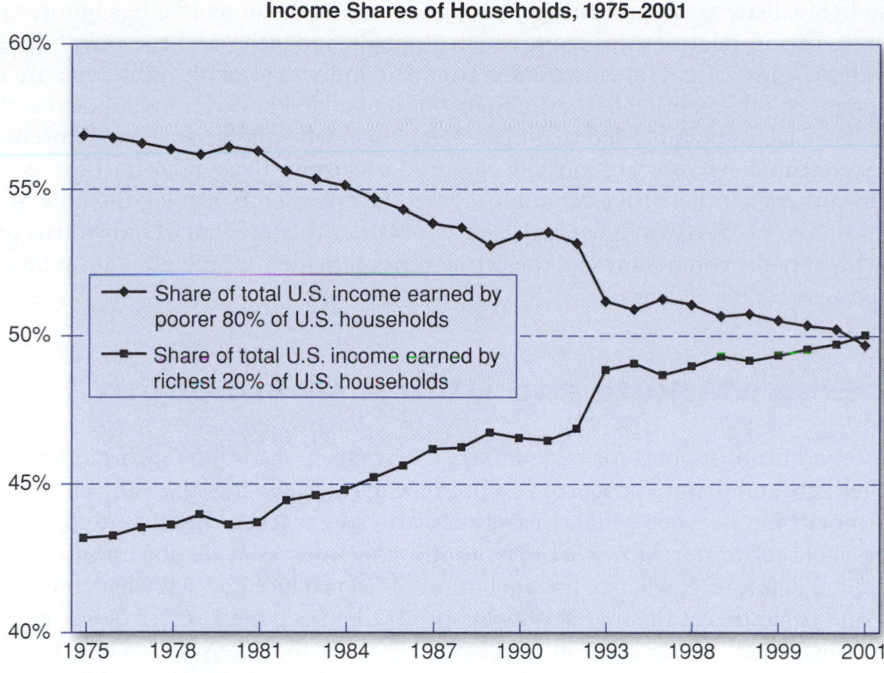

Figure 3.3
View the **Image** on **mythinkinglab.com**

Inequality on a global level has also increased, driven in part by the forces of globalization. Recall the case of Swingline, the company that manufactures staplers and staples. When the company left its workers behind in New York and moved to Mexico, the economic standing of the abandoned workers declined. When the company then left Mexico and moved to China because of its cheaper wage policies, the living standards of its abandoned workers once again went down. Thus, free trade agreements and globalization have enabled companies to move their operations from one country to another, and as a result the working poor of the world, many claim, keep getting poorer and this ultimately increases inequality.

Finally, critics have argued, Locke's argument assumes human beings are atomistic individuals with personal rights to liberty and property that flow from their individual nature independently of their relations to the larger community. Because these rights are assumed to be prior to and independent of the community, the community can make no claims on the property or freedom of the individual. However, critics claim that these individualistic assumptions are completely false: They ignore the key role of caring relationships in human societies and the demands of caring that arise from these relationships. Critics of Locke point out that humans are born dependent on the care of others; as they grow, they remain dependent on the care of others to acquire what they need to become able adults. Even when they become adults, they depend on the caring cooperation of others in their communities for virtually everything they do or produce. Even an individual's liberty depends on others. The degree of liberty a person has depends on what the person can do: The less a person can do, the less she is free to do. But a person's abilities depend on what the person learns from those who care for her, as well as on what others care to help her to do or allow her to do.

Similarly, the "property" that a person produces through labor depends ultimately on the skills acquired from those who cared for him or her and on the cooperative work of others in the community such as employees. Even one's identity—the sense of who one is as a member of the various communities and groups to which one belongs—depends on one's relationships with others in the community. In short,

Quick Review 3.2

Weaknesses of Locke's Views on Rights

- Locke does not demonstrate that individuals have "natural" rights to life, liberty, and property.
- Locke's natural rights are negative rights and he does not show these override conflicting positive rights.
- Locke's rights imply that markets should be free, but free markets can be unjust and can lead to inequalities.
- Locke wrongly assumes human beings are atomistic individuals.

the individualistic assumptions built into Locke's view of human beings ignores the concrete caring relationships from which a person's identity and the possibility of individual rights arise. Humans are not atomistic individuals with rights that are independent of others; instead, they are persons embedded in caring relationships that make those rights possible and that make the person who and what she is. Moreover, critics continue, persons are morally required to sustain these relationships and to care for others as others have cared for them. The community can legitimately make claims on the property of individuals and can restrict the freedom of individuals precisely because the community and the caring it has provided are the ultimate source of that property and freedom.

3.2 Free Markets and Utility: Adam Smith

The second major support for free markets derives from the utilitarian argument that free markets and private property will produce greater benefits than any amount of government interference could. In a system with free markets and private property, buyers will seek to purchase what they want for themselves at the lowest prices they can find. Therefore, it will pay private businesses to produce and sell what consumers want and to do this at the lowest possible prices. To keep their prices down, private businesses will try to cut back on the costly resources they consume. Thus, the free market, coupled with private property, ensures that the economy is producing what consumers want, that prices are at the lowest levels possible, and that resources are efficiently used. The economic utility of society's members is thereby maximized.

Adam Smith (1723–1790), the "father of modern economics," is the originator of this utilitarian argument for the free market.[47] According to Smith, when private individuals are left free to seek their own interests in free markets, they will inevitably be led to further the public welfare by an **invisible hand**:

invisible hand According to Adam Smith, the market competition that drives self-interested individuals to act in ways that serve society.

> By directing [his] industry in such a manner as its produce may be of the greatest value, [the individual] intends only his own gain, and he is in this, as in many other cases, led by an invisible hand to promote an end that was no part of his intention.... By pursuing his own interest he frequently promotes that of society more effectively than when he really intends to promote it.[48]

The "invisible hand," of course, is market competition. Every producer seeks to make a living by using private resources to produce and sell those goods that the producer perceives people want to buy. In a competitive market, a multiplicity of such private businesses must all compete with each other for the same buyers. To attract customers, therefore, each seller is forced not only to supply what consumers want, but to drop the price of goods as close as possible to "what it really costs the person who brings it to market."[49] To increase his or her profits, each producer will pare costs, thereby reducing the resources consumed. The competition produced by a multiplicity of self-interested private sellers serves to lower prices, conserve resources, and make producers respond to consumer desires. Motivated only by self-interest, private businesses are led to serve society. As Smith stated the matter in a famous passage:

> It is not from the benevolence of the butcher, the baker, and the brewer that we expect our dinner, but from their regard for their own self-interest. We address ourselves not to their humanity, but to their self-love, and never talk to them of our own necessities, but of their advantages.[50]

Smith also argued that a system of competitive markets allocates resources efficiently among the various industries of a society.[51] When the supply of a certain commodity is not enough to meet the demand, buyers bid the price of the commodity upward until it rises above what Smith called the *natural price* (i.e., the price that just covers the costs of producing the commodity, including the going rate of profit obtainable in other markets). Producers of that commodity then reap profits higher than those available to producers of other commodities. The higher profits induce producers of those other products to switch their resources into the production of the more profitable commodity. As a result, the shortage of that commodity disappears and its price sinks back to its natural level. Conversely, when the supply of a commodity is greater than the quantity demanded, the resulting surplus causes its price to fall, inducing its producers to switch their resources into the production of other, more profitable commodities. The fluctuating prices of commodities in a system of competitive markets then forces producers to allocate their resources to those industries where they are most in demand and to withdraw resources from industries where there is a relative oversupply of commodities. The market, in short, allocates resources so as to most efficiently meet consumer demand, thereby promoting social utility.

The best policy of a government that hopes to advance the public welfare, therefore, is to do nothing: to let each individual pursue his self-interest in "natural liberty" so he is free to buy and sell whatever he wishes.[52] Any interventions in the market by government can only serve to interrupt the self-regulating effect of competition and reduce its many beneficial consequences by creating either surpluses or shortages. The view that government interventions in the market are not beneficial, was the view that Abbott Laboratories adopted when it objected to Thailand's decision to manufacturer Abbott's patented drug. Abbott argued that the high prices it put on its drugs were necessary to recover the high costs of developing them, and if companies could not charge these high prices they would no longer have any incentive to continue developing new drugs, which would induce a shortage of new drug development. When Thailand's government intervened in the drug market by taking Abbott's patented drug, then, it interfered with Abbott's ability to recover its costs and to some extent, removed Abbott's incentive to continue developing new AIDS drugs, thereby potentially lowering the future supply of new AIDS drugs. Thus, in the long run, the government's intervention in the drug market was hurting its own people. Government interventions in the market, as Smith argued, will always end up harming consumers.

Quick Review 3.3

According to Adam Smith

- Market competition ensures the pursuit of self-interest in markets advances the public's welfare which is a utilitarian argument.
- Government interference in markets lowers the public's welfare by creating shortages or surpluses.

In the early twentieth century, economists Ludwig von Mises and Friedrich A. Hayek supplemented Smith's market theories by an ingenious argument.[53] They argued that not only does a system of free markets and private ownership serve to allocate resources efficiently, but it is in principle, impossible for the government or any human being to allocate resources with the same efficiency. Human beings cannot allocate resources efficiently because they can never have enough information nor calculate fast enough to coordinate in an efficient way the hundreds of thousands of daily exchanges required by a complex industrial economy. In a free market, high prices indicate that additional resources are needed to meet consumer demand, and they motivate producers to allocate their resources to those consumers. The market thereby allocates resources efficiently from day to day through the pricing mechanism. If a government were to try to do the same thing, von Mises and Hayek argued, it would have to know from day to day what things each consumer desired, what materials each producer would need to produce the countless things consumers desired, and would then have to calculate how best to allocate resources among interrelated producers so as to enable them to meet consumer desires. Von Mises and Hayek claimed that the infinite quantity of detailed bits

ON THE EDGE

Commodification or How Free Should Free Markets Be?

To "commodify" something is to treat it as, or turn it into, a commodity that can be bought and sold. Many people think we should be free to commodify whatever we want. Take Judge Richard Posner who sits on the U.S. Court of Appeals for the Seventh Circuit in Chicago. In an article, "The Economics of the Baby Shortage: A Modest Proposal," he pointed out that there are more couples who want to adopt a baby than there are babies up for adoption. He suggests that this "shortage" could be fixed by starting a "baby market" in which available babies could be sold and couples that want to adopt could buy them. In such a "baby market," he pointed out, a shortage of babies would cause their price to rise, and rising prices would lead to more babies being put up for sale and fewer couples stepping up to buy them, which would solve the shortage. There are other things besides babies that people would like to commodify but which the government does not allow such as body parts, sex, and hard drugs. In the United States, 80,000 sick people are on waiting lists for kidneys, but there are not enough donors willing to donate a kidney for free, (or enough recently deceased and suitable cadavers) so about 3,500 people on this list die each year. Some business entrepreneurs have started (illegal) brokerage services through which Americans can buy kidneys (or corneas, eyes, skin, and half-livers) from poor people in India, Pakistan, Iraq, Moldova, Romania, China, Peru, and Russia. The broker will charge the American $150,000 for a kidney transplant, pay about $10,000 to a poor person somewhere who is willing to sell a kidney for that price, and have the operation performed in South Africa. For example, an Iraqi, Raad Bader al-Muhssin, who was having trouble supporting his family when his wife got cancer, quickly accepted when he was offered $12,000 for one of his kidneys:

> I lived my whole life a poor man and was afraid my children were going to have the same fate and my wife would die because we do not have money to help her. It is [my] one chance in life. I still have a healthy kidney and with the money I got I will never be humiliated again. My sons returned to school and our life changed.

Many people would like government to allow the open sale of sexual intimacies and affection, but since selling sex is illegal in all states but Nevada, "sex workers" must secretly market their services online and in the Yellow Pages as "escorts." Others would like governments to allow people to freely buy and sell "hard" drugs like cocaine and heroin, as in some countries like Spain, Mexico, Portugal, and Italy.

1. Does commodification of a thing change the way we think of it? Is there anything that should not be commodified? Why or why not?
2. Explain why each of the above proposals for expanding the free market is a good, or a bad idea. What would John Locke and Adam Smith say about your explanations?

Sources: Afif Sarhan, "Helpless Iraquis Sell Their Organs," *QatarLiving.Com*, October 17, 2009 accessed June 15, 2010 at *http://www.qatarliving.com/node/754107*; Larry Rohter, "The Organ Trade: A Global Black Market," *The New York Times*, May 23, 2004; "The International Organ Trafficking Market," National Public Radio, July 30, 2009, transcript accessed June 15, 2010 at *http://www.npr.org/templates/story/story.php?storyId=111379908*; Larry Smith, "Does the War on Drugs Still Make Sense?", *The New Black Magazine*, accessed June 10, 2010 at *http://www.thenewblackmagazine.com/view.aspx?index=638*

of information and the astronomical number of calculations that such an government would need to make were beyond the capacity of any group of human beings. Thus, not only do free markets allocate goods efficiently, but it is quite impossible for government planners to duplicate their performance.

Although Adam Smith did not discuss the notion of private property at great length, it is a key assumption of his views. Before individuals can come together in markets to sell things to each other, they must have some agreement about what each individual "owns" and what each individual has the right to "sell" to others. Unless a society has a system of private property that allocates its goods to individuals, that society cannot have a free market system. For this reason, Adam Smith assumed that a society with free markets would have a private property system, although he gave no explicit arguments showing that a system of private property was better than, say, a system where all productive resources were "owned" in common by everyone or by government. Earlier philosophers, however, had provided arguments in support of a private property system that, like Smith's own arguments for free markets, were based on utilitarian considerations. In the thirteenth century, for example, philosopher Thomas Aquinas argued that society should not rely on a property system in which people own all things "in common." Instead, society would prosper best if its resources were owned by individuals who would have an interest in improving and caring for those resources. A private property system, Aquinas argued:

> ...is necessary to human life for three reasons. First because every man is more careful to procure what is for himself alone than that which is common to many or to all: since each one would shirk the labor and leave to another that which concerns the community.... Secondly, because human affairs are conducted in more orderly fashion if each man is charged with taking care of some particular thing himself, whereas there would be confusion if everyone had to look after any one thing indeterminately. Thirdly, because a more peaceful state is ensured to man if each one is contented with his own. Hence it is to be observed that quarrels arise more frequently where there is no division of the things possessed.[54]

In the view that Aquinas proposed, private property is not something that is "naturally" produced when labor is "mixed" into things, as Locke claims. Instead, private property is a social construct, an artificial, but beneficial, social institution that we create and that can be shaped in numerous ways. These utilitarian arguments in favor of a private property system over a system of common ownership have often been repeated. In particular, many philosophers have repeated the argument that, without a private property system in which individuals get the benefits that come from caring for the resources they own, individuals would stop working because they would have no incentive to work.[55] A private property system is best because it provides incentives for individuals to invest their time, work, and effort in improving and exploiting the resources they own and whose benefits they know they will personally receive.

Quick Review 3.4

Additional Support for Adam Smith

- Hayek and von Mises argued governments should not interfere in markets because they cannot have enough information to allocate resources as efficiently as free markets.
- Smith assumes a system of private property like Aquinas defends with the utilitarian argument that private ownership leads to better care and use of resources than common ownership.

Criticisms of Adam Smith

Critics of Smith's classic utilitarian argument in defense of free markets and his assumptions regarding private property have attacked him on a variety of fronts. The most common criticism is that the argument rests on unrealistic assumptions.[56] Smith's arguments assume, first, that the impersonal forces of supply and demand will force prices down to their lowest levels because the sellers of products are so numerous and each enterprise is so small that no one seller can control the price of a product. This assumption was perhaps true enough in Smith's day, when the largest firms employed only a few dozen men and a multitude of small shops and petty merchants competed for the consumer's attention. However, today many industries and markets are completely or partially monopolized, and the small firm is no longer the rule. In these monopolized industries, where one or a few large enterprises are able to set their own prices, it is no longer true that prices necessarily move to their lowest levels. The monopoly power of the industrial giants enables them to keep prices at artificially high levels and production at artificially low levels.

Many observers, for example, have pointed out that patents are a form of monopoly. A monopoly is a market in which there is only one seller. When a company is issued a patent for a drug it has developed, it alone has the right to sell that drug, so it has a monopoly in that drug. If the drug is able to cure some important disease, then the company will often be able to set the price for that drug as high as it wants to set it. In a free market, there are no limits on the price a monopolist can charge for its drugs. As we saw in the case of Abbott Laboratories who had patents on certain drugs that could help "cure" AIDS, the price at which it sold those drugs was so high that they were out of the reach of people in poor countries like Thailand. Abbott set the price of its AIDS drug Kaletra, for example, at $7,000 a year in most countries, and at $2,200 a year for Thailand. Other patented AIDs drugs could be sold for as much as $12,000 a year by companies that had patents that gave them a monopoly on those drugs. In monopolized "free markets" like these, prices do not move to their lowest levels as Adam Smith suggested they would.

Second, critics claim, Smith's arguments assume that all the resources used to produce a product will be paid for by the manufacturer who will try to reduce these costs to maximize profits. As a result, there is a tendency toward a more efficient utilization of society's resources. This assumption does not hold when manufacturers of a product consume resources for which they do not have to pay and on which they, therefore, do not try to economize. For example, when manufacturers use up clean air by polluting it, or when they impose health costs by dumping toxic chemicals into rivers, lakes, and seas, they are using resources of society for which they do not pay. Consequently, there is no reason for them to attempt to minimize these costs, and social waste is the result. Such waste is a particular instance of a more general problem that Smith's analysis ignored. Smith failed to take into account the external effects that business activities often have on parties in their surrounding environment. Pollution is one example of such effects, but there are others, such as the effects on society of introducing an advanced technology, the psychological effects increased mechanization has had on laborers, the harmful effects that handling dangerous products has on the health of workers, and the economic shocks that result when natural resources are depleted for short-term gains. For example, the U.S. workers that the Swingline stapler company abandoned in New York when it moved to Mexico, and the Mexican workers it abandoned in Nogales when it moved to China, paid the costs of Swingline's moves as it searched for cheaper labor. Smith ignored external costs like these which the firm imposes on other parties and he assumed, instead, that the firm is a self-contained agent whose activities affect only itself and its buyers. A firm's activities, however, often have spill-over effects that harm third parties, even as they help the firm lower its costs and increase its profits.

Third, critics claim, Smith's analysis wrongly assumes that every human being is motivated only by a "natural" and self-interested desire for profit. Smith, at least in *The Wealth of Nations*, assumes that in all dealings a person "intends only his own gain."[57] Human nature follows the rule of "economic rationality": Give away as little as you can in return for as much as you can get. Because a human being "intends only his own gain" anyway, the best economic arrangement is one that recognizes this "natural" motivation and allows it free play in competitive markets that force self-interest to serve the public interest. However, this theory of human nature, critics have claimed, is clearly false. First, human beings regularly show a concern for the good of others and constrain their self-interest for the sake of the rights of others. Even when buying and selling in markets, the constraints of honesty and fairness affect our conduct. Second, the critics claim, it is not necessarily "rational" to follow the rule "give away as little as you can for as much as you can get." In numerous situations, everyone is better off when everyone shows concern for others, and it is then rational to show such concern. Third, critics have argued, if human beings often behave like "rational economic men," this is not because such behavior is natural, but because the widespread adoption of competitive market relations forces humans to relate to each other as "rational economic men." The market system of a society makes humans selfish, and this widespread selfishness then makes us think the profit motive is "natural."[58] It is the institutions of capitalism that engender selfishness, materialism, and competitiveness. In actual fact, human beings are born with a natural tendency to show concern for other members of their species (e.g., in their families). A major moral defect of a society built around competitive markets, in fact, is that within such societies this natural benevolent tendency toward virtue is gradually replaced by self-interested tendencies toward vice. In short, such societies are morally defective because they encourage morally bad character.

Quick Review 3.5

Criticisms of Smith's Argument

- Rests on unrealistic assumption that there are no monopoly companies.
- Falsely assumes that all the costs of manufacturing something are paid by manufacturer, which ignores the costs of pollution.
- Falsely assumes human beings are motivated only by a self-interested desire for profit.
- Unlike what Hayek and von Mises said in support of Smith, some government planning and regulation of markets is possible and desirable.

As for the argument of von Mises and Hayek—that human planners cannot allocate resources efficiently—the examples of the French, Dutch, and Swedes have demonstrated that planning within some sectors of the economy is not quite as impossible as they imagined.[59] Moreover, the argument of von Mises and Hayek was answered on theoretical grounds by the socialist economist Oskar Lange, who demonstrated that a "central planning board" could efficiently allocate goods in an economy without having to know everything about consumers and producers and without engaging in impossibly elaborate calculations.[60] All that is necessary is for the central planners to receive reports on the sizes of the inventories of producers and price their commodities accordingly. Surplus inventories would indicate that lowering of prices was necessary, whereas inventory shortages would indicate that prices should be raised. By setting the prices of all commodities in this way, the central planning board could create an efficient flow of resources throughout the economy. Yet, even the critics of von Mises and Hayek must acknowledge that the kind of large-scale planning that has been attempted in some communist nations—particularly the former Soviet Union—has resulted in large-scale failure. It appears that planning is possible only if it is but one component within an economy in which exchanges are, for the most part, based on market forces.

The Keynesian Criticism

The most influential criticism of Adam Smith's classical assumptions came from John Maynard Keynes (1883–1946), an English economist.[61] Smith assumed that without any help from the government, the automatic play of market forces would ensure full employment of all economic resources including labor. If some resources are not being used, then their costs drop and entrepreneurs are induced to expand their output by using these cheapened resources. The purchase of these resources, in turn, creates the incomes that enable people to buy the products made from them. Thus, all available resources are used and demand always expands to absorb the supply of commodities made from them (a relationship that is now called **Say's Law**). Since Keynes, however, economists have argued that, without government intervention, the demand for goods may not be high enough to absorb the supply. The result is unemployment and a slide into economic depression.

Say's Law In an economy, all available resources are used and demand always expands to absorb the supply of commodities made from them.

aggregate demand According to John Maynard Keynes, the sum of the demand of three sectors of the economy: households, businesses, and government.

Keynesian economics The theory of John Maynard Keynes that free markets alone are not necessarily the most efficient means for coordinating the use of society's resources.

post-Keynesian school Economists who have sought to challenge and modify Keynesian economics.

Quick Review 3.6

Keynes' Criticism of Smith

- Keynes said Smith wrongly assumes demand is always enough to absorb the supply of goods.
- But if households forego spending, demand can be less than supply, leading to cutbacks, unemployment, and economic depression.
- Government spending can make up for such shortfalls in household spending, so government should intervene in markets.
- But Keynes' views were challenged when government spending did not cure high unemployment but created inflation.

Keynes argued that the total demand for goods and services is the sum of the demand of three sectors of the economy: households, businesses, and government.[62] The **aggregate demand** of these three sectors may be less than the aggregate amounts of goods and services supplied by the economy at the full employment level. This mismatch between aggregate demand and aggregate supply will occur when households prefer to save some of their income in liquid securities instead of spending it on goods and services. When, as a consequence, aggregate demand is less than aggregate supply, the result is a contraction of supply. Businesses realize they are not selling all their goods, so they cut back on production and thereby cut back on employment. As production falls, the incomes of households also fall, but the amounts households are willing to save fall even faster. Eventually, the economy reaches a stable point of equilibrium at which demand once again equals supply, but at which there is widespread unemployment of labor and other resources.

Government, according to Keynes, can influence the propensity to save, which lowers aggregate demand and creates unemployment. Government can prevent excess savings through its influence on interest rates, and it can influence interest rates by regulating the money supply: The higher the supply of money, the lower the rates at which it is lent. Second, government can directly affect the amount of money households have available to them by raising or lowering taxes. Third, government spending can close any gap between aggregate demand and aggregate supply by taking up the slack in demand from households and businesses (and, incidentally, creating inflation).

Thus, contrary to Smith's claims, government intervention in the economy is a necessary instrument for maximizing society's utility. Free markets alone are not necessarily the most efficient means for coordinating the use of society's resources. Government spending and fiscal policies can serve to create the demand needed to stave off unemployment. These views were the kernels of **Keynesian economics**.

Keynes's views, however, have to some extent fallen on hard times. During the 1970s, the U.S. economy (and other Western economies) was confronted with the simultaneous occurrence of inflation and unemployment, termed *stagflation*. The standard Keynesian analysis would have led us to believe that these two should not have occurred together. Increased government spending, although inflationary, should have enlarged demand and thereby alleviated unemployment. However, during the 1970s, the standard Keynesian remedy for unemployment (increased government spending) had the expected effect of causing more inflation, but it did not cure unemployment.

Various diagnoses have been offered for the apparent failure of Keynesian economics to deal with the twin problems of inflation and stubborn unemployment particularly during the 1970s.[63] Notable among these are the new Keynesian approaches being pioneered by the so-called **post-Keynesian school**.[64] John Hicks, a long-time Keynesian enthusiast and a "post-Keynesian," has suggested that in many industries today prices and wages are no longer determined by competitive market forces as Keynes assumed. Instead, they are set by conventional agreements among producers and unions.[65] The ultimate effect of these price-setting conventions is continuing inflation in the face of continued unemployment. Regardless of whether Hicks's analysis is correct, a flourishing post-Keynesian school has developed new approaches to Keynes that can more adequately account for the problems of stagflation. Post-Keynesian theories, like those of Hicks, retain the key claim of Keynes that unemployment can be cured by increasing aggregate demand (the "principle of effective demand") through government expenditures. Unlike Keynes, however, Hicks and other post-Keynesians take more seriously the oligopolistic nature of most modern industries and unionized labor markets, as well as the role that social conventions and agreements play in these oligopolistic markets as workers and companies struggle over income shares. The role for government, then, is even larger than that envisioned by Keynes. Not only must government boost aggregate demand through increased spending, it must also curb the power of large oligopolistic groups.

During the "Great Recession" of 2008–2009, governments around the world returned to Keynesian policies with a vengeance. The United States, for example, injected more than $700 billion into the U.S. economy to try to pull it out of recession. European and Asian governments also injected large amounts of money into their economies. While the world has gradually recovered from this "Great Recession," it is not completely clear that it did so because of the Keynesian measures that were used.

The Utility of Survival of the Fittest: Social Darwinism

Nineteenth-century social Darwinists added a new twist to utilitarian justifications of free markets by arguing that free markets have beneficial consequences over and above those that Adam Smith identified. They argued that economic competition produces human progress. The doctrines of **social Darwinism** were named after Charles Darwin (1809–1882), who argued that the various species of living things were evolving as the result of the action of an environment that favored the survival of some things while destroying others: "This preservation of favorable individual differences and variations, and the destruction of those which are injurious, I have called natural selection or the survival of the fittest."[66] The environmental factors that resulted in the ***survival of the fittest*** were the competitive pressures of the animal world. As a result of this competitive "struggle for existence," Darwin held, species gradually change because only the "fittest" survive to pass their favorable characteristics on to their progeny.

social Darwinism Belief that economic competition produces human progress.

survival of the fittest Charles Darwin's term for the process of natural selection.

Even before Darwin had published his theories, philosopher Herbert Spencer (1820–1903) and other thinkers had already begun to suggest that the evolutionary processes that Darwin described were also operative in human societies. Spencer claimed that just as competition in the animal world ensures that only the fittest survive, so free competition in the economic world ensures that only the most capable individuals survive and rise to the top. The implication is that:

> Inconvenience, suffering, and death are the penalties attached by Nature to ignorance as well as to incompetence and are also the means of remedying these. Partly by weeding out those of lowest development, and partly by subjecting those who remain to the never-ceasing discipline of experience, Nature secures the growth of a race who shall both understand the conditions of existence, and be able to act up to them.[67]

Those individuals whose aggressive business dealings enable them to succeed in the competitive world of business are the "fittest" and therefore, the best. Just as survival of the fittest ensures the continuing progress and improvement of an animal species, so the free competition that enriches some individuals and reduces others to poverty result in the gradual improvement of the human race. Government must not be allowed to interfere with this stern competition because this would only impede progress. In particular, government must not lend economic aid to those who fall behind in the competition for survival. If these economic misfits survive, they will pass on their inferior qualities and the human race will decline.

The shortcomings of Spencer's views were obvious even to his contemporaries. Critics were quick to point out that the skills and traits that help individuals and firms advance and "survive" in the business world are not necessarily those that help humanity survive on the planet. Advancement in the business world might be achieved through a ruthless disregard for other human beings. The survival of humanity, however, may well depend on the development of cooperative attitudes and the mutual willingness of people to help each other.

The basic problem underlying the views of the social Darwinist, however, is the fundamental normative assumption that *survival of the fittest* means *survival of the best.* That is, whatever results from the workings of nature is necessarily good. The fallacy, which modern authors call the ***naturalistic fallacy***, claims, that whatever happens naturally is always good. It is a basic failure of logic, however, to infer that what is should be, or that what nature does is what it ought to have been done.

naturalistic fallacy The assumption that what happens naturally is always what is good.

Quick Review 3.7

Views of Herbert Spencer

- Evolution operates in society when economic competition ensures the fittest survive and the unfit do not, which improves the human race.
- If government intervenes in the economy to shield people from competition, the unfit survive and the human race declines, so government should not do so.
- Spencer assumes those who survive in business are "better" people than those who do not.

In spite of its many shortcomings, however, many business people today firmly believe in a version of social Darwinism. That is, many business people believe that businesses must compete for their lives in an economic environment in which only the strong will survive. Modern versions of Spencerism hold that competition is good not because it destroys the weak individual, but because it weeds out weak firms. Economic competition ensures that the "best" business firms survive and, as a result, the economic system gradually improves. The conclusion of modern social Darwinists is the same: Government must stay out of the market because competition is beneficial. This is one of the reasons why many business people object to government "bailouts." During the last several decades, when very large businesses were failing and it looked like they might have to close and lay off all their workers, the U.S. government has stepped in and given those businesses enough money to "bail" them out of their troubles. This happened often during the 2008–2009 recession when government provided over $700 billion to prop up dozens of banks, insurance companies, automobile companies, and other businesses. Social Darwinists objected that all this did was prop up weak and inefficient companies that should have been allowed to go under.

3.3 Free Trade and Utility: David Ricardo

We have so far focused on the arguments for and against free markets. But utilitarian arguments have also been advanced in favor of free trade between nations. Adam Smith's major work, *The Wealth of Nations*, in fact, was primarily aimed at showing the benefits of free trade. There he wrote:

> It is the maxim of every prudent master of a family, never to attempt to make at home what it will cost him more to make than to buy. The tailor does not make his own shoes but buys them from the shoemaker.... What is prudence in the conduct of every family, can scarce be folly in that of a great kingdom. If a foreign country can supply us with a commodity cheaper than we ourselves can make it, better buy it of them with some part of the produce of our own industry, employed in a way in which we have some advantage.[68]

Adam Smith's point here is simple. Like individuals, countries differ in their ability to produce goods. One country can produce a good more cheaply than another and it is then said to have an "**absolute advantage**" in producing that good. These cost differences may be based on differences in labor costs, workers' skills, climate, technology, equipment, land, or natural resources. Suppose that because of these differences, our nation can make one product for less than a foreign nation can, and suppose the foreign nation can make some other product for less than we can. Then, clearly it would be best for both nations to specialize in making the product each has an "absolute advantage" in producing and to trade it for what the other country has an "absolute advantage" in producing.

absolute advantage A situation where the production costs (costs in terms of the resources consumed in producing the good) of making a commodity are lower for one country than for another.

But what if one country can produce everything more cheaply than another country? David Ricardo (1772–1823), a British economist, is usually credited with showing that even if one country has an absolute advantage at producing everything, it is still better for it to specialize and trade. In his major work, *On the Principles of Political Economy and Taxation*, Ricardo used the example of England and Portugal to show that even if England is better than Portugal at producing *both* cloth and wine, it is still better for both England and Portugal to specialize and trade:

> England may be so circumscribed that to produce the cloth may require the labor of 100 men for one year; and if she attempted to make the wine, it might require the labor of 120 men for the same time. England would therefore find it in her interest to import wine, and to purchase it by the exportation of cloth.
>
> To produce the wine in Portugal might require only the labor of 80 men for one year, and to produce the cloth in the same country, might require the labor of 90 men for the same time. It would therefore be advantageous for her to export wine in exchange for cloth. This exchange might even take place, notwithstanding that the commodity imported by Portugal could be produced there with less labor than in England. Though she could make the cloth with the labor of 90 men, she would import it from a country where it required the labor of 100 men to produce it, because it would be advantageous to her rather to employ her capital in the production of wine, for which she would obtain more cloth from England, than she could produce by diverting a portion of her capital from the cultivation of vines to the manufacture of cloth.[69]

Ricardo's argument asks us to imagine a world consisting of only two countries, England and Portugal. It costs England the labor of 120 men working 1 year to produce a certain amount of wine (let us arbitrarily assume that amount is 100 barrels), while it costs Portugal the year's labor of only 80 men to produce the same amount. And while it takes England the labor of 100 men to produce a certain amount of cloth (let us arbitrarily assume this is 100 rolls), it takes Portugal only 90 men to make the same amount of cloth. Clearly, Portugal has an absolute advantage in making both wine and cloth since it can make both more cheaply than England:

	100 Barrels of Wine	**100 Rolls of Cloth**
	Cost in Man-years	**Cost in Man-years**
England:	120	100
Portugal:	80	90

Suppose Portugal refused to trade with England because it can make both wine and cloth more cheaply. So both countries decide to produce everything on their own and neither trades with the other. Suppose that England has only 220 laborers whom it can put to work making either wine or cloth, while Portugal has 170 laborers who can also make either wine or cloth. And suppose both countries decide not to specialize, but to put their laborers to work to make 100 barrels of wine and 100 rolls of cloth each. Then, at the end of a year they would each have produced the amounts in the following table, yielding a total output of 200 barrels of wine and 200 rolls of cloth:

	Wine	**Cloth**
England:	100 barrels	100 rolls
Portugal:	100 barrels	100 rolls
Total output:	200 barrels	200 rolls

It was Ricardo's genius to realize that both countries could benefit from specialization and trade even though one can make everything more cheaply than the other. Consider that if England used the labor it costs to make a barrel of wine (1.2 man-years) to make cloth instead, it could make 1.2 rolls of cloth. So for England, to produce one barrel of wine it must give up 1.2 rolls of cloth (the so-called "opportunity cost" of a barrel of wine). In Portugal, the labor it costs to make a barrel of wine (0.8 man-years) could be used to make 0.89 rolls of cloth instead, so for Portugal to make a barrel of wine it must give up 0.89 rolls of cloth. Because Portugal gives up less (0.89 rolls of cloth) to make a barrel of wine than England gives up (1.2 rolls of cloth), Portugal has a "**comparative advantage**" in the production of wine. On the other hand, England could use the labor it takes to make a roll of cloth to instead make 0.83 barrels of wine, while Portugal could take the labor it uses to make a roll of cloth and use it to make 1.1 barrels of wine. Since England gives up less (0.83 barrels of wine) to make a roll of cloth than Portugal gives up (1.1 barrels of wine), England has the comparative advantage in the production of cloth. In short, compared to each other, Portugal is more efficient at making wine while England is more efficient at making cloth.

comparative advantage A situation where the opportunity costs (costs in terms of other goods given up) of making a commodity are lower for one country than for another.

Ricardo saw that both England and Portugal would benefit if each specialized in what each can make most efficiently and traded for what the other can make most efficiently. Suppose each country were to specialize, and we again assume that England has 220 laborers while Portugal has 170. Then, at the end of the year each would produce the amounts in the following table. Notice this yields a *larger* total output than when neither specialized:

	Wine	Cloth
England:	0	220 rolls
Portugal:	212 barrels	0
Total output:	212 barrels	220 rolls

Quick Review 3.8

Free Trade
- Advocated by Smith who showed everyone prospers if nations specialize in making and exporting goods whose production costs for them are lower than for other nations.
- Advocated by Ricardo who showed everyone prospers if nations specialize in making and exporting goods whose opportunity costs to them are lower than the opportunity costs other nations incur to make the same goods.
- The arguments of Smith and Ricardo provide support for globalization.

Now, if England trades 106 of its rolls of cloth for 102 of Portugal's barrels of wine (we suppose that the rate of exchange is about 1.04 rolls of cloth for 1 barrel of wine, which is right between the 1.2 rolls of cloth that it costs England to make one barrel of wine and the 0.89 rolls of cloth that it costs Portugal to make one barrel of wine), then both countries would end up with the amounts indicated in the following table:

	Wine	Cloth
England:	102 barrels	114 rolls
Portugal:	110 barrels	106 rolls
Total output:	212 barrels	220 rolls

Note that after specializing and trading, both countries have *more* of both products than either had when they did not specialize or trade. Specialization in comparative advantages increases the total output of goods countries produce, and through trade all countries can share in this added bounty.

Ricardo's ingenious argument has been hailed as the single "most important" and "most meaningful" economic discovery ever made. Some have said it is the most "surprising" and "counterintuitive" concept in economics. Comparative advantage is, without a doubt, the most important concept in international trade theory today and is at the heart of the most significant economic arguments people propose when they argue in favor of globalization. In fact, it is the key argument for globalization and free trade. All the arguments politicians and economists make in favor of globalization and free trade come down to Ricardo's point: Globalization is good because specialization and free trade boost total economic output and everyone can share in this increased output.

Criticisms of Ricardo

Although Ricardo's basic argument is accepted as correct in theory by most economists, many question whether his utilitarian argument applies in practice to today's real world. Of course, Ricardo makes a number of simplifying assumptions that clearly do not hold in the real world—such as that there are only two countries making only two products with only a fixed number of workers. But these are merely simplifying assumptions Ricardo made to get his point across more easily, and his conclusion could still be proved without these assumptions.

Quick Review 3.9

Objections to Ricardo's Theory

- His argument ignores the easy movement of capital by companies.
- He falsely assumed that a country's production costs are constant.
- He ignored the influence of international rule setters.

There are other assumptions, however, that are not so easy to get around. First, Ricardo assumes that the resources used to produce goods (labor, equipment, factories, etc.) do not move from one country to another. Yet today multinational companies can, and easily do, move their productive capital from one country to another. Second, Ricardo assumes that each country's production costs are constant and do not decline as countries expand their production (i.e., there are no "economies of scale") or as they acquire new technology. But we know that the costs of producing goods regularly decline as companies expand production and develop ever better production technologies.

Thirdly, Ricardo assumes that workers can easily and without cost move from one industry to another (from making wine, for example, to making cloth). Yet, when a company in a country closes down because it cannot compete with imports from another country that has a comparative advantage in those goods, the company's workers are laid off, suffer heavy costs, need retraining, and often cannot find comparable jobs. This is why many U.S. workers today reject globalization and free trade. As we saw above, for example, the U.S. workers of the Swingline stapler manufacturer had to bear significant burdens and costs when the manufacturer closed its factory in New York and moved to Nogales, Mexico. And a few years later, Swingline workers in Mexico suffered a similar fate when the company moved to China.

Finally, and perhaps most importantly, Ricardo ignores international rule-setters. International trade inevitably leads to disagreements and conflicts, and so countries must agree to abide by some set of rules. Today, the main organization that sets the rules that govern globalization and trade is the World Trade Organization, although both the World Bank, and the International Monetary Fund also impose rules on countries that borrow money from them. Critics claim that these organizations impose requirements that harm poor developing countries while benefiting the wealthy developed nations and their businesses. For example, during the late 1980s and the early 1990s, Abbott Laboratories and other large U.S. drug companies contributed millions of dollars to U.S. politicians and successfully got the U.S. government to seek world-wide acceptance of the patent protections they enjoyed in the United States. As a result, when the World Trade Organization agreements were negotiated in the 1980s and early 1990s, the United States insisted that all WTO countries had to recognize and enforce drug patents for 20 years. Because developing countries were too poor to engage in the expensive research needed to invent new drugs, enforcing drug patents would not benefit them. On the contrary, recognizing drug patents would force developing countries to pay the drug companies for the drugs that they had been freely copying. Nevertheless, developing countries went along with the requirement that they enforce drug patents because the WTO offered them the chance to sell their exports in the markets of the U.S. and other industrialized nations, by far the largest markets in the world. But in the end, the patent rules of the WTO forced the poor people of developing nations to pay about $60 billion a year to the drug companies of the rich industrialized nations.[70] Thailand, as we saw earlier, attempted to get around these expensive requirements by using an exception allowed by the TRIPS rules of the WTO.

It is difficult to say how telling these criticisms are. Many people today continue to be enthusiastic supporters of global free trade, repeating Ricardo's comparative advantage argument. Many others have become harsh critics of globalization. Indeed, there have been continuing and violent demonstrations against globalization on the streets of cities around the world, many of which have directly affected important meetings of the WTO.

3.4 Marx and Justice: Criticizing Markets and Free Trade

Karl Marx (1818–1883) is undoubtedly the harshest and most well-known critic of private property institutions, free markets, and free trade and the inequalities they are accused of creating. Writing at the height of the Industrial Revolution, Marx was an eyewitness to the wrenching and exploitative effects that industrialization had on the laboring peasant classes of England, Europe, and the rest of the world. Marx detailed the suffering and misery that capitalism was imposing on its workers: exploitative working hours, pulmonary diseases and premature deaths caused by unsanitary factory conditions, 7-year-olds working 12 to 15 hours a day; 30 seamstresses working 30 hours without a break in a room made for 10 people.[71]

Marx claimed that worker exploitation was merely a symptom of the underlying extremes of inequality that capitalism produces. According to Marx, capitalist systems offer only two sources of income: sale of one's own labor and ownership of the **means of production** (the buildings, machinery, land, and raw materials by means of which we produce goods). Because workers cannot produce anything without access to the means of production, they are forced to sell their labor to the owner in return for a wage. The owner, however, does not pay workers the full value of their labor, only what they need to subsist. The difference ("surplus") between the value of their labor and the subsistence wages they receive is retained by the owner and is the source of the owner's profits. Thus, the owner is able to exploit workers by appropriating from them the surplus they produce, using as leverage the ownership of the means of production. As a result, those who own the means of production gradually become wealthier, and workers become relatively poorer. Capitalism promotes unjust inequality.

means of production The buildings, machinery, land, and raw materials used in the production of goods and services.

Alienation

The living conditions that capitalism imposed on workers contrasted sharply with Marx's view of how human beings should live. In Marx's view, capitalism and its private property system creates **alienation** among workers. Marx used the word "alienation"—which means *separation* or *estrangement*—to refer to the condition of being separated or estranged from one's own true self or one's own true nature. Marx believed that it was the nature of a human being to be self-determined and able to satisfy one's true needs, i.e., to be in control of one's life, and able to fulfill one's true human needs. If a person lost control over her life and ability to be fulfilled through the satisfaction of her human needs, and was instead controlled by some external power and forced to meet its needs, this person was "alienated" from her own nature. Marx's fundamental criticism of capitalism was that it alienated workers by robbing them of control of their lives and forcing them to satisfy needs that were not their own.

alienation In Marx's view, the condition of being separated or estranged from one's true nature or true human self.

According to Marx, capitalist economies alienate workers in four ways.[72] First, capitalism alienates workers from their own productive work. In capitalism, a worker typically is forced to work for someone else and serves under the supervision and control of someone else. Because the purpose of his work is to make money for the owner or owners of his workplace, it is not designed to be a fulfilling form of productivity and to satisfy his own needs:

> In what, then, consists the alienation of labor? First, in the fact that labor is external to the worker, i.e., that it does not belong to his nature, that therefore he does not fulfill himself in his work, but denies himself in it, has a feeling of misery rather than satisfaction, does not develop freely his mental and physical energies but is physically exhausted and mentally depressed... His labor, therefore, is not voluntary, but forced—forced labor. It is not the gratification of his need, but only a means to gratify needs outside his work. Its alien nature shows itself clearly by the fact that work is shunned like the plague as soon as no physical or other kind of coercion exists. Lastly, the external character of labor for the worker appears in the fact that it is not his own, but someone else's, that it does not belong to him, that in it he belongs, not to himself, but to another.[73]

Quick Review 3.10

Marx on Alienation

- In capitalism, workers become alienated when they lose control of their own life activities and the ability to fulfill their true human needs.
- Capitalism alienates workers from their own productive work, the products of their work, their relationships with each other, and from themselves.
- Alienation also occurs when the value of everything is seen in terms of its market price.

Secondly, capitalist societies alienate workers from the products of their labor because workers have no control over the products they make with their own hands. When factory workers finish making something, their finished product is kept by their employer who uses it to add to his own profits by selling it. All the laborer is left with is the "wear and tear" labor inflicts on his body and mind:

> Labor, to be sure, produces marvelous things for the rich, but for the laborer it produces privation. It produces palaces for the wealthy, but hovels for the worker. It produces beauty, but cripples the worker. It replaces work by machines, but it throws part of the workforce back into a barbarous kind of work, while turning others into machines. It produces sophistication, but for the workers it produces feeble-mindedness and idiocy. [74]

Thirdly, capitalism alienates workers by giving them little control over how they must relate to each other and by forcing them into antagonistic relationships with each other. Workers are organized by the employer and must work with and alongside whomever their employer wants, not who they choose. Workers are pitted against each other when they are forced to compete with each other for jobs. And capitalist societies alienate human beings from each other by separating them into antagonistic and unequal social classes that break down community and caring relationships.[75] According to Marx, capitalism divides humanity into a "proletariat" working class and a "bourgeois" class of capitalist owners and employers: "Society as a whole is more and more splitting up into two great hostile camps, into two great classes directly facing each other: bourgeoisie and proletariat."[76]

And fourthly, capitalism alienates workers from themselves by instilling in them false views of what their real human needs are. Capitalism gets us to think that our fulfillment lies in making ever more money when in fact this will satisfy not our own needs, but the needs of capitalism itself. The more money you make, he says sarcastically, "the more you will be able to save and the greater will become your treasure which neither moth nor dust will corrupt—your capital. The less you are, the less you express your life, the more you have, the greater is your alienated life, and the greater is the saving of your alienated being."[77] Marx describes the alienation produced by this ceaseless striving for money and economic goods as "the renunciation of life and of human needs."[78]

A key cause of alienation, Marx claimed, was the way that capitalist societies come to see everything in terms of their market prices. Human interactions, he claimed, have been so commercialized and turned into commodities that everyone

Marx's Children

The terrible conditions under which workers—particularly child workers—of the nineteenth century had to labor inspired much of Marx's writing. Yet many of these conditions continue today. The International Labor Organization estimates that 218 million children work today. According to a 2010 report of Human Rights Watch, many U.S. farm companies have children working for them. Maria started working for a farm at age 11:

> You sweat. You walk until your feet hurt, you have blisters, and until you have cuts all over your hands... The ages [of fellow child workers] were always varied, 11 and 12 year olds, even10 year olds... The growers know that [children are there]. They see that—they would pass by when they drop off water. No one was going to say anything... The pay [less than minimum wage] was terrible... You had to go really fast... You had to bend down for hours until your next break... There were people who got sick [from pesticides]... They never told us they were spraying [pesticides], they would just say "watering"... One summer... they were spraying things we didn't know what they were. We heard it was chemicals...

In developing countries, child workers are common. In Uzbekistan, about 2 million children are forced to work on cotton farms each year, particularly during harvest season. During cotton growing season, children weed the cotton plants and spray them with pesticides. One child said, "It's so hot in the fields and the chemicals burn your skin if they touch it." Although many U.S. companies have agreed not to use cotton from Uzbekistan, others have refused to boycott cotton grown with forced child labor including Cargill and Fruit of the Loom.

In the soccer ball industry, child labor continues to be used to stitch soccer balls together in spite of a 1997 industry agreement to end the use of child workers. A 2010 report of the International Labor Rights Forum indicates that child labor occurs in China and India where stitching is done in workers' homes and not in a factory. Geeta, a 12 year-old girl stitcher from Kamalpur in India said, "I have been stitching footballs for as long as I can remember. My hands are constantly in pain. It feels like they are burning." Children must work in a hunched position for 5 to 7 hours to make two soccer balls for 3-4 rupees per ball (a total of 7.5 to 10 cents). Nike, Adidas, and Puma are among the largest companies that buy soccer balls from Indian manufacturers.

Children working in Uzbekistan cotton fields (above), Children weaving rugs in Nepal (right)

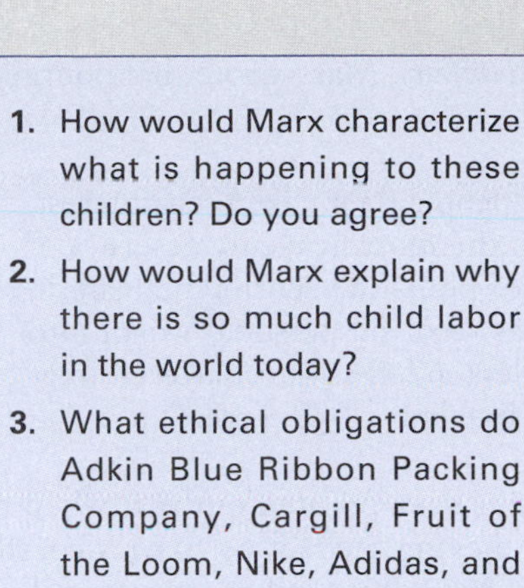

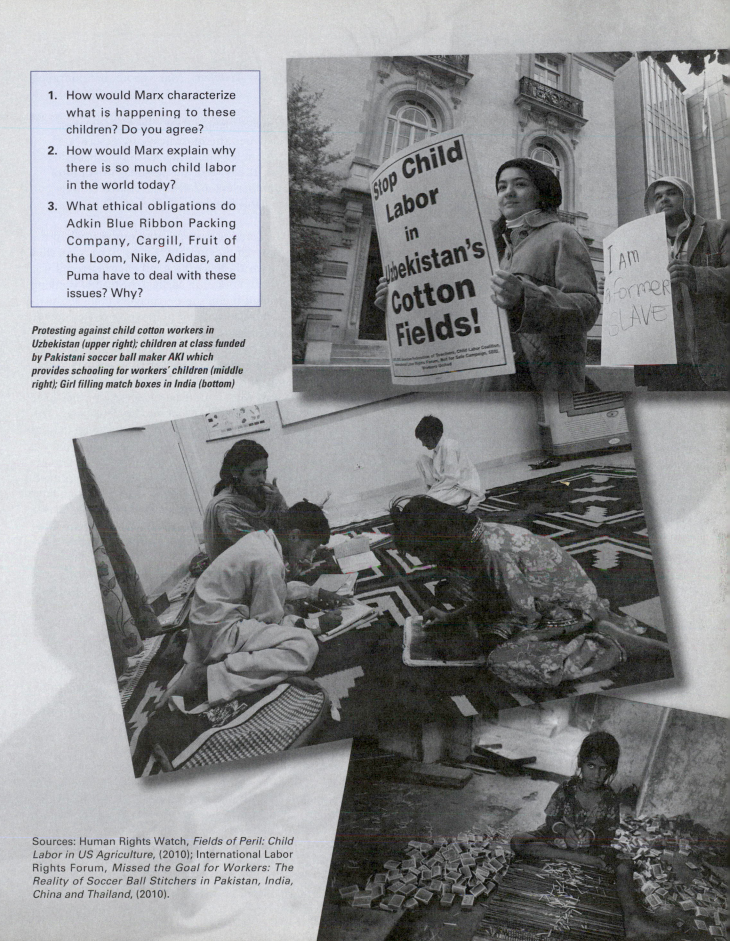

1. How would Marx characterize what is happening to these children? Do you agree?
2. How would Marx explain why there is so much child labor in the world today?
3. What ethical obligations do Adkin Blue Ribbon Packing Company, Cargill, Fruit of the Loom, Nike, Adidas, and Puma have to deal with these issues? Why?

Protesting against child cotton workers in Uzbekistan (upper right); children at class funded by Pakistani soccer ball maker AKI which provides schooling for workers' children (middle right); Girl filling match boxes in India (bottom)

Sources: Human Rights Watch, *Fields of Peril: Child Labor in US Agriculture*, (2010); International Labor Rights Forum, *Missed the Goal for Workers: The Reality of Soccer Ball Stitchers in Pakistan, India, China and Thailand*, (2010).

and everything has its price. In his *Communist Manifesto*, Marx wrote that bourgeois capitalism has:

> left remaining no other connection between people than naked self-interest, than callous 'cash payment.' It has drowned the most heavenly ecstasies of religious fervor, of chivalrous enthusiasm, of philistine sentimentalism, in the icy water of egotistical calculation. It has resolved personal worth into exchange value, and in place of the numberless indefeasible chartered freedoms, has set up that single, unconscionable freedom—free trade.[79]

As an example of what he meant, Marx might have pointed out that when the managers of the Swingline company considered moving the factory to Mexico, they did not think about their relationships with their workers; all that mattered was whether they would make more money in New York or in Mexico. Instead of thinking about their "connection" to the people around them, these managers used "egotistical calculation" to figure out whether the "cash payment" of moving to Mexico was greater than the "cash payment" of staying in New York. As another example, Marx might have pointed out how today we tend to value our "personal worth" in terms of how much we can earn, i.e., our "exchange value." Thus capitalism seems to value everything in terms of its market price and seemingly turns everything into a marketable commodity. Treating things in this way, Marx felt, makes it seem as if they have a value and life of their own, a process that Marx labeled "commodity fetishism."

Capitalism and its unregulated free markets, Marx argued, produce inequalities of wealth and power: a "bourgeois" class of owners who own the means of production and accumulate ever greater amounts of capital, and a "proletariat" class of workers who must sell their labor to subsist and who are alienated from what they produce, from heir own work, from their own human needs, and from the fellow human beings with whom they should form a caring community. Although private property and free markets may secure the "freedom" of the wealthy owner class, they do so by creating an alienated laboring class, and for both owner and worker everything is seen as having a price. Such alienation is unjust and in conflict with the demands of caring.

Marx did not hesitate to make clear that his views implied that private ownership of the means of production was wrong. A private property system that allows private control of productive property, he held, is the basis of the alienation and great inequalities that characterize capitalist societies:

> You are horrified at our intending to do away with private property. But in your existing society private property is already done away with for nine-tenths of the population; its existence for the few is solely due to its non-existence in the hands of those nine-tenths. You reproach us, therefore, with intending to do away with a form of property, the necessary condition for whose existence is the non-existence of any property for the immense majority of society.[80]

Quick Review 3.11

Marx and Private Property

- Private ownership of the means of production is the source of the worker's loss of control over work, products, relationships, and self.
- Productive property should serve the needs of all and should not be privately owned, but owned by everyone.

In this passage, Marx is not saying he wants people to do away with private ownership of their clothes, houses, or food, i.e., he does not object to "the power to appropriate the products of society."[81] He is objecting, instead, to private ownership of factories, companies, mines, farms, and other productive property, i.e., to "capital." Productive property should benefit everyone and so it should be owned by everyone. To the utilitarian argument that without private ownership of productive assets there would be no incentive for individuals to work, Marx replied:

> It has been objected that upon the abolition of private property all work will cease and universal laziness will overtake us. According to this, bourgeois

> society ought long ago to have gone to the dogs through sheer idleness; for those of its members who work, acquire nothing, and those who acquire anything, do not work.[82]

In Marx's view, productive property should be seen as having a social purpose: it belongs to the whole community and should serve the needs of all. Productive property should not be "private," but should be held in common and its fruits should be enjoyed by all. If there were no private ownership of the means of production, Marx believed, people would still continue to lead productive lives because the desire to be productive and to express ourselves through what we make with our hands and minds is an instinct that is built into our very nature.

The Real Purpose of Government

The actual function that governments have historically served, according to Marx, is to protect the interests of the ruling class. We may believe that modern government exists to protect freedom and equality and that it rules by consent (as Locke insisted), but, in fact, such beliefs are ideological myths that hide the reality: the wealthy class controls the political process and shapes our beliefs. To back up his claim, Marx offered a breathtakingly comprehensive analysis of society, which we can only sketch here.

economic substructure The materials and social controls that society uses to produce its economic goods.

social superstructure A society's government and its popular ideologies.

forces of production The materials (land, labor, natural resources, machinery, energy, technology) used in production.

relations of production The social controls used in producing goods (i.e., the social controls by which society organizes and controls its workers).

Marx claimed that every society can be analyzed in terms of two main components: its **economic substructure** and its **social superstructure**.[83] The economic substructure of a society consists of the materials and social controls it uses to produce its goods. Marx refers to the materials (land, labor, natural resources, machinery, energy, technology) used in production as the ***forces of production***. The societies of the Middle Ages, for example, were agricultural societies in which the forces of production were primitive farming methods, manual labor, and hand tools. The forces of production of modern industrialized societies are assembly-line manufacturing techniques, electricity, and factory machinery.

Marx called the controls a society uses to get people to produce goods (i.e., the social controls by which society organizes and controls its workers) the ***relations of production***. There are, Marx suggests, two main types of relations of production: (1) control based on ownership of the materials needed to produce goods, and (2) control based on authority to command. In modern industrial society, capitalist owners control their factory laborers because (1) the capitalists own the machinery on which laborers must work if they are to survive, and (2) laborers must enter a wage contract by which they give the owner (or manager) the legal authority to command them. According to Marx, a society's relations of production define the main classes that exist in that society. In medieval society, for example, the relations of production created the ruling class of lords and nobility, and the exploited serf class, whereas in industrial society, the relations of production created the capitalist class of owners (whom Marx called the *bourgeoisie*) and the exploited working class of wage earners (whom Marx called the *proletariat*).

Marx also claims that the kind of relations of production a society adopts depends on its forces of production. That is, the methods a society uses to produce goods determine the way that society organizes its workers. For example, the fact that medieval society had to depend on manual farming methods to survive forced it to adopt a social system in which a small class of lords organized and directed the large class of serfs who provided the manual labor society needed on its farms. Similarly, the fact that modern society depends on mass production methods has forced us to adopt a social system—capitalism—in which a small class of owners accumulates the capital needed to build large factories and in which a large class of workers provides the labor these mechanized factory assembly lines need. In short, a society's forces of

ON THE EDGE

Napster's Lost Revolution

When 18-year-old Shawn "Napster" Fanning, then a freshman at Northeastern University, founded Napster, Inc. in 1999, he started a property revolution. In college, Fanning developed software and a web site through which users could connect to each other and then copy ("download") for free the copyrighted music they had to pay for in stores. Many students felt the music they downloaded belonged to everyone and that copying was okay because it did not affect the original. Two music industry groups sued Napster, however, claiming that through its web site Napster was helping others steal their property and that if music property rights were not respected, musicians would have no incentive to produce music. On February 12, 2001, the courts ruled that Napster's web site actively contributed to copyright infringement and in 2002, the company was forced to block users from downloading copyrighted music. But Napster had paved the way for the development of decentralized "peer-to-peer" file sharing programs that let users connect to each other directly like Grokster, StreamCast, Freenet, Gnutella, eDonkey, Kazaa, Poisoned, Morpheus, BitTorrent, and LimeWire. Several music companies sued Grokster and StreamCast. In 2004, a federal district court ruled that because Grokster and StreamCast programs let users connect directly to each other without going through their web site, neither Grokster nor StreamCast could control what users did with their program. The music companies now turned to suing individual downloaders. One victim remarked, "It scares me. You have no power against these people." Moreover, the music companies appealed the Grokster/StreamCast decision to the U.S. Supreme Court and on June 23, 2005, the Supreme Court ruled that both Grokster and StreamCast had created their peer-to-peer software with the "intent" of "inducing" consumers to download copyrighted materials and so violated the laws protecting copyrights. In 2007, StreamCast was ordered to distribute new software that blocked users from downloading copyrighted material. Nevertheless, young people continued to download copyrighted materials by turning to other software suppliers such as BitTorrent and LimeWire. But record companies sued LimeWire in 2006, and on May 12, 2010 a Manhattan District Court ruled LimeWire had committed copyright infringement and induced others to do so as well. BitTorrent, anxious to change its business model, announced on February 25, 2007 that it would sell legal video material on its web site, with the cooperation of several studios, including Paramount which said "We look at this as a first step in the peer-to-peer world, to try to steer young people toward legitimate content." But in November 7, 2008, BitTorrent had to fire half its employees, and said it would close down its video web site to concentrate on distributing video games over the Internet. PirateBay, a file sharing web site in Sweden, continued to hold out, although on April 17, 2009 its founders were sentenced to prison for a year and fined $3.6 million for assisting in illegal copying in a case that was still in appeal as of this writing. As of 2011, PirateBay.org was still operating.

1. Although what Napster, Grokster, StreamCast, LimeWire, and PirateBay did was illegal, was it immoral? Explain.
2. Is it morally wrong to download copyrighted material without paying for it and without the authorization of the party that holds the copyright? Explain.
3. Should we treat digitized entertainment like online music, movies, or games in the way that Locke said property should be looked at, or like Aquinas said property should be looked at, or like the collectively-owned property that many socialists advocate? Is your view consistent in the sense of consistency defined in Chapter 1? How does the kind of free downloading that Napster, Grokster, StreamCast, LimeWire, and BitTorrent made possible fit with each of these three views on property?

production determine its relations of production, and these relations of production then determine its social classes.

For Marx, the "social superstructure" of a society consists of its government and its popular ideologies. Marx claims that the ruling class created by the economic substructure inevitably controls this superstructure. That is, the members of the ruling class will control the government and use it to protect "their property and interests" and to dominate the lower classes (Marx wrote: "Political power, properly so called, is merely the organized power of one class for oppressing another").[84] The ruling class will also popularize ideologies (e.g., through the media) that justify their position of privilege (as Marx put it: "the ideas of the ruling class are in every epoch the ruling ideas").[85] In modern societies, for example, the class of owners is instrumental in the selection of government officials and the government then enforces the private property system on which the owners' wealth depends and keeps the working class in line. Moreover, the class of owners popularizes the ideologies of "free enterprise" and "respect for private property," both of which support their own social class. Modern government, then, is not created by consent, as Locke had claimed, but by a kind of economic determination.

Marx's view, then, is that a society's government and its ideologies are designed to support its ruling economic class, which is created by its relations of production, which in turn are shaped by its forces of production. Ultimately, the forces of production determine what a society is like, i.e., its beliefs, its government, and its social classes. In fact, Marx claimed, all major historical changes are ultimately forced on society by changes in society's forces of production, i.e., its "material" forces. This has been particularly true of capitalism which is constantly inventing new innovative forces of production to expand and increase production. As we invent new forces of production (such as the steam engine, electricity, and factory assembly line), the old forces get pushed out of the way or destroyed (such as the water wheel, windmill, and individual handicrafts), and society reorganizes itself around these new innovative forces of production. New legal structures and social classes are created (such as the corporation and the managerial class), and the old legal structures and social classes are abandoned (such as the medieval manor and its lords and serfs). Great ideological battles take place for people's minds during these periods of transformation, but the new ways always triumph: History always follows the lead of the newest forces of production and wipes out the old. Capitalism, with its constant competitive struggles between businesses, is always innovating, and so continually destroys old forms of life and creates new ones. This Marxist view of history as determined by changes in the economic methods by which humanity produces the materials on which it must live is now generally referred to as **historical materialism**.

Quick Review 3.12

Marx's Historical Materialism

- The methods a society uses to produce its goods determines how that society organizes its workers.
- The way a society organizes its workers determines its social classes.
- A society's ruling social class controls society's government and ideologies and uses these to advance its own interests and control the working classes.

historical materialism
The Marxist view of history as determined by changes in the economic methods by which humanity produces the materials on which it must live.

Immiseration of Workers

Marx also claims that so long as production in modern economies is not planned, but is left to depend on private ownership and unrestrained free markets, the result could only be a series of related crises that would harm the working class.[86]

First, modern capitalist systems will exhibit an increasing concentration of global industrial power in a relatively few hands.[87] As self-interested private owners struggle to expand the businesses they control so they can better compete against other businesses, smaller firms will gradually be taken over by larger ones, which will keep expanding by growing and by acquiring more firms. As businesses expand, they eventually have to move beyond their nation of origin into international markets. International trade will do away with "national seclusion and self-sufficiency" and replace it with "the universal interdependence of nations," i.e., what we today call "globalization." As capitalism becomes globalized, ever greater economic power and wealth will continue to be concentrated in ever fewer hands.

Second, capitalist societies will experience repeated cycles of economic downturns.[88] Because workers are organized into mass assembly lines, the firm of each owner can produce large amounts of surplus. Because owners are self-interested and competitive, they each try to produce as much as they can without coordinating their production with that of other owners. As a result, firms periodically produce an oversupply of goods. These flood the market, and an economic depression or recession will result as the economy slows down to absorb the surplus.

Third, Marx argues, the position of the worker in capitalist societies will gradually worsen.[89] This gradual decline will result from the self-interested desire of capitalist owners to increase their profits at the expense of their workers. This self-interest will lead owners to replace workers with cheaper machines, thereby creating rising unemployment. Self-interest will also keep owners from increasing their workers' wages in proportion to the increase in productivity that mechanization makes possible. The combined effects of increased concentration, periodic economic downturns, rising unemployment, and declining relative compensation are what Marx refers to as the **immiseration** of the worker. The solution to all these problems, according to Marx, is collective ownership of society's productive assets and the use of rational planning to replace unregulated markets.[90]

immiseration of workers The combined effects of increased concentration, cyclic crises, rising unemployment, and declining relative compensation.

Marx's answer to capitalism is captured by the statement with which he ends his most famous work, *The Communist Manifesto*: "Workers of the world, unite!" The problems of capitalism arise from the conflict between classes—between the owner-class and the worker-class—so the only real solution is to get rid of classes. In other words, the way to overcome capitalism is to wipe away its class system and, in its place, establish a classless society. To get to the classless society, Marx thought, required a revolution in which the workers will overthrow the owners. He wrote that workers could achieve their ends "only by the forcible overthrow of all existing social conditions. Let the ruling classes tremble at a Communistic revolution. The workers have nothing to lose but their chains."

In the classless society, Marx thought, the means of production would no longer be an owner's private property, but would be collectively owned by all workers. Everyone would contribute according to their abilities, and receive according to their needs. This would be a society without exploitation, unemployment, poverty, and without inequality. It would be a society "where nobody has one exclusive sphere of activity but each can become accomplished in any branch he wishes, [where] society regulates the general production and thus makes it possible for me to do one thing today and another tomorrow, to hunt in the morning, fish in the afternoon, rear cattle in the evening, criticise after dinner, just as I have a mind, without ever becoming hunter, fisherman, herdsman or critic."[91]

Quick Review 3.13

Immiseration of Workers

- Marx claimed capitalism concentrates industrial power in the hands of a few who organize workers for mass production.
- Mass production in the hands of a few leads to surplus which causes economic depression.
- Factory owners replace workers with machines which creates unemployment; they keep wages low to increase profits.
- The combined effects of the above causes immiseration of workers.
- The only solution is a revolution that establishes a classless society where everyone owns the means of production.

The Replies to Marx's Criticisms

Critics have answered the Marxist criticism that free markets generate injustices by arguing that Marx wrongly assumes that justice means either equality or distribution according to need. This assumption is unprovable, some of his critics have claimed.[92] There are too many difficulties in the way of establishing acceptable principles of justice. Should distributive justice be determined in terms of effort, ability, or need? These questions cannot be answered in any objective way, they claim, so any attempt to replace free markets with some distributive principle will, in the final analysis, be an imposition of someone's subjective preferences on the other members of society. This, of course, will violate the (negative) right every individual has to be free of the coercion of others.

Other critics of Marx argue that justice can be given a clear meaning but one that supports free markets. Justice really means distribution according to contribution.[93] When markets are free and functioning competitively, some have argued, they will pay each worker the value of the worker's contribution because each person's wage will be determined by what the person adds to the output of the economy. Consequently, they argue, justice requires free markets.

A third kind of criticism that free market proponents have made is that, although inequalities may be endemic to private ownership and free markets, the benefits that private ownership and free markets make possible are more important.[94] The free market enables resources to be allocated efficiently without coercion, and this is a greater benefit than equality.

Free market proponents also have replied to the criticism that free capitalist markets break down communities. Free markets, they have argued, are based on the idea that the preferences of those in government should not determine the relationships of citizens. Government should not, for example, favor one kind of religious community or church relationship over another, or favor one community's values or forms of relationships over those of others. In societies characterized by such freedom, people are able to join together in associations in which they can pursue whatever values—religious or nonreligious—they choose.[95] In such free associations—supported by the right to freedom of association—true community and communal relationships can flourish. The freedom that underlies free markets, in short, provides the opportunity to freely form plural communities. Such communities are not possible in societies, such as the former Soviet Union, in which those in government decide which associations are allowed and which are prohibited. Thus, the persuasiveness of the argument that unregulated markets should be supported because they are efficient and protect the right to liberty and property depends, in the end, on the importance attributed to several ethical factors. How important are the rights to liberty and to property as compared with a just distribution of income and wealth? How important are the negative rights of liberty and property as compared with the positive rights of needy workers and of those who own no property? How important is efficiency as compared with the claims of justice? And finally, how important are the goods of community and of caring as compared with the rights of individuals?

Quick Review 3.14

Criticism of Marx

- Marx's claims that capitalism is unjust are unprovable.
- Justice requires free markets.
- The benefits of private property and free markets are more important than equality.
- Free markets can encourage community instead of causing alienation.
- Immiseration of workers has not occurred; instead their condition has improved.

The most telling criticism of Marx is that the immiseration of workers that he predicted did not in fact occur. Workers in capitalist countries are much better off now than their parents were a century ago. Nonetheless, contemporary Marxists argue that much of what Marx said remains true today. Many factory workers today find their work dehumanizing, meaningless, and lacking in personal satisfaction, i.e., work for them is alienating.[96] Moreover, as Marx claimed, unemployment, recessions, and other "crises" continue to plague our economy.[97] Advertisements attempt to instill in us desires for things we do not really need and false views of our real human needs and desires, so we become consumers centered on accumulating the material things businesses want to sell us. [98] Marx would have said that businesses' drive for profit creates "the renunciation of life and of human needs" through its use of advertising. Finally, a fundamental problem that Marx pointed to is still with us: inequality.[99] In fact, on an international scale, as free trade has expanded through globalization, the gulf between the "haves" and the "have-nots" around the world appears to have grown greater.[100]

3.5 Conclusion: The Mixed Economy, the New Property, and the End of Marxism

The debate for and against free markets, free trade, and private property still continues. Some people have claimed that the collapse of several communist regimes at the end of the twentieth century showed that capitalism, with its emphasis on free markets, was the clear winner.[101] Other observers, however, have held that the emergence of strong economies in nations that emphasize government intervention and collectivist property rights, such as China and Singapore, shows that free markets alone are not

mixed economy An economy that retains a market and private property system but relies heavily on government policies to remedy their deficiencies.

the key to prosperity.[102] It is inevitable, perhaps, that the controversy has led many economists to advocate retention of market systems and private ownership, but modification of their workings through government regulation that rid them of their most obvious defects. The resulting amalgam of government regulation, partially free markets, and limited property rights is appropriately referred to as the **mixed economy**.[103]

Basically, a mixed economy retains a market and private property system but relies heavily on government policies to remedy their deficiencies. Government transfers (of private income) are used to get rid of the worst aspects of inequality by drawing money from the wealthy in the form of income taxes and distributing it to the disadvantaged in the form of welfare payments or social services. Minimum wage laws, safety laws, union laws, and other forms of labor legislation are used to protect workers from exploitation. Monopolies are regulated, nationalized, or outlawed. Government monetary and fiscal policies attempt to ensure full employment. Government regulatory agencies police firms to ensure they do not engage in socially harmful behavior.

How effective are these sorts of policies? A comparison of the United States with other countries that have gone farther down the road toward implementing the policies of a "mixed economy" may be helpful. Sweden, Norway, France, Ireland, and Switzerland are all mixed economies with high levels of government regulation. Statistics are readily available comparing the performance of the economies of these countries to that of the United States. The statistics are interesting. To begin with, the United States has greater inequality than any of these countries: Based on CIA figures, the top 10 percent of all U.S. households, for example, receive 15 times as much income as the bottom 10 percent, whereas in Sweden and Norway the ratio is 6 times, in France it is 8 times, in Ireland and Switzerland it is 9 times.[104] Although the United States has a high level of inequality, it has not had a relatively high level of economic growth. According to the *CIA World Factbook* for 2010, the industrial productivity growth rates of Switzerland, Ireland, and Norway all surpass the U.S. growth rate, and the gross domestic product growth rates of Norway, Switzerland, and France likewise surpass the U.S. gross domestic product growth rate. The infant mortality rate of the United States (6.14 deaths per 1000 live births) is higher than that of Ireland (4.9 deaths), Denmark (4.29 deaths), Switzerland (4.12 deaths), France (3.31 deaths), and Sweden (2.74 deaths). The life expectancy at birth in the United States (78.2) is less than in Ireland (78.4), Denmark (78.4), Norway (80.1), Switzerland (81), Sweden (81), and France (81).

Although these brief comparisons do not tell the whole story, they indicate at least that a mixed economy may have some advantages. Moreover, comparisons of the performance of the U.S. economy during different periods of its history suggests a similar conclusion. Prior to the rise of government regulation and social welfare programs in the United States, the highest per capita growth rate in GDP that the United States experienced during a single decade was the 22 percent rate of growth that occurred between 1900 and 1910. During the 1940s, when the U.S. economy was being run as a command economy (because of its involvement in World War II), the growth rate in per capita GDP climbed to 36 percent (the highest ever). During the 1960s, when the United States introduced its major social welfare programs, the per capita GDP growth rate was at a 30 percent level. Again, these comparisons do not tell the whole story, but they suggest that the higher levels of government involvement characteristic of a mixed economy is not altogether a bad idea.

Property Systems and New Technologies

Debates have also swirled around the proper balance between property systems that emphasize Lockean notions of private ownership and those that emphasize socialist notions of collective ownership. Nowhere has this debate been more contentious than

intellectual property Nonphysical property that consists of knowledge or information such as formulas, plans, music, stories, texts, software, etc.

in regard to the new forms of **intellectual property** that modern technology—such as genetic engineering and information technologies—have created. *Intellectual property* is property that consists of a nonphysical object, such as a software program, a song, an idea, an invention, a recipe, a digital image or sound, a genetic code, or any form of information. Unlike physical objects, intellectual property is nonexclusive. That is, unlike physical objects, one person's use of intellectual property does not exclude other people's simultaneous use of that property. A physical object such as a house, a pizza, a car, or a square yard of land can be used only by one or a few parties at any single time, and what one party uses or consumes of the object cannot be used or consumed by another person. In contrast, intellectual property such as a song, an idea, or a piece of information can be copied, used, or consumed by countless individuals at the same time. If you create a digital program or image and store it on your computer, others can come along and make millions of exact copies of that program or image that work and look exactly like your original. Those millions of exact copies can be used and enjoyed by millions of people without limiting your own ability to use or enjoy your original copy.

What sort of property systems should societies adopt to determine ownership rights for intellectual property? On one side, are those who take either the Lockean or the utilitarian view that intellectual property should be treated like private property. Those who take a Lockean view argue that if I create a software program or a song, then it should be treated as my private property simply because it is a product of my own mental labor. If anyone tries to use or copy my program or song without my permission, they are violating my "natural" property rights. Utilitarians may also argue for private ownership of intellectual property, but for different reasons. Utilitarians can argue that private ownership of intellectual property provides a necessary incentive for people to work hard at generating new intellectual creations. It takes a lot of hard work for a company like Microsoft to create a word-processing program or for a musician to create an original piece of music. Companies and individuals would not put forth these efforts nor make these investments if they could not profit from their creations by being given rights of ownership that allow them the exclusive right to copy their creations and prevent others from making copies without their permission. Without such private property rights, intellectual creation would dry up.

On the other side of this debate are those who take a position that is more like Marx's, one that supports the collective or common ownership of intellectual property, particularly of property that can be used to produce additional value. Like Marx, many modern critics of private ownership of intellectual property claim that intellectual creativity does not require the financial incentives of a private property system. Before the modern period of history, the stories, poems, songs, inventions, and information that people created were considered common property that anyone could use or copy. Despite the lack of any financial returns, these artists, writers, and thinkers continued to produce their works. Even today, many people write software or music and make it freely available to others on the Internet—perhaps under the slogan "Information Wants To Be Free!"—despite receiving no financial incentives for their creativity. There is, in fact, a large group of computer software writers who promote "open-source software"—like Linux, Firefox, and OpenOffice—which is software that anyone can freely copy, use, or change. Others argue that the common good of society will be better served if intellectual property is treated as public or communal property that is freely available for others to use to develop new intellectual products or otherwise produce benefits for society. New scientific discoveries or new engineering developments should not be hoarded and hidden under the guise of private property, but should be freely available to benefit society. This is the position of many developing countries, where intellectual property is still seen as common property. Ethicist Paul Steidlmeir, for example, writes: "developing countries argue that individual claims on intellectual property are subordinate to more fundamental claims of social well-being... [and] that while people may have a right to the fruit of their labor, they have a duty to reward society which made the very fruitfulness of labor possible."[105] Not surprisingly, copying of copyrighted software is rampant in many developing countries where software that is priced at $300, $400, and $500 in the United States is available from street vendors for $5 or $10.

The property system for intellectual property in the United States is still evolving, although in many respects it tends more toward a Lockean/utilitarian system than a Marxist/socialist one. In the United States, an important distinction is made between an *idea* and the *expression* of the idea. Ideas cannot be owned nor become private property, but remain the common property of everyone. However, a particular *expression* of an idea, such as the text, words, or software used to express the idea is granted a ***copyright***, indicating that that particular expression of the idea is the private property of an individual or a company. Any tangible text or expression (i.e., one that can be physically seen or touched) can be copyrighted, including books, magazines, newspapers, speeches, music, plays, movies, radio and television shows, maps, paintings, drawings, photos, greeting cards, sound recordings on tapes or digital discs, software programs, and the masks used to imprint computer circuits. In a Lockean fashion, U.S. law says that registering a copyright with the government does not create the copyright, but that mere authorship of a work creates a copyright (i.e., ownership or property) in the work. Nevertheless, copyrights of things authored today expire 120 years after their creation or 95 years after publication, and then, like ideas, become common or public property.[106]

copyright A grant that indicates that a particular expression of an idea is the private property of an individual or a company.

A second way of creating property rights for intellectual property is through a *patent*. New, nonobvious, and useful inventions of machines, drugs, chemicals or other "compositions of matter," processes, software programs, manufactured articles, nonsexually reproduced plants, living material invented by a person, and product designs are also recognized to be private property when they are granted a patent. Patents, however, expire after 14 years (for patents of a new design of an existing product) or 20 years (for patents of new products) and then also become the common property of everyone.[107] Many people criticize this system, arguing that patents and copyrights prevent others from developing improved versions of protected software or from taking advantage of key new drug discoveries—a criticism that appeals to a kind of Marxist view that property should serve the good of the community. Yet, others counter that patents expire too quickly and that new inventions should remain the private property of the inventor for much longer—a view with Lockean connotations. The property debate between Locke and Marx thus continues to simmer.

The End of Marxism?

Defenders of free markets were greatly encouraged by what some called the complete abandonment of communism in several formerly communist nations, particularly the members of the former U.S.S.R. On September 24, 1990, the Soviet legislature voted to switch to a free market economy and to scrap 70 years of communist economics that had led to inefficiencies and consumer shortages. Then, during the summer of 1991, the Communist Party was outlawed after party leaders botched an attempt to take over the Soviet government. The Soviet Union broke up and its reorganized states discarded their radical Marxist-Leninist ideologies in favor of worldviews that incorporated both socialist and capitalist elements. The new nations embarked on experimental attempts to integrate private property and free markets into their still heavily socialist economies. These developments were hailed by some observers, such as Francis Fukuyama, as indicating "The End of History."[108] What Fukuyama and others were suggesting is that, with the end of communism, there will be no more "progress" toward a better or more perfect economic system: The whole world now agrees that the best system is capitalism.

Those historic communist reforms, however, did not signal the "complete abandonment" of Marx or socialism. Without exception, all of these reforms have been aimed at moving communist systems toward economies that are based on the best features of both socialism and capitalism. They have, in short, been aimed at moving the communist countries toward the same kind of mixed economy system that dominates Western nations. The debate today in the formerly communist world as in the United States is over the best mix of government regulation, private property rights, and free markets, and not over whether a pure market system is better or worse than a pure command system.

Followers of Smith and Locke continue to insist that the level of government intervention tolerated by the mixed economy does more harm than good. Their opponents continue to counter that, in our mixed economy, government still favors business interests and that allowing businesses to operate without regulatory oversight worsens our economic problems. On balance, however, it may be that the mixed economy comes closest to combining the utilitarian benefits of free markets with the respect for human rights, justice, and caring that are the characteristic strengths of government regulation.

Questions for Review and Discussion

Study and Review on mythinkinglab.com

1. Define the following: ideology, individualistic ideology, communitarian ideology, command economy, free market system, private property system, state of nature, natural rights, Locke's natural right to property, surplus value, alienation, bourgeois, proletariat, economic substructure, social superstructure, forces of production, relations of production, historical materialism, immiseration of workers, invisible hand, natural price, natural liberty, aggregate demand, aggregate supply, Keynesian economics, survival of the fittest, social Darwinism, naturalistic fallacy, mixed economy, intellectual property.
2. Contrast the views of Locke, Marx, Smith, Keynes, and Spencer on the nature and proper functions of government and on its relationship to business. Which views seem to you to provide the most adequate analysis of contemporary relations between business and government? Explain your answer fully.
3. "Locke's views on property, Smith's views on free markets, and Marx's views on capitalism obviously do not hold true when applied to the organizational structure and the operations of modern corporations." Comment on this statement. What reforms, if any, would Locke, Smith, and Marx advocate with respect to current corporate organization and performance?
4. "Equality, justice, and a respect for rights are characteristics of the U.S. economic system." Would you agree or disagree with this statement? Why?
5. "Free markets allocate economic goods in the most socially beneficial way and ensure progress." To what extent is this statement true? To what extent do you think it is false?

Web Resources

Readers interested in researching the topic of globalization can find on the Web both introductory discussions of globalization (*http://www.globalization101.org*) as well as more in-depth discussions (*http://www.globalissues.org* and *http://yaleglobal.yale.edu*);

statistics and data on globalization are also available (*http://globalization.kof.ethz.ch*); the Web also has materials on Locke, Marx, and Smith (*http://users.ox.ac.uk/~worc0337/philosophers.html* and *http://www.epistemelinks.com/index.aspx*).

CASES

Explore the Concept on mythinkinglab.com

The GM Bailout

By mid-December 2008, GM, the world's second largest auto manufacturer, was losing $2 billion a month. Rick Wagoner, CEO since 2000, knew that GM did not have enough money to survive much longer. The year 2008, GM's 100th anniversary, was turning out to be its worse ever.[1] Wagoner already knew GM would end the year with losses of about $31 billion. But that was an improvement from 2007 when the company lost $38.7 billion, the fourth-biggest corporate loss in history. Those losses, and losses of $1 billion in 2006 and $10 billion in 2005, meant that the company Wagoner led lost an astonishing $80 billion in four years.

Wagoner was a dedicated, affable, and likable man. In high school, he had excelled in all sports but his height of six feet four made him a star in basketball and upon graduation, he was secretly hoping to be a professional basketball player. But as a freshman basketball player at Duke University, it became clear to Wagoner that he did not have the talent and drive to be a professional athlete. Instead, he majored in economics and also began dating Kathleen Kaylor whom he eventually married. After graduating from Duke University and getting an MBA from Harvard University, Wagoner went to work for GM. He rapidly worked his way up through the company's ranks and in 2000, he was named CEO, the youngest person to ever hold that position in the company's history.

Wagoner blamed GM's misfortune on a number of factors. One of the most significant factors, he felt, was the "Great Recession" of 2008 that had hurt the sales of all the auto companies, particularly when the troubled banks stopped lending money so customers could no longer get car loans. Unfortunately, GM did not anticipate the "credit crunch," and by 2006, it had sold off a controlling interest in GMAC, the previously wholly-owned finance company that had provided cheap loans to its car buyers. After GM sold 51 percent of GMAC to Cerberus for $7.4 billion, Cerberus refused to let GMAC continue providing the same easy credit to GM's customers, which turned out to be a significant blow to GM's sales.

Yet another problem was GM's labor costs. In 2008, GM was paying an average of about $70 per hour for labor. That $70 included $30 that the worker actually received in wages, and $40 that went to fund other labor costs including the worker's benefits and pension, plus the cost of providing health care and pensions to about 432,000 GM retirees. Because GM had been operating for 100 years, the number of its retirees was much larger than those of new car companies. Toyota, for example, was paying about $53 per hour for labor in its U.S. manufacturing plants, of which $30 went to the worker as wages, and $23 went to pay for the worker's benefits and pension, but very little for retirees since the number was relatively low. In some of its plants, a Toyota spokesman said, it was paying as little as $48 per hour for labor.

But perhaps the major cause of GM's difficulties was its self-inflicted dependence on large SUVs (sport utility vehicles). Japanese car makers could make small and mid-sized cars for less than it cost GM to make comparable cars. To compete, GM had to lower its prices until the profit margins on its small and mid-sized cars were vanishingly thin. But during the 1980s, when gas was cheap, GM discovered that large SUVs were big hits with male customers and with couples with growing families. Moreover, unlike its smaller car models, profit margins on its large SUVs were hefty, as much as $10,000 to $15,000 per vehicle. As its SUV sales boomed during the 1990s, GM expanded its line and eagerly converted many of its plants over to the production of the lucrative big vehicles. By 2003, the bulk of its profits were coming from SUV sales. But when the price of gasoline gradually crept upward, the costs of owning an SUV also increased causing the SUV market to slow and then to decline. In 2004, unsold SUVs started piling up at car dealerships. When Hurricane Katrina made gasoline prices soar in 2005, sales of SUVs eventually collapsed. Thus, GM ended 2005 with a loss of $10.4 billion. Things improved somewhat in 2006, but then losses climbed to record levels: $38.7 billion in 2007, and $30.9 billion in 2008. Unfortunately, by now GM's plants, strategic plans, research and development programs, and its mindset, were all locked into the production of SUVs, and it would take years to change them.

Because of its reliance on SUVs, GM had put off investing in the small fuel-efficient cars a gas-conscious public had turned to in 2005. In the 1990s, GM had developed the technology for an all-electric car, the EV1. The EV1 was, in fact, the first mass-produced modern electric car made by a major car company. By 1999, GM had spent $500 million producing the EV1 and $400 million marketing it, yet had leased only 800 vehicles. Convinced that the car would never match the profitability of its SUVs, the company stopped making the cars and in 2002, it repossessed all the EV1s it had leased and phased out the project. At the same time, both Toyota and Honda were introducing their small hybrid electric-gas engine cars into the United States. The hybrids turned out to be a commercial success and, more importantly, production of the cars allowed both Toyota and Honda to gain almost a decade of experience in hybrid technology, while GM continued focusing on its gas-guzzling SUVs. In a June 2006 interview published in *Motor Trend*, Rick Wagoner confessed that his worst decision during his tenure at GM was "axing the EV1 electric-car program and not putting the right resources into hybrids."

All of these problems had culminated in the $80 billion loss that placed GM in the difficult situation Wagoner knew he had to deal with in the closing weeks of 2008. With many analysts predicting that GM would go bankrupt, banks—which themselves were barely surviving the worse financial crisis in decades—refused to loan the company more money. At the rate it was running through its cash reserves, Wagoner knew the risk of bankruptcy was growing daily. Given the company's dire straits, he decided that only a government bailout could save it.

Government bailouts were not popular. In September, 2008, the George W. Bush administration asked the U.S. Congress to pass legislation creating a $700 billion fund called the Troubled Asset Relief Program (TARP). A reluctant U.S. Congress approved the TARP bill which authorized the U.S. Treasury Department to use the funds "to purchase... troubled assets from any financial institution." The "troubled assets" were millions of mortgage loans that banks had extended to home buyers who were now unable to make their monthly mortgage payments, and whose homes were worth less than their mortgages because home prices had collapsed in early 2007. Since the homes were worth less than their mortgage loans, the mortgages could not be repaid in full when delinquent homeowners sold their homes or when banks confiscated them. Suffering huge losses, many U.S. banks were on the verge of failing as were European banks that earlier had taken over thousands of the now "troubled" U.S mortgages. Many economists predicted that these widespread bank failures would turn the deepening recession into a global depression worse than the worldwide Great Depression of the 1930s.

In spite of the looming financial crisis, many had opposed the plan to bail out the banks. A hundred leading economists signed a letter to the U.S. Congress that said lack of "fairness" was a "fatal pitfall" of the plan because it was "a subsidy to investors at taxpayers' expense. Investors who took risks to earn profits must also bear the losses."[2] Calling the bank bailouts "socialism for the rich," the Nobel prize-winning economist Joseph Stiglitz wrote "this new form of ersatz capitalism, in which losses are socialized and profits privatized, is doomed to failure. Incentives are distorted [and] there is no market discipline."[3]

Nevertheless, if U.S. banks were able to get bailout money from Washington, perhaps GM could do the same. So Rick Wagoner and two GM board members flew to Washington on October 13, 2008 to meet with officials of President George W. Bush's administration. During the meeting, Wagoner summarized the precarious position of the company and asked for a loan from the TARP fund. Bush's people balked at the request, saying the legislation explicitly said TARP funds were for financial institutions so they could not be used to provide loans to car manufacturers. Turned down by the administration, a desperate Wagoner turned to the U.S. Congress. On November 18 and 19, he and the CEOs of Chrysler and Ford—the two other U.S. auto companies were also going through difficult times—came before Congressional committees and asked for legislation authorizing government funds to aid the auto industry. Committee members, however, became angry, particularly when the auto executives admitted they had not prepared plans detailing how they would use the funds nor what changes they intended to make to ensure they could return to profitability. In the end, the three CEOs were told to come back in December with detailed financial plans for their companies. In early December, the CEOs dutifully returned to the U.S. Congress with plans in hand and repeated their requests for financial assistance. A few days later, both the U.S. House and the Senate proposed legislation to aid the auto companies. Unfortunately, while the House approved the auto aid bill on December 10, the Senate voted it down. Without the support of both the House and the Senate, the proposed legislation was dead.

Wagoner was stunned and despaired for the future of the company he had served for over thirty years. But his despair turned to elation when he got a telephone call from the Bush administration. The administration had decided the U.S. Treasury could, after all, use the TARP funds to provide loans to GM as well as to Chrysler. (Ford had decided it could survive without government money.) On December 19, 2008, President Bush announced that the U.S. Treasury would provide GM with a $13.4 billion loan from the TARP fund, while Chrysler would get a $4 billion loan. In announcing the assistance to the auto companies, the Bush administration said "the direct costs of American automakers failing and laying off their workers...would result in a more than one percent reduction in real GDP growth and about 1.1 million workers losing their jobs."[4] To get the money, Wagoner had to agree that by February 17, 2009, GM would hand over a detailed plan specifying how it would achieve "financial viability" and the plan had to be acceptable to U.S. Treasury officials. With his back to the wall, Wagoner agreed to the terms and on December 31, 2008, GM got a first installment of $4 billion from its allotted loan amount; it received another $5.4 billion on January 16, 2009, and a final installment of $4 billion on February 17, 2009.

Many objected that bailouts violated the free market philosophy embraced by many Americans and replaced it with a kind of socialism. Republican Senator Bob Corker said the GM bailout "should send a chill through all Americans who believe in free enterprise."[5] Several Republican members of Congress submitted a resolution on the bailouts that said they were "moving our free-market based economy another dangerous step closer toward socialism."[6]

By February 17, 2009, newly-elected President Barack Obama had taken office so his administration would end up finishing the auto bail-out that the previous administration had set in motion. As part of the "viability plan," that he had agreed to submit by February 17, Wagoner was to renegotiate GM's union contracts to make its labor costs competitive with foreign car makers in the U.S., reduce the number and models of cars it made, shrink its unsecured debt of $27.5 billion down to $9.2 billion by getting creditors to cancel part of their debt in exchange for GM stock, and invest in fuel-efficient hybrid and electric vehicles.[7]

Wagoner had quickly entered negotiations with the United Auto Workers (UAW), GM's major union, and with creditors. But GM's creditors had stubbornly refused to reduce their debt by the amount the government wanted. In the end, GM did not reach the debt reduction targets the U.S. Treasury wanted it to reach by February 17. Nevertheless, in the final "plan for viability" it submitted to the U.S. Treasury on February 17, GM said it would cut 37,000 blue-collar jobs and 10,000 white-collar jobs, close 14 plants over three years, eliminate four of its eight car brands, cut manager salaries by 10 per cent and all other salaries by 3 to 7 percent, and shift the costs of retiree health insurance to an independent trust funded in part with GM stock and in part with debt. However, the plan added, GM would need an additional $22.5 billion from the government to continue operating to 2011.[8]

The Auto Task Force Obama had put together to review GM's proposed plan was not happy with it. Steven Ratner, who headed up the task force said:

> It was clear to us from the "viability plans" that the companies had submitted on Feb. 17 that GM and Chrysler were in a state of denial. Both companies needed gigantic reductions in their costs and liabilities. They had way too many plants and workers for expected car volumes. And their labor costs were out of line with those of their most direct competitors ... I was shocked by the stunningly poor management that we found, particularly at GM, where we encountered, among other things, perhaps the weakest finance operation any of us had ever seen in a major company.[9]

"Team Auto," as the Obama task force called itself, spent over a month studying the plan and concluded that GM's optimistic assumptions that its market share would grow in the future, its costs would decline, and in a few years it would have positive cash flows, were out of touch with reality. On March 30, 2009, the Obama administration told the company that its plan was not acceptable and did "not warrant the substantial additional investments ... requested." Nevertheless, GM was given 60 days, until June 1, to try to extract deeper concessions from its creditors and was also given another loan of $6.36 billion to carry it through the next two months. Although GM continued trying to work with its creditors, the Obama task force soon realized that the only way GM would force its creditors to forgive GM's debt was by filing for bankruptcy.[10] This would give a federal judge the authority to cancel as much debt as was needed for the company to become a viable business again. On March 31, the U.S. Treasury informed the company's board of directors that if it filed for bankruptcy, the government would provide the funding it would need to emerge as a viable company.

By this time, Rick Wagoner's fate had been sealed. In mid-March, Steven Ratner asked Wagoner about his plans and he replied, "I'm not planning to stay until I'm 65 but I think I've got at least a few years left in me..., but I told the [Bush] administration that if my leaving would be helpful to saving General Motors, I'm prepared to do it."[11] On Friday, March 27, Wagoner attended a meeting with the Auto Task Force to discuss GM's restructuring plans. Before the meeting Steven Ratner pulled him aside and said, "In our last meeting you very graciously offered to step aside if it would be helpful. Unfortunately our conclusion is that it would be best if you did that." Wagoner agreed to step down, and on March 30 he submitted his resignation from GM.

On June 1, 2009, GM entered bankruptcy. The U.S. Treasury created a new company named "General Motors Company," and the now bankrupt "Old GM" sold its most profitable brands and most efficient manufacturing facilities to the new "General Motors Company" who used $30 billion of the government's money to buy them. The creditors of "Old GM" received a 10 percent share of the new company plus proceeds from the sale of the assets of "Old GM." A 17 percent share of the "New GM" was put into a trust to pay for union retiree health care benefits; the union trust also received a $2.5 billion note from "New GM" and $6.5 billion of its preferred stock. The government of Canada, which had contributed $10 billion to bail out several GM plants in Ottawa and Ontario, got 12 percent of the new company. The remaining 61 percent share of the company became the property of the U.S. government in return for a total of $50 billion it pumped into GM. The U.S. government also retained the right to elect 10 of the 12 members of the board of directors of the "New GM"; it was now the major owner of a car company.[12]

GM was not the only firm that became a (partially) state-owned company during the financial crisis. On February 27, 2009, it was announced that in exchange for $25 billion the U.S. Treasury was taking 36 percent ownership of Citigroup, Inc., a large banking company driven to the brink of failure by the financial crisis. On September 16, 2008, American International Group, an insurance company also brought to its knees by the financial crisis, announced that the government, through its Federal Reserve Bank, was taking ownership of 80 percent of the company in exchange for $85 billion.

Many observers claimed that government ownership of companies is the kind of government ownership of the "means of production" that Marx and other socialists advocate. For example, Robert Higgs, editor of *The Independent Review*, wrote that "the government is resorting to outright socialism by taking ownership positions in rescued firms."[13] And the Mackinac Center, a conservative research institute focused on promoting "the free market," published an article by Michael Winther that stated:

> There are only two economic systems in the world ... These two economic systems are generally described as "the free market" and "socialism." ... Socialism is characterized and defined by either of two qualities: Government ownership or control of capital, or forced pooling and redistribution of wealth. ... [T]he current bailout could be described as "super-socialism" because it involves every possible component of socialism: the forced redistribution of wealth, increased government control of capital, and even the extreme of socialism, which is government ownership of capital. Our federal government is not content to just regulate the markets (capital), but is also taking the next step of purchasing ownership interest in previously private companies.[14]

Questions

1. How would Locke, Smith, and Marx evaluate the various events in this case?
2. Explain the ideologies implied by the statements of: the letter to the U.S. Congress signed by 100 leading economists, Joseph Stiglitz, Bob Corker, the Republican resolution on the bailouts, Robert Higgs, and Michael Winther.
3. In your view should the GM bailout have been done? Explain why or why not. Was the bailout ethical in terms of utilitarianism, justice, rights, and caring?
4. In your judgment, was it good or bad for the government to take ownership of 61 percent of GM? Explain why or why not in terms of the theories of Lock, Smith, and Marx.

Notes

1. Tom Krisher and Kimberly S. Johnson, "GM Posts $9.6 Billion Loss," *Associated Press*, February 26, 2009; accessed May 30, 2010 at *http://www.thestar.com/Business/article/593350.*
2. Justin Wolfers, "Economists on the Bailout," *The New York Times*, September 23, 2008.
3. Joseph Stiglitz, "America's Socialism for the Rich," *The Guardian*, June 12, 2009.
4. Congressional Oversight Panel, *September Oversight Report, The Use of TARP Funds in the Support and Reorganization of the Domestic Automotive Industry*, September 9, 2009, p. 8.
5. Michael D. Shear and Peter Whoriskey, "Obama Touts Auto Bailout during Michigan Trip," *The Washington Post*, July 31, 2010.
6. Molly Henneberg, "Resolution Opposing Bailouts as 'Socialism' Airs Rift in GOP," *Fox News*, December 31, 2008.
7. Robert Snell, "GM's Wagoner, UAW's Gettelfinger Interviewed on 'Today'," *Detroit News*, January 9, 2009; Robert Snell, "Reaction Mixed to GM's Financial Plan, *Detroit News*, January 17, 2009.
8. See General Motors Corporation, *2019–2014 Restructuring Plan*, February 17, 2009, accessed January 19, 2011 at *http://www.treasury.gov/initiatives/financial-stability/investment-programs/aifp/Documents_Contracts_Agreements/GMRestructuring-Plan.pdf.*
9. Steven Ratner, "The Auto Bailout: How We Did It," *Fortune Magazine*, October 21, 2009.
10. Ibid.
11. Ibid.
12. General Motors Corporation, *2019–2014 Restructuring Plan*, p. 13.
13. Chris Mitchell, "The Great Bailout Brouhaha, Free Market Economists Weigh in on Paulson's Plan," *Reason Magazine*, September 25, 2008.
14. Michael R. Winther, "Five Principles that Are Violated by the Bailouts," Mackinac Center for Public Policy, March 13, 2009; accessed January 19 *at www.mackinac.org/10363.*

CASES

Accolade versus Sega[1]

Explore the Concept on mythinkinglab.com

Accolade, Inc. is a small software company located in San Jose, California, that had prospered by making and marketing games that could be played on Sega game consoles. Its most popular game so far was a game called "Ishido: The Way of Stones." Sega had not granted Accolade a license to make games for its consoles, and Sega derived no income from sales of Accolade's games.

In the early 1990s, Sega marketed a new game console called "Genesis," and Accolade engineers discovered that their games would no longer work on the new console because Sega had inserted new secret codes and security devices into its Genesis consoles that prevented other game programs from working on the console except those made by Sega. To get around this problem, Accolade engineers set to work reverse engineering Sega's new console and several of its games. Reverse engineering is the process of analyzing a product to discover how it was made and how it works. First, Accolade took several Genesis consoles apart to learn how its security mechanisms worked. Then, Accolade decompiled several of Sega's game programs.

To understand what this involved, it is necessary to understand that the software that makes up a game is produced in a two-step process. First, engineers write the program for the game using a software language that is easily understood by an engineer who knows the language and that consists of a series of comprehensible instructions such as "GOTO line 5." This version of the program is called the *source code*. Second, once they have finished writing the source code, the engineers enter the source code into a computer that compiles the code, essentially translating it into a machine language consisting of zeros and ones (such as "0001101100111 1001010"). Although the new compiled code is virtually impossible for a human to understand, the series of zeros and ones that make up a compiled code can be read by the game console computer and provides the basic instructions that make the game operate.

Software game programs (and, in fact, all software programs) that are sold in retail stores consist of such compiled code. Decompiling is an attempt to reverse the two-step process through which the program was originally produced. Basically, the compiled or "machine" code that makes up the software program is fed into a computer that attempts to translate the machine language (i.e., the series of zeros and ones) back into the original source code language (i.e., instructions such as "GOTO line 5") that can be understood by the engineer. The engineer can then examine the new source code and discover exactly how the program works and how it was put together. The process of decompiling is not always completely accurate, and sometimes engineers have to work hard to figure out exactly what the original source code was. Many engineers believe that reverse engineering, particularly decompiling, is inherently unethical.

Nevertheless, Accolade engineers succeeded in getting the information they wanted, and with this knowledge they were soon able to write games that would work on Sega's new Genesis consoles. Sega, however, immediately sued Accolade, claiming that the company had infringed on its copyright. Initially, the U.S. District Court in San Francisco agreed with Sega and issued an injunction forcing Accolade to withdraw its Sega-compatible games from the market.

Sega lawyers argued that when Accolade reversed engineered its software programs, Accolade had illegally made copies of Sega's source code. Because this source code was owned by Sega, Accolade had no right to copy or reverse engineer it, and Accolade in effect had stolen Sega's property by doing so. In addition, the new games that Accolade wrote had to include secret codes that were required to allow the software to work on the Genesis console. These secret codes, Sega claimed, were also owned and copyrighted by Sega and so could not be copied by Accolade and inserted into its game programs.

Accolade, however, appealed the decision of the U.S. District Court to a higher court, the Ninth Circuit Court of Appeals. Accolade claimed that the secret codes and security devices that Sega had used and that had to be known to allow games to play on the Genesis console were in effect a public interface standard. An *interface standard* is a standardized mechanism that one kind of product must use if it is to be able to work on another product. (The standard prongs that an electric cord must have if it is to fit into a standard outlet are an example of a simple interface standard.) Such interface standards cannot be privately owned by anyone, but are public property that can be used and duplicated by everyone. It was permissible, Accolade lawyers argued, to duplicate the source code because this was merely a way of getting access to the interface standard on the Genesis consoles. It was permissible for Accolade to include copies of these secret codes in its games because these were public property. Accolade's arguments eventually won out when it appealed the decision of the U.S. District Court in the Ninth Circuit Court of Appeals. The Ninth Circuit Court of Appeals overturned the earlier decision and essentially agreed with Accolade.

However, many legal experts disagreed with the Ninth Circuit Court of Appeals. They felt that Accolade's arguments were wrong and that the company had really stolen Sega's property. The security devices and secret codes that Sega had developed were not like the interface standards that different companies must agree on when working on products that must be compatible with each other. It is true that when companies are working on products that must be compatible with each other—like tires that must fit on cars, or electric plugs that must fit into electric sockets—they need to agree on a public standard interface that no one will own, but that everyone will be able to freely use. However, some legal experts have argued, Sega's Genesis console was a product that belonged to Sega alone and for which Sega wanted to be the sole provider of games. Thus, this was not a case of different companies having to reach an agreement over a public standard; it was a case of a single company making use of its own private technology to make its own games. So, critics of the court's decision have concluded, there was no public interface standard involved in the Accolade-Sega case.

Questions

1. Analyze this case from the perspective of each of the theories of private property described in this chapter (i.e., from the perspective of Locke's theory of private property, the utilitarian theory of private property, and the Marxist theory of private property). Which of these views do you most agree with and which do you think is most appropriate for this case?
2. Do you agree that Accolade had "really stolen" Sega's property? Explain why or why not.
3. In your judgment, did Accolade go too far in trying to discover the underlying source code of Sega's programs? Does a company have a right to reverse engineer any product it wants?

Note

1. This case is based on Richard A. Spinello, "Software Compatibility and Reverse Engineering," in Richard A. Spinello, *Case Studies in Information and Computer Ethics* (Upper Saddle River, NJ: Prentice Hall, 1997), pp. 142–145.

Mic

4

Ethics in the Marketplace

Why is a perfectly competitive free market said to be so desirable from an ethical point of view?

What is a monopoly market and why are such markets seen as ethically questionable?

How do oligopoly markets provide opportunities for anticompetitive behaviors that are ethically questionable?

Can we do anything to remedy the ethical shortcomings of monopolies and oligopolies?

Bill Gates is retired CEO and founder of Microsoft Corporation, which was subject to government oversight until May 2011 as the result of an April 2000 judgment by a U.S. District Court that it "maintained its monopoly power by anticompetitive means and attempted to monopolize the Web browser market." In March 2004 the European Union fined Microsoft $794 million, and an additional $448 million in 2006, and $1.44 billion more in 2008, for ongoing "abuse of its monopoly power."

INTRODUCTION

Listen to the Chapter Audio on mythinkinglab.com

Let's consider the following recent news stories:

> A South Korean executive with LG Display has agreed to plead guilty and serve a year in prison for participating in a global conspiracy to fix the prices of TFT-LCD (thin film transistor liquid crystal display) panels, the U.S. Department of Justice announced. Bock Kwon, who served in several executive roles at LG Display, conspired with employees from other TFT-LCD panel makers to fix prices between September 2001 and June 2006, the Department of Justice said.... "The participants in the LCD conspiracy committed a serious fraud upon American consumers by fixing the prices of a product that is in almost every American home." ... Four companies and nine individuals have been charged.... More than $616 million in criminal fines have been imposed, and four people have pleaded guilty and have been sentenced to serve jail time.... Kwon was accused of participating in meetings with competitors to discuss LCD prices and agreeing to abide by the prices they set.[1]
>
> The president of an Iowa ready-mix concrete company pleaded guilty to participating in a conspiracy to fix prices and rig bids for the sale of ready-mix concrete, the Department of Justice announced today. According to a one-count felony charge filed on May 6, 2010 in U.S. District Court in Sioux city, Iowa, Kent Robert Stewart, president of a ready-mix concrete company located in Iowa, participated in a conspiracy to fix prices and rig bids for ready-mix concrete sold to various companies in Iowa between approximately January 2008 and August 2009. According to the charge, Stewart participated in a conspiracy in which he engaged in discussions concerning project bids for sales of ready-mix concrete in Iowa, submitted rigged bids at collusive and noncompetitive prices and accepted payment for sales of ready-mix concrete at collusive and noncompetitive prices. Stewart is charged with violating the Sherman Act, which carries a maximum penalty of 10 years in prison and a fine of $1 million per count for individuals.[2]
>
> The former highest-ranking Qantas Airways Limited cargo executive employed in the United States has agreed to plead guilty, serve 8 months in jail, and pay a criminal fine for participating in a conspiracy to fix rates for international air cargo shipments, the Department of Justice announced today. According to the charges filed in U.S. District Court in the District of Columbia, Bruce McCaffrey, former Qantas Vice President of Freight for the Americas, and his co-conspirators, engaged in a conspiracy to fix rates on air cargo shipments charged to U.S. and international customers from at least as early as January 2000 and continuing until at least February 2006, in violation of the Sherman Act.[3]
>
> A federal grand jury in San Francisco today returned an indictment against a former executive of a large Taiwan-based color display tube (CDT) manufacturing company.... According to the charges Alex Yeh, a former director of sales, and his co-conspirators agreed to charge prices of CDTs at certain target levels or ranges and to reduce output of CDTs by shutting down CDT production lines for certain periods of time. The indictment alleges that Yeh and co-conspirators also agreed to allocate target market shares for the CDT market overall and for certain CDT customers. The conspirators are alleged to have exchanged CDT sales, production, market share and pricing information for the purpose of implementing, monitoring and enforcing their agreements. According to the indictment, Yeh and his co-conspirators implemented an auditing system that permitted co-conspirators to visit each other's production facilities to verify that CDT production lines had been shut down as agreed.[4]

In view of the key role of competition in the American economy, it is surprising that anticompetitive practices are so common. A report on New York Stock Exchange companies showed that 10 percent of the companies had been involved in antitrust suits during the previous 5 years.[5] A survey of major corporate executives indicated that 60 percent of those sampled believed that many businesses engage in price-fixing.[6] One study found that in a period of 2 years alone over 60 major firms were prosecuted by federal agencies for anticompetitive practices, and hundreds more were prosecuted by state officials.

If free markets are justified, it is because they allocate resources and distribute commodities in ways that are just, that maximize the economic utility of society's members, and that respect the freedom of choice of both buyers and sellers. These moral aspects of a market system depend crucially on the competitive nature of the system. If firms join together and use their combined power to fix prices, drive out competitors with unfair practices, or earn monopolistic profits at the expense of consumers, the market ceases to be competitive and the results are injustice, a decline in social utility, and a restriction of people's freedom of choice. This chapter examines the ethics of anticompetitive practices, the underlying rationales for prohibiting them, and the moral values that market competition is meant to achieve.

Before studying the ethics of anticompetitive practices, it is useful to have a clear understanding of the meaning of *market competition*, particularly of what we call *perfect competition*. Of course, we all have an intuitive understanding of competition: It is a rivalry between two or more parties trying to obtain something that only one of them can have. Competition exists in political elections, in football games, on the battlefield, and in courses in which grades are distributed "on the curve." Market competition, however, involves more than mere rivalry between two or more firms. To get a clearer idea of the nature of market competition, we are going to look at three economic models describing three degrees of competition in a market: **perfect competition, pure monopoly**, and **oligopoly**.

perfect competition A free market in which no buyer or seller has the power to significantly affect the prices at which goods are being exchanged.

pure monopoly A market in which a single firm is the only seller in the market and which new sellers are barred from entering.

oligopoly A market shared by a relatively small number of large firms that together can exercise some influence on prices.

If you are lucky enough to have taken a course in basic economics, you may already have seen some of these models of market competition. But your course in basic economics did not explain the ethical concepts related to these models of competition, particularly to the model of perfect competition. As we will see, the ethical concepts of utility, justice, and rights are closely tied to the model of perfect competition; that is, perfect market competition tends to result in just outcomes, to respect moral rights, and to satisfy utilitarianism (more precisely, perfectly competitive markets achieve a certain kind of justice, they satisfy a certain version of utilitarianism, and they respect certain kinds of moral rights). It is surprising and salutary that perfectly competitive markets have these three ethical features. Most nations of the world have embraced and tried hard to maintain competitive market systems precisely because competitive markets tend to maximize utility, because they are just, and because they respect people's moral rights. If we are going to understand why market competition is morally desirable then, we will have to understand why market competition maximizes utility, produces justice, and respects human rights. But to understand why perfect competition tends to have these results, we will need to understand how perfectly competitive markets operate. In particular, we have to understand how perfect competition tends to move toward an equilibrium point, and why this results in markets that maximize utility, establish justice, and respect people's moral rights.

Once we understand why perfectly competitive markets lead to these three moral outcomes, we will be able to see also why markets and market behaviors that *depart* from perfect competition tend to diminish utility, tend to be unjust, and tend to violate people's moral rights. That is, we will be able to see why departures from perfect competition tend to be morally defective. And that, in turn, should allow us to see why it is unethical to engage in those behaviors—like price fixing and other anticompetitive activities—that undermine or destroy market competition.

To truly understand the ethics of market behaviors, then, it is absolutely necessary to first understand why perfect market competition is morally desirable and this requires understanding some basic ideas of economics. There is, unfortunately, no shortcut path to a solid understanding of the ethics of markets and market behaviors. Any attempt to understand the ethics of, say, price-fixing, without a rudimentary understanding of some basic economic principles, will be superficial and easily dislodged when the opportunity to fix prices presents itself in real life. Without an understanding of some basic ideas of economics, we will not truly understand what is wrong with behaviors like price-fixing and can easily rationalize them. We noted in the news stories above that price-fixing and other anticompetitive behaviors are surprisingly common among business people. Part of the reason is because people involved in price-fixing conspiracies can often rationalize their behavior and say they did not think what they were doing was morally wrong.[7] In fact, they often say they were just trying to be morally upright citizens by preventing a "cut-throat competition" that would harm everyone, or that they were trying to establish a "reasonable return" or a "fair price" in the market, or that they were not trying to "gouge" consumers but just exercising their right to compete aggressively in a free enterprise economy. Without a good understanding of the ethics of market competition, it is easy to be taken in by such rationalizations which, after all, seem at first sight to make a lot of sense. But as we will now see, with a firm understanding of the ethics of market competition, it will be clear that price-fixing and other anticompetitive practices are exactly the opposite of what these rationalizations claim.

4.1 Perfect Competition

market A forum in which people come together to exchange ownership of goods; a place where goods or services are bought and sold.

A **market** is any forum in which people come together to exchange ownership of goods, services, or money. Markets can be small and very temporary (two friends trading clothes can constitute a tiny transient market) or quite large and relatively permanent (the oil market spans several continents and has been operating for decades).

A perfectly competitive free market is one in which no buyer or seller has the power to significantly affect the prices at which goods (we will use the term *goods* to include services and money) are being exchanged.[8] Perfectly competitive free markets are characterized by seven defining features:

(1) There are numerous buyers and sellers, none of whom has a substantial share of the market.
(2) All buyers and sellers can freely and immediately enter or leave the market.
(3) Every buyer and seller has full and perfect knowledge of what every other buyer and seller is doing, including knowledge of the prices, quantities, and quality of all goods being bought and sold.
(4) The goods being sold in the market are so similar to each other that no one cares from whom each buys or sells.
(5) The costs and benefits of producing or using the goods being exchanged are borne entirely by those buying or selling the goods and not by any other external parties.
(6) All buyers and sellers are utility maximizers: Each tries to get as much as possible for as little as possible.
(7) No external parties (such as the government) regulate the price, quantity, or quality of any of the goods being bought and sold in the market.

The first two features are the basic characteristics of a "competitive" market because they ensure that buyers and sellers are roughly equal in power and none can force the others to accept its terms. The seventh feature is what makes a market qualify as a "free" market: It is one that is free of any externally imposed regulations on price, quantity, or quality. (So-called *free* markets, however, are not necessarily free of all constraints, as we see later in this chapter.) Note that the term *free enterprise* is sometimes used to refer to perfectly competitive free markets.

In addition to these seven characteristics, free competitive markets also need an enforceable private property system (otherwise, buyers and sellers would not have any ownership rights to exchange), an underlying system of contracts (which allows buyers and sellers to forge agreements that transfer ownership), and an underlying system of production (that generates goods or services whose ownership can be exchanged).

In a perfectly competitive free market, the price buyers are willing to pay for goods rises when fewer goods are available, and these rising prices induce sellers to provide greater quantities of goods. Thus, as more goods are made available, prices tend to fall, and these falling prices lead sellers to decrease the quantities of goods they provide. These fluctuations produce a striking outcome: In a perfectly competitive market, prices and quantities always move toward what is called the ***equilibrium point***. The equilibrium point in a market is the point at which the amount of goods buyers want to buy equals the amount of goods sellers want to sell and at which the highest price buyers are willing to pay equals the lowest price sellers are willing to take. At the equilibrium point, every seller finds a willing buyer and every buyer finds a willing seller. Moreover, this surprising result of perfectly competitive free markets has an even more astonishing outcome: It satisfies three of the moral criteria—justice, utility, and rights. That is, perfectly competitive free markets achieve a certain kind of justice, satisfy a certain version of utilitarianism, and respect certain kinds of moral rights.

equilibrium point In a market, the point at which the quantity buyers want to buy equals the quantity sellers want to sell, and at which the highest price buyers are willing to pay equals the lowest price sellers are willing to take.

Why do perfectly competitive markets achieve these three surprising moral outcomes? The well-known supply and demand curves of economists can be used to explain the phenomenon. Our explanation proceeds in two stages. First, we see why perfectly competitive free markets always move toward the equilibrium point. Second, we see why markets that move toward equilibrium in this way achieve these three moral outcomes.

Equilibrium in Perfectly Competitive Markets

A **demand curve** is a line on a graph indicating the most that consumers (or buyers) would be willing to pay for a unit of some product when they buy different quantities of those products. As we mentioned, the fewer the units of a certain product consumers buy, the more they are willing to pay for those units, so the demand curve slopes down to the right. In the imaginary curve in Figure 4.1, for example, buyers are willing to pay $1 per basket of potatoes if they buy 600 million tons of potatoes, but they are willing to pay as much as $5 per basket if they buy only 100 million tons of potatoes.

demand curve A line on a graph indicating the *quantity* of a product buyers would purchase at each *price* at which it might be selling; the supply curve also can be understood as showing the highest price buyers on average would be willing to pay for a given amount of a product.

Notice that the demand curve slopes downward to the right, indicating that consumers are willing to pay less for each unit of a good as they buy more of those units; the value of a potato falls for consumers as they buy up more potatoes. Why is this? This phenomenon is explained by a principle we assume human nature always follows—the so-called **principle of diminishing marginal utility**. This principle states that each additional item a person consumes is less satisfying than each of the earlier items the person consumed: The more we consume the less utility or satisfaction we get from consuming more. The second pizza a person eats at lunch, for example, is much less satisfying than the first one; the third will be substantially less tasty than the second; while the fourth may be positively disgusting. Because of the principle of diminishing marginal utility, the more goods consumers purchase in a

principle of diminishing marginal utility The principle that generally each additional unit of a good a person consumes is less satisfying than each of the earlier units the person consumed.

Figure 4.1
Demand curve for potatoes.

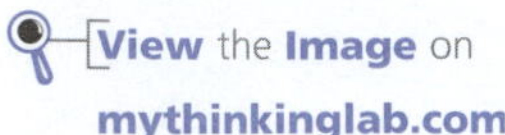
View the Image on mythinkinglab.com

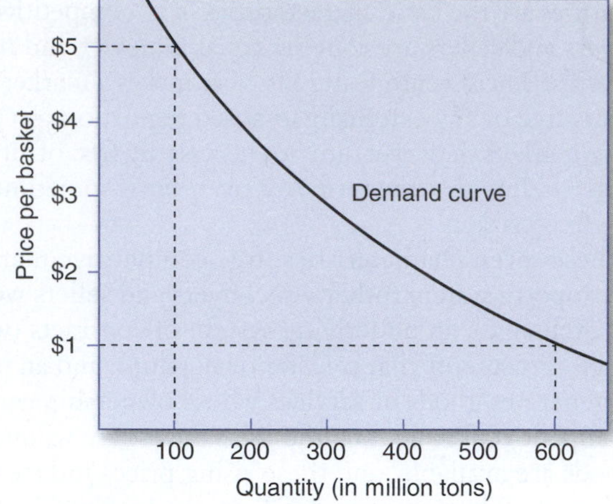

market, the less satisfying additional goods are to them and the less value they place on each additional good. Thus, the buyer's demand curve slopes downward to the right because the principle of diminishing marginal utility ensures that the price consumers are willing to pay for goods diminishes as the quantity they buy increases.

The demand curve thus indicates the value consumers place on each unit of a product as they purchase more units. Consequently, if the price of a product were to rise above their demand curve, average buyers would see themselves as losers—that is, as paying out more for the product than what it is worth to them. At any point below the demand curve, they would see themselves as winners—that is, as paying out less for a product than what it is worth to them. Therefore, if prices should rise above the demand curve, buyers would have little motive to buy, and they would tend to leave the market to spend their money in other markets. However, if prices were to fall below the demand curve, new buyers would tend to flock into the market because they would perceive a chance to buy the product for less than what it is worth to them.

supply curve A line on a graph indicating the *quantity* of a product sellers would provide for each *price* at which it might be selling; the supply curve also can be understood as showing the price sellers must charge to cover the average costs of supplying a given amount of a product.

Now, let us look at the other side of the market: the supply side. A **supply curve** is a line on a graph indicating the prices producers must charge to cover the average costs of supplying a given amount of a commodity. Beyond a certain point (which we explain shortly), the more units producers make, the higher the average costs of making each unit, so the curve slopes upward to the right. In the sample curve traced in Figure 4.2, for example, it costs farmers on average $1 a basket to grow 100 million tons of potatoes, but it costs them $4 per basket to grow 500 million tons.

principle of increasing marginal costs The principle that after a certain point, each additional unit a seller produces costs more to produce than earlier units.

At first sight, it may seem odd that producers or sellers must charge higher prices when they are producing large volumes than when producing smaller quantities. We are accustomed to thinking that it costs less to produce goods in large quantities than in small quantities. However, the increasing costs of production are explained by a principle that we call the **principle of increasing marginal costs**. This principle states that, after a certain point, each additional item the seller produces costs more to produce than earlier items. Why? Because of an unfortunate feature of our physical world: Its productive resources are limited. A producer will use the best and most productive resources to make the first few goods and at this point, costs will indeed decline as production expands. A potato grower farming in a valley, for example, will begin by planting the level fertile acres in the floor of the valley where the more acreage planted the more the costs per unit decline. But as the farm continues to expand, the farmer eventually runs out of these highly productive resources and must turn to using less productive land. As the acreage on the floor of the valley is used up, the farmer is forced to start planting the sloping and less fertile land at the edges of the

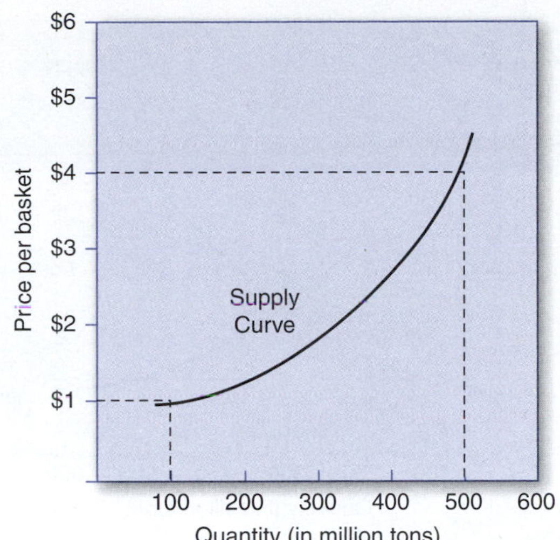

Figure 4.2
Supply curve for potatoes.

View the **Image** on **mythinkinglab.com**

valley, which may be rocky and may require more expensive irrigation. If production continues to increase, the farmer will eventually have to start planting the land on the mountainsides and costs will rise even higher. Eventually, the farmer reaches a situation where the more that is produced the more it costs to produce each unit because the farmer is forced to use increasingly unproductive materials. The predicament of the potato farmer illustrates the principle of increasing marginal costs: After a certain point, added production always entails increasing costs per unit. That is the situation illustrated by the supply curve. The supply curve rises upward to the right because it pictures the point at which sellers must begin to charge more per unit to cover the costs of supplying additional goods.

The supply curve, then, indicates what sellers must charge per unit to cover the costs of bringing given amounts of a product to market. It is important to note that these costs include more than the ordinary costs of labor, materials, distribution, and so on. The costs of producing a product also include the profits sellers must make to motivate them to invest in producing this product and forgo the profits they could have made by investing in other products. So the seller's costs include the costs of production plus the normal profits he could have made but gave up to make this product. These foregone normal profits are a cost of bringing a product to market. What is a "normal" profit? A normal profit is the average profit one could make in other markets with similar risks. The prices on the supply curve, then, must cover the ordinary costs of production plus the average profit the seller could have made by investing in other similar markets. A normal profit is part of the cost of bringing a product to market.

The prices on the supply curve, then, represent the minimum producers must receive to cover their ordinary costs and make a normal profit. When prices fall below the supply curve, producers see themselves as losers: They are receiving less than what it costs them to produce the product (keep in mind that "costs" include ordinary costs plus a normal profit). Consequently, if prices fall below the supply curve, producers will tend to leave the market and invest their resources in other, more profitable markets. However, if prices rise above the supply curve, then new producers will come crowding into the market, attracted by the opportunity to invest their resources in a market where they can derive higher profits than in other markets.

Sellers and buyers, of course, trade in the same markets, so their respective supply and demand curves can be superimposed on the same graph. Typically when this is done, the supply and demand curves will meet and cross at some point. The point at which they meet is the point at which the price buyers are willing to pay for a certain amount

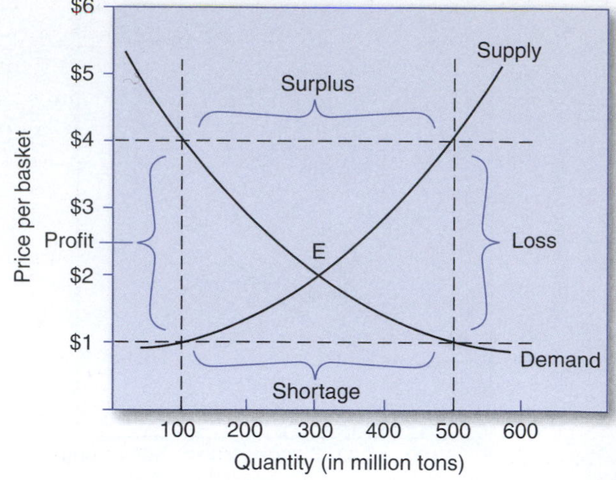

Figure 4.3
Supply and demand curves for potatoes.

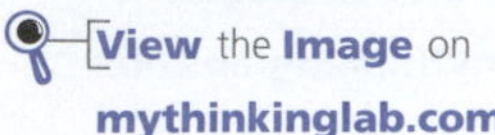
View the Image on mythinkinglab.com

point of equilibrium The point on a graph at which the supply and demand curves meet, so the quantity buyers want to buy equals the quantity sellers want to sell and the price buyers are willing to pay equals the price sellers are willing to take.

of goods exactly matches the price sellers must take to cover the costs of producing that same amount (i.e., the "equilibrium price"). This point of intersection, as indicated in Figure 4.3, where the point E at which the supply and demand curves meet, is the so-called **point of equilibrium** or equilibrium price. On the graph, it is at $2 per basket for 300 million tons.

We mentioned that in a perfectly competitive free market, prices, the amounts supplied, and the amounts demanded all tend to move toward the point of equilibrium. Why does this happen? Notice in Figure 4.3 that if the prices of potatoes rise above the point of equilibrium, say to $4 per basket, producers will supply more goods (500 million tons) than at the equilibrium price level (300 million tons). But at that high price, consumers will purchase fewer goods (only 100 million tons) than at the equilibrium price. The result will be a surplus of unsold goods (500 – 100 = 400 million tons of unsold potatoes). To get rid of their unsold surplus, sellers will be forced to lower their prices and decrease production. Eventually, equilibrium prices and amounts will be reached.

In contrast, if the price drops below the point of equilibrium in Figure 4.3, say to $1 per basket, then producers will start losing money and so will supply less than consumers want at that price. The result will be an excessive demand and shortages will appear. The shortages will lead buyers to bid up the price. Subsequently, prices will rise and the rising prices will attract more producers into the market, thereby raising supplies. Eventually, again, equilibrium will reassert itself.

Notice also what happens in Figure 4.3 if the amount being supplied, say 100 million tons, for some reason is less than the equilibrium amount. The cost of supplying such an amount ($1 per basket) is below what consumers are willing to pay ($4 per basket) for that same amount. Producers will be able to raise their prices up to the level the consumer is willing to pay ($4) and pocket the difference ($3) as abnormally high profits (i.e., profits above the normal profit, which we defined earlier). The abnormally high profits, however, will attract more producers into the market, thereby increasing the quantities supplied and bringing about a corresponding decrease in the price consumers are willing to pay for the larger quantities. Gradually, the amounts supplied will increase to the equilibrium point, and prices will drop to equilibrium prices.

The opposite happens if the amount being supplied, say 500 million tons, is for some reason more than the equilibrium amount. Under these circumstances, sellers will have to lower their prices to the very low levels that consumers are willing to pay for such large amounts. At such low price levels, producers will leave the market to invest their resources in other, more profitable markets, thereby lowering the supply, raising the price, and once again reestablishing equilibrium levels.

Quick Review 4.1

Equilibrium in Perfectly Competitive Market

Price and quantity move to equilibrium in perfectly competitive market because:

- If price rises above equilibrium, surplus appears and drives price down to equilibrium.
- If price falls below equilibrium, shortage appears and drives price up to equilibrium.
- If quantity is less than equilibrium, profits rise, attracting sellers who increase quantity to equilibrium.
- If quantity is more than equilibrium, prices fall, driving sellers out which lowers quantity to equilibrium.

At this point, the reader may be trying to think of an industry that fits the description of perfect competition we have just given. The reader will have some difficulty finding one. Only a few commodity markets, including agricultural markets such as grain and potato markets, come close to embodying the six features that characterize a perfectly competitive market.[9] The fact is that the model of perfect competition is a theoretical construct of the economist that characterizes only a few real-world markets. But although the model does not describe many real markets, as we will now see, it does provide us with a clear understanding of the moral advantages of competition and an understanding of why it is morally desirable to keep markets as competitive as possible.

Ethics and Perfectly Competitive Markets

As we have seen, perfectly competitive free markets incorporate forces that inevitably drive buyers and sellers toward the so-called *point of equilibrium*. In doing so, they achieve three major moral values: (1) they lead buyers and sellers to exchange their goods in a way that is just (in a certain sense of *just*); (2) they maximize the utility of buyers and sellers by leading them to allocate, use, and distribute their goods with perfect efficiency; and (3) they bring about these achievements in a way that respects buyers' and sellers' right of free consent. As we examine each of these moral characteristics of perfect competition, it is important to keep in mind that they are characteristics only of the perfectly competitive free market—that is, of markets that have the seven features we listed. Markets that fail to have one or the other of these features do not necessarily achieve these three moral values.

To understand why perfectly competitive free markets lead buyers and sellers to make exchanges that are just, we begin by recalling the capitalist meaning of *justice* described in Chapter 2. According to the capitalist criterion of justice, benefits and burdens are distributed justly when individuals receive in return at least the value of the contribution they made to an enterprise: Fairness is getting paid fully in return for what one contributes. It is this form of justice (and only this form) that is achieved in perfectly competitive free markets.

Perfectly competitive free markets embody capitalist justice because such markets necessarily converge on the equilibrium point, and the equilibrium point is the one (and only) point at which buyers and sellers on average receive the value of what they contribute. Why is this true? Consider the matter, first, from the seller's point of view. The supply curve indicates the price producers must receive to cover what it costs them to produce given quantities of a good. Consequently, if prices (and quantities) fall below the seller's supply curve, consumers are unfairly shortchanging the seller because they are paying him less than the seller contributed to produce those goods in those quantities. (Ordinarily, the seller would not supply those goods if he is getting less for them than it costs him to make them, but the seller can be forced to sell them if, for example, he has already produced them and he will lose even more money if he fails to sell them at all.) On the other hand, if prices rise above the seller's supply curve, the average seller is unfairly overcharging consumers because they are being charged more than what the seller knows those goods are worth in terms of what it costs to produce them. Thus, from the standpoint of the seller's contribution, the price is fair (i.e., the price equals the costs of the seller's contribution) only if it falls somewhere on the seller's supply curve.

Next, consider the matter from the standpoint of the average buyer or consumer. The demand curve indicates the highest price consumers are willing to pay for given quantities of goods, and so it indicates the full value of those quantities of goods to them. So, if the price (and quantity) of a good were to rise above the consumer's demand curve, the price would be more than the value of those goods (in those quantities)

Quick Review 4.2

Justice in Perfectly Competitive Market

- For buyer, prices are just (capitalist justice) only on the demand curve.
- For seller, prices are just (capitalist justice) only on the supply curve.
- Perfectly competitive markets move price to equilibrium point which is on both supply and demand curves and so is just for both buyer and seller.

to her. Ordinarily, the consumer would not buy goods when their price is above his or her demand curve and so is higher than what the goods are worth to her. If she were forced to buy the goods, (for example, because the seller will not sell her something else she desperately needs unless she buys the goods) then the consumer would unfairly be contributing to the seller more than what the goods are worth to her. On the other hand, if prices (and quantities) fall below the consumer's demand curve, the average consumer unfairly contributes less to sellers than the value (to the consumer) of the quantity of goods she receives. Thus, from the standpoint of the value the average consumer places on different quantities of goods, her contribution is fair (i.e., the price the consumer pays is equal to what the goods are worth to her) only if it falls somewhere on the consumer's demand curve.

Obviously, there is only a single point at which the price and quantity of a good lies both on the buyer's demand curve (and is thus fair from the standpoint of the value the average buyer places on the goods) and on the seller's supply curve (and is thus fair from the standpoint of what it costs the average seller to produce those goods), and that point is the equilibrium point. Thus, the equilibrium point is the one and only point at which prices are just (in terms of capitalist justice) both from the buyer's and the seller's point of view. When prices deviate from the equilibrium point, either the average buyer or the average seller is unjustly getting less than he or she contributes, or else one or the other is unjustly getting more than he or she contributes: in either case the outcome is unjust. But as we saw, in perfectly competitive markets prices and quantities are either at the equilibrium point, or forces drive them back to the equilibrium point. The perfectly competitive market thus continually—almost magically—reestablishes capitalist justice for its participants by continually leading them to buy and sell goods at the one quantity and the one price at which each receives the value of what he or she contributes, whether this value is calculated from the average buyer's or the average seller's point of view.[10]

In addition to establishing a form of justice, competitive markets also maximize the utility of buyers and sellers by leading them to allocate, use, and distribute goods with perfect efficiency. To understand this aspect of perfectly competitive markets, we must consider what happens not in a single isolated market, but in an economy that consists of a system of many markets. A market system is perfectly efficient when all goods in all markets are allocated, used, and distributed in a way that produces the highest level of satisfaction possible from these goods. A system of perfectly competitive markets achieves such efficiency in three main ways.[11]

Quick Review 4.3

Utility in Perfectly Competitive Market

- Prices in the system of perfectly competitive markets attract resources when demand is high and drives them away when demand is low, so resources are allocated efficiently.
- Perfectly competitive markets encourage firms to use resources efficiently to keep costs low and profits high.
- Perfectly competitive markets let consumers buy the most satisfying bundle of goods, so they distribute goods in way that maximizes utility.

First, a perfectly competitive market system motivates firms to invest resources in those industries where consumer demand is high and to move resources away from industries where consumer demand is low. Resources will be attracted into markets where high consumer demand creates shortages that raise prices above equilibrium, and they will flee markets where low consumer demand leads to surpluses that lower prices below equilibrium. The perfectly competitive market system allocates resources efficiently in accordance with consumer demands and needs; the consumer is "sovereign" over the market.

Second, perfectly competitive markets encourage firms to minimize the amount of resources consumed in producing a commodity and use the most efficient technology available. Firms are motivated to use resources sparingly because they want to lower their costs and thereby, increase their profit margin. Moreover, to not lose buyers to other firms, each firm will reduce its profits to the lowest levels consistent with the survival of the firm. The perfectly competitive market encourages an efficient use of the seller's resources as well.

Third, perfectly competitive markets distribute commodities among buyers in such a way that all buyers receive the most satisfying bundle of commodities they can purchase, given the commodities available to them and the money they can spend on these commodities. When faced by a system of perfectly competitive markets, each buyer will buy up those proportions of each commodity that correspond with the buyer's desire for the commodity when weighed against the buyer's desires for other commodities. When buyers have completed their buying, they will know that they cannot improve on their purchases by trading their goods with other consumers because all consumers can buy the same goods at the same prices. Thus, perfectly competitive markets enable consumers to attain a level of satisfaction on which they cannot improve given the constraints of their budgets and the range of available goods. An efficient distribution of commodities is thereby achieved.

Finally, perfectly competitive markets establish capitalist justice and maximize utility in a way that respects buyers' and sellers' negative rights. First, in a perfectly competitive market, buyers and sellers are free (by definition) to enter or leave the market as they choose. That is, individuals are neither forced into nor prevented from engaging in a certain business, provided they have the expertise and the financial resources required.[12] Perfectly competitive markets thus embody the negative right of freedom of opportunity.

Second, in the perfectly competitive free market, all exchanges are fully voluntary. That is, participants are not forced to buy or sell anything other than what they freely and knowingly consent to buy or sell. In a competitive free market, all participants have full and complete knowledge of what they are buying or selling, and no external agency (such as the government) forces them to buy or sell goods they do not want at prices they do not choose in quantities they do not desire.[13] Moreover, buyers and sellers in a perfectly competitive free market are not forced to pay for goods that others enjoy. In a perfectly competitive free market, by definition, the costs and benefits of producing or using goods are borne entirely by those buying or selling the goods and not by any other external parties. Free competitive markets thus embody the negative right of freedom of consent.

Quick Review 4.4

Rights in Perfectly Competitive Market

- Perfectly competitive market respects right to freely choose the business one enters.
- In perfectly competitive market, exchanges are voluntary so respect rights of free choice.
- In perfectly competitive market, no seller exerts coercion by dictating prices, quantities, or kinds of goods consumers must buy.

Third, no single seller or buyer will so dominate the perfectly competitive free market that others are forced to accept the terms or go without.[14] In a perfectly competitive market, industrial power is decentralized among numerous firms so that prices and quantities are not dependent on the dictates of one or a few businesses. In short, perfectly competitive free markets embody the negative right of freedom from coercion.

Thus, perfectly competitive free markets are perfectly moral in three important respects: (1) Each continuously establishes a capitalist form of justice; (2) together they maximize utility in the form of market efficiency; and (3) each respects certain important negative rights of buyers and sellers.

Several cautions are in order, however, when interpreting these moral features of perfectly competitive free markets. First, perfectly competitive free markets do not establish other forms of justice. Because they do not respond to the needs of those outside the market or those who have little to exchange, for example, they cannot establish a justice based on needs. Moreover, perfectly competitive free markets impose no restrictions on how much wealth each participant accumulates relative to the others, so they ignore egalitarian justice and may incorporate large inequalities.

Second, competitive markets maximize the utility of those who can participate in the market given the constraints of each participant's budget. However, this does not mean that *society's* total utility is necessarily maximized. The bundle of goods distributed to each individual by a competitive market system depends ultimately on that individual's ability to participate in the market and on how much that individual has to spend in the market. But this way of distributing goods may not produce the most satisfaction for everyone in society. Society's welfare might be increased, for example, by giving more goods to those who cannot participate in the market because they have nothing to exchange (perhaps they are too poor, too old, too sick, too disabled, or too young to have anything to trade in markets). Or the overall welfare might be increased by distributing more goods to those who have only a little to spend or by limiting the consumption of those who can spend a lot.

Third, although free competitive markets establish certain negative rights for those within the market, they may actually diminish the positive rights of those outside (those, for example, who cannot compete) or of those whose participation is minimal. People who have the money to participate in markets may consume goods (such as food or educational resources) that people outside the market, or those with very little money, need to develop and exercise their own freedom and rationality. Thus, although perfectly competitive free markets secure capitalist justice, although they maximize economic utility, and respect certain negative rights, they largely do this only for those who have the means (the money or the goods) to participate fully in those markets, and they necessarily ignore the needs, utility, and rights of those who are left out of the marketplace.

Fourth, free competitive markets ignore and can even conflict with the demands of caring. As we have seen in previous chapters, an ethic of care implies that people exist in a web of interdependent relationships and should care for those who are closely related to them. A free market system, however, operates as if individuals are completely independent of each other and takes no account of the human relationships that may exist among them. Moreover, as we mentioned, a free market pressures individuals to spend their resources (time, labor, money) efficiently. A system of competitive markets pressures individuals to invest, use, and distribute goods in ways that will produce the maximum economic returns. If individuals do not invest, use, and distribute their resources efficiently, they will lose out in the competition that free markets create. This means that if individuals divert their resources to spend them on caring for those with whom they have close relationships, instead of investing, using, and distributing them efficiently, they will lose out. For example, when an employer who likes and cares for her workers gives them higher wages than other employers are paying, her costs will rise. Then, the employer must either charge more for goods than other employers, which will drive customers away, or accept lower profits than other employers, which will allow other employers to make more money that they can then invest in improvements and may eventually enable them to drive the employer out of business. In short, the pressures toward economic efficiency that a system of perfectly competitive free markets creates not only ignore, but can regularly conflict with the demands of caring.[15]

Quick Review 4.5

Perfectly Competitive Free Markets

- Achieve capitalist justice (but not other kinds of justice like justice based on need)
- Satisfy a certain version of utilitarianism (by maximizing utility of market participants but not of all society)
- Respect some moral rights (negative rights but often not positive rights)
- Can lead to ignoring the demands of caring and value of human relationships
- Can encourage vices of greed and self-seeking and discourage virtues of kindness and caring
- Can be said to embody justice, utility, and rights only if seven defining features are present.

Fifth, free competitive markets may have a pernicious effect on people's moral character. The competitive pressures that are present in perfectly competitive markets can lead people to attend constantly to economic efficiency. Producers are constantly pressured to reduce their costs and increase their profit margins. Consumers are constantly pressured to patronize sellers that provide the highest value at the lowest cost. Employees are constantly pressured to seek out employers that pay higher wages and to abandon those with lower wages. Such pressures, it has been argued, lead people to develop character traits associated with maximizing individual economic well-being and neglect character traits associated with building close relationships to others. The virtues of loyalty, kindness, and caring may all diminish, whereas the vices of being greedy, self-seeking, avaricious, and calculating may be encouraged.

Finally, and most important, we should note that the three values of capitalist justice, utility, and negative rights are produced by free markets only if they embody the seven conditions that define perfect competition. If one or more of these conditions are not present in a given real market, then the claim can no longer be made that these three values are present. As we will see in the remainder of this chapter—and, in fact, throughout the rest of this book—this is the most crucial limitation of free market morality because real markets are not perfectly competitive, and consequently they may not achieve the three moral values that characterize perfect competition. Despite this critical limitation, however, the perfectly competitive free market provides us with a clear idea of how economic exchanges in a market economy should be structured if relationships among buyers and sellers are to secure the three moral achievements we indicated. We turn next to see what happens when some of the defining characteristics of perfect competition are absent.

4.2 Monopoly Competition

What happens when a free market (i.e., one without government intervention) ceases to be perfectly competitive? We begin to answer this question in this section by examining the opposite extreme of a perfectly competitive market: the free (unregulated) monopoly market. We then examine some less extreme varieties of noncompetition.

We noted earlier that a perfectly competitive market is characterized by seven conditions. In a monopoly, two of these conditions are not present.[16] First, instead of "numerous sellers, none of whom has a substantial share of the market," the monopoly market has only one dominant seller, and that dominant seller has a substantial share of the market. Technically, a company must have 100 percent of the market to be a monopoly, but in practice a company with less then 100 percent of the market can be considered a monopoly; that is, a monopoly market can consist of a single dominant firm with, say, 90 percent of the market and dozens of other companies each with less than one percent of the market. The key feature that determines whether a company has a monopoly is whether that one company has such control over a product that the company largely determines who can get some of the product and what the product will sell for.

The second way in which a monopoly differs from a perfectly competitive market is that instead of being a market that other companies "can freely and immediately enter or leave," the monopoly market is one that other companies cannot enter or that it is very difficult for other companies to enter. Other companies are blocked from entering by "barriers to entry" that keep other companies out, such as patent or copyright laws that do not allow other companies to make the patented product, or high entry costs that make it too costly or too risky for a new seller to try start a business in that industry. A monopoly company might itself create the barriers to entry that keep other companies out of its market. For example, a company might threaten to inflict substantial economic harm on any company that tries to enter its market (for example, by flooding the market with the product so that prices fall until it is no longer worth being in the market), or it might cultivate a reputation for being willing to retaliate viciously against any company that enters the market.

Two contemporary examples of monopoly markets are the worldwide market for operating systems for personal computers and the market for office suite software. The operating system market is dominated by Microsoft's Windows which had a total global market share of 92 percent in 2010. Microsoft also has a monopoly in the worldwide market for integrated office suite software where its MS Office suite commanded 94 percent of the market in 2010. While Microsoft does not hold 100 percent of either of these markets, most observers characterize its control of these markets as monopolies. There are several "barriers to entry" any company that wants to come into these markets has to overcome. One barrier is sheer total cost and risk: today it costs more than $10 billion to develop a new operating system like Windows and it would be extremely risky for a company to spend $10 billion on the gamble that it might overcome Microsoft's dominance of the market.[17] A second barrier is economies of scale which occur when the amount of product a company makes has grown so large that it costs it less to make each unit of its products than it would cost any smaller firm. Since Microsoft makes and sells many more units of Windows and MS Office than its competitors, Microsoft's costs per unit (for example, its research costs, its marketing and administrative costs, etc.) are lower than its competitors'. Another barrier is brand loyalty: if a company tried to take some of the 95 percent market share MS Office has, it would have to overcome the strong brand loyalty it commands, and this would require another large and risky investment in brand development.

Yet another barrier is the so-called "network effect" in which the value of a product increases as the number of users increases. Consumers prefer Windows over other operating systems like Unix because there are many more software programs available for Windows than for Unix. And the reason why there are many more programs for Windows is because software developers would much rather develop programs for Windows' many users, than for Unix's few users. So, the more Windows users there are, the more programs will be written for it, and the more valuable it is to users. A new operating system like Unix has a hard time competing with Windows because network effects continually make Windows more valuable to users than Unix. And, finally, we might note that some observers say that other companies are not eager to enter one of Microsoft's markets because it has a reputation of retaliating aggressively against companies that try to compete. That reputation serves as a barrier that keeps other companies away from Microsoft's markets.

Although there are few companies that have global monopolies like Microsoft, there are numerous companies that have local or regional monopolies, i.e., monopolies over markets that serve specific geographical areas such as a city, a county, or a state. Examples of companies with local or regional monopolies include public utilities, cable companies, trash collectors, road construction companies, postal services, water supply companies, phone companies, electrical power companies, etc.

Monopoly markets, then, are those in which a single dominant firm controls all or virtually the entire product in the market and which new sellers cannot enter or have great difficulty entering because of barriers to entry. A seller in a monopoly market can control the prices (within a certain range) of the available goods. Figure 4.4 illustrates the usual situation in a monopoly market: The monopoly firm is able to fix its output at a quantity that is less than the equilibrium quantity and at which demand is so high that it allows the firm to reap an excess monopoly profit by charging prices that are well above the supply curve and even above the equilibrium price. A monopoly seller, for example, can set prices above their equilibrium level—at, say, $3. By limiting supply to only those amounts buyers will purchase at the monopolist's high prices (at 300 units in Figure 4.4), the monopoly firm can ensure that it sells all its products and reaps substantial profits from its business. The monopoly firm will, of course, calculate the price-amount ratios that will secure the highest total profits (i.e., the profit-per-unit multiplied by the number of units), and it can then fix its prices and production volume at those levels. At the turn of the century, for example, the American Tobacco Company, with a monopoly in the sale of cigarettes, was making profits equal to about 56 percent of its sales.

Quick Review 4.6

Monopoly Markets

- One dominant seller controls all or most of the market's product, and there are barriers to entry that keep other companies out.
- Seller has the power to set quantity and price of its products on the market.
- Seller can extract monopoly profit by producing less than equilibrium quantity and setting price below demand curve but high above supply curve.
- High entry barriers keep other competitors from bringing more product to the market.

If entry into the market were open, of course, these excess profits would draw other producers into the market, resulting in an increased supply of goods and a drop in prices until equilibrium was attained. In a monopoly market, where "barriers to entry" make it virtually impossible or too costly for other firms to enter the market, this does not happen, and prices will remain high if the monopolist chooses to keep them high. As we have noted, barriers to entry can consist of legal barriers such as copyrights, patents, licenses, tariffs, quotas, grants, or other means by which government

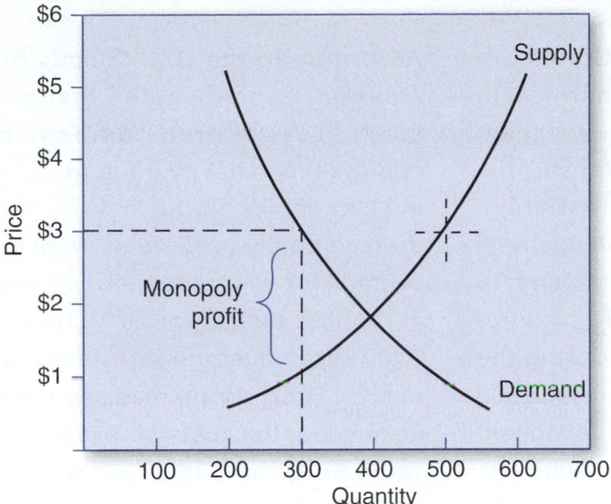

Figure 4.4

keeps new firms from entering a certain market. But as our discussion of Microsoft indicated, there are many other kinds of barriers to entry, including long-term customer contracts that make it too hard for a new entrant to capture the customers of an established incumbent; low manufacturing costs that allow the established incumbent to threaten to lower prices and win a price war if a new firm tries to enter the market; high start-up costs, high fixed costs, high advertising costs, or high research and development costs that the new entrant will not be able to recover if the firm has to leave the market, thus making entry too risky (firms risk huge losses if they try to enter); so-called "network effects" that give an established company with many users an advantage a new firm with few users will not have.

But will the monopolist necessarily choose to maximize its profits? If a seller sets its prices above what buyers are willing to pay (i.e., above the demand curve), or if the seller's costs are higher than buyers can pay, of course, then even if it is the only seller in the market it will not make a profit. There are limits (i.e., the demand curve) to how much even a monopoly can charge. But it is sometimes suggested that even when monopoly companies *can* make monopoly profits, they *actually* do not try to make monopoly profits.[18] Yet although it is conceivable that the managers of a monopoly firm may altruistically forgo potential profits and fix their prices at the equilibrium level—that is, the level that just gives them a normal rate of profit—this seems unlikely. It is difficult to see why a monopoly company would give up profits it could make for its shareholders. If a company has come to monopolize its market through legal means (perhaps it invented and now holds the patent on the only product known to be capable of meeting a consumer demand), then its monopoly profits are legal and shareholders will surely demand such profits. Of course, a monopolist might forgo some of its monopoly profits if government regulators force it to do so or if it is pressured to do so by an angry public. Drug company Burroughs Wellcome (now part of GlaxoSmithKline), for example, was pressured by angry activists to lower its price for AZT when it was the only treatment for AIDS. But in the absence of any external regulatory authority (such as the government), or of any external public pressures, monopolists are utility maximizers like every other company in a market and will, therefore, seek to maximize their profits if they are able to do so. If a monopoly can, then it actually will, seek monopoly profits. Is there any empirical evidence for this claim? There is an overwhelming amount of empirical statistical evidence which shows that, in fact, monopoly companies seek monopoly profits, although strong labor unions and executives can siphon off up to half of a company's monopoly profits as wages, benefits, salaries, and bonuses.[19]

Drug Company Monopolies and Profits

Drug companies in the United States are granted a patent on any new pharmaceutical drug they develop, which gives them a monopoly on that drug for 20 years. Not surprisingly, high monopoly profits (i.e., profits well beyond the average rate of profits in other industries) are characteristic of the pharmaceutical industry. In a 2003 study entitled *The Other Drug War II*, Public Citizen's Congress Watch noted that during the 1970s and 1980s, drug companies in the Fortune 500 had average profit rates (as a percent of revenues) that were double the average for all other industries in the Fortune 500. During the 1990s, drug company profit rates averaged 4 times the average profit rates of all other industries, and during the first 5 years of the twenty-first century, drug company profit rates were about 3 times the rates of other industries. According to the U.S. Census Bureau's *Quarterly Financial Reports*, in the first quarter of 2007 and 2008, average drug company profit rates were about 3 times the average for all other manufacturing companies. In the first quarter of 2009, average drug company profit rates were close to 7 times the average for all other manufacturing companies, and in the first quarter of 2010, they averaged close to 3 times the average for other manufacturing companies. Drug companies say they need these profits to cover the costs of research for new drugs. But while drug companies put only 14 percent of their revenues into research, they siphon off 17 percent of their revenues into dividends they hand out to shareholders and plow 31 percent into advertising and administration. A study of drug manufacturing costs (see *www.rense.com/general54/preco.htm*) found that prescription drugs have markups of 5,000 percent, 30,000 percent, and 500,000 percent over the cost of their ingredients. The ingredients in 100 tablets of Norvasc, which sold for $220, cost 14 cents; of Prozac, which sold for $247, 11 cents; of Tenormin, which sold for $104, 13 cents; of Xanax, which sold for $136, 3 cents, and so on.

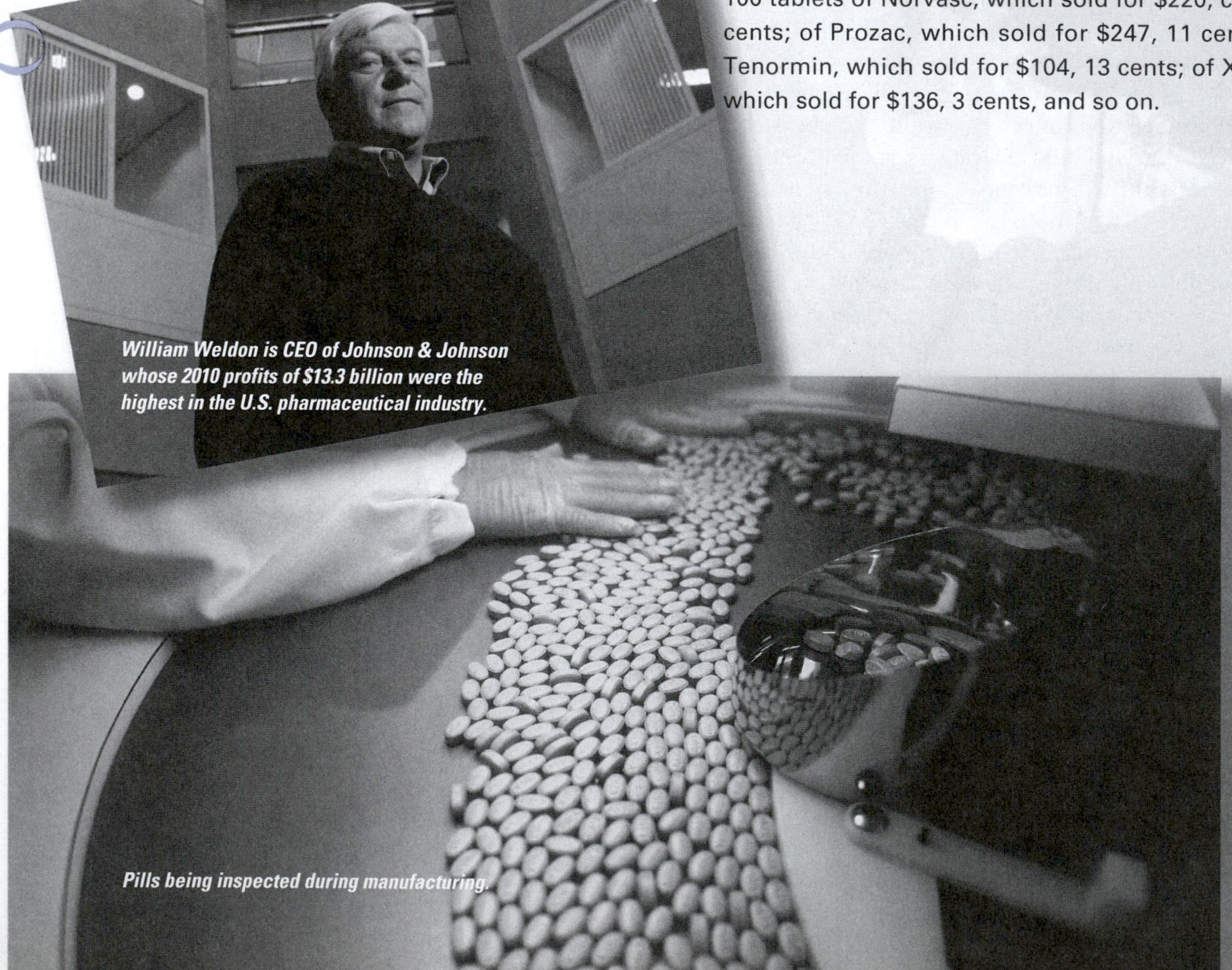

William Weldon is CEO of Johnson & Johnson whose 2010 profits of $13.3 billion were the highest in the U.S. pharmaceutical industry.

Pills being inspected during manufacturing.

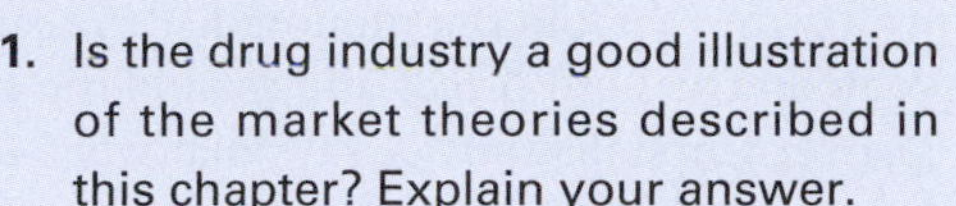

1. Is the drug industry a good illustration of the market theories described in this chapter? Explain your answer.
2. What changes, if any, do you think we should make to U.S. drug patent laws? Explain.
3. How should the relation between drugs and human life/health affect your views on drug industry monopoly profits? Explain.

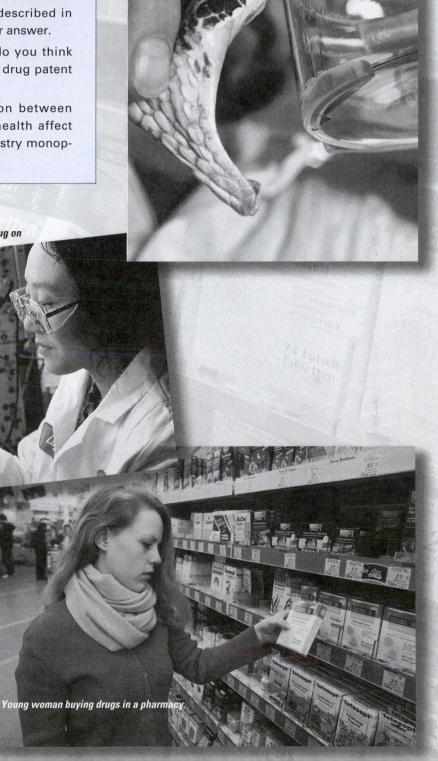

A drug researcher extracts venom from a Malaysian pit viper. The venom contains an anticoagulant drug that is being studied for use in treating stroke patients.

Researcher tests the effect of a new drug on living tissue.

Young woman buying drugs in a pharmacy.

Quick Review 4.7

Ethical Weaknesses of Monopolies

- Violate capitalist justice by charging more for products than producer knows they are worth
- Violate utilitarianism by keeping resources out of monopoly market where shortages show more are needed and diverting them to markets without such shortages; and by removing incentives to use resources efficiently
- Violate negative rights by forcing other companies to stay out of the market, by letting monopolist force buyers to purchase goods they do not want, and by letting monopolist makes price and quantity decisions that consumer is forced to accept.

Monopoly Competition: Justice, Utility, and Rights

How well does an unregulated monopoly market succeed in achieving the moral values that characterize perfectly competitive free markets? For the most part, not well. Unregulated monopoly markets can fall short of the three values of capitalist justice, economic efficiency, and respect for negative rights that perfect competition achieves.

The most obvious failure of monopoly markets lies in the high prices they enable the monopolist to charge and the high profits they enable the monopolist to reap—a failure that violates capitalist justice. Why do the high prices and profits the monopolist can command violate capitalist justice? Capitalist justice says that what each person receives should equal the value of the contribution they made. As we saw, the equilibrium point is the one (and only) point at which buyers and sellers each receive in return the value of what each contributes to the other, whether this value is determined from the average buyer's or the average seller's point of view. In a monopoly market, however, prices for goods can be set above the equilibrium level, and quantities can be set at less than the equilibrium amount. As a result, the seller can charge the buyer more than the goods are worth (from the average seller's point of view) because prices are more than the costs of making those goods. Thus, the high prices the seller can force the buyer to pay are unjust, and these unjustly high prices are the source of the seller's excess profits.

A monopoly market can also violate utilitarianism because it tends to allocate, distribute, and use resources inefficiently. First, the monopoly market allows resources to be used in ways that will produce shortages of those things buyers want and cause them to be sold at higher prices than necessary. The high profits in a monopoly market indicate a shortage of goods. However, because other firms are blocked from entering the market, their resources cannot be used to make up the shortages indicated by the high profits. This means that the resources of these other firms are deflected into other non-monopoly markets where they do less good because they do not have similar shortages. Moreover, the monopoly market allows the monopoly firm to set its prices well above costs instead of forcing the firm to lower its prices to cost levels. The resulting excess profits absorbed by the monopolist represent resources that are not needed to supply the amounts of goods it produces. Second, monopoly markets do not encourage the monopolist to minimize the resources consumed to produce its goods. A monopoly firm has little incentive to reduce its costs because it knows its monopoly profits can more than cover all its costs, and for the same reason it has little incentive to find less costly ways to make its product, and little incentive to invest a great deal in innovation and in improving its product. Because profits are high anyway, there is little incentive for it to develop new technology that might give it a competitive edge over other firms, for there are no other competing firms.

Third, monopoly markets place restrictions on the negative rights that perfectly free markets respect. First, monopoly markets by definition are markets that other sellers are not free to enter. Second, monopoly markets enable the monopoly firm to force on its buyers goods that they may not want in quantities they may not desire. The monopoly firm, for example, can force consumers to purchase product X only if they also purchase product Y from the firm. Third, monopoly markets are dominated by a single seller whose decisions determine the prices and quantities of a commodity offered for sale. The monopoly firm has considerable power over the market.

A monopoly market, then, is one that can, and generally will, deviate from the ideals of capitalist justice, economic utility, and negative rights. Instead of continually establishing a just equilibrium, the monopoly seller can impose unjustly high prices on the buyer and can generate unjustly high profits for him or herself. Instead of maximizing efficiency, monopoly markets provide sellers incentives for waste, misallocation of resources, and profit-gouging. Instead of protecting the negative rights of freedom, monopoly markets create an inequality of power that allows the monopoly firm to dictate terms to the consumer. The producer then replaces the consumer as "sovereign" of the market.

4.3 Oligopolistic Competition

Few industries are monopolies. Most major industrial markets are not dominated by a single firm, but more usually by a few—four, eight, or even more firms, depending on the market. Such markets lie somewhere on the spectrum between the two extremes of the perfectly competitive market with innumerable sellers and the pure monopoly market with only one seller. Market structures of this "impure" type are referred to as **imperfectly competitive markets**, of which the most important kind is the oligopoly.

imperfectly competitive markets Markets that lie somewhere on the spectrum between the two extremes of the perfectly competitive market with numerous sellers and the monopoly market with one dominant seller.

In an oligopoly market, two of the seven conditions that characterize the purely competitive market are once again not present. First, instead of many sellers, there are only a few significant sellers. That is, most of the market is shared by a relatively small number of large firms that together can exercise some influence on prices. The firms controlling the oligopoly market may be only 2 or as many as 50, depending on the industry. Second, other sellers are not able to easily enter the market. As with monopoly markets, barriers to entry may be due to the prohibitively high costs of starting a business in that industry, they may be the result of long-term contracts that have tied all the buyers to the firms already in the industry, or they may be due to enduring loyalties created by brand-name advertising.

Oligopoly markets, which are dominated by a few (e.g., three to eight) large firms, are said to be **highly concentrated**. Examples of such oligopoly markets are not hard to find because they include many of the largest manufacturing industries. Table 4.1 lists several highly concentrated U.S. industries, as indicated by the large share of the market that the biggest firms control. The firms that dominate the highly concentrated U.S. industries tend, by and large, to be among the largest corporations in the United States. Table 4.2 lists several major corporations dominant in various oligopoly industries, together with the approximate percentage of the markets controlled by these firms. These include many of the most well-known and largest U.S. firms operating in several of the most basic U.S. industries.

highly concentrated markets Oligopoly markets that are dominated by a few (e.g., three to eight) large firms.

Although oligopolies can form in a variety of ways, the most common causes of an oligopolistic market structure are **horizontal mergers**.[20] A horizontal merger is simply the unification of two or more companies that were formerly competing in the same line of business. If enough companies in a competitive industry merge, the industry can become an oligopoly composed of a few very large firms. During the 1950s, for example, the 108 competing banks in Philadelphia began to merge until, by 1963, the number of bank firms had been reduced to 42.[21] The Philadelphia National Bank emerged as the second-largest bank (as a result of nine mergers), and the Girard Bank emerged as the third-largest (as a result of six mergers). In the early 1960s, the Philadelphia National Bank and the Girard Bank proposed to merge into a single firm. If the merger had been approved (the government stopped it), the two banks together would have controlled well over one-third of the banking activities of metropolitan Philadelphia.

horizontal merger The unification of two or more companies that were formerly competing in the same line of business.

How do oligopoly markets affect consumers? Because a highly concentrated oligopoly has a relatively small number of firms, it is relatively easy for the managers of these firms to join forces and act as a unit. By explicitly or tacitly agreeing to set their prices at the same levels and to restrict their output accordingly, the oligopolists can function much like a single giant firm. This uniting of forces, together with the barriers to entry

Table 4.1 *Combined Market Shares of Largest Firms in Highly Concentrated Oligopoly Industries, 2002*

	Percent of Market Controlled by Largest Firms		
Product	**4 Largest**	**8 Largest**	**Herfindahl–Hirschman Index**
Cereal breakfast foods	82	93	2999
Cane sugar refining	78	99	2885
Beet sugar	85	98	2209
Breweries	91	94	(NA)
Chocolate	73	87	2268
Cigarettes	95	99	(NA)
Snack foods	64	72	2717
Thread	66	76	2434
Underwear	80	97	2400
Men's pants	84	90	2514
Botanical supplements	69	76	2704
Greeting cards	85	89	2830
House slippers	94	99	2944
Glass containers	87	96	2548
Small gun ammunition	84	90	2098
Computers	76	89	2662
Refrigerators and freezers	82	97	2025
Washers and driers	90	(NA)	2870
Electric bulbs	90	94	2848
Batteries	90	98	2507
Automobiles	87	97	2754
Vacuum cleaners	78	96	2096
Furniture	68	80	2913

Source: U.S. Census Bureau, *Concentration Ratios: 2002*, May 2006, Table 3. The Herfindahl–Hirschman index is a measure of market concentration calculated by squaring the individual market share (in percent) of each firm in the market and adding the squares together. An industry with a 4-firm combined share above 80 percent or a Herfindahl–Hirschman number above 1800 is considered to be highly concentrated.

that are characteristic of oligopoly industries, can result in the same high prices and low supply levels characteristic of monopoly markets. As a consequence, oligopoly markets, like monopolies, can fail to exhibit fair prices, can generate a decline in social utility, and can fail to respect basic economic freedoms. It has been shown, for example, that generally the more highly concentrated an oligopoly industry is, the higher the profits it is able to extract from its customers.[22] Studies also have estimated that the overall decline in consumer utility as a result of inefficient allocation of resources by highly concentrated oligopoly industries ranges between 0.5 percent and 4.0 percent of the nation's gross national product, or between $55 billion and $440 billion per year.[23]

Anticompetitive Behavior In a market economy like ours, and like most of the world now has, competition is what business is about. Everything a company does is normally aimed at making products or providing services that consumers will want to buy more than those competitors are trying to sell them. To succeed in that

Table 4.2 *Dominant Brands and Companies in Oligopoly Markets, 2010*

Brand/Company	Market	Market Share (%)
Gerber	Baby food	73%
Campbell's	Canned soup	70%
Kellogg's	Toaster pastry	72%
A-1	Marinades	79%
Gatorade	Sports drinks	82%
Levi's	Jeans	52%
Procter & Gamble	Laundry soap	57%
Clorox	Chlorine bleach	59%
Kiwi	Shoe polish	76%
General Electric	Light bulbs	79%
Tyco	Plastic pipe	60%
Reynolds	Aluminum foil	64%
Hewlett-Packard	Desktop laser printers	61%
Kitchen Aid	Stand-Alone mixers	83%
In-Sink-Erator	Garbage disposals	77%
Sony	Digital camcorders	68%
Kodak	Single-Use cameras	61%
Sony	Video game consoles	66%
Sony	Video games	64%
H&B	Wooden bats	65%

Source: Robert S. Lazich, *Market Share Reporter*, 2010 (Detroit, MI: Gale Research, 2011).

competition, a company has to provide consumers with products and services that are cheaper, or better, than competitors', or both. Companies normally prevail in this competition only if they can lower their costs below those of competitors (which lets them offer lower prices than competitors or make higher profits than competitors) or if they can develop products and services that are of higher quality than those of competitors. In either case, the company is competing in a way that ultimately benefits consumers and society: to cut costs companies make better and more efficient use of the resources they have, and to improve their products companies continually innovate and offer consumers and society increasingly better products.

Cutting costs and improving quality are the normal and honest ways in which companies in market economies compete and, as we have seen, competitive markets are fair, socially beneficial, and respectful of people's negative rights. But there are other ways to "compete" that are not aimed at lowering costs or improving quality, but instead aim at destroying competition itself. We are now going to turn to look at some of the specific ways in which employees and managers who operate in monopoly or oligopoly markets can manipulate the power they have in these markets to undermine competition and treat consumers unfairly, violate their rights, and diminish their utility. We are going to look, that is, at specific ways in which businesses can use their market power to unfairly harm consumers as well as competitors, instead of working at honestly lowering their costs and improving their products.

Explicit Agreements and Other Anticompetitive Tactics Prices in an oligopoly can be set at profitable levels through explicit agreements that restrain competition. The managers of the few firms operating in an oligopoly can meet and agree to act

ON THE EDGE

Fixing the Computer Memory Market

All personal computers need memory chips, called DRAM for "dynamic random access memory," which are sold in units of gigabytes (Gb) or megabytes (Mb). The $20 billion per year DRAM market is dominated by Micron, Infineon, Samsung, Hynix, and a few smaller companies who sell their DRAM to computer makers such as Dell, Compaq, Gateway, and Apple. In the late 1990s, the DRAM makers invested in bigger factories leading to a market glut, large inventories, and intense price competition. By February 2001, unsold inventories and a recession took DRAM prices into a steep fall (see graph), dropping to about $1 a unit by the end of 2001, a price well below manufacturing costs. In early 2002, while inventories were still high and the recession was in full swing, prices strangely rose and peaked at about $4.50 a unit in April (see chart). That month, Michael Dell of Dell Computers accused the companies of "cartel-like behavior," and the Department of Justice (DOJ) began to investigate the possibility of price-fixing. Prices now reversed, falling to $2 by the end of 2002, about 20 to 40 percent below manufacturing costs. The DOJ later released a November 26, 2001 e-mail written by Kathy Radford, a Micron manager, in which she described plans by Micron, Infineon, and Samsung to move their prices upward in unison: "the consensus from all [DRAM] suppliers is that if Micron makes the move, all of them will do the same and make it stick." On September, 2004, Infineon pled guilty to "participating in meetings, conversations, and communications" with other DRAM makers during 2001 and "agreeing during those meetings, conversations, and communications" to "fix the prices for DRAM." Infineon paid the U.S. government $160 million in fines. The DOJ announced it was investigating the other DRAM makers.

1. Estimate the equilibrium price from the graph.
2. Who ultimately paid for any monopoly profits above the equilibrium price?
3. Did the companies do anything unethical? Explain.

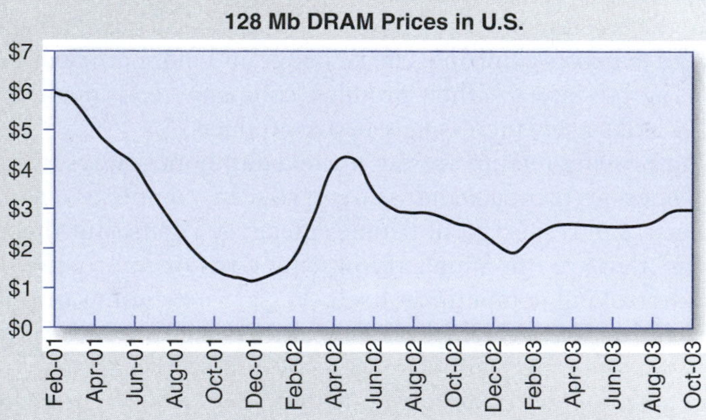

as a unit, for example, by charging the same price for their products. By uniting together, the oligopoly firms act like a single seller and, in effect, turn the oligopoly market into a monopoly. The greater the degree of market concentration present in an industry, the fewer the managers that have to be brought into the agreement, and the easier it is for them to, for example, fix their prices. Because such agreements reproduce the effects of a monopoly, they curtail market justice, market utility, and market rights as discussed in the first sections of this chapter.

Monopoly companies can also engage in anticompetitive behavior. A company, for example, who has a monopoly in one market may try to use its power to create a monopoly in another market. Microsoft, for example, who monopolized the market for personal computer operating systems with "Windows," was accused of trying to establish another monopoly in media players when it began to bundle "Windows Media Player" with each copy of Windows, so that a consumer could not buy "Windows" without also buying "Windows Media Player." Somewhat disingenuously Microsoft protested that it was "giving 'Windows Media Player' away for free." But, of course, Microsoft paid for the costs of developing "Windows Media Player" out of what consumers paid for "Windows," so part of what consumers were paying for "Windows" was really being used to pay for "Windows Media Player."

If the justice, freedom, and social utility that competitive markets achieve are important values for society, then it is morally wrong for the managers of oligopoly companies to unite together in a collusive agreement. Only if markets function competitively will they exhibit the justice, freedom, and utility that justify their existence. These beneficial aspects of a free market are reaped by society only as long as managers of oligopoly firms refrain from agreeing to practices that recreate a monopoly market. The following are several specific ways in which the managers of oligopoly companies can agree to act together in conspiracies that injure society and can unfairly destroy smaller competitors.

Price-Fixing When firms operate in an oligopoly market, their managers can meet secretly and agree to set their prices at artificially high levels, i.e., at prices well above the supply curve and generally above the equilibrium price. This is straightforward **price-fixing** which reproduces the effects of a monopoly. In 2010, for example, the managers of six companies—Sharp Corp., LG Display Co., Hitachi Displays Ltd., Epson Imaging Devices Corp., Chunghway Picture Tubes Ltd., and Chi Mei Optoelectronics—admitted they had put together a world-wide scheme to fix the prices of TFT-LCD panels which serve as the screens for flat televisions, computer monitors, laptop screens, cell phone displays, and media players. The managers confessed they got together several times in secret meetings in Japan, Korea, and the United States and there they discussed and agreed on the prices they would all charge for their TFT-LCD panels and agreed to limit the quantity of panels they would produce. By limiting their production, they created artificial shortages that let them raise their prices above the normal equilibrium level, thereby increasing their revenues even though throughout the period of the conspiracy their costs were constant and there was little competition on quality.[24] Through their price-fixing scheme they defrauded their buyers out of hundreds of millions of dollars. When this was discovered, their companies had to pay a record $860 million in fines and those managers who were involved in the price-fixing scheme were given jail sentences and fined thousands of dollars. In addition, each of their many direct buyers (e.g., television and cell-phone manufacturers) then had the legal right to sue their companies and recover *three times* the amount of money the managers overcharged them. Many of these suits are still going on.

price-fixing An agreement between firms to set their prices at artificially high levels.

Manipulation of Supply Managers in an oligopoly industry do not have to agree to fix prices to recreate the effects of a monopoly market. Instead they only need to agree to limit the quantity of goods they supply to the market at a level that is below the equilibrium quantity. Doing this will create a shortage because demand for the goods will be higher than the supply of goods (i.e., at the quantity they set, the demand curve is well above the supply curve). The shortages will make prices rise higher than the equilibrium prices that would result from free competition. This is called **manipulation of supply**. When hardwood manufacturers met periodically in trade associations early in this century, for example, they would often enter agreements to limit their output so they could secure high profits.[25] The American Column and Lumber Company was eventually prosecuted under the Sherman Antitrust Act to force it to desist from this practice. Manipulation of supply is often combined with price-fixing as happened in the global TFT-LCD price-fixing scheme described above.

manipulation of supply When firms in an oligopoly industry agree to limit their production so that prices rise to levels higher than those that would result from free competition.

Market Allocation Sometimes called "market division," market allocation occurs when companies in an oligopoly divide up the market among themselves and each agrees to sell only to customers within their own part of the market and not enter the parts allocated to the other companies. Managers can divide up the market by territory ("You get India and I get China"), or by customers ("You sell to hospitals and I'll sell to doctors"), or by time ("You have lower prices during the first half of the month and I'll have lower prices during the second half"). When markets are allocated among companies in this way, each section of the market has only one seller giving that company a monopoly in the section of the market allocated to it.

market allocation When companies in an oligopoly divide up the market among themselves and agree to sell only to customers in their part of the market.

Bid Rigging Large buyers, especially government buyers, who need to purchase a product or service often ask companies to submit secret bids which will indicate the quality of the product or service they are offering to sell and the price at which they will sell that product or service to the buyer. The buyer then chooses the seller that offers the best combination of quality and price. Bid rigging occurs when managers in an oligopoly market agree in advance which of them will submit the best or winning bid. The others may then not bid at all, or they may submit bids that they know are too high or that contain conditions they know the buyer will not accept. The sellers take turns offering the winning bid, or they may agree beforehand that whoever wins the bid will give each of the others a share of the buyer's business. Bid rigging, like price-fixing, eliminates competition. Because only one company will offer the buyer a satisfactory bid, the buyer unknowingly faces a monopoly and will get unfairly overcharged, while the companies can stop working at lowering their costs or innovating in quality.

bid rigging A prior agreement that a specific party will get a contract even though all parties will submit bids for the contract.

Exclusive Dealing Arrangements A firm institutes an exclusive dealing arrangement when it sells to a retailer on condition that the retailer will not purchase any products from competitors and/or will not do business outside of a certain geographical area. For several years, for instance, American Can Company would lease its can-closing machines (at low prices) only to those customers who agreed not to purchase any cans from Continental Can Company, its major competitor.[26] Exclusive dealing arrangements tend to remove price competition between retailers who are selling the company's products, and to this extent they reduce competition. However, sometimes an exclusive dealing arrangement may give retailers an incentive to become more aggressive in selling the products of the company with which they have the exclusive dealing arrangement. In such cases, an exclusive dealing arrangement may actually increase competition between retailers selling the products of different companies. For this reason, managers who require their buyers to enter exclusive dealing arrangements must carefully examine their actions and determine whether their overall effect is to dampen or promote competition.[27]

exclusive dealing arrangements When a firm sells to a retailer on condition that the retailer will not purchase any products from other companies and/or will not sell outside of a certain geographical area.

Tying Arrangements A firm enters into a tying arrangement when it sells a buyer a certain good only on condition that the buyer agrees to purchase a certain other good from the firm. Eastman Kodak Company, for example, makes photocopy machines and sells replacement parts to repair its machines. Kodak also sells repair services for its machines. When Kodak first began selling its photocopy machines, several small businesses stepped forward and began offering repair services for Kodak machines, often for less than Kodak charged for the same repair services.[28] So Kodak announced it would sell replacement parts only to those customers who also purchased their repair services from Kodak. Since other repair companies could not repair Kodak machines without the replacement parts, Kodak was able to effectively shut them out of the market even when they charged less for their services. Image Technical Services, Inc., and several other competing repair companies, sued Kodak for "tying" its services to its replacement parts. Image Technical Services won the case because, the Court said, Kodak's monopoly of the supply of replacement parts gave it enough monopoly power to force buyers to also buy its repair services and to shut out other sellers of repair services, and this was an abuse of its market power. In effect, Kodak was using the monopoly it had in one market (the market for repair parts for its machines) to create a monopoly in another market (the market for repair services for its machines) and thereby, eliminate competition in two markets.

tying arrangements When a firm sells a buyer a certain good only on condition that the buyer agrees to purchase certain other goods from the firm.

Retail Price Maintenance Agreements If a manufacturer sells to retailers only on condition that they agree to charge a certain set retail price for its goods, it is engaged in "retail price maintenance." Until 2007, retail price maintenance was automatically judged to be an illegal anticompetitive practice because it forces retailers to stop competing on price. In 2007, however, the U.S. Supreme Court, in the case of *Leegin Creative Leather Products, Inc. v. PSKS, Inc.*, pointed out that retail price maintenance is not always anticompetitive. It is possible, the Supreme Court held, that by forcing retailers to maintain a certain price for its products, a manufacturer could, in some circumstances, actually increase competition. For example, forcing retailers to sell a product at a premium price may give retailers enough funds to provide extra services, and these extra services may make the product more competitive than the products of other sellers. Many economists, however, have disagreed with the Supreme Court and continue to hold that retail price maintenance generally reduces competition between retailers and removes from the manufacturer the competitive pressure to lower prices and cut costs.

retail price maintenance agreements Occurs when a manufacturer sells to a retailer only on condition that the retailer agree to charge the same set retail prices for its goods.

Predatory Price Discrimination When a seller charges different prices to different buyers for identical products with identical costs, the seller is engaged in **price discrimination**. Price discrimination becomes **predatory price discrimination** when it is directed at destroying a competitor, particularly when a company tries to eliminate a competitor by selling the product in the competitor's market (but not in other markets) for less than it cost to make it. Predatory price discrimination was used by Continental Baking Company, the "predator," against Utah Pie Company, its "prey." Continental Baking Company operated in Salt Lake City, Utah when it tried to drive out Utah Pie Company, a competitor that had entered the market and managed to take away much of the Salt Lake City business of Continental Baking Company. Continental retaliated by selling its pies to Salt Lake City stores for less than the cost of making the pies, and at prices that were much lower than those it sold to stores in other areas, all in an attempt to undercut Utah Pie Company's sales and run it out of business. The predator, in short, was selectively cutting its prices only in the areas were its prey was operating precisely in order to drive it out of the market and thereby, create a local monopoly for itself. Although Continental sold

price discrimination To charge different prices to different buyers for identical goods or services.

predatory price discrimination Price discrimination aimed at running a competitor out of business.

its pies at a loss it planned to make up for the loss by raising prices when Utah Pie Company was gone. The Supreme Court ruled that price discrimination is "unfair" and illegal when its effect is "substantially to lessen competition or tends to create a monopoly in any line of commerce." In addition, Continental's below-cost pricing was "predatory" since it was intended to drive a competitor out of business. Price discrimination aimed at reducing competition or creating a monopoly by driving competitors out of business, particularly with below-cost prices, said the Court, is wrong unless the price differences are based on real differences in the company's costs of manufacturing, packaging, marketing, transporting, or servicing goods, or when the company is merely trying to match the lower prices of other competitors in the market.

Quick Review 4.8

Unethical Practices in Oligopoly Markets

- Price-fixing
- Manipulation of supply
- Market allocation
- Bid rigging
- Exclusive dealing arrangements
- Tying arrangements
- Retail price maintenance agreements
- Predatory price discrimination.

One of the most vicious examples of predatory pricing occurred in the late nineteenth century when John D. Rockefeller monopolized 91 percent of the oil refining industry by selectively cutting his prices in the local markets of his competitors, driving them into bankruptcy, and then buying them out.[29] In 1911 the U.S Supreme Court ruled that "unfair methods of competition, such as local price cutting ... to suppress competition" were illegal and broke up his "Oil Trust" into 34 separate companies.[30] Rockefeller's contemporary, James Buchanan Duke, also used predatory pricing to force 250 tobacco companies to become part of his "Tobacco Trust" and it too was broken up in 1911.[31]

Bribery Many a company has secretly bribed government officials so they will purchase goods from the company and not its competitors. From 2001 to 2007, for example, Siemens Corporation paid $1.4 billion in bribes to government officials in Venezuela, China, Russia, Argentina, Nigeria, and Israel, to get them to purchase Siemens equipment instead of buying from competitors. The U.S. Foreign Corrupt Practices Act (FCPA) makes it a crime for a company operating in the U.S. to bribe foreign government officials to make a sale. Because of the FCPA and a similar German law, Siemens paid more than $2.6 billion in fines.[32]

When a company bribes government officials to make a sale, the market is no longer competitive since the company no longer has to compete with other sellers. Instead, the bribe shuts competitors out of the market and serves as a barrier to entry. The bribing company becomes a monopoly seller and can engage in the unfairness and inefficiencies characteristic of monopolies: monopoly prices and shoddy quality. Moreover, the briber induces the government official to violate his moral obligation to act in his country's best interests. Government officials themselves, however, sometimes demand or "extort" a bribe from companies or threaten to harm a company unless it pays a bribe. Such extortion may mitigate a company's moral responsibility, but paying the bribe will still violate the FCPA. The FCPA, however, allows payment of "petty" bribes to low-level officials (like customs officials) who demand a bribe just to do their jobs.[33]

Incentives, Opportunities, and Rationalizations We have looked at several ways in which managers and employees can inflict serious injuries on society by trying to reduce or eliminate the competition they face. Instead of competing honestly by working to lower their costs or improve the quality of their products and services, they try to establish, maintain, or expand a monopolistic market position. But why do managers do this when they risk going to jail and destroying their own careers and families? Under what conditions do employees or managers decide to engage in such wrongful behaviors? The sociologist Donald Cressey has argued that employees and managers tend to engage in "white collar" crimes such as price-fixing, when the "fraud triangle" is present: (1) they are pressured or have strong incentives to engage in the wrongdoing, (2) they see an opportunity to do it, and (3) they can rationalize their actions.[34] Pressures and incentives for fraud can consist of organizational pressures to achieve objectives, pressures from peers, deteriorating business or market conditions, or more personal incentives such as medical bills, paying for an addiction, financial problems, or even simply greed. Opportunities arise when a person (a) has the ability to carry out the crime, (b) is presented with circumstances that allow the crime to be carried out, and (c) the risk of detection is low. Rationalizations, as we saw in Chapter 1, are the countless ways of framing or thinking about one's action so that it seems morally justified to oneself and/or others. For example, a wrongdoer may see his participation in a fraud as an attempt to help his company, or an attempt to get a "fair" profit from his customers, Or the wrongdoers may see financial fraud as "what everyone does," as "borrowing" money he or she will pay back, or as something he or she "deserves," or what "they" deserve, or something he or she will do "just this once."

In a detailed study of employees whose companies had been implicated in price-fixing arrangements, researchers Sonnenfeld and Lawrence found several industry and organizational factors that tended to lead individuals into price-fixing.[35] In terms of the "fraud triangle" some of the most important of the factors that tend to lead to price-fixing are:

Incentives and Pressures: (1) *A Crowded and Mature Market* Mature industries are sometimes subject to oversupply because demand begins to fall or companies all increase production at the same time, or many new companies come into the market. As prices fall and revenues decline, middle managers can feel pressured to do something to halt their losses and may respond by allowing, encouraging, and even ordering their sales teams to engage in price-fixing. (2) *Undifferentiated Products* In some industries, the products of each company are so similar to those of the other companies in the industry that the companies have no choice but to compete on price alone. This can lead to periodic price wars or a continuous slide in prices that makes salespeople feel that the only way to keep prices from collapsing and to protect themselves and their jobs is by getting together with the salespeople of competitor companies and forging an agreement to fix prices. (3) *Personnel Practices* In some companies, managers are evaluated and rewarded solely or primarily on the basis of revenues and sales volume, so that bonuses, commissions, advancement, and other rewards are dependent on achieving these objectives. Such incentive systems send the message that the company demands they achieve these objectives any way they can, thereby making managers feel pressured to take any means, including price fixing, to achieve their objectives.

Opportunities: (1) *The Job-Order Nature of the Business* In some industries, job orders are customized so salespeople are allowed to price their orders individually and are not closely monitored. When salespeople have the opportunity to make pricing decisions on their own with little oversight, they are more likely to start meeting with the salespeople of competitors and making agreements to fix their prices. (2) *Decentralized Pricing Decisions* Some organizations are so decentralized that pricing decisions are put into the hands of the lower divisions of the organization, and each division is allowed to operate more or less on its own. In such cases, price-fixing is more likely to happen at the divisional level particularly when such decisions are not monitored and the division is pressured to perform in a declining market. (3) *Industry or Trade Associations* Most industries have organized associations where the managers of the companies in the industry can meet and discuss common issues and problems. If salespeople are allowed to meet with the salespeople of competitors in trade association meetings,

Quick Review 4.9

The Fraud Triangle

- The pressures or strong incentives to do wrong, such as organizational pressure, peer pressure, company needs, personal incentives
- The opportunity to do wrong, which includes the ability to carry out the wrongdoing, being presented with circumstances that allow it, low risk of detection
- The ability to rationalize one's action by framing it as morally justified.

they are likely to talk about pricing and then are free to engage in price-setting arrangements with their counterparts in competing firms.

Rationalizations: (1) *Inactive Corporate Legal or H.R. Staff* When legal departments or human resource departments fail to provide guidance to sales staff until after a problem has occurred, sales staff may not understand that price-fixing is a seriously illegitimate sales activity. Sales staff may then believe that there is nothing inappropriate about meeting with competitors and making price-fixing agreements. (2) *Organizational Culture of the Business* Some companies have freewheeling cultures where wrongdoing is condoned and goes unpunished so long as bottom line objectives are met. Top management may provide a poor example of integrity, codes of ethics may serve as mere window dressing, sanctions for wrongdoing may be lacking, and corporate audits as well as performance appraisals may look only at purely economic measures. In such organizations, salespeople can be socialized into believing that price-fixing is a common and harmless practice that is desired, condoned, accepted, and even encouraged by the organization.

The failure of top managers to deal with these industry and organizational factors can put significant pressures on individuals who are otherwise striving to do what is best for a company. One chief executive officer describes the pressures that an irresponsible management can place on young new salespeople:

> I think we are particularly vulnerable where we have a salesman with two kids, plenty of financial demands, and a concern over the security of his job. There is a certain amount of looseness to a new set of rules. He may accept questionable practices feeling that he may just not know the system. There are no specific procedures for him to follow other than what other salesmen tell him. At the same time, he is in an industry where the acceptance for his product and the level of profitability are clearly dropping. Finally, we add to his pressures by letting him know who will take his job from him if he doesn't get good price and volume levels. I guess this will bring a lot of soul-searching out of an individual.[36]

Tacit Agreements

Although most of the forms of explicit market agreements enumerated above are illegal, price-setting in oligopolies is more often accomplished through some unspoken form of cooperation against which it is difficult to legislate. How does this take place? The managers of the major firms in an oligopoly can learn by hard experience that competition is not in their personal financial interests. Price-cutting competition, they find, will only lead to minimal profits. The firms in an oligopoly, therefore, may each come to the conclusion that cooperation is in the best interests of all. Each firm may then reach the independent conclusion that they will all benefit if, when one major firm raises its prices, all other firms set their prices at the same high levels. Through this process of "price-setting," all the major firms will retain their share of the market and they will all gain by the higher price. Since the 1930s, for example, the major tobacco companies have charged identical list prices for cigarettes. When one company decides it has a reason to raise or lower its cigarette prices, the other companies will always follow suit within a short period of time. The officials of these companies, however, have made no explicit agreement to act in concert; without ever having talked the matter over among themselves, each realizes that all will benefit so long as they continue to act in a unified fashion. In 1945, incidentally, the U.S. Supreme Court found the dominant cigarette companies guilty of tacit collusion, but the companies reverted to identical pricing after the case was settled.

To coordinate their prices, some oligopoly industries will recognize one firm as the industry's "**price leader**."[37] Each firm will tacitly agree to set its prices at the levels announced by the price leader, knowing that all other firms will also follow its price leadership. Because each oligopolist knows it will not have to compete with another firm's lower prices, it is not forced to reduce its margin of profit to the levels to which open competition would reduce them. There need be no overt collusion involved in this form of price-setting, only an unspoken understanding that all firms will follow the price leadership of the dominant firm and will not engage in the price-lowering tactics of competition.

price leader The firm recognized as the industry leader in oligopoly industries for the purpose of setting prices based on levels announced by that firm.

Whether prices in an oligopoly market are set by explicit agreements or implicit understandings, it is clear that social utility declines to the extent that prices are artificially raised above the levels that would be set by a perfectly competitive market. Consumers must pay the unjust prices of the oligopolists, resources are no longer efficiently allocated and used, and the freedom of both consumers and potential competitors diminishes.

4.4 Oligopolies and Public Policy

Oligopolies are not a modern phenomenon. Toward the end of the nineteenth century, as we suggested above, many businessmen began using anticompetitive practices to force competitors to sell out to them, eventually creating gigantic "**trusts**" that would then monopolize their markets, raise prices for consumers, cut prices for their suppliers such as farmers, and continually terrorize their remaining competitors with predatory pricing. Business people created trusts in the sugar, salt, whiskey, tobacco, and cottonseed oil industries. Earlier, competing railroads had been consolidated into huge enterprises by the so-called Robber Barons—Andrew Carnegie, Jay Gould, J. P. Morgan, and John D. Rockefeller. These gigantic trusts elicited the public's fear, suspicion, and hatred. Newspaper editorials and politicians railed against the unscrupulous ruthlessness with which the trusts ground down their competitors, monopolized crucial industries, and bullied the farmers who supplied them with raw materials. Intellectuals argued that the concentrated power of the trusts was dangerous and would give these businesses unfair political influence.

a trust An alliance of previously competitive oligopolists formed to take advantage of monopoly powers.

The rise of the trusts coincided with the Progressive movement, a political reform movement directed against big business abuses of power with the avowed aim of "busting" up the trusts. Responding to this movement, particularly the lobbying of struggling small farmers, the U.S. Congress in 1887 passed the Interstate Commerce Act to regulate the large railroad companies. Then, in 1890, Congress passed what was to become the most important single piece of antitrust legislation, the **Sherman Antitrust Act**. The two key sections of the act read:

Sherman Antitrust Act Federal law passed in 1890 that prohibits competitors from getting together to reduce competition or using monopoly power to keep or expand a monopoly.

> Section 1: Every contract, combination . . . , or conspiracy, in restraint of trade or commerce among the several States, or with foreign nations, is hereby declared illegal . . .
>
> Section 2: Every person who shall monopolize, or attempt to monopolize, or combine or conspire with any other person or persons to monopolize any part of the trade or commerce among the several States, or with foreign nations, shall be deemed guilty of a felony . . .

In the two decades following passage of the Sherman Antitrust Act, little was done to enforce it. But in 1908, the federal government filed suit against the Tobacco

Trust, claiming that its ruthless tactics against competitors had violated the Sherman Antitrust Act. In a May, 1911 decision, the Supreme Court agreed and ordered the Tobacco Trust to be broken up into 15 separate companies. Encouraged by the victory, the "trust busters" in government went on to successfully prosecute Standard Oil, DuPont, and other large trusts. The U.S. Supreme Court, in fact, went so far as to say that the Sherman Antitrust Act was "the Magna Carta of free enterprise, . . . as important to the preservation of economic freedom and our free-enterprise system as the Bill of Rights is to the protection of our fundamental personal freedoms."[38]

Since 1911, Section 1 of the Sherman Antitrust Act has been interpreted as prohibiting competing companies from making agreements to fix prices, to divide up territories or customers, or to restrict the quantity of goods they bring to market. Section 2 has been interpreted as prohibiting a company that already holds a monopoly from using its monopoly power to maintain its monopoly or to extend its monopoly into other markets. Thus, the Sherman Antitrust Act does not prohibit a company from acquiring a monopoly through legitimate business dealings (like having a better product, a shrewd strategy, or sheer luck). However, if a company that acquires a monopoly then tries to use its monopoly power to acquire a new monopoly, or to maintain its current monopoly, it is "guilty of a felony." In 1911, the U.S. Supreme Court ruled that although some agreements between competitors could be "reasonable" and legal if it "promotes competition," nevertheless, certain agreements (including agreements to fix prices or quantities) were so inherently ("per se") anticompetitive that they were always illegal.

The antitrust laws were expanded in 1914 by the Clayton Act, which prohibits price discrimination, exclusive dealing contracts, tying arrangements, and mergers between companies "where the effect may be to substantially lessen competition." This latter section of the Clayton Act also gives the federal government the power to prohibit two companies from merging if the government believes that their merger will "substantially lessen competition."

But although the United States has a long history of antitrust legislation, there is still a great deal of debate concerning what government should do about the power of oligopolies or monopolies. Some have argued that the economic power held by oligopoly corporations is actually quite small and insufficient to affect society, whereas others have claimed that it dominates modern economies, and still others have argued that several social factors inhibit the use of this power. These differences have given rise to three main views on oligopoly power.

The Do-Nothing View

Some economists hold that nothing should be done about the economic power held by oligopoly corporations because the power of large oligopoly corporations is actually not as large as it may first appear. Several arguments have been given to support this claim. First, it is argued that although competition within industries has declined, it has been replaced by competition between industries with substitutable products.[39] The steel industry, for example, is now in competition with the aluminum and cement industries. Consequently, although there may be a high degree of market concentration in a single industry like steel, a high level of competition is still maintained by its relation to other competing industries.

Second, as the economist John Kenneth Galbraith once argued, the economic power of any large corporation may be balanced and restrained by the "countervailing power" of other large corporate groups in society.[40] Government and unions, for example, both restrain the power of big businesses. Although a business corporation may have a large share of an industrial market, it is faced by buyers that are equally large and equally powerful. A large steel company, for example, must sell to equally large automobile companies. This balance of power between large corporate groups, Galbraith claims, effectively reduces the economic power any single corporate giant can exert.

Other economists have very different reasons for urging that we should not worry about the economic power of large oligopoly corporations. The so-called *Chicago School* of antitrust has argued that markets are economically efficient even when there are as few as three significant rivals in a market.[41] Although government should prohibit outright price-fixing and mergers that create a single-company monopoly, it should not become involved in trying to break down oligopolies that are providing consumers with products they freely choose to buy and that are, therefore, efficiently using economic resources to improve consumer welfare.[42]

Finally, yet others have argued that big is good particularly in light of the globalization of business that has taken place during recent decades. If U.S. companies are to compete with large foreign companies, they must be able to achieve the same economies of scale that are achievable by large foreign companies. Economies of scale are reductions in the cost of producing goods that result when larger quantities of goods are produced using the same fixed resources, such as the same machines, marketing programs, group of managers, or employees. If a company can make and sell larger quantities of products, it can spread these "fixed costs" over more units, thus reducing the cost of each unit and allowing it to sell its goods at lower prices. Thus, by expanding, companies are able to reduce their prices and thus compete more effectively against similarly large foreign companies. Although research suggests that in most industries expansion beyond a certain point will not lower costs but will instead increase costs, nevertheless many people continue to urge the *big is good* argument.[43]

The Antitrust View

The oldest view about the economic power oligopolies and monopolies possess is the view that lay behind the actions of the "trust busters" at the end of the nineteenth century. Like the trust busters, many contemporary economists and antitrust lawyers are suspicious of the economic power exerted by oligopoly corporations. They argue that prices and profits in concentrated industries are higher than they should be and that monopolists and oligopolists use unfair tactics against their competitors and suppliers. The solution, they argue, is to reinstate competitive pressures by forcing the large companies to divest themselves of their holdings, thereby breaking them up into smaller firms.

Clearly, the antitrust view is based on a number of assumptions. J. Fred Weston has summarized the basic propositions on which this traditional view is based:

1. If an industry is not atomistic with many small competitors, there is likely to be administrative discretion over prices.
2. Concentration results in recognized interdependence among companies, with no price competition in concentrated industries.
3. Concentration is due mostly to mergers because the most efficient scale of operation is not more than 3 to 5 percent of the industry. A high degree of concentration is unnecessary.

Quick Review 4.10

Main Views on Oligopoly Power

- Do-nothing view says do nothing since power of oligopolies is limited by competition between industries and by countervailing power of large groups; also oligopolies are competitive and big U.S. companies are good international competitors
- Antitrust view says large monopoly and oligopoly firms are anticompetitive and should be broken up into small companies
- Regulation view says big companies are beneficial but need to be restrained by government regulation.

4. There is a positive correlation between concentration and profitability that gives evidence of monopoly power in concentrated industries—the ability to elevate prices and the persistence of high profits. Entry does not take place to eliminate excessive profits.
5. Concentration is aggravated by product differentiation and advertising. Advertising is correlated with higher profits.
6. There is oligopolistic coordination by signaling through press releases or other means.[44]

On the basis of these assumptions, proponents of the antitrust view reach the conclusion that by breaking up large corporations into smaller units, higher levels of competition will emerge in those industries that are currently highly concentrated. The result is a decrease in explicit and tacit collusion, lower prices for consumers, greater innovation, and the increased development of cost-cutting technologies that will benefit us all.

The Regulation View

A third group of observers holds that oligopoly corporations should not be broken up because their large size has beneficial consequences that would be lost if they were forced to decentralize.[45] In particular, they argue, mass production and mass distribution of goods can be carried out only by using the highly centralized accumulation of assets and personnel that the large corporation makes possible. Moreover, the concentration of assets allows large firms to take advantage of the economies made possible by large-scale production in large plants. These savings are passed on to consumers in the form of cheaper and more plentiful products.

Although firms should not be broken up, it does not follow that they should not be regulated. According to this third view, concentration gives large firms an economic power that allows them to fix prices and engage in other forms of behavior that are not in the public interest. To ensure that consumers are not harmed by large firms, regulatory agencies and legislation should be set up to restrain and control the activities of large corporations.

Some observers, in fact, advocate that where large firms cannot be effectively controlled by the usual forms of regulation, then regulation should take the form of nationalization. That is, the government should take over the operation of firms in those industries[46] where only public ownership can ensure that firms operate in the public interest. Other advocates of regulation, however, argue that nationalization is not in the public interest. Public ownership of firms, they claim, is socialistic and inevitably leads to the creation of unresponsive and inefficient bureaucracies. Moreover, publicly owned enterprises are not subject to competitive market pressures, and this results in higher prices and higher costs.

Which of these three views is correct: the do-nothing view, the antitrust view, or the regulation view? Readers will have to decide this issue for themselves because at the moment there does not appear to be sufficient evidence to answer this question unequivocally. Whichever of these three views readers may find most persuasive, it is clear that the social benefits generated by free markets cannot be secured unless the managers of firms maintain competitive market relationships among themselves. The ethical rules prohibiting collusion are meant to ensure that markets are structured competitively. These rules may be voluntarily followed or legally enforced. They are justified insofar as society is justified in pursuing the utilitarian benefits, justice, and rights to negative freedom that free competitive markets can secure.

ON THE EDGE

Oracle and Peoplesoft

Oracle Corporation makes extremely complicated and large customized software programs that can support thousands of simultaneous users and that are capable of administering the personnel records and financial records of very large businesses (called "enterprise software"). Peoplesoft and SAP were the only two other major competitors making such massive enterprise software. Oracle held 18 percent of the market in customized software capable of handling the personnel records of very large businesses, SAP held 29 percent, and Peoplesoft held 51.5 percent. Moreover, Oracle held 17 percent, SAP held 39 percent, and Peoplesoft held 31 percent of the market for customized software capable of managing the financial records of very large businesses. On June 6, 2003, Oracle attempted a hostile takeover of Peoplesoft by offering to buy Peoplesoft's shares for $5.1 billion, or $16 a share. Peoplesoft's board of directors rejected Oracle's offer, and on June 18 Oracle raised its bid to $6.3 billion, or $19.50 per share, and then on February 4, 2004, raised its offer to $9.4 billion, or $26 per share. Peoplesoft stock was by then selling for $22 a share and its board rejected the new offer. Peoplesoft also passed a "poison pill" provision by promising customers cash refunds of up to 5 times what they paid for their software if Peoplesoft is taken over by another company.

On February 26, 2004, the U.S. Department of Justice (DOJ) sued to block Oracle's bid, claiming the takeover would reduce the market's competitors from three to two and "such a reduction in competition is likely to result in higher prices, less innovation, and decreased support" for large business customers. Oracle challenged the government's definition of the "enterprise software market" as too narrow and asserted that if the market was defined as the market for all "business software," then there were many dozens of companies competing in the market and not just three. Moreover, Oracle claimed, large companies like Microsoft planned to enter the enterprise software market, and anyway, large customers could negotiate low prices even when there were only two competing sellers in a market. On September 9, 2004, the Court ruled in Oracle's favor against the DOJ, and Oracle shortly acquired Peoplesoft.

1. Does an Oracle takeover of Peoplesoft leave the market too concentrated?
2. Do large companies do more good than bad?

Questions for Review and Discussion

Study and **Review** on **mythinkinglab.com**

1. Define the following concepts: perfect competition, demand curve, supply curve, equilibrium point, monopoly competition, oligopolistic competition, price-fixing, manipulation of supply, market allocation, bid rigging, exclusive dealing arrangements, tying arrangements, retail price maintenance agreements, price discrimination, price-setting, price leadership, the fraud triangle, countervailing power, do-nothing view on oligopoly power, antitrust view on oligopoly power, regulation view on oligopoly power.
2. "From an ethical point of view, big business is always bad business." Discuss the pros and cons of this statement.
3. What kind of public policy do you think the United States should have with respect to business competition? Develop moral arguments to support your answer

(i.e., arguments showing that the kinds of policies you favor will advance the public welfare, or secure certain important rights, or ensure certain forms of justice).

4. In your judgment, should a U.S. company operating in a foreign country in which collusive price-fixing is not illegal obey the U.S. laws against collusion? Explain your answer.

Web Resources

Readers who want to conduct research on the market issues in this chapter through the Internet might want to start with the American Antitrust Institute, which provides cases, articles, and links on price-fixing, mergers, vertical price restraints, and so on at their web site (*http://www.antitrustinstitute.org*). Also excellent is Oligopoly Watch, which provides a continually updated web site with current information on price-fixing activity, mergers, and so on (*http://www.oligopolywatch.com*). The Federal Trade Commission (FTC) provides access to its antitrust decisions and proceedings (*http://www.ftc.gov*), and the U.S. Justice Department does the same (*http://www.usdoj.gov/atr/index.html*). Additional links and important legal cases relating to all these issues can be found through the excellently organized and copious resources of Hieros Gamos (*http://hg.org/antitrust.html*), or through the American Bar Association (*http://www.abanet.org/antitrust*).

CASES

Intel's "Rebates" and Other Ways It "Helped" Customers

Explore the **Concept** on **mythinkinglab.com**

On November 12, 2009, Intel Corp. gave Advanced Micro Devices (AMD) $1.25 billion to settle a lawsuit AMD filed against it in 2005. Intel's CEO Paul Otellini said he agreed to pay $1.25 billion to settle AMD's lawsuit because he no longer felt the "time and money [spent fighting it] makes sense."[1] AMD's lawsuit accused Intel of being a monopoly and of using its monopoly power to unfairly keep computer companies from buying AMD's microprocessors. With about 70 percent of the market, Intel Corp. is the world's largest manufacturer of personal computer (PC) "microprocessors"—also called "computer chips," "microchips," or "processors"—tiny electronic devices that serve as the "brain" of a personal computer and carries out its basic operations. As the world's second largest maker of PC microprocessors, AMD is Intel's only real competitor, although it holds only about 20 percent of the PC processor market. It is difficult for other companies to get into the business of making PC microprocessors because of several "barriers to entry." First, Intel and AMD hold the patents for making the kind of microprocessors almost all personal computers use. Second, it costs several billion dollars to build facilities for making microprocessors. Third, Intel and AMD are so big and experienced that they can now make microprocessors for a lot less than a new company could, so if a new company tried to enter the market its prices would likely not be competitive with Intel's or AMD's.

AMD was not the only one that had accused Intel of using monopoly power to stifle competition. On May 5, 2009, the European Commission fined Intel a record $1.5 billion and said the company had used its monopoly power to unfairly block AMD from the market. On November 4, 2009, New York Attorney General Andrew Cuomo sued Intel for harming New York's consumers by using its monopoly power to keep computer makers from buying better AMD microprocessors. In June, 2008, South Korea's Fair Trade Commission ruled that Intel had used its monopoly power in violation of its antitrust laws. In 2005, Japan's Fair Trade Commission ruled that Intel had violated Japanese antitrust laws by paying companies to buy all or almost all of their processors exclusively from Intel.

Many of the activities Intel was being blamed for originated in a strategic mistake the company made in the late 1990s when it invested hundreds of millions of dollars developing a new type of microprocessor that would not use "x86 technology." x86 technology consists of certain instructions that are built into so-called "x86 microprocessors." All microprocessors must contain "instructions" that allow them to "read" and run software programs like games, word-processors, or web browsers. Because all x86 microprocessors contain the same instructions, the newest x86 microprocessors can generally read and use the same data and programs that ran on older x86 microprocessors. This means that when a customer who has been using a computer with an x86 processor buys a new computer with a more advanced x86 microprocessor, he or she does not have to throw away all his or her old programs and data because they will still work on the new computer.

This ability of each new generation of x86 microprocessors to run most of the programs that previous generations of x86 microprocessors could run is a major advantage for both consumers and businesses alike. However, from Intel's perspective, x86 microprocessors have a major disadvantage: AMD can legally make x86 microprocessors so Intel is forced to compete with AMD. Intel's biggest nightmare was that AMD someday might come up with an x86 microprocessor that was faster and more powerful than any of Intel's and then take over the market.

So when it invested in a new generation of microprocessors in the 1990s, Intel decided to develop and patent a microprocessor that did not use x86 technology. Since Intel alone would hold the patent for this new non-x86 processor, AMD would be legally barred from making it. With luck, Intel might eventually have the entire pc processor market to itself.

Intel called its new pc processor the "Itanium" and it was faster and more powerful than all previous generations of pc processors, but there was a problem. Since the Itanium processor did not use x86 technology, all software designed to run on current and older x86 processors would not work on the new Itanium unless the user first ran an "emulation" program that, in effect, forced the Itanium to imitate an x86 processor. But the emulation program slowed down the programs designed for x86 processors, sometimes to a frustrating crawl. This meant that when a consumer or business bought a new computer with the Itanium processor inside, its current software and data would not work at all well on the new computer. This was a major deterrent for buyers.

AMD had also developed a more advanced generation of PC processors during the 1990s. But AMD decided to stick with the x86 technology so its new processor could run software designed for x86 processors without using an emulation program. AMD called its new processor the Athlon. Since the Athlon was not slowed down by an emulation program when it ran x86 programs, all x86 programs ran extremely fast and smoothly on computers equipped with AMD's new processor. Not only could AMD's Athlon run x86 programs much faster and better than Intel's Itanium, it also used less electricity and AMD sold it for less than the Itanium. Intel's worse nightmare had come true.

When AMD and Intel marketed their new microprocessors in 1999, reviewers and users raved about AMD's fast and low-priced Athlon and heaped scorn on Intel's clunky Itanium. PC manufacturers flocked to put AMD's processor into their new computers and AMD's market share grew from about 9 percent to about 25 percent of the PC processor market, while Intel's fell from 90 percent to 74 percent.

But in 2003 and 2004, AMD's sales hit a wall. Computer manufacturers suddenly refused to buy AMD's processors. In 2002, Sony had put AMD's Athlon into 23 percent of its computers; by 2004 it had stopped using the Athlon completely. NEC went from using the Athlon in 84 percent of its desktop computers, to using it in virtually none. Toshiba went from using it in 15 percent of its computers in 2000, to using it in none by 2001.[2] Altogether, AMD's share of the Japanese PC processor market fell from 25 percent in 2002 to 9 percent in 2004.

What had happened? Tom McCoy, AMD's executive vice president for legal affairs, claimed in an article that the drop in orders for Athlon chips was "a matter of sheer exercise of monopoly power" by Intel.[3] McCoy claimed that Intel paid the Japanese companies—Sony, NEC, and Toshiba—millions of dollars in "rebates" provided they stopped buying AMD's microprocessors and used only Intel microprocessors inside their computers. But these payments, McCoy claimed, were not really rebates. A true rebate is a payment based on the number of products a customer purchases, and so are in effect discounts that are paid after the customer buys the product, unlike regular discounts which are subtracted from the price before the purchase. But the payments Intel was giving computer makers, McCoy asserted, were not related to the number of processors they bought. Instead, Intel handed over these payments when a company agreed to stop buying from AMD, regardless of the number of processors they subsequently purchased.

Moreover, McCoy wrote, Intel threatened companies by warning them that if they did not stop using AMD's microprocessors, Intel might stop supplying them with any microprocessors at all. The threat was a powerful one because even if they used AMD's microprocessors on some of their top-quality computers, every computer manufacturer still depended on Intel for the microprocessors in all their other computers.[4] Because of its small size, AMD could not provide the full range of microprocessors that the larger companies needed.

Convinced that Intel was using unfair and illegal means to block them out of the market, AMD sued Intel on June 27, 2005. Intel's general legal counsel, Bruce Sewell, responded to AMD's claims by arguing that the reason computer makers stopped buying AMD's microchips was because once they started using them in large numbers and running many different programs on them, they found AMD chips did not run the programs as fast as they had first appeared to. "When AMD has good parts, they do fine," said Bruce Sewell, "When AMD has lousy parts, they don't do so well. That's what a competitive market is all about."

Bruce Sewell also defended Intel's rebates. If it is not wrong, he said, for a small company to build loyal customers by giving them more rebates when they agree to use your products exclusively, why should it be wrong for a larger company to do the same? Moreover, rebates in effect lowered the price of its computer chips and what was wrong with that? Ultimately, didn't that benefit the consumer? And why was it so important to relate rebates to the number of units a customer buys? If Intel gave larger rebates to those companies that agreed to use its products exclusively, and smaller rebates to those companies that would not make the same commitment, what was wrong with that? Wasn't a company's agreement to use Intel as its exclusive supplier valuable to Intel and so shouldn't Intel be allowed to reward that company with larger rebates than the discounts it offered other companies?

Because the AMD lawsuit was complicated and required gathering and reviewing a great deal of documentary evidence, it had still not gone to trial by the end of 2009. By then, however, AMD's allegations had convinced several foreign governments—including the European Union, South Korea, and Japan—that they should investigate Intel and their investigations ended with substantial fines of Intel for violating antitrust laws. The United States, however, did very little until, toward the end of 2009, the U.S. Federal Trade Commission (FTC) sued Intel for "illegal monopolization," "unfair methods of competition," and "deceptive acts and practices in commerce."[5]

The FTC said in its suit that its investigations had discovered what Intel's legal counsel Bruce Sewell had suggested: some software programs ran slowly on AMD's processors. But the reason was not because AMD's processors were inherently slow. They had found that Intel had changed the programs sold by software companies so that their programs would not work well on computers using AMD's computer chips. All software companies use "compilers" to convert their programs into a form that will run on particular kinds of computer chips. The compilers are provided by the companies that make the chips, in this case Intel and AMD, who are each supposed to provide compilers that will allow programs to run on both their processors. But in 2003, the FTC said, Intel changed its compilers so that programs compiled with Intel's compilers would run fine on Intel processors, but would run slowly or poorly on AMD's. Without their knowledge, when software companies used Intel's compilers to process one of their programs, Intel's compiler secretly inserted bugs into the program that slowed it when it ran on an AMD processor, but not on an Intel processor. Customers and reviewers blamed AMD's processor when their new programs did not run well on a computer that had an AMD chip inside.[6]

The FTC also claimed that Intel had provided software companies with "libraries" of software code that were also designed to trip up programs when they ran on AMD microchips. The software code the FTC was talking about were short bits of software that carry out certain frequently used, but routine operations on x-86 processors. Software engineers insert these short bits of code into their programs instead of writing them out each time they need them. Intel provided software engineers with "libraries" consisting of dozens of these bits of code. However, the FTC claimed, Intel changed the software codes in its library so they would not work well on AMD processors. Consumers and reviewers again blamed AMD's chips when a program containing Intel's codes did not run well on a computer that used an AMD microchips.[7]

The FTC also said that Intel had paid computer makers to boycott AMD's processors by giving them what Intel called "rebates" although these payments required only that a company agree not to buy AMD processors and were unrelated to the amount the company bought. The computer manufacturer Dell, Inc., was a good example of how Intel paid computer makers to boycott AMD. Intel had began making significant quarterly "rebates" to computer manufacturer Dell, Inc. in 2001, and Dell at that time stopped using AMD's processors even though many of its customers said they wanted computers with AMD's processor.

Dell, which was founded in 1984 by its current CEO, Michael Dell, who was then a student at the University of Texas at Austin, began when he started selling computers out of his dorm room. By 2001, Dell had become the largest PC manufacturer in the world and held 13 percent of the worldwide PC market. The company finished 2001 with a net income of $2.24 billion, its largest so far.

In 2002, according to a Dell memo, Dell's chief operating officer (COO) met with several Intel officials. Before the meeting, Dell's lead negotiator had explained what he expected Intel's officials would say to Dell's COO: "without being blatant [Intel] will make it clear that Dell won't get more [payments] if we do [use] AMD [processors]. We'll get less and someone else will get ours."[8] During the meeting Intel officials said they were willing to do "whatever it takes" to get Dell not to use any AMD processors in its computers. According to the memo, Intel agreed at the meeting that its quarterly payments to Dell "should increase from the $70 million this quarter to $100 million."[9] But Dell had to continue to refuse to use AMD's processors.[10]

It was not difficult for Intel to pay the hundreds of millions of dollars it was giving Dell. Intel had unusually high profit margins of 50 percent that allowed it to accumulate $10.3 billion of cash at the end of 2001, and by the end of 2005 it held $14.8 billion of cash. In a February, 2004 email, Michael Dell remarked on Intel's profitability:

> [Intel's] profits in the 2nd half of 2001 were $1.397 billion on revenues of $13.528 billion. In the 2nd half of 2003 they were $4.885 billion on revenues of $16.574 billion. In other words their sales went up 22.5% and their profits went up 350%! Or said another way, their revenues went up $3.046 billion and their profits went up $3,488 billion!! Not even Microsoft can do that.[11]

Although many smaller companies started using AMD's chips, Dell feared retaliation from Intel if it tried to do the same. In an email, a Dell executive noted that if "Dell joins the AMD exodus" the consequences would be costly for Dell. He noted that Intel's CEO and Chairman "are prepared for jihad if Dell joins the AMD exodus. We will get ZERO [payments] for at least one quarter while Intel 'investigates the details'—there's no legal/moral/threatening means for us to apply and avoid this."[12]

Although Dell complained that its refusal to use ADM processors was hurting its sales, Intel kept Dell loyal, throughout 2004, by increasing its quarterly payments to $300 million per quarter, an amount equal to almost a third of Dell's quarterly net income and apparently enough to compensate Dell for any sales declines.

But Dell continued to lose market share and its CEO, Michael Dell, became increasingly frustrated. On November 4, 2005, Intel's CEO, Paul Otellini wrote an email saying that he had just received "one of the most emotional calls I have ever, ever had with [Michael Dell]." Otellini noted that "[Michael Dell] opened by saying 'I am tired of losing business'... He repeated it 3–4 times. I said nothing and waited. [He said] he has been traveling around the USA. He feels they are losing all the high margin business to AMD-based [computers]. Dell is no longer seen as a thought leader."[13] A week later, Michael Dell sent an email to Otellini complaining that "We have lost the performance leadership and it's seriously impacting our business in several areas." Otellini responded to Dell's complaints by pointing out how much Intel was paying Dell: "We are [now] transferring over $1 billion per year to Dell for its efforts. This was judged by your team to be more than sufficient to compensate for the competitive issue."[14] On November 25, Michael Dell wrote in an email to Otellini that "None of the current benchmarks and reviews say that Intel-based systems are better than AMD. We are losing the hearts, minds and wallets of our best customers."[15]

In spite of realizing that boycotting AMD's processors was hurting its revenues, Dell remained so loyal to Intel that in February, 2006, Otellini joked that Dell's CEO was "The best friend money can buy."[16] Intel continued to increase its payments to Dell through 2005 and 2006 until they reached a high of $805 million a quarter in early 2006, an amount equal to 104 percent of Dell's net income per quarter that year.

But 2006 was the year Dell finally broke away from its agreement to not use AMD processors. That year it purchased Alienware, a computer manufacturer that made high-end gaming computers with AMD microprocessors. In April of that year Michael Dell sent an email to his top executives which said: "We have been looking at the situation for a long time, and have decided to introduce a broad range of AMD based systems into our product line to provide the choice our customers are asking for." In the second quarter of the year, perhaps testing Intel's reaction, Dell announced a single new line of high-end computers with AMD chips inside. That quarter its payments from Intel dropped to $554 million. The next quarter Dell announced additional lines of PCs with AMD processors inside and Intel paid it only $200 million.

Intel's Board Chair told Intel's CEO that the company should respond harshly to Dell's actions: "I think you should reply in kind. Not a time for weakness on our part. Stop writing checks immediately and put them back on list prices [i.e., on prices with no discounts or rebates].[17] The next day Intel CEO Otellini instructed his people that "We should be prepared to remove all [payments] and related programs. Post haste ... then we ought to enter negotiations."

Now subject to Intel's punishment, Dell received no more "rebates." In 2007, Dell's net income fell to $2.58 billion, down from $3.57 billion in 2006. The company recovered a bit in 2008 when it posted a net income of $2.95 billion, but then it began a downward slide to $2.48 billion in 2009 and $1.43 billion in 2010. Between 2001 and 2006, Intel had pumped an estimated total of about $6 billion into Dell's income figures. Because Dell had not reported that most of its profits during those years were cash it was receiving from Intel, the U.S. Securities and Exchange Commission (SEC) accused Dell and its officers of deceiving investors who had been told by the company that it's high profits were due to its ultra-efficient management of its supply chain, its direct-sales strategy, its cost reduction initiatives, and the declining costs of computer parts.[18] Dell had become one of the most admired companies in America because it was falsely assumed that its strong profits were due to the company's management skills.

Intel pressured other big companies, like HP and IBM, into refusing to use AMD processors. Unlike Dell, HP and IBM did not agree to completely boycott AMD's processors. In HP's case, Intel got HP to agree to limit its purchases of AMD processors to 5 percent or less, and Intel agreed to give HP a "rebate" of $130 million, spread out over a year.[19] IBM agreed to only use AMD processors in its "High Performance Computers."[20]

The FTC's lawsuit against Intel never made it to court. On Wednesday, August 4, 2010, the FTC announced that without admitting guilt, Intel had agreed to settle the FTC's antitrust lawsuit. In a press release the FTC wrote that under the settlement, "Intel will be prohibited from conditioning benefits to computer makers in exchange for their promise to buy chips from Intel exclusively or to refuse to buy chips from others; and [from] retaliating against computer makers if they do business with non-Intel suppliers by withholding benefits from them." In addition, Intel was prohibited from using its compilers or its libraries of software code to inhibit the ability of programs to run on competitors' microprocessors. Some observers argued that the restrictions of the settlement no longer mattered since Intel had once again taken the lead in the x86 processor market and AMD was again a trailing competitor. In the first quarter of 2006, according to CPU Benchmarks, AMD's market share had climbed as high as 48 percent and Intel's had fallen to 51 percent. But AMD's share dropped after that and by 2011, Intel had 71 percent of the x86 microprocessor market while AMD was down to 25 percent.

Questions

1. In your judgment is Intel a "monopoly"? Did Intel use monopoly-like power; in other words, did Intel achieve its objectives by relying on power that it had due to its control of a large portion of the market? Explain your answers.
2. In your judgment, were Intel's rebates ethical or unethical? Explain your answer.
3. Was it unethical for Intel to use its compilers and its libraries of software code in the way it did, or is this permissible for companies in a free market economy? Explain your answer.
4. Were Intel's rebates unethical? Explain why or why not.
5. In your view, did Intel violate either of the two key sections of the Sherman Antitrust Act? Explain.

Notes

1. David Goldman, "Intel and AMD Reach $1.25B Settlement," *CNNMoney.com*, November 12, 2009.
2. Roger Parloff, "Intel's Worst Nightmare: Dwindling Market Share Isn't the No. 1 Chipmaker's only Problem, says *Fortune's* Roger Parloff. It needs to Mount a Fierce Defense to AMD's Epic Antitrust Lawsuit," *Fortune Magazine*, November 16, 2006.
3. Ibid.
4. Ibid.
5. David Goldman, "FTC Sues Intel Over Chip Dominance," *CNNMoney.com*, December 16, 2009.
6. *In the Matter of Intel Corporation, a Corporation, The United States of America Before the Federal Trade Commission*, Docket No. 9341, Complaint, December 16, 2009, paragraphs 56–61.
7. Ibid., paragraphs 62–71.
8. *State of New York, by Attorney General Andrew W. M. Cuoma, Plaintiff, vs. Intel Corporation, a Delaware Corporation, Defendant*, Complaint in the United States District Court for the District of Delaware, November 3, 2009, paragraph 90.
9. Roger Parloff, "Intel Settlement: The Power of Emails," *Fortune Magazine*, November 13, 2009.
10. Ibid.
11. Ibid., paragraph 27.
12. Ibid., paragraph 105.
13. Ibid., paragraph 135.
14. Ibid., paragraph 136.
15. Ibid., paragraph 137.
16. Parloff, "Intel Settlement: The Power of Emails."
17. Ibid., paragraph 142.
18. Justin Scheck and Kara Scannell, "SEC: Intel Cash Inflated Dell," *The Wall Street Journal*, July 23, 2010.
19. *New York v. Intel*, Complaint, paragraph 170.
20. Ibid., paragraph 211.

CASES

Archer Daniels Midland and the Friendly Competitors

Explore the **Concept** on **mythinkinglab.com**

By 1995, Archer Daniels Midland Company (ADM) had become one of the world's largest agricultural companies. ADM processes corn, wheat, soybeans, peanuts, and other oilseeds to make products used by the food, beverage, and chemical industries. Its global sales in 1994 were about $13 billion. Since 1966, the company had been headed by Dwayne Andreas, a hard-driving executive who pushed the company toward greater productivity and rapid expansion. Dwayne brought in his son, Michael D. Andreas, who became the company's executive vice president of sales and marketing.

In early 1989, Dwayne and Michael Andreas decided that ADM should enter the lysine business. Lysine is an amino acid derived from corn that is used as an additive in animal feed because it promotes the growth of lean muscle. Because lysine is an undifferentiated commodity buyers are price-sensitive, a characteristic that is normally indicative of a highly competitive market. But Dwayne and his son had noticed that the world market in lysine was dominated by only three companies: Ajinomoto (a Japanese company), Kyowa (also Japanese), and Miwon (a Korean company). Cheil, a Korean company, had plans to enter the market by 1991. The fact that there were only a handful of players supplying the market attracted the two Andreas: the market looked more like a staid gentlemen's club than an aggressive rivalry.

To manage ADM's entry into the lysine business, Dwayne Andreas and his son, Michael, hired an extremely bright and energetic young man named Mark Whitacre. Whitacre would run ADM's lysine business and would report to Michael Andreas. Only 32 years old, Whitacre had a B.S. and an M.S. in animal science from Ohio State University, had earned a Ph.D. in nutritional biochemistry at Cornell University, and had worked 5 years for Degussa, a German chemical company. Married to Ginger Gilbert, his girlfriend at the high school where he had been senior class president, Whitacre now became president of ADM's new lysine division.[1] He thrived at ADM, where he enjoyed the absence of bureaucracy and the dynamic and quick moving "can-do" company culture:

> For the first few years I loved working at the company. I was very proud of ADM and how it operated. I was very enthusiastic about my work, very excited. (Statement of Mark Whitacre)[2]

ADM started building its new $100 million lysine production plant in September, 1989 and finished in February, 1991, a surprisingly short period of 17 months. Capable of producing 250 million tons of lysine a year—enough to supply half of the annual worldwide demand—the new plant was the largest in the world. With the resources of ADM behind him, Whitacre could hire the best people from around the world to work for him in ADM's new lysine business.

When Whitacre began selling lysine, it was selling for $1.30 a pound. ADM's large new plant, however, brought a huge volume of new product into the market, and prices quickly began to fall. (See the Figure "Timeline of Meetings and Prices in Lysine Price-Fixing Case.") Whitacre felt that in order to get customers to buy from a newcomer, he had to price his product below established competitors. But his tactic led to a disastrous and costly price war among the five companies in the industry:

> When we started selling, prices started falling, and there was a tremendous price war. Lysine went from about $1.30 a pound down to about 60 cents a pound. At that point we were losing money, a few million dollars a month. (Statement of Mark Whitacre)[3]

ADM was in fact losing about $7 million a month. Managers at all five lysine-producing companies—all of whom were also losing money—felt the devastating situation could not continue. Whitacre knew something had to change or his new career would be over just as it was starting. Then, he learned that ADM had a method of dealing with such situations. Terry Wilson, president of ADM's Corn Processing Division, had developed the "method" and then introduced it to the managers at other divisions of ADM. Michael Andreas talked with Whitacre and asked him to go and learn from Terry Wilson "how ADM does business."

> It was during my first year or so at the company that I started hearing about price fixing at ADM—in four or five other divisions. People said it was fairly common. I didn't see it, but I heard about it from people who were involved with it either directly or indirectly.... Around February 1992 ... they told me that they wanted me to work closer with Terry Wilson.... I should look to Terry as a mentor, someone to teach me some things about how ADM does business.... When they told me that, I had a strong feeling about what they were getting at, about what was coming next. (Statement of Mark Whitacre)[4]

Whitacre began discussing his problems with Terry Wilson and learned that the company had often had to deal with tight markets. Wilson proposed that he and Whitacre meet with top managers of the other four companies producing lysine. He would show Whitacre what to

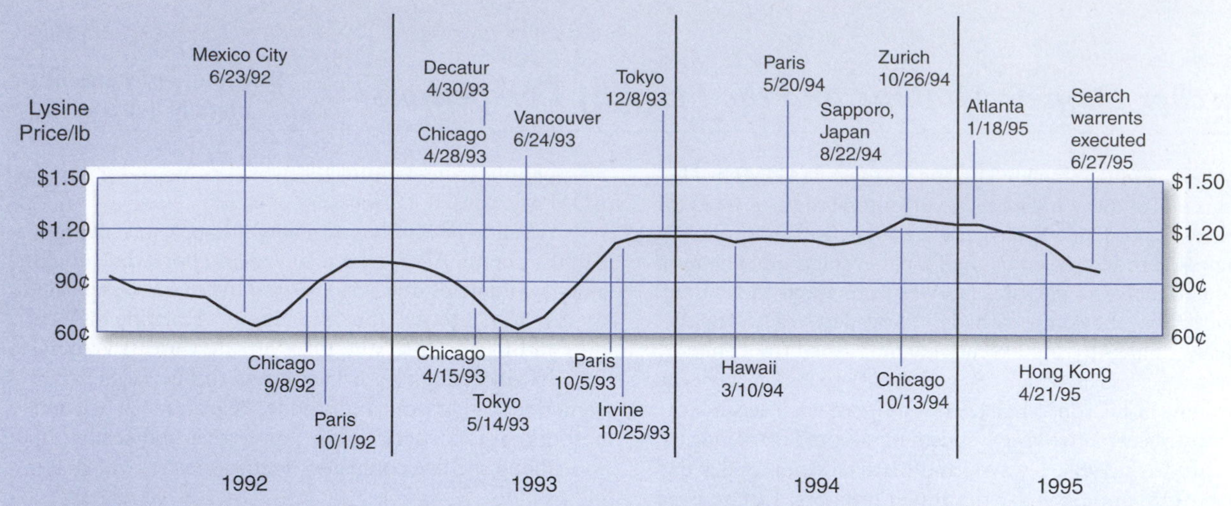

Figure 4.5
Timeline of Meetings and Prices in Lysine Price Fixing Case.

do. A meeting was arranged, and on June, 1992, Wilson and Whitacre met in a Mexico City hotel with the managers of Ajinomoto and Kyowa, the two Japanese producers of lysine.[5] Absent from the meeting were managers from the two Korean companies, Miwon and Cheil. Among them, however, ADM, Ajinomoto, and Kyowa controlled most of the world's lysine market.

During the June, 1992 Mexico City meeting, Terry Wilson stood in front of a flip chart and asked the representatives of the companies how many million pounds of lysine each of them produced in a year in their plants. He wrote the quantities on the flip chart and added them together, including estimates for the two absent Korean companies. Wilson then turned the page over. He now asked the group for their estimates of how many million pounds of lysine were actually purchased each year in Europe, Latin America, Asia, and the United States. He wrote down these quantities and added them together on a second page. Finally, he compared the amounts on the two pages and pointed to "our problem": The total amount they were producing was 25 percent more than the total amount of worldwide demand. Wilson next multiplied their estimate of worldwide demand by 60 cents, the current price of a pound of lysine. He also multiplied their estimate of worldwide demand by $1.30, the price the Japanese companies were maintaining before ADM had entered the market. The difference was $200 million. Wilson declared that $200 million was the amount that the five companies were giving away to their customers. This meant, he continued, that the benefits were going to their customers, not to the five competing companies who had each spent hundreds of millions of dollars building their plants. At ADM, Wilson said, "We believe the competitor is our friend and the customer is our enemy." Whitacre was listening. "We should be trusting," Wilson added, "and have competitive friendliness" among the companies.

Whitacre joined the conversation when Wilson and the representatives of the two Japanese companies turned to discussing a "target" price at which the companies could agree to sell lysine "if we stop the competition." The purpose of their meeting, it was noted, was to end the price war among them that had driven prices downward. Their aim could be achieved, however, only if all five companies agreed to sell lysine at the same price, without undercutting each other. The managers of the two Japanese companies volunteered to contact the two absent Korean companies and talk them into coming on board and joining their agreement. Toward the end of the meeting, the representative of Ajinomoto summed up the agreement: "if the discussions [with the Korean companies] go smoothly, we will aim for prices at the level of $1.05/lb for North America and Europe … by October, and $1.20/lb in December." Terry Wilson suggested that to hide the real purpose of any future meetings, they should form a "trade association" that would meet periodically with a fake public agenda. This, he said, was how ADM had arranged secret price-fixing meetings for other commodities the company produced.

After the meeting, Whitacre and Wilson flew home. Over the next few days, Mark gradually raised his prices as they had agreed. So did the other four companies, including the Koreans, who had evidently been talked into joining the agreement. In the United States, the price of lysine rose to $1.05/lb by the end of the summer of 1992 (see Figure). For a while, Whitacre felt that the price wars had ended.

When Whitacre was contacted by managers of the four other lysine companies, he agreed they should all meet in Paris in October, 1992 to launch the newly formed

International Amino Acid Producers Association. They published a fake agenda stating that they would discuss animal rights and other environmental concerns. But they never discussed those topics. Instead, Whitacre and the other managers spent their meeting time congratulating themselves on the success of their earlier agreement and working to reach a new agreement on future prices for each region of the world where they sold lysine.

After the Paris meeting, however, Whitacre realized they still had a problem. Instead of rising, the price of lysine stayed at $1.05 through the end of 1992, and then began to gradually decline. The price fell through January, February, and March of 1993, and reached 70 cents by April (see Figure). In April, Whitacre met with Michael Andreas and Terry Wilson, and discussed scheduling an urgent meeting with the representatives of the other companies to talk about the deteriorating situation. Since Anjimoto was the largest lycine producer, they decided to began by meeting with officials of Ajinomoto. The meeting took place in Decatur and continued in Chicago. At the meeting, Andreas and Wilson explained to the Ajinomoto managers that the major problem with their price-fixing agreement was that the five companies had not agreed to limit their production quantity. In the absence of any quantity agreement "from the supply side," each of the companies had tried to produce and sell as much lysine as it could. Together, they had flooded the market with more product than was being demanded, and so could not hold to their price agreements. The only way to bring "stability" to the market was by controlling volume on the supply side. Unless volume is controlled, Wilson noted, "prices go down." The Ajinomoto representatives said they would think about it.

With prices still falling, Whitacre, Wilson, and the Ajinomoto officials again met—this time in Tokyo—on May 14, 1993 and they again discussed limiting the quantity they were producing in order to improve prices. At the meeting, Wilson explained that in other markets ADM had met with competitors and each competitor had agreed to sell only a specific quantity of the product to ensure that their cumulative supply did not outstrip demand. Once specific volumes are allocated to each company, he pointed out, there is no need to even monitor prices because "as long as the volume [of each company] turns out okay, if they want to sell [their assigned volume] for less money, that's their business." The Ajinomoto people were still hesitant.

Whitacre realized, moreover, that an agreement to limit the volume of lysine each company could sell would require an agreement with all four companies, not just Ajinomoto. He was feeling increasingly stressed because by now the price of lysine had dropped to 60 cents a pound, so that ADM as well as the other companies were losing money (see Figure). He talked by phone with the managers of the other companies and they agreed to meet on June 24, 1993 in Vancouver, Canada. But the meeting only frustrated Whitacre. Although they again reached an agreement on prices, the managers quarreled over accepting restrictions on the amount each could sell because "everybody wanted a bigger share." Ajinomoto, especially, was still not willing to limit how much it could sell. They all agreed, however, to at least hold to their current levels of production and to raise their prices together to the newly agreed levels.

After the Vancouver meeting, Whitacre breathed a sigh of relief as he watched prices gradually move upward in tune with their agreement. The experience of the past several months, however, had convinced him that the companies would have to agree on a volume allocation if they were to hold the line on prices. On October 25, 1993, Andreas, Wilson, and Whitacre set up another meeting with officials of Ajinomoto in Irvine, California so they could again try to hammer out a volume agreement. The representatives of the two companies finally agreed that in 1994 each company would limit itself to selling the same quantity it had sold in 1993, plus a certain amount of the quantity by which they estimated the industry would grow in 1994. If they did not stick to this agreement to limit their volumes, Michael Andreas warned, then ADM would use its huge lysine capacity to again flood the market and drive down prices for everyone and "there becomes a free-for-all." The next step was to bring the other companies into their volume agreement.

On December 8, 1993, representatives of ADM, Ajinomoto, Kyowa, and Miwon met in Tokyo; Cheil was not represented at the meeting. In Tokyo, the companies agreed on prices for the coming quarter. More importantly, they finally also agreed to a schedule indicating the amount of lysine (in tons) that each could sell in each region of the world. They also agreed on a method of ensuring that none of them would be tempted to sell more than they were allowed to sell: If a company sold more than its allocated share, then at the end of the year, it would have to make amends by buying that amount of lysine from another company that had sold less than its allocated share. Moreover, every month each company would send a report to an official at Ajinomoto indicating the amount of lysine it had sold the previous month. These reports would be audited and Ajinomoto would distribute the reports to the other companies.

A few months later, on March 10, 1994, the companies met in Hawaii where Cheil joined the group and also agreed to limit its sales volume to a specified amount. Now, at last all five companies had succeeded in reaching an agreement to set both their prices and their production volumes.

Whitacre and, sometimes, Wilson and Andreas, continued to meet once a quarter with top managers of Ajinomoto, Kyowa, Miwon, and Cheil for the rest of 1994 and through the first half of 1995. Lysine prices from December 1993 until April 1995 remained at about $1.20 per pound in accordance with the agreements the companies had hammered out (see Figure).

The agreement ended abruptly on June 27, 1995 when FBI officials raided the offices of ADM and questioned Michael Andreas at his home about price-fixing in the lysine market. Andreas said that it was impossible to fix prices in the lysine industry and denied that ADM had ever exchanged price or production information with competitors. A few days later, however, the FBI revealed that in November, 1992, they had convinced Mark Whitacre to become an FBI informer. Subsequently, when Whitacre attended price-fixing meetings, he had carried hidden audio or video recorders that had recorded the discussions among the companies. All the conversations among Andreas, Wilson, Whitacre, and the managers of Ajinomoto, Kyowa, Miwon, and Cheil had been recorded on audio tapes, and some had even been videotaped.

A month later came another surprise. It was revealed that while Whitacre was recording the price-fixing discussions between ADM and the competitors, he had secretly been taking money from ADM. Altogether he had taken $2.5 million from the company, Whitacre claimed that this was a "bonus" and that the company often let its executives pay themselves such bonuses under the table to avoid taxes.

Based on the tapes that Whitacre turned over to the FBI, ADM was indicted as a company for price-fixing and fined $100 million. On July 9, 1999, Andreas and Wilson were each fined $350,000 and given 20-month prison sentences for price-fixing, a sentence the court reaffirmed on June 26, 2000. Whitacre, whose theft of money from ADM nullified the immunity agreement he had worked out with the FBI, was sentenced to 9 years in prison for embezzlement, plus 20 months for price-fixing and forced to return the money he took. The managers of the Korean and Japanese companies that participated in the price-fixing meetings were fined $75,000 each, but were granted immunity from serving time in prison in exchange for agreeing to testify against ADM and its executives. On July 6, 2000, the European Union fined ADM an additional $46 million for fixing lysine prices in Europe.

Mark Whitacre spent eight and a half years in federal prison and was released on December 2006. He was given what he calls "a second chance" when Cypress Systems, Inc., a California biotechnology company, agreed to hire him. He is now chief operating officer for the company. And he greatly regrets what he did. In a 2009 interview, Whitacre said:

> I made some horrific decisions and broke some serious federal laws. In fact, ego and greed were behind many of these poorly made decisions. Others have said that ultimately the corporate culture of ADM played a primary role in my decision making at the time. Alas, not true. These were decisions of my own making. When trying to win so hard that truth and ethics do not matter anymore, then one is in a bad place in his or her life. That is exactly where I was in the early and mid-1990s. I cannot explain how I lost my way, but I did.[6]

Questions

1. According to the case, the ADM plant could produce "250 million tons of lysine a year—enough to supply half of the annual worldwide demand," so the average worldwide demand for lysine was about 41.7 tons a month. Calculate how much the lysine companies were making each month their price-fixing scheme was actually working (i.e., when lysine was selling for $1.20 per pound). Next, based on the price lysine sold for when the price-fixing schemes broke down, estimate what you think the equilibrium price of lysine was during the period of the case. Calculate how much the lysine companies would have made each month if lysine had sold for the equilibrium price. Now calculate the difference between what the companies made each month their price-fixing scheme actually worked, and what they should have made each month if lysine had sold for the equilibrium price, in order to get the "monopoly profit" the companies made each month they successfully fixed prices. Finally, estimate the total number of months that you think the price-fixing scheme was actually working. In light of your estimate of the total number of months their price-fixing worked, what was the total amount of "monopoly profit" the companies took from their customers? Explain fully the ethics of extracting this monopoly profit from customers. Did the U.S. and European government fines fully recover the total amount of monopoly profits the companies made?
2. This chapter of your text cites a number of factors that cause companies to engage in price-fixing. Identify the factors that you think were present in the ADM case. Explain your answer and be specific.
3. In your view, was Mark Whitacre to blame (i.e., morally responsible) for what he did? Explain. Were any of the obstacles to moral behavior (see Chapter 1) operating in his situation? Explain. Do you agree with Whitacre's own assessment that although "others have said that ultimately the corporate culture of ADM played a primary role in my decision making at the time" this is, "Alas, not true"?
4. Do you believe that in the end Mark Whitacre was treated justly? Explain.

Notes

1. James B. Lieber, *Rats in the Grain* (New York: Four Walls Eight Windows, 2000), pp. 8–11.
2. Mark Whitacre and Ronald Henkoff, "My Life as a Corporate Mole for the FBI," *Fortune*, September 1995, v. 132, n. 5, pp. 52–59.
3. Ibid.
4. Ibid.
5. The times and contents of the discussions at the various meetings described here and in what follows are based on the sources

above plus the following additional sources: *U.S. vs. Michael D. Andreas, Mark E. Whitacre, and Terrance S. Wilson*, Brief for Appellee and Cross-Appellant United States of America, in the United States Court of Appeals for the Seventh Circuit, No. 99–3097, October 19, 1999, accessed on June 5, 2004 at *http://www.usdoj.gov/atr/cases/f3700/3757.htm*; and *USA v. Michael D. Andreas and Terrance S. Wilson*, Appeals from the United States Court for the Northern District of Illinois, Eastern Division, No. 96 CR 762, June 26, 2000, accessed on June 6, 2004 at *http://www.justice.gov/atr/cases/f220000/220009.htm*. Some details are also drawn from: Angela Wissman, "ADM Execs Nailed on Price-Fixing," *Illinois Legal Times*, October, 1998, p. 1; James B. Lieber, op. cit.; Kurt Eichenwald, *The Informant: A True Story* (New York: Random House, 2000).

6. Feedinfo News Service, "Interview: Mark Whitacre—Lysine Cartel Whistleblower on Price-Fixing and Rebuilding his Life after Prison," June 13, 2009, accessed July 28, 2010 at *http://www.feedinfo.com/console/PageViewer.aspx?page=1202114&public=yes*

PART **THREE**

Business and Its External Exchanges: Ecology and Consumers

THE PROCESS OF PRODUCING GOODS FORCES BUSINESSES TO ENGAGE IN EXCHANGES AND INTERACTIONS WITH TWO MAIN EXTERNAL ENVIRONMENTS: THE NATURAL ENVIRONMENT AND A CONSUMER ENVIRONMENT. IT IS FROM THE NATURAL ENVIRONMENT THAT BUSINESS ULTIMATELY DRAWS THE RAW MATERIALS THAT IT TRANSFORMS INTO ITS FINISHED PRODUCTS. THESE FINISHED PRODUCTS ARE THEN EXTERNALLY PROMOTED AND SOLD TO CONSUMERS. THUS, THE NATURAL ENVIRONMENT PROVIDES THE RAW MATERIAL INPUT OF BUSINESS, WHEREAS THE CONSUMER ENVIRONMENT ABSORBS ITS FINISHED OUTPUT.

THE NEXT TWO CHAPTERS EXPLORE THE ETHICAL ISSUES RAISED BY THESE EXCHANGES AND INTERACTIONS. CHAPTER 5 DISCUSSES THE TWO BASIC ISSUES RELATED TO THE NATURAL ENVIRONMENT: POLLUTION AND RESOURCE DEPLETION. CHAPTER 6 DISCUSSES SEVERAL CONSUMER ISSUES, INCLUDING PRODUCT SAFETY AND ADVERTISING.

5

Ethics and the Environment

What are the two main threats to the environment and how serious are they?

What ethical issues are raised by pollution from commercial and industrial enterprises?

What obligations, if any, do we have to conserve our resources?

Workers clean tarballs washing up on the beach of Waveland, Mississippi from the BP oil well that exploded in the Gulf of Mexico on April 20, 2010, killing 11 men and spilling 205 million gallons of oil onto wildlife habitats. The oil spill killed hundreds of sea turtles, thousands of birds and land animals, millions of sea organisms and cost BP $40 billion. The National Commission on the BP Oil Spill said the company had a history of oil spills and safety violations and to save money it had failed to take measures to reduce known risks.

INTRODUCTION

Listen to the Chapter Audio on mythinkinglab.com

Modern industry has provided us with a material prosperity unequaled in our history. It has also created unparalleled environmental threats to ourselves and to future generations. The very technology that has enabled us to manipulate and control nature has also polluted our environment and rapidly depleted our natural resources. According to the U.S. Environmental Protection Agency (EPA) emissions inventories, the United States in 2008 pumped more than 130 million tons of "common air pollutants" (such as smoke, lead, and carbon monoxide) into the air, in addition to the 7.7 billion tons of carbon dioxide emissions with which we seem to be heating up our atmosphere. We produced 3.9 billion tons of toxic wastes, of which 247 million pounds was released as surface water discharge. Our total energy consumption for the year was 100 quadrillion BTUs (British Thermal Units) which is equivalent to about 17.24 billion barrels of oil or 721 billion gallons of gasoline.[1] Each U.S. citizen annually accounts for the consumption of about 1,300 pounds of metal and 18,500 pounds of other minerals, and each produces over 7 pounds of garbage every day of the year.

Although the nation has made significant progress in controlling certain types of pollution and in conserving energy, significant environmental problems still remain, especially at an international level. In a summary of its report, *Global Environment Outlook: GEO4*, the UN Environment Program wrote:

> We now have evidence of unprecedented environmental changes at global and regional levels. These unprecedented changes are due to human activities in an increasingly globalized, industrialized and interconnected world, driven by expanding flows of goods, services, capital, people, technologies, information, ideas and labor, even affecting isolated populations. The key changes [include]:
>
> Climate change is under way, and an average temperature increase of 0.74°C over the past century has been recorded. … 11 of the last 12 years (1995–2006) rank among the 12 warmest years since 1850. … Impacts are already evident and include changes in water availability, spread of waterborne disease vectors, food security, sea-level and ice cover changes as exemplified by melting of the Greenland ice sheet. Anthropogenic GHG [human-generated Green House Gas] emissions (principally carbon dioxide) are the main drivers of change. The projected increase in frequency and intensity of heat waves, storms, floods and droughts would dramatically affect many millions of people. The Intergovernmental Panel on Climate Change (IPCC) projects an increase in the global temperature of 1.8–4°C by the end of this century. …
>
> More than 2 million people are estimated to die prematurely each year due to indoor and outdoor air pollution. Severe indoor air pollution occurs in many poor communities when biomass and coal are used for cooking and heating in enclosed places without adequate ventilation. Outdoor air pollution arises from many sources, including industrial processes, motor vehicles, energy generation, and wildfires. …
>
> The "hole" in the stratospheric ozone layer over the Antarctic–the layer that protects people from harmful ultraviolet radiation–is now the largest it has ever been. Due to decreased emissions of ozone depleting substances, the ozone layer is expected to recover, assuming full Montreal Protocol compliance, but not until between 2060 and 2075. …
>
> Unsustainable land and water use, and the impacts of climate change are driving land degradation, including soil erosion, nutrient depletion, water scarcity, salinity, chemical contamination and disruption of biological cycles. The cumulative effects of these changes threaten food security, biodiversity, and carbon fixation and storage.…

> [D]eforestation in the tropics has continued at an average annual rate of 130,000 km^2, with serious implications for GHG gas concentrations and biodiversity loss. ...
>
> The release of harmful and persistent pollutants, such as heavy metals and organic chemicals, from mining, manufacturing, sewage, energy and transport emissions, the use of agro-chemicals, and from leaking stockpiles of obsolete chemicals and products, remains a problem for terrestrial and aquatic ecosystems. ...
>
> Contaminated water remains the greatest cause of human sickness and death on a global scale. The per capita availability of freshwater is declining, in part because of excessive withdrawals of surface and groundwater. If present trends continue ... 1.8 billion people will be living in countries or regions with absolute water scarcity by 2025 and two-thirds of the people in the world could be subject to water stress. ...
>
> The world's oceans are the primary regulator of global climate and an important sink for GHGs. ... At watershed, regional and ocean basin scales, the water cycle is being affected by long-term changes in climate, altering precipitation patterns. Climate changes are also causing major reductions in Arctic sea ice cover, and the accelerated melting of permafrost and mountain glaciers, and Arctic land ice. ...
>
> Eutrophication of inland and coastal waters caused by excessive nutrient loads from sources such as agricultural fertilizer causes sporadic major fish kills, and threatens human health and livelihoods. The deterioration of inland and coastal water quality is being exacerbated by other pollutants from land-based sources, particularly, municipal wastewater, and urban run-off. ...
>
> The reduction in distribution and functioning of land, freshwater and marine biodiversity is more rapid than at any time in human history. Ecosystems such as forests, wetlands, and drylands are being transformed and, in some cases, irreversibly degraded. Rates of species extinction are increasing. The great majority of well-studied species, including commercially important fish stocks, are declining in distribution or abundance or both.[2]

The severity of these environmental problems is exacerbated by the continuing growth of the world's population which stood at about one billion in 1800, increased to 3 billion by 1960, to 6.7 billion by 2010, and is predicted to reach 10 billion by 2050. As environmental stresses put pressure on our capacity to sustain humanity, population growth can only add to those pressures. So intractable and difficult are the problems raised by these environmental threats that many observers believe that they cannot be solved. For example, William Pollard, a physicist, despaired of our ability to deal with these problems:

> My own view is that [mankind] will not do so until he has suffered greatly and much that he now relies upon has been destroyed. As the earth in a short few decades becomes twice as crowded with human beings as it is now, and as human societies are confronted with dwindling resources in the midst of mounting accumulations of wastes, and a steadily deteriorating environment, we can only foresee social paroxysms of an intensity greater than any we have so far known. The problems are so varied and so vast and the means for their solutions so far beyond the resources of the scientific and technological know-how on which we have relied that there simply is not time to avoid the impending catastrophe. We stand, therefore, on the threshold of a time of judgment more severe, undoubtedly, than any mankind has ever faced before in history.[3]

Environmental issues, then, raise large and complicated ethical and technological questions for our business society. What is the extent of the environmental damage produced by the processes through which we manufacture our products, grow our food, and power our cities? How large a threat does this damage pose to our well being? What values must we give up to halt or slow such damage? Whose rights are violated by pollution and who should be responsible for paying for the costs of polluting the environment? How long will our natural resources last? What obligations do firms have to future generations to preserve the environment and conserve our resources?

This chapter explores these environmental issues. It begins with an overview of various technical aspects of environmental resource use. This is followed by a discussion of the ethical basis of environment protection. The final sections discuss two controversial issues: our obligations to future generations and the prospects for continued economic growth.

5.1 The Dimensions of Pollution and Resource Depletion

Environmental damage inevitably threatens the welfare of human beings as well as plants and animals. Threats to the environment come from two sources: pollution and resource depletion. **Pollution** refers to the undesirable and unintended contamination of the environment by human activities, such as manufacturing, waste disposal, burning fossil fuels, etc. **Resource depletion** refers to the consumption of finite or scarce resources. In a certain sense, pollution is really a type of resource depletion because contamination of air, water, or land diminishes their beneficial qualities. But for purposes of discussion, we keep the two issues distinct.

pollution The undesirable and unintended contamination of the environment by human activity such as manufacturing, waste disposal, burning fossil fuels, etc.

resource depletion The consumption of finite or scarce resources.

Air Pollution

Air pollution is not new—it has been with us since the Industrial Revolution introduced the world to the belching factory smokestack. However, the costs of air pollution increased exponentially as industrialization expanded. Today, air pollutants affect vegetation, decreasing agricultural yields and inflicting losses on the timber industry; they deteriorate exposed construction materials through corrosion, discoloration, and rot; they are hazardous to health and life, raising medical costs and lessening the enjoyment of living; and they threaten catastrophic global damage in the form of global warming and destruction of the stratospheric ozone layer.[4]

global warming The increase in temperatures around the globe due to rising levels of greenhouse gases.

greenhouse gases Carbon dioxide, nitrous oxide, methane, and chlorofluorocarbons—gases that absorb and hold heat from the Sun, preventing it from escaping back into space, much like a greenhouse absorbs and holds the Sun's heat.

Global Warming **Greenhouse Gases**—carbon dioxide, nitrous oxide, methane, and chlorofluorocarbons—are gases that absorb and hold heat from the Sun, preventing it from escaping back into space, much like a greenhouse absorbs and holds the Sun's heat. Of these gases, methane is able to capture more heat than an equal amount of any of the others, but there is much more carbon dioxide so it is the gas that actually makes the greatest contribution to heating the atmosphere. Greenhouse gases occur naturally in the atmosphere and, in fact, they have kept the Earth's temperature about 33°C warmer than it would otherwise be, enabling life to evolve and flourish. However, industrial, agricultural, and other human activities during the last 150 years have released substantially more greenhouse gases into the atmosphere, particularly by the burning of fossil fuels such as oil, gas, and coal, all of which emit carbon dioxide. Since the beginning of the industrial era, the amount of carbon dioxide in the atmosphere has increased by 27 percent to 390 ppm (parts per million, by volume) and so is now more than the natural range of 180–300 ppm that prevailed during the last 650,000 years. Measurements at Mauna Loa, Hawaii, since 1958 indicate that carbon dioxide in the atmosphere is currently increasing at the rate of about 2 ppm a year (see Figure 5.1).[5] We have known since the late-nineteenth-century work of the scientist Svante Arrhenius that carbon dioxide traps heat and so is capable of heating the Earth's atmosphere. The rising levels of greenhouse gases that we have produced since the beginning of the Industrial Revolution have in fact raised temperatures around the globe by measurable amounts. Average global temperatures today are already .7° C higher than in 1900 and are expected to rise by 1.5°C to 4.5°C by the year 2100 as they track our growing carbon emissions. In the southwestern United States, average temperatures have risen by 1.5°C above the average that prevailed in the years 1900–1970. This rising heat is expanding the world's deserts; it is melting glaciers and the polar ice caps; it is causing sea levels to rise; it is intensifying heat waves, droughts and other extreme weather events; and it is driving species of plants and animals into extinction.[6]

The UN Intergovernmental Panel on Climate Change (IPCC) is an international group of scientists that studies and monitors global warming.[7] The IPCC forecasts large shifts of vegetation into higher latitudes and elevations and rapid changes in the mix of species in these areas, as a result of global warming. Because forest species grow, reproduce, and evolve much more slowly than the climate is changing, entire forests and forest species will likely disappear. Bodies of water such as lakes and oceans will warm, and this will dramatically shift the geographical distribution of fish and other marine species.

Currently some 1.1 billion people do not have safe supplies of drinking water that is the direct cause each year of 1.6 million deaths (of which 1.4 million are of children under 5); climate change has increased the frequency and magnitude of droughts, thereby increasing the number of people without water. Currently, 750 million people

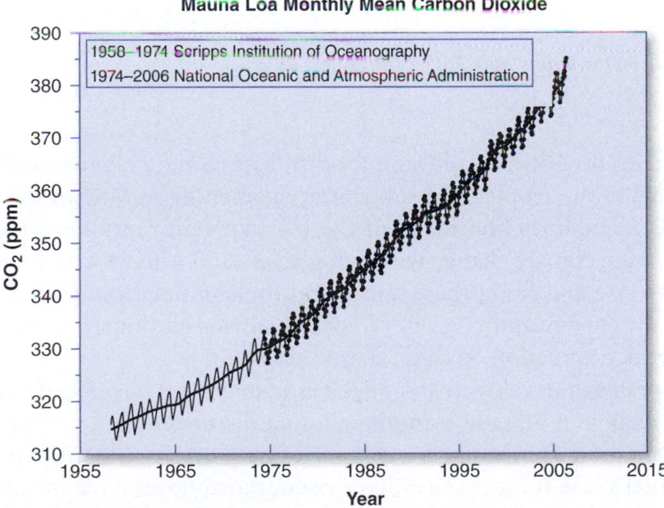

Figure 5.1
The Mauna Loa Atmospheric Carbon Dioxide Record shown here indicates an average increase each year of 0.53 percent, or two parts per million, of carbon dioxide in the atmosphere. The regular rise and fall of the line indicates annual seasonal variations. Scripps analyzed the data during 1958–1974, then NOAA took over.

Source: U.S. National Oceanic and Atmospheric Administration.

View the Image on mythinkinglab.com

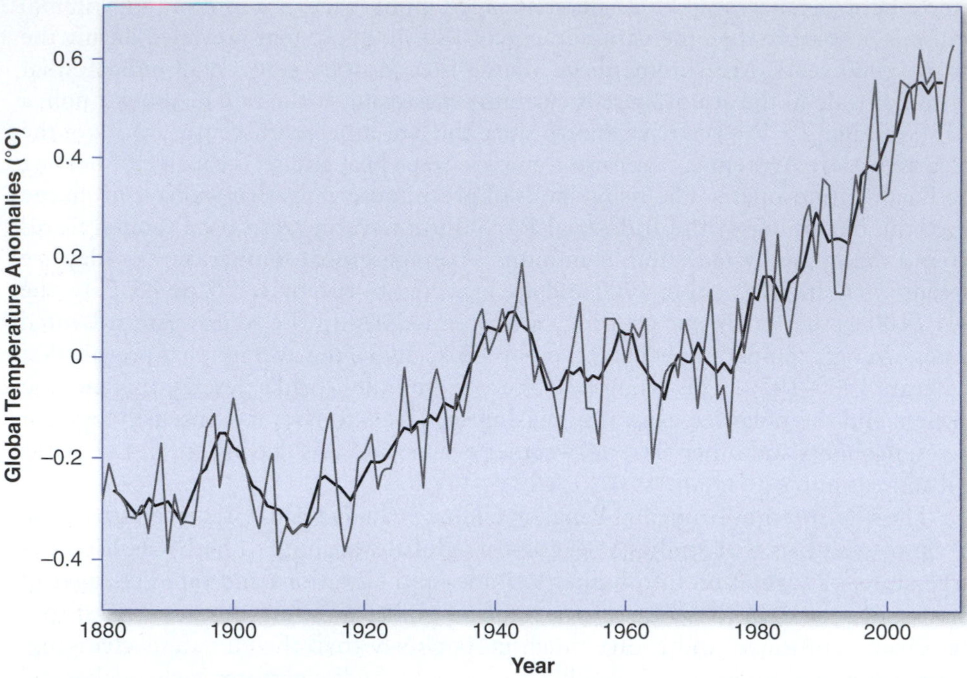

View the Image on mythinkinglab.com

Figure 5.2
Rising global temperatures from 1880 to 2010 as indicated by temperature anomalies. A temperature anomaly is a temperature that differs from a baseline average. Here the thin line indicates the amount by which each year's temperature differed from the average temperature during the base period 1951–1980; the thick line is a five-year running average. The graph indicates 2010 was 1.34° F. hotter than the average during 1951–1980, and that each decade since the 1970s the global average temperature has risen by 0.36° F. The year 2010 tied with 2005 as the hottest on record; tied for second hottest were 2002, 2003, 2006, 2007, and 2009.

Source: National Aeronautics and Space Administration.

in poor countries do not have enough food to eat; climate change will decrease agricultural yields in the tropics and subtropics, worsening famine in these areas. Half of the world's population and many of the world's major cities are located in low-lying coastal zones; climate change will melt glaciers and Antarctic and Arctic ice sheets causing seas to rise and flood these zones and their population. Climate change has increased the frequency and severity of coastal storms and hurricanes and the storm surges that wreak destruction on these coastal areas.

Mortality rates in developed and developing countries have been dropping; however, climate change is already bringing about a disturbing and widespread increase in vector-borne infectious diseases such as dengue, malaria, Hantavirus, West Nile virus, and cholera.[8] As temperatures have risen, mosquitoes have invaded previously cool regions, carrying malaria and dengue fever with them. The entire United States has now seen the emergence of West Nile virus, a disease transmitted by mosquitoes; California, Washington, Texas, Arizona, Colorado, Idaho, Montana and other Western states have seen the outbreak of Hantavirus, an often lethal infection carried by rodents whose natural predators have been killed by drought.

Though its effects are increasingly easy to see, global warming is an extremely difficult problem to solve for technological, economic, and political reasons. The IPCC calculates that halting the increase in levels of greenhouse gases would require reducing current worldwide emissions of greenhouse gases by 60 to 70 percent—an amount that would seriously affect the economies of both developed and developing nations and that would require the development of new energy sources and technologies. This is such a large reduction, in fact, that few governments are ready to attempt the political negotiations required to mandate such a reduction, and so most nations are still increasing their carbon dioxide emissions by substantial amounts. In 2010, President Obama, without full congressional support, pledged that the United States would aim at cutting carbon emissions by 17 percent from 2005 levels by the year 2020. That same year, Canada announced it, too, would aim at a 17 percent reduction from 2005 levels by 2020 while China announced it would cut its emissions by 40 to 45 percent from 2005 levels by 2020 and Brazil said it would aim at a 39 percent reduction. Such measures, however, will certainly not be sufficient to achieve the 60 to 70 percent reduction in global emissions the IPCC says are necessary. Some environmentalists have suggested that making these kinds of emissions reductions will require a wholesale change in our lifestyles and values.

The main sources of greenhouse gas emissions are power generation (21.3 percent), industrial processes (16.8 percent), transportation (14 percent), farming (12.5 percent), and drilling for oil and processing it (11.3 percent). These are all activities in which business is heavily involved. If greenhouse gas emissions are going to be reduced, business is going to have to play a major role in making those reductions. Many businesses are already working hard at reducing their so-called "carbon footprint" (the amount of greenhouse gases their activities directly or indirectly produce). Ford, Volvo, Walmart, HP, PepsiCo, and many other companies are working not only to reduce their own emissions, but are helping their suppliers reduce theirs and working to make products that will enable their customers to do the same. But other companies have done little and some companies, particularly energy companies, have opposed attempts to reduce greenhouse gas emissions.

Ozone Depletion Chlorofluorocarbons (CFCs) are gases that gradually break down ozone gas in the stratosphere above us. This layer of ozone in the stratosphere screens life on Earth from the harmful ultraviolet radiation the Sun emits. The ozone layer is destroyed by CFC gases, which have been used in aerosol cans, refrigerators, air conditioners, industrial solvents, and industrial foam blowers. When released into the air, CFC gases rise and in 7 to 10 years, they reach the stratosphere, where they destroy ozone molecules and remain for 75 to 130 years, continuing all the while to break down additional ozone molecules. Studies predict that the shrinking of the ozone layer and the subsequent increase of ultraviolet rays may cause several hundred thousand new cases of skin cancer and injure the 75 percent of the world's major crops that are sensitive to ultraviolet light. Other studies suggest that the plankton that float on the surface layers of the Earth's oceans and on which the entire food chain of the world's oceans ultimately depends, is sensitive to ultraviolet light and may suffer widespread destruction. International agreements to which the United States is a party pledged to gradually phase out the use of CFC gases by 2000, and emissions of CFCs have dropped by 87 percent from their peak in 1988.[9] However, scientists warn that even if the use of CFC gases were completely halted, CFC levels in the atmosphere would still continue their dangerous upward climb because those gases already released will continue to rise upward for many years and will persist for perhaps a century.[10] Moreover, not all countries have agreed to cease making and producing CFC gases, and CFC gases are often released when refrigeration or air-conditioning systems built many years ago are repaired or disposed of.[11]

ozone depletion The gradual breakdown of ozone gas in the stratosphere above us caused by the release of chlorofluorocarbons (CFCs) into the air.

ON THE EDGE

Ford's Toxic Wastes

Making cars produces a steady stream of toxic liquids and solids, and during the 1960s and early 1970s Ford Motor Company dumped tons of its Mahwah factory wastes on a wooded hilly 500 acre area of Ringwood, N.J., including unused paints, solvents, paint thinners, battery acids, and other chemicals. It was legal to dump wastes on bare land then, and Ford owned the wooded area. The colorful sludge, which contained benzene, lead, arsenic, antimony, xylenes, and other poisonous substances—some carcinogenic, like chromium which causes nosebleeds—was dumped on what locals call "Sludge Hill." The slippery goo attracted local children who played with it and often came home with bad nosebleeds. A resident, Wayne Mann, said in 2009: "I was one of those children who used to go up on Sludge Hill. I would take a car hood and ride down, hand steering in the wet sludge. You paint your face. You lick it, whatever." Many residents, including Mann, are sick. Some have already died of cancer. Adults and children suffer mysterious rashes, rare blood disorders, cancers, asthma, and other unusual diseases. The 600 people living in the area think the toxic sludge caused their illnesses and that too many are sick or dying to blame the sicknesses on chance. The area is populated by Ramapough, an impoverished Indian group who say they are victims of environmental injustice.

Although Ford admits they dumped the chemicals, John Holt, a company spokesperson, said in 2009 that the chemicals did not cause the sicknesses: "They've found no higher incidence of cancer or anything else here besides lung cancer." Moreover, he points out, Ford spent ten years cleaning up the site and in 1994, the U.S. Federal Environmental Protection Agency (EPA) and the New Jersey Department of Environmental Protection certified Ford did an adequate job. But in 2006, when the EPA checked the site again, they decided they made a mistake in 1994, relisted the site as contaminated, and Ford launched another clean-up which continues to this day. Pointing to the woods, in 2009 John Holt said, "This site was done and excavated and restored to its natural state ... according to the requirements of the state of New Jersey and the EPA." But Federal officials said much of the sludge remains. A state official said "Ford made false or misleading submissions to federal regulators" about earlier clean-ups. Federal officials have also reported that lung cancer rates are significantly higher than normal in the area. Bladder cancer and non-Hodgkin's lymphoma rates are also elevated but their numbers are too small to rule out coincidence. Statistics do not show cause-and-effect, so there is no way to know for sure what caused the diseases. Rain has now carried the chemicals into streams, rivers, and underground. They have also entered the local food chain. As of 2011, Ford had not completed the cleanup begun in 2006, although it had hauled out 50,000 more tons of the sludge. Much of the sludge had been poured into deep underground caves that are almost impossible to access.

1. Should Ford be held responsible for the sicknesses of the residents? Check the videos at *http://www.northjersey.com/specialreports/ringwood5yearslater.html and at http://toxiclegacy.northjersey.com.* Do the videos suggest the contamination should concern you? What would the various forms of environmental ethics described in this chapter say about Ford's actions?

Source: *NorthJersey.com*, "Toxic Landscape: Ringwood–Five Years Later," accessed January 19, 2011 at *http://www.northjersey.com/specialreports/ringwood5yearslater.html.*

Acid Rain Acid rain occurs when coal containing high levels of sulfur is burned and releases large quantities of sulfur oxides and nitrogen oxides into the atmosphere. Coal-burning electric power plants account for 70 percent of annual sulfur oxide emissions and 30 percent of nitrogen oxides.[12] When these gases are carried into the air, they combine with water vapor in clouds to form nitric acid and sulfuric acid. These acids are then carried down in rain, which often falls hundreds of miles away from the original sources of the oxides. The acidic rainfall—sometimes as acidic as vinegar—is carried into lakes and rivers, where it raises the acidity of the water. Many fish populations and other aquatic organisms—including algae, zooplankton, and amphibians—are unable to survive in lakes and rivers that have become highly acidic due to acid rain.[13] Acid rain directly damages or destroys trees, plants, lichens, and mosses. Acidic rainwater can also leach toxic metals—cadmium, nickel, lead, manganese, and mercury—from soil and carry these into waterways, where they contaminate drinking water or fish. Finally, acid rain can corrode and damage buildings, statues, and other objects, particularly those made of iron, limestone, and marble. Dozens of people were killed in West Virginia when a steel bridge collapsed as a result of acid rain corrosion, and priceless monuments such as the Acropolis in Athens and the Taj Mahal in India have been corroded by acid rain.

acid rain Occurs when sulfur oxides and nitrogen oxides are combined with water vapor in clouds to form nitric acid and sulfuric acid. These acids are then carried down in rainfall.

Airborne Toxics Less catastrophic but still worrisome air pollution threats are the 2.4 billion pounds of airborne toxic substances released annually into our nation's atmosphere, including phosgene, a nerve gas used in warfare, and methyl isocyanate, which killed more than 2,000 Indians in Bhopal. The chemical brew released into the air annually includes 235 million pounds of carcinogens, such as benzene and formaldehyde, and 527 million pounds of such neurotoxins as toluene and trichloroethylene. Although levels of most airborne toxics have been declining gradually across the nation, some states have registered increases in the levels of several carcinogenic toxics in the air.[14] The Environmental Protection Agency (EPA) has estimated that 20 of the more than 329 toxics released into the air alone cause more than 2,000 cases of cancer each year and that living near chemical plants raises a person's chances of cancer to more than 1 in 1,000. Exceptionally high cancer rates have been found near plants in several states, including West Virginia and Louisiana.

Common Air Pollutants The most prevalent forms of air pollution, however, are the six kinds of gases and particulates spewed out mostly by autos and industrial processes that the EPA calls "common air pollutants." These six affect the quality of the air we breathe, injure human health, harm the environment, and damage property. The six "common air pollutants" are carbon monoxide, sulfur oxides, nitrogen oxides, airborne lead, ozone (or "smog"), and particulates (airborne mixtures of extremely small particles and liquid droplets). The effects of these pollutants, which were recognized more than four decades ago, are summarized in Figure 5.3.[15]

More recent long-range studies have indicated that the deterioration of lung function in human beings caused by their chronic exposure to air pollutants, whether it be auto smog or industrial smokestack emissions, is long lasting and often irreversible.[16] Some of the 2,500 subjects in the studies suffered as much as 75 percent loss of lung capacity during a 10-year period of living in Los Angeles communities—a region with very high levels of air pollution—leaving them vulnerable to respiratory disease, emphysema, and impairment of their stamina. Damage to the still-developing lungs of children was especially serious.

Quick Review 5.1

Major Types of Air Pollution

- Greenhouse gases: carbon dioxide, methane, nitrous oxide,
- Ozone depleting gases: chlorofluorocarbons
- Acid rain gases: sulfur oxides
- Airborne toxics: benzene, formaldehyde, toluene, trichloroethylene, and 329 others
- Common air pollutants: carbon monoxide, sulfur oxides, nitrogen oxides, airborne lead, ozone, particulates.

Pollutant	Health Effects	Environmental and Climate Effects
Ozone (O_3)	Decreases lung function and causes respiratory symptoms, such as coughing and shortness of breath; aggravates asthma and other lung diseases leading to increased medication use, hospital admissions, emergency department (ED) visits, and premature mortality.	Damages vegetation by visibly injuring leaves, reducing photosynthesis, impairing reproduction and growth, and decreasing crop yields. Ozone damage to plants may alter ecosystem structure, reduce biodiversity, and decrease plant uptake of CO_2. Ozone is also a greenhouse gas that contributes to the warming of the atmosphere.
Particulate Matter (PM)	Short-term exposures can aggravate heart or lung diseases leading to symptoms, increased medication use, hospital admissions, ED visits, and premature mortality; long-term exposures can lead to the development of heart or lung disease and premature mortality.	Impairs visibility, adversely affects ecosystem processes, and damages and/or soils structures and property. Variable climate impacts depending on particle type. Most particles are reflective and lead to net cooling, while some (especially black carbon) absorb energy and lead to warming. Other impacts include changing the timing and location of traditional rainfall patterns.
Lead (Pb)	Damages the developing nervous system, resulting in IQ loss and impacts on learning, memory, and behavior in children. Cardiovascular and renal effects in adults and early effects related to anemia.	Harms plants and wildlife, accumulates in soils, and adversely impacts both terrestrial and aquatic systems.
Oxides of Sulfur (SO_x)	Aggravate asthma, leading to wheezing, chest tightness and shortness of breath, increased medication use, hospital admissions, and ED visits; very high levels can cause respiratory symptoms in people without lung disease.	Contributes to the acidification of soil and surface water and mercury methylation in wetland areas. Causes injury to vegetation and local species losses in aquatic and terrrestrial systems. Contributes to particle formation with associated environmental effects. Sulfate particles contribute to the cooling of the atmosphere.
Oxides of Nitrogen (NO_x)	Aggravate lung diseases leading to respiratory symptoms, hospital admissions, and ED visits; increase susceptibility to respiratory infection.	Contributes to the acidification and nutrient enrichment (eutrophication, nitrogen saturation) of soil and surface water. Leads to biodiversity losses. Impacts levels of ozone, particles, and methane with associated environmental and climate effects.
Carbon Monoxide (CO)	Reduces the amount of oxygen reaching the body's organs and tissues; aggravates heart disease, resulting in chest pain and other symptoms leading to hospital admissions and ED visits.	Contributes to the formation of CO_2 and ozone, greenhouse gases that warm the atmosphere.
Ammonia (NH_3)	Contributes to particle formation with associated health effects.	Contributes to eutrophication of surface water and nitrate contamination of ground water. Contributes to the formation of nitrate and sulfate particles with associated environmental and climate effects.

Pollutant	Health Effects	Environmental and Climate Effects
Volatile Organic Compounds (VOCs)	Some are toxic air pollutants that cause cancer and other serious health problems. Contribute to ozone formation with associated health effects.	Contributes to ozone formation with associated environmental and climate effects. Contributes to the formation of CO_2 and ozone, greenhouse gases that warm the atmosphere.
Mercury (Hg)	Causes liver, kidney, and brain damage and neurological and developmental damage.	Deposits into rivers, lakes, and oceans where it accumulates in fish, resulting in exposure to humans and wildlife.
Other Toxic Air Pollutants	Cause cancer; immune system damage; and neurological, reproductive, developmental, respiratory, and other health problems. Some toxic air pollutants contribute to ozone and particle pollution with associated health effects.	Harmful to wildlife and livestock. Some toxic air pollutants accumulate in the food chain. Some toxic air pollutants contribute to ozone and particle pollution with associated environmental and climate effects.

Figure 5.3
Health, Environmental, and Climate Effects of Various Air Pollutants.

Source: U.S. Environmental Protection Agency, *Our Nation's Air: Status and Trends Through* 2008, February 2010.

The major sources of the common air pollutants are utilities, industrial smokestacks, and automobiles. In congested urban areas such as Los Angeles, automobiles cause about 80 percent of the air pollution. Industrial pollution is derived principally from power plants and plants that refine and manufacture basic metals. Electrical power plants that depend on fossil fuels—such as oil, coal, or natural gas—throw tons of sulfur oxides, nitrogen oxides, and ashes into the air. The last decade has seen considerable improvement in the air quality of most regions of the United States, primarily as a result of environmental legislation and regulation. Emissions of four of the six common air pollutants have been substantially reduced, particularly of airborne lead (78 percent reduction from 1990 levels), sulfur dioxide (59 percent reduction), and carbon monoxide (68 percent reduction), although reductions in ozone (14 percent), particulates (31 percent), and nitrogen oxide (35 percent) were smaller.[17] As Figure 5.4 indicates, aggregate reductions in the six common air pollutants have decreased in spite of increases in driving, population, and economic production. Since 1990, total emissions of toxic air pollutants also fell by 40 percent, and acid rain deposits declined by 30 percent.

The health costs of low air quality are known to be high. Studies have indicated that when the concentrations of sulfur oxides over our major cities were cut in half from their 1960 levels, this added an average of 1 year to the life of each resident.[18] If air quality in urban areas were similar to the levels of rural regions with clean air, the death rates for asthma, bronchitis, and emphysema would drop by about 50 percent, and deaths from heart disease would drop by about 15 percent.[19] Improvements in air quality since 1970, it is believed, now save about 14,000 lives per year.[20] The U.S. Office of Management and Budget estimated that between 1992 and 2002 regulations that reduced or eliminated air pollution annually produced benefits of $117–$177 billion while imposing costs of only $18–$21 billion, which means that annual benefits outweighed costs to a significant degree.[21]

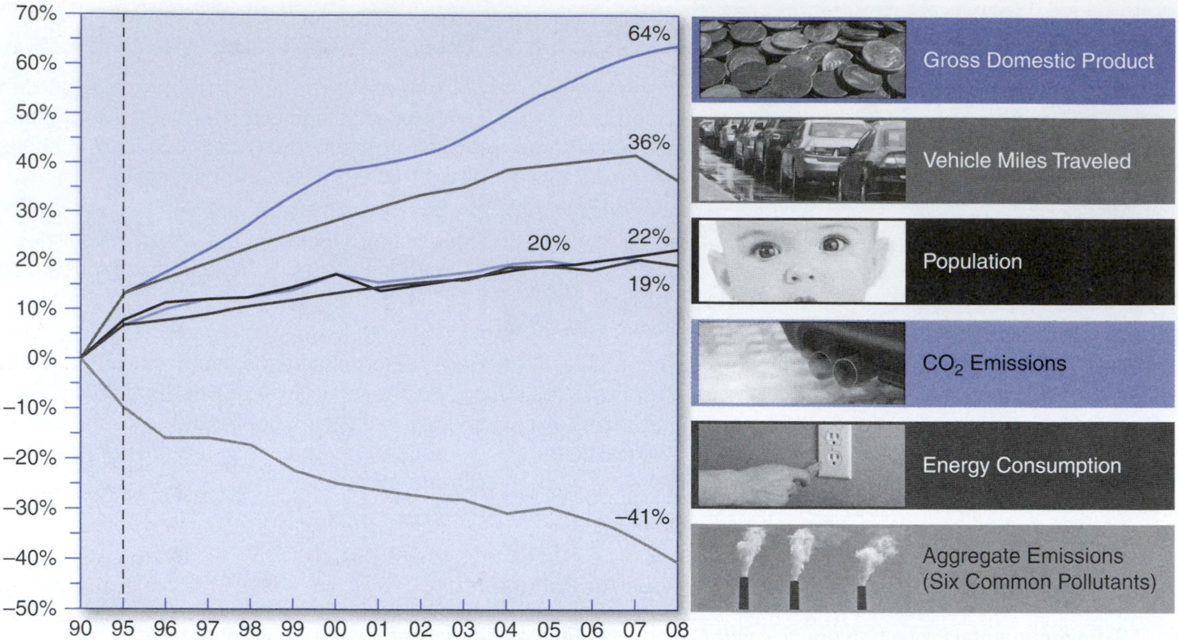

Figure 5.4
Comparison of aggregate reduction in emissions of the six common air pollutants (bottom line) between 1990 and 2008, with increases during the same period of gross domestic product, vehicle miles traveled, population, etc.

View the **Image** on **mythinkinglab.com**

Source: U.S. Environmental Protection Agency, *Our Nation's Air: Status and Trends Through* 2008, February 2010.

Water Pollution

The contamination of water sources is an old problem—one that has been with us since civilization began using water to dispose of its wastes and sewage. Water pollutants today, however, are much more diverse, consisting not only of organic wastes, but also dissolved salts, metals, and radioactive materials as well as suspended materials such as bacteria, viruses, and sediments. These can impair or destroy aquatic life, threaten human health, and foul the water. About 40 percent of our surface water is too polluted to fish or swim in.[22] Water pollutants enter surface water or underground water basins either from a single point source, such as a pipe or a well carrying sewage or industrial wastes, or they enter from a diffused or nonpoint source covering a large area, such as crop pesticides or animal wastes carried in rainwater or runoff.[23]

Salt brines from mines and oil wells, as well as mixtures of sodium chloride and calcium chloride used to keep winter roads clear of snow; all eventually drain into water sources, where they raise the saline content.[24] The high saline levels in ponds, lakes, and rivers kill whatever fish, vegetation, or other organisms inhabit them. Highly salinated water also poses major health hazards when it finds its way into city water supplies and is drunk by persons with heart disease, hypertension, cirrhosis of the liver, or renal disease.

organic wastes Largely untreated human waste, sewage, and industrial waste from processing various food products, from the pulp and paper industry, and from animal feedlots.

Water drainage from coal mining operations contains sulfuric acid as well as iron and sulfate particles. Continuous-casting and hot-rolling mills employ acids to scrub metals, and these acids are then rinsed off with water. The acidic water from these sources is sometimes flushed into streams and rivers. The high acid levels produced in waterways by these practices are lethal to most organisms living within the aquatic environment.[25]

Organic wastes consist of untreated human wastes and sewage, as well as wastes derived from industrial processing of various food products, and wastes from the pulp and paper industry, and animal feedlot wastes.[26] Various types of bacteria consume organic wastes that find their way into water resources and in the process they deplete the water of its oxygen. The oxygen-depleted water then becomes incapable of supporting fish life and other organisms.

Phosphorus compounds also contaminate many of our water sources.[27] Phosphorus compounds are found in detergents used both domestically and industrially, in fertilizers used for agricultural purposes, and in untreated human and animal sewage. Lakes with high concentrations of phosphorus give rise to explosive expansions of algae populations that choke waterways, drive out other forms of life, deplete the water of its oxygen, and severely restrict water visibility.

Various inorganic pollutants pose serious health hazards when they make their way into water used for drinking and eating purposes. Mercury has been finding its way into fresh water supplies and the oceans. It comes from burning coal which is naturally contaminated with mercury, from chlorine plants which use mercury to extract chlorine from salt, from mining activities and smelting processes, and from mercury-based fungicides and pesticides.[28] Mercury is transformed into organic compounds by microorganisms and becomes increasingly concentrated as it moves up the food chain to fish and birds. When consumed by humans—for example by eating mercury-contaminated fish—these compounds can cause brain damage, paralysis, and death.

Quick Review 5.2

Major Types of Water Pollution

- Organic wastes: human sewage, animal wastes, bacteria, oil,
- Inorganic pollutants: salt brines, acids, phosphates, heavy metals, asbestos, PCBs, radioactive chemicals.

Businesses still sometimes discharge liquids containing toxic substances into the nation's rivers.[29] Cadmium from zinc refineries, the agricultural use of certain fertilizers, and disposed electrical batteries makes its way into water sources, where it becomes concentrated in the tissues of fish and shellfish.[30] Cadmium causes a degenerate bone disease that cripples some victims and kills others; it induces severe cramps, vomiting, and diarrhea, and causes high blood pressure and heart disease. Asbestos fibers are another dangerous pollutant which, if swallowed, can cause cancer of the gastrointestinal tract. Mining companies are notorious for depositing asbestos-contaminated wastes into fresh water sources.[31]

Oil spills are a form of water pollution whose occurrence became more frequent as our dependence on oil increased. Oil spills result from offshore drilling, discharges of sludge from oil tankers, and oil tanker accidents. There are numerous examples of such spills, discharges, and oil tanker accidents that occurred in the last decade alone. In 2002, the *Prestige* sank off the Spanish coast spilling 616,000 barrels of oil and carrying 20 million gallons of oil down with it into the sea; in 2004, a storm drove an oil carrier into the rocks off the Aleutian islands, Alaska causing it to disintegrate and release 337,000 gallons of oil; in 2005, Hurricane Katrina struck New Orleans and released more than 7 million gallons of oil from various oil storage sites; on July 15, 2006, Israeli bombs hit a power station near Beirut, Lebanon causing it to leak between 3 million and 10 million gallons of oil into the sea; in 2007, a ship off of South Korea's coast hit a steel cable and spilled 2.8 million gallons of crude oil destroying 12 miles of South Korean beaches; on July 25, 2008, a barge collided with a tanker ship and spilled most of the 419,000 gallons of oil it was carrying into the Mississippi River near New Orleans; in January, 2010, the oil tanker Eagle Otome collided with a barge and spilled 462,000 gallons of oil into the bay at Port Arthur, Texas; in April, 2010, the explosion of a British Petroleum (BP) oil rig in the Gulf of Mexico released between 92 million and 184 million gallons of crude oil into the waters of the Gulf making it the largest oil spill in U.S. history; and in Nigeria's Niger River Delta roughly 400 oil spills over the past decade have poured a total of about 100 million gallons of oil into the Delta.[32] The contamination produced by oil spills is directly lethal to sea life, including fish, seals, plants, and aquatic birds; it requires expensive cleanup operations for residents, and imposes costly losses on nearby tourist and fishing industries.

In the past, the oceans have been used as disposal sites for intermediate- and low-level radioactive wastes. Oceanographers have examined seawater and found traces of plutonium, cesium, and other radioactive materials that have apparently leaked from the sealed drums in which radioactive wastes are disposed.[33] Coastal estuaries and marine sediments also have been found to contain unusually high concentrations of cadmium, chromium, copper, lead, mercury, and silver. Polychlorinated biphenyls (PCBs), which were used as cooling fluids in electrical transformers, as lubricants, and as flame retardants until their production was completely banned in the United States in 1979, have become widespread in the environment and have gradually accumulated in the oceans, especially in coastal areas. Minute amounts of PCBs are deadly to human beings and other life forms, and traces can engender a variety of toxic effects, including reproductive failures, birth defects, tumors, liver disorders, skin lesions, and immune suppression. PCBs, which continue to be produced by other countries and still are often improperly disposed of in the United States, are a cause of profound concern because they are persistent and become increasingly concentrated as they move up the food chain.[34]

Underground water supplies are also becoming more polluted. According to a government report, "Incidents of ground-water contamination—by organic chemicals, inorganic chemicals, radionuclides [radioactive wastes], or microorganisms—are being reported with increasing frequency and have now occurred ... in every state in the nation."[35] The sources of contamination have included landfills, waste piles, legal and illegal dumps, and surface reservoirs. More than 50 percent of the U.S. population depends on underground sources for drinking water. Underground water contaminants have been linked to cancers, liver and kidney diseases, and damage to the central nervous system. Unfortunately, exposure frequently occurs unknowingly over periods of years because contaminated groundwater is usually odorless, colorless, and tasteless.

Today, about 884 million people in the world lack access to safe drinking water, about a third of them live in Sub-Saharan Africa and most of rest live in rural areas of poor developing countries.[36] Fresh water is essential not only to human life as well as plant and animal life, but also to agriculture, industry, and economic development.[37] There is no substitute for water in most of its uses. Nevertheless, the world's *per capita* supply of fresh water (of which only a small part is safe drinking water) declines as population rises because the total annual supply of fresh water is fixed. Increases in population, farming, and economic activity have increased the demands put on our water resources, while pollution, climate change, and aquifer depletion have reduced the supply. As urban areas have grown and increased their demands for water, water has been increasingly diverted from agricultural irrigation to provide water for cities, a conflict that is predicted to expand.

How much does water pollution cost us, and what benefits might we expect from its removal? The U.S. Office of Management and Budget estimates that on average in each of the years between 1992 and 2002, clean water regulations cost between \$2.9 and \$2.4 billion (in 2001 dollars) and produced benefits (in the form of pollution costs avoided) ranging somewhere between \$8.0 and \$1.0 billion, not counting important nonquantifiable benefits.[38]

Land Pollution

Toxic Substances Hazardous or toxic substances are those that can cause an increase in mortality rates or irreversible or incapacitating illness or those that have other seriously adverse health or environmental effects. Toxic substances that have been released on land include acidic chemicals, inorganic metals (such as mercury or arsenic), flammable solvents, pesticides, herbicides, phenols, explosives, and so on. (Radioactive wastes are also classified as hazardous substances, but we will discuss these separately.) Silvex and 2, 4, 5-T, for example, are two widely used herbicides that contain dioxin—a deadly poison (100 times more deadly than strychnine) and a carcinogen.

Coal ash from coal-fired power plants that collect the ash before it escapes through exhaust stacks, contains several toxic metals and other cancer-causing wastes, but was unregulated until late 2010 when the Environmental Protection Agency (EPA) issued the first national regulations covering coal ash. In Caledonia, Wisconsin residents discovered in June, 2010 that their wells were contaminated with molybdenum, a toxic ingredient of coal ash, that probably leaked from a nearby landfill or a nearby coal plant; that same month the residents of Colstrip, Montana, discovered that their well water—which they drank although it had tasted bad for years—was also contaminated by toxic coal ash wastes stored in waste ponds by a local coal plant.[39] In 2007, the EPA published a report listing 24 other neighborhoods around the nation that had been "proven" to have been contaminated by coal plant or oil plant toxic wastes, and an additional 43 neighborhoods that were also contaminated by coal plant toxic wastes, but the wastes had not yet "migrated to the extent that they could cause human health concerns."[40] At 1 A.M. on December 22, 2008, in Roane County, Tennessee, the dam of a pond filled with coal ash and water broke, releasing 1.1 billion gallons of the coal ash slurry which flooded a nearby neighborhood, destroying homes, poisoning the land, and polluting the Emory River. It is estimated that scattered across the nation there are about 1,300 other coal plant waste dumps containing billions of gallons of water and coal ash slurry. Until 2010, most of these dumps were neither regulated nor monitored and all contain significant amounts of toxic heavy metals like arsenic, cadmium, lead, mercury, boron, thallium, and selenium that can migrate into groundwater and surrounding areas.[41]

About 70,000 different chemical compounds are currently being used in the United States, of which well over a thousand are probably toxic.[42] Their number is growing each year. Among the most common of the toxic chemicals produced by industry is acrylonitrile, which is used in the manufacture of plastics (used in appliances, luggage, telephones, and numerous common household and industrial products) and whose production is currently rising by 3 percent a year. Acrylonitrile is a suspected carcinogen; it releases the toxic chemical hydrogen cyanide when plastic containing it is burned.[43]

Benzene is a common industrial chemical that is also used in plastics, as well as dyes, nylon, food additives, detergents, drugs, fungicides, and gasoline. Benzene is toxic and a cause of anemia, bone marrow damage, and leukemia. Studies have shown that benzene workers are several times more likely than the general population to get leukemia.[44]

Vinyl chloride is another common toxic chemical used to make plastics, whose production is rising by 3 percent per year. Vinyl chloride, which is released in small amounts when plastic products deteriorate, causes liver damage; birth anomalies; liver, respiratory, brain, and lymph cancers; and bone damage. Cancer mortality for vinyl chloride workers is 50 percent higher than for the general population, and communities located around plants where it is used also have higher cancer rates than the general population.[45]

Solid Wastes Americans today produce more residential garbage than do the citizens of any other country in the world. Each year people living in U.S. cities produce 250 million tons of municipal solid waste—enough to fill a 226,000-mile-long convoy of 10-ton garbage trucks, about the distance from the Earth to the Moon.[46] Each person reading this book produces, on average, more than three-fourths of a ton of garbage a year—about 4.5 pounds a day. Only about a third of residential wastes are recovered through recycling—a low proportion that is due to the lack of financial backing for recycling operations, the small size of markets for recycled products, and toxic chemicals present in recyclable garbage.

Although the total amount of garbage we produce has been increasing each year, the facilities to handle it have decreased. In 1978, there were about 20,000 municipal garbage dumps in operation; by 1989, there were less than 8,000; in 1995 there were 3,500; and by 2008, there were only about 1,800. Many have had to be closed for safety reasons. Florida, Massachusetts, New Hampshire, and New Jersey are a few of the states that closed most of their garbage dumps during the 1990s. Moreover, fewer and fewer dumps are opened each year.

City garbage dumps are significant sources of pollution, containing toxic substances such as cadmium (from rechargeable batteries), mercury, lead (from car batteries and TV picture tubes), vanadium, copper, zinc, and PCBs (from refrigerators, stoves, engines, and appliances built before 1980 and since dumped). Only about one-fourth of all city dumps test groundwater for possible contamination, less than 16 percent have insulating liners, only 5 percent collect polluting liquid wastes before they percolate into groundwater, and less than half impose any restrictions on the kinds of liquid wastes that can be poured into them. Not surprisingly, almost one-fourth of the nonmilitary sites identified in the Superfund National Priorities List as posing the greatest chemical hazards to public health and the environment are city dumps.[47]

Quick Review 5.3

Major Types of Land Pollution

- Toxic substances: acids, heavy metals, solvents, pesticides, herbicides, phenols
- Solid wastes: residential garbage, industrial wastes, agricultural wastes, mining wastes,
- Nuclear wastes: high-level (cesium, strontium, plutonium), transuranic (diluted high-level wastes), low-level (contaminated reactor equipment, uranium mine tailings)

The quantity of residential garbage that Americans produce, however, is dwarfed by the quantities of solid waste produced through industrial, agricultural, and mining processes. Although residential garbage, as mentioned, is 250 million tons a year, American industries generate over 7.6 billion tons of solid waste a year, oil and gas producers generate 2 to 3 billion tons, and mining operations about 1.4 billion tons.[48] These wastes are dumped into some 220,000 industrial waste heaps, the vast majority of which are unlined surface dumps.

Thousands of abandoned industrial dumps have been discovered containing hazardous wastes, most created by the chemical and petroleum industries.[49] The majority of hazardous waste sites are located in industrial regions. Altogether, about 80 percent of industrial wastes are estimated to have been deposited in ponds, lagoons, and landfills that are not secure.[50] The cost of cleaning up these dumps was estimated to be between $28.4 billion and $55 billion.[51]

The total amount of hazardous waste currently being produced has been difficult to establish. The EPA has estimated that 10 to 15 percent of the industrial wastes being produced each year were toxic—an estimated total of 15 million tons per year. More recently, the agency announced that nearly six times more hazardous waste was being generated each year than it had previously estimated. Some studies have concluded that in a single year 290 million tons of toxic wastes are produced.[52]

Nuclear Wastes Light-water nuclear reactors contain radioactive materials, including known carcinogens such as strontium 90, cesium 137, barium 140, and iodine 131. Extremely high levels of radiation from these elements can kill a person; lower dosages (especially if radioactive dust particles are inhaled or ingested) can cause thyroid, lung, or bone cancer as well as genetic damage that will be transmitted to future generations. To this date, nuclear plants in this country have operated safely without any catastrophic release of large quantities of radioactive materials. Estimates of the probable risk of such a catastrophic accident are highly controversial, and significant doubts surround these risk estimates, especially in light of the accidents at Three Mile Island in the United States, Chernobyl in Russia, and the earthquake and tsunami induced accident in Fukashima, Japan, all of which defied earlier probability estimates.[53] Even without catastrophic accidents, however, small amounts of radioactive materials are routinely released into the environment during the normal operations of a nuclear plant and during the mining, processing, and transporting of nuclear fuels. The U.S. government has estimated that, by the year 2000 (about four decades after nuclear plants began to be built in the United States), about 1,000 people had died of cancer from these routine emissions; other estimates, however, place these figures at higher levels.[54]

Plutonium is produced as a waste by-product in the spent fuel of light-water reactors. A 1,000-megawatt reactor, for example, will generate about 265 pounds (120 kilograms) of plutonium wastes each year that must be disposed of Plutonium is a highly toxic and extremely carcinogenic substance. A particle weighing 10 millionths of a gram, if inhaled, can cause death within a few weeks. Twenty pounds, if properly distributed, could give lung cancer to everyone on Earth. Plutonium is also the basic constituent of atomic bombs. Therefore, as nuclear power plants proliferate around the world, the probability has increased that plutonium will fall into the hands of criminal terrorists or other hostile groups, who may use it to construct an atomic weapon or lethally contaminate large, populated areas.[55] Nevertheless, many groups have called for the construction of more nuclear power plants because nuclear plants have the significant advantage of producing energy without releasing any greenhouse gases.

Nuclear power plant wastes are of three main types: high-level wastes, transuranic wastes, and low-level wastes. High-level wastes emit gamma rays, which can penetrate all but the thickest shielding. These include cesium 137 and strontium 90, which both become harmless after about 1,000 years, and plutonium, which remains hazardous for 250,000 to 1,000,000 years. All of these are highly carcinogenic. Nuclear reactors produce about 612,000 gallons of liquid and 2,300 tons of solid high-level wastes each year. These wastes must be isolated from the environment until they are no longer hazardous. It is unknown at this time whether there is any safe and permanent method for disposing of these wastes.[56]

Transuranic wastes contain smaller quantities of the elements found in high-level wastes. These come from spent fuel processing and various military weapons processes. Until recently, transuranic wastes were buried in shallow trenches. When it was discovered that radioactive materials had been migrating out of these trenches, they had to be exhumed and redisposed of at a cost of several hundred million dollars.[57]

Low-level wastes consist of contaminated clothing and used equipment from reactor sites and the tailings from mining and milling uranium. About 16 million cubic feet of these wastes have been produced at reactor sites, and an additional 500 million cubic feet of uranium tailings (about 140 million tons) have accumulated in the open at mine sites. About 10 million additional tons of mill tailings are produced each year. Uranium tailings continue to emit radioactive radon for several hundred thousand years. In addition, all nuclear plants (including equipment, buildings, and land) become low-level nuclear wastes after an operating life of 30 to 35 years. The entire plant must then be decommissioned because it remains radioactive for thousands of years; the dismantled plant and land site must be maintained under constant security for the next several centuries.[58]

More than one author has suggested that the safe disposal of nuclear wastes is soluble only if we assume that none of our descendants will ever accidentally drill into nuclear repositories or enter them during times of war; that records of their locations will be preserved for the next several centuries; that the wastes will not accidentally flow together and begin reacting; that geological events, ice sheets, or other unforeseen earth movements will never uncover the wastes; that our engineering estimates of the properties of metal, glass, and cement containers are accurate; and that our medical predictions concerning safe levels of radiation exposure prove correct.[59] Although no new nuclear power plants have been constructed in the United States for several years, those built decades ago are still producing wastes, and their past wastes have been accumulating. How these will be disposed of is still uncertain. Of the 65 nuclear plants currently operating in the United States, 59 reactors have been approved to continue operating for an additional 20 years, and they will likely be joined by several newly constructed ones during the next few years. While the United States generates about 20 percent of its electricity with nuclear plants, other countries have a much higher stake in nuclear power, including France (76%), Belgium (54%), Armenia (44%), Hungary (37%), Slovakia (56%), Slovenia (42%), Sweden (42%), Switzerland (39%), and Ukraine (47%).

Depletion of Species and Habitats

Human activity has rendered dozens of plant and animal species extinct. Since 1600, at least 96 known species of mammals and 88 major identifiable species of birds are known to have become extinct.[60] Several hundred more species, such as whales and salmon, today find themselves threatened by commercial fishing. Forest habitats on which the bulk of species depend are also being decimated by the timber industry. Between the years 1600 and 1900, half of the forested land area in the United States was cleared.[61] Experts estimate that the planet's rain forests are being destroyed at the rate of about 1 percent a year.[62] The loss of forest habitats combined with the effects of pollution is thought to have led to the extinction of a large number of unidentified species. The International Union for Conservation's "Red List of Threatened Species," the most comprehensive database of species and subspecies known to be extinct or threatened with extinction, concludes that out of the 47,978 species (all known life forms including birds, animals, plants, insects, fungi, mollusks, etc.) specifically known in 2010 to have existed during the last 500 years, 17,315 or 36 percent were threatened with extinction, and 840 are now extinct.[63]

Nowhere has the depletion of living organisms been as significant as in the oceans. Fish stocks around the world have collapsed because of over-fishing, resulting in a serious decline in the fish protein available to local populations. In the Northwest Atlantic, for example, the stocks of haddock, red hake, and Atlantic cod all collapsed during the 1990s. The United Nations estimated in 2007 that 19 percent of all fish stocks were being overfished and 9 percent were already depleted, while a 2009 study estimated that 14 percent had collapsed.[64] Polluted runoff that has entered the oceans has also created large "dead zones" devoid of most fish and shell fish. More than 400 dead zones have been documented off the coasts of countries around the world.[65]

Depletion of Fossil Fuels

Until the early 1980s, fossil fuels were being depleted at an exponentially rising rate. That is, the rate at which they were being used had doubled with the passage of a regular fixed time period. This type of exponential depletion is illustrated in Figure 5.4. Some early predictions of resource depletion assumed that fossil fuels would continue to be depleted at these exponentially rising rates. If continued, an exponentially rising rate of depletion would end with the complete and catastrophic depletion of the resource in a relatively short time.[66] Estimated world resources of coal would be depleted in about 100 years, estimated world reserves of oil would be exhausted in about 40 years, and estimated reserves of natural gas would last only about 25 years.[67]

Experts point out, however, that our consumption of a resource cannot continue rising at exponential rates.[68] As reserves of any resource shrink, they become increasingly difficult, and therefore more costly, to extract, which in turn slows down their depletion rates. Consequently, although the rates at which reserves

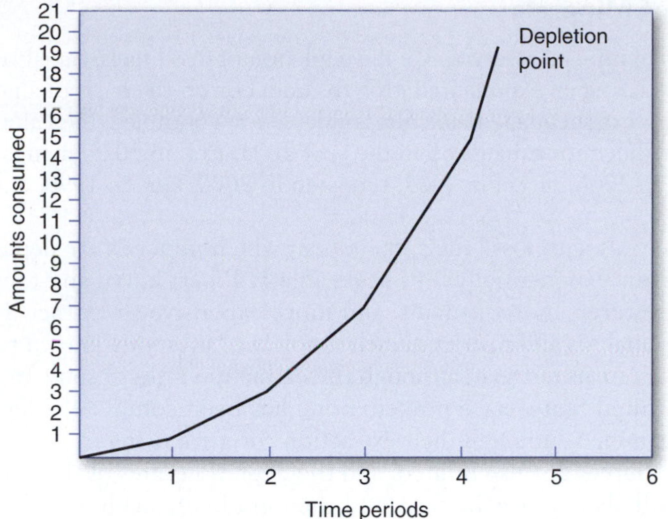

Figure 5.5
Exponential depletion rate.

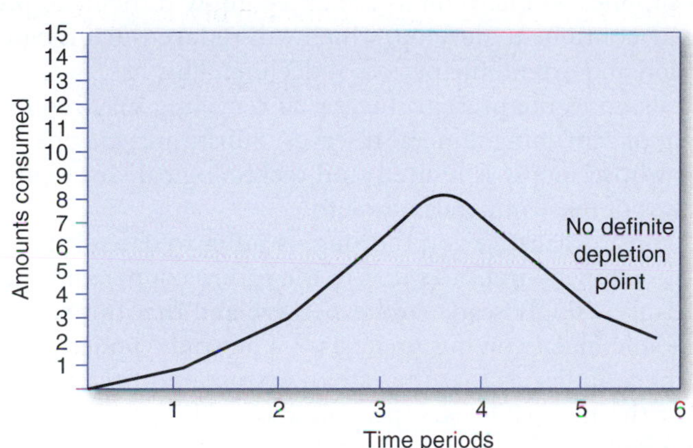

Figure 5.6
Peaked depletion rate.

of a resource are depleted may rise exponentially for a period, the rising costs of extraction eventually cause the rates to peak and then begin to decline without complete depletion ever being attained (as prices continue to rise ever more steeply). Figure 5.6 illustrates this type of peaked depletion curve, sometimes called a "Hubbert curve" after M. King Hubbert, a geologist who used the curve to correctly predict in 1956 that extraction of U.S. oil would peak in 1970 and then decline thereafter.[69]

If we assume that the rate at which we deplete our resources is more adequately mirrored by the peaked Hubbert model than by the exponential model, then fossil fuels will not be depleted within the short time frame predicted by earlier exponential growth models. The extraction of estimated reserves of coal will probably peak in about 150 years and then continue, but at a declining rate coupled with rising prices, for another 150 years; the extraction of estimated U.S. reserves of natural gas has already peaked and is expected to decline gradually over the next 30 or 40 years. The extraction of U.S. reserves of oil peaked in about 1970 and has steadily declined since then (as the peaked model would predict). Estimates of the depletion rates of world reserves of oil are controversial and vary widely.[70] Cambell estimates the peak probably began in 2004 and certainly occurred before 2010; Laherrère and Ivanhoe both predicted the peak would begin around 2010; Greene predicts the peak may not begin until 2040.[71]

Depletion of Minerals

The depletion of mineral reserves, like the depletion of fossil fuels, can also be calculated either on the basis of an exponential growth model or on the basis of a peaked growth model. If earlier exponentially rising rates of depletion continued, then aluminum would have been scheduled for exhaustion in the year 2003, iron in 2025, manganese in 2018, molybdenum in 2006, nickel in 2025, tungsten in 2000, zinc in 1990, and copper and lead in 1993.[72]

Fortunately, as with fossil fuels, the rate at which minerals are depleted does not continue to grow exponentially, but peaks in a Hubbert curve and then declines as metals become rarer, more difficult, and more expensive to extract. If we use this peaked model analysis and restrict ourselves solely to presently known reserves in the United States, it turns out that, although the extraction rates of some important minerals in the United States have peaked, none has been completely depleted and all continue to be mined, although their extraction costs are rising.[73]

World resources are also limited, and the depletion rates of the world's supplies of minerals will also eventually peak and then gradually decline as remaining supplies become harder and more expensive to mine.[74] The precise impact the limitations of world supplies will have on us are exceedingly difficult to predict. Mining technologies may continue to develop, which will reduce the difficulty and costs of mineral extraction and extend the period of decline. This has, in fact, been the case for most minerals up to the present. Increased recycling may reduce the need for intensive mining of remaining mineral reserves. Substitutes may be found for many of the minerals whose supply is limited, and technological development may make many current uses of these minerals obsolete.

Quick Review 5.4

Depletion of Nonrenewable Resources

- Several species have lost habitats and become extinct
- Natural resources depleted at peaked rate, not exponential rate
- Fossil fuel depletion: coal likely peaks in 150 years, natural gas in 30–40 years, oil between 2010 and 2040
- Mineral depletion: copper and mercury peak in about 2100, aluminum during 21st century, indium and antimony in about 10 years, tantalum in 20–116 years

One of the most exhaustive and thorough studies to date of the world limits of a single mineral—copper—indicates that in the future copper and the other minerals will become increasingly scarce and expensive and that this scarcity will have a noticeable economic impact on our societies.[75] The study, undertaken by Robert B. Gordon and others, indicates that the rate of extraction of the world's copper will rise rapidly over the next 100 years, peak in about 2100, and then slowly decline. Rich copper ores will be exhausted by about 2070. Thereafter, copper must be mined from common rock, an expensive process that will force dramatic rises of copper prices from about $2 per kilogram to $120 per kilogram, even with intense recycling and even assuming other materials can be substituted for all but a handful of the essential uses of copper. According to Gordon and his coauthors: "Similar arguments can be raised for other metals, such as lead, zinc, tin, tungsten, and silver. . . .We have not made a complete analysis for any other scarce metal, but we strongly suspect that if we did a pattern of future use similar to that predicted for copper would emerge."[76]

In a 2000 study, the U.S. Geological Survey of the U.S. Department of the Interior concluded that world reserves of conventional aluminum resources (bauxite) are sufficient to meet world demand for aluminum "well into the 21st century"; world reserves of manganese total 5 billion tons, which are being mined at the rate of about 7 million tons a year; world reserves of mercury are estimated at nearly 600,000 tons, which are "sufficient for another century or more"; world reserves of copper total 2.3 billion tons, which are currently being mined at the rate of 13,000 tons a year; world resources of iron are estimated at more than 250 billion tons, which are being mined at a rate of about 1 billion tons a year; and lead world resources total more than 1.5 billion tons, which are being mined at about 3 million tons a year.[77] These estimates suggest we can rely on a steady supply of these metals for many years to come. Somewhat more pessimistic conclusions, however, were drawn in a 2007 study of several essential minerals which estimated that, depending on how much consumption rates increase from 2007 rates, indium, a key component of flat-screen TVs and certain solar cells, will run out in 4–13 years (from year 2007); antimony, which is used in certain drugs and flame retardant materials will run out in 13–30 years; tantalum, a component of cell phones and camera lenses, in 20–116 years; uranium, which will be in high demand if the world begins building more nuclear power plants, in 19–59 years; tin in 17–40 years; silver in 9–29 years; gold in 36–45 years; zinc in 34–46 years; and nickel in 57–90 years.[78]

There are physical limits, then, to our natural resources: Although many are abundant, none can be exploited indefinitely. Eventually each will peter out and the costs of extraction will rise significantly. More plentiful substitute materials may be found for many of these resources, but it is likely that substitutes cannot be found for all of them. Whatever substitutes are developed will also be limited, so the day of reckoning will only be delayed.

5.2 The Ethics of Pollution Control

For centuries, business institutions were able to ignore their impact on the natural environment, an indulgence created by a number of causes. First, business was able to treat air and water as free goods—that is, as goods that no one owns and that each firm can therefore use without reimbursing anyone for their use. For several years, for example, a DuPont plant in West Virginia had been dumping 10,000 tons of chemical wastes each month into the Gulf of Mexico until it was forced to stop. The waters of the Gulf provided a free dumping site for whose damages DuPont did not have to pay. Because such resources are not privately owned, they lack the protection that a private owner would normally provide, and businesses were able to ignore the damages they inflicted on them. Second, businesses have seen the environment as an unlimited good. That is, the "carrying capacity" of air and water is relatively large, and each firm's contribution of pollution to these resources seems relatively small and insignificant.[79] The amount of chemicals DuPont was dumping into the Gulf, for example, was relatively small compared with the size of the Gulf and the effects were seen as negligible. When the effects of its activities are seen as so slight, a firm will tend to ignore these effects. However, when every firm reasons in this way, the combined negligible effects of each firm's activities may become enormous and potentially disastrous. The carrying capacity of the air and water is soon exceeded, and these free and unlimited goods rapidly deteriorate.

Of course, pollution problems are not rooted only in business activities. Pollution also results from the use that consumers make of products and from human waste products.[80] A primary source of air pollution, for example, is automobile use, and a primary source of water pollution is sewage. We are truly all polluters.[81] Because every human being pollutes, pollution problems have increased as our population has multiplied. The world's population grew from 1 billion in 1850 to 2 billion in 1930 to 6.3 billion in 2003 and is projected to grow to 9 billion by 2050.[82] This population explosion has put severe strains on the air and water resources into which we dump our share of pollutants. Moreover, these strains have been aggravated by our tendency to concentrate our populations in urban centers. All over the world, urban areas are growing rapidly, and the high-population densities that urbanization has created multiplies the pollution burdens placed on air and water resources.[83]

The problems of pollution, then, have a variety of origins, and their treatment requires a similarly variegated set of solutions. Our focus in what follows, however, concentrates on a single range of problems: the ethical issues raised by pollution from commercial and industrial enterprises.

The Auto Companies in China

In 2000, China's car market began to expand dramatically due to the increasing wealth of the country, the encouragement of the government, and a growing middle class that wanted the comfort, convenience, and pride of car ownership. By 2010 China had become the largest car market in the world with over 18 million cars sold that year. With a population of 1.2 billion people and double-digit growth rates, China estimated that by 2035 as many as 300 million cars would be traveling on its highways. Foreign car companies eagerly flocked to help China expand its car industry, including Volkswagen, General Motors (GM), Honda, Toyota, Ford, Citroen, and BMW, who together invested more than $20 billion to kick-start China's auto industry in 2000. In 2011, Volkswagen announced it had sold 2 million cars in China the previous year and GM announced it had sold 2.3 million and would be selling 5 million a year by 2015. Critics suggested, however, that the overzealous auto companies unwittingly might be inflicting serious harms on the global environment. To begin with, the pollution from so many new cars promised to have severe environmental impacts. Even "clean" cars will generate carbon dioxide as they burn fuel, thus worsening the greenhouse effect. Cars also produce smog and other health hazards (tuberculosis cases will double; emphysema and lung cancers will rise), and China's form of gasoline contains lead, a toxic metal. Expanding China's car production will increase oil consumption, placing heavy pressures on the world's dwindling oil resources. China's rising oil consumption was partly responsible for continuing oil prices of over $100 a barrel in 2011 (the high price was also due to civil unrest in the Middle East) that drove the price of gas in the U.S. to over $4 a gallon. If car ownership in China continues to rise, by 2020 China's oil consumption could be two thirds of the United States' (the U.S. consumes one-fourth of the world's oil), a level the world's oil supplies probably cannot support. Some experts claim world oil production peaked in 2010, leaving declining and more expensive oil supplies to meet the rising demands of China, the United

Worker on an assembly line building the GM Chevrolet Sail in Shandong province, China.

General Motors displays its revolutionary Hy-Wire car at the Great Wall of China.

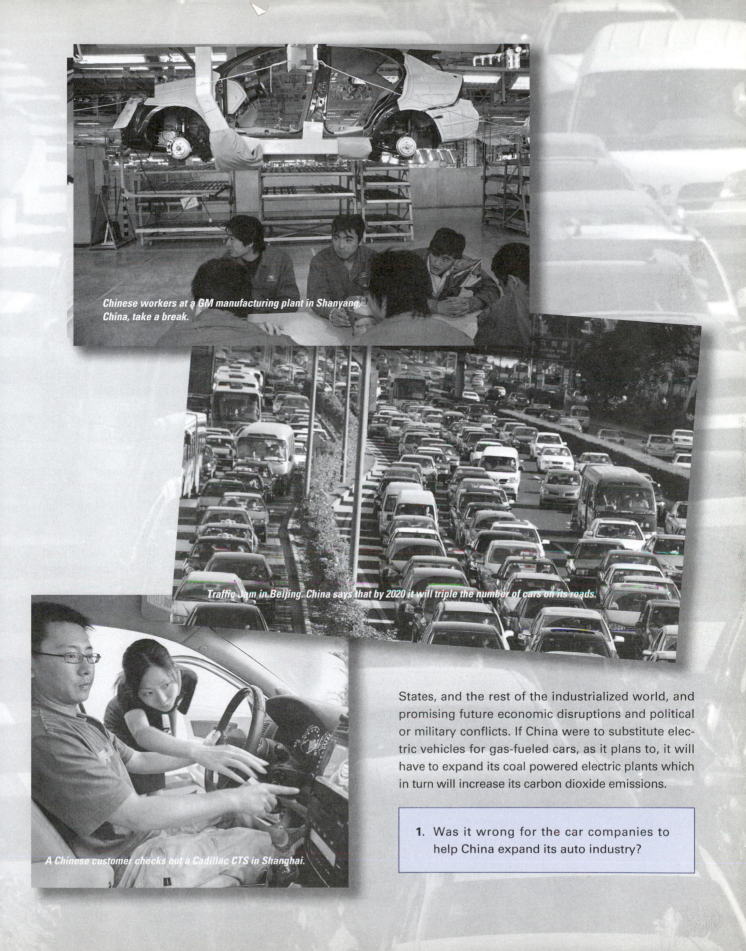

Chinese workers at a GM manufacturing plant in Shanyang, China, take a break.

Traffic Jam in Beijing. China says that by 2020 it will triple the number of cars on its roads.

A Chinese customer checks out a Cadillac CTS in Shanghai.

States, and the rest of the industrialized world, and promising future economic disruptions and political or military conflicts. If China were to substitute electric vehicles for gas-fueled cars, as it plans to, it will have to expand its coal powered electric plants which in turn will increase its carbon dioxide emissions.

1. Was it wrong for the car companies to help China expand its auto industry?

Ecological Ethics

Concern for the environment has a long history. During the thirteenth century, for example, Arabic thinkers discussed air and water pollution and how these were linked to human health[84] while in England, King Edward I outlawed the burning of sea coal because its smoke polluted the air of London. Early concern for the environment, however, was for the most part ***anthropocentric*** (human-centered), i.e., concern for the environment was based on how it affected the interests of human beings. The natural environment was largely seen as a resource that should serve the interests of human beings and which has only an instrumental value, i.e., it is valuable to the extent that it serves human interests. In the Old Testament book of *Genesis*, for example, God declares that humans are to "have dominion over the fish of the sea, and over the birds of the air, and over every living thing that moves upon the earth," and the ancient Greek philosopher Aristotle wrote that "nature has made all things specifically for the sake of man," while Thomas Aquinas, a thirteenth century philosopher-theologian wrote that nonhumans are "ordered to man's use."[85] The view that nature has value to the extent that it serves human interests continued into the modern period (with a few exceptions). The philosopher Immanuel Kant, for example, famously wrote that the reason why it is wrong for a person to be cruel to animals is because "cruelty to animals is contrary to man's duty to *himself*, since it deadens in him the feeling of sympathy for their sufferings and thus weakens a natural tendency that is very useful to morality in relation to other humans." The idea here is that a person's cruelty toward animals is not wrong because of the pain it inflicts on the animal itself, but because of the effect it has on the person's moral relationships with other humans.

As we will see shortly, the view that the natural environment is valuable only because it serves human interests continues to our own day. Many people today, in fact, work to protect the environment precisely because they hold this view: To them, damage to the environment is morally wrong because it ultimately harms human beings. Those who hold an anthropocentric view of the environment can still believe that air, water, and land pollution, the extinction of species, climate change, the release of radioactive wastes, and the destruction of the ozone layer are all harmful to us and for that reason we must work to stop them. But environmental critics of anthropocentric views argue that holding an anthropocentric view is itself part of the problem. Because we see nature as something that is there to serve us, we pollute and consume it as if it has no value in itself. Critics of anthropocentric views claim that if we do not change our anthropocentric views we will continue to exploit, pollute, and consume nature until it is too late. We will take care of nature only if we accept the view that nature is valuable in itself and that by virtue of its intrinsic value we are obligated to respect and preserve it.

ecological system An interrelated and interdependent set of organisms and environments.

Some opponents of anthropocentrism claim that the problem of pollution (and environmental issues in general) can best be framed in terms of our duty to recognize and preserve the **ecological systems** within which we live.[86] An ecological system is an interrelated and interdependent set of organisms and environments, such as a lake in which the fish depend on small aquatic organisms, which in turn live off decaying plant and fish waste products.[87] Because the various parts of an ecological system are interdependent, the activities of one of its parts will affect all the other parts and the well-being of each part depends on the wellbeing of the other parts. Business firms (and all other social institutions) are parts of a larger ecological system, "spaceship earth."[88] Business firms depend on the natural environment for their energy, material resources, and waste disposal, and that environment in turn is affected by the commercial activities of business firms. For example, the activities of eighteenth-century European manufacturers of beaver hats led to the wholesale destruction of beavers in the United States, which in turn led to the drying up of the innumerable swamp lands that had been created by beaver dams.[89] Businesses must recognize the interrelationships and interdependencies of the ecological systems within which they operate.

Recognition of the fact that we are only an interdependent part of a larger ecological system, some writers have argued, should lead us to recognize that we have a moral duty to protect the interests not only of human beings, but also of other nonhuman parts of this system.[90] This insistence on what is sometimes called ***ecological ethics*** or *deep ecology* is not based on the idea that the environment should be protected *for the sake of human beings*. Instead, ecological ethics is based on the idea that nonhuman parts of the environment deserve to be preserved *for their own sake*, regardless of how this may benefit human beings. As opposed to the view that only humans have intrinsic value and that other things are only instrumentally valuable to the extent that they support or enhance human well-being, an ecological ethic claims that nonhuman parts of the environment—such as animals—have an intrinsic value that is independent of what they contribute to human beings. Thus, we have a moral duty to respect and refrain from harming these nonhumans regardless of whether they make any contribution to our human welfare. Several supporters of this approach have formulated their views in a platform consisting of the following statements:

ecological ethics The ethical view that nonhuman parts of the environment deserve to be preserved for their own sake, regardless of whether this benefits human beings.

1. The well-being and flourishing of human and nonhuman life on earth have value in themselves. ... These values are independent of the usefulness of the nonhuman world for human purposes.
2. Richness and diversity of life forms contribute to the realization of these values and are also values in themselves.
3. Humans have no right to reduce this richness and diversity except to satisfy vital needs.
4. The flourishing of human life and cultures is compatible with a substantial decrease of the human population. The flourishing of nonhuman life requires such a decrease.
5. Present human interference with the nonhuman world is excessive, and the situation is rapidly worsening.
6. Policies must therefore be changed. The changes in policies affect basic economic, technological, and ideological structures. The resulting state of affairs will be deeply different from the present.
7. The ideological change is mainly that of appreciating life quality ... rather than adhering to an increasingly higher standard of living.
8. Those who subscribe to the foregoing points have an obligation directly or indirectly to participate in the attempt to implement the necessary changes.[91]

An ecological ethic is thus an ethic that claims that because at least some nonhumans are intrinsically valuable, we humans have a duty not to harm them without a sufficiently serious reason. The philosopher Richard Routley has proposed a "mental experiment" to show that nature is intrinsically valuable and should not be harmed without serious reason: Suppose some catastrophic event has killed all human beings but one.[92] Suppose this "last man" had the power to do something that would ensure that every other living thing on Earth, and all Earth's landscapes, would be destroyed after he himself died. From an anthropocentric view it would not be wrong for him to carry out such a destructive act since no humans would be affected. Yet, Routley argues, we recognize that it would indeed be wrong for the "last man" to destroy everything on the Earth's surface. This means that we must feel that these other nonhuman things have intrinsic value that is independent of their value to humans. The claims of an ecological ethic then must be correct: at least some nonhumans are

Quick Review 5.5

The "Last Man" Argument for Ecological Ethics

- Routley asks us to imagine a man who is Earth's last survivor.
- We recognize it is wrong for the last man to destroy all nonhumans.
- So we must recognize some nonhumans have intrinsic value apart from humans.

intrinsically valuable and we have a moral duty to refrain from harming them without a sufficiently weighty reason.

The claims of ecological ethics clearly have significant implications for those businesses whose activities affect the natural environment and its nonhuman organisms. In June, 1990, for example, environmentalists successfully petitioned the U.S. Fish and Wildlife Service to bar the timber industry from logging potentially lucrative old-growth forests of northern California to save the habitat of an endangered species, the dark-brown northern spotted owl that lived in the lush "old growth" 200-year-old forests of the Pacific Northwest.[93] The decision of the U.S. Fish and Wildlife Service (and the U.S. "Endangered Species Act" on which it was based) was consistent with ecological ethics, although it was estimated to have cost the timber industry millions of dollars, to have lost workers as many as 36,000 lumber jobs, and to have raised the costs of consumer prices for fine wood products such as furniture and musical instruments. Members of the Sea Shepherd Conservation Society have sabotaged whale processing plants, sunk several ships, and otherwise imposed costs on the whaling industry to protect whales.[94] Members of Earth First! have driven nails into randomly selected trees of forest areas scheduled to be logged so that power logging saws are destroyed when they bite into the spiked trees in order to protect forests. All these activities are based on the idea that nature and its parts have an intrinsic value that we have a moral duty to protect and that this value is at least sometimes more weighty than human interests.

There are several varieties of ecological ethics, some more radical and far-reaching than others. Perhaps the most popular version claims that, in addition to human beings, other animals have intrinsic value and are deserving of our respect and protection. Some utilitarians, such as Peter Singer, for example, have claimed that pain is an evil whether it is inflicted on humans or on members of other animal species. In fact, Singer argues, the pain experienced by an animal is as great an evil as a *comparable* pain experienced by a human being. He grants that a human may be more sensitive to pain than an animal, and a human may suffer more from anticipating the pain than an animal would, so an animal's pain may have to be more intense to be "comparable to" a human's pain. Nevertheless, at some level of intensity the pain of the animal would become comparable to the pain of the human being, and at that level the animal's pain would be as great an evil as the human's pain. It follows, Singer concludes, that if is morally wrong to inflict the pain on a human, it is equally wrong to inflict the comparable pain on an animal. It is a form of *speciesism* (akin to racism or sexism, i.e., a prejudice against members of another group) to think that the moral duty to avoid inflicting pain on members of other species is not equal to our duty to avoid inflicting comparable pain on members of our own species.[95]

Certain nonutilitarians have reached similar conclusions by a different route. They have claimed that the life of every animal "itself has value" apart from the interests of human beings. Because of the intrinsic value of its life, each animal has certain moral rights, in particular the right to be treated with respect.[96] Humans have a duty generally to respect this right, although in some special cases a human's right might override an animal's right.

Supporters of views that animals have intrinsic value have imposed substantial costs on cattle ranchers, slaughterhouses, chicken farms, fur companies, and pharmaceutical and cosmetic corporations that use animals to test chemicals. Both the utilitarian and the rights arguments in support of human duties toward animals imply that it is wrong to raise animals for food in the crowded and painful circumstances in which agricultural business enterprises currently raise cows, pigs, and chickens, and wrong to slaughter them in the painful ways in which they are slaughtered. It is wrong, they claim, because there are other ways of raising and slaughtering animals that do not inflict such pain on them. The utilitarian and rights arguments also imply that it is wrong to use animals in painful test procedures—as millions are currently still used in some industries—when there are alternative kinds of test procedures or when the benefits that come from using the tests cannot justify the animal pains they produce.[97] Companies like Procter & Gamble, Clorox, L'Oreal, Unilever, Dial, Johnson & Johnson, Shiseido, and S.C. Johnson have been singled out by groups like PETA (People for the Ethical Treatment of Animals) as companies that unethically test the toxicity of cosmetics and household products on animals in their labs. For example, experiments in these labs include forcing household cleaners into the stomachs of animals or squirting chemicals into their eyes or spraying hairsprays into their lungs.[98] PETA insists that the benefits of cosmetics and many household products cannot justify inflicting the kind of extreme pain, suffering, and death that such tests inflict on animals. Moreover, they claim, there are alternatives to many animal tests such as testing with computer models, testing on cell cultures, and testing on human volunteers.

Broader versions of ecological ethics would extend our duties beyond the animal world to include plants. Thus, some ecological ethicians have claimed that it is arbitrary and hedonistic to confine our duties to creatures that can feel pain. Instead, they urge, we should acknowledge that all living things including plants have "an interest in remaining alive" and that consequently they deserve moral consideration for their own sakes.[99] Other environmentalists such as Aldo Leopold have claimed that not only living things, but even a natural species or a natural structure—such as a lake, a wild river, a mountain, and even an entire "biotic community"—has a right to have its "integrity, stability, and beauty" preserved.[100] If correct, these views would have important implications for businesses engaged in strip-mining or logging operations.

Some versions of ecological ethics have turned away from talk of duties and obligations and have instead urged an approach toward nature more closely linked to notions of virtue and character. An early version of such an approach was fashioned by Albert Schweitzer, who wrote that when traveling on a river in Africa, "at the very moment when, at sunset, we were making our way through a herd of hippopotamuses, there flashed upon my mind, unforeseen and unsought, the phrase, 'Reverence for Life'."[101] As Schweitzer later articulated it, to be a person who has reverence for life is to see life itself, in all its forms, as having inherent worth, a worth that inspires an unwillingness to destroy and a desire to preserve:

> The man who has become a thinking being feels a compulsion to give to every will-to-live the same reverence for life that he gives to his own. He experiences that other life in his own. He accepts as being good: to preserve life, to promote life, to raise to its highest value life which is capable of development; and as being evil: to destroy life, to injure life, to repress life which is capable of development. This is the absolute, fundamental principle of the moral.[102]

More recently, the philosopher Paul Taylor urged a similar approach, writing that "character traits are morally good in virtue of their expressing or embodying a certain ultimate moral attitude, which I call respect for nature."[103] This respect for nature, Taylor argued, is based on the fact that each living thing seeks its own good and so is a "teleological center of a life":

> To say it is a teleological center of a life is to say that its internal functioning as well as its external activities are all goal-oriented, having the constant tendency to maintain the organism's existence through time and to enable it successfully to perform those biological operations whereby it reproduces its kind and continually adapts to changing environmental events and conditions.[104]

The goal-oriented nature of all living things, Taylor argued, implies that all living things have an inherent "good of their own" that should be respected. Such respect is the only attitude consistent with a biocentric outlook that realizes that we ourselves are living members of Earth's community of life, that we are part of a system of interdependence with other living things, that living things have their own good, and that we are not inherently superior to other living things within that system.

However, these attempts to extend moral rights to nonhumans or claim that an attitude of respect for all nature is morally demanded are still controversial, and some authors have labeled them "incredible."[105] It is difficult, for example, to see why the fact that something *is* alive implies that it *ought to be* alive and that we, therefore, have a duty to keep it alive or to express respect or even reverence for it. It is also difficult to see why the fact that a river or a mountain exists implies that it *ought to* exist and that we have a duty to keep it in existence or revere it. Facts do not imply values in this easy way.[106] It is also controversial whether we can claim that animals have rights or intrinsic value.[107] But we do not have to rely on these views to develop an environmental ethic. As we mentioned earlier, there are other more traditional, although anthropocentric, approaches to environmental issues.[108] One is based on a theory of human rights, and the other is based on utilitarian considerations.

Environmental Rights and Absolute Bans

Quick Review 5.6

Environmental Rights
- Blackstone argues humans have a right to fulfill their capacities as free and rational and a livable environment is essential to such fulfillment.
- So humans have a right to a livable environment which is violated by practices that destroy the environment.
- Such environmental rights can lead to absolute bans on pollution even when the costs far outweigh the benefits.

In an influential article, William T. Blackstone argued that the possession of a livable environment is not merely a desirable state of affairs, but something to which each human being has a right.[109] That is, a livable environment is not merely something that we would all like to have: It is something that others have a duty to allow us to have. They have this duty, Blackstone argued, because we each have a right to a livable environment, and our right imposes on others the correlative duty of not interfering in our exercise of that right. This is a right, moreover, that should be incorporated into our legal system.

Why do human beings have this right? According to Blackstone, a person has a moral right to a thing when possession of that thing is "essential in permitting him to live a human life" (i.e., in permitting him to fulfill his capacities as a rational and free being).[110] At this time in our history, it has become clear that a livable environment is essential to the fulfillment of our human capacities. Consequently, human beings have a moral right to a decent environment, and it should become a legal right. Moreover, Blackstone adds, this moral and legal right should override people's legal property rights. Our great and increasing ability to manipulate the environment has revealed that, unless we limit the legal freedom to engage in practices that destroy the environment, we shall lose the very possibility of human life and the possibility of exercising other rights, such as the right to liberty and equality.

Several states have introduced amendments to their constitutions that grant to their citizens an environmental right, much like Blackstone advocated. Article One of the Constitution of Pennsylvania, for example, was amended several years ago to read:

> The people have a right to clean air, pure water, and to the preservation of the natural scenic, historic, and aesthetic values of the environment. Pennsylvania's natural resources ... are the common property of all the people, including generations yet to come. As trustee of these resources, the commonwealth shall preserve and maintain them for the benefit of all people.

To a large extent, something like Blackstone's concept of *environmental rights* is recognized in federal law. Section 101(b) of the National Environmental Policy Act of

1969, for example, states that one of its purposes is to "assure for all Americans safe, healthful, productive, and aesthetically and culturally pleasing surroundings." Subsequent acts tried to achieve this purpose. For example, the Water Pollution Control Act of 1972 required firms, by 1977, to use the "best practicable technology" to get rid of pollution (i.e., technology used by several of the least-polluting plants in an industry); the Clean Water Act of 1977 required that, by 1984, firms must eliminate all toxic and nonconventional wastes with the use of the "best available technology" (i.e., technology used by the one least-polluting plant). The Air Quality Act of 1967 and the Clean Air Amendments of 1970 and 1990 established similar limits to air pollution from stationary sources and automobiles and provided the machinery for enforcing these limits. These federal laws did not rest on a utilitarian cost-benefit analysis. That is, they did not say that firms should reduce pollution so long as the benefits outweigh the costs. Instead, they simply imposed absolute bans on pollution regardless of the costs involved. Such absolute restrictions can best be justified by an appeal to people's rights.

Federal statutes in effect impose absolute limits on the property rights of owners of firms, and Blackstone's arguments provide a plausible rationale for limiting property rights in these absolute ways for the sake of a human right to a clean environment. Blackstone's argument obviously rests on a Kantian theory of rights: Because humans have a moral duty to treat each other as ends and not as means, they have a correlative duty to respect and promote the development of each person's capacity to freely and rationally choose for himself or herself.

The main difficulty with Blackstone's view, however, is that it fails to provide any nuanced guidance on several pressing environmental choices. How much pollution control is really needed? Should we have an absolute ban on pollution? How far should we go in limiting property rights for the sake of the environment? What goods, if any, should we cease manufacturing to halt or slow environmental damage? Who should pay for the costs of preserving the environment? Blackstone's theory gives us no way of handling these questions because it imposes a simple and absolute ban on pollution.

This lack of nuance in the absolute rights approach is especially problematic when the costs of removing certain minimal amounts of pollution are high and the results are insignificant. Consider the situation of a pulp company as reported by its president:

> Surveys conducted along the lower Columbia River since completion of primary treatment facilities at our mills show that water-quality standards are being met and that the river is being used for fishing, swimming, water supply, and recreation. In all respects, therefore, the 1985 goals of the [Federal Water Pollution Control] act are presently being met. But the technical requirements of the act call for installation of secondary treatment facilities at our mills at Camas and Wauna. The cost will be about $20 million and will not result in any measurable improvement of water quality on the river. On the contrary, the total environmental effect will be negative. We calculate that it will take about 57 million kwh of electricity and nearly 8000 tons of chemicals to operate these unnecessary facilities. Total power requirements will involve burning 90,000 bbl/yr of scarce oil, in turn creating 900,000 lb of pollutants at the generating source.[111]

It has been suggested that there is a way of thinking about the "right to a clean environment" that would answer, at least partially, the problem this pulp company president points out. As he suggests, once the waters of a lake or a stream, for example, have been cleansed of 99.999999 percent of all pollutants, removing the remaining .000001 percent may provide insignificant benefits. Beyond a certain point, additional removal of pollutants is hardly worth the investment to remove them. But what is this point? If we return to Blackstone's claim that we have a right to a clean environment, we can see that the basis of this right is the more basic right to "live a human life," i.e., a right to fulfill our capacities as free and rational persons. This reasoning suggests that the right to a clean environment is a right to an environment that is clean enough to allow all of us to live a full human life, i.e., an environment in which pollution does not prevent us from living healthy and fulfilled lives. This idea that the environment must be cleaned only up to the point at which it allows us to live healthy and fulfilled human lives has sometimes been called the "safety standard." It implies that once the environment is "safe" enough for us to live healthy and fulfilled lives, more cleansing is not morally required.

At what point is the environment "safe" enough? Governments have struggled with this question as they have attempted to implement the many laws that seem to require absolutely no pollution. The U.S. government has often decided that when exposure to pollution during one year poses a risk of death of 1 in 1 million or less, it is safe enough; and when, during a year, exposure poses a risk of death of 3 in 10,000 or more, it is unsafe and must be cleaned up. Risks that lie in-between are handled on a case-by-case basis.[112] This means that when pollution kills no more than 1 person out of a million who were exposed to it during a year, it is safe enough; when it kills 3 or more persons out of 10,000 who were exposed to it during a year, it is unsafe and must be addressed. But this way of dealing with the problem of how safe is safe enough, has not been acceptable to everyone. Many people claim that if 1 person out of a million dies every year from exposure to pollution, then the pollution is still too high: that one person also had a right to a healthy environment and that right was violated. But is this claim justified? It seems unrealistic to demand the complete elimination of absolutely all risks to life and health because fulfilling that demand would impose unacceptable costs and burdens on all of us.

Another different kind of problem "absolute bans" on pollution raise is their potential impact on plant closings and jobs.[113] Some politicians have claimed that pollution control legislation costs as much as 160,000 jobs a year. However, the EPA studied the period between 1971 and 1981 and found only 153 plant closings that possibly could be attributed to environmental legislation, and these closings accounted for only 32,611 jobs, for an average of 3,200 jobs lost a year.[114] A U.S. Department of Labor study of layoffs during 1987 to 1991 found that of 2,546 layoff events only 4 were attributable to environmental and safety regulations.[115] Many, perhaps most, of the workers affected by these closings found other jobs, and many new jobs have been created by companies that design, manufacture, and install pollution-control devices. Nevertheless, environmental legislation clearly imposes some minimal level of costs on those workers who are at least temporarily displaced by those layoffs attributable to environmental regulations.

Because of the objections raised against absolute bans, the U.S. federal government in the early 1980s began to turn to methods of pollution control that tried to balance the costs and benefits of controlling pollution and that did not impose absolute bans. Since then cost-benefit analyses have played a much bigger role in environmental regulations.[116] These regulatory approaches are not based on the notion that people have absolute environmental rights, but on a utilitarian/economic approach to the environment.

Markets and Partial Controls

One way to answer the questions that Blackstone's theory of environmental rights raises is to see environmental problems as market defects. If an industry pollutes the environment, the market prices of its commodities will no longer reflect the full costs of producing the commodities; the result is a misallocation of resources, a rise in waste, and an inefficient distribution of commodities. Consequently, society as a whole is harmed as its overall economic welfare declines.[117] Individuals, then, should avoid pollution because they should avoid harming society's welfare. The following paragraphs explain this argument in greater detail and explain the more nuanced approach to pollution that this market analysis is said to provide.

Private Costs and Social Costs

Economists often distinguish between what it cost a private manufacturer to make a product and what the manufacture of that product cost society as a whole. Suppose, for example, that an electric firm consumes a certain amount of fuel, labor, and equipment to produce 1 kilowatt of electricity. The cost of these resources is its **private cost**: The price it must pay out of its own pocket to manufacture 1 kilowatt of electricity. However, producing the kilowatt of electricity may also involve other external costs for which the firm does not pay.[118] When the firm burns fuel, for example, it may generate smoke and soot that settles on surrounding neighbors, who have to bear the costs of cleaning up the grime and paying for any medical problems the smoke creates. From the viewpoint of society as a whole, then, the costs of producing the kilowatt of electricity include not only the internal costs of fuel, labor, and equipment for which the manufacturer pays, but also the external costs of cleanup and medical care that the neighbors pay. This sum total of costs (the private internal costs plus the external costs the neighbors must pay) are the **social costs** of producing the kilowatt of electricity: the total price society must pay to manufacture 1 kilowatt of electricity. Of course, private costs and social costs do not always diverge as in this example; sometimes the two coincide. If a producer pays for all the costs involved in manufacturing a product, for example, or if manufacturing a product imposes no external costs, then the producer's costs and the total social costs are the same.

private cost The cost an individual or company must pay out of its own pocket to engage in a particular economic activity.

social cost The private internal costs plus the external costs of engaging in a particular economic activity.

Thus, when a firm pollutes its environment in any way, the firm's private costs are always less than the total social costs involved. Whether the pollution is localized and immediate, as in the neighborhood effects described in this example, or whether the pollution is global and long-range, as in the hot-house effects predicted to follow from introducing too much carbon dioxide into the atmosphere, pollution always imposes external costs—that is, costs for which the person who produces the pollution does not have to pay. Pollution is fundamentally a problem of this divergence between private and social costs.

Why should this divergence be a problem? It is a problem because when the private costs of manufacturing a product diverge from the social costs involved in its manufacture, markets no longer price commodities accurately. Consequently, they no longer allocate resources efficiently. As a result, society's welfare declines. To understand why markets become inefficient when private and social costs diverge, let us suppose that the electrical power industry is perfectly competitive (it is not, but let us suppose it is).[119] Suppose, then, that market supply curve S in Figure 5.7 reflects the private costs producers must pay to manufacture each kilowatt of electricity. The market price will then be at the equilibrium point E, where the supply curve based on these private costs crosses the demand curve.

In the hypothetical situation in Figure 5.7, the curves intersect at the market price of 3.5 cents and at an output of 600 million kilowatt hours. Suppose that, besides the private costs that producers incur in manufacturing electricity, the manufacture of electricity also imposes external costs on their neighbors in the form of environmental pollution. If these external costs were added to the private costs of producers, then

Figure 5.7

Figure 5.8

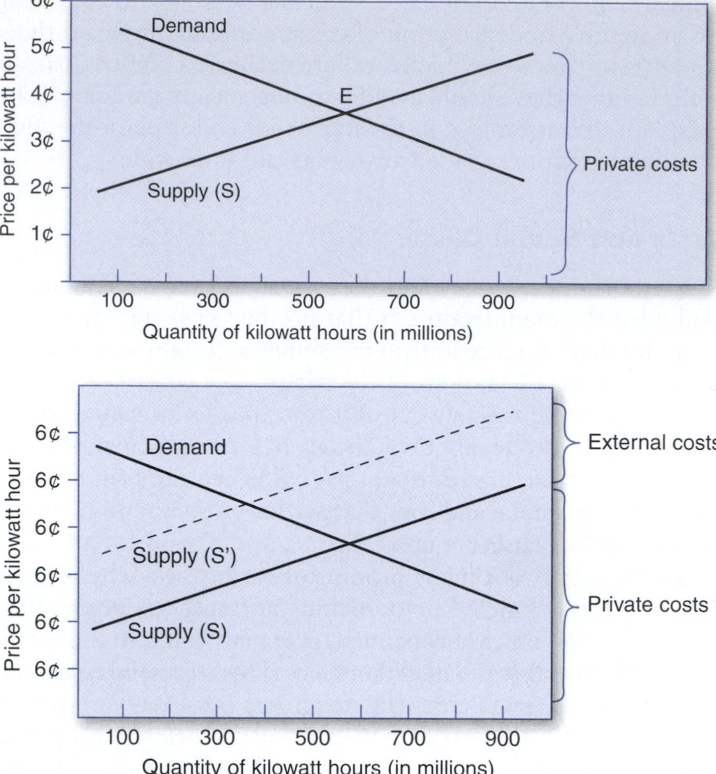

a new supply curve, S´, would result that would take into account all the costs of manufacturing each kilowatt hour of electricity, as in Figure 5.8.

> *Quick Review 5.7*
>
> **Markets and Pollution**
>
> - Total costs of making a product include a seller's internal private costs and the external costs of pollution paid by society.
> - A supply curve based on all costs of making a product lies higher than one based only on sellers' internal private costs and the higher supply curve crosses the demand curve at a lower quantity and a higher price than the lower supply curve.
> - So when sellers' costs include only private costs, too much is produced and price is too low (compared to when all costs are included), which lowers utility, and violates rights, and justice.

The new supply curve in Figure 5.7, S´, which is above the supply curve S (which includes only the manufacturer's private costs), shows the quantities of electricity that would be supplied if all the costs of producing the electricity were taken into account and the prices that would have to be charged for each kilowatt hour if all costs were thus taken into account. As the new curve, S´, indicates, when all the costs are taken into account, the market price of the commodity, 4.5 cents, will be higher, and the output, 350 million kilowatt hours, will be lower than when only private costs are incorporated. Thus, when only private costs are taken into account, the electricity is underpriced and overproduced. This, in turn, means that the electricity market is no longer allocating resources and distributing commodities so as to maximize utility. Three ethical deficiencies can be noted.

First, allocation of resources in markets that do not take all costs into account is not optimal because, from the point of view of society as a whole, more of the commodity is being produced than society would demand if society had an accurate measure available of what it is actually paying to produce the commodity. Because the commodity is being overproduced, more of society's resources are being consumed to produce the commodity than is optimal. The resources being consumed by overproduction of the commodity are resources that could be used to produce other commodities for which there would be greater demand if prices accurately reflected costs. Resources are thereby being misallocated.

Second, when external costs are not taken into account by producers, producers ignore these costs and make no attempt to minimize them like they minimize their other costs. Because the firm does not have to pay for external costs, it uses up and wastes the resources being consumed by these external costs (such as clean air). There may be technologically feasible ways of producing the same commodities without polluting or by polluting less, but the producer will have no incentive to find them.

Third, when the production of a commodity imposes external costs on third parties, goods are no longer efficiently distributed to consumers. External costs introduce effective price differentials into markets: Everyone does not pay equal prices for the same commodities. The neighbors who live near our imaginary electric plant, for example, pay not only the prices the plant charges everyone else for electricity, but also the costs the smoke from the burning fuel imposes on them in the form of extra cleaning bills, medical bills, painting bills, and so forth. Because they must pay for these extra external costs, of course, they have fewer funds to pay for their share of market commodities. Consequently, their share of goods is not proportioned to their desires and needs as compared with the shares of those who do not have to pay the extra external costs.

Pollution, then, imposes external costs, and this in turn means that the private costs of production are less than the social costs. As a consequence, markets with pollution do not impose an optimal discipline on producers, and the result is a drop in social utility. Pollution of the environment, then, is a violation of the utilitarian principles that underlie a market system.

Quick Review 5.8

Ethical Approaches to Environmental Protection

- Ecological approach: nonhumans have intrinsic value
- Environmental rights approach: humans have a right to a livable environment
- Market approach: external costs violate utility, rights, and justice so they should be internalized.

Pollution also violates the kind of justice or fairness that characterizes a free competitive market. In a well-functioning competitive market, as we saw in Chapter 4, the value of what buyers and sellers on average receive from their market exchanges equals the value of what they contribute. But when a market generates pollution, there are external costs that some people have to pay in addition to what they pay for the goods they receive from the market. These costs are unfair: They are costs the producer imposes on people (for example, the people who live near an electric plant that rains coal soot on them, forcing them to pay higher doctor bills and cleaning bills and to accept declining property values) and for which these people unfairly get nothing in return. (Pollution is also related to other forms of justice, as we will see later.)

Finally, it is also clear that pollution violates the rights that characterize a free competitive market. In a free competitive market, we noted in Chapter 4, all market exchanges are voluntary and so the market respects participants' negative right to choose the exchanges they will make. Moreover, people are free to enter or leave the market and no producer so dominates the market that it can force others to accept its terms. However, when a producer generates pollution, that producer imposes costs on people that they did not voluntarily choose, thereby violating their right to choose. Moreover, the victims of pollution were never given the choice to enter or leave the "market" in which they find themselves burdened with costs for which they get nothing in return. And because the producer dominates the exchange, the producer in effect forces its victims to accept its terms: i.e., pay its costs and get nothing in return.

Pollution, then, not only violates utility, but also violates justice and rights.

Remedies: The Duties of the Firm

The remedy for external costs, according to the preceding market analysis, is to ensure that the **costs of pollution are internalized**—that is, that they are absorbed by the producer and taken into account when determining the price of its goods.[120] In this way, goods will be accurately priced, market forces will provide the incentives that will encourage producers to minimize external costs, and some consumers will no longer end up paying more than others for the same commodities. Justice will once more reassert itself because the people who were being victimized by pollution costs no longer have to pay those costs, and people's rights will no longer be violated because they are no longer forced into exchanges they did not voluntarily choose.

internalization of the costs of pollution Absorption of external costs by the producer, who then takes them into account when determining the price of goods.

There are various ways to internalize the external costs of pollution. One way is for the polluting agent to pay to all of those being harmed, voluntarily or by law, an amount equal to the costs the pollution imposes on them. When Union Oil's drilling in the Santa Barbara channel on the California coast led to an oil spill, the total costs that the spill imposed on local residents and state and federal agencies were estimated at about $16,400,000 (including costs of cleanup, containment, administration, damage to tourism and fishing, recreational and property damages, and loss of marine life). Union Oil paid about $10,400,000 of these costs voluntarily by paying for all cleanup and containment of the oil, and it paid about $6,300,000 in damages to the affected parties as the result of litigation.[121] Thus, the costs of the oil spill were internalized, in part voluntarily and in part through legal enforcement. When the polluting firm pays those on whom its manufacturing processes impose costs, as Union Oil did, it is led to figure these costs into its own subsequent price determinations. Market mechanisms then lead it to come up with ways of cutting down pollution to cut down its costs. After the Santa Barbara oil spill, for example, Union Oil invested considerable amounts of money in developing methods to minimize pollution damage from its own oil spills. (Yet, as the British Petroleum Oil Spill in the Gulf of Mexico during the summer of 2010 showed, not all oil companies have made similar investments in the technology needed to deal with oil spills.)

A problem with this way of internalizing the costs of pollution, however, is that when several polluters are involved, it is not always clear just who is being damaged by whom. How much of the environmental damage caused by several polluters should be counted as damages to my property and how much should be counted as damages to your property, when the damages are inflicted on things such as air or public bodies of water, and for how much of the damage should each polluter be held responsible? Moreover, the administrative and legal costs of assessing damages for each distinct polluter and granting separate compensation to each distinct claimant (i.e., the transaction costs) can become substantial.

A second way of internalizing the costs of pollution is for the polluter to stop pollution at its source by installing pollution-control devices. In this way, the external costs of polluting the environment are translated into the internal costs the firm pays to install pollution controls. Once costs are internalized in this way, market mechanisms again provide cost-cutting incentives and ensure that prices reflect the true costs of producing the commodity. In addition, the installation of pollution-control devices serves to eliminate the long-range effects of pollution.

Justice

This way of dealing with pollution (i.e., by internalizing costs) also seems to be consistent with the requirements of distributive justice insofar as distributive justice favors equality. Observers have noted that pollution can increase inequality.[122] If a firm pollutes, its stockholders benefit because their firm does not have to absorb the external costs of pollution; this leaves them with greater profits. And those customers who purchase the firm's products also benefit because the firm does not charge them for all the social costs required to make the product. Therefore, the beneficiaries of pollution tend to be those who can afford to buy a firm's stock and its products. However, the external costs of pollution are borne largely by the poor—a phenomenon some have termed ***environmental injustice***.[123] Property values in polluted neighborhoods are generally lower, and consequently they are inhabited by the poor (not by choice but because they have no other option) and abandoned by the wealthy. Thus, pollution can produce a net flow of benefits away from the poor and toward the well-off, thereby increasing inequality. In addition, several studies have supported claims of ***environmental racism***: claims that pollution levels tend to be

environmental injustice The bearing of external costs of pollution largely by those who do not enjoy a net benefit from the activity that produces the pollution.

correlated with race so that the higher the proportion of racial minorities living in an area, the higher the likelihood that the area is subject to pollution. To the extent that pollution is correlated with income and race, pollution violates distributive justice. Internalizing the costs of pollution, as utilitarianism requires, would rectify matters by removing the burdens of external costs from the backs of minorities and the poor and placing them in the hands of the more wealthy: the firm's stockholders and its customers. By and large, therefore, the utilitarian claim that the external costs of pollution should be internalized is consistent with the requirements of distributive justice.

We must add an important qualification, however: if a firm makes basic goods (food products, clothing, gasoline, automobiles) for which the poor must allocate a larger portion of their budgets than the affluent, then internalizing costs may place a proportionately greater burden on the poor than on the affluent because the prices of these basic goods will rise. The poor may also suffer if the costs of pollution control rise so high that unemployment results (although as noted earlier, current studies indicate that the unemployment effects of pollution-control programs are transitory and minimal).[124] There is some rudimentary evidence that tends to show that current pollution-control measures place greater burdens on the poor than on the wealthy.[125] This suggests the need to integrate distributional criteria into our pollution-control programs.

Internalizing external costs also seems to be consistent with the requirements of retributive and compensatory justice.[126] Retributive justice requires that those who are responsible for and benefit from an injury should bear the burdens of rectifying the injury, whereas compensatory justice requires that those who have been injured should be compensated by those who injure them. Taken together, these requirements imply that (a) the costs of pollution control should be paid by those who cause pollution and who have benefited from pollution activities, whereas (b) the benefits of pollution control should flow to those who have had to bear the external costs of pollution. Internalizing external costs seems to meet these two requirements: (1) The costs of pollution control are borne by stockholders and customers, both of whom benefit from the polluting activities of the firm, and (2) the benefits of pollution control flow to those neighbors who once had to put up with the firm's pollution.

Costs and Benefits

The technology for pollution control has developed effective, but sometimes costly methods for reducing pollution. Up to 60 percent of water pollutants can be removed through primary screening and sedimentation processes, up to 90 percent can be removed through more expensive secondary biological and chemical processes, and amounts over 95 percent can be removed through even more expensive tertiary chemical treatment.[127] Air pollution abatement techniques include the use of fuels and combustion procedures that burn more cleanly; mechanical filters that screen or isolate dust particles in the air; scrubbing processes that pass polluted air through liquids that remove pollutants; and, most expensive of all, chemical treatment that transforms gases into more easily removed compounds.

It is possible, however, for a firm to invest too much in pollution-control devices, an issue that we briefly noted when discussing "absolute bans" on pollution. Suppose, for example, that the pollution from a certain firm causes $100 worth of environmental damage, and suppose that the only device that can eliminate this pollution would cost the firm at least $1,000. Then it would seem—at least from a utilitarian point of view—that the firm should not install the device; if it does so, the economic utility of society will decline: The costs of eliminating the pollution will be greater than the benefits society will reap, thereby resulting in a shrinkage of total utility.

How much should a firm invest in pollution control then? Consider that the costs of controlling pollution and the benefits derived from pollution control are inversely related.[128] As one rises, the other falls. Why is this so? Think for a moment that if a body of water is highly polluted, it will probably be quite easy and consequently, quite cheap to filter out a certain limited amount of pollutants. To filter out a few more pollutants, however, will require finer and, therefore, additional and more expensive filters. Costs will keep climbing for each additional level of purity desired, and getting out the last few molecules of impurities would require astronomically expensive additional equipment. However, getting out those last traces of impurities will probably not matter much to people and will be of little benefit. At the other end of the scale, however, getting rid of the first gross amounts of pollutants will be highly beneficial to people: The costs of damages from these pollutants are substantial. Consequently, if we plot as curves on a graph the costs of removing pollution and the benefits of removing pollution (which are equivalent to the external costs removed), the result will be two intersecting curves, as illustrated in Figure 5.9. What is the optimal amount of pollution control? Obviously, the point at which the two lines cross. At this point, the costs of pollution control exactly equal its benefits. If the firm invests additional resources in removing pollution, society's net utility will decline. Beyond this point, the firm should resort to directly or indirectly (i.e., through taxes or other forms of social investment) paying society for the costs of polluting the environment.

To enable the firm to make such cost-benefit analyses, researchers have devised an array of theoretical methods and techniques for calculating the costs and benefits of removing pollution. These make use of estimates of consumer surplus, rents, market prices and shadow prices, adjustment for transfers, discounted future values, and recognition of risk factors.[129] Thomas Klein summarized the procedures for cost-benefit analysis as follows:

1. Identify costs and benefits of the proposed program and the person or sectors incurring or receiving them. Trace transfers.
2. Evaluate the costs and benefits in terms of their value to beneficiaries and donors. The standard of measure is the value of each marginal unit to demanders and suppliers ideally captured in competitive prices. Useful refinements involve:
   (a) Incorporating time values through the use of a discount rate.
   (b) Recognizing risk by factoring possible outcomes according to probabilities and, where dependent, probability trees.
3. Add up costs and benefits to determine the net social benefit of a project or program.[130]

Figure 5.9

View the **Image** on **mythinkinglab.com**

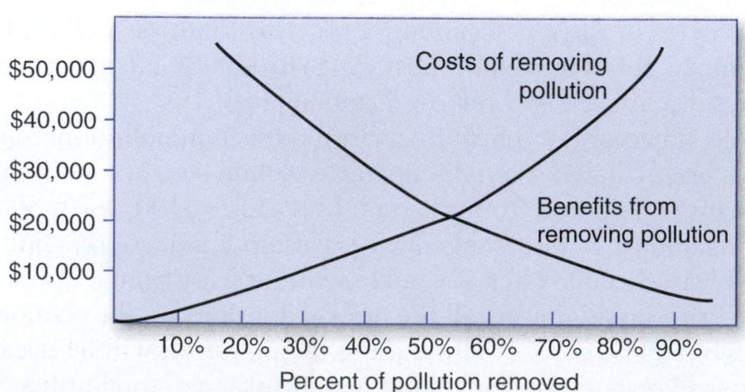

To avoid erratic and costly use of these procedures, Klein recommended that firms introduce a system of social accounting that "routinely measures, records, and reports external effects to management and other parties."[131]

It is at this point, however, that a fundamental difficulty in the utilitarian approach to pollution emerges. The cost-benefit analyses just described assume that the costs and benefits of reducing pollution can be accurately measured.[132] In some cases (limited and local in character), cost-benefit measurements are available. The costs and benefits of cleaning up the oil spilled by Union Oil at Santa Barbara several years ago, for example, were more or less measurable. However, the costs and benefits of pollution removal are difficult to measure when they involve damages to human health and loss of life: What is the price of life?[133]

Measurement is also difficult when the effects of pollution are uncertain and, consequently, difficult to predict: What will be the effects of increasing the carbon dioxide content of our atmosphere by burning more coal, as the United States is now starting to do? In fact, perhaps the major problem involved in obtaining the measurements needed to apply cost-benefit analysis to pollution problems is the problem of estimating and evaluating risk (i.e., the probability of future costly consequences).[134] Many new technologies carry with them unknown degrees of risk to present and future generations. Moreover, even if the risk associated with a new technology were known, it is unclear how much weight it should be given in a social cost-benefit analysis. Imagine, for example, that society currently accepts with some indifference a 0.01 risk of death associated with driving. Does it then follow that society also should be indifferent to accepting a 0.01 risk of death from the introduction of a certain new technology? Obviously not, because risk is cumulative: The new technology will *double* society's risk of death to 0.02. Although society may be indifferent to carrying a 0.01 risk of death, it may find a 0.02 risk unacceptable. Knowing the risk of a certain costly future event does not, then, necessarily tell us the value that society will place on that risk once it is added to the other risks society already runs. To add to the difficulties, individuals differ substantially in their aversion to risk: Some individuals like to gamble, whereas others find it distasteful.

Quick Review 5.9

Optimal Level of Pollution Removal in Utilitarian Approach

- Costs of removing pollutants rise as benefits of removal fall
- Optimal level of removal is point where its costs equal its benefits
- But when costs and benefits are not measurable, utilitarian approach fails
- When costs and benefits are not measurable some use the precautionary principle, others the maximin rule.

The almost insurmountable problems involved in getting accurate pollution measurements are illustrated by the few federal estimates of the benefits produced by pollution-control activities. The present financial *costs* of pollution control are fairly easy to obtain by examining reports on expenditures for pollution equipment. However, the *benefits* that these expenditures produce are difficult to measure accurately because these benefits are often unquantifiable. For example, the White House Office of Management and Budget (OMB) each year compiles estimates of the annual benefits and costs of major federal regulations (entitled *Report to Congress on the Costs and Benefits of Federal Regulations*). The OMB estimated that between 2000 and 2010, regulations limiting air pollution produced annual benefits of $77,300–$535,130 million and imposed costs of $19,500–$24,600 million, while regulations limiting water pollution produced annual benefits of $1,300–$3,900 million and imposed costs of $1,100–$1,200 million. Clearly, the OMB analysis showed that our air pollution laws generate significantly more benefits than costs, and that our water pollution laws probably generate more benefits than costs. Yet, the estimates of the OMB are based on uncertain methodologies, and they omit many of the important effects of pollution, such as the future costs imposed by long-range global effects of pollution like the effects of carbon dioxide buildup and ozone depletion, as well as the aesthetic benefits from the elimination of pollution. In addition, many regulations save lives, or extend life, or reduce the risk of death, and in all of these cases, the OMB is forced to make controversial assumptions about the value of human life.

social audit A report of the social costs and social benefits of the firm's activities.

The problems involved in getting accurate measurements of the benefits and costs of pollution control are also illustrated by the difficulties businesses have encountered in trying to construct a **social audit** (a report of the social costs and social benefits of the firm's activities). Those who advocate that a corporation should measure and report the social impacts of its activities have been forced to "recognize that the goal of measuring all impacts of all actions on all conditions and all publics, using standard techniques and units, considerably exceeds current capabilities and that compromises and modifications are inevitable."[135] As a result of this inability to measure benefits, so-called social audits are often nothing more than qualitative descriptions of what a firm is doing. Without definite quantitative measurements of the benefits deriving from its attempts to reduce pollution, however, a firm has no way of knowing whether its efforts are cost-effective from a social point of view.

These measurement difficulties pose significant technical problems for utilitarian approaches to pollution. In addition, the use of utilitarian cost-benefit analysis is sometimes based on assumptions that are inconsistent with people's moral rights. Advocates of utilitarian cost-benefit analysis sometimes assume that if the benefits of a certain technology or manufacturing process clearly outweigh its costs, then it is morally permissible to impose the process on unwilling citizens. For example, a government report makes the following recommendations:

> Because nuclear problems are such highly emotional issues and becoming even more so, as evidenced by the states that have indicated an unwillingness to permit nuclear waste disposal within their boundaries, it may be impossible to get the public and political support necessary for a given state to accept nuclear waste. Ultimately, if state approval for waste repository sites cannot be obtained within an established time, the federal government might have to mandate selections. While such action would not be easy it may be necessary if the waste problem is to be solved in a reasonable time.[136]

However, recommendations of this type seem to violate the basic moral right that underlies democratic societies: Persons have a moral right to be treated only as they have consented to be treated (see Chapter 2, second section). If people have not consented to take on the costs of a technology (and indicate this unwillingness, e.g., through local legislation, hearings, or opinion surveys), then their moral right of consent is violated when these costs are imposed on them anyway. Using only cost-benefit analysis to determine whether a new technology or manufacturing process should be adopted, then, ignores the question of whether the costs involved are voluntarily accepted by those who must bear them or whether they are unilaterally imposed on them by others in violation of their rights.

It should be noted that although the right of consent seems to imply that decisions concerning pollution control should always be left in the hands of the ordinary citizen, this implication is not always necessarily correct. People can give their informed consent to a risky project only if they have an adequate understanding of the project and its attendant risks. However, contemporary technology is often so complex that even experts disagree when estimating and assessing the risks it may involve (e.g., in the past scientists have disagreed wildly over the safety of using nuclear power). Therefore, it may be impossible for ordinary citizens to understand and assess the risks that a certain polluting technology will impose on them. Consequently, it may be impossible, in principle, for them to give their informed consent to it.

In view of all the problems raised by market or cost-benefit approaches to pollution, it may be that alternative approaches are more adequate. In particular, in light of all the uncertainties that cost-benefit analysis involves, it may be that the absolute bans on pollution that are still incorporated in many federal laws, and the rights theory on which these absolute bans rest, are a more adequate approach to pollution issues than utilitarian cost-benefit analysis, at least when costs and benefits are uncertain. That is, when the costs and benefits of cleaning up our pollution are uncertain, we should simply clean it up, provided only that it is feasible and affordable for us to do so.

Some argue that a similarly stringent approach is particularly necessary when the costs of a practice or technology are potentially catastrophic and irreversible (e.g., climate change). When potentially catastrophic and irreversible costs are involved, they claim, we should adopt the "precautionary principle." The ***precautionary principle*** says that if a practice or technology carries an unknown risk of catastrophic and irreversible consequences, but we are uncertain how large that risk is (maybe uncertain even whether there is any risk at all), then the practice or technology should be rejected until we are certain that the risk is nonexistent or insignificant. The precautionary principle has been adopted as a legal principle by the European Union (which includes almost all European nations), and has been endorsed in several environmental treaties. A weak version of the principle says it does not apply to a practice or technology unless there is scientific evidence that shows there is some likelihood it will lead to catastrophic harm. A strong version says the principle applies to any proposed practice or technology unless those who propose it provide scientific evidence that the practice or technology carries no risk of catastrophic harm. The weak version places the burden of proof (that there is some risk) on those who want to reject a possibly risky technology, while the strong version places the burden of proof (that there is no risk) on those who want to adopt possibly risky technology.

precautionary principle The principle that if a practice carries an unknown risk of catastrophic and irreversible consequences, but it is uncertain how large that risk is, then the practice should be rejected until it is certain the risk is nonexistent or insignificant.

Others suggest that when risks cannot be assessed, justice requires we identify those who are most vulnerable and who would have to bear the heaviest costs if things should go wrong, and then choose the option that will protect them from having to bear these costs. For example, future generations and those who are currently children are vulnerable to the choices we now make about greenhouse gas emissions and they will have to pay the most for global warming, so we should choose now only those options that we know will protect them from having to bear the costs of global warming. Finally, yet others suggest that when risks cannot be measured, the most rational procedure is to first assume that the worst will happen and then choose the option that leaves us best off when the worst happens (this is the so-called *maximin rule* of probability theory). For example, in making decisions about greenhouse gas emissions, we should first assume that the worst predictions about global warming are correct. Then, we should choose that option that will leave us best off on the assumption that the worse predictions about global warming will turn out to be correct.

It is unclear which, if any, of these alternative approaches should be adopted when we are uncertain whether the costs of our choices will be catastrophic. But it is clear that many environmental issues carry this kind of uncertainty, including: climate change, species extinctions, loss of biodiversity, spread of genetically modified organisms, and severe pollution.

Social Ecology, Ecofeminism, and the Demands of Caring

The difficulties inherent in cost-benefit and rights-based approaches to the ethical issues raised by environmental degradation have led many to look for alternative approaches. Some have argued, in fact, that cost-benefit and rights-based theories embody a kind of calculative and rationalistic way of thinking that is responsible for environmental crises. Cost-benefit thinking assumes that nature is to be measured and used efficiently, whereas rights-based theories see humans and other entities in individualistic terms and ignore their relationships with the rest of nature. These ways of thinking, it has been argued, are tightly linked to the kind of society in which we live.

social ecology The environmental crises we face are rooted in the social systems of hierarchy and domination that characterize our society.

Many thinkers have argued that the environmental crises we face are rooted in the social systems of hierarchy and domination that characterize our society. This view, now referred to as **social ecology**, holds that until those patterns of hierarchy and domination are changed, we will be unable to deal with environmental crises. In a hierarchical social system, one group holds power over another and members of the superior group are able to dominate those of the inferior group and get them to serve their ends. Examples of such systems of hierarchy include social practices such as racism, sexism, and caste systems, as well as social institutions such as property rights, capitalism, bureaucracies, and the mechanisms of government. Such systems of hierarchy and domination go hand in hand with the widespread environmental destruction taking place all around us and with economic ways of managing the environment. Murray Bookchin, the most well-known proponent of this view, wrote:

> We must look into the cultural forms of domination that exist in the family, between generations, sexes, racial and ethnic groups, in all institutions of political, economic, and social management, and, very significantly, in the way we experience reality as a whole, including nature and nonhuman life forms.[137]

Systems of hierarchy and domination, Bookchin suggested, facilitate the rise of a broad cultural mentality that encourages domination in many forms, including the domination of nature. Success becomes identified with dominance and control: The greater the number of people who work for a person, the greater that person's wealth, power, and status, and the more successful the person is deemed to be. Success also becomes identified with the domination of nature as society comes to identify "progress" with the increasing ability to control and dominate nature and its processes. Science, technology, and agriculture all join hands in this attempt to dominate and control nature. Weighing the costs and benefits of destroying nature is inevitable in this perspective. The widespread destruction of nature that results, then, cannot be halted until our societies become less hierarchical, less dominating, and less oppressive. The ideal society is one that rejects all domination and in which all power is decentralized. Agriculture and technology would be restricted to those kinds that are sustainable and which allow humans to live in harmony with nature.

ecofeminism Belief that the root of our ecological crisis lies in a pattern of domination of nature that is tightly linked to the social practices and institutions through which women have been subordinated to men.

Several feminist thinkers have argued that the key form of hierarchy connected to destruction of the environment is the domination of women by men. **Ecofeminism** has been described as "the position that there are important connections—historical, experiential, symbolic, theoretical—between the domination of women and the domination of nature, an understanding of which is crucial to both feminism and environmental ethics."[138] Ecofeminists have argued that the root of our ecological crisis lies in a pattern of domination of nature that is tightly linked to the social practices and institutions through which women have been subordinated to men. Underlying this subordination of women to men are ways of thinking that justify and perpetuate the subordination. One key pattern of thinking—the "logic of domination"—sets up dualisms (masculine–feminine, reason–emotion, artificial–natural, mind–body, objective–subjective) that are used to characterize men and women. Because of their roles in childbearing, childraising, and human sexuality, women are seen as more emotional, closer to nature and the body, and more subjective and passive, whereas men are masculine, more rational, builders of artifacts, and more objective and active. The masculine characteristics are then seen as superior to and more valuable than the feminine characteristics (reason, objectivity, and the mind are superior to emotion, subjectivity, and bodily feelings), and this is taken as justifying the subordination of women to men. This subordination of what is feminine in turn is transferred to nature, which is seen as feminine (for example, we refer to nature as "mother nature") and with which women are felt to be more closely associated. Thus, the domination of nature accompanies the domination of women, and as women are exploited for the interests of men, so too is nature.

If the forms of thinking that accompany hierarchy and domination are responsible for the destruction of the environment, with what should they be replaced? Social ecologists such as Bookchin have argued that humans should see themselves as stewards of nature, not as masters who should dominate nature. Some ecofeminists have argued that women should strive for an androgynous culture, which eradicates traditional gender roles and does away with the distinction between *feminine* and *masculine* that justifies a destructive domination of nature. Many ecofeminists have argued that instead one should try "to remedy ecological and other problems through the creation of an alternative 'women's culture'... based on revaluing, celebrating and defending what patriarchy has devalued, including the feminine, nonhuman nature, the body and the emotions."[139] In particular, some have argued, the destructive masculine perspective of domination and hierarchy must be replaced with the feminine perspective of caring.

From the perspective of an ethic of caring, the destruction of nature that has (supposedly) accompanied male hierarchies of domination must be replaced with caring for and nurturing our relationships to nature and living things. Nel Noddings, a feminist proponent of an ethic of care, argued that "when my caring is directed to living things, I must consider their natures, ways of life, needs, and desires. And, although I can never accomplish it entirely, I try to apprehend the reality of the other."[140] Although Noddings holds that the demands of caring extend only to those parts of nature that are living and with which one is directly related, others have extended the ethic of care to encompass relationships with all of nature. Karen Warren, for example, claims that ecofeminism gives a central role to "care, love, friendship, trust, and appropriate reciprocity," and that these relationships can be extended to nonhumans.[141] She suggests, for example, that a rock climber can have a "conqueror-type relationship" toward the rock or can, more appropriately, see it as a partner "whom one can come to care about and treat respectfully."

Quick Review 5.10

Alternative Approaches to Pollution

- Social Ecology says to get rid of social systems of hierarchy and domination
- Ecofeminism says change male pattern of dominating nature and women
- Some feminists say we should extend the ethic of care toward nature

Ecofeminists like Warren would hold that, although the concepts of utilitarianism, rights, and justice have a limited role to play in environmental ethics, an adequate environmental ethic must also take into account in a central manner the perspectives of an ethic of care. Nature must be seen as an "other" that can be cared for and with which one has a relationship that must be nurtured and attended to. Nature must not be seen as an object to be dominated, controlled, and manipulated.

Although social ecology and ecofeminist approaches to the environment are thought provoking, it is unclear what their specific implications may turn out to be. These approaches are still too recent to have been fully articulated. The shortcomings of utilitarian cost-benefit and rights-based approaches to the environment, however, may prompt a much fuller development of these approaches in the future.

5.3 The Ethics of Conserving Depletable Resources

Conservation refers to the saving or rationing of natural resources for later uses. Conservation, therefore, looks primarily to the future: to the need to limit consumption now to have resources available for tomorrow.

conservation The saving or rationing of natural resources for later uses.

In a sense, reducing pollution is a form of conservation. Pollution "consumes" pure air and water, and reducing pollution "conserves" them for the future. However, there are basic differences between the problems of pollution and the problems of resource depletion that makes the term *conservation* more applicable to the latter problems than to the former. With some notable exceptions (such as nuclear waste and, perhaps, greenhouse gases), most forms of pollution affect present generations, and reducing them will benefit present generations. The depletion of most scarce resources, however, lies far in the future, and the effects of their depletion will be felt primarily by posterity and not by present generations. Consequently, our concern over the depletion of resources is to a large extent a concern for future generations and for the benefits that will be available to them. For this reason, conservation is more applicable to the problems of resource depletion than to those of pollution. Moreover (again with notable exceptions), pollution is a problem concerned primarily with "renewable" resources, insofar as air and water can be "renewed" by ceasing to dump pollutants into them and allowing them time to recover. Tomorrow's supply, therefore, will be created anew over and over if we take the proper precautions. Resource depletion, however, is concerned with finite, nonrenewable resources. The only store of a finite, nonrenewable resource that will be around tomorrow is that which is left over from today. Conservation, therefore, is the only way of ensuring a supply for tomorrow's generations. Resource depletion forces two main kinds of questions on us: Why should we conserve resources for future generations? How much should we conserve?

Rights of Future Generations

Quick Review 5.11

Arguments Against Attributing Rights to Future Generations

- Future generations do not now exist and may never exist.
- If future generations have rights then the present must be sacrificed for the future.
- Because we do not know what interests future generations will have, we cannot say what rights they have.

It might appear that we have an obligation to conserve resources for future generations because they have an equal right to the limited resources of this planet. If future generations have an equal right to the world's resources, then by depleting these resources, we are taking what is actually theirs and violating their right to these resources.

A number of writers, however, have claimed that although we should have concern for future generations, it is a mistake to think that the reason why we should have concern for them is because future generations have rights.[142] Consequently, it is a mistake to think that the reason we should refrain from consuming natural resources is because we are taking what future generations have a "right" to. Three main arguments have been advanced to show that it is wrong to justify our concern for future generations by attributing rights to those generations.

First, future generations cannot coherently be said to have rights because they do not now exist and may never exist.[143] I may be able to think about future people, but I cannot hit them, punish them, injure them, or treat them wrongly. Future people presently exist only in the imagination, and imaginary entities cannot be acted on in any way whatsoever except in imagination. Similarly, we cannot say that future people possess things now when they do not yet exist to possess or have them. Because there is a possibility that future generations may never exist, they cannot "possess" rights.

Second, if future generations did have rights, we might be led to the absurd conclusion that we must sacrifice our entire civilization for their sake.[144] Suppose that each of the infinite number of future generations had an equal right to the world's supply of oil. Then, we would have to divide the oil equally among them all, and our share would be a few quarts at the most. We would then be put in the absurd position of having to shut down our entire Western civilization so that each future person might be able to possess a few quarts of oil.

Third, we can say that someone has a certain right only if we know that he or she has a certain interest which that right protects. The purpose of a right, after all, is to protect the interests of the right holder, but we are virtually ignorant of what interests future generations will have. What wants will they have? The men and women of the future may be genetically fabricated to order, with desires, pleasures, and needs vastly different from our own. What kinds of resources will future technology require for supplying their wants? Science might come up with technologies for creating products from raw materials that we have in abundance—minerals in seawater, for example—and might find potentially unlimited energy sources such as nuclear fusion. Moreover, future generations might develop cheap and plentiful substitutes for the scarce resources that we now need. Because we are uncertain about these matters, we must remain ignorant about the interests future generations will want to protect. (Who could have guessed 80 years ago that uranium rocks would one day be considered a "resource" in which people would have an interest?) Consequently, we are unable to say what rights future people might have.[145]

If these arguments are correct, then to the extent that we are uncertain what future generations will exist or what they will be like, they cannot be said to have rights. It does not follow, however, that we have no obligations to future generations because we may have obligations that are based not on rights, but on other kinds of moral considerations.

Justice to Future Generations

John Rawls argued that, although it is unjust to impose disproportionately heavy burdens on present generations for the sake of future generations, it is also unjust for present generations to leave nothing for future generations. To determine a just way of distributing resources between generations, he suggested, the members of each generation should put themselves in the "original position" and, without knowing what generation they belong to, they should do the following:

> ask what is reasonable for members of adjacent generations to expect of one another at each level of (historical) advance. They should try to piece together a just savings schedule by balancing how much at each stage (of history) they would be willing to save for their immediate descendants against what they would feel entitled to claim of their immediate predecessors. Thus, imagining themselves to be parents, say, they are to ascertain how much they would set aside for their children by noting what they would believe themselves entitled to claim of their own parents.[146]

In general, Rawls claims that this method of ascertaining what earlier generations in justice owe to later generations will lead to the conclusion that what justice demands of us is merely that we hand to the next generation a situation no worse than we received from the generation before us:

> Each generation must not only preserve the gains of culture and civilization, and maintain intact those just institutions that have been established, but it must also put aside in each period of time a suitable amount of real capital accumulation. . . . (It should be kept in mind here that capital is not only factories, and machines, and so on, but also the knowledge and culture, as well as the techniques and skills, that make possible just institutions and the fair value of liberty.) This . . . is in return for what is received from previous generations that enables the later ones to enjoy better life in a more just society.[147]

Justice, then, requires that we hand over to our immediate successors a world that is not in worse condition than the one we received from our ancestors.[148]

The demands of caring that arise from an ethic of care would also suggest conservation policies that are similar to those advocated by Rawls's views on justice. Although

Quick Review 5.12

Conservation Based on Justice

- Rawls: Leave the world no worse than we found it
- Care Ethic: Leave our children a world no worse than we received
- Attfield: Leave the world as productive as we found it.

most people would agree that they have a fairly direct relationship of care and concern with the generation that immediately succeeds their own, such a direct relationship does not exist with more distant and so more abstract generations. The generation that immediately succeeds our own, for example, consists of our own children. The demands of caring, we have seen, imply that one should attempt to see matters from the perspective of those with whom we are thus directly related and that we attempt to care for their specific needs. Such caring would imply that we should at least leave the immediately succeeding generation a world that is not worse than the one we received.

Rawls's conclusion is also supported by some utilitarian reasoning. For example, Robin Attfield, a utilitarian, argued that utilitarianism favors what he called the *Lockean principle* that "each should leave enough and as good for others."[149] Attfield interpreted this principle to mean that each generation must leave for future generations a world whose output capacity is no less than that generation received from previous generations.[150] That is, each generation must leave the world no less productive than it found it. Attfield suggested that leaving the world with the same output capacity does not necessarily mean leaving the world with the same resources. Instead, maintaining the same level of output can be achieved either through conservation, recycling, or technological innovation.

ON THE EDGE

Exporting Poison

According to a 2001 study by the Foundation for Advancements in Science and Education in the *International Journal of Occupational and Environmental Health*, U.S. companies export 45 tons of pesticides per hour to other nations, including highly toxic chemicals such as alachlor, chlordane, heptachlor, and metribuzin. The United States banned the use of chlordane and heptachlor as an insecticide on crops or around residences 10 to 20 years ago. Velsicol Chemical Corporation, however, reported in 1997 that it was still manufacturing chlordane and heptachlor for export. It exported these chemicals to Africa for use on roads, to Australia and Far Eastern countries to spray in residences, and to South America to use on crops. Between 1997 and 2000, U.S. companies exported about 65 million pounds of pesticides that are banned or severely restricted in the United States—including captafol, chlordane, isazofos, monocrotophos, and mirex—and about 30 tons a day of pesticides the World Health Organization (WHO) classifies as "extremely hazardous." Every hour, U.S. companies export about 16 tons of pesticides known or suspected to cause cancer. Sixty percent of these pesticides are shipped to developing nations for use in agriculture. Over 75 percent of working children in developing nations work in agriculture, including 80 million in Africa, 152 million in Asia, and 17 million in Latin America. They are exposed daily to U.S. pesticides in the fields, in their drinking water, and on their clothes. Farmers in developing nations pour pesticides labeled "poison" into small containers without labels, which many workers in developing nations cannot read anyway.

1. Does an American company like Velsicol have any obligation to refrain from selling pesticides that are banned in the United States to developing nations where they are not banned?
2. Does a U.S. company like Velsicol have an obligation to refrain from exporting chemicals that are only suspected of causing cancer?
3. Whose responsibility is it to ensure citizens of developing nations are not harmed by exports of pesticides?

Other utilitarians have reached slightly different but still similar conclusions by relying on other basic utilitarian principles. Utilitarians have argued that each generation has a duty to maximize the future beneficial consequences of its actions and to minimize their future injurious consequences.[151] However, utilitarians have claimed that these future consequences should be "discounted" (given less weight) in proportion to their uncertainty and to their distance in the future.[152] Together, these utilitarian principles imply that we at least have an obligation to avoid those practices whose harmful consequences for the generation that immediately follows us are certain to outweigh the beneficial consequences our own generation derives from them. Our responsibility for more distant future generations, however, is diminished especially insofar as we are unable to foresee what effects our present actions will have on them because we do not know what needs or technology they will have.

When considering problems of resource depletion, some observers have suggested that we should rely on market forces to determine what we should do with the resources we have. Unfortunately, we cannot rely on market mechanisms (e.g., rising prices) to ensure that scarce resources are conserved for future generations. The market registers only the effective demands of present participants and the actual supplies presently being made available in the market. The needs and demands of future generations, as well as the potential scarcities that lie far in the future, are so heavily "discounted" by markets that they hardly affect prices at all.[153] William Shepherd and Clair Wilcox provide several other reasons why the private choices of businesses in markets will fail to take into account the future scarcity of resources including: (1) businesses try to consume resources quickly before competitors do, (2) businesses have short time horizons, (3) the future is difficult for businesses to predict, and (4) businesses tend to ignore externalities.[154] The only means of conserving for the future, then, appear to be voluntary (or politically enforced) policies of conservation.

In practical terms, Rawls's view implies that, although we should not sacrifice the advances we have made, we should adopt voluntary or legal measures to conserve those resources and environmental benefits that we can reasonably assume our immediate posterity will need if they are to live lives comparable, at least, to our own. In particular, this would mean that we should preserve wildlife and endangered species, that we should take steps to ensure that the rate of consumption of fossil fuels and minerals does not continue to rise, that we should cut down our consumption and production of those goods that depend on nonrenewable resources, that we should recycle nonrenewable resources, and that we should search for substitutes for materials that we are too rapidly depleting.

Sustainability The conclusion that Rawls, Attfield, and others have arrived at, then, is that we are obligated to do what we can to ensure that we leave the next generation a world that is no worse than the one we received from the generation previous to ours. This conclusion is very similar to what has been characterized as the obligation of sustainability. Unfortunately, there are hundreds of definitions of sustainability.[155] Generally, sustainability means the ability to sustain—i.e., to continue or to maintain—something into the future. ***Sustainability***, then, refers to the capacity something (a thing, a quality, an activity, a system, etc.) has to continue to function into the future. The term was popularized by the UN Commission on Development and the Environment that said in its 1987 Brundtland Report: "Humanity has the ability to make development sustainable—to ensure that it meets the needs of the present without compromising the ability of future generations to meet their own needs."[156] The Brundtland Report specified the kind of functioning that we want to continue into the future when we talk about sutainability, i.e., the function of meeting present and future needs. In light of this report, sustainability is now

Sustainability The capacity something has to continue to function into the future.

environmental sustainability The capacity of the natural environment to continue to meet the needs of present generations without compromising the ability of future generations to meet their needs from that environment.

Quick Review 5.13

Sustainability

- It is the view that we must deal with the environment, society, and economy so that they have the capacity to continue to meet the needs of present generations without compromising the ability of future generations to meet their own needs.
- Environmental sustainability, economic sustainability, and social sustainability are interdependent.
- Environmental sustainability implies not depleting renewable resources faster than their replacement; not creating more pollution than environment can absorb; not depleting non-renewable resources faster than we find replacements.
- Technology pessimists say science will not find substitutes for all renewable resources so we must conserve and reduce consumption to achieve sustainability.
- Technology optimists say science will find such substitutes so sustainability requires neither conservation nor reducing consumption.

widely understood to refer to the capacity something has to continue to meet the needs of present generations without compromising the ability of future generations to also meet their needs. Here we are concerned with the environment and in this context, we can say that ***environmental sustainability*** refers to the capacity of the natural environment to continue to meet the needs of present generations without compromising the ability of future generations to meet their needs from that environment.

The concept of sustainability, however, is now commonly interpreted as encompassing more than just environmental concerns. Sustainability is often said to depend on "three pillars": our economic activities, our social activities, and our environmental activities. These three domains are seen as interrelated and dependent on each other, so that sustainability in any one domain is possible only if the other domains are sustainable. The way that we organize and carry out our economic activities, for example, affects the environment, yet what happens to the environment in turn affects our economic activities. We can, for example, pursue economic growth through manufacturing processes that rapidly deplete our natural resources and pollute the natural world, while the depletion of our environmental resources and continued degradation of the environment, in turn, can limit or prevent us from pursuing economic growth. Our social arrangements similarly affect and are affected by the environment. The lifestyles we adopt, the number of children we have, and the kinds of things our society teaches us to want, for example, can all produce levels of consumption that ravage the environment, and, in turn, a ravaged environment can lead to impoverished and unhealthy lives, families, and societies. Economic sustainability, then, requires structuring our economy so that we produce and distribute goods on a scale and in a way that does not undercut environmental sustainability, and social sustainability requires creating societies that allow us to develop cultures, communities, and ways of life that respect and nurture environmental sustainability so that the environment continues to provide that on which our lives depend.

It is important to see that environmental sustainability depends on social and economic sustainability. It is also important to grasp how our social arrangements—our lifestyles and consumption patterns—as well as our economic practices—the way we manufacture goods and use our resources—all affect the environment. But in this chapter on the environment, our focus has been and will continue to be environmental sustainability. What, exactly, does the obligation of environmental sustainability require? The environmentalist Herman Daly argued that environmental sustainability requires three specific things:[157]

1. renewable resources should not be depleted at a rate that is greater than their rate of replacement;
2. the emission rate of pollution should not exceed the capacity of the environment to cleanse and assimilate that pollution;
3. non-renewable resources should be depleted at a rate no greater than the creation of renewable alternatives.

The first two items on this list are widely accepted. That is, most people accept that we should not use up renewable resources faster than they can be renewed. We should not consume fish stocks, forests, clean air, and so on, faster than they can renew themselves or they will eventually completely disappear, as many of these already have. Most people also accept the second item, i.e., that we should not generate more pollution than the environment can absorb for otherwise it will start to pile up and eventually suffocate us. However, the third item on this list is more controversial.

Many people reject the third item if it is interpreted to mean that we should limit our use of nonrenewable resources such as oil and minerals until we have found substitutes that are "renewable." Technology optimists, in particular, believe that as we deplete our natural non-renewable resources (iron, copper, oil, etc.), science will develop new synthetic substitutes for them. As we use up a resource like oil, for example, its supply will fall and it will become more expensive. This will provide economic incentives that will prompt us to develop a technology capable of serving as a cheaper substitute for oil like, perhaps, nuclear fusion. So we do not have to worry about the rate at which we use up our non-renewable resources because science will find substitutes for them if and when they start to run out. Moreover, technology optimists believe that we must not hamper the development of new technologies since that is what will enable us to find the substitutes we may need. Sustainability, then, does not require conservation of nonrenewable resources, while it does require encouraging the development of new technologies.

On the other hand, technology pessimists accept item number 3 because they believe that as we deplete our nonrenewable resources, we are unlikely to be able to develop adequate technological substitutes. As we use up our nonrenewable resources, human welfare may simply decline. Technology pessimists, then, believe that because our nonrenewable resources are limited and because we will likely find no technological substitutes for many of them, our future is bleak unless we reduce our use of these resources by significantly cutting consumption and simplifying our lifestyles. Moreover, we can stretch out the time before things run out by trying not to deplete any nonrenewable resource for which we have not yet actually found a substitute. And this, of course, requires conservation. For the technology pessimist, then, sustainability requires significantly lowering our levels of consumption and conserving our nonrenewable resources. Many technology pessimists also believe that technology is not a future solution, but is, in fact, part of our current problem because it is what has led us to increase our consumption and pollute our environment.

Although there is some controversy about how sustainability can be achieved, it is clear that the idea of sustainability is consistent with the ethical judgment of Rawls and Attfield that we should leave our children a world that is no worse than the one our parents left us. This means, specifically, that we must not consume renewable resources faster than they can renew themselves, and that we must not produce more pollution than the environment can absorb. How we interpret a third point—that we should not deplete nonrenewable resources faster than our technology can develop adequate substitutes—depends on whether you are a technological optimist or a technological pessimist.

Economic Growth?

To many observers, even conservation measures will fall far short of what is needed to ensure sustainability. Several environmentalists have argued that if we are to preserve enough of our limited nonrenewable and non-substitutable resources so that future generations can maintain their quality of life at a level similar to ours, we shall have to change our economies substantially, particularly by scaling down our pursuit of economic growth. E. F. Schumacher, for example, claimed that the industrialized nations will have to convert from growth-oriented, capital-intensive technologies to much more labor-intensive technologies in which humans do work machines now do.[158] Others argue that economic systems will have to abandon their goal of steadily increasing production and put in its place the goal of decreasing production until it has been scaled down to "a steady state"—that is, a point at which "the total population and the total stock of physical wealth are maintained constant at some desired levels by a 'minimal'

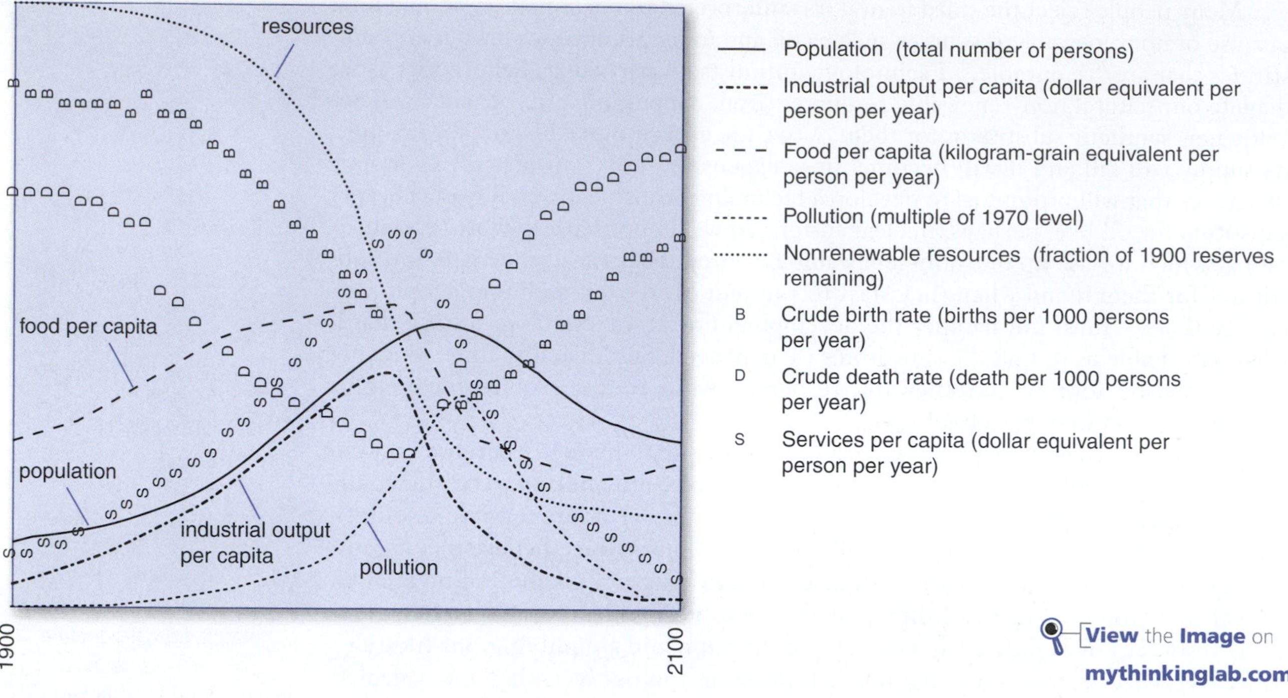

View the Image on mythinkinglab.com

Figure 5.10
The "standard" world model run assumes no major change in the physical, economic, or social relationships that have historically governed the development of the world system. All variables plotted here follow historical values from 1900 to 1970. Food, industrial output, and population grow exponentially until the rapidly diminishing resource base forces a slowdown in industrial growth. Because of natural delays in the system, both population and pollution continue to increase for some time after the peak of industrialization. Population growth is finally halted by a rise in the death rate due to decreased food and medical services.

Source: From Donella H. Meadows et al., *The Limits to Growth* (New York: Universe Books, 1974), pp. 123–24. Reprinted by permission of Universe Books.

rate of maintenance throughout (that is, by birth and death rates that are equal at the lowest feasible level, and by physical production and consumption rates that are equal at the lowest feasible level)."[159] The conclusion that economic growth must be abandoned if society is to be able to deal with the problems of diminishing resources, however, has been challenged.[160] On the other hand, it is at least arguable that adherence to continual economic growth will end up degrading the quality of life of future generations and possibly the later life of the current generation.[161]

The arguments for this last claim are simple, stark, and controversial. If the world's economies continue to pursue the goal of economic growth, the demand for nonrenewable resources will continue to rise. Because the stock of nonrenewable resources are finite and some, at least, will have no substitutes, at some point supplies will simply run out, many pessimists claim. At this point, if the world's nations are still based on growth economies, we can expect a collapse of their major economic institutions (i.e., of manufacturing and financial institutions, communication networks, the service industries), which in turn will bring down their political and social institutions (i.e., centralized governments, education and cultural programs, scientific and technological development, health care).[162] Living standards will then decline sharply in the wake of widespread starvation and political dislocations. Various scenarios for this sequence of events have been constructed, all of them more or less speculative and necessarily based on uncertain assumptions.[163] The most famous and oldest of these are the studies of the Club of Rome, which three decades ago projected on computers the catastrophic results of continuing the economic growth patterns of the past in the face of declining resources and rising pollution.[164] Later studies came to similar conclusions.[165] Figure 5.10 reproduces one of the original computer projections of the Club of Rome.

In the computer-based graph of Figure 5.10, the horizontal axis represents time; as we run from the year A.D. 1900 at the left to the year A.D. 2100 at the right, we see what will happen to the world's population, industrial output, food, pollution levels, nonrenewable resources, and so on as time passes. During the first half of the 1900s, population, output, food, and services continue to grow while death rates, birth rates, and resources decline. At some point after 2050, however, a catastrophic collapse of output and services occurs as key resources decline. Population continues to rise, but a climbing death rate and declining food supply soon brings it down. The decline in industrial output causes a decline in pollution, but food supplies, industrial output, and population by 2100 are below 1900 levels. "We can thus say with some confidence that, under the assumption of no major change in the present system, population and industrial growth will certainly stop within the next century at the latest."[166]

The assumptions on which the doomsday scenarios of the Club of Rome and other groups were based have often been criticized.[167] The computer programs and underlying equations on which the predictions were based made controversial and highly uncertain assumptions about future population growth rates, the absence of future increases in output per unit of input, our inability to find substitutes for nonrenewable resources, and the ineffectiveness of recycling. These assumptions can all be challenged. Although future generations will certainly have fewer of the nonrenewable resources on which we depend, we cannot be sure exactly what impact this will have on them. Perhaps, the impact will not be as catastrophic nor will it occur as early as the forecasts of the Club of Rome indicated (although the number of researchers predicting a catastrophic future is rising, due particularly to a growing belief that we will not be able to control our emissions of greenhouse gases and the consequent rise in global temperatures).[168] On the other hand, we cannot assume that the impact will be entirely benign, or that there will be no major environmental disruptions in our lifetimes.[169] Some observers are again coming to the conclusion that the Club of Rome may have been substantially correct, even if its timetables were quite obviously mistaken. The increasing pace of species extinctions, the global rise in temperature attributable to rising levels of greenhouse gases, the continuing decimation of forests, and the still increasing rates of population growth all point to a difficult future for us. Given the extreme uncertainties in our situation, at the very least a commitment to conservation seems to be in order. Whether a wholesale transformation of our economy is also necessary if civilization is to survive is a difficult and disturbing question that we may soon have to face.

Just as troubling are the moral questions raised by the distribution of dwindling energy supplies and other resources among the world's peoples that policies of economic growth in developed nations have created. The United States, European nations, and Japan are among the world's richest developed nations and the highest consumers of energy. The 6 percent of the world's population that lives within the United States, for example, consumes 25 percent of the world's annual energy supplies, whereas the 50 percent of the world's people who inhabit less-developed nations must get along with about 8 percent of its energy supplies. Each person in the United States, in fact, consumes 15 times more energy than a native South American, 24 times more than a native Asian, and 31 times more than a native African.

The high energy consumption rates of Americans, Europeans, and the Japanese are not paralleled by similarly high rates of energy production. In fact, their energy

Quick Review 5.14

Economic Growth

- Schumacher claims we must abandon the goal of economic growth if we are to allow future generations to live as we do.
- Some argue we must achieve a "steady state" where births equal deaths and production equals consumption and these remain constant at their lowest feasible level.
- Club of Rome computer models suggested continued economic growth will deplete resources and increase pollution until industrial output, food production, and services decline, causing catastrophic population loss sometime during the twenty-first century.
- Troubling moral questions are raised by the economic growth policies that have led to high rates of energy and resource consumption in developed nations while developing nations are left to consume at low rates.

consumption is subsidized by other countries, in particular by the Caribbean, the Middle East, and Africa. That is, there is a net flow of energy out of these less-consuming populations and into the high-consumption population of the United States and other developing nations. Moreover, the people of the developed world use much of the energy supplies available to them for inessentials (unneeded products, unnecessary travel, household comforts, and conveniences), whereas the more frugal nations tend to use their supplies to meet basic needs (food, clothing, housing).

In view of the approaching scarcity of energy resources, these comparisons cannot help but raise the question of whether the high-consumption nations are morally justified in continuing the economic growth policies that lead them to appropriate for their own use the nonrenewable resources of other, more frugal nations that are too weak economically to use these resources or too weak militarily to protect them. Any attempt to answer this question obviously requires a detailed inquiry into the nature of the world's social, economic, and political systems—an inquiry that is beyond the scope of this book. The question, however, is one that events may also soon force us to face.[170]

Study and **Review** on **mythinkinglab.com**

Questions for Review and Discussion

1. Define the following concepts: pollution, toxic substance, nuclear waste, exponential depletion, peaked depletion, free good, unlimited good, ecological system, ecological ethic, right to a livable environment, absolute ban, private costs, social costs, external costs, to internalize costs, cost-benefit analysis, risk, social audit, right of consent, conservation, rights of future generations, justice toward future generations, multiple access, time preference, doomsday scenario, high-consumption nation.
2. Define the main forms of pollution and resource depletion and identify the major problems associated with each form.
3. Compare and contrast the views of (a) an ecological ethic, (b) Blackstone's ethic of environmental rights, and (c) a utilitarian ethic of pollution control. Which view seems to you to be the more adequate? Explain your answer.
4. Do you agree with the claims that (a) future generations have no rights, and (2) the future generations to which we have obligations actually include only the generation that will immediately succeed us? Explain your answer. If you do not agree with these claims, state your own views, and provide arguments to support them.
5. In your judgment, should the major decisions on pollution and resource depletion (especially energy policy) be made by government experts? By scientific experts? By everyone? Provide moral arguments in support of your judgment.
6. "Any pollution law is unjust because it necessarily violates people's right to liberty and right to property." Discuss.
7. In their book *Energy Future*, R. Strobaugh and D. Yergin claimed that in the debate over nuclear power "the resolution of differing opinions over how to deal with uncertainty, over how much risk is acceptable, or how safe is safe enough—all require judgments in which values play as large a role as scientific facts" (p. 100). Discuss this claim.

Web Resources

Readers interested in researching environmental issues through the Internet should begin with the Envirolink web page, which has links to numerous Internet resources (*http://www.envirolink.org*). The EPA also provides numerous links and its own ample database (*http://www.epa.gov*), as does the Office of Ocean and Coastal Resource Management (*http://oceanservice.noaa.gov*) and the UN Environment Program (*http://www.unep.org*). Several environmental organizations and journals are accessible through the Essential Organization web page (*http://www.essential.org*). Other links are provided by the Greenmoney fund (*http://www.greenmoney.com*), the Worldwatch Institute (*http://www.worldwatch.org*), and Solcomhouse (*http://www.solcomhouse.com*).

CASES

Explore the Concept on mythinkinglab.com

The Ok Tedi Copper Mine[1]

Paul Anderson, chief executive officer of Broken Hill Proprietary Company Limited (BHP) was unsure what to do. In November. 1998. he had left Duke Energy Corporation in the United States and moved to Australia with his wife, Kathy, to take over as CEO of BHP, a global mining company. Only a year and a half later, he was faced with having to decide how to manage what was being called one of the world's greatest ongoing "environmental disasters," a pollution catastrophe that was even then being created by BHP's Ok Tedi copper mine in the western part of Papua New Guinea. BHP owned 52 percent of the mine, the government of Papua New Guinea owned 30 percent, and Inmet Mining Corporation, a Canadian company, owned 18 percent.

For almost two decades, the mine had been discharging 80,000 tons of mine tailings and 120,000 tons of waste rock a day into the Ok Tedi River, which flows into the Fly River, which in turn meanders through the western part of Papua New Guinea before flowing through a large delta into the sea. The ongoing buildup of wastes was destroying the ecology of the tropical rain forests and wetlands through which the rivers flowed and had already devastated 120 riverside villages, whose 50,000 inhabitants had depended on the rivers for subsistence fishing and farming. The villagers and the government of Papua New Guinea were now economically dependent on the mine. Because of their dependence on the mine, they did not want the mine to shut down even though it continued to dump 200,000 tons of waste daily into the Ok Tedi River and continued wreaking havoc on the environment. In September, 1999, BHP had begun discussing its options with the government of Papua New Guinea, but by January, 2000, the company had not yet decided what it would do about the growing tragedy. Anderson was anxious to resolve the issue by the end of the year.

BHP (renamed BHP Billiton since its 2001 merger with Billiton PLC.) was founded in Australia in 1885 as a natural resources company engaged in the discovery, development, production, and marketing of iron ore, steel, coal, copper, oil and gas, diamonds, silver, gold, lead, zinc, and other natural resources. By the twentieth century, the company had become a global leader in its three main operating businesses: minerals, petroleum, and steel. Headquartered in Melbourne, Australia, the company had about 30,000 employees worldwide.

In 1976, Papua New Guinea chose BHP to develop a mine to exploit the large copper deposits discovered in 1963 on the western side of Papua New Guinea in the interior highlands. Papua New Guinea occupies the eastern half of the island of New Guinea (the other half belongs to Indonesia), just 150 miles from the northernmost tip of Australia. The deposits were located in the Star Mountains region in the center of the island along the border with Indonesia. The mine would be located on Mount Fubilan, which is about 1,800 meters above sea level at the headwaters of the Ok Tedi River, whose waters flow south, down into the Fly River, through lowlands, and on over an immense delta to finally empty into the Gulf of Papua on the Coral Sea.

The previous year, in 1975, Papua New Guinea had won its independence from Australia. Its new and inexperienced government was eager to prove itself in the face of high expectations from its people and pressures from the World Bank and the International Monetary Fund. The government wanted to use the income from mining to develop infrastructure and services for its people.

Papua New Guinea is a rugged tropical island covered with rain forests inhabited by several population groups. Isolated from each other by the high rugged mountains and dense forests, the groups had developed fascinating and distinctive tribal cultures and different languages. The tribes living on the southern part of the island, for example, were once notorious for cannibalism and headhunting, whereas the Huli, discovered in 1954 in the interior, were peaceful people who wore spectacular wigs embellished with feathers, human hair, flowers, and fur. Many tribespeople today continue to live traditional lives in hundreds of small villages scattered in virtually inaccessible areas throughout the island. Along the Ok Tedi and Fly River drainage area lived an estimated 73,500 villagers whose subsistence life style was based on traditional gardening, hunting, and fishing centered on the river. There were few schools, no health care, and little infrastructure such as paved highways, public buildings, electricity, etc. Child mortality was high and life expectancy short. Ecologists called the island a "botanical treasure" because its pristine rain forests, mountains, rivers, and surrounding coral reefs are home to a multitude of rare plants, animals, birds, and insects. Fish abounded in its rivers, which are used as waterways by canoeing natives who grow food gardens along the banks.

In 1976, the government of Papua New Guinea passed the Ok Tedi Agreement Mining Act, which defined the obligations and rights related to the development of the Ok Tedi Mine. In 1980, the government officially granted permission for the formation of the group that became the Ok Tedi Mining Limited Company (OTML), a joint-venture company established to develop the Ok Tedi Mine. The mine would use conventional open-pit mining techniques to extract annually about 30 million tons of copper ore and 55 million tons of waste rock. The 1976 Mining Act required that conventional environmental controls would be used by the Ok Tedi Mining Limited Company to minimize environmental damage, including a large storage facility behind a dam that would be used to hold about 80 percent of the tailings and waste produced by the mine. (Tailings are fine sands left over after the ore containing a mineral is crushed and the mineral removed.) Construction of the tailings storage facility began in 1983, about a year before the mine was scheduled to open. However, in 1984, a large landslide destroyed the foundations of the storage dam. The Ok Tedi Mining Limited Company proposed to the government that it be allowed to proceed temporarily without the storage facility since otherwise the mine would not be able to open as scheduled. The government of Papua New Guinea agreed and passed the Interim Tailings License Act, which allowed the mine to begin operation without a waste storage facility.

In 1984, the mine started operating and began discharging its waste rock and tailings into the Ok Tedi River. The ore not only contained copper but had significant quantities of gold and silver. BHP now commissioned a study of the area where the storage facility was to be built and discovered that a storage dam built in the vicinity would probably collapse again. The area was prone to landslides, frequent earthquakes of magnitude 7.0 on the Richter scale, and huge quantities of rainfall throughout the year. The company reported this to the government, which agreed in 1986 to pass the "Eighth Supplemental Agreement," which licensed the company to defer construction of a permanent waste storage facility; this license was renewed in 1988 and was never revoked. All water, rock, and tailings produced by the mining operations were now flowing directly into the Ok Tedi River and downstream into the Fly River.

The effects on the rain forests surrounding the Ok Tedi and Fly Rivers were evident by the late 1980s when the sediment levels of the rivers more than quadrupled, from their previous natural level of 100 parts per million to 450–500 parts per million. In many places, the sediment and rock raised the level of the river bed by 5–6 meters, increasing the frequency of flooding and overflows. Over the years, repeated rains and floods carried the sediment onto the floor of the forests surrounding the rivers. The sediment on the forest floors was waterlogged, reducing the oxygen level in the soil, starving the roots of trees and vegetation, and gradually killing them (an effect called *dieback*). The area of forest dieback grew from 18 square kilometers in 1992 to 480 square kilometers in 2000 and was predicted to eventually increase to between 1,278 square kilometers and 2,725 square kilometers.

Since the mining operations extracted only 80 percent of the copper, the rest was flowing into the river, where dissolved copper levels now rose, sometimes exceeding 0.02 milligrams per liter. Fish in the rivers declined by 90 percent, a possible result of the increased copper levels, or of sedimentation, or of a loss of food supplies.

The sediments and mud deposited by flooding ruined the garden crops of villagers (mostly from the Yonggom tribe) living along the rivers. Canoes became difficult to navigate in the river because the raised river beds created shallows in which the canoes got stuck and created rapids in other areas where water was funneled into narrow, rock-strewn channels. Fishing collapsed as the fish levels declined. Several unique species of fish and aquatic organisms had disappeared from the river waters. Where a simple trade economy had existed prior to the mine, the new roads and money flowing from the mine introduced supermarkets and a money economy to the highlands. Villagers abandoned their previous simple dress for Western-style clothes.

The mine brought other changes to the Papua New Guinea, many of them beneficial. Since the mine had begun operations, it contributed about $155 million a year in royalties and taxes to the national government. Between 1985 and 2000, the mine had produced 9.2 million tons of copper, 228 tons of gold, and 382 tons of silver. The copper, gold, and silver production of the mine made up about 18 percent of the nation's exports and constituted 10 percent of its gross domestic product. Half of the revenues of the government for the Western Province (the province where the mine was located) came from the mine. In addition, the mine employed about 2,000 workers directly and another 1,000 who worked for contractors hired to provide support services to the mine, plus a few thousand others who provided goods and services to the miners and their families. The training programs of the Ok Tedi Mine were considered exemplary, and many former employees had found other companies who were interested in their newly developed skills. The mine had sponsored several health projects, and as a result infant mortality in the area around the mine fell from 27 percent to about 2 percent, while life expectancy grew from about 30 years to over 50 years. The incidence of malaria in children of the surrounding area decreased from 70 percent to less than 15 percent, and in adults it fell from 35 percent to less than 6 percent. The mine had also set up the Fly River Development Trust to ensure that downstream residents along the Fly River received some of the economic benefits of the mine. The company had contributed about $3 million annually to the trust, which developed the area by building 133 community halls, 40 classrooms, 2 school libraries, 400 solar lights and pumps, 600 water tanks, 23 women's clubs, and 15 clinics. In effect, the mine had become the principle social agent in the Ok Tedi and Fly River areas, providing local social services such as health, education, training programs, infrastructure development, and local business development.

In 1989, a number of the landowners living along the polluted Ok Tedi and Fly Rivers began petitioning the government to take some action to prevent the discharge of the tailings into the river and to provide them with some compensation for their losses. In 1992, over 30,000 of these landowners joined together and sued BHP, the major nongovernment owner of the mine. After a great deal of legal wrangling, the case was settled out of court on June 12, 1996 when BHP agreed to give the landowners a total of $500 million: $90 million would be paid in cash to the 30,000 people who were living along the Ok Tedi and Fly Rivers; $35 million would be paid to the villagers living along the lower Ok Tedi River, the area that had been most devastated by the mine. And a 10 percent ownership share in the mine, valued at about $375 million, would be held by the government of Papua New Guinea in trust for the people of the Western Province, the province where the mine and the rivers were located. In addition, BHP agreed to implement a tailings containment plan if practical, after commissioning a 2-year study to assess the practicality of a containment facility and to recommend a plan for the mine.

The study examining the engineering, environmental, social, and risk aspects of managing the mine and its wastes was launched in 1996. As part of the study, a dredging operation was begun in 1998 along the lower section of the Ok Tedi River to see if dredging could mitigate the effects of the sediment accumulations.

On June 4, 1999, several months past the deadline, Ok Tedi Mining Limited announced that it had received a draft of the study of the environmental and social aspects of the mine operations. The report was passed on to Paul Anderson at BHP's headquarters. The study had found that the environmental impact of the mine, as well as the area affected by the pollution, was significantly greater than had been indicated by earlier studies the mine had commissioned. In addition, the study found that even if the mine were to close immediately, the sediments already deposited in the river would continue to kill the surrounding forests for perhaps 40 more years. Over the next 10 to 15 years, dieback would expand from the Ok Tedi River well into the forests of the downstream Fly River. The study had examined four possible options:

1. continue operating the mine and continue the current dredging in the lower Ok Tedi River
2. continue operating the mine and continue dredging, and in addition construct a new storage facility for future mine tailings
3. continue operating the mine and do nothing else
4. close down the mine immediately

None of these four options offered a good solution to the environmental impacts of the mine.

The study found that the ongoing dredging would lower the sand levels in the Ok Tedi, which would decrease flooding. But sediment would continue to accumulate downstream from the dredging, and dredging would not significantly halt the continuing degradation of the forests. In addition, dredging absorbed funds (see the following Table) that could be invested in health, education, or worker training.

Construction of a new storage facility would involve significant expenses (see Table) and would also create social problems because the amount of land required would destroy the whole area of one of the tribal clans. In addition, a storage facility might rupture, creating even more damage, and the stored tailings would generate acids that themselves would become an environmental threat.

To continue operating the mine while doing nothing would allow the environmental damage to continue unabated. If the mine continued operating until its originally scheduled date of 2010, an additional 200–300 million tons of tailings and rock would be created and these would be added to the sediments already in the rivers. This would significantly lengthen the already long period before the rivers would recover.

Closing down the mine immediately would limit the environmental damage that continued operations would create and would shorten the time the river would need to recover. But immediate closing of the mine would be an economic and social blow to national, provincial, and local communities. The study predicted that if the mine closed immediately, the many workers who had migrated into the mine area would suffer shortages in food supply resulting from overhunting and increases in store food prices. The high population around the mine would probably not decline until driven away by rising hunger and malnutrition. The national government would see its exports decline by almost 20 percent, its gross national product would decline by 10 percent, and its annual tax revenues would drop by more than 100 million dollars. The provincial government of the Western Province would lose half of its revenues, which came from the mine, and this would degrade its education and health services. In short, the economic, health, and social benefits that the mine was producing would end, and because the area had become dependent on the mine and had not prepared itself for life without the mine, the risk of social and economic decline was high.

The study also estimated the costs the mine itself would lose under each of the options by first calculating the basic cost of the option, then adding to it the potential additional costs that the option risked. The following table summarizes these costs in millions of 1999 U.S. dollars:

Option	Basic Cost	Potential Added Costs	Total Likely Costs
Mine and dredge	$294	$20–$70	$300–$400
Mine only	$177	$30–$140	$200–$300
Mine and dredge and store	$426	$20–$70	$400–$500
Early closure	$479	$30–$90	$500–$600

When Paul Anderson and BHP were presented with these options, he was uncertain how to weigh them. By now the situation at Ok Tedi had become international news. Anderson convened a committee of top-level managers from BHP and initiated a series of discussions with them. The committee discussed the four options proposed in the study and suggested others, such as simply walking away from the mine, giving the government of Papua New Guinea the 52 percent share of the mine that BHP still owned, gradually phasing down operation of the mine over several years, etc. As the discussions progressed through the summer of 2000, however, the BHP managers came to feel that if the company was to limit the environmental disaster that its operations were creating, the best option was to immediately close the mine. Only this option, Paul Anderson felt, was consistent with the environmental stewardship that he wanted BHP to demonstrate during his tenure as CEO. This option was also the option that various international groups were recommending, including the World Bank and virtually every environmental group familiar with the issues.

On August, 1999, Paul Anderson communicated to the government of Papua New Guinea BHP's view that the best option was to close down the mine. The government, however, was not favorable to his view. On August 28, Anderson commented to a group of analysts: "Ok Tedi is not an easy one to reach a simple conclusion on because the other shareholders in Ok Tedi, and the government of Papua New Guinea, in its role as a regulator, as opposed to as a shareholder, but in addition to its role as a shareholder, are not in favor of early closure. So you get into a situation where it's very hard to play out exactly how this is going to come to an end. . . ." (Financial Markets Presentation, Melbourne Australia, Monday August 28, 2000; taken from BHP archives).

The view of the government of Papua New Guinea was that the mine had to continue to operate because of the human and economic costs that closing the mine would inflict on the people. Villagers downriver from the mine supported the government's view. As one villager put it: "If the mine shuts, I will revert to wearing penis gourds [the traditional form of male dress.]"[2] The government also favored continued dredging since this would mitigate flooding for people living along the rivers. However, because constructing a storage facility carried additional risks and would absorb a major portion of the profits the mine would produce, the government did not support building a storage facility for tailings. In this, too, the villagers supported their government. Said one tribesman: "If it [the water] is safe for people, then they should continue to dump tailings into the river. They will never fix this river—it is already dead. They should give us money instead."[3]

On November, 2000, BHP reported that although it understood why the government wanted the mine to remain open, BHP's own continued involvement with the mine "would not be appropriate," and so the company had decided to "exit" its stake in the mine "in a way that ensures a smooth transition, minimizes the environmental impact, maximizes the social benefits," and ensures that BHP "does not incur liabilities for the future operations of the mine."[4] On February 8, 2001, BHP announced that it had reached an agreement with the government of Papua New Guinea and with the other shareholders of the Ok Tedi Mine. BHP had agreed to transfer its entire share of the mine (52 percent) to a trust (the Papua New Guinea Sustainable Development Program) that would use the money generated by BHP's former share of the mine to fund social projects for the government of Papua New Guinea. The mine would continue to operate at least until 2010 (with dredging but without a containment facility for tailings). It was expected that the next several years of the mine would be its most productive and lucrative years. BHP wrote down the transfer of its share of mine revenues as a one-time loss. In return, the government of Papua New Guinea passed legislation releasing BHP from any and all liability stemming from its past actions at the mine.

In 2011 the government of Papua New Guinea announced the mine would continue operating until 2013 and possibly until 2022, which would allow it to produce an additional 700,000 tons of copper and 2.3 million ounces of gold. The mine continued to discharge about 90 million tons of waste rock and tailings into the Ok Tedi river each year, raising the river bed by several more meters and causing the dieback area to expand. It was expected that dieback would eventually cover about 3,000 square meters and would take about two centuries years to recover. A statement on the Ok Tedi Mining web site indicated that despite the mine's impact on the "river system and their subsistence livelihoods," the people of the Ok Tedi and Fly River "strongly endorsed its continued operation" and their losses were "compensated under a number of compensation arrangements."

Notes

1. Sources used throughout this case include: International Institute for Environment and Development, "Ok Tedi Riverine Disposal Case" in Dirk van Zyl, Meredith Sassoon, Anne-Marie Fleury, and Silvia Kyeyune, eds., *Mining for the Future*, a report commissioned by the Mining, Minerals and Sustainable Development Project of the International Institute for Environment and Development, accessed June 2, 2004 at *http://www.iied.org/mmsd/mmsd_pdfs/068a_mftf-h.pdf*; Polly Ghazi, "Ok Tedi Mine: Unearthing Controversy," in World Resource Institute, *World Resources 2002–2004: Decisions for the Earth: Balance, Voice and Power* (July 2003), United Nations Development Program, accessed June 2, 2004 at *http://www.governance.wri.org/pubs_content_text.cfm?ContentID=1860*; World Bank, *Ok Tedi Mining Ltd. Mine Waste Management Project Risk Assessment and Supporting Documents* (1999), accessed June 2, 2004, at *http://www.mpi.org.au/oktedi/world_bank_full_report.html*; and the Ok Tedi Mining web site at *http://www.oktedi.com*, accessed April 15, 2011.
2. Kevin Pamba, "Ok Tedi: What to Do about the Damage Done," September 17, 1999, *Asia Times Online*, accessed July 25, 2004 at *http://www.atimes.com/oceana/AI17Ah01.html*.
3. Stuart Kirsch, "An Incomplete Victory at Ok Tedi," article accessed June 15, 2004 at *http://www.carnegiecouncil.org/viewMedia.php/prmTemplateID/8/prmID/614*.
4. Broken Hill Proprietary Company Limited, "Case Study: Ok Tedi," *BHP Environment and Community Report 2000* (November 2000), accessed June 19, 2004 at *http://www.envcommreport.bhp.com/Closure/okTedi.html*.
5. November, 1999: BHP consults with the government of PNG.

CASES

Gas or Grouse?

During the summer of 2008, people living near the Pinedale Mesa (sometimes called the Pinedale Anticline) in Wyoming were anxiously waiting for the Bureau of Land Management (BLM) to issue a decision regarding whether Questar and other energy companies would be allowed to drill thousands of ugly natural gas wells all over the serene wilderness that lay atop the mesa. The Pinedale Mesa is a 40-mile-long, 300-square-mile plateau extending north and south along the eastern side of Wyoming's Green River Basin, an area that is famous as the gateway to the hunting, fishing, and hiking treasures of the Bridger-Teton wilderness. The city of Pinedale, which sits below the mesa, a short distance from its northern end, was already surrounded by hundreds of recently drilled wells that ceaselessly pumped natural gas from the vast pockets that are buried underneath the region and which are estimated to contain 25 trillion cubit feet of gas worth billions of dollars.

Questar Corporation, an energy company with assets valued at about $4 billion, is the main developer of the gas wells around the city and had already drilled several wells up on the mesa that overlooked the city. Occasionally elk, mule deer, pronghorn antelope, and other wildlife, including the imperiled greater sage grouse, descend from their habitats atop the mesa and gingerly pick their way around and between the wells Questar drilled around Pinedale. Not surprisingly, environmentalists were at war with Questar and the other energy companies, whose plans to expand their operations on the mesa, they claimed, would have serious negative effects on the wildlife on the mesa as well as on the beauty of the area.

The federal government's Bureau of Land Management (BLM) was responsible for deciding what was done with the acreage on the mesa. Of 198,034 acres on the mesa, the federal government owns 158,000, Wyoming owns 9,800, and 29,800 are privately owned. In 2000, the

BLM had authorized limited drilling on the mesa, but had imposed several restrictions that protected wildlife from the full impact of the drilling. In 2008, the Bureau was being asked by Questar and the other companies who wanted to drill on the mesa to remove its limits on drilling by allowing more than 4,300 additional wells, as well as to lift one of the restrictions that cushioned the drilling's impact on wildlife but had proven very costly to the companies.

Headquartered in Salt Lake City, Questar Corporation drilled its first successful test well on the Pinedale Mesa in 1998. Extracting the gas under the mesa was not feasible earlier because the gas was trapped in tightly packed sandstone that prevented it from flowing to the wells and no one knew how to get it out. It was not until the mid-1990s that the industry developed techniques for fracturing the sandstone and freeing the gas. Full-scale drilling had to await the completion of an environmental impact statement, which the Bureau of Land Management (BLM) finished in mid-2000 when it approved drilling up to 900 wells on the federally owned acreage on the Pinedale Mesa. By the beginning of 2004, Questar had drilled 76 wells on the 14,800 acres it leased from the federal government and from the state of Wyoming and the company had plans to eventually drill at least 400 more wells. Energy experts around the country welcomed the new supply of natural gas, which, because of its simple molecular structure (CH_4), burns much more cleanly than any other fossil fuels. Moreover, because natural gas is extracted in the United States, its use reduces U.S. reliance on foreign energy supplies. Businesses in and around Pinedale also welcomed the drilling activity, which brought numerous benefits, including jobs, increased tax revenues, and a booming local economy. Wyoming's state government likewise supported the activity since 60 percent of the state budget is based on royalties the state receives from coal, gas, and oil operations.

Questar's wells on the mesa averaged 13,000 feet deep and cost \$2.8 to \$3.6 million each, depending on the amount of fracturing that had to be done.[1] Drilling a well typically required clearing and leveling a 2- to 4-acre "pad" to support the drilling rig and other equipment. One or two wells could be drilled at each pad. Access roads had to be run to the pad, and the well had to be connected to a network of pipes that drew the gas from the wells and carried it to where it could be stored and distributed. Each well produced waste liquids that had to be stored in tanks at the pad and periodically hauled away on tanker trucks.

The BLM, however, had imposed a significant restriction on Questar's operations on the mesa. Large areas of the mesa provide habitat for mule deer, pronghorn sheep, sage grouse, and other species, and the BLM imposed drilling rules that were designed to protect this. Chief among these species was the sage grouse.

The sage grouse is a colorful bird that today survives only in scattered pockets in 11 states. The grouse, which lives at elevations of 4,000 to 9,000 feet and is dependent on increasingly rare old-growth sagebrush for food and to screen itself from predators, is extremely sensitive to human activity. Houses, telephone poles, or fences can draw hawks and ravens, which prey on the ground-nesting grouse. It is estimated that 200 years ago the birds—known for their distinctive spring "strutting" mating dance—numbered 2 million and were common across the western United States. By the 1970s, their numbers had fallen to about 400,000. A study completed in June, 2004 by the Western Association of Fish and Wildlife Agencies concluded that there were only between 140,000 and 250,000 of the birds left and that "we are not optimistic about the future." The dramatic decline in their number was blamed primarily on the destruction of 50 percent of their sagebrush nesting and mating grounds (called *leks*), which in turn was blamed on livestock grazing, new home construction, fires, and the expanding acreage being given over to gas drilling and other mining activities. Biologists believe that if its sagebrush habitats are not protected, the bird will be so reduced in number by 2050 that it will never recover. According to Pat Deibert, a U.S. Fish and Wildlife Service biologist, "they need large stands of unbroken sagebrush" and anything that breaks up those stands such as roads, pipelines, or houses, affects them.[2]

In order to protect the sage grouse, whose last robust population had nested for thousands of years on the ideal sagebrush fields up on the mesa, the BLM required that Questar's roads, wells, and other structures had to be located a quarter mile or more from grouse breeding grounds, and at least 2 miles from nesting areas during breeding season. Some studies, however, concluded that these protections were not sufficient to arrest the decline in the grouse population. As wells proliferated in the area, they were increasingly taking up land on which the grouse foraged and nested and were disturbing the sensitive birds. Conservationists said that the BLM should increase the quarter-mile buffer areas around the grouse breeding grounds to at least 2-mile buffers.

In May, 2004, the U.S. Fish and Wildlife Service announced that it would begin the process of studying whether the sage grouse should be categorized as an endangered species, which would bring it under the protection of the Endangered Species Act, something conservationists had been urging the Service to do since 2000. Questar and other gas, oil, and mining companies adamantly opposed having the grouse listed as an endangered species because once listed, the grouse would make large areas of federal land off-limits to drilling, mining, and development. Since 80 percent of Wyoming is considered sage grouse habitat, including much of the Pinedale Mesa, Questar's drilling plans would be severely compromised.

Questar and other companies formed a coalition—the Partnership for the West—to lobby the Bush administration to keep the grouse off the endangered species list. Led by Jim Sims, a former communications director for President George W. Bush's Energy Task Force, the coalition established a web site where they called on members to lobby "key administration players in Washington" and to "unleash grass-roots opposition to a listing, thus providing some cover to the political leadership at Department of Interior and throughout the administration." The coalition also suggested "funding scientific studies" that would be designed to show that the sage grouse was not endangered. According to Sims, the attempt to categorize the grouse as an endangered species was spearheaded by "environmental extremists who have converged on the American West in an effort to stop virtually all economic growth and development. They want to restrict business and industry at every turn. They want to put our Western lands off-limits to all of us."[3] Dru Bower, vice president of the Petroleum Association of Wyoming, said, "[endangered species] listings are not good for the oil and gas industry, so anything we can do to prevent a species from being listed is good for the industry. If the sage grouse is listed, it would have a dramatic effect on oil and gas development in the state of Wyoming."[4]

The sage grouse was not the only species affected by Questar's drilling operations. The gas fields to which Questar wanted additional drilling rights was an area 8 miles long and 3 miles wide, located on the northern end of the mesa. This property was located in the middle of the winter range used by mule deer and pronghorn antelope, some of which migrate to the mesa area from as far away as the Grand Teton National Park, 170 miles to the north. Although the mesa was elevated and winters there were harsh, it was much lower than the mountains where the mule deer and pronghorn antelope lived in spring and summer, and the mesa provided large fields of sagebrush that fed the animals. Migration studies conducted between 1998 and 2001 revealed that the pronghorn antelope herds make one of the longest annual migrations among North American big game animals. The area around Pinedale is laced with migration corridors used by thousands of mule deer and pronghorn every fall as they make their way south to their winter grounds on the mesa and the Green River Basin. Traffic on Highway 191 which cuts across some of the migration corridors sometimes has to be stopped to let bunched-up pronghorn herds pass.[5] Environmentalists feared that if the animals were prevented from reaching their winter ranges or if the winter ranges became inhospitable, the large herds would wither as the animals died off.

Unfortunately, drilling operations create a great deal of noise and require the constant movement of many trucks and other large machines, all of which can severely impact animals during the winter when they are already physically stressed and vulnerable due to their low calorie intake. Some studies had suggested that even the mere presence of humans disturbed the animals and led them to avoid an area. Consequently, the BLM required Questar to cease all drilling operations on the mesa each winter from November 15 to May 1. In fact, to protect the animals the BLM prohibited all persons, whether on foot or on automobile, from venturing into the area during winter. The BLM, however, made an exception for Questar trucks and personnel who had to continue to haul off liquid wastes from wells that had already been drilled and that continued to operate during the winter (the winter moratorium prohibited only drilling operations, and completed wells were allowed to continue to pump gas throughout the year).

Being forced to stop drilling operations during the winter months was extremely frustrating and costly to Questar. Drilling crews had to be laid off at the beginning of winter, and new crews had to be hired and retrained every spring. Every fall the company had to pack up several tons of equipment, drilling rigs, and trucks and move them off the mesa. Because of the seasonal interruption in its drilling schedule, the full development of its oil fields was projected to take 18 years, much longer than the company wanted.

In 2004, Questar submitted a proposal to the Bureau of Land Management. Questar proposed to invest in a new kind of drilling rig that allowed up to 16 wells to be dug from a single pad, instead of the traditional 1 or 2. The new technology (called *directional drilling*) aimed the drill underground at a slanted angle away from the pad, so that by placing wells around the perimeter of the pad, all at an underground slant leading away from the pad—like the outstretched tentacles on an octopus—multiple distant locations could be tapped by several wells branching out from a single pad. This minimized the surface land occupied by the wells: while traditional drilling required 16 separate 2–4 acre pads to support 16 wells, the new "directional drilling" technology allowed a single pad to hold 16 wells. The technology also reduced the number of required roadways and distribution pipes since a single access road and pipe could now service the same number of wells that traditionally required 16 different roads and 16 different pipes. Questar also proposed that instead of carrying liquid wastes away from operating wells on noisy tanker trucks, the company would build a second pipe system that would pump liquid wastes away automatically. These innovations, Questar pointed out, would substantially reduce any harmful impact that drilling and pumping had on the wildlife inhabiting the mesa. Using the new technology for the additional 400 wells the company wanted to drill would require 61 pads instead of 150, and the pads would occupy 533 acres instead of 1,474.

The new directional drilling technology added about $500,000 to the cost of each well and required investing in several new drilling rigs. The added cost for the 400 additional wells Questar planned would total $185 million. Questar noted, however, that "the company anticipates that it can justify the extra cost if it can drill and complete all the wells on a pad in one continuous operation" that continued through the winter.[6] If the company was allowed to drill continuously through the winter, it would be able to finish drilling all its wells in 9 years instead of 18, thereby almost doubling the company's revenues from the project over those 9 years. This acceleration in its revenues, coupled with other savings resulting from putting 16 wells on each pad, would enable it to justify the added costs of directional drilling. In short, the company would invest in the new technology that reduced the impact on wildlife, but only if it was allowed to drill on the mesa during the winter months.

In addition, Questar had requested that it be allowed to increase the number of wells it was allowed to drill on the mesa. By now, several other energy companies were trying to get permission to drill on the mesa, including Ultra Resources, Shell, BP, Stone Energy, Newfield Exploration, Yates Petroleum, and Anschutz. Together, the companies asked the BLM that they be allowed to drill an additional 4,399 natural gas wells on the mesa. And all of them were also requesting they be allowed to drill through the winter.

Although environmentalists welcomed Questar's willingness to invest in directional drilling, they strongly opposed allowing it or the other companies to operate on the mesa during the winter when mule deer and antelope were there foraging for food and struggling to survive. The Upper Green River Valley Coalition, a coalition of environmental groups, issued a statement that read: "The company should be lauded for using directional drilling, but technological improvements should not come at the sacrifice of important safeguards for Wyomings's wildlife heritage."

In order to allow Questar to test the feasability of directional drilling and to study its effects on wintering deer herds, the Bureau of Land Management decided to let Questar drill wells at a single pad through the winter of 2002–2003 and again through the winter of 2003–2004. The Bureau would launch a 5-year study of the impact of the drilling which would continue until 2007 (later extended beyond 2010). Questar was glad it was at least being given the chance to show that drilling through the winter was compatible with the wildlife living on the mesa. Two of the other companies, Shell and Ultra were also allowed to test winter drilling in 2005.

Before the Bureau made a final decision about whether it would approve the companies' requests to drill thousands of additional wells and to drill them through the winters, it had to again prepare an environmental impact statement, this one called a "supplemental environmental impact statement" or SEIS.[7] The Bureau therefore began collecting information about the impact of increasing the number of wells and allowing year-round drilling. Its 5-year study of the impact of winter drilling was expanded to include on-going monitoring of wildlife on the mesa. In a preliminary 2004 report on the results of its study, the Bureau of Land Management said that it had found "no conclusive data to indicate quantifiable, adverse effects to deer" due to drilling. The Bureau was clearly anxious to avoid the public dismay that it had created when it had first opened up the mesa to drilling by Questar and it was trying to be as open as possible. During the winter of 2005 and the spring of 2006, the Bureau held several open meetings at which the public was invited to comment on the requests of Quesar and the other companies. In December, 2006, the Bureau completed the first draft of its environmental statement and released it to the public for more comments. Based on this additional input, a second preliminary draft was issued for public comment in December, 2007 and the Bureau held additional public meetings on the second draft during early 2008.

Finally, on September 12, 2008, the Bureau issued its decision on the requests of the drilling companies, along with the final draft of its environmental impact statement. Its decision assumed that future drilling would use the new drilling technology Quesar had proposed. According to the Bureau, it had studied the impact of five main alternative decisions it could render: (1) continue to prohibit winter drilling and allow no additional wells; (2) allow winter drilling and allow 4,399 more wells on a maximum of 600 drilling pads all located within a large "core area" in the central part of the mesa; (3) allow winter drilling and 4,399 more wells on a maximum 600 pads *plus*: confine drilling to specific parts of the "core area" and prohibit drilling or disturbance of any areas that were "crucial winter ranges" for mule deer and pronghorn antelope, or mating and nesting areas of the sage grouse; (4) allow winter drilling and 4,399 wells on 600 pads, confine drilling to parts of the core area, prohibit drilling or disturbance of winter ranges of mule deer or pronghorn antelope or mating and nesting areas of sage grouse, *plus:* prohibit drilling on the thousands of acres (the "flank area") surrounding the "core area" where drilling was allowed, require annual review of wildlife impacts, and require the companies to establish a fund (with an initial contribution of $4.2 million and annual payments of $7,500 per well) to monitor wildlife and to pay for the costs of mitigating any impacts on wildlife that monitoring detected; (5) Allow drilling only within the "core area" and prohibit drilling in the area around the periphery, *but:* permit fewer than 4,399 wells and less than 600 pads and limit the total acreage devoted to wells.

The BLM admitted that under all alternatives but (1), the deer and antelope "would continue to be adversely affected," and "decreased habitat" would result for the sage grouse. Also "surface disturbance is expected to adversely affect migratory birds," and sediment from drilling that entered rivers could lead to "decreased reproductive success in spring-spawning native salmon species." Nevertheless, the BLM decided to choose alternative (4), saying that it provided the best balance between protecting the natural environment and allowing access to the natural gas that was so valuable to the United States. In its official statement of its decision, the BLM added, in an important "appendix B," that if the number of mule deer or antelope declined by 15 percent in any one year or from their levels in 2005/2006, or if the number of sage grouse declined by 30 percent in any two-year period, then the BLM was required, and had the right, to take a number of "mitigation responses." Specifically, the BLM had to first try to expand the habitat of the declining species by removing all human disturbances from the large "flank area" surrounding the "core" and by enhancing these areas so they could provide additional habitat by, for example, planting more sagebrush and other edible vegetation. But if this did not work, then the BLM could change where wells were allowed and how fast new wells could be added, as needed to protect wildlife.

Questar and the other companies were pleased with the outcome. They had, essentially, gotten what they had asked for, even if there were limits to where they could drill their wells. The companies quickly moved into the "core areas" and began building and drilling, and continued through the winter of 2009. But on October 28, 2010, Western Ecosystems Technology, the group monitoring wildlife on the Pinedale Mesa, announced that in 2009 mule deer on the mesa had declined by 60 percent compared to their numbers in 2001, and by 28 percent compared to their number in 2005.[8] The Western Ecosystem Technology study also found that in 2009 less than 70 percent of adult female mule deer survived the winter on the mesa, compared to a normal survival rate of 85 percent. A representative of Shell, one of the companies drilling on the mesa, reacted by saying more research was needed: "Let's see what the results are before we start reacting too much to what could be naturally caused variation." But a local Bureau official responded that since the decline in deer numbers had passed the threshold of 15 percent, "aggressive and positive action" on mitigation measures was required.

Questions

1. What are the systemic, corporate, and individual issues raised in this case?
2. How should wildlife species like grouse or deer be valued, and how should that value be balanced against the economic interests of a society or of a company like Questar? What principles or rules would you propose we use to balance the value of wildlife species against economic interests?
3. In light of the fact that natural gas reduces the U.S.'s undesirable dependence on foreign oil and the fact that natural gas produces less greenhouse gases than coal, oil, and other fuels, should Questar continue its drilling operations? Does the environmental impact of Questar's drilling operations imply that Questar is morally obligated to stop drilling wells on the Pinedale Mesa? Explain.
4. What, if anything, should Questar and the other companies be doing differently?
5. From an ethical point of view, was alternative (4) the best option among those from which the BLM chose? Is another alternative better from an ethical point of view? Explain your answer.
6. Should the loss of species produced by the drilling operations of Questar be considered a problem of pollution or a problem of conservation? Can the loss of species by evaluated as an "external cost"? Explain.

Notes

1. Peggy Williams, "The Pinedale Anticline," *Oil and Gas Investor*, December 2001, pp. 2–5.
2. Tom Kenworthy, "Battle Brewing Over Sage Grouse Protection," *USA Today*, July 13, 2004, p. 2a; Todd Wilkinson, "Sage Grouse of Western Plains Seen as Next 'Spotted Owl,'" *Christian Science Monitor*, June 25, 2004, p. 1.
3. Julie Cart, "Bird's Fate Tied to Future of Drilling," *Los Angeles Times*, June 10, 2004, p. 11.
4. Ibid.
5. Rebecca Huntington, "Cowboy Enterprise: Wildlife Find Less Room in Energy Boom," *Associated Press State and Local Wire*, December 2, 2003.
6. Questar, "The Pinedale Anticline: A Story of Responsible Development of a Major Natural Gas Resource," proposal available on Questar web site.
7. The information in this and all the following paragraphs is drawn from: Bureau of Land Management Wyoming State Office, *Final Supplemental Environmental Impact Statement for the Pinedale Anticline Oil and Gas Exploration and Development Project*, Sublette County, Wyoming, June 2008, and U.S. Department of the Interior, Bureau of Land Management, Cheyenne, Wyoming, *Record of Decision, Final Supplemental Environmental Impact Statement for the Pinedale Anticline Oil and Gas Exploration and Development Project*, Sublette County, Wyoming, September 2008, both documents accessed January 19, 2011 at ***http://www.blm.gov/wy/st/en/info/NEPA/documents/pfo/anticline/seis.html***.
8. Cat Urbigkit, "Pinedale Mesa Deer Population Drops," *Casper Star Tribune*, October 28, 2010, accessed January 19, 2011 at ***http://trib.com/news/state-and-regional/article_fa6d49fa-a7b6-5335-82bf-8cc7d217ea69.html***.

伙
記
奥运用酒
合作店
GREATWALL
可口可乐

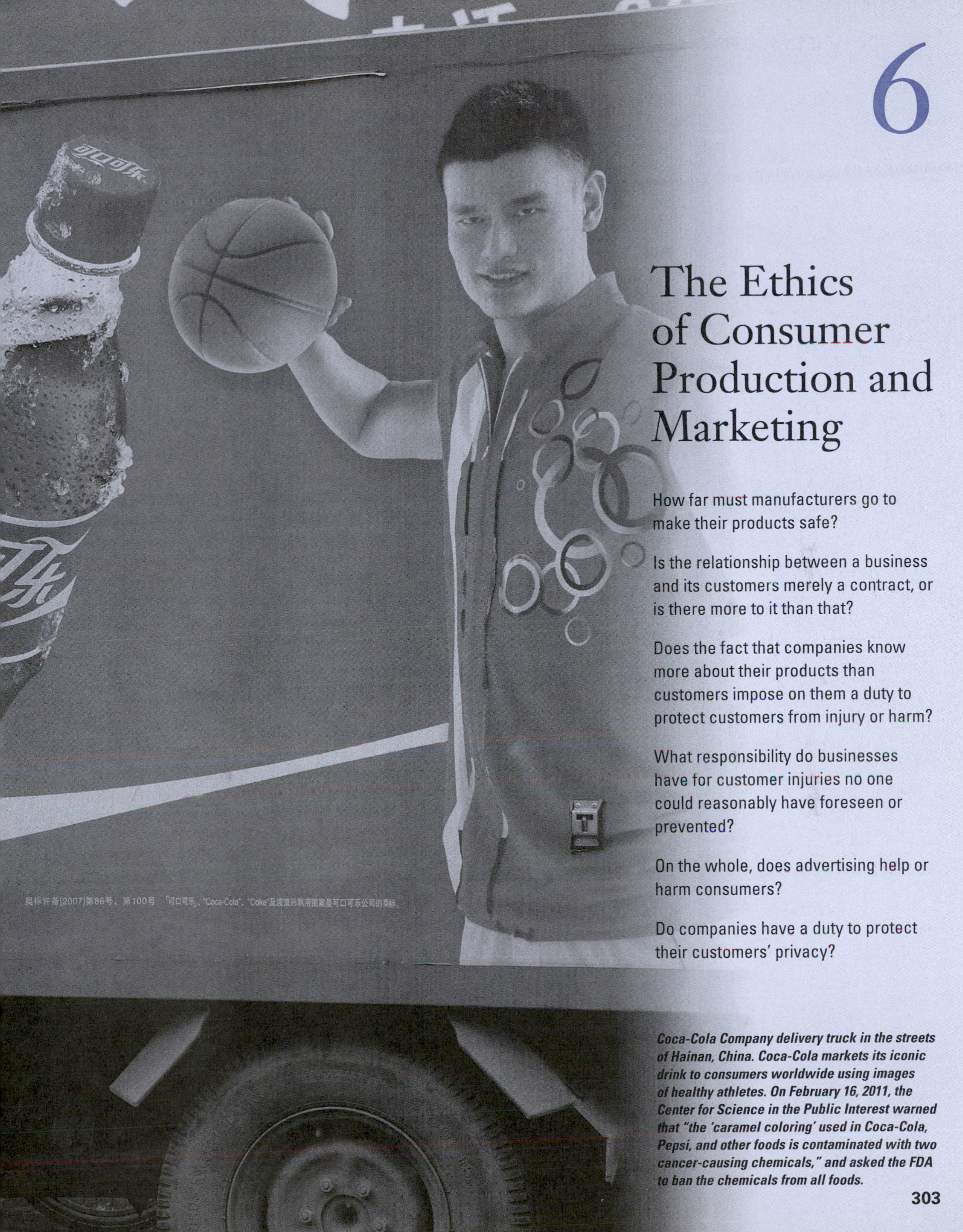

6

The Ethics of Consumer Production and Marketing

How far must manufacturers go to make their products safe?

Is the relationship between a business and its customers merely a contract, or is there more to it than that?

Does the fact that companies know more about their products than customers impose on them a duty to protect customers from injury or harm?

What responsibility do businesses have for customer injuries no one could reasonably have foreseen or prevented?

On the whole, does advertising help or harm consumers?

Do companies have a duty to protect their customers' privacy?

Coca-Cola Company delivery truck in the streets of Hainan, China. Coca-Cola markets its iconic drink to consumers worldwide using images of healthy athletes. On February 16, 2011, the Center for Science in the Public Interest warned that "the 'caramel coloring' used in Coca-Cola, Pepsi, and other foods is contaminated with two cancer-causing chemicals," and asked the FDA to ban the chemicals from all foods.

INTRODUCTION

Listen to the **Chapter Audio** on **mythinkinglab.com**

Motor vehicles annually kill 34,000 Americans including pedestrians (traffic crashes are the leading cause of death for Americans between 2 and 34 years of age), incapacitate 260,000, and injure 2.2 million others,[1] while firearms kill 32,000 and injure an additional 65,000.[2] The cigarettes that Phillip Morris, American Brands, RJ Reynolds, B. A. T., Loews, and Liggett companies sell kill 440,000 of their U.S. customers each year, almost as many Americans as AIDS has killed during its *entire 30-year* history.[3] Worldwide cigarettes kill 5 million customers a year, more than twice what AIDS kills. Prescription painkillers cause about 12,000 U.S. deaths each year and hospitalize another 300,000 people.[4] Two hundred thousand children are injured annually by playground equipment and 147 die of their injuries.[5] All-terrain vehicles (ATVs) kill between 600 and 800 people a year and injure about 130,000.[6]

The number of product deaths and injuries would be much greater if the U.S. government did not regularly require companies to recall defective or harmful products. Here is a small sample from among the millions of defective products that have to be recalled each year:

> **Baby Slings – Infantino (2010)** In this recent case, approximately 1 million Infantino baby slings were recalled due to breathing hazards that arise from the product's design. Infantino's "SlingRider" and "Wendy Bellissimo" models were called back because the soft material and "C" curve could push a baby's head forward, making it very difficult—if not impossible—for a baby to breathe.
>
> **High Chairs – Graco (2010)** The U.S. Consumer Product Safety Commission (CPSC) issued a recall of Graco's Harmony model of high chair after the chair's design was deemed unsafe. Approximately 1.2 million high chairs were recalled in March 2010, in response to the reported 24 injuries. In January, Graco recalled approximately 1.5 million strollers due to fingertip amputation and laceration hazards.
>
> **Faulty Pedals and Floor Mats – Toyota (2010)** In January 2010, Toyota issued a second recall in three months for various models of Toyota and Lexus cars due to problems with faulty pedals and floor mats that, in some cases, led to sudden and unintended acceleration. The automaking giant recalled a total of more than 9 million vehicles, and the company faced congressional probes looking into the matter.
>
> **Window Blinds – 2009** In December 2009, all Roman-style shades and roll-up blinds were recalled after reports that babies and toddlers had died of strangulation after getting caught in the loose cords of the window coverings.... In total, nearly 50 million blinds were affected and recalled.
>
> **Cruise Control – Ford (2009)** In October 2009, Ford added an additional 4.5 million vehicles to its largest ever product recall, which spanned an entire decade. The models recalled in October 2009 brought the staggering grand total to more than 14 million recalled vehicles. The cars were recalled due to faulty cruise-control switches that were linked to an estimated 550 vehicle fires across the U.S.[7]

Americans are exposed daily to astonishingly high levels of risk from the use of consumer products. Each year on average 33.6 million people suffer injuries related to consumer products (not counting motor vehicles) and about 28,200 of them are killed.[8] The Consumer Product Safety Commission estimates that the total cost of product related injuries in a single year is about $800 billion.

However, product injuries make up only one category of costs imposed on unwary consumers. Consumers must also bear the costs of deceptive selling practices, shoddy product construction, products that immediately break down, and warranties that are not honored. For example, several years ago, the engine of Martha and George Rose's General Motors (GM) station wagon began hissing and white smoke poured out of the tailpipe as she drove it 6 miles to work. When their mechanic inspected it, he found a crack in the engine block so the car needed an expensive new engine. But they were not worried since the engine was still under GM's "5-year or 50,000-mile" warranty. However, when a GM mechanic inspected their car, he concluded that the radiator thermostat had stuck shut so no coolant had reached the engine. Because the thermostat was only under a "12-month or 12,000-miles" warranty that had by then expired, and because the faulty thermostat had caused the engine to overheat and the engine block to crack, GM concluded it had no responsibility under its "5-year or 50,000-mile" warranty.[9]

The practices of AT&T Inc. and its subsidiaries illustrate the difficulties consumers face. In 2003, AT&T's California division, then called "Pacific Bell," paid $15 million in fines for "deceptive" marketing of its telephone services. The deception was almost identical to what the company had done a few years earlier, when it had to pay a $17 million fine for duping telephone customers into buying an expensive package of optional features without telling them the features did not have to be purchased as part of the company's basic service. The company's policy, according to one of its sales representatives, was that "People should be intelligent enough to ask; why should it be PacBell's job to tell them?"[10] In 2003 the company renamed an expensive package of optional services "The Basics" so that when new customers called asking for "basic" telephone service, sales representatives sold them the expensive package without telling them cheaper basic service was available. In 2010 AT&T was accused of "fraud and deceit" in a class action lawsuit that claimed the company "intentionally, knowingly and artificially inflates the data usage" of its cell phone customers by "an amount that is three to five times the actual data usage … then bills the customer based upon the inflated data usage … not the actual data used … by that customer."[11] According to the lawsuit, when Guardian Corporation, an AT&T customer, became suspicious of its cell phone bills, it hired an expert to go through AT&T's internal engineering reports and discovered that Guardian's "actual data usage and data transfer … were, as a matter of corporate policy, being misrepresented by AT&T's system." By inflating a customer's usage, the suit said, AT&T was also able to charge higher "overage" fees for usage beyond the amount the customer's plan contract allowed, even when the customer stayed within the usage allowed by the plan. Ordinary consumers could not check the accuracy of their bills because they did not have access to AT&T's internal engineering reports nor to an expert who could understand those reports. AT&T has had to settle other charges of deceptive consumer practices in New York, Florida, Washington, Texas, Louisiana, West Virginia, North Carolina, and several other states as well as charges of nationwide deceptive practices.

Consumers are also bombarded daily by an endless series of advertisements urging them to buy numerous products. Although sometimes defended as sources of information, advertisements are also criticized on the grounds that they rarely do more than give the barest indications of the basic function a product is meant to serve and sometimes misrepresent and exaggerate its qualities. Economists argue that advertising expenditures are a waste of resources and sociologists bemoan the cultural effects of advertising.[12]

This chapter examines the many ethical issues raised by product quality and advertising. The first few sections discuss various approaches to consumer issues, and the last sections deal with consumer advertising. We begin with a focus on what is perhaps the most urgent issue: consumer product injuries and the responsibilities of manufacturers.

Quick Review 6.1

Problems consumers face
- Dangerous and risky products
- Deceptive selling practices
- Poorly constructed products
- Failure to honor warranties
- Deceptive and unpleasant advertising

Quick Review 6.2

Market Approach to Consumer Protection
- Claims safety is a commodity that should not be mandated by government.
- Safety should instead be provided through the market.
- In a market, sellers will provide safety if consumers demand it.
- In a market, the price of safety and the amount sellers provide will be determined by the costs of providing it and the value consumers place on it.
- Government intervention in consumer markets makes them unfair, inefficient, and coercive.

rational utility maximizer A person who has a well-defined and consistent set of preferences, and who knows how personal choices will affect those preferences.

6.1 Markets and Consumer Protection

Consumer advocates point out that each year there are more than 500,000 injuries requiring hospital treatment inflicted on youngsters and adults using toys, nursery equipment, and playground equipment; close to 290,000 people are mangled using home workshop equipment; over 2,800,000 people need emergency treatment for injuries involving home furnishings; and over 3,000,000 people require treatment for injuries involving home construction materials.[13] Non-fatal injuries from motor vehicle accidents in 2009 averaged 51,000 each week and deaths averaged over 90 people per day.[14] A 2010 study concluded that the financial losses from motor vehicle accidents total more than $99 billion a year.[15]

It is sometimes argued that consumers will be protected from injury by the operations of the free market and that neither governments nor businesspeople should intervene in markets to require product safety.[16] The market approach to consumer protection argues that consumer safety can be provided efficiently through the free market because sellers must respond to consumer demands if they are to make a profit. If consumers want products to be safer, they will indicate this preference in markets by willingly paying more for safer products and showing a preference for manufacturers of safe products while turning down the goods of those who make unsafe products. Manufacturers will respond to this demand by building more safety into their products or they risk losing customers to competitors who cater to the safety preferences of consumers. Thus, if consumers want safety the market will provide it and sellers will price it according to how much it costs to provide it (indicated by their supply curve) and how much consumers think its worth (indicated by their demand curve). As a result, the market will provide safety at a fair price, in a way that respects customers' free choices, and with an efficient use of society's resources.

On the other hand, if consumers do not place a high value on safety and demonstrate neither a willingness to pay more for safety nor a preference for safer products, then it is wrong for government to force manufacturers to build more safety into their products. Forcing manufacturers to provide more safety than consumers want increases manufacturing costs which leads to higher consumer prices so that ultimately consumers are forced to pay for a product feature they did not want in the first place. Such government interference also distorts markets by leading manufacturers to invest society's resources where there is little demand, and forcing consumers to pay prices that unfairly charge them for a product quality they do not value. Only consumers can say what value they place on safety, the market approach argues, and they should be allowed to register their preferences through their free choices in markets and not be coerced by businesses or governments into paying for safety levels they do not want. Such coercion leads to unfairness, does not respect the consumer's right of free choice, and reduces society's utility.

Critics of this market approach to safety respond, however, that the market approach assumes consumer markets are perfectly competitive, but in fact they rarely are. As we saw in Chapter 4, we can claim that markets are fair, respectful of negative rights, and efficiently maximize utility only when they have the seven characteristics that make them perfectly competitive. When markets are not perfectly competitive because they lack some of these characteristics, it's hard to say whether they are fair, are respectful of rights, or maximize utility. In particular, we can say consumer markets will respond efficiently and fairly to consumer preferences only if buyers have adequate information about what they are buying, are **rational utility maximizers**, and have the other characteristics of the perfectly competitive market. However, buyers are not always adequately informed about the goods they are buying, nor are they always rational, and most markets lack some of the other characteristics of perfectly competitive markets.

Consumers are often uninformed about the products they buy simply because many products are so complex only an expert can be knowledgeable about them, and because the manufacturer, who is most knowledgeable about the product, may not voluntarily share this knowledge with consumers. And it may be too expensive and impractical for consumers to conduct the research needed to learn enough about a particular product to make an informed purchase decision.[17]

Moreover, research shows that we become highly inept, irrational, and inconsistent when we make purchase decisions based on estimates about the probability that a product carries no major risk of injury or the probability it will serve our purposes.[18] We typically underestimate the risks of common life-threatening activities, such as driving, smoking, eating fried foods, or being injured by the products we use, and we overestimate the probabilities of unlikely but memorable events such as tornadoes or attacks by grizzly bears in national parks.[19] Studies have shown that our probability judgments go astray for a number of reasons, including: we ignore or discount important information about a product, we make broad generalizations on the basis of small samples, we believe in a self-correcting but nonexistent "law of averages," and we believe that we exert control over purely chance events.[20] A number of researchers have also shown that people are irrational and inconsistent when weighing choices based on probability estimates about the future, sometimes ranking one future choice as being both better and worse than another and sometimes paying more for the choice they least prefer.[21]

Quick Review 6.3

Problems with the Market Approach

Assumes markets are perfectly competitive but they are not because:

- Buyers do not have adequate information when products are complex and information is costly and hard to find
- Buyers are often not rational about product risk or probabilities and are often inconsistent
- Many consumer markets are monopolies or oligopolies.

Finally, as several critics have pointed out, many, perhaps most, consumer markets are not competitive but are, instead, monopolies or oligopolies in which sellers can manipulate price and supply. For example, the markets for automobiles, cigarettes, air travel, soft drinks, televisions, cell phones, gasoline, movies, music, books, breakfast cereals, beer, health insurance, fast food, electronic goods, television cable services, wireless phone service, pharmaceutical drugs, computers, television entertainment, etc., are all oligopolies.

On balance, then, it does not appear that market forces by themselves can deal with all consumer concerns for safety, freedom from risk, and value. Market failures, characterized by inadequate consumer information, irrationality in the choices of consumers, and concentrated markets, undercut arguments that try to show that markets alone can provide adequate consumer protection. Instead, consumers must be protected through the legal structures of government and through the voluntary initiatives of responsible businesspeople. We turn then to examining several views about the responsibilities of businesses toward consumers—views that have formed the basis of many of our consumer laws and of increased calls for greater acceptance of responsibility for consumer protection on the part of business.

It is clear, of course, that part of the responsibility for consumer injuries must rest on consumers. Individuals are often careless in their use of products. "Do-it-yourselfers" use power saws without guards attached or use flammable liquids near open flames. People often use tools and instruments that they do not have the skill, knowledge, or experience to handle. But consumer responsibility is only part of the story. Injuries also arise from flaws in product design, in the materials out of which products are made, and in the processes used to construct products. Insofar as manufacturing defects are the source of product-related injuries, consumer advocates claim, minimizing injuries is the responsibility of manufacturers because they are in the best position to know the hazards a product carries and to eliminate the hazards at the point of manufacture.

Where, then, does the consumers' duty to protect his or her own interests end, and where does the manufacturer's duty to protect consumers' interests begin?

Three different theories on the ethical duties of manufacturers have been developed, each of which strikes a different balance between consumers' duty to protect themselves and the manufacturer's duty to protect consumers: the contract view, the "due care" view, and the social costs view. The contract view would place the greater responsibility on the consumer, whereas the due care and social costs views place the larger measure of responsibility on the manufacturer. We examine each of these in turn.

6.2 The Contract View of Business Firm's Duties to Consumers

contract view of the business firm's duties to its customers The view that the relationship between a business firm and its customers is essentially a contractual relationship, and the firm's moral duties to the customer are those created by this contractual relationship.

According to the **contract view of the business firm's duties to its customers**, the relationship between a business firm and its customers is essentially a contractual relationship, and the firm's moral duties to the customer are those created by this contractual relationship.[22] When a consumer buys a product, this view holds, the consumer voluntarily enters into a "sales contract" with the business firm. The firm freely and knowingly agrees to give the consumer a product with certain characteristics, and the consumer in turn freely and knowingly agrees to pay a certain sum of money to the firm for the product. By virtue of having voluntarily entered this agreement, the firm then has a duty to provide a product with those characteristics, and the consumer has a correlative right to get a product with those characteristics.

The contract theory of the business firm's duties to its customers rests on the view that a contract is a free agreement that imposes on the parties the basic duty of complying with the terms of the agreement. We examined this view earlier (Chapter 2) and noted the two justifications Kant provided for the view: A person has a duty to do what the person contracts to do because failure to adhere to the terms of a contract is a practice that (a) cannot be universalized, and (b) treats the other person as a means and not as an end.[23] Rawls's theory also provides a justification for the view, but one that is based on the idea that our freedom is expanded by the recognition of contractual rights and duties: An enforced system of social rules that requires people to do what they contract to do will provide them with the assurance that contracts will be kept. Only if they have such assurance will people feel able to trust each other's word and, on that basis, to secure the benefits of the institution of contracts.[24]

We also noted in Chapter 2 that traditional moralists have argued that the act of entering into a contract is subject to several secondary moral constraints:

1. Both of the parties to the contract must have full knowledge of the nature of the agreement they are entering.
2. Neither party to a contract must intentionally misrepresent the facts of the contractual situation to the other party.
3. Neither party to a contract must be forced to enter the contract under duress or undue influence.

These secondary constraints can be justified by the same sorts of arguments that Kant and Rawls use to justify the basic duty to perform one's contracts. Kant, for example, easily shows that misrepresentation in the making of a contract cannot be universalized, and Rawls argues that if misrepresentation were not prohibited, fear of deception would make members of a society feel less free to enter contracts. However, these secondary constraints can also be justified on the grounds that a contract cannot exist unless these constraints are fulfilled. A contract is essentially a free agreement struck between two parties. Because an agreement cannot exist unless both parties know what they are agreeing to, contracts require full knowledge and the absence of misrepresentation. Because freedom implies the absence of coercion, contracts must be made without duress or undue influence.

Hence, the contractual theory of business firms' duties to consumers claims that a business has four main moral duties: the basic duty of (1) complying with the terms of the sales contract and the secondary duties of (2) disclosing the nature of the product, (3) avoiding misrepresentation, and (4) avoiding the use of duress and undue influence. By acting in accordance with these duties, a business respects the right of consumers to be treated as free and equal persons—that is, in accordance with their right to be treated only as they have freely consented to be treated.

The Duty to Comply

The most basic moral duty that a business firm owes its customers, according to the contract view, is the duty to provide consumers with a product that lives up to those claims that the firm expressly made about the product, which led the customers to enter the contract freely and which formed the customers' understanding concerning what they were agreeing to buy. Winthrop Laboratories, for example, marketed a painkiller that it advertised as nonaddictive. Subsequently, a patient using the painkiller became addicted to it and shortly died from an overdose. A court found Winthrop Laboratories liable for the patient's death because, although it had expressly stated that the drug was nonaddictive, Winthrop Laboratories had failed to live up to its duty to comply with this express contractual claim.[25] As this example suggests, our legal system has incorporated the moral view that firms have a duty to live up to the express claims they make about their products. The Uniform Commercial Code (a model set of laws regulating commercial transactions that have been completely or partially adopted by all 50 states), for example, states in Section 2-314:

> Any affirmation of fact or promise made by the seller to the buyer that related to the goods and becomes part of the basis of the bargain creates an express warranty that the goods shall conform to the affirmation or promise.

In addition to the duties that result from the express claims a seller makes about the product, the contract view also holds that the seller has a duty to carry through on any implied claims knowingly made about the product. For example, the seller has the moral duty to provide a product that can be used safely for the ordinary and expected purposes for which the customer, relying on the seller's judgment, has been led to believe it can be used. Sellers are morally bound to do whatever they know the buyers understood the sellers were promising because at the point of sale, sellers should have corrected any misunderstandings of which they were aware.[26] This idea of an implied agreement has also been incorporated into the law. Section 2-315 of the Uniform Commercial Code, for example, reads:

> Where the seller at the time of contracting has reason to know any particular purpose for which the goods are required and that the buyer is relying on the seller's skill or judgment to select or furnish suitable goods, there is ... an implied warranty that the goods shall be fit for such purpose.

The express or implied claims that a seller might make about the qualities possessed by the product range over a variety of areas and are affected by a number of factors. Frederick Sturdivant classified these areas in terms of four variables: "The definition of product quality used here is: the degree to which product performance meets predetermined expectations with respect to (1) reliability, (2) service life, (3) maintainability, and (4) safety."[27]

reliability The probability that a product will function as the consumer is led to expect that it will function.

Reliability Claims of reliability refer to the probability that a product will function as the consumer is led to expect that it will function. If a product incorporates a number of interdependent components, then the probability that it will function properly is equal to the result of multiplying together each component's probability of proper functioning.[28] As the number of components in a product multiplies, therefore, the manufacturer has a corresponding duty to ensure that each component functions in such a manner that the total product is as reliable as it is implicitly or expressly claimed to be. This is especially the case when malfunction poses health or safety hazards. The U.S. Consumer Product Safety Commission lists hundreds of examples of product hazards on its web site.[29]

service life The period of time during which the product will function as effectively as the consumer is led to expect it to function.

Service Life Claims concerning the life of a product refer to the period of time during which the product will function as effectively as the consumer is led to expect it to function. Generally, the consumer implicitly understands that service life will depend on the amount of wear and tear to which one subjects the product. In addition, consumers also base some of their expectations of service life on the explicit guarantees the manufacturer attaches to the product.

A more subtle factor that influences service life is the factor of obsolescence.[30] Technological advances may render some products obsolete when a new product appears that carries out the same functions more efficiently. Purely stylistic changes may make last year's product appear dated and less desirable. The contract view implies that sellers who know that a certain product will become obsolete have a duty to correct any mistaken beliefs they know buyers will form concerning the service life they may expect from the product.

maintainability The ease with which the product can be repaired and kept in operating condition.

Maintainability Claims of maintainability are claims concerning the ease with which the product can be repaired and kept in operating condition. Claims of maintainability are often made in the form of an express warranty. Whirlpool Corporation, for example, appended this express warranty on one of its products:

> During your first year of ownership, all parts of the appliance (except the light bulbs) that we find are defective in materials or workmanship will be repaired or replaced by Whirlpool free of charge, and we will pay all labor charges. During the second year, we will continue to assume the same responsibility as stated above except you pay any labor charges.[31]

But sellers often also imply that a product may be easily repaired even after the expiration date of an express warranty. In fact, however, product repairs may be costly, or even impossible, because of the unavailability of parts.

product safety The degree of risk associated with using a product.

Product Safety Implied and express claims of product safety refer to the degree of risk associated with using a product. Because the use of virtually any product involves some degree of risk, questions of safety are essentially questions of acceptable and known levels of risk. That is, a product is safe if its attendant risks are known and judged to be "acceptable" or "reasonable" by the buyer in view of the benefits the buyer expects to derive from using the product. This implies that sellers comply with their part of a free agreement if the sellers provide a product that involves only those risks they say it involves, and buyers purchase it with that understanding. The National Commission on Product Safety, for example, has characterized *reasonable risk* in these terms:

> Risks of bodily harm to users are not unreasonable when consumers understand that risks exist, can appraise their probability and severity, know how to cope with them, and voluntarily accept them to get benefits they could not obtain in less risky ways. When there is a risk of this character, consumers have reasonable opportunity to protect themselves; and public authorities should hesitate to substitute their value judgments about the desirability of the risk for those of the consumers who choose to incur it. But preventable risk is not reasonable (a) when consumers do not know that it exists; or (b) when, though aware of it, consumers are unable to estimate its frequency and severity; or (c) when consumers do not know how to cope with it, and hence are likely to incur harm unnecessarily; or (d) when risk is unnecessary in that it could be reduced or eliminated at a cost in money or in the performance of the product that consumers would willingly incur if they knew the facts and were given the choice.[32]

Thus, the seller of a product (according to the contractual theory) has a moral duty to provide a product whose use involves no greater risks than those the seller expressly communicates to the buyer, or those the seller implicitly communicates by the implicit claims made when marketing the product for a use whose normal risk level is well known. If the label on a bottle, for example, indicates only that the contents are highly toxic ("Danger: Poison"), the product should not include additional risks from flammability. If a firm makes and sells skis, use of the skis should not carry risks other than the well-known risks that attend skiing (e.g., it should not involve the added possibility of being pierced by splinters should the skis fracture). In short, sellers have a duty to provide a product with a level of risk that is no higher than they expressly or implicitly claim it to be and that consumers freely and knowingly contract to assume.

The Duty of Disclosure

An agreement cannot bind unless both parties to the agreement know what they are doing and freely choose to do it. This implies that the seller who intends to enter a contract with a customer has a duty to disclose exactly what the customer is buying and what the terms of the sale are. At a minimum, this means the seller has a duty to inform the buyer of any characteristics of the product that could affect the customer's decision to purchase the product. For example, if the product the consumer is buying possesses a defect that poses a risk to the user's health or safety, the consumer should be so informed. Some have argued that sellers should also disclose a product's components or ingredients, its performance characteristics, costs of operation, product ratings, and any other applicable standards.[33]

Behind the claim that entry into a sales contract requires full disclosure is the idea that an agreement is free only to the extent that one knows what alternatives are available: Freedom depends on knowledge. The more the buyer knows about the various products available on the market and the more comparisons the buyer is able to make among them, the more one can say that the buyer's agreement is voluntary.[34]

The view that sellers should provide a great deal of information for buyers, however, has been criticized on the grounds that information is costly and, therefore, should be treated as a product for which the consumer should either pay or do without. In short, consumers should freely contract to purchase information as they freely contract to purchase goods, and producers should not have to provide it for them.[35] The problem with this criticism is that the information on which a person

Quick Review 6.4

Moral Duties to Consumers Under Contractual Theory

- Duty to comply with express and implied claims of reliability, service life, maintainability, and safety
- Duty of disclosure
- Duty not to misrepresent
- Duty not to coerce.

bases a decision to enter a contract is a rather different kind of entity from the product exchanged through the contract. Because a contract must be entered into freely and free choice depends on knowledge, contractual transactions must be based on an open exchange of information. If consumers had to bargain for such information, the resulting contract would hardly be free.

The Duty Not to Misrepresent

Misrepresentation, even more than the failure to disclose information, renders freedom of choice impossible. That is, misrepresentation is coercive: The person who is intentionally misled acts as the deceiver wants the person to act and not as the person would freely have chosen to act if the person had known the truth. Because free choice is an essential ingredient of a binding contract, intentionally misrepresenting the nature of a commodity is ethically wrong.

Sellers misrepresent a commodity when they represent it in a way deliberately intended to deceive the buyer into thinking something about the product that the seller knows is false. The deception may be created by a verbal lie, as when a used model is described as new, or it may be created by a gesture, as when an unmarked used model is displayed together with several new models. The deliberate intent to misrepresent by false implication is as wrong as the explicit lie.

The varieties of misrepresentation seem to be limited only by the ingenuity of the greed that creates them.[36] A computer software or hardware manufacturer may market a product it knows contains "bugs" without informing buyers of that fact; a manufacturer may give a product a name that the manufacturer knows consumers will confuse with the brand name of a higher-quality competing product; the manufacturer may write *wool* or *silk* on material made wholly or partly of cotton; the manufacturer may mark a fictitious "regular price" on an article that is always sold at a much lower "sale" price; a business may advertise an unusually low price for an object that the business actually intends to sell at a much higher price once the consumer is lured into the store; a store may advertise an object at an unusually low price, intending to "bait and switch" the unwary buyer over to a more expensive product; and a producer may solicit paid "testimonials" from professionals who have never really used the product. Sellers can be astonishingly creative. We return to some of these issues when we discuss advertising.

The Duty Not to Coerce

People often act irrationally when under the influence of fear or emotional stress. When a seller takes advantage of a buyer's fear or emotional stress to extract consent to an agreement that the buyer would not make if the buyer were thinking rationally, the seller is using duress or undue influence to coerce. An unscrupulous funeral director, for example, may skillfully induce guilt-ridden and grief-stricken survivors to invest in funeral services they cannot afford. Because entry into a contract requires freely given consent, the seller has a duty to refrain from exploiting emotional states that may induce buyers to act irrationally against their own best interests. For similar reasons, the seller also has the duty not to take advantage of gullibility, immaturity, ignorance, or any other factors that reduce or eliminate the buyer's ability to make free rational choices.

Problems with the Contractual Theory

The main objections to the contract theory focus on the unreality of the assumptions on which the theory is based. First, critics argue, the theory unrealistically assumes that manufacturers make direct agreements with consumers. Nothing could be farther from the truth. Normally, a series of wholesalers and retailers stands between the manufacturer and the ultimate consumer. The manufacturer sells the product to the wholesaler, who sells it to the retailer, who finally sells it to the consumer. The manufacturer never enters into any direct contract with the consumer. How then can one say that manufacturers have contractual duties to the consumer?

Quick Review 6.5

Problems with Contractual Theory

- Assumes makers of products deal directly with consumers but they do not; however manufacturer's advertisements do form a kind of direct promise to consumers.
- Sellers can remove all their duties to buyers by getting them to agree to disclaimers of responsibility.
- Assumes consumer and seller meet as equals, but seller has more knowledge so consumer must rely on the seller.

Advocates of the contract view of manufacturers' duties have tried to respond to this criticism by arguing that manufacturers enter into *indirect* agreements with consumers. Manufacturers promote their products through their own advertising campaigns. These advertisements supply the promises that lead people to purchase products from retailers, who merely function as "conduits" for the manufacturer's product. Consequently, through these advertisements, the manufacturer forges an indirect contractual relationship not only with the immediate retailers who purchase the manufacturer's product, but also with the ultimate consumers of the product. The most famous application of this doctrine of broadened indirect contractual relationships is to be found in a 1960 court opinion, *Henningsen v. Bloomfield Motors*.[37] Mrs. Henningsen was driving a new Plymouth when it suddenly gave off a loud cracking noise. The steering wheel spun out of her hands and the car lurched to the right and crashed into a brick wall. Mrs. Henningsen sued the manufacturer, Chrysler Corporation. The court opinion read:

> Under modern conditions the ordinary layman, on responding to the importuning of colorful advertising, has neither the opportunity nor the capacity to inspect or to determine the fitness of an automobile for use; he must rely on the manufacturer who has control of its construction, and to some degree on the dealer who, to the limited extent called for by the manufacturer's instructions, inspects and services it before delivery. In such a marketing milieu his remedies and those of persons who properly claim through him should not depend "upon the intricacies of the law of sales. The obligation of the manufacturer should not be based alone on privity of contract [that is, on a direct contractual relationship]. It should rest, as was once said, upon "'the demands of social justice'" *Mazetti v. Armous & Co.* (1913). "If privity of contract is required," then, under the circumstances of modern merchandising, "privity of contract exists in the consciousness and understanding of all right-thinking persons. . . ." Accordingly, we hold that under modern marketing conditions, when a manufacturer puts a new automobile in the stream of trade and promotes its purchase by the public, an implied warranty that it is reasonably suitable for use as such accompanies it into the hands of the ultimate purchaser.

Thus, the car manufacturer was found liable for Mrs. Henningsen's injuries on the grounds that its advertising had created a contractual relationship with Mrs. Henningsen and this contract created an "implied warranty" about the car, which the manufacturer had a duty to fulfill.

A second objection to the contract theory focuses on the fact that a contract is a two-edged sword. If a consumer can freely agree to buy a product with certain qualities, the consumer can also freely agree to buy a product without those qualities. That is, freedom of contract allows a manufacturer to be released from contractual obligations by explicitly disclaiming that the product is reliable, serviceable, safe, and so on. Many manufacturers put such disclaimers on their products. The Uniform Commercial Code, in fact, stipulates in Section 2-316:

> a. Unless the circumstances indicate otherwise, all implied warranties are excluded by expressions like "as is," "with all faults," or other language that in common understanding calls the buyer's attention to the exclusion of warranties and makes plain that there is no warranty, and

b. When the buyer before entering into the contract has examined the goods or the sample or model as fully as he desired, or has refused to examine the goods, there is no implied warranty with regard to defects that on examination ought in the circumstances to have been revealed to him.

The contract view, then, implies that if the consumer has ample opportunity to examine the product and the seller's disclaimers of responsibility and voluntarily consents to buy it anyway, the consumer assumes the responsibility for the defects disclaimed by the manufacturer, as well as for any defects the customer may carelessly have overlooked. Disclaimers can effectively nullify all contractual duties of the manufacturer.

A third objection to the contract theory criticizes the assumption that buyer and seller meet each other as equals in the sales agreement. The contractual theory assumes that buyers and sellers are equally skilled at evaluating the quality of a product and that buyers are able to adequately protect their interests against the seller. This is the assumption built into the requirement that contracts must be freely and knowingly entered into: Both parties must know what they are doing and neither must be coerced into doing it. This equality between buyer and seller that the contractual theory assumes derives from the laissez-faire ideology that accompanied the historical development of contract theory.[38] Classical laissez-faire ideology held that the economy's markets are competitive and that in competitive markets the consumer's bargaining power is equal to that of the seller. Competition forces the seller to offer the consumer as good or better terms than the consumer could get from other competing sellers, so the consumer has the power to threaten to take business to other sellers. Because of this equality between buyer and seller, it was fair that each be allowed to try to outbargain the other and unfair to place restrictions on either. In practice, this laissez-faire ideology gave birth to the doctrine of *caveat emptor:* Let the buyer beware.

In fact, sellers and buyers do not exhibit the equality that these doctrines assume. A consumer who must purchase hundreds of different kinds of commodities cannot hope to be as knowledgeable as a manufacturer who specializes in producing a single product and who has greater bargaining power. Consumers generally have neither the expertise nor the time to acquire and process the information on which they must base their purchase decisions. Consequently, consumers must usually rely on the word and the judgment of the seller in making their purchase decisions and are particularly vulnerable to being harmed by the seller. Equality, far from being the rule, as the contract theory assumes, is usually the exception.

due care theory of the manufacturer's duties to consumers The view that because manufacturers are in a more advantaged position and consumers must rely on them, they have a duty to take special care to ensure that consumers' interests are not harmed by the products that they offer them.

caveat emptor Let the buyer take care.

caveat vendor Let the seller take care.

6.3 The Due Care Theory

The **"due care" theory of the manufacturer's duties to consumers** is based on the idea that consumers and sellers do not meet as equals and that the consumer's interests are particularly vulnerable to being harmed by the manufacturer who has a knowledge and an expertise that the consumer lacks. Because manufacturers are in a more advantaged position, they have a duty to take special care to ensure that consumers' interests are not harmed by the products that they offer them. The doctrine of ***caveat emptor*** is here replaced with a weak version of the doctrine of ***caveat vendor***: Let the seller beware. A New York court decision neatly described the advantaged position of the manufacturer and the consequent vulnerability of the consumer:

> Today as never before the product in the hands of the consumer is often a most sophisticated and even mysterious article. Not only does it usually emerge as a sealed unit with an alluring exterior rather than as a visible assembly of component parts, but its functional validity and usefulness often

> depend on the application of electronic, chemical, or hydraulic principles far beyond the ken of the average consumer. Advances in the technologies of materials, of processes, of operational means have put it almost entirely out of the reach of the consumer to comprehend why or how the article operates, and thus even farther out of his reach to detect when there may be a defect or a danger present in its design or manufacture. In today's world it is often only the manufacturer who can fairly be said to know and to understand when an article is suitably designed and safely made for its intended purpose. Once floated on the market, many articles in a very real practical sense defy detection of defect, except possibly in the hands of an expert after laborious, and perhaps even destructive, disassembly. By way of direct illustration, how many automobile purchasers or users have any idea how a power steering mechanism operates or is intended to operate, with its "circulating work and piston assembly and its cross shaft splined to the Pitman arm"? We are accordingly persuaded that from the standpoint of justice as regards the operating aspect of today's products, responsibility should be laid on the manufacturer, subject to the limitations we set forth.[39]

The "due care" view holds, then, that because consumers must depend on the greater expertise of the manufacturer, the manufacturer not only has a duty to deliver a product that lives up to the express and implied claims about it, but also has a duty to exercise due care to prevent others from being injured by the product even if the manufacturer explicitly disclaims such responsibility and the buyer agrees to the disclaimer. The manufacturer violates this duty and is negligent when there is a failure to exercise the care that a reasonable person could have foreseen would be necessary to prevent others from being harmed by use of the product. Due care must enter into the design of the product, the choice of reliable materials for constructing the product, the manufacturing processes involved in putting the product together, the quality control used to test and monitor production, and the warnings, labels, and instructions attached to the product. In each of these areas, according to the due care view, the manufacturer, in virtue of a greater expertise and knowledge, has a positive duty to take whatever steps are necessary to ensure that when the product leaves the plant it is as safe as possible, and the customer has a right to such assurance. Failure to take such steps is a breach of the moral duty to exercise due care and a violation of the injured person's right to expect such care—a right that rests on the consumer's need to rely on the manufacturer's expertise.

The respected scholar of management, Edgar Schein, sketched out the basic elements of the "due care" theory when he noted that "it is the *vulnerability of the client* that has necessitated the development of moral and ethical codes surrounding the relationship" between a professional and his client. A professional—like a lawyer, a doctor, a real estate agent, or an engineer—has knowledge or expertise that he or she exercises in the interests of the client and the client has to trust the professional to protect and advance those interests. But this makes the client vulnerable to being exploited by the more knowledgeable professional. This vulnerability, Schein claims, led to the development of professional codes of ethics that impose on professionals the ethical duty to use their skills only to serve and protect the interests of the client. But the consumer is likewise "in a relatively vulnerable position" relative to the manager of a company from which the consumer buys a product, since the consumer lacks the expertise to adequately evaluate the product. Managers have "knowledge and skills" that they exercise on behalf of the consumer and they can use their knowledge and skills to take advantage of the vulnerable consumer's lack of expertise. Therefore, Schein argues, managers, like professionals, must be charged with the ethical duty

ON THE EDGE

The Tobacco Companies and Product Safety

On June 28, 2010, a mammoth case that had begun more than 10 years earlier finally came to a definitive end. The case, *U.S. v. Philip Morris et al.*, pitted the U.S. Department of Justice (DOJ) against Philip Morris and eight other cigarette companies, and had the DOJ asking that the companies be forced to "disgorge" and give to the government the hundreds of billions of dollars they had earned since 1953. The DOJ argued that since 1953 the companies had conspired to deceive the public about the risks of smoking and its addictive nature, and so had operated as outlaw companies as defined by the Racketeer-Influenced and Corrupt Organizations Act (RICO) which requires convicted companies to "disgorge" the profits they had earned. In 1953, the DOJ showed, the companies met in New York and formed a group called the Tobacco Industry Research Committee (TIRC) that began a "conspiracy to deny that smoking caused disease and to maintain that whether smoking caused disease was an 'open question' despite having actual knowledge that smoking did cause disease." In the 1950s, despite published research showing that smoking causes cancer, the group spent millions of dollars advertising that "there is no proof that cigarette smoking is one of the causes" of lung cancer. For example, one ad virtually shouted: "MORE DOCTORS SMOKE CAMELS THAN ANY OTHER CIGARETTE! Family physicians, surgeons, diagnosticians, nose and throat specialists, doctors in every branch of medicine ... a total of 113,597 doctors ... were asked the question: "What cigarette do you smoke?" And more of them named Camel as their smoke than any other cigarette! Three independent research groups found this to be a fact."

From the 1960s to the 1990s, the companies spent hundreds of millions more advertising that "a cause and effect relationship between smoking and disease has not been established." According to the DOJ's evidence, the tobacco companies advertised that nicotine is not addictive even as they adjusted the amount of nicotine in cigarettes and "controlled the nicotine delivery of cigarettes so that they could addict new users." The DOJ also provided evidence showing the companies "researched how to target their marketing at children and actively marketed cigarettes to children." Finally, the DOJ claimed that the companies had a duty to test their product, to design a safe product, and to warn users of its dangers, yet the companies instead did no research and tried to suppress research on smoking risks, even as they marketed a product that killed 400,000 to 500,000 Americans a year. And until forced to do so in 1969, they did not warn smokers of the health risks and addictive nature of smoking and they targeted children who could not adequately assess the true risks of smoking. In 2006, in a 1652-page opinion, Judge Gladys Kessler of the U.S. District Court for the District of Columbia ruled that the DOJ had fully proved its case against the tobacco companies. However, she also ruled against the DOJ's demand that the companies should be forced to turn over all the profits they had made by conspiring to deceive and harm the public since 1953. Instead, she ruled, the companies would only be "prevented and restrained" from "committing future RICO violations." Almost immediately after Judge Kessler's decision, both the DOJ and the tobacco companies appealed her decision to the U.S. Supreme Court. Four years later, on June 28, 2010, the U.S. Supreme Court decided that Judge Kessler's decision should not be overturned and so rejected the appeals, bringing the decade-long case to an end.

1. If the DOJ claims are true, as Judge Gladys Kessler determined, what do the three theories of manufacturers' duties imply with respect to the ethical obligations of the tobacco companies and the extent to which they met these obligations?
2. Should the tobacco companies have been forced to turn over the profits they made from their "conspiracy"?

to use their knowledge and skills to serve and protect the interests of the vulnerable consumer.[40]

The due care view, of course, rests on the principle that agents have a moral duty not to harm or injure other parties by their acts and that this duty is particularly stringent when those other parties are vulnerable and dependent on the judgment of the agent. This principle can be supported from a variety of different moral perspectives, but it is most clearly implied by the requirements of an ethic of care. The principle follows almost immediately, in fact, from the requirement that one should care for the well-being of those with whom one has a special relationship, particularly a relationship of dependence, such as a child has on its mother. Moreover, an ethic of care imposes the requirement that one should carefully examine the particular needs and characteristics of the person with whom one has a special relationship to ensure that one's care for that person is tailored to that person's particular needs and qualities. This emphasis on carefully examining the specific needs and characteristics of a vulnerable party is also an explicit and essential part of the due care view.

Although the demands of an ethic of care are aligned with the due care principle that manufacturers have a duty to protect vulnerable consumers, the principle has also been defended from other moral perspectives. Rule utilitarians have defended the principle on the grounds that if the rule is accepted, everyone's welfare will be advanced.[41] It also has been argued for on the basis of Kant's theory because the principle seems to follow from the categorical imperative that people should be treated as ends and not merely as means—that is, from the principle that people have a positive right to be helped when they cannot help themselves.[42] Rawls has argued that individuals in the "original position" would agree to the principle because it would provide the basis for a secure social environment.[43] The judgment that individual producers have a duty not to harm or injure vulnerable parties, therefore, is solidly based on several ethical perspectives.

The Duty to Exercise Due Care

According to the due care theory, manufacturers exercise sufficient care only when they take adequate steps to prevent whatever injurious effects they can foresee that the use of their product may have on consumers after having conducted inquiries into the way the product will be used and after having attempted to anticipate possible misuses of the product. A manufacturer is not morally negligent, however, when others are harmed by a product and the harm was not one that the manufacturer could have possibly foreseen or prevented. Nor is a manufacturer morally negligent after having taken all reasonable steps to protect the consumer and ensure that the consumer is informed of any irremovable risks that might still attend the use of the product. For example, a car manufacturer cannot be said to be negligent from a moral point of view when people carelessly misuse the cars the manufacturer produces. A car manufacturer would be morally negligent only if it had allowed unreasonable dangers to remain in the design of the car, i.e., dangers that consumers cannot be expected to know about or cannot guard against on their own.

What specific responsibilities does the duty to exercise due care impose on the producer? In general, the producer's responsibilities would extend to the following three areas:[44]

Quick Review 6.6

Manufacturers' Duties in Due Care Theory

- When designing product, research its risks in conditions of use, design it so risks are minimized, take capacities of users into account.
- In production, use strict quality control to eliminate defects and ensure materials and manufacturing do not add defects or risk.
- When marketing provide users with information about using product safely, warn of all dangers, do not market to those unable to avoid risk.

Design The manufacturer should ascertain whether the design of an article conceals any dangers, whether it incorporates all feasible safety devices, and whether it uses materials that are adequate for the purposes the product is intended to serve. The manufacturer is responsible for being thoroughly acquainted with the design of the item and to conduct research and tests extensive enough to uncover any risks that may be involved in employing the article under various conditions of use. This requires researching consumers and analyzing their behavior, testing the product under different conditions of consumer use, and selecting materials strong enough to stand up to all probable usages. The effects of aging and wear should also be analyzed and taken into account in designing an article.

In determining the safeguards that should be designed into a product, the manufacturer must also take into consideration the capacities of the persons who will use the product. If a manufacturer anticipates that a product will be used by persons who are immature, mentally deficient, or too inexperienced to be aware of the dangers attendant on the use of the product, the manufacturer owes them a greater degree of care than if the anticipated users were of ordinary intelligence and prudence. For example, children cannot be expected to realize the dangers involved in using electrical equipment. Consequently, if a manufacturer anticipates that an electrical item will probably be used by children, steps must be taken to ensure that a person with a child's understanding will not be injured by the product.

Production The production manager should control the manufacturing processes so as to eliminate any defective items, identify any weaknesses that become apparent during production, and ensure that shortcuts, substitution of weaker materials, or other economizing measures are not taken during manufacture that would compromise the safety of the final product. To ensure this, there should be adequate quality controls over materials that are to be used in the manufacture of the product and over the various stages of manufacture.

Marketing The manufacturer should attach labels, notices, or instructions on the product that will warn the user of all dangers involved in using or misusing the item and that will enable the user to adequately guard against harm or injury. These instructions should be clear and simple, and warnings of any hazards involved in using or misusing the product should also be clear, simple, and prominent. In the case of drugs, manufacturers have a duty to warn physicians of any risks or dangerous side effects that research or prolonged use have revealed. It is a breach of the duty not to harm or injure if the manufacturer attempts to conceal or downplay the dangers related to drug usage. A firm should not oppose regulation of the sale of a product when regulation is the only effective means of ensuring that the users of the product are fully aware of the risks its use involves.

If the possible harmful effects of using a product are serious or if they cannot be adequately understood without expert opinion, then sale of the product should be carefully controlled. Products should not be marketed to users who do not have the capacity to understand the dangers of the product or are unable to protect themselves against its risks or are otherwise unable to use the product safely.

Problems with "Due Care"

The basic difficulty raised by the "due care" theory is that there is no clear method for determining when one has exercised enough "due care." That is, there is no hard-and-fast rule for determining how far a firm must go to ensure the safety of its product. Some authors have proposed this general utilitarian rule: The greater the probability of harm and the larger the population that might be harmed, the more the firm is obligated to do. However, this fails to resolve some important issues. Every product involves at least some small risk of injury. If the manufacturer should try to eliminate even low-level risks, this would require that the manufacturer invest so much in each product that the product would be priced out of the reach of most consumers. Moreover, even attempting to balance higher risks against added costs involves measurement problems; for example, how does one quantify risks to health and life?

A second difficulty raised by the "due care" theory is that it assumes that the manufacturer can discover the risks that attend the use of a product before the consumer buys and uses it. In fact, in a technologically innovative society, new products whose defects cannot emerge until years or decades have passed will continually be introduced into the market. Only years after thousands of people were using and being exposed to asbestos, for example, did a clear correlation emerge between the incidence of cancer and exposure to asbestos. Although manufacturers may have greater expertise than consumers, their expertise does not make them omniscient. Who, then, is to bear the costs of injuries sustained from products whose defects neither the manufacturer nor the consumer could have uncovered beforehand?

Third, the "due care" view appears to some to be paternalistic: It assumes that the manufacturer should be the one who makes the important decisions for the consumer, at least with respect to the levels of risks that are proper for consumers to bear. One may wonder whether such decisions should not be left up to the free choice of consumers, who can decide for themselves whether they want to pay for additional risk reduction.

Quick Review 6.7

Problems with Due Care Theory

- Does not limit what producer must spend to eliminate risk
- Does not indicate who should pay for product injuries that cannot be foreseen
- Puts manufacturer in paternalistic position of deciding how much risk is best for consumers.

6.4 The Social Costs View of the Manufacturer's Duties

A third theory on the duties of the manufacturer would extend the manufacturer's duties beyond those imposed by contractual relationships and beyond those imposed by the duty to exercise due care in preventing injury or harm. This third theory, ***the social costs view of the manufacturer's duties to consumers*** holds that a manufacturer should pay the costs of any injuries sustained through any defects in the product, even when the manufacturer exercised all due care in the design and manufacture of the product and has taken all reasonable precautions to warn users of every foreseen danger. According to this third theory, a manufacturer has a duty to assume the risks of even those injuries that arise out of defects in the product that no one could reasonably have foreseen or eliminated. The theory is a strong version of the doctrine of *caveat vendor:* Let the seller beware.

This third theory, which has formed the basis of the legal doctrine of ***strict liability***, is founded on utilitarian arguments.[45] The utilitarian arguments for this third theory hold that the "external" costs of injuries resulting from unavoidable defects in the design of an artifact constitute part of the costs society must pay for producing and using an artifact. By having the manufacturer bear the external costs that result from these injuries as well as the ordinary internal costs of design and manufacture, all costs are internalized and added on as part of the price of the product. Internalizing all costs in this way, according to proponents of this theory, will lead to a more efficient use of society's resources. First, because the price will reflect all the costs of producing and using the artifact, market forces will ensure that the product is not overproduced and resources are not wasted on it. (Whereas if some costs were not included in the price, then manufacturers would tend to consume resources to produce more than is needed.) Second, because manufacturers have to pay the costs of injuries, they will be motivated to exercise greater care and thereby reduce the number of accidents. Therefore, manufacturers will strive to cut down the social costs of injuries, and this means a more efficient use of our resources. To produce the maximum benefits possible from our limited resources, therefore, the social costs of injuries from defective

social costs view of the manufacturer's duties to consumers The view that a manufacturer should pay the costs of any injuries caused by defects in the product, even if the manufacturer exercised all due care in designing, making, and marketing it, and the injury could not have been foreseen.

strict liability A legal doctrine that holds that manufacturers must bear the costs of injuries resulting from product defects regardless of fault.

ON THE EDGE

Selling Personalized Genetics

Several companies on the Internet sell genetic tests directly to consumers including 23andMe, Navigenics, decode Genetics, DNA Tribes, Genelex, ScientificMatch, Consumer Genetics, Salugen, DNAprint Genomics, Genova Diagnostics, Suracell, and many more. The companies ask customers to collect a sample of their genes with a cheek swab and send it to them for testing. Most test by putting the customer's gene sample on a small flat "DNA microarray chip" that already contains pieces of DNA matching known genes (or gene mutations). If one of the customer's genes matches one of the pieces of DNA on the chip, it binds to the DNA fragment which creates a tiny fluorescent glow showing that the gene indicated by the DNA fragment is in the sample. A computer then analyzes the pattern of glowing spots on the chip and prints out a list of the genes (or gene mutations) in the customer's sample. Scientists have discovered a few genes that are associated with specific diseases or personal characteristics. Studies found, for example, genes that are linked to cystic fibrosis, Tay Sachs disease, and Lou Gehrig's disease, genes that increase the risk of certain breast, colon, and thyroid cancers, and genes associated with sensation seeking, eye color, obesity, and lactose intolerance. They also found that some genes are more often found in people whose ancestors came from certain regions of the world. The companies say that based on these studies and their own gene tests, they can give customers valuable personalized information (for a price, of course). One company, Sciona, (no longer operating) said on its web site: "Sciona is a leader in nutrigenomics, the science of personalizing your nutrition and lifestyle choices to match your genes"; Sciona gave customers "a personalized preventative dietary regime" that was supposed to prevent the diseases their genes put them at risk for. Another site promises: "Based upon the ... [genetic] analysis, Suracell recommends to each client a personalized regimen of nutraceuticals [vitamin supplements]." Another states: "DNA Tribes ... uses genetic material ... to measure your genetic connections to individual ethnic groups and major world regions." Another company claims to do it all: "With a simple saliva sample we'll help you gain insight into your traits, from baldness to muscle performance. Discover risk factors for 95 diseases. Know your predicted response to drugs, from blood thinners to coffee. And uncover your ancestral origins." Critics claim, however, that with a few exceptions, most studies have shown only weak connections between genes and specific traits, disease risks, drug responses, nutritional or vitamin needs, or ancestral origins. Many studies that link specific genes to a disease are only preliminary and the full picture has not yet been worked out. Moreover, critics say, it is wrong to tell customers their genes put them at risk of a deadly disease without proper counseling, especially when the scientific studies are weak and many other environmental, demographic, and lifestyle factors determine actual onset of a disease. Ordinary consumers, they conclude, are being sold a product that they do not have the expertise to interpret. But defenders of the tests say consumers have a right to know what genes they carry and what science has learned about those genes. The companies charge from $140 to test for two or three genes, up to $999 to test for a full suite of genes.

1. Evaluate the ethics of selling gene tests directly to consumers like these companies are doing. What would each of the three theories of a business's duties to consumers say about what the companies are doing? Under what conditions do you think selling the tests would be ethically legitimate?
2. Check out the video of GAO interviews of gene-test company sales people at *http://www.gao.gov/products/gao-10-847t.* Evaluate the selling practices shown on the video.

products should be internalized by passing them on to the manufacturer even when the manufacturer has done all that could be done to eliminate such defects. Third, internalizing the costs of injury in this way enables the manufacturer to distribute losses among all the users of a product instead of allowing losses to fall on a few injured individuals who otherwise would have to bear all the costs of injury. Such a distribution of costs would seem to be more fair than imposing the costs on a few victims.

Underlying this third theory on the duties of the manufacturer are the standard utilitarian assumptions about the values of efficiency. The theory assumes that an efficient use of resources is so important for society that social costs should be allocated in whatever way will lead to a more efficient use and care of our resources. On this basis, the theory argues that a manufacturer should bear the social costs for injuries caused by defects in a product even when no negligence was involved and no contractual relationship existed between the manufacturer and user.

Quick Review 6.8

The Social Costs View

- Claims manufacturer should pay the costs of all injuries caused by defects in a product even if the manufacturer exercised all due care and the injury could not have been foreseen
- Argues product injuries are external costs that should be internalized as a cost of bringing the product to market, this maximizes utility and distributes costs more fairly.

Criticisms of the Social Costs View

The major criticism of the social costs view of the manufacturer's duties is that it is unjust.[46] It is unjust, the critics charge, because it violates the basic canons of compensatory justice. Compensatory justice implies that a person should have to compensate an injured party only if the person could have foreseen and prevented the injury. By forcing manufacturers to pay for injuries they could neither foresee nor prevent, the social costs theory (and the legal theory of "strict liability" that flows from it) treats manufacturers unjustly. Moreover, insofar as the social costs theory encourages passing the costs of injuries on to all consumers (in the form of higher prices), consumers are also being treated unfairly since they had nothing to do with the injuries.

A second criticism of the social costs theory attacks the assumption that passing the costs of all injuries on to manufacturers will reduce the number of accidents.[47] On the contrary, critics claim, by relieving consumers of the responsibility of paying for their own injuries, the social costs theory will encourage carelessness in consumers. An increase in consumer carelessness will lead to an increase in consumer injuries.

A third argument against the social costs theory focuses on the financial burdens the theory imposes on manufacturers and insurance carriers. Critics claim that a growing number of consumers successfully sue manufacturers for compensation for any injuries sustained while using a product even when the manufacturer took all due care to ensure that the product was safe.[48] Not only have the number of "strict liability" suits increased, critics claim, but the amounts awarded to injured consumers have also escalated. Moreover, they continue, the rising costs of the many liability suits that the theory of "strict liability" has created have precipitated a crisis in the insurance industry because insurance companies end up paying the liability suits brought against manufacturers. These high costs have imposed heavy losses on insurance companies and have forced many insurance companies to raise their rates to levels that are so high that many manufacturers can no longer afford insurance. Thus, critics claim, the social costs or "strict liability" theory wreaks havoc with the insurance industry, forces the costs of insurance to climb to unreasonable heights, and forces many valuable firms out of business because they can no longer afford liability insurance, nor can they afford to pay for the many and expensive liability suits they must now face.

Defenders of the social costs view, however, have replied that in reality the costs of consumer liability suits are not large. Studies have shown that the number of liability suits filed in state courts has increased at a fairly low rate.[49] Less than 1 percent of product-related injuries results in suits, and successful suits average payments of only a few thousand dollars.[50] Defenders of the social costs theory also point out that insurance companies and the insurance industry as a whole have remained quite

Quick Review 6.9

Criticisms of the Social Cost View

- Unjust to manufacturers since compensatory justice says one should compensate injured parties only if the injury was foreseeable and preventable
- Falsely assumes that the social cost view prevents accidents; instead, encourages consumer carelessness by relieving them of responsibility for their injuries
- Has increased the number of successful consumer lawsuits which imposes heavy losses on insurance companies, and makes insurance too expensive for many firms; however studies show only small increase in lawsuits and insurance firms remain profitable.

profitable; they also claim that higher insurance costs are due to factors other than an increase in the amount of liability claims.[51]

The arguments for and against the social costs theory deserve much more discussion than we can give them here. The theory is essentially an attempt to come to grips with the problem of allocating the costs of injuries between two morally innocent parties: the manufacturer who could not foresee or prevent a product-related injury and the consumer who could not guard against the injury because the hazard was unknown. This allocation problem will arise in any society that, like ours, has come to rely on technology whose effects do not become evident until years after the technology is introduced. Unfortunately, it is also a problem that may have no "fair" solution.

Quick Review 6.10

Characteristics of Advertising

- A public communication aimed at a large social group intended to induce members of this audience to buy the seller's products.
- It succeeds by creating a desire for the seller's product or a belief that a product will satisfy a preexisting desire.

6.5 Advertising Ethics

The advertising industry is a massive business. Over $188 billion was spent in 2008 on advertising.[52] More than $55 billion was spent on broadcast and cable television advertising alone; another $54 billion was spent on newspaper and magazine advertisements; and $23 billion was spent on Internet advertising.[53] There are over 6,000 advertising agencies doing business in the United States, many of which employ several thousand people.

Who pays for these advertising expenditures? In the end, advertising costs must be covered by the prices consumers pay for the goods they buy—the consumer pays. What do consumers get for their advertising dollar? According to most consumers, they get very little. Surveys have shown that 66 percent of consumers feel that advertising does not reduce prices, 65 percent believe it makes people buy things they should not buy, 54 percent feel advertisements insult their intelligence, and 63 percent feel advertisements do not present the truth.[54] However, defenders of the advertising industry see things differently. Advertising, they claim, "is, before all else, communication."[55] Its basic function is to provide consumers with information about the products available to them—a beneficial service.[56]

Is advertising, then, a waste or a benefit? Does it harm consumers or help them?

A Definition

commercial advertising Communication between a seller and potential buyers that is publicly addressed to a mass audience and is intended to induce members of this audience to buy the seller's products.

Commercial advertising is sometimes defined as a form of "information" and an advertiser as "one who gives information." The implication is that the defining function of advertising is to provide information to consumers. This definition of advertising, however, fails to distinguish advertisements from, say, articles in publications like *Consumer Reports*, which compare, test, and objectively evaluate the durability, safety, defects, and usefulness of various products. One study found that more than half of all television ads contained no consumer information whatsoever about the advertised product and that only half of all magazine ads contained more than one informational cue.[57] Consider how much information is conveyed by the following advertisements:

"Got Milk?" (America's Dairy Farmers and Milk Processors)

"Be late" (Neiman Marcus watches)

"Embrace your demons" (cinnamon-flavored Altoids)

"For the way it's made" (KitchenAid home appliances)

"Connect with style" (Nokia cell phones)

"Have it your way" (Burger King)

"Inside every woman is a glow just waiting to come out" (Dove soap)

"It is, in the end, the simple idea that one plus one can, and must, equal more than two" (Chrysler cars)

"Doing what we do best" (American Airlines)

"The United Colors of Benetton" (Benetton)

"Before there was a Land Rover there was a dream" (Land Rover S.U.V.)

Advertisements often do not include much objective information for the simple reason that their primary function is not that of providing unbiased information. The primary function of commercial advertisements, rather, is to sell a product to prospective buyers, and whatever information they happen to carry is subsidiary to this basic function and usually determined by it.

A more helpful way of characterizing commercial advertising is in terms of the buyer–seller relationship: Commercial advertising can be defined as a certain kind of communication between a seller and potential buyers. It is distinguished from other forms of communication by two features. First, it is publicly addressed to a mass audience as distinct from a private message to a specific individual. Because of this public feature, advertising can have widespread social effects.

Second, advertising is intended to induce members of its audience to buy the seller's products. An advertisement can succeed in this intent in two main ways: (1) by creating a desire for the seller's product in consumers and (2) by creating a belief in consumers that the product is a means of satisfying some desire the buyer already has.

Discussion of the ethical aspects of advertising can be organized around the various features identified in the prior definition: its social effects, its creation of consumer desires, and its effects on consumer beliefs. We begin by discussing the social effects of advertising.

Social Effects of Advertising

Critics of advertising claim that it has several adverse effects on society: It degrades people's tastes, it wastes valuable resources, and it creates monopoly power. We examine these criticisms one by one.

Psychological Effects of Advertising A familiar criticism of advertising is that it debases the tastes of the public by presenting irritating and aesthetically unpleasant displays.[58] To be effective, advertisements must often be intrusive, strident, and repetitive. Therefore, so that they are understood by the most simple-minded person, advertisements are often boring, insipid, and insult the intelligence of viewers. In illustrating the use of toothpaste, mouthwashes, deodorants, and underwear, for example, advertisements sometimes employ images that many people find vulgar, offensive, disgusting, and tasteless. However, although these sorts of criticisms may be accurate, they do not seem to raise truly ethical issues. It is certainly unfortunate that advertisements do not measure up to our aesthetic norms, but this does not imply that they also violate our ethical norms.

More to the point is the criticism that advertising debases the tastes of consumers by gradually and subtly inculcating materialistic values and ideas about how happiness is achieved.[59] Because advertising necessarily emphasizes the consumption of material goods, people are led to forget the importance of their other, more basic needs and of other, more realistic ways of achieving self-fulfillment. As a result, personal efforts

ON THE EDGE

Advertising Death to Kids?

Because 4 million of their worldwide customers die each year, tobacco companies like R .J. Reynolds have to keep recruiting new smokers. Few people start smoking after they reach adulthood (88 percent of smokers start before they are 18), so new recruits have to come from the ranks of children. As an internal report by a cigarette company stated: "Today's teenager is tomorrow's potential regular customer, and the overwhelming majority of smokers first begin to smoke while still in their teens." So in spite of a 1998 legal settlement prohibiting cigarette promotions aimed at children, R. J. Reynolds (RJR) has run large multi-page ads promoting a "collaboration between Camel and independent artists and record labels" in *Rolling Stone* magazine whose readers include more than 1.5 million teenagers. The tobacco ads featured cartoons of animals, monsters, aliens, and space ships and references to "an alternate dimension where everyone wears Black Converse." In 2007, RJR marketed Camel cigarettes flavored with tastes of cocoa, Asian mint, sweet apple, and toasted honey. Earlier, an internal RJR memo suggested making "a cigarette which is obviously youth oriented ... for example, a flavor which would be candy-like but give the satisfaction of a cigarette." RJR has also promoted a new product, "Camel No. 9," packaged in a pink wrapper, in women's magazines whose readers include a high percentage of young girls. The number of teen girls who now say Camel ads are their favorite ads has doubled since the promotion began.

RJR and other tobacco companies are spending more money (now a record 90 percent of the $12.5 billion they spend on tobacco promotions) advertising in retail stores and other places where their ads will be visible to children, placing them at childrens' eye level or next to candy shelves. At least once a week most teens (75 percent) visit retail stores, 80 percent of which post tobacco ads inside, and 60 percent of which post them outside. Advertisements for those cigarette brands most popular with children reach 80 percent of children an average of 17 times a year. According to the U.S. Surgeon General, cigarettes are known to injure nearly every bodily organ by inducing deadly cancerous tumors inside the mouth, lungs, throat, larynx, esophagus, bladder, stomach, cervix, kidney, and

Source: Meg Riordan, "Tobacco Industry Continues to Market to Kids," Campaign for Tobacco-Free Kids, *http://tobaccofreekids.org/research/factsheets.*

RJR promoted this pink-colored "Camel No 9" cigarette box in magazines whose readers included a high percentage of young girls.

The number of teenage girls who say Camel ads are their favorite doubled when RJR began promoting "Camel No 9" in magazines read by young girls.

pancreas and by causing emphysema and heart attacks. Joe Tye, an industry critic, notes: "No advertising is more deceptive than that used to sell cigarettes. Images of independence are used to sell a product that creates profound dependence. Images of health and vitality are used to sell a product that causes disease and suffering. Images of life are used to sell a product that causes death." Numerous studies show banning cigarette ads would significantly reduce teen smoking. But tobacco companies oppose ad restrictions, arguing that they violate free speech, that cigarette ads are not deceptive and smokers know the risks which are on every pack and ad, that people have a right to smoke and to have information about cigarette brands, that ads do not make people start smoking or smoke more but only keep smokers from changing brand, and that their ads do not intentionally target children.

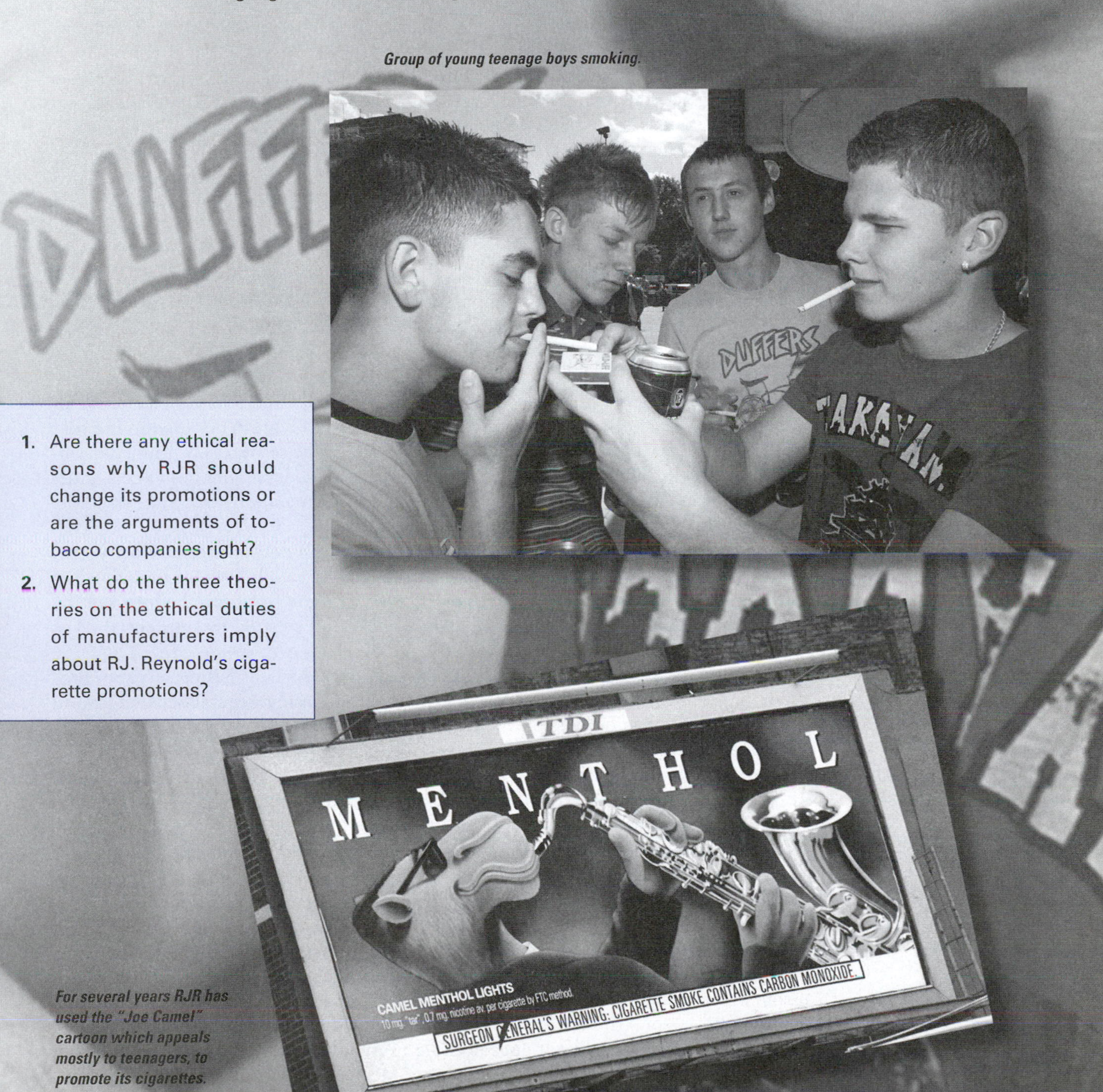

Group of young teenage boys smoking.

For several years RJR has used the "Joe Camel" cartoon which appeals mostly to teenagers, to promote its cigarettes.

1. Are there any ethical reasons why RJR should change its promotions or are the arguments of tobacco companies right?
2. What do the three theories on the ethical duties of manufacturers imply about RJ. Reynold's cigarette promotions?

are diverted from "nonmaterialistic" aims and objectives, which are more likely to increase the happiness of people, and are instead channeled into expanded material consumption. Consumer advocate Mary Gardiner Jones once wrote, for example, that the message of any television advertisement has two basic premises. The first is that it is by acquiring things that we will "gratify our basic and inner needs and aspirations." That is, all of our problems will be "instantly eliminated by the use of a product." The second premise is that everyone is "externally motivated," in the sense that we all want to emulate "our neighbors" or "popular successful individuals" and that personal success comes from having external things instead of being "the product of years of study and training." Advertisements lead us to adopt this "essentially materialistic" message.[60]

The difficulty with this kind of criticism, however, is that it is uncertain whether advertising actually has the large psychological effects the criticism attributes to it.[61] A person's beliefs and attitudes are notoriously difficult to change without their willingness to accept the message being offered. Thus, the success of advertising may depend more on its appeal to the values consumers already possess than on its ability to instill new values. If this is so, then advertising does not so much create society's values as reflect them.

Advertising and Waste A second major criticism brought against advertising is that it is wasteful and so violates utilitarian principles.[62] Economists sometimes distinguish between ***production costs*** and ***selling costs***. Production costs are the costs of the resources consumed in producing or improving a product. Selling costs are the additional costs of resources that do not go into changing the product, but are invested instead in getting people to buy the product. The costs of resources consumed by advertising, critics claim, are essentially "selling costs": They are not used to improve the product, but to merely persuade people to buy it. The resources consumed by advertisements do not add anything to the utility of the product. Such resources, critics conclude, are "wasted" because they are expended without adding to consumer utility in any way.

production costs The costs of the resources consumed in producing or improving a product.

selling costs The additional costs of resources that do not go into changing the product, but are invested instead in getting people to buy the product.

One reply made to this argument is that advertising does in fact produce something: It produces and transmits information on the availability and the nature of products.[63] Yet as many have pointed out, even in these respects, the information content of advertisements is minimal and could be transmitted by substantially less expensive means.[64]

Another more persuasive reply to the argument is that advertising serves to produce a beneficial rise in demand for all products. This rising general demand in turn makes mass production possible. The end result is a gradually expanding economy in which products are manufactured with ever greater efficiency and ever more cheaply. Advertising adds to consumer utility by serving as an incentive to greater consumption and thereby, indirectly motivating a greater productivity and efficiency and a lower price structure.[65]

However, there is substantial uncertainty surrounding the question of whether advertising is responsible for a rise in the total consumption of goods.[66] Studies have shown that advertising frequently fails to stimulate consumption of a product, and consumption in many industries has increased despite minimal advertising expenditures. Thus, advertising appears to be effective for individual companies not because it expands consumption, but only because it shifts consumption away from one product to another. If this is true, then economists are correct when they claim that, beyond the level needed to impart information, advertising becomes a waste of resources because it does nothing more than shift demand from one firm to another.[67]

Moreover, even if advertising were an effective spur to consumption, many authors have argued, this is not necessarily a blessing. E. F. Schumacher, Herman E. Daly, and other economists have claimed that the most pressing social need at present is finding ways to *decrease* consumption.[68] Increasing consumption has led to a rapid industrial expansion that has polluted much of the natural environment and has rapidly depleted our nonrenewable resources. Unless we limit consumption, we will soon outrun the finite natural resources our planet possesses with disastrous consequences for us all. If this is so, then the claim that advertising induces ever higher levels of consumption is not in its favor.

Quick Review 6.11

Criticisms of Advertising Based on its Social Effects

- It debases the tastes of the public; but this criticism is not a moral criticism.
- It inculcates materialistic values; but this criticism ignores the lack of evidence that advertisements can change people's values.
- Its costs are selling costs that, unlike production costs, do not add to the utility of products and so waste resources; but this criticism ignores how advertising can increase consumption which is good; however, studies suggest advertising does not increase consumption and anyway increasing consumption is not necessarily good.
- It is used by big firms to create brand loyalties which let them become monopolies or oligopolies; however this criticism ignores studies showing big monopoly or oligopoly firms do not advertise more than little firms.

Advertising and Market Power For many decades, Nicholas Kaldor and others have claimed that the massive advertising campaigns of modern manufacturers enable them to achieve and maintain a monopoly (or oligopoly) power over their markets.[69] Monopolies, as we have seen, lead to higher consumer prices. Kaldor's argument was simple. Large manufacturers have the financial resources to mount massive and expensive advertising campaigns to introduce their products. These campaigns create in consumers a "loyalty" to the brand name of the manufacturer, giving the manufacturer control of a major portion of the market. Small firms are then unable to break into the market because they cannot finance the expensive advertising campaigns that would be required to get consumers to switch their brand loyalties. As a result, a few large oligopoly firms emerge in control of consumer markets from which small firms are effectively barred. Advertising, then, is supposed to reduce competition and raise barriers to entry into markets.

However, is there a connection between advertising and market power? If advertising does raise costs for consumers by encouraging monopoly markets, there should be a statistical connection between the amount of advertising revenues spent by an industry and the degree of market concentration in that industry. The more concentrated and less competitive industries should exhibit high levels of advertising, whereas less concentrated and more competitive industries should exhibit correspondingly lower levels. Unfortunately, the statistical studies aimed at uncovering a connection between advertising intensity and market concentration have been inconclusive.[70] Some concentrated industries (soaps, cigarettes, breakfast cereals) expend large amounts on advertising, but others (drugs, cosmetics) do not. Moreover, in at least some oligopoly industries (e.g., the auto industry), smaller firms spend more per unit on advertising than the large major firms. Whether advertising harms consumers by diminishing competition is an interesting but unsettled question.

The criticisms of advertising based on its social effects are inconclusive. They are inconclusive because it is unknown whether advertising has the capacity to produce the effects that the critics assume it has. To establish the case for or against advertising on the basis of its effects on society will require a great deal more research on the exact nature of the psychological and economic effects advertising has.

Advertising and the Creation of Consumer Desires

John K. Galbraith and others have argued that advertising is manipulative: It is the creation of desires in consumers for the sole purpose of absorbing industrial output.[71] Galbraith distinguished two kinds of desires: those that have a "physical" basis, such as desires for food and shelter, and those that are "psychological in origin," such as the individual's desires for goods that "give him a sense of personal achievement, accord him a feeling of equality with his neighbors, direct his mind from thought, serve sexual aspiration, promise social acceptability, enhance his subjective feeling of health, contribute by conventional canons to personal beauty, or are otherwise

Quick Review 6.12

Criticism of Advertising Based on its Effects on Desires

- Galbraith claimed advertising creates psychic desires which, unlike physical desires, are pliable and unlimited.
- Psychic desires are created so firms can use us to absorb their output.
- Using us this way treats us as means and not as ends and so is unethical.
- However, this criticism ignores studies which suggest advertising cannot create and manipulate desires; on the other hand, subliminal ads can manipulate our desires and children's desires can be manipulated.

psychologically rewarding."[72] The physically based desires originate in the buyer and are relatively immune to being changed by persuasion. The psychic desires, however, are capable of being managed, controlled, and expanded by advertising. Because the demand created by physical needs is finite, producers soon produce enough to meet these needs. If production is to expand, therefore, producers must create new demand by manipulating the pliable psychic desires through advertising. Advertising is therefore used to create psychic desires for the sole purpose of "ensuring that people buy what is produced"—that is, to absorb the output of an expanding industrial system.

The effect of this management of demand through advertising is to shift the focus of decision in the purchase of goods from the consumer, where it is beyond control, to the firm, where it is subject to control.[73] Production is not molded to serve human desires; rather, human desires are molded to serve the needs of production. If this view of Galbraith's is correct, then advertising violates the individual's right to choose: Advertising manipulates the consumer. The consumer is used merely as a means for advancing the ends and purposes of producers, and this diminishes the consumer's capacity to freely choose.[74]

It is not clear that Galbraith's argument is correct. As we have already seen, the psychological effects of advertising are still unclear. Consequently, it is unclear whether psychic desires can be manipulated by advertising in the wholesale way that Galbraith's argument assumes.[75] Moreover, as F. A. von Hayek and others have pointed out, the "creation" of psychic wants did not originate with modern advertising.[76] New wants have always been "created" by the invention of novel and attractive products (such as the first bow and arrow, the first painting, the first perfume), and such a creation of wants seems harmless enough.

However, although it is unclear whether advertising as a whole has the massive manipulative effects that Galbraith attributes to it, it is clear that some particular advertisements are at least intended to manipulate. They are intended to arouse in consumers a psychological desire for the product without consumers' knowledge and without consumers being able to rationally weigh whether the product is in their own best interests. Advertisements that intentionally rely on "subliminal suggestion," or that attempt to make consumers associate unreal sexual or social fulfillment with a product, fall into this class, as do advertisements that are aimed at children.

Suppa Corporation in Fallbrook, California, for example, briefly tested candy advertisements printed on paper on which the word *buy* was written so it would register subconsciously, but could not be consciously perceived unless one specifically looked for it. Subsequent tests showed that the ads created more of a desire to buy candy than those printed on paper on which the word *no* appeared in a similar subliminal manner.[77] Manipulative ads aimed at children are exemplified by a criticism the National Advertising Division of the Council of Better Business Bureaus recently leveled at a Mattel, Inc. television commercial aimed at children, which mixed animation sequences with group shots of dolls. Children who are still learning to distinguish between fantasy and reality, the council felt, would not be given "an accurate depiction of the products" pictured in the advertisements.[78] The council also criticized a Walt Disney Music Co. advertisement of a limited-time offer that conveyed a "sense of urgency" that children might find "overwhelming." Critics have also claimed that television shows of animated characters resembling toy dolls and figures that are advertised on the same show are, in effect, prolonged advertisements for these toys. The effect of such "half-hour advertisements," they allege, is to manipulate vulnerable children by feeding them commercials under the guise of entertainment.[79] Moreover, such advertisement programs often contain high levels of violence because their cartoon superhero characters such as "He-Man," "Rambo," "GI Joe," and "Transformers," are violent. Advertising that promotes toys modeled on violent characters or promotes military toys indirectly promotes aggression and violent behavior in children who are highly suggestible and easily manipulated, critics claim, and it is therefore unethical.[80] Advertisements of this sort are manipulative insofar as they circumvent conscious reasoning and seek to influence the consumer to do what the advertiser wants and not what is in the consumer's interests.[81] They violate, that is, the consumer's right to be treated as a free and equal rational being.

Advertising and Its Deceptive Effects on Beliefs

The most common criticism of advertising concerns its effect on the consumer's beliefs. Because advertising is a form of communication, it can be as truthful or deceptive as any other form of communication. Most criticisms of advertising focus on the deceptive aspects of modern advertising.

Deceptive advertising can take several forms. An advertisement can misrepresent the nature of the product by using deceptive mock-ups, using untrue paid testimonials, inserting the word *guarantee* where nothing is guaranteed, quoting misleading prices, failing to disclose defects in a product, misleadingly disparaging a competitor's goods, or simulating well-known brand names. Some deceptive forms of advertising involve more complex schemes. For example, bait advertisements announce the sale of goods that later prove not to be available or to be defective. Once consumers are lured into the store, they are pressured to purchase another, more expensive item.

A long ethical tradition has consistently condemned deception in advertising on the grounds that it violates consumers' rights to choose for themselves (a Kantian argument) and on the grounds that it generates a public distrust of advertising that diminishes the utility of this form and even of other forms of communication (a utilitarian argument).[82] The central problem, then, is not understanding why deceptive advertising is wrong, but understanding at what point it becomes deceptive and, therefore, unethical.

All communication involves three elements: (1) the author(s) who originates the communication, (2) the medium that carries the communication, and (3) the audience who receives the communication. Because advertising is a form of communication, it involves these three elements, and the various ethical problems raised by the fact that it is a form of communication can be organized around them.

Quick Review 6.13

Deceptive Advertising Requires

- An author who (unethically) intends to make the audience believe what he or she knows is false by means of an intentional act or utterance.
- Media or intermediaries who communicate the false message of the advertisement and so are also responsible for its deceptive effects.
- An audience who is vulnerable to the deception and who lacks the capacity to recognize the deceptive nature of the advertisement.

The Authors Deception involves three necessary conditions in the author of a communication: (1) The author must intend to have the audience believe something false, (2) the author must know it is false, and (3) the author must intentionally utter or do something that leads the audience to believe the falsehood. This means that the deliberate intent to have an audience believe something false by merely implying it is already a deception. It also means, however, that the advertiser cannot be held morally responsible for misinterpretations of an advertisement when these are the unintended and unforeseen results of unreasonable carelessness on the part of the audience. The "author" of an advertisement should be taken to include not only the heads of an advertising agency, but also the persons who create advertising copy and those who "endorse" a product. By offering their positive cooperation in the making of an advertisement, they become morally responsible for its deceptive effects so long as they knew what they were doing and could have opted out of doing it.

The Media Part of the responsibility for truth in advertising rests on the media or intermediaries that carry or transmit the message of the advertisements. As active participants in the communication of a message, they also lend their positive cooperation to the success of the advertisement and so they, too, become morally responsible for its effects. Therefore, they should take steps to ensure that the contents of their advertisements are true and not misleading. In the drug industry, retail agents who serve as company sales agents to doctors and hospitals are in effect a form of advertising "media" and are morally responsible for not carrying misleading information to doctors about the safety and risks of the drugs their company wants them to promote.

The Audience Whether an advertisement is deceptive depends in part on the capacities of the person or persons who receive the message. A clever and knowledgeable audience, for example, may be capable of correctly interpreting an advertisement that may be misleading to a less-knowledgeable or less-educated group. Consequently, advertisers should take into account the interpretive capacities of the audience when they design an advertisement. Most buyers can be expected to be reasonably intelligent and possess a healthy skepticism concerning the exaggerated claims advertisers make for their products. Advertisements that will reach the ignorant, credulous, immature, and unthinking, however, should be designed to avoid misleading even those potential buyers whose judgment is limited. When matters of health or safety, or the possibility of significant injury to buyers is involved, special care should be exercised to ensure that advertisements do not mislead users into ignoring possible dangers.

This third category of issues ("The Audience") raises what is perhaps the most troubling problem in advertising ethics: To what extent do consumers possess the capacity to filter out the puffery and bias most advertising messages carry? When an advertisement for a Norelco electric shaver proclaims, "You can't get any closer," do consumers automatically discount the vague, nonspecific, and false implication that Norelco was tested against every possible method of shaving and was found to leave facial hair shorter than any other method? Unfortunately, we have little knowledge of the extent to which consumers are able to filter out the exaggerations advertisements contain.

The moral issues raised by advertising are complex and involve several still unsolved problems. However, the following summarizes the main factors that should be taken into consideration when determining the ethical nature of a given advertisement:

Social Effects

1. What does the advertiser intend the effect of the advertisement to be?
2. What are the actual effects of the advertisement on individuals and on society as a whole?

Effects on Desire

1. Does the advertisement inform or does it also seek to persuade?
2. If it is persuasive, does it attempt to create an irrational and possibly injurious desire?

Effects on Belief

1. Is the content of the advertisement truthful?
2. Does the advertisement have a tendency to mislead those to whom it is directed?

6.6 Consumer Privacy

Advances in computer processing power, database software, and communication technologies have given us the power to collect, manipulate, and disseminate personal information about consumers on an unprecedented scale. This new power over the collection, manipulation, and dissemination of personal information has enabled mass invasions of the privacy of consumers and has created the potential for significant harm arising from the spread of mistaken or false information. For example, a pair of British investigators reported that in England, where companies register with the government the kind of information they will collect, businesses were collecting highly detailed and very personal information about their customers. The Midland Bank, for example, was given approval to collect information about the sex lives of customers who were applying for insurance; another company was cleared to collect and store sexual and political information about any of its customers; a retailer, W.H. Smith, had permission to collect sexual data for "personnel and employee administration; a leisure company, Grand Metropolitan, could store similar information for use by its corporate lawyers; and BT was approved to collect information about political party affiliation "as a reference tool."[83]

In the United States, fairly complete files on the medical history of consumers is maintained by the Medical Information Bureau (MIB), a company founded in 1902 to provide insurance companies with information about the health of individuals applying for life insurance to detect fraudulent applications. The MIB currently has medical histories on about 15 million people. Information is collected from the forms consumers fill out when applying for life insurance, the applicant's physician, hospitals, employment records, the Department of Motor Vehicles (DMV), and even interviews with employers or friends. But information in these files is sometimes inaccurate. One individual was erroneously reported to have AIDS and to be gay, whereas another was wrongly reported to be an alcoholic.[84]

The most complete files on consumers are those maintained by credit bureaus. Credit bureaus provide credit reports about specific individuals to banks, retailers, employers, and other businesses who ask for information about specific customers. These credit reports include information about a person's credit card accounts, mortgages, bank loans, student loans, history of payments on these with special notes on late payments, foreclosures, bankruptcies, details about loan amounts, nonpayment of property taxes, personal or property liens, divorce proceedings, marriage licenses, driver licenses, civil lawsuits, present and past employers, present and previous addresses, and other personal information compiled from various sources. There are currently three main bureaus—Experian (formerly TRW), Equifax, and Trans Union LLC—that together compile information on about 150 million consumers. Every day fresh credit data come into each bureau that must be entered into the appropriate files. Equifax has estimated that its staff must input some 65 million updates each day. Not surprisingly, a study by *Consumer Reports* found errors in 43 percent of the reports they analyzed.[85] These errors can result in being refused a loan, credit card, or job. Beyond the problems created by errors in the data files maintained on them, consumers worry that the detailed information that credit bureaus compile will be given to inappropriate parties. For example, until a few years ago, credit bureaus would sell names from their files to junk mailers. The potential for invading consumers' privacy is clearly quite high. To discuss this issue, however, it is important to have a clearer idea about what privacy is and why consumers and others have a right to privacy.

Speaking broadly, the right to privacy is the right to be left alone. We do not discuss this broad characterization of the right to privacy, however, but concentrate on privacy as the right of individuals not to have others spy on their private life. In this more narrow sense, the **right to privacy** can be defined as the right of persons to determine what, to whom, and how much information about themselves will be disclosed to other parties.[86]

right to privacy The right of persons to determine what, to whom, and how much information about themselves will be disclosed to other parties.

psychological privacy Privacy with respect to a person's inner life.

physical privacy Privacy with respect to a person's physical activities.

There are two basic types of privacy: *psychological* and *physical*.[87] **Psychological privacy** is privacy with respect to a person's inner life. This includes the person's thoughts and plans, personal beliefs and values, feelings, and wants. These inner aspects of a person are so intimately connected with the person that to invade them is almost an invasion of the very person. **Physical privacy** is privacy with respect to a person's physical activities. Because people's inner lives are revealed by their physical activities and expressions, physical privacy is important in part because it is a means for protecting psychological privacy. However, many of our physical activities are considered "private" apart from their connection to our inner life. What kinds of activities are considered private depends to some extent on the conventions of one's culture. For example, a person in our culture normally feels degraded if forced to disrobe publicly or perform biological or sexual functions in public. Physical privacy, therefore, is also valued for its own sake.

The purpose of rights, as analyzed in Chapter 2, is to enable individuals to pursue their significant interests and to protect these interests from the intrusions of other individuals. To say that persons have a moral right to something is to say at least that they have a substantial interest in that "something." Why is our interest in privacy considered important enough to surround it with the protection of a right?[88] To begin with, privacy has several protective functions. First, privacy ensures that others do not acquire information about us that, if revealed, would expose us to shame, ridicule, embarrassment, blackmail, or other harm. Second, privacy also prevents others from interfering in our plans simply because they do not hold the same values we hold. Our private plans may involve activities that, although harming no one, might be viewed with distaste by other people. Privacy protects us against their intrusions and thereby allows us the freedom to behave in unconventional ways. Third, privacy protects those whom we love from being injured by having their beliefs about us shaken. There may be things about ourselves that, if revealed, might hurt those whom we love. Privacy ensures that such matters are not made public. Fourth, privacy also protects individuals from being led to incriminate themselves. By protecting their privacy, people are protected against involuntarily harming their own reputations.

Quick Review 6.14

Importance of Privacy

- Protects individuals from disclosures that can shame, can encourage interference in one's private life, hurt loved ones, and lead to self-incrimination.
- Enables the intimacy that develops personal relationships, the trust and confidentiality that underlies client-professional relationships, the ability to maintain distinct social roles, and the ability to determine how others will see us.

Privacy is also important because it has several enabling functions. First, privacy enables a person to develop ties of friendship, love, and trust. Without intimacy, these relationships could not flourish. Intimacy, however, requires both sharing information about oneself that is not shared with everyone and engaging in special activities with others that are not publicly performed. Therefore, without privacy, intimacy would be impossible and relationships of friendship, love, and trust could not exist. Second, privacy enables certain professional relationships to exist. Insofar as the relationships between doctor and patient, lawyer and client, and psychiatrist and patient all require trust and confidentiality, they could not exist without privacy. Third, privacy also enables a person to sustain distinct social roles. The executive of a corporation, for example, may want, as a private citizen, to support a cause that is unpopular with the firm. Privacy enables the executive to do so without fear of reprisal. Fourth, privacy enables people to determine who they are by giving them control of the way they present themselves to society in general and of the way that society in general looks upon them. At the same time, privacy enables people to present themselves in a special way to those whom they select. In both cases, this self-determination is secured by one's right to determine the nature and extent of disclosure of information about oneself.

It is clear, then, that our interest in privacy is important enough to recognize it as a right that all people have, including consumers. However, this right must be balanced against the rights and legitimate needs of others. If banks are to provide loans to consumers, for example, they need to know something about the credit history of the individuals to whom they are providing loans and how diligent they have been in repaying previous loans. Consumers ultimately benefit from such a banking system. Insurance companies that want to provide life insurance to individuals need to know whether they have any life-threatening illnesses, and so they must have access to their medical information. Consumers benefit from having life insurance available to them. Thus, there are significant consumer benefits that businesses can provide, but that they can provide only if there exist agencies that can collect information about individuals and make that information available to those businesses. Thus, consumers' rights to privacy have to be balanced with these legitimate needs of businesses. Several considerations have been suggested as key to balancing legitimate business needs with the right to privacy, including (a) purpose, (b) relevance, (c) informing, (d) consent, (e) accuracy, and (f) security and recipients.

Purpose The purpose for which information about specific consumers is collected must be a legitimate business need. In this context, a purpose is legitimate if it results in benefits that are generally enjoyed by the people about whom the information is being collected. Consumers benefit, for example, if banks are generally willing to extend loans, insurers are generally willing to insure them, and credit card companies are generally willing to provide credit. This does not mean that a specific individual will benefit from having personal information available to, say, a bank, because the bank may refuse to give that specific person a loan on the basis of the person's credit record. It merely means that consumers benefit generally from having available a banking system (or credit card or insurance companies) that is willing to provide loans, and such a system requires a mechanism for collecting information on its potential customers.

Quick Review 6.15

Balancing Right to Privacy and Business Needs

- Is the *purpose* of collecting information a legitimate business need that benefits the consumer?
- Is the information that is collected *relevant* to the business need?
- Is the consumer *informed* the information is being collected and the purpose?
- Did the consumer *consent* to the information disclosure?
- Is the information *accurate*?
- Is the information *secure* and not disclosed to *recipients* or *used* in ways to which the consumer did not consent?

Relevance Databases containing information on consumers should include only information that is directly relevant to the purpose for which the database is being compiled. Thus, credit information provided to banks or credit card issuing agencies should not include information about sexual orientation, political affiliations, medical history, or other information not directly relevant to determining an individual's creditworthiness.

Informing Entities collecting information on consumers should inform consumers that the information is being collected and inform them about the purpose for which the information is being collected. This enables consumers to voluntarily choose not to engage in those transactions that will result in revealing information about themselves that they do not want to reveal.

Consent A business should collect information about an individual person only if that person has explicitly or implicitly consented to provide that information to that business and only if the information is to be used for the purpose for which the person consented to have it used. Consent may be explicit, such as when a person provides information on a credit card application. But consent may be implicit, such as when a person makes a purchase with a credit card knowing that a record of that purchase will be kept by the company issuing the credit card and the record will be collected by a credit bureau. In the latter case, the very act of using the credit card constitutes acceptance of the conditions the credit card company imposes on use of the card, particularly if the credit card company has explicitly advised the consumer that such information will be collected and reported to a credit bureau.

Accuracy Agencies collecting information on a person must take reasonable steps to ensure that the information they store is accurate and that any inaccuracies called to their attention are corrected. Toward this end, agencies should allow individuals to see what information they have collected on them and allow them to bring inaccuracies to their attention.

Security, Recipients and Uses Agencies that collect information on specific individuals must ensure that information is secure and not revealed to parties that the individual has not explicitly or implicitly consented to be a recipient of that information or used in ways to which the consumer did not consent. If an individual provides information to one business so that the business can better serve that individual, it is wrong for that business to give or sell that information to another business without the individual's consent.

Study and Review on mythinkinglab.com

Questions for Review and Discussion

1. Define the following concepts: contractual theory (of a seller's duties), duty to comply, implied claim, reliability, service life, maintainability, product safety, reasonable risk, duty of disclosure, duty not to misrepresent, duty not to coerce, manufacturer's implied warranty, disclaimer, caveat emptor, due care theory (of a seller's duties), caveat vendor, professional, manufacturer's duty to exercise due care, social costs theory (of a seller's duties), advertisement, production costs, selling costs, to expand consumption, to shift consumption, Kaldor's theory of advertising and market power, brand loyalty, Galbraith's theory of the creation of consumer desires, bait advertisements, deception.
2. Discuss the arguments for and against the three main theories of a producer's duties to the consumer. In your judgment, which theory is most adequate? Are there any marketing areas where one theory is more appropriate than the others?
3. Who should decide (a) how much information should be provided by manufacturers, (b) how good products should be, and (c) how truthful advertisements should be? The government? Manufacturers? Consumer groups? The free market? Explain your views.
4. Carefully examine two or more advertisements taken from current newspapers or magazines and assess the extent to which they meet what you would consider adequate ethical standards for advertising. Be prepared to defend your standards.

Web Resources

Readers who want to conduct research on consumer issues through the Internet might begin by turning to the web sites of the following organizations: the National Safety Council (*http://www.nsc.org*), the Consumer Product Safety Commission (*http://www.cpsc.gov*), the Consumer Law Page (*http://consumerlawpage.com*), the Federal Trade Commission (*http://www.ftc.gov*). Articles on consumer law can be found at the Nolo Press (*http://www.nolo.com*), and *Consumer World* (*http://www.consumerworld.org*). Statistics on consumer injuries can be found at Fatality Analysis Reporting system (*http://www-fars.nhtsa.dot.gov*), National Highway Traffic Safety Administration (*http://www.nhtsa.dot.gov*), FedStats (*http://www.fedstats.gov*), The National Center for Health Statistics (*http://www.cdc.gov/nchs*), and the Centers for Disease Control and Prevention Web-based Injury Statistics Query and Reporting System (WISQARS) (*http://www.cdc.gov/injury/wisqars/index.html*)

CASES

Explore the Concept on mythinkinglab.com

Becton Dickinson and Needle Sticks

In 2004, Becton Dickinson, the world's largest manufacturer of medical supplies and equipment agreed to pay Retractable, a small innovative company making safety syringes, $100 million dollars for damages it had inflicted on the small manufacturer. The year before, Premier and Novation, two of the largest GPOs (general purchasing organizations that buy supplies for hospitals and clinics), had paid Retractable an undisclosed sum of money for damages they had inflicted on the small company by cooperating with Becton Dickinson. Much more important, and uncompensated, however, were the injuries the three companies were said to have inflicted on countless health workers who had contracted AIDS and other blood-borne diseases because the three companies had blocked Retractable from selling its safety syringes to the hospitals, medical clinics, and other health organizations where they worked. To add insult to injury, in 2009, Becton Dickinson was found by a jury to have copied Retractable's patented safety syringes and to have sold them to the very organizations whom earlier it had not allowed to have access to Retractable's revolutionary safety syringes.

During the last decade of the twentieth century, safety syringes had become an issue when the AIDS epidemic started to pose peculiarly acute dilemmas for health workers. After routinely removing an intravenous system, drawing blood, or delivering an injection to an AIDS patient, nurses could easily stick themselves with the needle they were using. "Rarely a day goes by in any large hospital where a needle stick incident is not reported."[1] In fact, needlestick injuries accounted for about 80 percent of reported occupational exposures to the AIDS virus among health care workers.[2] It was conservatively estimated in 1991 that about 64 health care workers were infected with the AIDS virus each year as a result of needlestick injuries.[3]

AIDS was not the only risk posed by needlestick injuries. Hepatitis B, hepatitis C, and other lethal diseases were also being contracted through accidental needlesticks. In 1990, the Center for Disease Control (CDC) estimated that at least 12,000 health care workers were annually being exposed to blood contaminated with the hepatitis B virus, and of these 250 died as a consequence while many others were seriously incapacitated.[4] Because the hepatitis C virus had been identified only in 1988, estimates for infection rates of health care workers were still guesswork, but were estimated by some observers to be around 9,600 per year. In addition to AIDS, hepatitis B, and hepatitis C, needlestick injuries can also transmit numerous viral, bacterial, fungal, and parasitic infections, as well as toxic drugs or other agents that are delivered through a syringe and needle. The cost of all such injuries was estimated at $400 million to $1 billion a year.[5]

Several agencies stepped in to set guidelines for nurses, including the Occupational Safety and Health Administration (OSHA). On December 6, 1991, OSHA required hospitals and other employers of health workers to (a) make sharps containers (safe needle containers) available to workers, (b) prohibit the practice of recapping needles by holding the cap in one hand and inserting the needle with the other, and (c) provide information and training on needlestick prevention to employees.[6]

The usefulness of these guidelines was disputed.[7] Nurses worked in high-stress emergency situations requiring quick action, and they were often pressed for time both because of the large number of patients they cared for and the highly variable needs and demands of these patients. In such workplace environments, it was difficult to adhere to the guidelines recommended by the agencies. For example, a high-risk source of needlesticks is the technique of replacing the cap on a needle (after it has been used) by holding the cap in one hand and inserting the needle into the cap with the other hand. OSHA guidelines warned against this two-handed technique of recapping and recommended instead that the cap be placed on a surface and the nurse use a one-handed "spearing" technique to replace the cap. However, nurses were often pressed for time and, knowing that carrying an exposed contaminated needle is extremely dangerous, yet seeing no ready surface on which to place the needle cap, they would recap the needle using the two-handed technique.

Several analysts suggested that the nurse's work environment made it unlikely that needlesticks would be prevented through mere guidelines. Dr. Janine Jaegger, an expert on needlestick injuries, argued that "trying to teach health care workers to use a hazardous device safely is the equivalent of trying to teach someone how to drive a defective automobile safely.... Until now the focus has been on the health care worker, with finger wagging at mistakes, rather than focusing on the hazardous product design.... We need a whole new array of devices in which safety is an integral part of the design."[8] The U.S. Department of Labor and Department of Health and Human Services in a joint advisory agreed that "engineering controls should be used as the primary method to reduce worker exposure to harmful substances."[9]

The risk of contracting life-threatening diseases by the use of needles and syringes in health care settings had been well documented since the early 1980s. Articles in medical journals in 1980 and 1981, for example, reported on the "problem" of "needle stick and puncture wounds" among health care workers.[10] Several articles in 1983 reported on the growing risk of injuries hospital workers were sustaining from needles and sharp objects.[11] Articles in 1984 and 1985 were sounding higher-pitched alarms on the growing number of hepatitis B and AIDS cases resulting from needlesticks.

About 70 percent of all the needles and syringes used by U.S. health care workers were manufactured by Becton Dickinson. Despite the emerging crisis, Becton Dickinson decided not to change the design of its needles and syringes during the early 1980s. To offer a new design would not only require major engineering, retooling, and marketing investments, but would mean offering a new product that would compete with its flagship product, the standard syringe. According to Robert Stathopulos, who was an engineer at Becton Dickinson from 1972 to 1986, the company wanted "to minimize the capital outlay" on any new device.[12] During most of the 1980s, therefore, Becton Dickinson opted to do no more than include in each box of needled syringes an insert warning of the danger of needlesticks and of the dangers of two-handed recapping.

On December 23, 1986, the U.S. Patent office had issued patent number 4,631,057 to Norma Sampson, a nurse, and Charles B. Mitchell, an engineer, for a syringe with a tube surrounding the body of the syringe that could be pulled down to cover and protect the needle on the syringe. It was Sampson and Mitchell's assessment that their invention was the most effective, easily usable, and easily manufactured device capable of protecting users from needlesticks, particularly in "emergency periods or other times of high stress."[13] Unlike other syringe designs, theirs was shaped and sized like a standard syringe so nurses already familiar with standard syringe design would have little difficulty adapting to it.

The year after Sampson and Mitchell patented their syringe, Becton Dickinson purchased from them an exclusive license to manufacture it. A few months later, Becton Dickinson began field tests of early models of the syringe using a 3-cc model. Nurses and hospital personnel were enthusiastic when shown the product. However, they warned that if the company priced the product too high, hospitals, with pressures on their budgets rising, could not buy the safety syringes. With concerns about AIDS increasing, the company decided to market the product.

In 1988, with the field tests completed, Becton Dickinson had to decide which syringes would be marketed with the protective sleeves. Sleeves could be put on all of the major syringe sizes, including 1-cc, 3-cc, 5-cc, and 10-cc syringes. However, the company decided to market only a 3-cc version of the protective sleeve. The 3-cc syringes accounted for about half of all syringes used, although the larger sizes—5-cc and 10-cc syringes—were preferred by nurses when drawing blood.

This 3-cc syringe was marketed in 1988 under the trademarked name *Safety-Lok Syringe* and sold to hospitals and doctors' offices for between 50 and 75 cents, a price that Becton Dickinson characterized as a "premium" price. By 1991, the company had dropped the price to 26 cents a unit. At the time, a regular syringe without any protective device was priced at 8 cents a unit and cost 4 cents to make. Information about the cost of manufacturing the new safety syringe was proprietary, but an educated estimate would put the costs of manufacturing each Safety-Lok syringe in 1991 at 13 to 20 cents.[14]

The difference between the price of a standard syringe and the "premium" price of the safety syringe was an obstacle for hospital buyers. To switch to the new safety syringe would increase the hospital's costs for 3-cc syringes by a factor of 3 to 7. An equally important impediment to adoption was the fact that the syringe was available in only one 3-cc size, and so, as one study suggested, it had "limited applications."[15] Hospitals are reluctant to adopt, and adapt to, a product that is not available for the whole range of applications the hospital must confront. In particular, hospitals often needed the larger 5-cc and 10-cc sizes to draw blood, and Becton Dickinson had not made these available with a sleeve.

In 1992, a nurse, Maryann Rockwood (her name is disguised to protect her privacy), was working in a San Diego, California, clinic that served AIDS patients. That day she used a Becton Dickinson standard 5-cc syringe and needle to draw blood from a patient known to be infected with AIDS. After drawing the blood, she transferred the AIDS-contaminated blood to a sterile test tube called a Vacutainer tube by sticking the needle through the rubber stopper of the test tube, which she was holding with her other hand. She accidently pricked her finger with the contaminated needle. A short time later, she was diagnosed as HIV positive.

Maryann Rockwood sued Becton Dickinson, alleging that, because it alone had an exclusive right to Sampson and Mitchell's patented design, the company had a duty to provide the safety syringe in all its sizes and that by withholding other sizes from the market it had contributed to her injury. Another contributing factor, she claimed, was the premium price Becton Dickinson had put on its product, which prevented employers like hers from purchasing even those sizes that Becton Dickinson did make. Becton Dickinson quietly settled this and several other, similar cases out of court for undisclosed sums.

By 1992, OSHA had finally required that hospitals and clinics give their workers free hepatitis B vaccines and provide safe needle disposal boxes, protective clothing, gloves, and masks. The U.S. Food and Drug Administration (FDA) also was considering requiring that employers phase in the use of safety needles to prevent needlesticks, such as the new self-sheathing syringes that Becton Dickinson was now providing. If the FDA or OSHA required safety syringes and needles, however, this would hurt the U.S. market for Becton Dickinson's standard syringes and needles, forcing it to invest heavily in new manufacturing equipment and a new technology. Becton Dickinson, therefore, sent its marketing director, Gary Cohen, and two other top executives to Washington, D.C., to convey privately to government officials that the company strongly opposed a safety needle requirement and that the matter should be left to "the market." The FDA subsequently decided not to require hospitals to buy safety needles.[16]

The following year, a major competitor of Becton Dickinson announced that it was planning to market a safety syringe based on a new patent that was remarkably like Becton Dickinson's. Unlike Becton Dickinson, however, the competitor indicated that it would market its safety device in all sizes and that it would be priced well below what Becton Dickinson had been charging. Shortly after the announcement, Becton Dickinson declared that it, too, had decided to provide its Safety-Lok syringe in the full range of common syringe sizes. Becton Dickinson now proclaimed itself the "leader" in the safety syringe market.

However, in 1994, the most trusted evaluator of medical devices, a nonprofit group named ECRI, issued a report stating that after testing it had determined that although Becton Dickinson's Safety-Lok Syringe was safer than Becton Dickinson's own standard syringe, nevertheless the Safety-Lok "offers poor needlestick protection." The following year this low evaluation of the Safety-Lok Syringe was reinforced by the U.S. Veteran's Administration, which ranked the Safety-Lok Syringe below the safety products of other manufacturers.

The technology for safety needles took a giant step forward in 1998 when Retractable Technologies, Inc., unveiled a new safety syringe that rendered needlesticks a virtual impossibility. The new safety syringe, invented by Thomas Shaw, a passionate engineer and founder of Retractable Technologies, featured a syringe with a needle attached to an internal spring that automatically pulled the needle into the barrel of the syringe after it was used. When the plunger of the syringe was pushed all the way in, the needle snapped back into the syringe faster than the eye could see. Called the Vanishpoint syringe, the new safety syringe required only one hand to operate and was acclaimed by nursing groups and doctors. Unfortunately, it was difficult for Retractable Technologies to sell its new automatic syringe because of a new phenomenon that had emerged in the medical industry.

During the 1990s, hospitals and clinics had attempted to cut costs by reorganizing themselves around a few large distributors called Group Purchasing Organizations or GPOs. A GPO is an agent that negotiates prices for medical supplies on behalf of its member hospitals. Hospitals became members of the GPO by agreeing to buy 85 percent to 95 percent of their medical supplies from the manufacturers designated by the GPO, and their pooled buying power then enabled the GPO to negotiate lower prices for them. The two largest GPOs were Premier, a GPO with 1,700 member hospitals, and Novation, a GPO with 650 member hospitals. GPOs were accused, however, of being prey to "conflicts of interest" because they were paid not by the hospitals for which they worked, but by the manufacturers with whom they negotiated prices (the GPO received from each manufacturer a negotiated percentage of the total purchases its member companies made from that manufacturer). Critics claimed that manufacturers of medical products in effect were paying off GPOs to get access to the GPO-member hospitals. In fact, critics alleged, GPOs such as Premier and Novation no longer tried to bring their member hospitals the best medical products nor the lowest-priced products. Instead, critics alleged, GPOs chose manufacturers for their members based on how much a manufacturer was willing to pay the GPO. The more money (the higher percentage of sales) a manufacturer gave the GPO, the more willing the GPO was to put that manufacturer on the list of manufacturers from which its member hospitals had to buy their medical supplies.[17]

When Retractable tried to sell its new syringe, which was recognized as the best safety syringe on the market and as the only safety syringe capable of completely eliminating all needlesticks in a nursing environment, it found itself blocked from doing so. In 1996, Becton Dickinson had gotten Premier GPO to sign an exclusive, 7 1/2-year, $1.8 billion deal that required Premier's member hospitals to buy at least 90 percent of their syringes and needles from Becton Dickinson. Around the same time, Becton Dickinson had signed a similar deal with Novation that required its member hospitals to buy at least 95 percent of their syringes and needles from Becton Dickinson. Because hospitals were now locked into buying their syringes and needles from Becton Dickinson, or suffer substantial financial penalties, they turned away Retractable's salespeople, even when their own nursing staffs recommended Retractable's safety product as better and more cost-effective than Becton Dickinson's.

Although Retractable's safety syringe was almost double the cost of Becton Dickinson's, hospitals that adopted Retractable's syringe would save money over the long run because they would not have to pay any of the substantial costs associated with having their workers suffer frequent needlesticks and needlestick infections. The Center for Disease Control (CDC) estimated that each needlestick in which the worker was not infected by any disease cost a hospital as much as $2,000 for testing, treatment, counseling, medical costs, and lost wages, plus unmeasurable emotional trauma, anxiety, and abstention from sexual intercourse for up to a year. Those needlesticks in which the victim was infected by HIV, hepatitis B or C, or some other potentially lethal infection, cost a hospital between $500,000 to more than $1 million and cost the victim anxiety, sickness from drug therapy, and, potentially, life itself. Retractable's syringe completely eliminated all of these costs. Because all of the other syringes then on the market, including Becton Dickinson's Safety-Lok, still allowed some needlesticks to occur, they could not completely eliminate all the costs associated with needlesticks and so were not as cost-effective. (A CDC study found that Becton Dickinson's Safety-Lok, when tested by hospital health workers in three cities from 1993 to 1995, had cut needlestick injuries only from 4 per 100,000 injections down to 3.1 per 100,000 injections, a reduction of only 23 percent, the worst performance of all the safety devices tested.) An econometric study commissioned by Retractable proved that its safety syringe was the most cost-effective syringe on the market.

In October 1999, ECRI, the nation's most respected laboratory for testing medical products, rated Becton Dickinson's Safety-Lok syringe "unacceptable" as a safety syringe, saying it might actually cause an increase in needlesticks because it required two hands to use it and one hand might accidently touch the needle. It simultaneously gave Retractable's Vanishpoint syringe its highest rating as a safety syringe, the only safety syringe to achieve this highest level. Becton Dickinson objected strenuously to the low rating of its own syringe, and in 2001, the testing lab raised the rating for the Safety-Lok a notch to "not recommended." Retractable's Vanishpoint syringe, however, continued to receive the highest rating. In spite of being recognized as the best and most cost-effective technology for protecting health care workers from being infected through needlesticks, Retractable still found itself blocked out of the market by the long-term deals that Becton Dickinson had negotiated with the major GPOs.[18]

In 1999, California became the first state to require its hospitals to provide safety syringes to its workers. Then, in November, 2000, the Needlestick Safety and Prevention Act was signed into law. The act required the use of safety syringes in hospitals and doctor's offices. In 2001, OSHA incorporated the provisions of the Needlestick Safety and Prevention Act, finally requiring hospitals and employers to use safety syringes and significantly expanding the market for safety syringes, a development that is expected to bring lower prices. None of this legislation required a specific type or brand of syringe and Becton Dickinson's safety devices were stocked by most GPO member hospitals.

Continuing to find itself locked out of the market by Becton Dickinson's contracts with Premier and Novation, Retractable sued Premier, Novation, and Becton Dickinson in federal court alleging that they violated antitrust laws and harmed consumers and numerous health care workers by using the GPO system to monopolize the safety needle market.[19] In 2003, Premier and Novation settled with Retractable out of court, agreeing to henceforth allow its member hospitals to purchase Retractable's safety syringes when they wanted. In 2004, Becton Dickinson also settled out of court, agreeing to pay $100 million in compensation for the damage it inflicted on Retractable. During the 6 years that Becton Dickinson's contracts prevented Retractable and other manufacturers from selling their safety needles to hospitals and clinics, thousands of health workers continued to be infected by needlesticks each year.

Ironically, in November, 2009, a jury found Becton Dickinson guilty of infringing on Retractable's safety syringe patents by copying Retractable's design and then manufacturing and selling the syringes under its own name. When ECRI had judged Becton Dickinson's own safety needle technology "unacceptable," and "not recommended," sales had dropped off. To compensate for the drop in sales, Becton Dickinson had apparently taken a short-cut. The jury that found Becton Dickinson guilty of patent infringement ordered it to pay Retractable $5 million and to cease infringing on its patents.[20]

Questions

1. In your judgment, did Becton Dickinson have an obligation to provide the safety syringe in all its sizes in 1991? Explain your position, using the materials from this chapter and the principles of utilitarianism, rights, justice, and caring.
2. Should manufacturers be held liable for failing to market all the products for which they hold exclusive patents when someone's injury would have been avoided if they had marketed those products? Explain your answer.
3. Evaluate the ethics of Becton Dickinson's use of the GPO system in the late 1990s. Are the GPOs monopolies? Are they ethical? Explain.

Notes

1. J. R. Roberts, "Accidental Needle Stick," *EM & ACM*, May 1987, pp. 6–7.
2. R. Marcus, "Surveillance of Health Care Workers Exposed to Blood from Patients Infected with the Human Immunodeficiency Virus,"*N. Eng. J. Med.*, October 1988, v. 319, n. 17, pp. 1118–23.
3. "Special Report and Product Review; Needle Stick-Prevention Devices," *Health Devices*, May 1991, v. 20, n. 5, p. 155.
4. Ibid.
5. Kathy Sullivan and Diana Schnell, "Needleless Systems," *Infusion*, October 1994, pp. 17–19.
6. "Rules and Regulations," *Federal Register*, December 6, 1991 v. 58, n. 235, pp. 64175–64182.
7. "Needle Stick Injuries Tied to Poor Design," *Internal Medicine*, December 1, 1987.
8. Ibid.
9. Quoted in *Health Devices*, p. 154.

10. J. S. Reed et al., "Needle Stick and Puncture Wounds: Definition of the Problem," *Am. J. Infect. Control*, 1980, v. 8, pp. 101–106; R. D. McCormick et al., "Epidemiology of Needle Stick Injuries in Hospital Personnel," *Am J. Med.*, 1981, v. 70, pp. 928–932.
11. J. T. Jacobson et al., "Injuries of Hospital Employees from Needles and Sharp Objects," *Infectious Control*, 1983, v. 4, pp. 100–102; F. L. Reuben et al., "Epidemiology of Accidental Needle Puncture Wounds in Hospital Workers," *American J. Med. Sci.*, 1983, v. 286, n. 1, pp. 26–30; B. Kirkman-Liff et al., "Hepatitis B—What Price Exposure?" *Am J. Nurs*, August 1984, pp. 988–990; S. H. Weiss et al., "HTLV-III Infection Among Health Care Workers: Association with Needle-Stick Injuries," *JAMA*, 1985, v. 254, n. 15, pp. 2089–2093.
12. Reynolds Holding and William Carlsen, "High Profits—At What Cost? Company markets unsafe needles despite reported risks," *The San Francisco Chronicle*, April 14, 1998, p. A1.
13. U.S. Patent 4,631,057, Mitchell.
14. In 1991, the device carried a published list price of 26 cents; see *Health Devices*, p. 170. Assuming an extremely conservative 20 percent margin, this would imply a manufacturing cost of about 20 cents; assuming a margin similar to its regular syringes of 50 percent would imply a manufacturing cost of about 12 cents.
15. *Health Devices*, p. 170.
16. Reynolds Holding and William Carlsen, "Watchdogs Fail Health Workers: How safer needles were kept out of hospitals," *The San Francisco Chronicle*, April 15, 1998, p. A-1.
17. Barry Meier and Mary Williams Walsh, "Questioning $1 Million Fee in a Needle Deal," *The New York Times*, July 19, 2002, p. 1.
18. Ibid.
19. Mark Smith, "Medical Innovations: Clash of Blood, Money; Patients Take Back Seat to Costs, Critics Say," *The Houston Chronicle*, April 18, 1999, p. 1.
20. Mariah Blake, "Dirty Medicine: How Medical Supply Behemoths Stick It To the Little Guy, Making America's Health Care System More Dangerous and Expensive," *Washington Monthly*, July/August 2010, accessed August 25, 2010 at *http://www.washingtonmonthly.com/features/2010/1007.blake.html.*

CASES

Reducing Debts at Credit Solutions of America

Doug Van Arsdale began Credit Solutions of America (CSA) in 2003 in Richardson, Texas with 5 employees.[1] Now headquartered in Dallas, Texas, his company has more than 1000 employees, operates in several states, and has tens of thousands of customers enrolled in its debt reduction programs. Company revenues in 2007 were $77,354,088, double its 2006 revenues of $40,333,517. When Doug Van Arsdale founded CSA he used his own funds, and developed its programs, processes, and procedures on his own. In 2007, the company won the prestigious J. D. Power and Associates award for "An Outstanding Customer Service Experience." Why is it that such an outstanding company, so devoted to serving its customers, had been sued or was being sued by the Attorney Generals of eight states for customer fraud?

CSA is part of the "debt settlement" or "debt management" industry. Debt settlement companies help consumers who have accumulated a large amount of debt and who are now unable to continue making monthly payments on their debt and who also cannot pay their debts off in full.[2] One option for such consumers is to file for personal bankruptcy in a federal court. Filing for personal bankruptcy stops all collection efforts by creditors and allows a judge to have the debtor's assets sold to pay off as much of his debt as possible, and then to issue a court order that eliminates any remaining debts. When a debtor reaches the point of bankruptcy, he or she will usually have little or no assets left, so creditors often get nothing. Bankruptcy, in effect, allows a person who has been overwhelmed by debt to have his or her debts forgiven and to start over with a clean slate. However, bankruptcy has some long-lasting serious consequences. The bankruptcy will stay on a person's credit report for ten years and during that time it will be almost impossible for the person to get a loan, a credit card, buy a home, buy anything on credit such as a car, get life insurance, and will make even getting a job difficult. Because of these serious negative consequences, most debtors are reluctant to file for bankruptcy and will first try to find some other way to settle their debts. That is where debt settlement companies come in.

There are several different kinds of debt settlement companies. Some companies provide traditional "credit counseling," which consists of showing their customers how to put together a budget and a plan for paying off their debts, and helping them work with creditors to reduce their interest rates or their penalty fees. Other companies provide "debt consolidation loans" which provide the customer with a single loan that they use to pay off all their other debts, but that allows repayment over several years so that each month's payment is low enough for the customer to afford. A third group of debt settlement companies provide "debt management," which consists of negotiating directly with the customer's creditors on behalf of the customer, and trying to convince the creditors to reduce the customer's monthly payments to an affordable level, usually by making the pay-off period longer but sometimes by forgiving part of the debt.

But these options seemed inadequate to Doug Van Arsdale. Before he founded CSA he had spent nine months researching and studying the industry.[3] He discovered, he said, that there was a need for an "effective alternative to both bankruptcy and consumer credit counseling." The main problem, he said, was that "In our society, most customers with debt problems are treated poorly [and] I saw that consumers needed someone who was exclusively on their side." So he decided to establish a different kind of debt settlement company, one that would provide more vigorous help to consumers who were being swamped by their debt.

CSA initiated a fourth category of debt settlement companies. This fourth category consists of companies that engage in an aggressive kind of debt relief that tries to *force* creditors to reduce the customer's debt. Companies in this category work primarily with customers who have unsecured debt, i.e., debt that is not backed by an asset—like a house, a car, or shares of stock—that the creditor can repossess if the customer cannot repay the debt. Since the main form of unsecured debt is credit card debt, most of CSA's customers have credit card debts that they cannot repay and whose monthly payments they can no longer afford. A person must have at least $6,000 of unsecured debt to become a customer of CSA.

Companies like CSA operate by suggesting their customers stop making all monthly payments on their unsecured debts.[4] CSA tells its customers that although it cannot legally advise them to stop paying their creditors, the CSA "program" will not work unless they stop making payments. Customers are instructed to open a savings account and each month deposit there the money they would have used to make their payments. They must also agree to let CSA handle all contacts with their creditors from that point on. After several months of failing to make their regular payments, the customer's debts go into default and the creditors begin demanding their money, calling and writing letters trying to collect, and even threatening to sue. After a period of time, the debt settlement company, CSA, contacts the creditors and negotiates a substantial reduction of the loan, perhaps suggesting that if the loan is not reduced the creditor may not get any of their money back because the customer may file for bankruptcy. Although creditors are unwilling to discuss reductions when they are getting their monthly payments, they are more open to doing so when they are not getting any money from the customer anyway—which is why this kind of debt management works only if customers stop making payments on their debts. In many cases, creditors at this point will agree to a settlement, i.e., agree to reduce the debt, perhaps by 30 percent, but very often by as much as 40 percent or even 60 percent, depending on the circumstances and the skills of the negotiator. This part of its program is a feature that Van Arsdale's company often advertised on its web site:

> Debt settlement specifically reduces your current outstanding total balances 40–60% . . . A typical settlement can be accomplished within 36 months or less with a lower monthly payment than any other debt resolutions option . . . More than 200,000 people from every walk of life have entrusted us to help them become debt free. Credit Solutions is the industry leader, managing more than $2.25 billion of debt for our clients.[5]

If the negotiations are successful, the customer's debt is reduced to a level he or she can manage but without the negative consequences of a bankruptcy. The customer uses the money he or she has been putting in a savings account to make a beginning lump-sum payment to the creditor and then usually gets back to making monthly payments. Often the reduced debt is low enough for the customer to pay off in a matter of months.

In return for its services, CSA charges a fee of 15 percent of the total debt the customer wants reduced, and the customer pays this fee in three large payments made in the first three months and then in smaller monthly installments spread over the next fourteen months. CSA takes these monthly fees out of the savings account the customer opened when he or she first stopped paying creditors. CSA starts drawing its fees out of the customer's savings account at the beginning of the program, which is right when the customer stops making monthly payments on his or her debts, but before the debts have defaulted and so before CSA begins to actively negotiate settlements. CSA does not start to negotiate with creditors until several months later when the creditors are anxious to get at least some of their debt back, and the customer has saved up enough money to make the initial lump sum payments creditors will demand.

Customers sign up with CSA by calling one of their salespeople. The company, in fact, has twice as many people working on sales as are working to resolve their customer's credit problems. The company gives its sales people a "script" to follow when talking to customers, although the company also advised salespeople that: "We are NOT EXCLUSIVELY SCRIPTED! Formulate your own artillery of rebuttals! Don't be a robot! Be creative!"[6] The sales script tells sales people to explain that CSA's debt settlement is better than debt consolidation or credit counseling and that debt settlement can "dramatically reduce your debt and get you out in 3 years or less."

If a customer asks "Will I get sued?" the script suggests a response: "We want to reassure the client that there is nothing that can happen that we will not try to assist them with." If a customer asks "What is this going to do to my credit?" the script suggests asking "What's your current credit score?" which will distract the customer from their own question since most consumers will not know their score. The salesperson can also say, "After you're out of the program, your score will be as good if not better than it is now ..." If the customer asks, "Can you guarantee that my creditors will settle with you?" the script suggests answering: "We guarantee our service fee because we know that your creditors will negotiate settlement with us. (Let them know that we are currently building relationships with as many creditors as possible.) Some creditors actually set aside certain days of the week just to work with us. Notice, we do not say we "don't guarantee," but rather tell them what we can and do guarantee."

Doug Van Arsdale felt that his company was able to provide help right when indebted consumers were at their lowest. "That's where we come into play and ultimately make a difference," he said.[7] Moreover, the company had even become a helpful resource for the creditors themselves. "Working with us on behalf of our mutual clients is very beneficial to them," he noted. "They save time and money that would have been spent on ineffective collection efforts."

The methods CSA uses to get creditors to reduce their customer's debts puts considerable stress on the customer. When a customer stops making his or her monthly payments, creditors start calling constantly, sending threatening letters and adding "late fees" and other penalties to the debt; then creditors may turn the debt over to a collection agency that is even more aggressive and harassing. Eventually the customer is threatened with lawsuits, or the creditor gets a court order that allows it to "garnish" (to take) part of the customer's wages. The creditor also will report the customer's failure to pay his or her debt to a credit agency so the customer's credit rating falls which makes it much more difficult for the customer to get credit again. In the extreme, the creditor will actually sue the customer. Nevertheless, although the process can be traumatic, the final outcome can leave CSA's customers satisfied.

One of CSA's satisfied customers, "Tiffany of Orlando," posted a comment about her experience with CSA on *ConsumerAffairs.com*, a web site that collects comments about debt settlement:

> I lost my job ... and joined Credit Solutions in June 2009 after trouble paying all my credit card bills.... The first six months of the program was the hardest. I was receiving creditor calls, letters, etc. since I [had] stopped paying my monthly credit card bills.... Then, after 6 months an offer came in from a credit card I owed over $5K on ... and I was able to settle my first account for less than half of what I actually owed. A few months later I paid off two more accounts ... so I personally think it has been worth it.... Plus I have already saved twice as much as their total service fee ... It is not easy, and yes your credit score will be destroyed, but in my situation, it seemed like the only way to get out of debt. Paying the rent and buying food for the kids seemed more important than my credit score at the time.
>
> Tiffany of Orlando, FL Feb. 9, 2010[8]

Another satisfied CSA customer using the name "Anonymous" posted this comment on a different web site entitled "Pissed Consumer":

> I used Credit Solutions to eliminate my debt and it did work and I was able to get out of $10,000 worth of credit card debt in just less than a year. They are horrible to try to get a hold of.... They are a bit unorganized ... I was told to close my accounts. I was just told to call them when I had saved a specific percentage of my [debt] balance, and they would try to negotiate at that point. I saved, and called, and it did work out, even though the card balance had gone to lawyers, they still negotiated a better deal for me. I felt they did their job on that one, but my other credit card company just offered me a deal about 6 months into the program for half the balance and I took it ... So ... they did help me, ..., but there definitely are some frustrating customer service factors.[9]

Yet for each satisfied customer that posts a comment on web sites dedicated to customer complaints like these, there seem to be ten to twenty CSA customers that are extremely upset with the way the company treated their credit problems, with what they perceive as inaction on the part of CSA, with the fees they paid CSA for work they felt did not merit the fees, or with the fallout of CSA's methods. On *ConsumerAffairs.com*, one customer calling himself Jamie wrote:

> When I was in college I first started to use credit cards. A credit card with a $25,000 dollar credit limit was easier to find in college than a keg party.... I was way over my head, and way immature to understand debts and to use credit wisely. I could no longer pay my bills ... Credit Solutions states they can easily help you. All you have to do

> is stop paying your bills ... Then when they go to collection agencies you can settle it for pennies on the dollar! All you had to do was pay Credit Solutions ... What did they do? Nothing.... All they do is take your money. After the creditors were trying to sue me, I had to finally do what Credit Solutions was paid to do. Start calling and talking to them to set up payment plans. I finally just paid off all my credit card debt. However I am still upset that this company talked me into such a stupid, idiotic way to work through my debt.
>
> Jamie of Pittsburgh , PA Dec. 21, 2009[10]

Another dissatisfied CSA customer posted this comment on *ConsumerAffairs.com*:

> When I signed up with Credit Solutions they told me not to answer or talk to any of our creditors, that they would work with our creditors. We have paid Credit Solutions over $4000 dollars and my credit is worse than when I enrolled in their program. I am being taken to court and received a writ of garnishment from one of my creditors.... I now am filing for bankruptcy because I am so behind and in debt that this is the only alternative I have to protect my family from living on the streets.... Creditors are garnishing my wages [and] I cannot support my family when my livelihood is being taken.
>
> Bruce of Alamosa, CO Feb. 21, 2009[11]

A student left this distressing comment on *ConsumerAffairs.com*:

> I enrolled in Credit Solutions in July of 2008. I was a student, trying to make ends meet. I thought Credit Solutions was a life saver. Finally be debt free ... I could finally get a better student loan and didn't have to hold 2 full time jobs anymore just to pay min. payments on a credit card.... What they don't tell you is when you're waiting for things to be settled your credit hurts even more. All my credit cards were put in collections. I would get harassed everyday by creditors. When I would contact Credit Solutions they would say that they were handling it. I finally ... contacted all my credit card companies, they NEVER RECIEVED ANYTHING FROM CREDIT SOLUTIONS!!! I paid for nothing ... I went from owing $1700 on one credit card to $2600! I'm a 21 yo med student ... I can't qualify for any loans because of this ... My future and dreams are ruined.
>
> Nicole of West Palm Beach, FL Jan. 2, 2009[12]

The "Debt Consolidation Care Forum," which provides a web site for comments, opened a forum entitled "Credit Solutions—Is it a scam company?" and quickly received over a hundred posts. Some were favorable to the company, like that of the writer who had almost finished paying off his debts and who "had nothing but good things from them." But most comments were negative, including one from a writer who signed up with Credit Solutions and then was harassed daily by debt collectors and threatened with lawsuits until "I was near suicidal."[13]

Many of CSA's dissatisfied customers lodged complaints with the Better Business Bureau. In the middle of 2010, the Bureau noted on its web site that it had received more than 1,400 complaints about CSA during the previous 36 months. According to its report on CSA posted on the Bureau's web site, "customers complain that paying the company fee and following the debt negotiation program does not reduce debt, as stated by company representatives. As a result of the program, customers complain, they have an increase in debt, due to late fees or additional interest and negative credit reporting."[14]

Many dissatisfied customers also lodged complaints with state officials. By 2011, the attorney generals of Texas, New York, Oregon, Idaho, Florida, Illinois, Maine, and Missouri had all filed lawsuits against the company on behalf of state residents. Some of the lawsuits alleged that CSA had engaged in deception by promising, but failing to deliver, 60-percent debt reductions. The company was also accused of engaging in fraudulent business practices by getting its customers to stop paying their debts knowing that this would lead to late fees and other financial penalties including lower credit ratings, but failing to inform them of this. And CSA was accused of making its customers pay fees when in fact it was doing nothing for them. Oregon banned CSA from doing business in the state for three years. Idaho ruled that debt settlement companies could not operate in the state unless they were non-profits, which disqualified CSA.

CSA had several ready defenses against such accusations. Many customers who complained were probably just unhappy with the stresses of going through the early months of the CSA program when creditors first start calling because they are not being paid. But this was an important and necessary step toward getting creditors to agree to debt reductions, and customers knew that they would have to endure this period. CSA helped customers through this period by asking them to not contact creditors and to let CSA handle all contacts and letters with creditors. Those customers who complained that the company had not negotiated any debt reductions for them were perhaps also referring to those first several months of the program when CSA deliberately does not do any negotiating with creditors. And when customers said that they were paying CSA yet CSA was doing nothing for them, perhaps this was because CSA required customers to begin paying its 15 percent fee from the first month, when the company deliberately refrained from engaging in any active negotiations with creditors.

CSA did not hide that although it said on its web site and in its discussions with customers that debt reductions could be as much as 60 percent, not all customers received such large debt reductions. However, CSA never promised customers that they would receive reductions of that magnitude. The company only agreed to try to negotiate a reduction, and such reductions could, but need not, be as much as 60 percent of the customer's debt. And in fact, CSA was regularly able to negotiate large reductions of 60 percent for many of its customers. While there were customers whose creditors would agree to reduce their debts by only a smaller amount, the creditors of other customers were very open to negotiating significant debt reductions with CSA.

Finally, some customer complaints came from customers who had not adhered to their agreement to not contact creditors. Instead of letting CSA handle all creditor contacts, some customers contacted creditors before they should have and had thereby interfered in the negotiations that were involved. When customers became impatient and contacted creditors on their own, they often did so prematurely and so CSA was not able to get the kind of concessions from creditors that waiting longer could produce. Any actions a creditor took, such as filing a lawsuit or garnishing a customer's wages, could be done away with as part of CSA's negotiations with the creditor provided the customer was willing to be patient. Even late fees and other financial penalties creditors tacked on to a customer's debt could be removed during negotiations.

Nevertheless, many customers complained that even though they had followed all of CSA's instructions, and paid all its fees, in the end their debts were not reduced or were reduced by less than they had paid CSA. In New York, the state Attorney General said that Credit Solutions had enrolled 18,000 New York customers yet the company had settled the debts of less than 2,000 of them. Evelyn Mazzella, a New York customer of CSA said "I ended up paying them a couple of thousand dollars, but they only settled one card" with Best Buy, an electronics retailer.[15] In 2009, customers also complained that when they had trouble trying to both pay CSA's fees and save up enough money to make the lump sum payment required in any potential settlement, the company gave them a list of useless suggestions including: "Refinance home," "Get a second mortgage," "Baby sit," "Sell plasma," "Ask for a raise," "Get off the station before your usual stop and walk," "Cut down your drinking," "Drink tap water," and "Buy frozen."[16] Other customers complained that CSA salespeople did not tell them that any money deducted from their debts would be counted and taxed as income by the IRS, nor that for seven years the deduction would appear on their credit report as a "charge-off," a negative mark that would reduce their ability to get future credit. Many credit experts pointed out that when consumers got in trouble with their credit card debts, they could go directly to their credit card company and negotiate a reduction themselves without the help of CSA.

Doug Van Arsdale, who remained CEO of Credit Solutions in 2011, said in a statement that Credit Solutions of America (CSA) "subscribes to the highest ethical standards" and remained focused on its customers.[17] The company, he said, "treats them with respect and assists them with getting their lives back in order, regardless of their situation."[18]

Notes

1. *State of Texas, Plaintiff, v. CSA-Credit Solutions of America, Inc., Defendant*, case no. D-1-GV-09-000417, Filed 09 March 26, in the District Court of Travis County, Texas, 261st Judicial District, Plaintiff's Original Petition., p. 6; revenue data and information on Doug Van Arsdale is from the web site of "The American Business Awards," accessed January 30 at *http://www.stevieawards.com/pubs/awards/403_2591_19325.cfm.*
2. Federal Trade Commission, "Facts for Consumers, Knee Deep in Debt," accessed January 13, 2011 at *http://www.ftc.gov/bcp/edu/pubs/consumer/credit/cre19.shtm.*
3. All Van Arsdale quotations from "Ernst & Young's Entrepreneur of the Year Finalists," *D Magazine*, [online], June 11, 2008 [From D CEO, July 2008], accessed January 30 at *http://www.dmagazine.com/Home/2008/06/05/Ernst__Youngs_Entrepreneur_of_the_Year_Finalists.aspx?redirected=1.*
4. *State of Texas v. CSA*, op. cit., p. 2.
5. Ibid., p. 7.
6. Ibid., pp. 8–12.
7. Quotes are from "Ernst & Young's Entrepreneur of the Year Finalists," *loc.cit.*
8. *ConsumerAffairs.com*, accessed January 30 at *http://www.consumeraffairs.com/debt_counsel/credit_solutions.html#ixzz0xejZbTyl.*
9. *PissedConsumer.com*, accessed January 30, 2011 at *http://credit-solutions-of-america.pissedconsumer.com/helped-me-out-but-have-mixed-feelings-20080722128582.html.*
10. *ConsumerAffairs.com*, Ibid.
11. Ibid.
12. Ibid.
13. See *http://www.debtconsolidationcare.com/settlement/credit-solutions-scam.html.*
14. Better Business Bureau, "BBB Reliability Report for Credit Solutions," accessed January 30 at *http://www.bbb.org/dallas/business-reviews/debt-relief-services/credit-solutions-in-dallas-tx-90005445.*
15. David Streitfeld, "2 Firms Accused of Fraud in Debt Settlement," *The New York Times*, May 19, 2009.
16. Ibid.
17. "Cuomo Targets Debt Settlement Companies," *CNYcentral.com*, May 8, 2009, accessed January 17, 2011 at *http://www.cnycentral.com/news/story.aspx?list=190258&id=297298.*
18. Quote is from "Ernst & Young's Entrepreneur of the Year Finalists," *loc.cit.*

PART FOUR

Ethics and Employees

THE PROCESS OF PRODUCING GOODS FORCES BUSINESSES NOT ONLY TO ENGAGE IN EXTERNAL EXCHANGES, BUT ALSO TO COORDINATE THE ACTIVITIES OF THE VARIOUS INTERNAL CONSTITUENCIES THAT MUST BE BROUGHT TOGETHER AND ORGANIZED INTO THE PROCESSES OF PRODUCTION. EMPLOYEES MUST BE HIRED AND ORGANIZED, STOCKHOLDERS AND CREDITORS MUST BE SOLICITED, AND MANAGERIAL TALENT MUST BE TAPPED. INEVITABLY, CONFLICTS ARISE WITHIN AND BETWEEN THESE INTERNAL CONSTITUENCIES AS THEY INTERACT WITH EACH OTHER AND AS THEY SEEK TO DISTRIBUTE BENEFITS AMONG THEMSELVES. THE NEXT TWO CHAPTERS EXPLORE SOME OF THE ETHICAL ISSUES RAISED BY THESE INTERNAL CONFLICTS. CHAPTER 7 DISCUSSES THE ISSUE OF JOB DISCRIMINATION. CHAPTER 8 DISCUSSES THE ISSUE OF CONFLICTS BETWEEN THE INDIVIDUAL AND THE ORGANIZATION.

7

The Ethics of Job Discrimination

What distinctions can companies reasonably make between job applicants without engaging in discrimination?

How widespread is job discrimination?

Why is it wrong to discriminate?

What is affirmative action and why is it so controversial?

Female and minority workers are the fastest growing demographic group of new employees.

INTRODUCTION

Listen to the Chapter Audio on mythinkinglab.com

In 2011, the U.S. Court of Appeals for the Fifth Circuit ruled that the University of Texas at Austin did not engage in racial discrimination, although it used race as one of the criteria for determining which students would be admitted into the University.[1] The admissions process the University used was an "affirmative action" plan aimed at ensuring that the student body of the University included people from a diverse range of geographical areas, socio-economic classes, experiences, backgrounds, and, of course, races. The ruling of the Fifth Circuit Court was unusual because 15 years earlier the same Court had ruled that it was illegal and discriminatory for the University to take race into account in its admissions programs. Thus, in its 2011 decision the Court in effect reversed its own earlier decision. This reversal was based on a 2003 U.S. Supreme Court decision that had considered the claims of Barbara Grutter who argued that the University of Michigan had unlawfully discriminated against her when it turned down her application for admission because she was white.

When Grutter was denied admission to the University of Michigan Law School, she sued both the University and Lee Bollinger, president of the University at the time (*Grutter v. Bollinger*). Many companies took notice because they used hiring programs that were in some respects like those of the University. Grutter claimed that the university's affirmative action program had unfairly given preference to minority students with "similar credentials" to her own. The U.S. District Court for the Eastern District of Michigan first heard her case in the winter of 2001. The District Court agreed with Grutter and ruled on March 27, 2001 that the University of Michigan had engaged in a form of racial discrimination by showing preference to minority students in violation of Grutter's right to equal treatment. The University of Michigan appealed the District Court's ruling to the Court of Appeals for the Sixth Circuit. In a split decision on May 14, 2002, the judges of the Court of Appeals overturned the earlier District Court's ruling. The Court of Appeals held that the University of Michigan's preferential program was both fair and constitutional to the extent that it sought "diversity"—i.e., a student population that possesses a diverse range of ages, ethnicities, genders, races, talents, experiences, and other significant human qualities. Grutter was not satisfied with this decision, so she took her case to the nation's highest court, the U.S. Supreme Court. The Supreme Court, in a separate case (*Gratz v. Bollinger*), had ruled that an affirmative action program used by the University of Michigan in its *undergraduate* programs was unconstitutional because it was not "narrowly tailored" and so gave *too much* weight to race. Would the Supreme Court also reject the *law school's* affirmative action program? On June 23, 2003, the Supreme Court reached its decision: It is fair and constitutional, the Supreme Court held, for a university to show preference to minorities in admissions if its goal is to achieve "diversity" in a way that is "narrowly tailored" to achieve this goal and the University of Michigan's Law School program met these criteria.

> Student body diversity is a compelling state interest that can justify using race in university admissions.... Major American businesses have made clear that the skills needed in today's increasingly global marketplace can only be developed through exposure to widely diverse people, cultures, ideas, and viewpoints.... Moreover, because universities, and in particular, law schools, represent the training ground for a large number of the Nation's leaders, the path to leadership must be visibly open to talented and qualified individuals of every race and ethnicity. Thus, the Law School has a compelling interest in attaining a diverse student body. The Law School's admissions program bears the hallmarks of a narrowly tailored plan.... Universities cannot establish quotas for members of certain racial or ethnic groups or put them on

> separate admissions tracks. . . . The Law School's admissions program, [however,] . . . is flexible enough to ensure that each applicant is evaluated as an individual and not in a way that makes race or ethnicity the defining feature of the application.[2]

Earlier, more than five dozen major U.S. corporations had urged the court to protect the University of Michigan's goal of achieving diversity through its affirmative action program. In an "amicus" brief, the companies—including 3M, Intel, Microsoft, Hewlett-Packard, Nike, Coca-Cola, Shell, Ernst & Young, Kellogg, Procter & Gamble, General Motors, and over 50 others—argued:

> In the experience of [these companies], individuals who have been educated in a diverse setting are more likely to succeed, because they can make valuable contributions to the workforce in several important and concrete ways. First, a diverse group of individuals educated in a cross-cultural environment has the ability to facilitate unique and creative approaches to problem-solving arising from the integration of different perspectives. Second, such individuals are better able to develop products and services that appeal to a variety of consumers and to market offerings in ways that appeal to those consumers. Third, a racially diverse group of managers with cross-cultural experience is better able to work with business partners, employees, and clientele in the United States and around the world. Fourth, individuals who have been educated in a diverse setting are likely to contribute to a positive work environment, by decreasing incidents of discrimination and stereotyping. Overall, an educational environment that ensures participation by diverse people, viewpoints and ideas will help produce the most talented workforce.[3]

While most of the judges of the U.S. Supreme Court agreed with these companies and their affirmation of the importance of diversity, their decision was not unanimous. Like the judges who had earlier disagreed over the Grutter case, the judges on the Supreme Court were also divided about the fairness of affirmative action programs and the legitimacy of pursuing diversity. Although five of the Supreme Court's nine judges held that affirmative action was fair and not a form of unconstitutional "discrimination," four of the judges, including Clarence Thomas, a black man, were harshly critical of that opinion. Thomas asserted that showing preference to minorities was harmful "racial discrimination":

> I believe what lies beneath the Court's decision today are the benighted notions that one can tell when racial discrimination benefits (rather than hurts) minority groups, and that racial discrimination is necessary to remedy general societal ills. . . . Clearly the majority still cannot commit to the principle that racial classifications are per se harmful and that almost no amount of benefit in the eye of the beholder can justify such classifications. . . . This discrimination engender[s] attitudes of superiority or, alternatively, provoke[s] resentment among those who believe that they have been wronged by the government's use of race. These programs stamp minorities with a badge of inferiority and may cause them to develop dependencies or to adopt an attitude that they are "entitled" to preferences.[4]

The decision of the U.S. Supreme Court did not end the controversy. After the Supreme Court's decision was announced, the Michigan state legislature began a divisive and rancorous debate over whether to pass a law that would withhold state funds from public universities—including the University of Michigan—that used affirmative action programs. The debate over the issue was so heated and belligerent that a fistfight broke out on the floor of the legislature between opponents and supporters of the measure. In the end, a deeply divided legislature passed the law. Even then the matter did not end. In 2004, a group of Michigan residents began a drive in support of a statewide vote on a measure that would make it illegal for universities and other public institutions in Michigan to use affirmative action programs; in 2006, the drive succeeded with the passage of the Michigan Civil Rights Initiative. California had already passed such a law, and Washington, Florida, Nebraska, and Arizona had passed similar laws by 2011. Yet citizens in other states, like Colorado, voted against banning affirmative action programs.

As the 2011 University of Texas Court of Appeals decision, the 2003 Supreme Court decision in the University of Michigan Law School case, and the polarizing campaigns to pass state laws banning affirmative action all indicate, our nation today remains bitterly divided over our legacy of discrimination and over the justice of dealing with the effects of past discrimination through affirmative action programs. Many businesses, like the Fortune 500 companies that supported the goal of diversity, believe that it is key to competing in a rapidly globalizing world because, as the Supreme Court stated, "the skills needed in today's increasingly global marketplace can only be developed through exposure to widely diverse people, cultures, ideas, and viewpoints." Many, however, believe that attempts to achieve diversity through affirmative action programs are themselves forms of unjust "reverse discrimination."

The debates over equality, diversity, and discrimination have been prolonged and acrimonious. Controversy continues to swirl around the nature of the plight of racial minorities, the inequality of women, and the harm that whites or males have suffered as a result of preference shown to women and minorities. These continuing debates over racial and sexual diversity have often focused on business and its needs. This is inevitable: Racial and sexual discrimination have had a long history in business, and diversity now promises to have significant benefits for business.

Perhaps more than any other contemporary social issue, public discussions of discrimination and diversity have clearly approached the subject in ethical terms: The words *justice*, *equality*, *racism*, *rights*, and *discrimination* inevitably find their way into the debate. This chapter analyzes the various sides of this ethical issue. The chapter begins by examining the nature and extent of discrimination. It then turns to discussing the ethical aspects of discriminatory behavior in employment and ends with a discussion of diversity and affirmative action programs in business.

7.1 Job Discrimination: Its Nature

A few years ago, the American Broadcasting Company (ABC) sent a male and female, Chris and Julie, on an "experiment" to apply in person for jobs several companies were advertising. Chris and Julie were both blonde, trim, neatly dressed college graduates in their 20s, with identical resumes indicating management experience. Unknown to the companies, however, both were secretly wired for sound and had hidden cameras. One company indicated in its help-wanted ad that it had several open positions. However, when the company recruiter spoke with Julie, the only job he brought up was a job answering telephones. A few minutes later, the same recruiter spoke with Chris. He was offered a management job. When interviewed afterward by ABC, the company recruiter said he would never want a man answering his telephone. Another company had advertised positions as territory managers for lawn-care services. The owner of the company gave Julie a typing test, discussed her fiance's business with her, and then offered her a job as a receptionist at $6 an hour. When the owner interviewed Chris, however, he gave him an aptitude test, chatted with him about how he kept fit, and offered him a job as territory manager paying $300 to $500 a week. When the owner was later interviewed by ABC, he commented that women "do not do well as territory managers, which involves some physical labor." According to the owner, he had also hired one other woman as a receptionist and had hired several other males as territory managers.[5] Several other researchers have replicated the findings of the ABC study and came up with similar results.[6]

The experience of young Chris and Julie suggests that sexual discrimination is alive and well. Numerous similar experiments suggest that racial discrimination also continues to thrive. In one study, researchers at the Urban Institute paired several young black men with similar young white men, matching them in openness, energy level, articulateness, physical characteristics, clothing, and job experience. Young Hispanic males fluent in English were likewise matched with young white males. Each member of each pair was trained and coached in mock interviews to act exactly like the other, then they applied in person for the same jobs, ranging from general laborer to management trainee in manufacturing, hotels, restaurants, retail sales, and office work. Despite the fact that all were equally qualified for the same jobs, blacks and Hispanics were offered jobs 50 percent fewer times than the young white males. In another study, white students paired with black students applied for low-wage, entry-level jobs in Milwaukee. While the white applicants told employers they had been in jail for 18 months, the black applicants presented themselves with a clean record. Yet the white ex-cons were called back for interviews 17 percent of the time, while their crime-free black equivalents were called back only 14 percent of the time. In short, being black is about equivalent to having an 18-month jail conviction. In yet another study, identical resumes were sent to random help-wanted ads in Boston and Chicago. Half of the resumes carried the "white-sounding" names "Emily" and "Greg" while the other half carried the "African-American-sounding" names "Lakisha" and "Jamal." The white-sounding names received 50 percent more callbacks for interviews.[7]

Today, outright sexist and racist bigotry are usually not openly exhibited or expressed; on the contrary, virtually everyone will sincerely and forcefully deny that they are prejudiced against women or minorities. Yet, the studies described above suggest that both minorities and women today continue to be treated differently from their white or male counterparts. Studies like these, as it were, catch us in the very act of discriminating against minorities or women, perhaps without us even realizing what we are doing.

The root meaning of the term ***discriminate*** is "to distinguish one object from another," a morally neutral and not necessarily wrongful activity. However, in modern usage, the term is not morally neutral; it is usually intended to refer to the wrongful act of distinguishing illicitly among people not on the basis of individual merit, but on the basis of prejudice or some other *invidious* or morally reprehensible attitude.[8] This morally charged notion of invidious discrimination, as it applies to employment, is what is at issue in this chapter. In this sense, to discriminate in employment is to make an adverse decision (or set of decisions) against employees (or prospective employees) who belong to a certain class because of morally unjustified prejudice toward members of that class, whether or not that prejudice is consciously held. Discrimination can be based on an overt and conscious racist bias against a group, or it can arise from unconscious stereotypes about the members of a group. Thus, discrimination in employment must involve three basic elements. First, it is a decision against one or more employees (or prospective employees) that is not based on individual merit, such as the ability to perform a given job, seniority, or other morally legitimate qualifications. Second, the decision

discrimination
The wrongful act of distinguishing illicitly among people not on the basis of individual merit, but on the basis of prejudice or some other *invidious* or morally reprehensible attitude.

derives solely or in part from racial or sexual prejudice, false stereotypes, or some other kind of morally unjustified attitude, whether consciously held or not, against members of the class to which the employee belongs. Third, the decision (or set of decisions) has a harmful or negative impact on the interests of the employees against whom the decision is made, in hiring, compensation, promotion, job assignments, or termination of those employees.

Employment discrimination in the United States historically has been directed at a surprisingly large number of groups. These have included religious groups (such as Jews and Catholics), ethnic groups (such as Italians, Poles, and Irish), racial groups (such as blacks, Asians, and Hispanics), and sexual groups (such as women and homosexuals). We have an embarrassingly rich history of discrimination.

Quick Review 7.1

Forms of Discrimination

- Intentional discrimination is conscious and deliberate discrimination.
- Unintentional discrimination is discrimination that is not consciously or deliberately sought, but is brought about by stereotypes or as an unintended outcome.
- Individual discrimination is the discrimination of one or a few individuals acting on their own.
- Institutional discrimination is discrimination that is the result of the actions of all or many of the people in an institution and of their routine processes and policies.

Forms of Discrimination: Intentional and Institutional Aspects

A helpful framework for analyzing different forms of discrimination can be constructed by distinguishing the extent to which a discriminatory act is intentional (conscious) or unintentional (unconscious), and the extent to which it is an individual (isolated) or institutional (systematic) act.[9] *Intentional discrimination* is carried out consciously and deliberately, while *unintentional discrimination* is not consciously or deliberately sought, but is the result of unconscious factors such as stereotypes or processes that have unintended outcomes. *Individual discrimination* consists of the discriminatory act or acts of one or a few individuals acting on their own and so has a one-time or limited effect, while *institutional or institutionalized discrimination* consists of the discriminatory act or acts that are the frequent outcomes of the actions of all or many members of an institution and of the regular processes and policies of the institution. While individual discrimination has a one-time or limited effect, institutionalized discrimination tends to have recurring and widespread effects within the institution and even beyond. There are, then, four categories of discriminatory actions. First, a discriminatory act may be the isolated act of a single *individual* who *intentionally* discriminates out of personal prejudice. In the ABC experiment, for example, the attitudes that the male interviewer is described as having may not be characteristic of other company interviewers: His behavior toward female job seekers may be an intentional, but isolated instance of sexism in hiring. Second, a discriminatory act may be part of the routine *institutional* behavior of a group that *intentionally* discriminates because of the shared prejudices of its members. Aryan Nations, Stormfront, and the White Aryan Resistance, for example, are organizations that engage in intentional institutionalized discriminatory behavior against minorities of virtually every kind. Third, an act of discrimination may be the isolated act of a single (or a few) *individual(s)* who *unintentionally* discriminates against women or minorities because the individual has unconscious stereotypes about the abilities of women or minorities, perhaps absorbed from surrounding society. If the interviewer quoted in the ABC experiment, for example, acted unintentionally, then he would fall into this third category. Fourth, a discriminatory act may be the result of the *institutionalized* routines of a corporate organization whose procedures and practices *unintentionally* discriminate against women or minorities. The companies studied in the ABC experiment, for example, were organizations in which the best-paying jobs were routinely assigned to men and the worst-paying jobs were routinely assigned to women—on the stereotypical assumption that women are fit for some jobs and not for others. There may be no conscious intent to discriminate, but the result is the same: a recurring and widespread pattern of racially or sexually based preferences biased against minority or female candidates.

During the last century, an important shift in emphasis occurred—from seeing discrimination primarily as an intentional and individual matter to seeing it as an institutionalized and perhaps, unintentional outcome of routine corporate behavior. During the early 1960s, employment discrimination was seen primarily as an intentional act performed by one individual on another. Title VII of the Civil Rights Act of 1964 (amended in 1972 and 1991)—the fundamental U.S. law against discrimination—seems to have had this notion of discrimination in mind when it stated:

> It shall be an unlawful employment practice for an employer (1) to fail or refuse to hire or to discharge any individual, or otherwise discriminate against any individual with respect to his compensation, terms, conditions, or privileges of employment because of such individual's race, color, religion, sex, or national origin; or (2) to limit, segregate, or classify his employees or applicants for employment in any way that would deprive or tend to deprive any individual of employment opportunities or otherwise adversely affect his status as an employee because of such individual's race, color, sex, or national origin.[10]

However, in the late 1960s, the concept of discrimination was enlarged to include more than the traditionally recognized intentional forms of individual discrimination. Executive Order 11246, issued in 1965, required companies doing business with the federal government to not discriminate and to take steps to correct any "racial imbalances" in their workforce. By the 1970s, the term *discrimination* was being used regularly to include disparities of minority representation within the ranks of a firm regardless of whether the disparity had been intentionally created. An organization was "discriminatory" when minority group representation within its ranks was significantly disproportional to the group's local availability—for example if a company hired for certain positions from an area in which qualified minorities made up 30 percent of the people in the pool of available workers, then qualified minorities should make up about 25–35 percent of the company's workers in those positions, and not, say, 5 or 10 percent. The "discrimination" would be remedied when the proportions of minorities within the organization more or less matched their proportions in the available pool of workers. To remedy any imbalances, companies were asked to use **"affirmative action" programs**. For example, a U.S. Department of Labor guidebook for employers issued in February, 1970 stated:

> An acceptable affirmative action program must include an analysis of areas within which the contractor is deficient in the utilization of minority groups and women, and further, goals and timetables to which the contractor's good faith efforts must be directed to correct the deficiencies and thus to increase materially the utilization of minorities and women at all levels and in all segments of his work force where deficiencies exist.... "Underutilization" is defined as having fewer minorities or women in a particular job classification than would reasonably be expected by their availability.[11]

The Equal Employment Opportunity Act of 1972 gave the **Equal Employment Opportunity Commission** increased power to combat this form of discrimination and to even require affirmative action programs to correct any deficiencies.

Some people, however, criticized the view that an institution is "discriminatory" if a minority group is underrepresented within its ranks. Discrimination is the intentional act of individuals, they argued, and it is individual women and minorities whom it mistreats. Consequently, these critics concluded, we should not say discrimination exists until we know that a specific individual intentionally discriminated against another individual in a specific instance. The problem with this criticism is that it is generally impossible to know when, or even whether, a specific individual

affirmative action program Any program designed to ensure that minorities, women, or members of some other group, are adequately represented within an organization and its various levels by taking positive steps to increase their number when underrepresented; what counts as "adequate representation" depends on the objectives of the program: some aim at having the same proportion of women or minorities as exists in the pool from which new members are drawn, others aim at achieving the diversity needed to meet organizational objectives.

Equal Employment Opportunity Commission A federal agency that investigates claims of on-the-job discrimination.

Quick Review 7.2

Controversy over Forms of Discrimination

- Four possible kinds of discrimination are (1) individual and intentional, (2) institutional and intentional, (3) individual and unintentional, and (4) institutional and unintentional.
- In the 1960s, discrimination is seen as individual and intentional; by the 1970s, it is seen to have institutional and unintentional forms, as indicated by "underrepresentation" of minorities or women, and to be remedied with affirmative action.
- In the 1980s, some insist discrimination is only individual and intentional, but in the 1990s, the view prevails it can also be institutional and unintentional.

Quick Review 7.3

Discrimination and the Law

- Civil Rights Act of 1964 made it illegal to base hiring, firing, or compensation decisions on race, color, religion, sex, or national origin; created the Equal Employment Opportunity Commission (EEOC) to administer the Act.
- Executive Order 11246 required companies doing business with the federal government to take steps to redress racial imbalance in workforce.
- Equal Employment Opportunity Act of 1972 gave EEOC increased power to combat "under representation" and to require affirmative action programs.

was discriminated against in a particular instance. Individuals compete with other individuals for jobs and promotions. Whether a specific individual wins a specific job or promotion depends on a number of variable factors that include not only his or her qualifications, but also the fairness of the hiring manager and the unconscious stereotypes he or she may hold, as well as numerous chance factors, such as who the other competitors happened to be, what qualifications the competitors happened to have, how the manager happened to feel the day he or she made the decision, and how the applicant happened to perform at the moment of the interview. Consequently, when a minority individual loses in this competitive process, there is generally no way of knowing whether that individual's loss was the result of his or her qualifications or some chance factor or unconscious (or conscious) discrimination. The only way of knowing whether a process is discriminating is by looking at what happens to minorities as a group over a period of time: If minorities as a group regularly lose out in a competitive process in which their abilities as a group match those of non-minorities, then we may conclude that the process itself is systematically discriminating even though we may not know which particular individuals were discriminated against.[12]

Nevertheless, during the 1980s, government policy under the Reagan administration shifted toward the view that the focus of society should not be on discrimination in its institutionalized forms. Starting in about 1981, the federal government began to actively oppose affirmative action programs based on statistical analyses of systematic discrimination. The Reagan administration held that only individuals who could prove that they had been the victims of discrimination aimed specifically and intentionally at them should be eligible for special treatment in hiring or promotions. Although the administration was largely unsuccessful in its efforts to dismantle affirmative action programs altogether, it did succeed in naming a majority of U.S. Supreme Court justices who rendered decisions that tended to undermine some legal supports of affirmative action programs. These trends were reversed once again in the 1990s, when George H. W. Bush became president and pledged to "knock down the barriers left by past discrimination." In 1991, the U.S. Congress passed, and the President signed, legislation that supported affirmative action programs and reversed the U.S. Supreme Court rulings that had undermined them. As we saw earlier, in 2003 the Supreme Court approved the use of "preferential treatment" programs to achieve diversity in educational institutions. Thus, our society has wavered and continues to waver on the question of whether discrimination should be seen only as an intentional and individual act or also as an unintentional and institutionalized pattern of actions revealed by statistics, and whether we should bend our efforts to combating only the former or should also try to overcome the latter with affirmative action programs.

For purposes of analysis, it is also important to keep separate the ethical issues raised by policies that aim at *preventing discrimination before it happens again*, whether intentional or unintentional, from those raised by policies like affirmative action that aim at *remedying discrimination after it has already happened* by, say, achieving a proportional representation of minorities within a business. We will discuss each of these issues separately since each raises distinct ethical issues.

First, however, we must examine whether and to what extent our business institutions today are discriminatory. It is a commonly held belief that, although our institutions used to be discriminatory, this is no longer the case because of the great strides minorities and women have made during the last few years. For example, Barack Obama was elected President in 2008, Edward Brooke in 1966 became the first African-American to be elected Senator since Reconstruction, Edward Hidalgo became the first Hispanic Secretary of the Navy in 1979, Sandra Day O'Connor became the first female Supreme Court Justice in 1981, Dr. Antonia Novello was named the first Hispanic U.S. Surgeon General in 1990, Colin Powell was named the first African-American Chair of the Joint Chiefs of Staff in 1989 and the first African-American Secretary of State in 2001, Nancy Pelosi became the

Helping Patients at Plainfield Healthcare Center

Plainfield Healthcare Center is an Indiana nursing home that cares for elderly women in frail health who live there fulltime. Brenda Chaney, a black certified nurse's aid (CNA) worked at the Center. Each day, the Center gave Brenda a sheet that assigned specific patients to her and she was responsible for attending to the needs of her patients along with any other CNAs assigned the same patients. Next to each patient's name on the assignment sheet was an indication of the care they needed and various notes about each patient's condition, special needs, or special requests. Marjorie Latshaw, a white elderly woman, was a patient who had lived at the Center for several months and who suspected she would live there until her death. Latshaw felt that since the Center was her home, she had a right to have things arranged as she would have arranged them for herself in the privacy of her own home. Indiana laws state that residents in nursing homes have a right to "choose a personal attending physician and other providers of services." So when she was admitted to the nursing home, Lashaw insisted that she be attended only by white caretakers. The nursing home had a policy of honoring each resident's requests so far as possible, and this included honoring their racial preferences in caretakers. Consequently, the daily assignment sheets that Chaney received each day indicated, next to Latshaw's name, "Prefers No Black CNAs." The managers of the nursing home were clear that this meant that all black CNAs were "banned" from assisting Latshaw or any other white patient that made a similar request. The managers of Plainfield Healthcare Center said that if they did not honor Latshaw's requests, they would not be following Indiana state laws which said residents of nursing homes have the right to have access to the providers they choose, the right to privacy, and the right to bodily autonomy (i.e., the right to determine what is done to one's body). Federal civil rights laws on equal employment opportunity normally overrule state laws, and federal civil rights laws prohibit employers from accommodating the discriminatory preferences of their customers. However, federal courts had ruled that those laws do not prohibit *nursing homes* from accommodating their patient's privacy rights when patients asked that their providers be members of their *own sex*. Plainfield Healthcare Center's managers decided that this same reasoning meant that a nursing home could accommodate its patients when they requested that their caretakers be of their *own race*.

Chaney was extremely upset by the policy of the nursing home, but because she feared being fired and needed the job, she went along with it. Although Latshaw was sometimes on her assignment sheet, she refrained from assisting her. Once when Latshaw fell to the ground, Chaney was forced to search the facility looking for a white nurse's aid to help Latshaw get up, as she had insisted. Other white patients had also said they wanted only white CNAs to help them and also regularly rejected Chaney's offers of assistance. These racially-based rejections of her offers to help humiliated and depressed Chaney and often reduced her to tears. Moreover, the policy seemed to encourage some of her white co-workers who had made racial slurs; one co-worker once called her a "black bitch" and another asked why the Center "keeps on hiring all of these black niggers? They're not gonna stay anyway." Another co-worker reminded her several times that she could not touch certain patients because she was black. But the managers of the Center immediately responded when Chaney complained by reprimanding the co-workers and the slurs stopped. Nevertheless, Chaney was fired when one of her co-workers alleged that she had used profanity while helping a patient, although another patient who witnessed the event denied the allegation and although Chaney's supervisor pointed out she had never heard her use profanity at work.

1. Is it unethical for the managers of Plainfield Healthcare Center to honor their white patients' requests to be helped only by members of their own race? Was Brenda Chaney subjected to a "hostile workplace" on the basis of her race? Did the managers of Plainfield Healthcare Center unethically discriminate against Chaney?

Source: *Brenda Chaney v. Plainfield Healthcare Center*, U.S. Court of Appeals for the 7th Circuit, no. 09-3661, July 20, 2010.

first female Speaker of the House of Representatives in 2007, and Sonia Sotomayor became the first Hispanic Supreme Court Justice in 2009. There are now several examples of female heads of large companies including: Meg Whitman, CEO of eBay; Anne Mulcahy, CEO of Xerox; Indra Nooyi, CEO of Pepsi; and Christina Gold, CEO of Western Union. And there are some examples of Hispanic heads of Fortune 500 companies: Antonio Perez, CEO of Kodak; Fernando Aquirre, CEO of Chiquita; Alvaro de Molina, CEO of GMAC; and William Perez, CEO of Wrigley. And the African Americans who likewise are heads of Fortune 500 companies include Kenneth Chenault, CEO of American Express; Clarence Otis, CEO of Darden Restaurants; Rodney O'Neal, CEO of Delphi; and John Thompson, CEO of Symantec. If the belief that discrimination is a thing of the past is correct—and it is at least challenged by the experiments described earlier, in which matched pairs of male and female or white and minority people applied for the same job—then there is not much point in discussing the issue of discrimination. But is it correct?

7.2 Discrimination: Its Extent

Quick Review 7.4

Prima Facie Indicators of Discrimination

- Average benefits minorities and women receive compared to others
- Proportions of minorities and women at lowest economic levels
- Proportions of minorities and women at highest economic levels.

How do we determine whether an institution or a set of institutions is discriminating against a certain group? We do so by looking at statistical indicators of how the members of that group are being distributed within the institution. A prima facie indication of discrimination exists when a disproportionate number of the members of a certain group hold the less desirable positions within the institution despite their preferences and abilities.[13] Looking at three kinds of comparisons can show whether such disproportionate distributions affect minorities or women today: (1) examining the average benefits our institutions bestow on minorities and females compared to the average benefits they bestow on other groups, (2) examining the proportion of minorities and women found in the lowest levels of the institutions compared to the proportions of other groups found at those levels, and (3) examining the proportions of women and minorities that hold the more advantageous positions in our institutions compared to the proportions of other groups in those positions. If we look at U.S. society in terms of these three kinds of comparisons, it becomes clear that some form of racial and sexual discrimination is present in U.S. institutions today.

Average Income Comparisons

Income comparisons provide the most revealing indications that some kind of sexual and racial discrimination takes place in our society. Although these comparisons do not imply that such discrimination is intentional, they do suggest it is at least institutionalized. If we compare the average total incomes of non-white U.S. families, for example, with the average total incomes of white American families, we see that white family incomes are substantially above those of non-whites, as Figure 7.1 indicates.

Contrary to a commonly held belief, the average family income gap between whites and minorities has not decreased, but has actually increased somewhat in absolute terms. Since 1970, even during periods when all incomes have increased, real minority family incomes have not caught up with white incomes. In 1975, as Figure 7.1 indicates, the average income for a black family was 63 percent of a white family's average income and the average Hispanic family income was 67 percent of the average white family income; in 2008, the average black family's income was still only 64 percent of the average white family's income, while the average Hispanic family income had declined to 65 percent of the average high family income.[14]

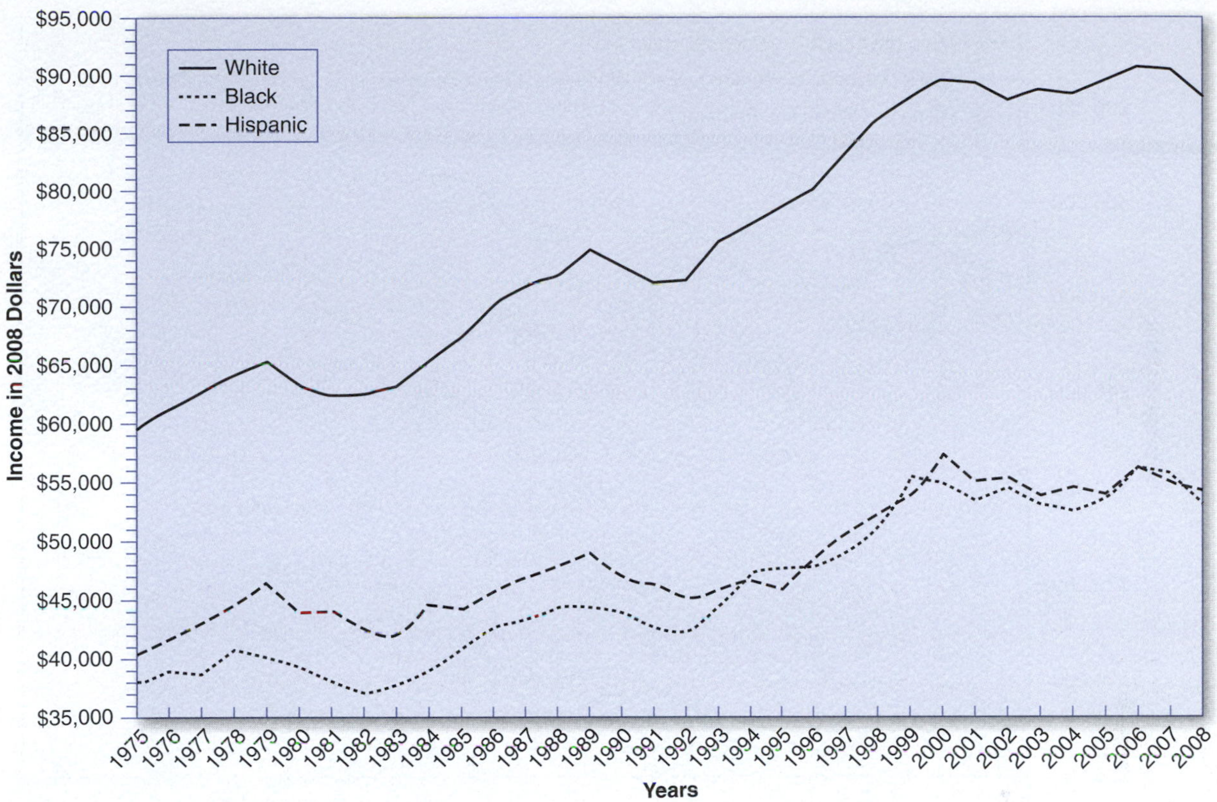

Figure 7.1
Average Family Incomes by Race (2008 Dollars).

View the Image on mythinkinglab.com

Source: U.S. Census Bureau Historical Income Tables – Table F-23. Families by Total Money Income, Race, and Hispanic Origin of Householder, 1967–2008 (Income in 2008 dollars).

Comparisons of the incomes of individuals also reveal large inequalities based on sex and race. A comparison of average incomes for men and women shows that women receive only a portion of what men receive. One study found that firms employing mostly men paid their workers on average 40 percent more than those employing mostly women.[15] The gap between the *median* earnings of men and the *median* earnings of women narrowed from 65 percent in 1968 to 77 percent in 2008 (the median earnings level for a group is the amount of earnings at which half of the people in the group have higher earnings, and half have lower earnings), but it took 40 years for women to make that 12 percent improvement.[16] Moreover, as Figure 7.2 indicates, a comparison of 2008 men and women's *average* earnings shows women earned only about 70 cents of average earnings for every dollar of average earnings of men (average earnings are the total earnings of a group divided by the number of people in the group). And some of the improvement in the ratio of female and male earnings has come about not as a result of declining discrimination, but as a result of declines in the average earnings of men due to an ongoing decline in the number of manufacturing jobs traditionally occupied by men.[17]

As studies show, the disparities in earnings between men and women begin as soon as men and women graduate from college, contrary to the optimistic and legitimate hope held by each generation of graduating women that "our generation will be different." A 2007 study by the American Association of University Women, for example, found that a year out of college, women were earning only 80 percent of what their

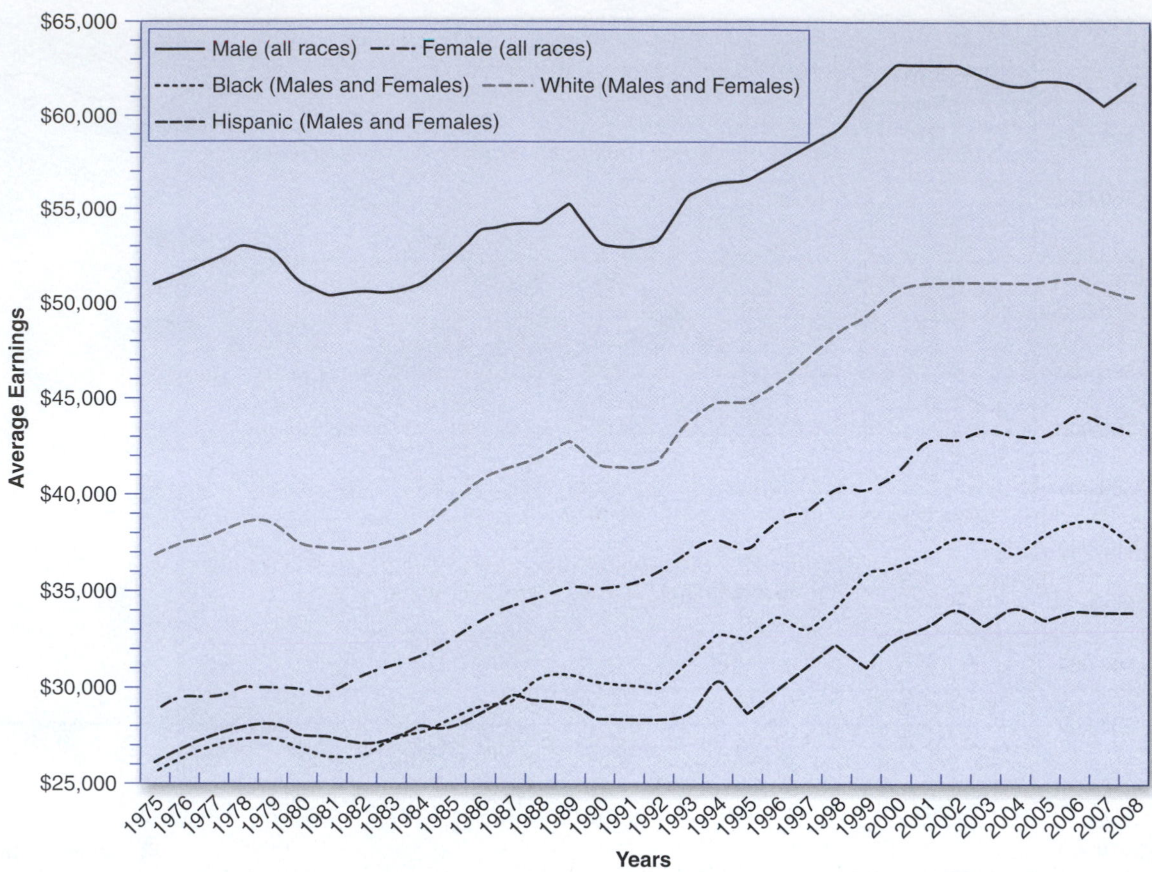

Figure 7.2
Average Earnings of Male, Female, white, Black and Hispanic Full Time Workers, 1975–2008 (in 2008 dollars).

View the **Image** on **mythinkinglab.com**

Source: Census Bureau, Historical Tables, Table P-39. Full-Time, Year-Round Workers by Mean Earnings and Sex: 1967 to 2008 (15 years old and over), and Table P-43. Full-Time, Year-Round Workers (Both Sexes Combined) by Median and Mean Earnings: 1974 to 2008 (15 years old and over).

male colleagues earned, whether they had specialized in a female-dominated major such as education where they earned only 95 percent of what their male counterparts earned, or in a male-dominated major such as mathematics where they ended up earning only 75 percent of what their male colleagues earned. [18] The study also found that ten years after graduation women had fallen even father behind their male cohort, earning only 69 percent of what their male colleagues earned. This has been the case for decades. An early study in 1980—more than a decade and a half after our civil rights laws were enacted—of white men and women ages 21 to 22 found that although their qualifications had increased substantially relative to men's, women's starting salaries were 83 percent of men's—an actual *decline* from 1970, when women of that age earned 86 percent of what men earned.[19] In 2008, as Table 7.1 indicates, a young woman aged 18 to 24 who had just graduated from college with a bachelor's degree got a job with an average salary of $34,898, whereas her male counterpart was given one with a salary of $44,656; a young woman aged 25 to 34 with a new master's degree on average could expect to earn $56,715 whereas her male counterpart would be earning an average of $71,637. If she had a professional degree (such as a law degree or an MBA), she would earn an average of $78,765, whereas her male counterpart would earn an average of $109,109.

Table 7.1 *Average Earnings of Year-Round Full-Time Working Men and Women Recently Out of School, 2008*

	Average Earnings of 18- to 24-Year-Olds		Average Earnings of 25- to 34-Year-Olds	
Education	**Men**	**Women**	**Men**	**Women**
Elementary	$19,896	NA	$24,211	$17,923
High school				
some, no diploma	21,305	$17,228	32,212	18,107
diploma	26,218	22,814	36,742	27,607
College				
some, no degree	27,591	24,953	44,597	31,592
associate degree	31,992	26,814	48,089	35,091
bachelor's degree	44,656	34,898	62,840	46,415
master's degree	NA	NA	71,637	56,715
professional degree	NA	NA	109,109	78,765

Source: U.S. Census Bureau, Table P-32. "Educational Attainment—Full-Time Year-Round Workers 18 Years Old and Over, by Mean Earnings, Age, and Sex: 1991–2008."

Table 7.2 *Average Total Earnings of Year-Round Full-Time Workers, 18 Years Old and Over, by Education, Race and Sex, 2008*

			Both Men and Women		
Education	**Men's Average Earnings**	**Women's Average Earnings**	**Whites' Average Earnings**	**Blacks' Average Earnings**	**Hispanics' Average Earnings**
Elementary	$28,375	$21,376	$31,557	$23,348	$25,514
High school					
some, no diploma	33,457	22,246	33,995	27,657	26,444
diploma	43,493	31,666	41,545	33,410	32,696
College	50,433	36,019	46,521	36,890	37,563
some, no degree					
associate degree	54,830	39,935	49,051	41,332	43,910
bachelor's degree	81,975	54,207	72,938	51,787	56,470
master's degree	99,177	65,133	85,305	66,005	82,987
professional degree	164,785	100,518	148,636	116,658	97,863
doctorate degree	128,114	83,616	113,908	NA	NA

Source: U.S. Census Bureau, Table PINC-04. "Educational Attainment—People 18 Years Old and Over, by Total Money Earnings in 2008, Work Experience in 2008, Age, Race, Hispanic Origin, and Sex."

As Table 7.2 shows, female college graduates over the course of their lives have lower average yearly earnings ($54,207) than male graduates ($81,975); in fact, the average earnings of a woman who has graduated with a master's degree ($65,133) will be significantly less than the average earnings of a man with only an undergraduate bachelor's degree ($81,975). The average earnings of a woman with a high school degree ($31,666) will not only be less than the average earnings of a man with a high school degree ($43,493), but she will even earn less than a man who never graduated from high school ($33,457).

Table 7.3 *Median Weekly Earnings of Full-Time Male and Female Workers by Major Occupational Group, 2009*

Occupational Group	Median Weekly Earnings		Women's as Percent of Men's
	Men	Women	
Management, business & financial operations	$1334	$955	72%
Professional & related	1191	880	74
Healthcare support	544	464	85
Protective service	798	599	75
Food preparation and serving related	416	378	90
Building and grounds cleaning & maintenance	488	388	79
Personal care & service	546	415	76
Sales & related	793	525	66
Office & administrative support	657	602	91
Farming, fishing, & forestry	428	372	86
Construction & extraction (mining)	719	673	93
Installation, maintenance & repair	787	644	81
Production	678	472	69
Transportation & material moving	618	472	76

Source: U.S. Bureau Of Labor Statistics, *Current Population Survey*, Household Data, Annual Averages, Table 39. Median Weekly Earnings Of Full-Time Wage And Salary Workers By Detailed Occupation And Sex, 2009.

The earning disparities between men and women extend to all occupations, as Table 7.3 indicates. In every major occupational group, women's weekly earnings are only a portion of men's, ranging from sales occupations where women earn only 66 percent of what men earn, to construction and mining in which the few women who work in those occupations earn 93 percent of what men earn.

Black and Hispanic minorities do not fare much better than females. Figure 7.2 above shows that both the earnings of blacks and Hispanics are consistently less than the earnings of whites. Since 1990, the average earnings of blacks have stayed at around 73 percent of the average earnings of whites. In fact, in 2008 the average earnings of blacks at 74 percent of the average earnings of whites had hardly moved from their 1990 level when they were 73 percent of the average earnings of whites. The average earnings of Hispanics have also failed to increase; they have remained at about 67 percent of the average earnings of whites since 1990.

Like the gap between the earnings of males and females, there is also a gap between the earnings of whites and minorities that education does not eradicate. As Table 7.2 above indicates, the earnings of a black person with a master's graduate degree ($66,005) are significantly less than the earnings of a white person with an undergraduate degree ($72,938), and a black person with an associate college degree earns slightly less ($41,332) than a white person with a high school diploma ($41,545). Hispanics fare even worse; an Hispanic who graduates from high school earns only slightly more ($32,696) than a white person who completes elementary school ($31,557), and a male Hispanic who graduates from college earns much less ($56,470) than his white counterpart ($72,938).

Lowest Income Group Comparisons

The lowest identified income group in the United States consists of those people whose annual income falls below the poverty level. In 2008, the poverty level was set at $22,025 for a family of four (by comparison, the average tuition, room, and board costs of attending a public or private 4-year college during the 2007–2008 school year was about $19,400, plus another $2,500 in books and miscellaneous, for a total of about $21,900).[20] As Figure 7.3 indicates, the poverty rate among minorities has consistently been 2 to 3 times higher than among whites. This is not surprising, since, as we have seen, minorities have lower average incomes.

In view of the lower average incomes of women, it also comes as no surprise that families headed by single women fall below the poverty level at a much greater rate than families headed by single men. As Figure 7.4 indicates, families headed by single women are now more than twice as likely to be poor compared to families headed by single men. This is an improvement since, as Figure 7.4 also shows, until the late 1980s families headed by women were *three* times as likely to be poor as families headed by men. Although it has narrowed over the past several decades, the gap between the poverty rate of male-headed and female-headed families has persisted to the present day.

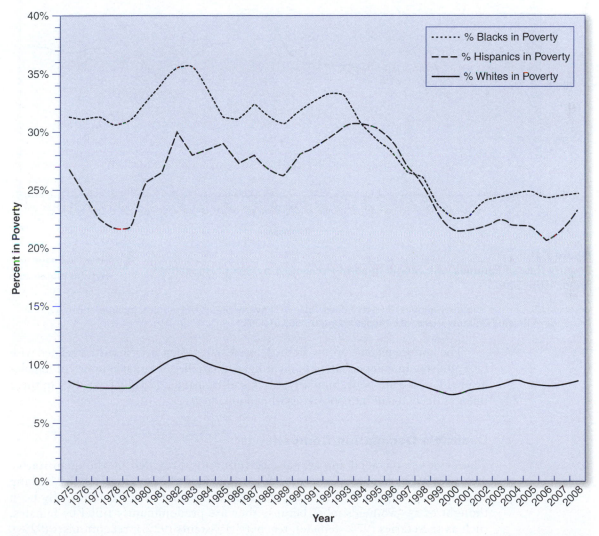

Figure 7.3
Percent of Whites, Blacks, and Hispanics Living in Poverty, 1975–2008.

Source: U.S. Census Bureau, Historical Poverty Tables, Table 2. "Poverty Status of People by Family Relationship, Race, and Hispanic Origin: 1959 to 2008."

View the **Image** on **mythinkinglab.com**

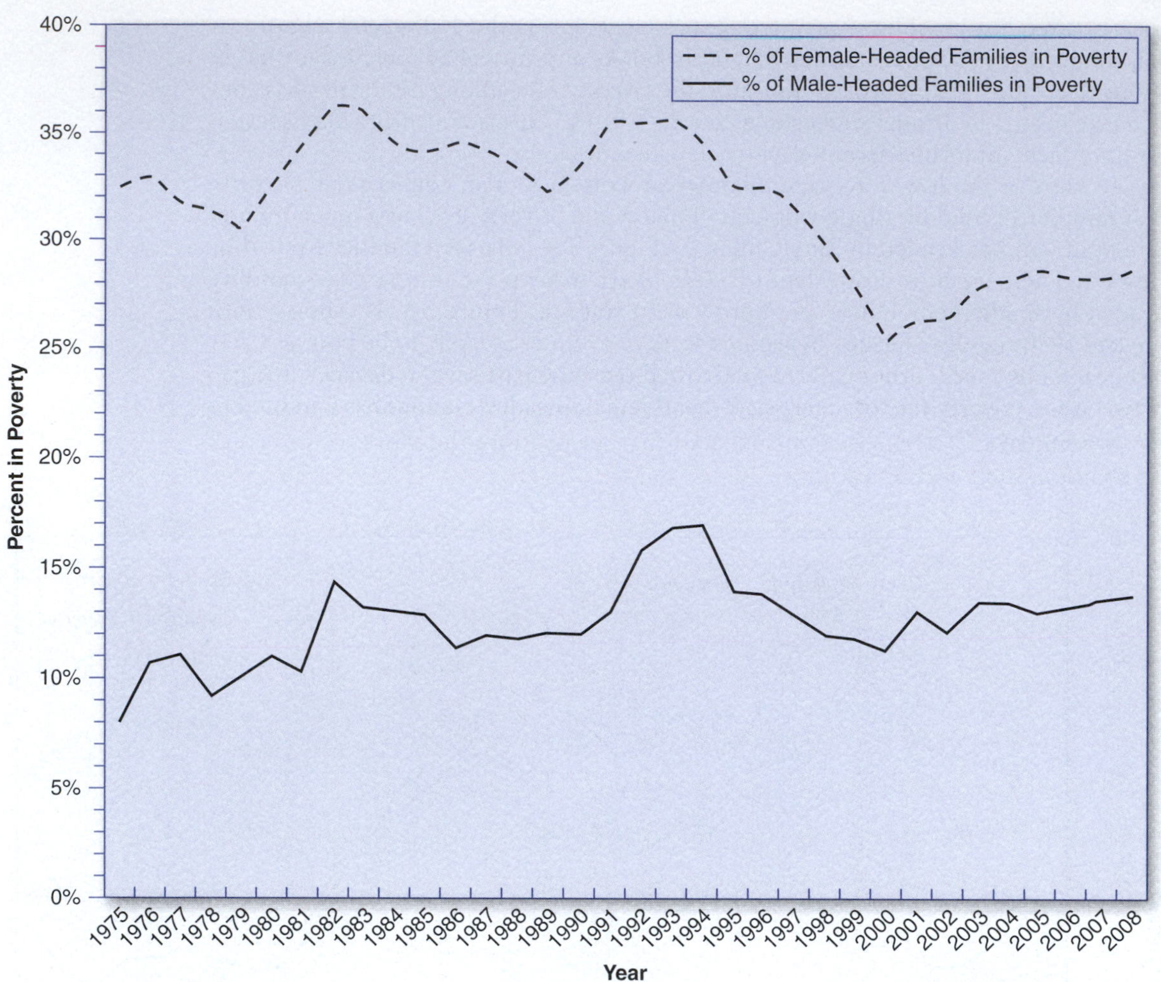

Figure 7.4
Poverty Rate of Families with Single Head-of-Household by Sex of Household Head, 1975–2008.

View the **Image** on **mythinkinglab.com**

Source: U.S. Census Bureau, Historical Poverty Tables, Table 4. "Poverty Status of Families, by Type of Family, Presence of Related Children, Race, and Hispanic Origin: 1959 to 2008."

The bottom income groups in the United States, then, are closely correlated with race and sex. In comparison with male-headed families, a larger number of female-headed families are poor. Similarly, black and Hispanic individuals are two to three times as likely to fall into poverty as white individuals.

Desirable Occupation Comparisons

The evidence of racial and sexual discrimination provided by the quantitative measures we have presented can be filled out somewhat qualitatively by looking at people's occupations. For many decades, certain jobs have traditionally been thought of as "women's jobs" because they are predominantly filled by females, such as secretaries (97% female), teachers' assistants (92%), receptionists (92%), dental assistants (98%), child care workers (95%), and hairdressers (90%); while other jobs have been thought of as "men's jobs" because they are predominantly filled by males such as mechanics (99% male), electrical power-line workers (99%), crane operators (99%), brick layers (100%), welders (96%), and roofers (99%). But salaries for the women's jobs are noticeably lower (secretaries, $32,240; teachers' assistants, $24,544; receptionists, $26,884; dental assistants, $27,716; child care workers, $19,084; hairdressers, $22,100) in comparison to the salaries for the men's jobs (power line workers, $52,936; crane operators, $40,456; brick layers, $36,452; roofers, $31,200; welders, $35,100; mechanics, $34,684), although both sets of jobs require about the same amount of education and training. In fact, many of the more well-paying occupations tend to be "men's jobs," while many of the lower-paying occupations tend to be "women's jobs." As Table 7.4 suggests, the higher the proportion of women in an occupation, the lower the pay for that occupation tends to be. Although there are a large number of exceptions, (some of which occur in the Table) there is a fairly close negative correlation between the proportion of women in an occupation and the earnings level of that occupation: the more women in an occupation, the lower its earnings.[21]

Table 7.4 *Median Weekly Earnings of Selected Occupations and Percent of Men and Women in Those Occupations, 2009*

Occupation	Weekly Earnings	Percent of Total in Occupation Who Are	
		Men	Women
Child-care workers	$367	5%	95%
Receptionists	517	8	92
Bookkeepers	633	8	92
Licensed practical nurses	710	9	91
Legal assistants	846	14	86
Social workers	787	19	81
Clinical lab technicians	829	25	75
Tax collectors	922	26	74
Human resources managers	1234	33	67
Accountants	1003	38	62
High school teachers	1169	45	55
College teachers	1169	51	49
Artists	1085	54	46
Management analysts	1247	57	43
Marketing managers	1330	57	43
Producers and Directors	1070	60	40
Lawyers	1757	68	32
Physicians	1738	68	32
Computer systems analysts	1245	73	27
Chief executives	1916	75	25
Computer software engineers	1493	80	20
Aerospace engineers	1488	90	10
Electrical engineers	1502	91	9
Engineering managers	1773	92	8
Airplane pilots	1650	95	5

Source: U.S. Bureau of Labor Statistics, Table 39. Median Weekly Earnings of Full-Time Wage and Salary Workers by Detailed Occupation and Sex, 2009, Household Data Annual Averages, and Table 11. Employed Persons by Detailed Occupation, Sex, Race, and Hispanic or Latino Ethnicity, 2009, Household Data Annual Averages.

glass ceiling
An invisible, but impenetrable, barrier to further promotion sometimes encountered by women or minorities.

Quick Review 7.5

Discrimination in the United States

- Gap between average family incomes of whites and minorities has not decreased.
- Gaps between average incomes and median earnings of men and women have decreased but are still large; women earn less than less-educated men; women earn less in every occupational group.
- Gaps between the average earnings of minorities and of whites have hardly narrowed; minorities earn less than less-educated whites; percent of minorities in poverty is 2 to 3 times the white percentage.
- Poverty rate of families headed by women is twice that of male-headed families.
- Salaries of "women's jobs" are significantly lower than "men's jobs."
- Top-paying executive positions are filled by men; a "glass ceiling" stops women.
- The earnings gaps are not explained by education, career choices, preferences, work history, training, or absenteeism.

Studies also indicate that, despite two decades of women entering the workforce in record numbers, women managers still are not being promoted from middle-management positions into senior or top-management positions, because they encounter an impenetrable **"glass ceiling"** through which they may "look but not enter."[22] Consequently, although many women have moved into middle-management positions in recent years, all but a very few have been blocked from entering the top-paying executive positions. Blacks and Hispanics are in a similar situation. We noted above that there are women and minorities serving as CEOs of large companies, but their number is miniscule. As of 2009, only 12 (2.4 percent) of the Fortune 500 companies had women as president or chief executive officer, only 5 (1 percent) of the Fortune 500 companies had black CEOs, and only 7 (1.4 percent) had Hispanic CEOs.

The fact that women and minorities end up in positions that earn less than white males is not explainable in terms of the lower educational levels of minorities and women.[23] If we return to Table 7.2 above, we see that in 2008, the average full-time, year-round working male who graduated junior college earned $54,830—more than the $54,207 earned by a similar female who graduated from a four-year college. The same year, a white, full-time, year-round worker who attended high school but never graduated made $33,995, more than the $33,410 earned by a black, full-time, year-round worker who likewise attended high school but graduated; and whereas a white worker with a college degree made $72,938, a black worker with both a college and a graduate master's degree made only $66,005 (Table 7.2).

Nor can the large disparities in earnings between white males and women or minorities be wholly accounted for by the preferences or qualifications of the two latter groups.[24] It is sometimes suggested that women *voluntarily choose* to work in those jobs that have relatively low pay and low prestige. It is suggested, for example, that women believe only certain jobs (such as secretary or kindergarten teacher) are appropriate for women, that many women choose courses of study that suit them only for such jobs, that many women choose those jobs because they plan to raise children and these jobs are relatively easy to leave and reenter, that many women choose these jobs because they have limited demands and allow them time to raise children, and that many women defer to the demands of their husbands' careers and choose to forgo developing their own careers. Although choice plays some role in pay differentials, however, researchers who have studied the differences in earnings between men and women have all concluded that the wage differences between men and women and between whites and minorities cannot be accounted for simply on the basis of such factors. One study found that only half of the earnings gap between men and women might be accounted for by women's choices, whereas other studies have found it could account for somewhat more or somewhat less.[25]

All studies, however, have demonstrated that only a portion of the gap can be accounted for on the basis of male and female differences in education, work experience, work continuity, self-imposed work restrictions, and absenteeism.[26] These studies show that, even after taking such differences into account, a gap between the earnings of men and women remains that can only be accounted for by discrimination in the labor market. A report of the National Academy of Sciences concluded that "about 35 to 40 percent of the disparity in average earnings is due to sex segregation because women are essentially steered into lower-paying 'women's jobs.'"[27] Some studies have shown that perhaps only one-tenth of the wage differences between men and women can be accounted for by differences in their personalities and tastes.[28] Similar studies have shown that half of the earning differences between white and minority workers cannot be accounted for by differences of work history, on-the-job training, absenteeism, or self-imposed restrictions on work hours and location.[29] A 2007 study arrived at the conclusion that although "discrimination cannot be measured directly" because "it is illegal," nevertheless "one way to discover discrimination is to eliminate other explanations for the pay gap" between men and women. After all, "the 'explanations' for the pay gap [between men and women] are included" in a statistical analysis, the study concludes, "they cannot fully explain the pay disparity" and so "while discrimination cannot be measured directly, it is reasonable to assume that this pay gap is the product of gender discrimination."[30]

Several trends that emerged toward the end of the twentieth century have increased the difficulties facing women and minorities in job markets. To begin with, most new workers now entering the labor force are not white males, but women and minorities. Although two decades ago white males held the largest share of the job market, by the beginning of the twenty-first century, white males were only 15 percent of the new workers entering the labor force. Three-fifths of new workers were women—a trend created by sheer economic necessity as well as cultural redefinitions of the role of women. Native minorities and immigrants now make up some 40 percent of all new workers.[31]

This large influx of women and minorities has encountered major difficulties in the job market. First, as we mentioned, cultural stereotypes, prejudice, and conscious and unconscious biases steer a sizable proportion of women into traditionally "female jobs" that pay less than traditionally "male jobs."

Second, as women advance in their careers, they encounter barriers (like the so-called *glass ceiling*) when attempting to advance into highest-paying, top management positions. As Table 7.4 indicates, men predominantly take the highest-paying jobs. Surveys have found that over 90 percent of newly promoted corporation chairs, presidents, and vice presidents are men. In fact, some studies have suggested that the percentage of women being promoted to the top corporate level is declining. In 2005, the percentage of corporate officers who were women in Fortune 500 companies peaked at 16.4 percent and by 2009, had declined to 15.7 percent.

Third, married women who want children, unlike married men who want children, currently encounter major difficulties in their career advancement. One survey found that 52 percent of the few married women who were promoted to vice president remained childless, whereas only 7 percent of the married men had no children. Another survey found that during the 10 years following their college graduation, 54 percent of those women who had made significant advances up the corporate ladder had done so by remaining childless. Several studies have found that women with professional careers are 6 times more likely than their husbands to be the one who stays home with a sick child; even women at the level of corporate vice president report that they must carry a greater share of such burdens than their husbands.[32]

The large numbers of minorities entering the workforce also encounter significant disadvantages. As these large waves of minorities hit the labor market, they find that most of the well-paying jobs awaiting them require greater skills and education than they have. Of all the new jobs that have been created during the past two decades, more than half require some education beyond high school and almost a third require a college degree. Among the fastest-growing fields are professions with extremely high education requirements, such as technicians, engineers, social scientists, lawyers, mathematicians, scientists, and health professionals. In contrast, jobs that require relatively low levels of education and skills, such as machine tenders and operators, blue-collar supervisors, assemblers, hand workers, miners, and farmers, have actually been declining in number. Even many jobs that require relatively low levels of skill now have tough requirements: Secretaries, clerks, and cashiers need the ability to read and write clearly, understand directions, and use computers; assembly-line workers are being required to learn statistical process control methods employing basic algebra and statistics. Thus, most good new jobs demand more education and higher levels of language, math, and reasoning skills.

Quick Review 7.6

Increasing Problems for Women and Minorities

- Women and minorities make up most new workers, but face significant disadvantages.
- Women are steered into low-paying jobs and face a "glass ceiling" and sexual harassment.
- Minorities need skills and education but lack them.

Unfortunately, minorities are currently the least advantaged in terms of skill levels and education. Studies have shown that only about three-fifths of whites, two-fifths of Hispanics, and one-fourth of blacks could find information in a news article or almanac; only 25 percent of whites, 7 percent of Hispanics, and 3 percent of blacks could interpret a bus schedule; and only 44 percent of whites, 20 percent of Hispanics, and 8 percent of blacks could figure out the change they were owed from buying two items.[33] While the skill levels of whites in general are not very high, those of blacks and Hispanics are even lower. Minorities are also much more disadvantaged in terms of education. In 2007, when 89 percent of all white adults had graduated from high school, only 80 percent of blacks, and 60 percent of Hispanics had graduated from high school.[34] That same year, 30 percent of whites had graduated from college, but only 17 percent of blacks and 12 percent of Hispanics had graduated from college.[35] Some studies have indicated that because official statistics do not accurately count all students who drop out of school, real graduation rates are much lower.[36] Thus, although future new jobs will require increasing levels of skills and education, minorities are falling behind whites in their educational levels.

Working women, especially, face another troubling issue in the workplace (although as we will see, some men are also forced to deal with this issue). Forty-two percent of all women working for the federal government report that they experienced some form of uninvited and unwanted sexual attention, ranging from sexual remarks to attempted rape or assault. Women working as executives, prison guards, and even rabbis have reported being sexually harassed.[37] Victims of verbal or physical forms of sexual harassment were most likely to be single or divorced, between the ages of 20 and 44, have some college education, and work in a predominantly male environment or for a male supervisor.[38] An early study of sexual harassment in business found that 10 percent of 7,000 people surveyed reported that they had heard of or observed a situation in their organizations as extreme as: "Mr. X has asked me to have sex with him. I refused, but now I learn that he's given me a poor evaluation...."[39] A federal court vividly described the injuries that sexual harassment can inflict on a person:

> Cheryl Mathis's relationship with Mr. Sanders began on terms she described as good, but it later became clear that Sanders sought some kind of personal relationship with her. Whenever Mathis was in his office he wanted the door to outside offices closed, and he began discussing very personal matters with her, such as the lack of a sexual relationship with his wife. He then began bombarding her with unwelcome invitations for drinks, lunch, dinner, breakfast, and asking himself to her house. Mathis made it clear that she was not interested in a personal relationship with her married boss.... Sanders also commented on Mathis's appearance, making lewd references to parts of her body. As Mathis rejected Sanders's advances, he would become belligerent. By the spring of 1983 Mathis began to suffer from severe bouts of trembling and crying which became progressively worse and eventually caused her to be hospitalized on two separate occasions, once for a week in June, 1983, and again in July for a few days. During this entire summer Mathis remained out on sick leave, not returning to work until September, 1983.... As soon as she returned to work, Sanders's harassment resumed... and once again she was forced to seek medical help and did not work.... The harassment not only tormented... Mathis, it created hostility between her and other members of the department who apparently resented the plaintiff's familiarity with Sanders.[40]

Every year thousands of complaints of sexual harassment are filed with the Equal Employment Opportunity Commission (EEOC), a national (federal) government agency established in 1964 to enforce our federal civil rights laws. Thousands of other complaints are lodged with state civil rights commissions that enforce state civil rights laws. While the great majority of these complaints are filed by women, an increasing number are being filed by men who find themselves being forced to endure sexual advances they do not want.[41] In 2009, about 16 percent of the 12,700 claims filed with the EEOC were filed by men.

The various statistical comparisons that we have examined, together with the extensive research showing that these differences are not due in any simple way to differences in the preferences or qualifications of women and minorities, strongly suggest that many business organizations still harbor some degree of probably unintentional yet institutionalized discrimination, much of it no doubt a relic of the past. Whether we compare average incomes, representation in the highest economic positions, or representation in the lowest economic positions, it turns out that women and minorities do not yet have opportunities equal to those of white males, even if during the last 30 years the racial and sexual gaps have somewhat narrowed. Moreover, a number of troubling trends indicate that, unless we change the way we hire and promote people in our organizations, the situation for minorities and women will not improve.

It is important to recognize that finding that our institutions as a whole still embody a degree of unintentional but institutionalized discrimination does not show that any particular business organization is discriminatory. To find out whether a particular firm is perhaps unconsciously engaging in discriminatory behavior, we would have to make the same sorts of comparisons among the various employment levels of the firm that we made earlier among the various economic and occupational levels of U.S. society as a whole. To facilitate such comparisons within firms, employers today are required to report to the government the number of minorities and women their firm employs in each of nine categories: officials and managers, professionals, technicians, sales workers, office and clerical workers, skilled craftworkers, semiskilled operatives, unskilled laborers, and service workers.

7.3 Discrimination: Utility, Rights, and Justice

Given the statistics on the comparative incomes and low-status positions of minorities and women in the United States, the question we must ask ourselves is this: Are these inequalities wrong, and if so, how should businesses and managers deal with them? To be sure, these inequalities directly contradict the fundamental principles on which the United States was founded: "We hold these truths to be self-evident: that all men are created equal and endowed by their creator with certain inalienable rights."[42] However, historically we have often tolerated large discrepancies between these ideals and reality. The ancestors of most black Americans living today, for example, were brought to this country as slaves, treated like cattle, and lived out their lives in bondage, despite our ideals of equality. As the personal property of a white owner, blacks prior to the Civil War were not recognized as people and consequently had no legal powers, and no claims on their bodies or their labors. They were regarded by the U.S. Supreme Court in its 1857 Dred Scott decision as "beings of an inferior order...and so far inferior that they had no rights that the White man was bound to respect."[43] Women were treated almost in a similar way. Through much of the nineteenth century, women could not hold office, could not vote, could not serve on juries, nor bring suit in their own names. A married woman lost control over her property (which was acquired by her husband), she was considered incapable of making binding contracts, and, in an important 1873 decision (*Bradwell v. Illinois*), a married woman was declared by the U.S. Supreme Court to have "no legal existence, separate from her husband, who was regarded as her head and representative in the social state."[44] Why are these forms of inequality wrong? Why is it wrong to discriminate?

The arguments mustered against discrimination generally fall into three groups: (1) utilitarian arguments, which claim that discrimination leads to an inefficient use of human resources; (2) rights arguments, which claim that discrimination violates basic human rights; and (3) justice arguments, which claim that discrimination results in an unjust distribution of society's benefits and burdens.

Utilitarian Arguments

The standard utilitarian argument against racial and sexual discrimination is based on the idea that a society's productivity will be optimized to the extent that jobs are awarded on the basis of competency (or "merit").[45] Different jobs, the argument goes, require different skills and personality traits if they are to be carried out in as productive a manner as possible. Furthermore, different people have different skills and personality traits. Consequently, to ensure that jobs are maximally productive, they must be assigned to those individuals whose skills and personality traits qualify them as the most competent for the job. Insofar as jobs are assigned to individuals on the basis of other criteria unrelated to competency, productivity must necessarily decline. Discriminating among job applicants on the basis of race, sex, religion, or other characteristics unrelated to job performance is necessarily inefficient and, therefore, contrary to utilitarian principles.[46]

Utilitarian arguments of this sort, however, have encountered two kinds of objections. First, if the argument is correct, then jobs should be assigned on the basis of job-related qualifications only so long as such assignments will advance the public welfare. If, in a certain situation, the public welfare would be advanced to a greater degree by assigning jobs on the basis of some factor not related to job performance, then the utilitarian would have to hold that in those situations jobs should not be assigned on the basis of job-related qualifications, but on the basis of that other factor. For example, if society's welfare would be promoted more by assigning certain jobs on the basis of need (or sex or race) instead of on the basis of job qualifications, then the utilitarian would have to concede that need (or sex or race), and not job qualifications, is the proper basis for assigning those jobs.[47]

Second, the utilitarian argument must also answer the charge of opponents who hold that society as a whole may benefit from some forms of sexual discrimination. Opponents might claim, for example, that society will function most efficiently if one sex is socialized into acquiring the personality traits required for raising a family (nonaggressive, cooperative, caring, submissive, etc.) and the other sex is socialized into acquiring the personality traits required for earning a living (aggressive, competitive, assertive, independent).[48] One might hold that one sex ends up with the traits suited for raising a family as a result of its inborn biological nature, whereas the other sex ends up with the traits suited for earning a living as a result of its own biology. In either case, whether sexual differences are acquired or natural, one might argue that jobs that call for one set of sexually based traits rather than another should be assigned on the basis of sex because placing people in jobs that suit their personality traits promotes society's welfare.[49]

The utilitarian argument against discrimination has been attacked on several fronts. None of these attacks, however, seems to have defeated its proponents. Utilitarians have countered that using factors other than job-related qualifications never provides greater benefits than the use of job-related qualifications.[50] Moreover, they claim, studies have demonstrated that there are few, or no, morally significant differences between the sexes.[51]

Rights-based Arguments

Nonutilitarian arguments against racial and sexual discrimination may take the approach that discrimination is wrong because it violates a person's basic moral rights.[52] Kantian theory, for example, holds that human beings should be treated as *ends* and never used merely as *means*. At a minimum, this principle means that each individual has a moral right to be treated as a free person equal to any other person and that all individuals have a correlative moral duty to treat each individual as a free and equal person. Discriminatory practices violate the principle in two ways. First, discrimination is based on the belief that one group is inferior to other groups, that blacks, for example, are less competent or less worthy of respect than whites or perhaps that women are less competent or worthy of respect than men.[53] Racial and sexual discrimination, for instance, may be based on stereotypes that see minorities as "lazy" or "shiftless" and see women as "emotional" and "weak." Such degrading stereotypes undermine the self-esteem of those groups against whom the stereotypes are directed and thereby, violate their right to be treated as equals. Second, discrimination places the members of groups that are discriminated against in lower social and economic positions: Women and minorities have fewer job opportunities and are given lower salaries. Again, the right to be treated as a free and equal person is violated.[54]

A group of Kantian arguments, related to those mentioned, holds that discrimination is wrong because the person who discriminates would not want to see his or her behavior universalized.[55] In particular, the person would not want to be discriminated against on the basis of characteristics that have nothing whatever to do with the person's own ability to perform a given job. Because the person who discriminates would not want to see his or her own behavior universalized, according to Kant's first categorical imperative, it is morally wrong for that person to discriminate against others.

Quick Review 7.7

Arguments Against Discrimination

- Utilitarian: Discrimination leads to inefficient use of human resources, but opponents reply that some forms of discrimination may actually benefit society.
- Rights-based: Discrimination violates basic human rights by holding minorities and women as "inferior," assigning them lower social and economic positions; discrimination cannot be universalized.
- Justice-based: Discrimination results in unjust distributions of benefits and burdens according to John Rawls, and it violates the formal principle of equality by differentiating between people on the basis of characteristics that are not relevant to job performance.

Justice-based Arguments

A second group of nonutilitarian arguments against discrimination views it as a violation of the principles of justice. For example, John Rawls argued that among the principles of justice that the enlightened parties to the "original position" would choose for themselves is the principle of equal opportunity: "Social and economic inequalities are to be arranged so that they are attached to offices and positions open to all under conditions of fair equality of opportunity."[56] Discrimination violates this principle by arbitrarily closing off to minorities and women the more desirable positions in an institution, thereby not giving them an opportunity equal to that of others. Arbitrarily giving some individuals less of an opportunity to compete for jobs than others is unjust, according to Rawls.

Another approach to the morality of discrimination that also views it as a form of injustice is based on the formal **principle of equality**: Individuals who are equal in all respects relevant to the kind of treatment in question should be treated equally even if they are dissimilar in other, nonrelevant respects. To many people, as indicated in Chapter 2, this principle is the defining feature of justice.[57] Discrimination in employment is wrong because it violates the basic principle of justice by differentiating between people on the basis of characteristics (race or sex) that are not relevant to the tasks they must perform. A major problem faced by this kind of argument against discrimination, however, is that of defining precisely what counts as a *relevant respect* for treating people differently and explaining why race and sex are not relevant, whereas something like intelligence or war service may be counted as relevant.

principle of equality Individuals who are equal in all respects relevant to the kind of treatment in question should be treated equally even if they are dissimilar in other, nonrelevant respects.

Discriminatory Practices

Regardless of the problems inherent in some of the arguments against discrimination, it is clear that there are strong reasons for holding that discrimination is wrong. It is consequently understandable that our laws have gradually been changed to conform to these moral requirements and that there has been a growing recognition of the various ways in which discrimination in employment occurs. Among the practices now widely recognized as having discriminatory outcomes and so as practices that business managers should strive to remove to ensure their companies are not engaged in discrimination are the following:[58]

Recruitment Practices Firms that rely solely on the word-of-mouth referrals of present employees to recruit new workers tend to recruit only from those racial and sexual groups that are already represented in their labor force. When a firm's labor force is composed of only white males, this recruitment policy will tend to discriminate against minorities and women. Also, when desirable job positions are only advertised in media (or by job-referral agencies) that are not used by minorities or women (such as in English newspapers not read by Spanish-speaking minorities) or are classified as *for men only*, recruitment will also be discriminatory.

Screening Practices Job qualifications are discriminatory when they are not relevant to the job to be performed (e.g., requiring a high school diploma or a credential for an essentially manual task in places where minorities statistically have had high secondary school dropout rates). Aptitude or intelligence tests used to screen applicants become discriminatory when they serve to disqualify members from minority cultures who are unfamiliar with the language, concepts, and social situations used in the tests, but who are in fact fully qualified for the job. Job interviews are discriminatory if the interviewer routinely disqualifies women and minorities by relying on sexual or racial stereotypes. These stereotypes may include assumptions about the sort of occupations "proper" for women, the sort of work and time burdens that may fittingly be "imposed" on women, the ability of a woman or minority person to maintain "commitment" to a job, the propriety of putting women in "male" environments, the assumed effects women or minorities would have on employee morale or on customers, and the extent to which women or minorities are assumed to have personality and aptitude traits that make them unsuitable for a job. Such generalizations about women or minorities are not only discriminatory, they are also false.

Promotion Practices Promotion, job progression, and transfer practices have discriminatory outcomes when employers place white males on job tracks separate from those open to women and minorities. Seniority systems will be discriminatory if past discrimination has eliminated minorities and women from the higher, more senior positions on the advancement ladder. To rectify the situation, individuals who have specifically suffered from discrimination in seniority systems should be given their rightful place in the seniority system and provided with whatever training is necessary for them to have. Also, when promotions rely on the subjective recommendations of immediate supervisors, promotion policy will tend to be discriminatory to the extent that supervisors rely on racial or sexual stereotypes. Supervisors should be trained to recognize such unconscious stereotypes and, where needed, should be given targets or benchmarks by which they can assess whether their practices are having discriminatory outcomes.

Conditions of Employment Wages and salaries are discriminatory to the extent that equal wages and salaries are not given to people who are doing essentially the same work. If past discrimination or present cultural traditions result in some job classifications being disproportionately filled with women or minorities (such as secretarial, clerical, or part-time positions), steps should be taken to make their compensation and benefits comparable to those of other classifications. All job classifications should periodically be examined to make sure that compensation is not influenced by stereotypes, assumptions, or biases that result in women or minorities receiving generally lower compensation levels.

Discharge Firing an employee on the basis of race or sex is a clear form of discrimination. Less blatant but still discriminatory are layoff policies that rely on a seniority system in which women and minorities have the lowest seniority because of past discrimination and so are last to be considered for promotion and first to be considered for layoffs. The records of women and minorities should periodically be examined to ensure that past discrimination has not resulted in disadvantages—such as low seniority—that make them more vulnerable to layoffs, and if necessary they should be moved upward in rankings so that they will not be as vulnerable.

Sexual Harassment

Women, as noted earlier, are victims of a particularly troublesome kind of discrimination that is both overt and coercive: They are subjected to **sexual harassment**. Although males are also subjected to some instances of sexual harassment, it is women who are by far the most frequent victims. For all its acknowledged frequency, sexual harassment still remains difficult to define and to police and prevent. In 1978, the Equal Employment Opportunity Commission (EEOC) published a set of "guidelines" defining sexual harassment and setting out what, in its view, was prohibited by the law. In their current form, the guidelines state:

sexual harassment Under certain conditions, unwelcome sexual advances, requests for sexual favors, and other verbal or physical contact of a sexual nature.

> Unwelcome sexual advances, requests for sexual favors and other verbal or physical contact of a sexual nature constitute sexual harassment when (1) submission to such conduct is made either explicitly or implicitly a term or condition of an individual's employment, (2) submission to or rejection of such conduct by an individual is used as the basis for employment decisions affecting such individual, or (3) such conduct has the purpose or effect of unreasonably interfering with an individual's work performance or creating an intimidating, hostile or offensive working environment.[59]

The guidelines go on to prohibit sexual harassment and explain that an employer is responsible for all sexual harassment engaged in by employees, "regardless of whether the employer knew" the harassment was occurring and regardless of whether it was "forbidden by the employer."

In several major respects, the guidelines are clearly morally justified. They are intended to outlaw those situations in which an employee is coerced into giving in to another employee's sexual demands by the threat of losing some significant job benefit, such as a promotion, raise, or even the job. This kind of degrading coercion exerted on employees who are vulnerable and defenseless inflicts great psychological harms on the employee, violates the employee's most basic rights to freedom and dignity, and is an outrageously unjust misuse of the unequal power that an employer

ON THE EDGE

Driving for Old Dominion

Old Dominion Freight Line is a trucking company that hires two kinds of drivers. "Line Haul" drivers drive long distances and spend nights and weekends on the road. "Pickup and Delivery" drivers only drive locally and stay home, but they have to carry and stack heavy loads so their job is more physically demanding. Out of 3,100 Pickup and Delivery drivers in the company, only five were women. Deborah Merritt worked for six years as a Line Haul driver, making long trips across the United States, sometimes driving over five hundred miles a day. Still, she never complained and did her job well. But Merritt wanted a Pickup and Delivery job so she would not have to spend time away from home. To show she could do the job, she filled in for Pickup and Delivery drivers when needed. Her supervisor said Merritt did a good job on Pickup and Delivery and several clients complimented her work. When a full-time Pickup and Delivery job finally was available, Merritt told Bobby Howard, her Lynchburg, Virginia terminal manager, that she wanted the job. Howard said he did not have the authority to fill the position. But later, he in fact hired someone else to take the job: a male driver with less truck-driving experience. Merritt did not complain however. A year later, a Pickup and Delivery job became available again. Again, Howard hired a less-experienced male driver. When Merritt asked why he passed her over twice, Howard said it "had been discussed and it was decided that they could not let a woman have that position." He pointed out that "the company did not really have women... [Pickup and Delivery] drivers." An Old Dominion driver put it simply: "We don't have no females." Howard also told her that Old Dominion's Regional Vice President "was afraid [a female] would get hurt" and "didn't think a girl should have that position." An operations manager agreed, saying "this is not a woman's place."

Another year passed and a Pickup and Delivery job again became available. This time the company gave the position to Merritt, but told her that she would be on probation for ninety days and she would lose the job if she had any performance problems. No male drivers had ever been required to go through a probation period. Merritt worked as a Pickup and Delivery driver for ninety days, and had no problems carrying freight or doing anything else required of the position. But seven months later, she injured her ankle while moving boxes. Her doctor said she could not do Pickup and Delivery until it healed. Three months later, Merritt's ankle was well and her doctor told her "nothing... prevented her from performing her duties as a Pickup and Delivery driver.... [Her ankle was] as well, if not better,... than before her injury." So Merritt asked to have her Pickup and Delivery job back. But Brian Stoddard, Vice President of Safety and Personnel said that she first had to take a "physical ability test" that would evaluate her strength, agility, and cardiovascular endurance and have her perform the tasks of a Pickup and Delivery driver. Merritt did not pass the test; but the test had been used only rarely and only when hiring new people. If male employees were injured while on the job, Stoddard admitted, he was "not necessarily going to send them for a [physical fitness] test." Moreover, Merritt said, she could obviously do the job since she did it for seven months and filled in for other drivers even longer. Nevertheless, Stoddard fired her because of her "inability to perform [the] job" as indicated by the test and later replaced her with a male driver.

1. Was the fact that Deborah Merritt did not pass the physical ability test sufficient justification for firing her? Did Old Dominion Freight Line discriminate unjustly against Merritt? If you think firing her was unjust discrimination, then was it individual or institutionalized discrimination? Explain your answers.

Source: *Deborah Merritt v. Old Dominion Freight Line, Inc.*, U.S. Court of Appeals for the 4th Circuit, no. 09-1498, April 9, 2010.

can exercise over the employee. It is thus a crude violation of the moral standards of utilitarianism, rights, justice, and care.

However, several aspects of these guidelines merit further discussion. First, the guidelines prohibit more than particular acts of harassment. In addition to prohibiting harassing acts, they also prohibit conduct that "creates" an "intimidating, hostile or offensive working environment." That means that an employer is guilty of sexual harassment when the employer allows an environment that is hostile or offensive to women even in the absence of any particular incidents of sexual harassment. This raises some difficult questions. If the mechanics in a garage are accustomed to placing pin-ups in their place of work and are accustomed to recounting off-color jokes and using off-color language, are they guilty of creating an environment that is "hostile and offensive" to a female coworker? In a well-known case, for example, a federal court described the following real situation:

> For seven years the [female] plaintiff worked at Osceola as the sole woman in a salaried management position. In common work areas [she] and other female employees were exposed daily to displays of nude or partially clad women belonging to a number of male employees at Osceola. One poster, which remained on the wall for eight years, showed a prone woman who had a gold ball on her breasts with a man standing over her, golf club in hand, yelling "Fore!" And one desk plaque declared "Even male chauvinist pigs need love...." In addition, Computer Division Supervisor Dough Henry regularly spewed anti-female obscenity. Henry routinely referred to women as "whores," "cunt," "pussy," and "tits...." Of plaintiff, Henry specifically remarked, "All that bitch needs is a good lay" and called her "fat ass."[60]

Should this kind of situation count as the kind of "intimidating, hostile, or offensive working environment" that the guidelines prohibit as sexual harassment? The answer to this legal question is unclear, and different courts have taken different positions on the question. But a different question and one that is more relevant to our inquiry is this: Is it morally wrong to create or allow this kind of environment? The answer to this question seems in general to be "yes" because such an environment is degrading, it is usually imposed by more powerful male parties upon more vulnerable female employees, and it imposes heavy costs on women because such environments tend to belittle them and make it more difficult for them to compete with males as equals.

Nevertheless, some critics object that these kinds of environments were not created to intentionally degrade women, but that they are part of the "social mores of [male] American workers," that it is hopeless to try to change them, and that they do not unjustly harm women because women have the power to take care of themselves.[61] A *Forbes* magazine article, for example, asked rhetorically, "Can women really think they have the right to a pristine work environment free of rude behavior?"[62] Such sentiments are indicative of the uncertainties surrounding this issue.

A second important point to note is that the guidelines indicate that "verbal or physical contact of a sexual nature" constitutes sexual harassment when it has the "effect of unreasonably interfering with an individual's work performance." Many critics have argued that this means that what counts as sexual harassment depends on the purely subjective judgments of the victim. According to the guidelines, verbal contacts—presumably conversations—of a sexual nature count as prohibited sexual harassment when they "unreasonably" interfere with work performance. But sexual conversations that are "unreasonable" interferences to one person, critics claim, may be well within reasonable limits to another person because people's tolerance, even enjoyment, of sexual conversations differs. What one person believes is innocent innuendo, flirting, or an enjoyable sexual joke may be taken by another as an offensive and debilitating "come-on." The critics claim that a person who, in all innocence, makes a comment that is taken wrongly by another person may find himself the target of a sexual harassment complaint. However, supporters of the guidelines reply that our law courts are well experienced with defining what is *reasonable* in the more or less objective terms of what an average competent adult would feel to be reasonable, so this concept should present no major difficulties. Critics, however, have countered that this still leaves open the question of whether the guidelines should prohibit sexual conversations that the average woman would find unreasonable or that the average man would find unreasonable—two standards, they claim, that would have drastically different implications.

Quick Review 7.8

Moral Objections to Sexual Harassment Guidelines

- Guidelines prohibit "intimidating, hostile, or offensive working environment," but it is sometimes hard to distinguish this from male rudeness not intended to degrade women.
- Guidelines prohibit "verbal or physical contact of a sexual nature" when it has the "effect of unreasonably interfering with an individual's work performance," but this seems to require use of purely subjective judgments.
- Guidelines prohibit "verbal conduct" that creates an "intimidating, hostile or offensive working environment," but this can conflict with the right to free speech.
- Guidelines hold employer guilty of employee's sexual harassment even if employer did not know nor could have prevented it, but some respond that eradicating sexual harassment justifies forcing employer to be responsible for preventing it, and it is an "external cost" employers should internalize.

A more fundamental objection to the prohibition of "verbal conduct" that creates an "intimidating, hostile, or offensive working environment" is that these kinds of prohibitions in effect violate people's right to free speech. This objection is frequently made on university campuses, where prohibitions of speech that creates a hostile or offensive environment for women or minorities are not unusual and where such prohibitions are generally characterized as requiring "politically correct speech." Students and faculty alike have objected that free speech must be preserved on university campuses because truth is found only through the free discussion and examination of all opinions, no matter how offensive, and truth is the objective of the university. Similar claims cannot usually be made about a business corporation, of course, because its objective is not the attainment of truth through the free discussion and examination of all opinions. Nevertheless, it can be argued that employees and employers have a right to free speech and that prohibitions of speech that create an environment that some feel to be offensive are wrong even in corporate contexts because such prohibitions violate this basic right. The reader will have to decide whether such arguments have much merit.

A third important feature of the guidelines to note is that an employer is guilty of sexual harassment even if the employer did not know and could not have been expected to know that it was going on and even if the employer had explicitly forbidden it. This violates the common moral norm that people cannot be held morally responsible for something of which they had no knowledge and which they had tried to prevent. Many people have suggested that the guidelines are deficient on this point. However, supporters reply that the guidelines are morally justified from a utilitarian point of view for two reasons. First, over the long run, they provide a strong incentive for employers to take steps that will guarantee that the harm of sexual harassment is eradicated from their companies, even in those areas of the company of which they usually have little knowledge. Moreover, the harms inflicted by sexual harassment are so devastating that any costs imposed by such steps will be balanced by the benefits. Second, the guidelines in effect ensure that the harms inflicted by sexual harassment are always transferred to the shoulders of the employer, thereby making such harms part of the costs of doing business that the employer will want to minimize to remain competitive with other businesses. Thus, the guidelines in effect internalize the costs of sexual harassment so that competitive market mechanisms can deal with them efficiently. The guidelines are also just, supporters claim, because the employer is usually better able to absorb the costs of sexual harassment than the innocent injured employee who would otherwise have to suffer the losses of harassment alone.

Beyond Race and Sex: Other Groups

Are there other groups that deserve protection from discrimination? The Age Discrimination in Employment Act of 1967 prohibited discriminating against older workers merely because of their age, until they reached age 65. This Act was modified in 1978 to prohibit age discrimination until workers reach age 70.[63] On October 17, 1986, new legislation was enacted prohibiting forced retirement at any specific age. Thus, in theory, older workers are protected against discrimination by federal laws. The disabled are also now protected by the **Americans with Disabilities Act of 1990**, which bars discrimination on the basis of disability and which requires that employers make reasonable accommodation for their disabled employees and customers. Nevertheless, because of widespread stereotypes about the abilities and capacities of older workers and the disabled, subtle and overt discrimination against these groups continues to pervade the United States.[64]

Americans with Disabilities Act of 1990 Bars discrimination on the basis of disability and requires that employers make reasonable accommodation for their disabled employees and customers.

Although older and disabled workers at least have some legal protections against discrimination, such protections are rare for workers with unusual sexual preferences. There are no federal laws that prohibit discrimination on the basis of sexual orientation, and only a few states and some cities have laws prohibiting discrimination against gays or transsexuals. A court held, for example, that Liberty Mutual Insurance Company was not acting illegally when it refused to hire a male merely on the grounds that he was "effeminate," and a court also cleared Budget Marketing, Inc., of acting illegally when that company fired a male who began to dress as a female prior to a sex-change operation.[65]

Although it is illegal to do so, many companies have found reasons to fire or cancel the health benefits of workers found to have the virus for acquired immune deficiency syndrome (AIDS).[66] The Centers for Disease Control (CDC) reports that in 2002 some 384,906 persons were living with AIDS in the United States and an additional 144,129 had been diagnosed with HIV that had not yet developed into AIDS.[67] Only a portion of these were suffering symptoms or debilitation that affected their ability to perform well on the job. Several court decisions have held that AIDS qualifies as a "handicap" (under the federal Vocational Rehabilitation Act of 1973 and, more recently, under the Americans with Disabilities Act), and federal law prohibits federal contractors, subcontractors, or employers who participate in federally funded programs from firing such handicapped persons, so long as they can perform their jobs if some "reasonable" accommodation is made. Some states and cities have enacted local laws to prevent discrimination against AIDS victims, but many employers are not monitored, and some continue to discriminate against the victims of this terrible disease.

Quick Review 7.9

Besides Race and Sex, Discrimination can be Based on

- Age, which is protected by the Age Discrimination in Employment Act
- Sexual orientation, which has few protections against discrimination
- Transsexual status, which has few protections
- Disability, which is protected by the Americans with Disabilities Act
- Obesity, which has no protections.

Many managers are reluctant to hire overweight persons—a class of people that the laws of most states do not protect. For example, Philadelphia Electric Company refused to hire Joyce English on the grounds that she weighed 300 pounds and not because she was unable to perform the duties of the position for which she applied.[68] Should any of these groups—gays, transsexuals, obese persons—be protected against job discrimination? Some have argued that they should be protected on the same grounds that women and ethnic minorities are currently protected.[69] At the present time, these groups remain as vulnerable as women, minorities, and older workers once were.

Peter Oiler and Winn-Dixie Stores

Winn-Dixie Stores fired Peter Oiler, a truck driver who had worked for the Louisiana supermarket chain for 21 years. Oiler loaded groceries from the company's warehouse and drove them to Winn-Dixie stores in Louisiana and Mississippi. A good worker, he received above-average performance ratings and was promoted three times. Oiler had been married to his wife, Shirley, for 23 years.

Two years before he was fired, Oiler asked his supervisor, Greg Miles, to squelch a company rumor that he was gay. A year later, Miles met with Oiler and asked him if the rumor still bothered him. Oiler said it did because he was not gay, but a "transgender," a person whose anatomical sex is inconsistent with their feelings about their gender. Oiler said he had no intention of changing his sex or of "transitioning" to live full-time as a woman.

A month later, Miles again met with Oiler. Miles said a supervisor had seen Oiler off-duty dressed as a woman. Oiler responded he sometimes dressed as a woman but never on company time. Miles replied he might harm the company image, and so he should resign and look for another job. Oiler said he was happy at Winn-Dixie and did not want another job. When consulted, Michael Istre, president of Winn-Dixie, agreed with firing Oiler because "I was concerned about my business and what kind of impact and effect that this type of behavior would have on my business and my customer base if my customers saw him."

Over the next three months, Oiler met five times with Winn-Dixie managers and was told repeatedly to look for another job because he was to be fired. Although his job performance was fine, they said, his off-work dressing as a woman could harm the company's image with the public. At the final meeting, Oiler was terminated while continuing to protest that he adhered to company policy for at-work dress. Said Oiler: "To be fired after 21 years with the company felt like a knife in my chest. I showed up for work on time, did a good job and followed all the rules, but I was fired because I cross-dress off-duty. We lost our health insurance, and nearly had our home foreclosed. The unbearable stress took, and still takes, a toll on our health and continues to affect our 24-year marriage." Although Oiler sued, a U.S. district judge decided federal laws against discrimination do not apply to transgendered people.

With more than 500 stores in Florida, Alabama, Louisiana, Georgia, and Mississippi, Winn-Dixie Stores, Inc. says it aspires to be the "leading neighborhood grocer in every market it serves."

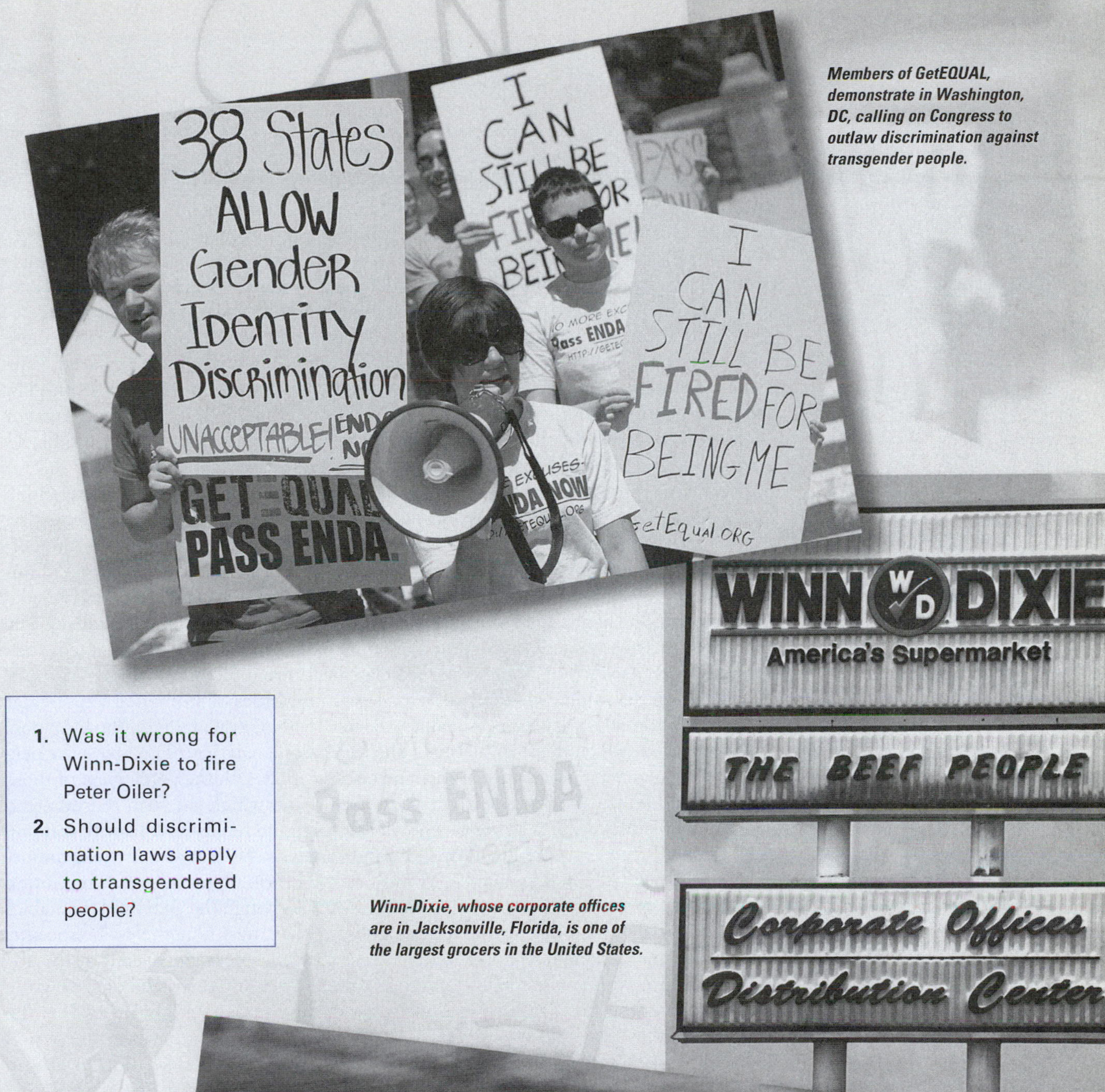

Members of GetEQUAL, demonstrate in Washington, DC, calling on Congress to outlaw discrimination against transgender people.

Winn-Dixie, whose corporate offices are in Jacksonville, Florida, is one of the largest grocers in the United States.

Peter Oiler drove a 50-foot truck with a trailer delivering groceries throughout southeastern Louisiana and the Gulf Coast of Mississippi.

1. Was it wrong for Winn-Dixie to fire Peter Oiler?
2. Should discrimination laws apply to transgendered people?

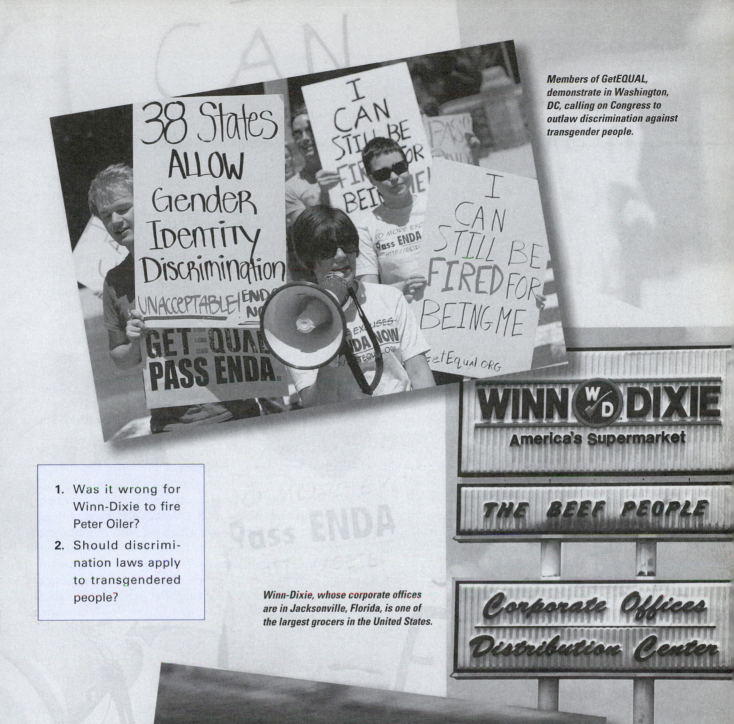

7.4 Affirmative Action

All of the equal opportunity policies discussed above are ways of making employment decisions blind with respect to sex and race. These policies are all negative: They aim to prevent any further discrimination. Therefore, they ignore how past discrimination has left minorities and women disadvantaged in comparison to non-minorities and men. Because of past discrimination, minorities and women do not have the kind of work skills and workplace qualifications that their more advantaged white and male counterparts have been able to acquire. Women and minorities are still underrepresented in the more prestigious and well-paying economic positions which creates stereotypical impressions that they are not well-suited for these positions or that these positions are appropriate for whites or males. Past discrimination has also placed white and male employees in decision-making positions that determine who will be hired or promoted, and, psychologists have found, from early childhood people tend to favor those who are most like themselves (although in U.S. society both whites and blacks tend to be biased toward lighter skin).[70] The policies discussed so far do not call for any positive steps to eliminate these lingering effects of past discrimination that tend to reproduce similar (perhaps unconscious) discriminatory behaviors in the present.

To rectify the effects of past discrimination, many employers have instituted affirmative action programs designed to achieve a more representative distribution of minorities and women within the firm by giving some degree of preference to women and minorities. What does an affirmative action program in employment involve? The heart of an affirmative action program that applies to the workplace is a detailed study (a "utilization analysis") of all the major job classifications in the firm.[71] The purpose of the study is to determine whether there are fewer minorities or women in a particular job classification than could be reasonably expected by their availability in the local pool of workers from which the firm recruits. The utilization analysis will compare the percentage of women and minorities in each job classification with the percentage of those minority and female workers available in the area from which the firm recruits who have the requisite skills or who are capable of acquiring the requisite skills with training the firm could reasonably supply. If the utilization analysis shows that women or minorities are underutilized in certain job classifications, the firm then establishes recruiting goals and timetables for correcting these deficiencies. Although the goals and timetables must not be rigid and inflexible numerical "quotas," they must nonetheless be specific, measurable, and designed in good faith to correct the deficiencies uncovered by the utilization analysis within a reasonable length of time. For example, instead of setting the goal of making the "next 10 hires" minority hires, the company might instead set the goal of increasing its minority employees by "8 percent to 12 percent over the period of a year" and do so by using race as one of several different considerations it uses in hiring. The firm appoints an officer to coordinate and administer the affirmative action program, and it undertakes special efforts and programs to increase the recruitment of women and minorities so as to meet the goals and timetables it has established for itself.

U.S. Supreme Court decisions have not been completely clear about the legality of affirmative action programs. A large number of federal court decisions have agreed that the use of affirmative action programs to redress racial or gender imbalances that are the result of previous discriminatory hiring practices is legitimate. Moreover, the U.S. Supreme Court has ruled that companies can legally use affirmative action programs to remedy a "manifest racial imbalance" or a "historic," "persistent," and "egregious" underrepresentation of women or minorities, even if the representation was not the result of past discriminatory job practices.[72] Over the years the Supreme Court has placed additional conditions on affirmative action programs. Race or gender can be only one of several factors affirmative action programs consider when making decisions about individuals; affirmative action targets cannot be inflexible "quotas"; affirmative action programs must be temporary and must be "narrowly tailored" to achieve their objectives. And finally, as we have seen, affirmative action can be used to achieve "diversity," at least by educational institutions and, apparently, even by the government when it distributes broadcast licenses.

In June, 1984, however, the Court ruled that companies may not set aside the seniority of white workers during layoffs in favor of women and minority workers hired under affirmative action plans so long as the seniority system was adopted without a discriminatory motive. Thus, although affirmative action programs that give preferences to women or minorities as a group were not declared illegal, their effects could disappear during hard times because *the last hired, first-fired* rule of seniority would hit strongest at women and minorities recently hired through the programs.[73] The 1984 Supreme Court decision also included a nonbinding advisory statement that

> If individual members of a . . . class demonstrate that they have been actual victims of the discriminatory practice, they may be awarded competitive seniority and given their rightful place on the seniority roster. However, . . . mere membership in the disadvantaged class is insufficient to warrant a seniority award; each individual must prove that the discriminatory practice had an impact on him.[74]

To many this seemed to imply that affirmative action programs that awarded jobs on the basis of membership in a disadvantaged class were not completely legal. However, others interpreted the "advisory" more narrowly to mean merely that awarding seniority could not be based on mere membership in a disadvantaged class.[75] This latter interpretation seemed to be supported by another Supreme Court ruling on May 19, 1986, which held that, although layoffs based on race were unconstitutional, racial hiring goals were a legally allowable means to remedy past discrimination. The 1986 Supreme Court majority opinion stated that layoffs based on race "impose the entire burden of achieving racial equality on particular (White) individuals, often resulting in serious disruption of their lives. . . . On the other hand, racial preferences in hiring merely deny a future employment opportunity, not the loss of an existing job, and may be used to cure the effects of past discrimination."[76]

In 1989, the Supreme Court issued several decisions that interpreted previous civil rights laws in a manner that substantially weakened the ability of minorities and women to seek redress against discrimination, particularly through affirmative action programs. In 1991, however, the U.S. Congress passed the Civil Rights Act of 1991, which stated explicitly how those laws should be interpreted and in effect overruled the Supreme Court decisions of 1989. One important decision was left standing, however. In January 1989, in *City of Richmond v. J. A. Croson Co.*, the Court ruled that the affirmative action plan of a state or local government that operates by setting aside a certain percentage of its public monies for minority contractors is unconstitutional. Such set-aside programs, the Court ruled, could be used by public bodies only as "a last resort" in an "extreme case" and only if there was hard and specific proof of previous racial bias by that governmental body. *Adarand Construction, Inc. v. Pena*, a case the Supreme Court heard in 1995, reinforced this decision when it ruled that the federal government is also bound by its ruling in *City of Richmond v. J. A. Croson Co.* As we noted in the introduction to this chapter, in *Grutter v. Bollinger* the Supreme Court held in 2003 that universities may use affirmative action programs to achieve the goal of diversity so long as race or gender is but one of several other criteria used to determine admissions.

Quick Review 7.10

Legal Status of Affirmative Action

- Affirmative action is legal when used to correct a racial or sexual imbalance that is the result of previous discrimination, or to correct an "egregious," "persistent," and "manifest racial imbalance" not caused by previous discrimination; can be used in hiring but not in layoffs; cannot use "inflexible" quotas; must be "narrowly tailored" to their objectives; can be used to achieve "educational diversity" and "broadcast diversity."
- Affirmative action cannot overrule seniority, cannot be used in government set-aside programs except as a "last resort" in an "extreme case" involving previous racial bias by the government.

Thus, the U.S. Supreme Court has vacillated on the constitutionality of affirmative action programs. Depending on the period in question, the issue at stake, and the current makeup of the Court, it has tended at times to support and at other times to undermine affirmative action programs. Like the public, which remains deeply divided on the issue, the Supreme Court has had trouble making up its mind whether to support or disallow these programs.[77]

Of course, affirmative action programs are not found only in the United States. In Canada affirmative action programs are widely used for women, the disabled, aboriginal people, and persons whose visible features identify them as members of a minority group. India uses affirmative action programs particularly for members of the lowest castes who are underrepresented in schools and within government jobs. India's lowest castes, sometimes called the "Depressed Classes," include those once popularly referred to as "untouchables," people who have long been (and who in many parts of India still are) humiliated, shunned, oppressed, segregated, and impoverished, but for whom the government now reserves a certain percentage of places in schools and universities plus jobs in government. Many Chinese universities have affirmative action policies directed at several of their own ethnic minorities, while Romania uses affirmative action for the Roma people otherwise known as "gypsies. " The South African government supports affirmative action programs for blacks, Indians, and coloreds, and Israel uses such programs for Jewish Ethiopians. But as in the United States, affirmative action in other countries is highly controversial and it has been attacked in foreign nations just as in the United States.

Affirmative action programs have been attacked mainly on the grounds that, in attempting to correct the effects of past discrimination, these programs have become racially or sexually discriminatory.[78] By showing preference to minorities or women, critics argue, the programs institute a form of reverse discrimination against White males.[79] A 45-year-old electrical worker at a Westinghouse plant, for example, is quoted as saying:

> What does bother me is the colored getting the preference because they're black. This I am against. I say, I don't care what his color is. If he has the ability to do the job, he should get the job—not because of his color. They shouldn't hire 20 percent just because they're black. This is discrimination in reverse as far as I'm concerned.... If they want it, they can earn it like I did. I am not saying deprive them of something—not at all.[80]

Affirmative action programs are said to discriminate against white males by using a nonrelevant characteristic—race or sex—to make employment decisions, and this violates justice by violating the principles of equality and equal opportunity.

The arguments used to justify affirmative action programs in the face of these objections tend to fall into two main groups.[81] One group of arguments interprets the preferential treatment accorded to women and minorities as a form of compensation for past injuries they have suffered. A second set of arguments interprets preferential treatment as an instrument for achieving certain social goals. Whereas compensation arguments for affirmative action are backward looking insofar as they focus on the wrongness of past acts, the instrumentalist arguments are forward looking insofar as they focus on the goodness of a future state (and the wrongness of what happened in the past is irrelevant).[82] We begin by examining the compensation arguments and then turn to the instrumentalist arguments.

Compensation Argument for Affirmative Action

Arguments that defend affirmative action as a form of compensation are based on the concept of compensatory justice.[83] Compensatory justice, as noted in Chapter 2, implies that people have an obligation to compensate those whom they have intentionally and unjustly wronged. Affirmative action programs are then interpreted as a form of reparation by which white male majorities now compensate women and minorities for unjustly injuring them by discriminating against them in the past. One version of this argument holds, for example, that blacks were wronged in the past by U.S. whites and that consequently the former should now receive compensation from whites.[84] Programs of preferential treatment provide that compensation.

Quick Review 7.11

Compensation Argument for Affirmative Action

- Claims affirmative action compensates groups for past discrimination
- Criticized as unfair because those who benefit were not harmed and those who pay did not injure, which are requirements of compensatory justice
- Some argue in response to criticism that discrimination has harmed all minorities and women, and all whites and males have benefited from it.

The difficulty with arguments that defend affirmative action on the basis of the principle of compensation is that the principle requires that compensation should come only from those specific individuals who intentionally inflicted a wrong, and it requires them to compensate only those specific individuals whom they wronged. For example, if five red-haired persons wrongfully injure five black-haired persons, then compensatory justice obligates only the five red-haired persons to give to only the five black-haired persons whatever the black-haired persons would have had if the five red-heads had not injured them. Compensatory justice, however, does not require that compensation should come from all the members of a group that contains some wrongdoers, nor does it require that compensation should go to all the members of a group that contains some injured parties. In this example, although justice requires that the five red-haired persons must compensate the five black-haired persons, it does not require that all red-haired persons should compensate all black-haired persons. By analogy, only the specific individuals who discriminated against minorities or women in the past should now be forced to make reparation of some sort, and they should make reparation only to those specific individuals against whom they discriminated.[85]

Although affirmative action programs usually benefit all the members of a racial or sexual group, regardless of whether they specifically were discriminated against in the past, and because these programs hinder every white male regardless of whether he specifically discriminated against someone in the past, it follows that such preferential programs cannot be justified on the basis of compensatory justice.[86] In short, affirmative action programs are unfair because the beneficiaries of affirmative action are not the same individuals who were injured by past discrimination, and the people who must pay for their injuries are usually not the ones who inflicted those injuries.[87]

Various authors have tried to counter this objection to the "affirmative action as compensation" argument by claiming that actually *every* black person (or every woman) living today has been injured by discrimination and that *every* white person (or every male) has benefited from those injuries. For example, the well-known philosopher Judith Jarvis Thomson wrote:

> But it is absurd to suppose that the young blacks and women now of an age to apply for jobs have not been wronged.... Even young blacks and women have lived through downgrading for being black or female.... And even those who were not themselves downgraded for being black or female have suffered the consequences of the downgrading of other blacks and women: lack of self-confidence and lack of self-respect.[88]

And the philosopher Martin Redish wrote:

> It might also be argued that, whether or not the [white males] of this country have themselves participated in acts of discrimination, they have been the

beneficiaries—conscious or unconscious—of a fundamentally racist society. They thus may be held independently "liable" to suppressed minorities for a form of unjust enrichment.[89]

It is unclear whether these arguments succeed in justifying affirmative action programs that benefit groups (all blacks and all women) instead of specific injured individuals and that penalize groups (white males) instead of specific wrongdoers.[90] Has every minority and woman really been injured, as Thomson claims, and are all white males really beneficiaries of discrimination as Redish implies? Even if a white male happens (through no fault of his own) to benefit from someone else's injury, does this make him "liable" for that injury?

Affirmative Action as an Instrument for Increasing Utility

A second set of justifications advanced in support of affirmative action programs is based on the idea that these programs are morally legitimate instruments for achieving morally legitimate ends. For example, utilitarians have claimed that affirmative action programs are justified because they promote the public welfare.[91] They have argued that past discrimination has produced a high degree of correlation between race and poverty.[92] As racial minorities were systematically excluded from better-paying and more prestigious jobs, their members have become impoverished. The kinds of statistics cited earlier in this chapter provide evidence of this inequality. Impoverishment in turn has led to unmet needs, lack of self-respect, resentment, social discontent, and crime. Therefore, the public welfare is promoted if the position of these impoverished persons is improved by giving them special educational and employment opportunities. If opponents object that such affirmative action programs are unjust because they distribute benefits on the basis of an irrelevant criterion such as race, the utilitarian can answer that *need*, not race, is the criterion by which affirmative action programs distribute benefits. Race provides an inexpensive *indicator* of need because past discrimination has created a high correlation between race and need. Need, of course, is a just criterion of distribution.[93] Appealing to the reduction of need is consistent with utilitarian principles because reducing need will increase total utility.

Quick Review 7.12

Utilitarian Argument for Affirmative Action

- Claims affirmative action reduces need by benefiting minorities and women in need, and so increases utility
- Criticized on grounds that its costs outweigh its benefits and that other ways of reducing need will produce greater utility.

The major difficulties encountered by these utilitarian justifications of affirmative action have concerned, first, the question of whether the social costs of affirmative action programs (such as the frustrations felt by white males) outweigh their obvious benefits.[94] The utilitarian defender of affirmative action, of course, will reply that the benefits far outweigh the costs. Second, and more important, opponents of these utilitarian justifications of affirmative action have questioned the assumption that race is an appropriate indicator of need. It may be inconvenient and expensive to identify the needy directly, critics argue, but the costs might be small compared to the gains that would result from having a more accurate way to identify the needy.[95] Utilitarians answer this criticism by arguing that all minorities (and women) have been impoverished and psychologically harmed by past discrimination. Consequently, race (and sex) provide accurate indicators of need.

Equal Justice Argument for Affirmative Action

Although utilitarian arguments in favor of affirmative action programs are quite convincing, the most elaborate and persuasive array of arguments advanced in support of affirmative action have proceeded in two steps. First, they argue that the end envisioned by affirmative action programs is equal justice. Second, they argue that affirmative action programs are morally legitimate means for achieving this end.

The end that affirmative action programs are supposed to achieve is phrased in various ways. In our present society, it is argued, jobs are not distributed justly because they are not distributed according to the relevant criteria of ability, effort, contribution, or need.[96] Statistics show that jobs are in fact still distributed according to race and sex. One end of affirmative action is to bring about a distribution of society's benefits and burdens that is consistent with the principles of distributive justice and that eliminates the important position race and sex currently have in the assignment of jobs.[97] In our present society, women and minorities do not have the equal opportunities that white males have and that justice demands. Statistics prove this. This lack of equal opportunity is because of subtle racist and sexist attitudes that bias the judgments of those (usually white males) who evaluate job applicants and that are so deeply entrenched that they are virtually ineradicable by good-faith measures in any reasonable period of time.[98] A second end of affirmative action programs is to neutralize such conscious and unconscious bias to ensure equal opportunity to women and minorities. The lack of equal opportunity under which women and minorities currently labor has also been attributed to the privations they suffered as children. Economic privation hindered minorities from acquiring the skills, experience, training, and education they needed to compete equally with white males.[99] Furthermore, because women and minorities have not been represented in society's prestigious positions, young men and women have had no role models to motivate them to compete for such positions as young white males have. Carl Callahan, for example, has argued that few black youths are motivated to enter the legal profession because they have been "denied an inspiring image of the Negro Lawyer," and they likewise shun law enforcement because they know "in what lack of regard the Negro, if employed in law enforcement at all, is held."[100]

A third end of affirmative action programs is to neutralize these competitive disadvantages with which women and minorities are currently burdened when they compete with white males and thereby, bring women and minorities to the same starting point in their competitive race with others. The aim is to ensure an equal ability to compete with white males.[101]

The basic end that affirmative action programs seek is a more just society—a society in which an individual's opportunities are not limited by race or sex. This goal is morally legitimate insofar as it is morally legitimate to strive for a society with greater equality of opportunity. The means by which affirmative action programs attempt to achieve a just society is giving qualified minorities and females preference over qualified white males in hiring and promotion and instituting special training programs for minorities and females that will qualify them for better jobs. By these means, it is hoped, the more just society outlined will eventually be born. Without some form of affirmative action, it is argued, this end could not be achieved.[102] But is preferential treatment a morally legitimate means for attaining this end? Three reasons have been advanced to show that it is not.

First, it is often claimed that affirmative action programs are a form of "reverse discrimination" against white males.[103] Supporters of affirmative action programs, however, have pointed out that there are crucial differences between the treatment accorded to whites by affirmative action programs and unjust discrimination.[104] To discriminate, as we indicated earlier, is to make an adverse decision against the member of a group because members of that group are considered inferior or less worthy of respect. Preferential treatment programs, however, are not based on invidious contempt for white males. On the contrary, they are based on the judgment that white males are currently in an advantaged position and that others should have an equal opportunity to achieve the same advantages. Moreover, racist or sexist discrimination is aimed at destroying equal opportunity. Preferential treatment programs are aimed at restoring equal opportunity where it is absent. Thus, preferential treatment programs cannot accurately be described as "discriminatory" in the same immoral sense that racist or sexist behavior is discriminatory.

Second, it is sometimes claimed that preferential treatment violates the principle of equality ("Individuals who are equal in all respects relevant to the kind of treatment in question should be treated equally") by allowing a nonrelevant characteristic (race and sex) to determine employment decisions.[105] Defenders of affirmative action programs have replied that sexual and racial differences are now relevant to making employment decisions. These differences are relevant because when society distributes a scarce resource (such as jobs), it may legitimately choose to allocate it to those groups that will best advance its legitimate ends. In our present society, allocating scarce jobs to women and minorities will best achieve equality of opportunity, thus race and sex are now relevant characteristics to use for this purpose. Moreover, as we have seen, the reason that we hold that jobs should be allocated on the basis of job-related qualifications is that such an allocation will achieve a socially desirable (utilitarian) end: maximum productivity. When this end (productivity) conflicts with another socially desirable end (a just society), it is legitimate to pursue the second end even if doing so means that the first end will not be as fully achieved.

Quick Review 7.13

Equal Justice Argument for Affirmative Action

- Claims affirmative action will secure equal opportunity by a fairer distribution of jobs, by neutralizing the effects of unconscious bias that affects judgments about minorities and women, and by placing women and minorities in less disadvantaged and more competitive positions in competitions with males and whites.
- Claims affirmative action is a morally legitimate means for securing equal opportunity, since it is not a form of "reverse discrimination" because it is not based on invidious judgments of male inferiority nor aims at destroying equal opportunity; it does not use a non-relevant characteristic since race and sex are relevant in this limited context; it does not harm minorities and women and any harm would be less than the harms inflicted by current unconscious discrimination.

Third, some critics have objected that affirmative action programs actually harm women and minorities because such programs imply that women and minorities are so inferior to white males that they need special help to compete.[106] This attribution of inferiority, critics claim, is debilitating to minorities and women and ultimately inflicts harms that are so great they far outweigh the benefits provided by such programs. In a widely read and much-acclaimed book, for example, black author Shelby Steele criticized affirmative action in business and education because, he wrote, after twenty years, it has proved to be "more bad than good."[107] Specifically, he writes, in affirmative action programs "the quality that earns us preferential treatment is an implied inferiority." According to Steel, even when a black person does not see such implied inferiority in preferential treatment, "he knows that whites do" so "the result is virtually the same." Preferential treatment he claims is "the lowering of normal standards" in order to increase black representation and such a lowering of standards leads blacks who are measured by those lower standards, to suffer a "debilitating doubt" that may be "unrecognized" but nevertheless becomes a "preoccupation" that "undermines their ability to perform, especially in integrated situations." Steele's eloquently expressed view is not idiosyncratic. It is a view that many other minorities have come to hold.[108]

This third objection to affirmative action programs has met with several responses. First, although many minorities concede that affirmative action carries some costs for minorities, they also hold that the benefits of such programs still outweigh the costs. For example, a black worker who won several jobs through affirmative action is reported as saying, "I had to deal with the grief it brought, but it was well worth it."[109]

Second, proponents of affirmative action programs also argue that these programs are based not on an assumption of minority or female inferiority, but on recognition of the fact that white males, often unconsciously, will bias their decisions in favor of other white males. As studies repeatedly show, even when women and minorities are more qualified, white males are still granted higher salaries and positions by their white male counterparts. The only remedy for this, they argue, is some kind of affirmative action program that requires white males to counter this bias by insisting they hire that proportion of minority applicants that research shows are qualified and willing to work. Moreover, they claim, the unjustified attributions of inferiority that many minorities experience are the result of lingering racism on the part of coworkers and employees, and such racism is precisely what affirmative action programs are meant to eradicate.

A third response that supporters of affirmative action make is that although a portion of minorities may be made to feel inferior by current affirmative action programs, nevertheless many more minorities were made to feel much more devastatingly inferior by the overt and covert racism that affirmative action is gradually eroding. The overt and covert racism that pervaded the workplace prior to the implementation of affirmative action programs systematically disadvantaged, shamed, and undermined the self-esteem of all minorities to a much higher degree than is currently the case.

Finally, proponents argue that it is simply false that showing preference toward a group makes members of that group feel inferior: For centuries, white males have been the beneficiaries of racial and sexual discrimination without apparent loss of their self-esteem. If minority or female beneficiaries of affirmative action programs are made to feel inferior, it is because of lingering racism and sexism, not because of the preference extended to them and their fellows. Several studies have, in fact, shown that almost no minority and female beneficiaries of affirmative action programs feel inferior because they benefitted from affirmative action programs. One survey of blacks and women who had benefited from affirmative action, for example, found that 90 percent of them reported they did not feel any loss of self-esteem due to having benefitted from affirmative action.[110] This is not surprising since affirmative action programs do not select women and minorities solely because of their gender or race. Affirmative actions programs typically show preference for women and minorities on the basis of their qualifications, as well as their gender or race; that is, the qualifications of women and minorities must pass certain thresholds before they will be chosen to participate in an affirmative action program. Since they know that they have been selected to participate in affirmative action on the basis of their qualifications, minorities and women typically are not made to feel inferior by their selection.

Strong arguments can be made in support of affirmative action programs, and strong objections can be lodged against them. Because there are such powerful arguments on both sides of the issue, the debate over the legitimacy of affirmative action programs continues to rage without resolution. However, the review of the arguments seems to suggest that affirmative action programs are at least a morally permissible means for achieving just ends, even if they may not show that they are a morally required means for achieving those ends.

Implementing Affirmative Action and Managing Diversity

Opponents of affirmative action programs have argued that other criteria besides race and sex have to be weighed when making job decisions in an affirmative action program. First, if sex and race are the only criteria used, this will result in the hiring of unqualified workers and a consequent decline in productivity.[111] Second, many jobs have significant impacts on the lives of others or are critical to the success of the firm. Consequently, if a job has significant impact on life or health, (e.g., it affects the safety of others such as the job of flight controller or surgeon) or the entire success of the company, then criteria other than race or sex should have a prominent place and can override affirmative action.[112] Third, opponents have argued that affirmative action programs, if continued, will turn us into a more racially and sexually conscious nation.[113] Consequently, the programs should cease as soon as the defects they are meant to remedy are corrected.

The following guidelines have been suggested as a way to fold these sorts of considerations into an affirmative action program when minorities are underrepresented in a firm:[114]

1. Both minorities and nonminorities should be hired or promoted only if they reach certain minimum levels of competency or are capable—after training or education—of reaching such levels in a reasonable time.
2. If the qualifications of the minority candidate are equal to (or higher or only slightly less than) than those of the nonminority, then the minority should be given preference.
3. If both the minority and nonminority candidates are adequately qualified for a position but the nonminority candidate is clearly more qualified, then:
   a. if performance in the job directly affects the lives and safety of people (such as a surgeon or an airline pilot) or if performance on the job has a substantial and critical effect on the entire firm's success (such as head comptroller), then the more qualified nonminority should be given preference; but
   b. if the position (like most positions in a firm) does not directly involve safety factors and does not have a substantial and highly critical effect on a firm's success, then the minority person should be given preference.
4. Preference should be extended to minority candidates only so long as their representation throughout the various levels of the firm is not proportional to their availability.

The success or failure of an affirmative action program also depends in part on the accommodations a company makes to the special needs of a racially and sexually diverse workforce. Both women and minorities encounter special workplace problems, as we noted above, and companies need to devise innovative means for addressing these needs. The major problems faced by women relate to the fact that a large number of married couples have children, and it is women who physically bear children and who, in our culture, carry most of the burden of raising and caring for them. Some people have suggested that companies respond by creating two career tracks for women: one track for women who indicate that they plan to have and actively participate in raising their own children while pursuing their careers, and the other track for women who either plan not to have children or plan to have others (husbands or child-care providers) raise their children while they devote themselves to pursuing their careers by putting in extra hours, making sacrifices in their personal lives, traveling, transferring, and relocating to advance their careers, and taking every opportunity for professional development.[115]

This approach, however, has been criticized as unjust because it may force women, unlike men, to choose between their careers and their families, and it may result in a lower status cohort of women on a "Mommy Track" who are discriminated against in favor of a high-status cohort of women on a "Career Track." Others have suggested that so long as our culture continues to put child-care tasks primarily on women, companies should help women by providing more generous family leave policies (IBM provides up to 8 weeks of paid maternity leave, up to an additional year of unpaid leave for a new parent with the option of part-time work during that year and a guarantee of their jobs when they return, and pays a portion of the employee's adoption expenses); more flexible work schedules (allowing parents to schedule their arrival and departure times to fit the needs of their children's schedules or work four 10-hour days in a week instead of five 8-hour days, allowing mothers of school-age children to work full-time during the school year and either rely on temporary replacements during vacations or allow mothers to only work part-time); sick leave for parents whose children are sick (or for nonparents who have special needs); special job arrangements for parents (letting new parents spend several years working part-time while their children are growing up and guaranteeing their jobs when they return, or letting two parents share the same job); and child-care support (setting up a child-care facility at or near the workplace, reimbursing employees for child-care expenses, setting up a child-care referral service, providing special day-care personnel who can care for employees' sick children, or providing an onsite clinic that can care for sick children while parents work).[116]

The special needs of minorities differ from those of women. Minorities are much more economically and educationally disadvantaged than nonminorities, with fewer work skills, fewer years of formal education, poor-quality educations, and poor or nonexistent English language skills. To meet their needs, companies have to begin providing on-the-job education in work skills, basic reading, writing, and computational skills, and English language skills. Newark, New Jersey's Prudential Insurance, for example, provides computer-assisted training in reading and math for entry-level applicants. Northeast Utilities in Hartford, Connecticut, provides 5 weeks of training in vocational skills and English language skills for its Hispanic recruits. Amtek Systems in Arlington, Virginia, provides similar programs for Asians. Minorities often have cultural values and beliefs that can give rise to misunderstandings, conflicts, and poor work performance. To deal with this issue, companies have to train their managers to manage a culturally diverse workforce by educating them (minority managers as well as nonminorities) on those minority cultures represented in their workforce and helping managers learn to become more aware of, to listen to, communicate with, and understand people from diverse backgrounds.[117]

comparable worth program A program designed to ensure that jobs of equal value to an organization are paid the same regardless of external labor markets.

The controversy over the moral propriety of affirmative action programs has not yet disappeared. The U.S. Supreme Court has ruled that such programs do not violate the Civil Rights Act of 1964. It does not follow that these programs do not violate any moral principles. If the arguments examined are correct, however, then affirmative action programs are at least consistent with moral principles. However, the arguments continue to be the subject of intense debate.

Conclusions

Earlier sections of this chapter examined several future trends that will affect the status of women and minorities in the workforce. Of particular significance is the fact that only a small proportion of new workers will be white males. Most new workers will be women and minorities. Unless major changes are made to accommodate their needs and special characteristics, they will not be incorporated smoothly into the workplace.

We have reviewed a number of programs that provide special assistance to women and minorities on moral grounds. However, it should be clear, in view of the future demographic trends, that enlightened self-interest should also prompt business to give women and minorities a special hand. The costs of not assisting the coming influx of women and minorities with their special needs will not be borne entirely by women and minorities. Unfortunately, if U.S. businesses do not accommodate themselves to these new workers, businesses will not be able to find the workers they need and will suffer recurrent and crippling shortages over the next decade. The pool of traditional white male workers simply will be so small that businesses will not be able to rely on them to fill all their requirements for skilled and managerial positions.

Many businesses, aware of these trends, have undertaken programs to prepare themselves now to respond to the special needs of women and minorities. To respond to women's needs, for example, many companies have instituted day-care services and flexible working hours that allow women with children to care for their needs. Other companies have instituted aggressive affirmative action programs aimed at integrating large groups of minorities into their firms where they are provided with education, job training, skills, counseling, and other assistance designed to enable them to assimilate into the workforce. The belief of such companies is that if they act now to recruit women and minorities, they will be familiar with their special needs and will have a large cadre of women and minorities capable of bringing other women and minorities along. James R. Houghton, chairman of Corning Glass Works, is quoted as saying:

> Valuing and managing a diverse work force is more than ethically and morally correct. It's also a business necessity. Work force demographics for the next decade make it absolutely clear that companies which fail to do an excellent job of recruiting, retaining, developing and promoting women and minorities simply will be unable to meet their staffing needs.[118]

Study and **Review** on **mythinkinglab.com**

Questions for Review and Discussion

1. Define the following concepts: job discrimination, institutionalized/isolated discrimination, intentional/nonintentional discrimination, statistical indicators of discrimination, utilitarian argument against discrimination, Kantian arguments against discrimination, formal principle of "equality," discriminatory practices, affirmative action program, utilization analysis, "reverse discrimination," compensation argument for preferential treatment, instrumental argument for preferential treatment, utilitarian argument for preferential treatment, the end goals of affirmative action programs, invidious contempt.
2. In your judgment, was the historical shift in emphasis from intentional/isolated discrimination to nonintentional/institutionalized discrimination good or bad? Justify your judgment.
3. Research your library or the Internet (e.g., the U.S. Census Bureau puts its statistics on the Web at *http://www.census.gov*) for statistics published during the last year that tend to support or refute the statistical picture of racism and sexism developed in Section 7.2 of the text. In view of your research and the materials in the text, do you agree or disagree with the statement, "There is no longer evidence that discrimination is widely practiced in the United States"? Explain your position fully.
4. Compare and contrast the three main kinds of arguments against racial and sexual job discrimination. Which of these seem to you to be the strongest? The weakest? Can you think of different kinds of arguments not discussed in the text? Are there important differences between racial discrimination and sexual discrimination?
5. Compare and contrast the main arguments used to support affirmative action programs. Do you agree or disagree with these arguments? If you disagree with an argument, state clearly which part of the argument you think is wrong, and explain why it is wrong. (It is not enough to say, "I just don't think it is right.")
6. "If employers only want to hire the best-qualified, young white males, then they have a right to do so without interference, because these are their businesses." Comment on this statement.

Web Resources

Readers interested in researching the topic of discrimination might want to begin by accessing the Web page of the U.S. Census Bureau for current detailed statistics on income, earnings, poverty, and other topics (*http://www.census.gov*) or the Bureau of Labor Statistics (*http://www.bls.gov*) or the Equal Employment

Opportunity Commission (*http://www.eeoc.gov*). The legal aspects of discrimination can be researched by searching the civil rights section of Hieros Gamos web site (*http://www.hg.org/civilrgt.html*). Patrick McCarthy's Review of Court Decisions on Workplace Discrimination provides useful summaries and links to key U.S. Supreme Court cases on job discrimination, although it is no longer regularly updated (*http://www.mtsu.edu/~pmccarth/eeocourt.htm*); EEO News provides ongoing summaries and links to key stories on discrimination cases and developments (*http://www.eeonews.com*); the Oyez directory on civil rights and discrimination provides useful summaries and links on current and previous U.S. Supreme Court cases on discrimination (*http://www.oyez.org/oyez/portlet/directory/200/222*). For materials on affirmative action and racial discrimination in general, check out Vernellia R. Randall's web site (*http://academic.udayton.edu/race/04needs/affirmat.htm*).

CASES

Explore the Concept on mythinkinglab.com

Should Kroger Pay Now for What a Ralphs' Employee Did in the Past?

The Kroger Company, a Cincinnati-based firm that operates 2,500 supermarkets in 32 states, acquired the Ralphs chain of 450 supermarkets in 1998 when it bought Fred Meyer Inc., which had acquired Ralphs the year before. Kroger had a reputation for being a well-run company, with progressive and exemplary employee policies. According to company spokesman Gary Rhodes, for example, "Kroger has had a written policy prohibiting sexual harassment since the 1980s. It includes a procedure that enables employees to point out any concerns to the company. All complaints are thoroughly investigated."[1] The company had a zero-tolerance policy for sexual harassment.

On Friday, April 5, 2002, managers of Kroger were stunned to learn that its relatively new subsidiary, Ralphs, was being told to pay compensatory and punitive damages totaling $30.6 million—the largest sexual harassment verdict ever in California, and the second-largest in the history of the United States—for the actions of Roger Misiolek, a Ralphs store manager accused of harassing six female employees at a Ralphs supermarket in Escondido, California, during 1995 and 1996. It seemed especially unfair that Kroger would have to pay for alleged injustices that had occurred before Kroger even owned Ralphs.

The harassment suit against Ralphs had been filed in 1996 by six women—Dianne Gober, Sarah Lange, Terri Finton, Peggy Noland, Suzanne Pipiro, and Tina Swann—all of whom were employees of a Ralphs store in Escondido, California. Four of the women worked as grocery cashiers, one was a bookkeeper, and one was the manager of the bakery department in the Escondido market. The trial began in April, 1998 and concluded on June 1, 1998. During the trial, the women testified that Roger Misiolek, manager of the store where they worked, began to harass them immediately after he took over the store in 1995. The harassment continued through the rest of 1995 and into 1996. The women claimed that he touched them inappropriately, verbally abused them with profanity, and that on certain occasions, he shoved shopping carts at them, and threw objects at them including telephones, clipboards, and, in one instance, a 30-pound mailbag. One woman testified that Misiolek used foul language and racial slurs against her, fondled her against her will, and threw pens and a 12-pack of soda at her. A cashier testified that Misiolek suggestively touched, grabbed, hugged, and patted her. Another testified that he repeatedly asked her about her sex life. According to the four cashiers, Misiolek would come to their grocery checkout stand, squeeze into the small area with them so body-to-body touching would occur, and grab them around the waist.

Several of the women said they complained to Ralphs management. The women claimed, however, that the company did not remove Misiolek from his store manager's position, but instead moved the complaining women to other stores. The women submitted evidence showing that more than 80 harassment complaints had been filed against Misiolek at four different stores since 1985.

In April, 1996, events came to a head when Misiolek grabbed Dianne Gober and threw her into a chair with so much force that the chair was sent rolling across the room and slammed into a desk. She subsequently complained to the senior vice president for human resources at the company's headquarters in Compton, California. At this point, according to Ralphs, the company disciplined Misiolek and transferred him to another Ralphs store in nearby Mission Viejo. Ralphs made him manager over that store, where he supervised 80 store employees. Female employees and customers there allegedly again complained about him. Ralphs now moved Misiolek to another store, but this time demoted him to the position of receiving clerk.

Misiolek denied the allegations of the female employees. It was true, he later said, that he did "become angry on occasion." But when he did so, he said, "it was not in any undue fashion." Whatever his failings as a supervisor, Misiolek had a reputation for being quite skilled at turning a store around. Evidence submitted at the trial showed that Misiolek had a history of boosting profits at the stores that he managed and of achieving excellent bottom-line figures at those stores. Ralphs highly valued these qualities in its store managers. The company also claimed that it did not know about Misiolek's conduct. According to Ralphs, the first time that company headquarters learned of Misiolek's harassment was when Dianne Gober and her husband—who also worked for Ralphs—complained to human resources at its company headquarters in Compton, right after Misiolek slammed her into a chair and pushed her into a desk. At that time, Ralphs said, it had moved Misiolek to Mission Viejo where he would no longer be supervising any employees whom he might have been harassing.

On June 1, 1998, the jury reached a two-part verdict. In the first phase of the trial, they found the supermarket chain liable for gender harassment, failure to prevent gender harassment, and malice or oppression based on a conscious disregard of the rights or safety of others. In the second, penalty, phase of the trial, the jury awarded the six women $550,000 in compensatory damages and $3.325 million in punitive damages. Kroger Co., of course, would ultimately have to pay those damages.

Part of the June 1, 1998 verdict, however, was set aside almost immediately. California Judge Joan Weber, who presided over the trial, discovered that one of the jurors was a shareholder of Ralphs. Moreover, during their deliberations, that juror had looked up Ralphs' net worth and shared his information with other jurors, disputing the expert testimony that had been offered in court on what Ralphs' real net worth was. The jurors had relied on information about the company's net worth to decide what punitive damages they should impose on the company during the penalty phase of the trial.

Ralphs asked that the case be retried. Judge Weber, however, ruled that the juror's misconduct affected only the penalty phase of the trial and so only the penalty for punitive damages needed to be retried. Judge Weber's decision was upheld on appeal. The six women and their lawyers would have to return to court to retry the penalty phase of the trial.

In 1999, Misiolek had been demoted to working on a loading dock. However, he continued working for Ralphs for more than a year after Kroger took over Ralphs. In early 2000, Ralphs' management sent Misiolek a disciplinary letter, claiming that he had continued to make sex- and race-based insults against Ralphs' employees and had continued to touch women inappropriately. Fourteen months after Kroger acquired Ralphs, the company finally suspended Misiolek and he subsequently quit. In his resignation letter to Ralphs, Misiolek continued to deny the accusations against him.

The 1-month trial for the penalty phase of the case took place in 2002 and was presided over by Judge Michael Anello. This time, there was less dispute over the net worth of Ralphs because the jurors had available the exact price that Fred Meyer Inc. had paid for Ralphs in 1996 and that Krogers had subsequently paid in 1997. The penalty phase concluded on April 5, 2002, when the jury announced that it had awarded each of the six women $550,000 as compensation for emotional damage the harassment had caused them and $5 million each in punitive damages, for a total award of $33.3 million.

The award was among the largest ever for a sexual harassment case in the United States, and came as a surprise to Kroger, who had hoped it would be substantially less. The women's lawyer declared that the award was appropriate since the company "knew it was happening, but chose not to take any effective action. All they would do was transfer the victims away." After the trial, the lawyer for the women told jurors that the judge had not allowed him to present evidence that Misiolek had been harassing women for 10 years before he was put in charge of the Ralphs store in Escondido. One woman who worked for Misiolek in 1985 allegedly said he called her a "dirty Mexican" and threw things at her, while a black woman said he had told her in 1992, "You can call me, 'Yessuh, boss.'" One of the jurors, John Adair, declared that he felt the penalty was too small because the company should have been penalized at least 1 percent of its $3.7 billion net worth.

Nevertheless, a few months after the trial ended, the verdict of the jurors was set aside again. Judge Michael Anello issued an order on July 15, 2002, which argued that the damages awarded to the six women was "grossly excessive" and the result of the jury's "passion and prejudice." In his order Judge Anello conceded that Misiolek's behavior was "utterly despicable." However, he continued, "there was no evidence to support the conclusion that Misiolek was a managing agent of Ralphs, and the evidence was insufficient to support the conclusion that Ralphs approved of or ratified Misiolek's conduct." Misiolek was not acting on behalf of Ralphs when he harassed the women, claimed the judge, nor was the harassment ordered by the company's management. It was, instead, the isolated action of a single manager.

The company as a whole should therefore not be held responsible for his actions, the judge argued. Instead, the jury should have punished the company only for the specific actions of Misiolek's supervisors who allowed him to run the Escondido store after they had received complaints from other women about his behavior. The actions of this handful of managers did not merit a penalty of $30.6 million against the entire company. Moreover, said Judge Anello, the punitive damages (which were about 60 times the $550,000 awarded as compensatory damages by the second jury) were not reasonably related to the compensatory damages. And the compensatory damages the second jury had awarded each woman ($550,000) were themselves excessive and should also be set aside.

Finally, the $30.6 million exceeded the amount needed to punish Ralphs and to deter other companies from doing the same in the future. Anello concluded by reducing the $30.6 million award to $8.25 million. According to the judge, the punitive damages each of the women should receive should be no more than 15 times the amount of compensatory damages the first jury had awarded them. This meant that Dianne Gober should receive $3 million, Tina Swann should receive $1.5 million, Finton and Lang should each receive $934,500, Noland should get $750,000, and Papiro should receive $1.125 million. The judge gave the six women 10 days to make up their minds whether to accept his reduced award, or to agree to a third trial.

On July 24, 2002, two of the women, Dianne Gober and Tina Swann, agreed to accept the judge's reduced award equal to 15 times the compensatory damages awarded by the jury in their first trial. The other four women decided to reject the smaller awards and to return to the courtroom for yet another trial as the judge promised they could do. One of the lawyers for the women angrily stated that the reduced awards failed to punish Ralphs, would fail to deter similar activity from other companies, and failed to serve as an example to others, as punitive damages are supposed to do.

For four years the case slowly wound its way through the court system as both sides filed repeated appeals. But the ten-year old case reached its final conclusion on March 1, 2006 when the case came before the Court of Appeal for the Fourth District, Division 1, of California. The Court of Appeal, in what appeared to be a reprimand to the four remaining female victims, ruled that they were entitled to punitive damages equal to only 6 times the compensatory damages awarded by the jury in their first trial, much less than the punitive award of 15 times the compensatory damages which had been offered by the judge four years earlier on July 24, 2002! This meant that instead of the $934,500 Finton and Lang had each been offered in 2002, they each would now receive only $375,000; instead of the $750,000 Noland was offered in 2002, she would now receive $300,000; and instead of the $1.25 million Papiro was offered in 2002, she would now receive $450,000. If the women's lawyers had thought that the 2002 punitive amounts were such negligible sums to a company the size of Kroger that they neither punished the company nor served as a deterrent, then the 2006 amounts the women were given for what they had gone through while working at Ralph's perhaps did not even register as a slap on the company's figurative wrists.

Questions

1. Assuming that the store and district managers of Ralphs received complaints about Misiolek's behavior starting in 1985, but that these complaints did not reach Ralphs' headquarters in Compton, do you believe that the judge is right in holding that the company as a whole should not be held responsible for his actions? Should the company be held responsible for policies that prevent complaints from reaching headquarters?
2. What kind of penalty do you believe would be appropriate for Ralphs? In your view, was the $33.3 million penalty excessive? Explain. Was the final 2006 judgment fair? Explain.
3. Should Kroger have to pay for events that happened before it took over the chain of supermarkets?
4. What can a company do to make sure that a situation like Misiolek's does not occur? Why do you think Ralphs allowed Misiolek to continue managing stores?

Note

1. This case is base on the following sources: Jim McNair, "Subsidiary of Kroger Loses $30.6 M Lawsuit," *Cincinnati Enquirer*; Alexei Oreskovic, "$30M Awarded in Sex Harassment Suit," *The Recorder*, April 10, 2002; "Post-Verdict, Jury Learns of Other Allegations," ABCNEWS.com, June 20, 2002; Davan Maharaj, "$3.3-Million Judgment Against Ralphs Tossed Out," *Los Angeles Times*, July 24, 1998; Onell Soto, "Ralphs to Pay $30 Million over Sexual Harassment," *San Diego Union-Tribune*, April 7, 2002; Onell Soto, "Harassment Award Against Ralphs Cut," *San Diego Union-Tribune*, July 17, 2002; Lisa Girion, "$30.6 million Judgement Against Ralphs Slashed," *Los Angeles Times*, July 17, 2002; Lisa Girion, "Harassment Verdict Prompts Review," *Los Angeles Times*, April 9, 2002; Davan Maharaj, "Ralphs Fights Record Award," *Los Angeles Times*, July 23, 1998; Lisa Girion, "6 Women Win Suit Against Employer Ralphs," *Los Angeles Times*, April 6, 2002; Margaret Fisk, "$3.3 M Award Swells to $30 M," *National Law Journal*, April 15, 2002; Alexei Oreskovic, "$30 Million Verdict Cut," *National Law Journal*, July 22, 2002; "Harassment In The Supermarket," ABCNEWS.Com, June 30, 2002; and the court decisions online at *www.nosexualharassment.com* including particularly *Gober v. Ralphs Grocery Co.* (2006) 137 Cal.App.4th.

CASES

Explore the Concept on mythinkinglab.com

Wal-Mart's Women[1]

On April 26, 2010, the full eleven-member Nineth Circuit U.S. Court of Appeals in San Francisco ruled in a 137-page opinion (*Betty Dukes et al. v. Wal-Mart Stores, Inc*), that a case accusing Wal-Mart Stores, Inc. of discriminating against its U.S. female workers could proceed to trial as a class action lawsuit, thereby reaffirming most of the earlier 2007 and 2004 rulings of three members of the Nineth Circuit Court of Appeals as well as earlier district court rulings. The women, according to the 2010 Court of Appeals opinion, "allege that women employed in [domestic] Wal-Mart stores: (1) are paid less than men in comparable positions, despite having higher performance ratings and greater seniority; and (2) receive fewer—and wait longer for—promotions to in-store management positions than men." The case, the largest ever in American civil rights history, had been launched almost a decade earlier by six American women who had worked in 13 Wal-Mart stores. They were asking the company to compensate them and any other women who had worked for Wal-Mart in the United States since December 26, 1998 for the many years of injury they had suffered as a result of the company's sexual discrimination. Several analysts noted that if Wal-Mart were to lose the case, it would cost the company many billions of dollars since the allegedly injured group would include all women employees subjected to discrimination at Wal-Mart's 3,400 stores hired since December 26, 1998, a group estimated to include as many as 1.5 million to 2 million women. While the 2010 decision allowed all women who were working for Wal-Mart when the lawsuit was filed to be part of this injured group, it ruled that a lower district court would have to decide how to handle any women who worked for Wal-Mart after December 26, 1998 but who were no longer working for Wal-Mart the day the lawsuit was filed.

Wal-Mart Stores, Inc., the world's biggest retailer, owns more than 8,400 stores, including 800 discount stores, 2,747 Wal-Mart Supercenter combination discount and grocery stores, and 596 Sam's Club warehouse stores. It is the leading retailer in both Canada (317 stores) and Mexico (1,469), owns almost 40 percent of SEIYU, a Japanese supermarket chain, and has stores in Argentina (43), Brazil (434), China (279), Chile (252), Costa Rica (170), El Salvador (77), Guate-mala (164), Honduras (53), Japan (371), Nicaragua (55), Puerto Rico (56), and the United Kingdom (371). At the end of its fiscal year, January 2010, Wal-Mart posted sales of $408.2 billion (64 percent from U.S. sales) and net profits of $14.3 billion. The company had over 2,100,000 employees worldwide.

The "Always Low Prices" company is famous for its strong and distinctive corporate culture, which it actively promotes. New employees get videos, classes, and literature on Wal-Mart's culture, such as the "Three Basic Beliefs" ("Respect for the Individual," "Service to Our Customers," and "Strive for Excellence"). Employees read founder Sam Walton's personal biography and learn how his personal values became core beliefs of the company. Weekly training on company culture is mandatory for managers and employees. Managers get continuing lessons on the company's culture and impart these lessons to subordinates. Managers are evaluated on their knowledge of the culture and employees are rewarded when they demonstrate a strong commitment to it.[2] Some of the company's cultural traditions are male-oriented. Senior managers attend an annual corporate retreat, for example, that always includes fishing and quail hunting. Managers sometimes scheduled district meetings at Hooter's restaurants, and annual sales meetings sometimes featured side trips to strip clubs.

Although the staunchly antiunion company is known as a benevolent employer, its reputation suffered during the opening decade of the twenty-first century. In July, 2000, an internal audit uncovered violations of state labor laws concerning time for breaks and violations of federal child-labor laws. In October, 2003, the Immigration and Naturalization Service (INS) conducted several midnight raids and discovered that the cleaning companies Wal-Mart hired to clean its stores at night had hundreds of illegal immigrants working as janitors. Wal-Mart was charged with conspiring with the cleaning companies to cheat immigrants out of their wages. In February, 2004, the company was found guilty of failing to pay overtime wages to workers who claimed they had to work overtime without pay between 1994 and 1999. In 2005, a California jury made Wal-Mart pay $172 million to employees forced to work without meal breaks. In 2006, Wal-Mart ended up paying $188 million to settle a Pennsylvania lawsuit over off-the-clock work. In December 2008, Wal-Mart announced it had agreed to pay between $352 million and $640 million to settle 63 cases in 42 states involving hundreds of thousands of employees forced to work off the clock so the company could save money on wages.[3] The settlement, announced two weeks after a $54 million wage-and-hour lawsuit settlement with 100,000 other workers, left 12 other similar lawsuits still pending against Wal-Mart.

Wal-Mart's biggest employee headache, however, was the class action lawsuit (*Dukes et al. v. Wal-Mart Stores, Inc.*) claiming the company discriminated against female employees in promotions, pay, management training, and job assignments. The lawsuit was launched in June, 2001 by six female Wal-Mart employees and on June 22, 2004, U.S. District Court Judge Martin Jenkins ruled that the six women could sue on behalf of all female employees of Wal-Mart who worked at its U.S. stores anytime since December 26, 1998. The women asked for back pay and compensation for all 1.6 million female employees against whom Wal-Mart had discriminated. In 1995, six years before the lawsuit was filed, Wal-Mart had paid a law firm to assess its compensation practices and the law firm reported that in 1993 Wal-Mart's male department managers earned $236.80 while females earned $223.70; males in salaried jobs earned $644.20 a week while females got $540.50. These and other disparities, the law firm concluded, "are statistically significant and sufficient to warrant a finding of discrimination unless the company can demonstrate at trial that the statistical disparities are caused by legitimate, nondiscriminatory factors."

The six women who filed the discrimination lawsuit in 2001 hired a statistical expert, Richard Drogin, a professor at California State University at Hayward, to analyze Wal-Mart's computerized employee records of 3,945,151 employees who had worked any time during 1996–2002.[4] The professor's findings supported some of the allegations of the women.

Drogin's report noted that Wal-Mart employees are divided into two main groups: hourly employees at the lower levels and salaried management employees at the higher levels. Hourly employees include store cashiers, associates, stock people, department heads, and support managers. Salaried management employees are divided into two groups: At the lower level are those who manage a single store, and at the higher level are those who manage an entire district or region or who enter corporate management. At the store level, salaried managers include store managers and assistant managers; above them are district managers, regional vice presidents, and senior vice presidents. Since Wal-Mart promotes predominantly from within, workers typically progress from being an upper hourly employee (usually a "support manager"), to management trainee, to store manager or assistant manager, and finally to district, regional, or corporate manager.

Compensation increases from one level to the next. In 2001, salaried managers made about $50,000 a year while hourly employees made $18,000. Drogin found that 65 percent of hourly employees were women, but only 33 percent of salaried managers were. At both levels, women earned less than men. The 2001 average annual earnings, for example, were as follows:

Group	% Female	Male Earnings	Female Earnings
Hourly	70.2%	$18,609	$17,459
Salaried managers	33.5	55,443	40,905

Drogin found this pattern repeated in all 41 of Wal-Mart's American regions.

Drogin also found that, on average, women earned less than men at each in-store salaried management job. During the years 1999–2001, for example, he found the following average annual salaries among salaried managers:

Job	% Female	Male Salary	Female Salary
Regional VP	10.3%	$419,435	$279,772
District manager	9.8	239,519	177,149
Store manager	14.3	105,682	89,280
Comanager	23	59,535	56,317
Asst. manager	35.7	39,790	37,322
Mgmt. trainee	41.3	23,175	22,371

Drogin found a similar gap in hourly pay rates. In 2001, for example, he found that in the three largest hourly jobs, average hourly wages were as follows:

Job	% Female	Male Hourly Pay	Female Hourly Pay
Dept. head	78.3%	$11.13	$10.62
Sales associate	67.8	8.73	8.27
Cashier	92.5	8.33	8.05

Drogan concluded that for a single year "the total earnings paid to men is about $5,000 more than earnings paid to women, among full-time employees working at least 45 weeks, on average, in 2001."

Drogin analyzed whether the discrepancies could be accounted for by the assumption that women left their jobs more than men, perhaps to raise children or for some other reason. This would give women higher turnover rates and men greater experience and seniority. He found that women stayed in the workforce longer than men at Wal-Mart and so had more on-the-job experience on average than men did. For example, at the end of 2001, the average number of years since their date of hire for men and women was as follows:

Job	Men	Women
All hourly	3.13 years	4.47 years
All managers	6.69	7.39
Sales associates	2.53	3.41
Dept. managers	5.29	7.49
Cashiers	1.86	2.53

Drogin discovered also that while it took women 4.38 years from their date of hire to be promoted to assistant manager, men were promoted after only 2.86 years, and while it took women 10.12 years to become store managers, it took men only 8.64 years.

Drogin next checked whether the wage and promotion discrepancies could be accounted for by the performance records of males and females; perhaps males performed better than females. He found that, on average, women had higher performance ratings than men. In 2001, for example, the performance ratings (on a scale of 1–7, where 1 is low and 7 high) were as follows:

Job	Men's Ratings	Women's Ratings
All hourly	3.84	3.91
Sales associates	3.68	3.75
Dept. manager	4.28	4.38
Cashier	3.58	3.49

Drogin also examined whether the pay gap between male and female compensation at Wal-Mart stayed the same over the years. He found that women who were hired into hourly jobs in 1996 were paid $0.35 less per hour than men hired into hourly jobs that same year. By 2001, the gap between the wages of these same employees had increased to $1.16 per hour. Also, women hired as sales associates in 1996 received $0.20 per hour less than men hired as sales associates that year. By 2001, the difference had grown to $1.17 per hour.

Finally, Drogin performed several statistical tests to determine whether the discrepancies in promotions and pay could be the result of women not being available (not in the "feeder pools") when promotions came up or of some other factors. He found, instead, that

- Women received 2,891 fewer promotions into Support Manager [the step before Management Trainee] than would be expected from their representation in the feeder pools.
- Women received 2,952 fewer promotions into Management Trainee than would be expected from their representation in the feeder pools.
- Women received 346 fewer promotions into Co-Manager than would be expected from their representation in the feeder pools.
- Women received 155 fewer promotions into Store Manager than would be expected from their representation in the feeder pools.
- Total earnings paid to women ranged between 5 and 15 percent less than total earnings paid to similarly situated men in each year 1996–2001, even when accounting for factors such as seniority, status, and store.

Drogin noted two factors that might affect women's promotion into management. First, many store managers believed that employees going into salaried management positions had to be willing to relocate geographically, and they communicated this belief to women. In practice, however, only a small proportion of managers were required to relocate their homes, and the company had programs that allowed women to opt out of this requirement. Second, while the company had a policy of posting available management positions, managers had the discretion to not post some positions and to communicate the availability of these positions by word of mouth to potential candidates they picked.

Another expert hired by the six women who brought the discrimination lawsuit against Wal-Mart, Marc Bendick, a labor economist, noted that Wal-Mart's top retail competitors had no trouble promoting women into management. While Wal-Mart's in-store salaried managers were 34.5 percent women, salaried managers at 20 comparable large retail chains were 56.5 percent female. If Wal-Mart had achieved the same female manager-to-nonmanager ratios as comparable chains in 1999, it would have had at least 4,004 more in-store female managers, 466 more female managers at corporate headquarters, 144 more at "blue-collar" nonstore establishments, 107 more in other nonstore establishments, and 97 more in separately reporting establishments.

The six women suing Wal-Mart also hired an expert in sociology, William T. Bielby, a professor at the University of California, Santa Barbara, to analyze and report on Wal-Mart's hiring practices.[5] Based on numerous hours of testimony under oath given by Wal-Mart managers, Bielby concluded that although company guidelines stated minimum criteria for promotions, managers had no written policies to guide them in selecting among candidates who met the minimum criteria, nor did they have guidelines to guide them in setting exact salaries. He noted that "a large body of social science research demonstrates that gender stereotypes are especially likely to influence personnel decisions when they are based on subjective factors, because substantial decision-maker discretion tends to allow people to seek out and retain stereotype-confirming information and ignore or minimize information that defies stereotypes." Moreover, he added, "In such settings stereotypes can bias assessments of women's qualifications, contributions, and advancement potential, because perceptions are shaped by stereotypical beliefs about women generally, not by the actual skills and accomplishments of the person as an individual." In his report he noted:

> For example, Store Manager Arturo Mireles testified that he was aware of no written criteria to be used in making decisions about promotion to Department Manager or Support Manager. His practice was to rely on a range of unwritten criteria, including subjective factors such as teamwork, ethics, integrity, ability to get along with others, and willingness to volunteer to come in to assist in the store or at another store outside of regular work hours. While factors like these might have common sense appeal and some might in fact be appropriate to consider in making promotion decisions, assessments will be biased [by stereotypes] unless they are assessed in a systematic and valid manner, with clear criteria and careful attention to the integrity of the decision-making process. . . . The same kind of discretion is allowed in decisions about compensation for hourly employees. . . . [A]ccording to company policy the Store Manager can pay up to two dollars an hour above the stated rate, based on his or her assessment of factors such as previous pay and experience. There is no company guideline and no training on when and how to adjust pay upwards and while overall payroll is monitored, there is no monitoring of these individual adjustments . . . A Store Manager can give a raise larger than the specified amount at his or her own discretion. In addition, employees can be given merit increases for "exceptional performance." . . . However, there is no guideline for assessing "exceptional performance" and no monitoring of the number of people who receive increases and how frequently they are given to any specific employee.

Bielby also noted, however, that Wal-Mart's "managers testified consistently that they did not believe that women were less qualified than men for management positions in the company." Wal-Mart insisted, in fact, that it explicitly prohibited any form of discriminatory behavior and that its managers all believed that women were as qualified as men. Any discriminatory behavior would have to be based on an individual manager's personal decision to contravene company policy and should not be attributed to anything Wal-Mart had done. On the contrary, the company worked hard to ensure equal opportunity for all its employees.

More than 100 female Wal-Mart employees came forward to provide sworn declarations detailing their treatment by the company.[6] These included:

- A female assistant manager in Utah was told by her store manager that retail is "tough" and "not appropriate" for women.
- A manager in Texas told a female employee that women have to be "bitches" to survive Wal-Mart management.
- A Sam's Club manager in California told a woman that to get promoted she should "doll up," dress a little better, and "blow the cobwebs off her make up."
- Male managers in several states repeatedly told numerous women employees in virtually identical words that men "need to be paid more than women because they have families to support."
- A male manager in South Carolina told a female employee that "God made Adam first, so women will always be second to men."
- A female personnel manager in Florida was told by her manager that men were paid more than women because "men are here to make a career and women aren't. Retail is for housewives who just need to earn extra money."
- A female corporate manager in Arkansas was told by a senior VP that it would be better if she "were at home raising a family" and that since she did not hunt, fish, or do other typically male activities, she would not advance any further: "you aren't a part of the boy's club, and you should raise a family and stay in the kitchen."
- A female management trainee in Texas was told by her supervisor, "I don't like college graduates, and I don't like female managers" and was told by her next manager that she should "resign and find a husband to settle down with and have children."

The company's lawyers claimed that the group of allegedly injured women was too large to handle in a single trial and that the experiences of the six women who brought the suit could not possibly be representative of the diverse and varied experiences of the millions of women that had worked for Wal-Mart. Moreover, they argued, Wal-Mart used many different systems for compensating and promoting employees, depending on the position and the particular store. Pay and promotion decisions were independently determined by individual managers at the store level and were not based on a uniform company policy. The company as a whole should not be penalized, they said, because of the independent decisions of some of its managers. The company had instituted many equal opportunity programs to ensure that everyone was treated the same regardless of race or gender.

As early as the 1990s, in fact, Wal-Mart had started a number of programs to achieve diversity. The company had a written antidiscrimination policy posted everywhere. Managers got reports on the gender composition of their hourly and salaried positions. Managers were told that women's representation should "reflect the community." Managers had to set an annual goal of increasing female representation in their areas and were supposed to be evaluated on the progress they made toward reaching the goals they set for themselves. Although this evaluation did not affect the compensation of in-store salaried managers, all higher-level managers were evaluated on the progress they made toward the diversity goals they had set themselves, and this evaluation was then averaged with their progress toward three other kinds of "people" goals. Each manager's "people average" constituted 5 percent of the final evaluation on which their compensation for the following year was based. The managers testified that they tried to set goals that were "realistic," "achievable," "made sense," and "weren't worse than the year before." A program that allowed women to enter salaried management jobs without having to relocate their homes had been begun by the late Sam Walton. After Walton's death, however, the program was not widely used nor known.

Although the Ninth Circuit Court of Appeals ruled in April, 2010 that the women's case could finally go forward as a class action, Wal-Mart's management appealed the ruling to the U.S. Supreme Court. On Monday, December 6, 2010, the Supreme Court announced that it had decided to hear the Wal-Mart case and to make a final determination about whether the case could be tried as a class action suit that would end up involving some 1.5 million female workers. Wal-Mart management believed that if the lawsuit were to succeed, it could have a significant material financial impact on the company. Some analysts speculated that Wal-Mart might choose to reach a settlement with the women either before or after the Supreme Court decided what it would do to "put the case behind it," although even a negotiated settlement would not be cheap.

Jeff Gearhart, Executive Vice President and General Counsel for Wal-Mart said "We are proud of the strides we have made to advance and support our female associates and have been recognized for our efforts to advance women through a number of awards and accolades. In 2008, Walmart was named in the 'Top 40 Greatest Organizations for Women of Color to Work' by *Women of Color* magazine as well as one of the 'Top 10 Best Companies for Women' by *PINK* magazine." On May, 2007, Wal-Mart announced it was named one of the "Top 50 Companies for Diversity" by *DiversityInc* magazine. "We remain committed to maintaining diversity in all aspects of our business," said a company spokesperson.

Questions

1. What financial impact do you think the lawsuit could potentially have on Wal-Mart? Do you think the women deserve to win their lawsuit? What if the outcome of the case cost Wal-Mart so much it had to lay off thousands of its workers and close stores?
2. What are the major moral complaints of the females suing Wal-Mart? Do you believe these complaints are justified? Why? Wal-Mart has said that the case should not be heard as a class-action, but that each woman should be considered individually and an individual determination should be made regarding whether she specifically was discriminated against by Wal-Mart, because each woman's situation is different. Do you agree?
3. What factors do you think might account for the discrepancies the Drogin report uncovered?
4. What, if anything, do you think Wal-Mart should do to correct these discrepancies? Should the company institute an "affirmative action" promotion program for female employees? If so, what should this program be like?

Notes

1. Much of this case is based on the documents the plaintiffs in *Dukes et al. v. Wal-Mart Stores, Inc* have made available at *http://www.walmartclass.com/walmartclass_forthepress.html*. In particular, the materials cited in notes 4, 5, and 6 are available at this web site and can be accessed there.
2. See M. J. Schneider, "The Wal-Mart Annual Meeting: From Small-Town America to a Global Corporate Culture," *Human Organization*, v. 57, 1998, pp. 292–299, and "Saturday Morning Fever: Wal-Mart's Weekly Meeting," *The Economist*, December 8, 2001.
3. Steven Greenhouse and Stephanie Rosenbloom, "Wal-Mart Settles 63 Lawsuits Over Wages," *The New York Times*, December 23, 2008; see also Wal-Mart Stores, Inc., *2004 Annual Report*, accessed August 3, 2004 at *http://www.walmartstores.com/Files/annualreport_2004.pdf*; and Steven Greenhouse, "Report Warned Wal-Mart of Risks Before Bias Suit," The New York Times, June 3, 2010.
4. Richard Drogin, "Statistical Analysis of Gender Patterns in Wal-Mart Workforce," February 2003, accessed August 1, 2004 on Wal-Mart Class web site (see note 1); all information and quotations attributed to Drogin in this case are drawn from this report.
5. William T. Bielby, "Expert Report of William T. Bielby, Ph.D.," February 3, 2003, accessed August 1, 2004 on Wal-Mart Class web site (see note 1); all information and quotations attributed to Bielby in this case are drawn from this report.
6. This summary of the 100 declarations is taken in part from the April 28, 2003 news release, "Women Present Evidence of Widespread Discrimination at Wal-Mart; Ask Judge to Expand Case to be Largest Ever Sex Discrimination Case," accessed August 2, 2004 on Wal-Mart Class web site (see note 1); all 100 declarations are available on the Wal-Mart Class web site and my summary includes some materials drawn from these declarations.

8

Ethics and the Employee

How does the rational model define a business organization?

What is a conflict of interest and how can it be avoided?

What factors should be considered when determining a "fair wage"?

How does the political model of the organization differ from the rational model?

In what ways is a modern corporation like a government?

What kinds of political tactics are most often encountered in business organizations?

What are the key ethical issues from the perspective of the caring organization?

Every morning millions of workers hurry off to work. Psychologists tell us we define ourselves by the work we do, and that our health, both physical and emotional, depends on whether our work is fulfilling or a source of meaningless stress.

INTRODUCTION

Listen to the Chapter Audio on mythinkinglab.com

What are organizations like? Here are descriptions of life inside organizations by three people at different organizational levels:

Spot-welder at a Ford Assembly Plant

I start the automobile, the first welds. . . . The welding gun's got a square handle, with a button on the top for high voltage and a button on the bottom for low. . . . We do about thirty-two jobs per car, per unit. Forty-eight units an hour, eight hours a day. Thirty-two times forty-eight times eight. Figure it out. That's how many times I push that button. . . . It don't stop. It just goes and goes and goes. . . . I don't like the pressure, the intimidation. How would you like to go up to someone and say, "I would like to go to the bathroom?" If the foreman doesn't like you, he'll make you hold it, just ignore you. . . . Oh, yeah, the foreman's got somebody knuckling down on him, putting the screws to him. But a foreman is still free to go the bathroom, go get a cup of coffee. He doesn't face the penalties. . . . When a man becomes a foreman, he has to forget about even being human, as far as feelings are concerned. You see a guy there bleeding to death. So what, buddy? That line's gotta keep goin'.[1]

Plant Manager at a Ford Assembly Plant

I'm usually here at seven o'clock. . . . Then I go out on the floor, tour the plant. . . . I'll change my tour so they can't tell every day I'm going to be in the same place at the same time. The worst thing I could do is set a pattern where they'll always know where I'll be. I'm always stopping to talk to foremen or hourly fellas. . . . I may see a water leak, I say to the foreman, "Did you call maintenance?" Not do it myself, let him go do it. By the time I get back in the office, I have three or four calls, "Can you help me on this?" This is how you keep in contact. . . . The operating committee meets usually every other day: my assistant plant managers; an operations manager, he has two production managers; a controller; an engineering manager; a quality control manager; and a materials manager. That's the eight key figures in the plant. . . . You can't run a business sitting in the office 'cause you get divorced too much from the people. The people are the key to the whole thing. If you aren't in touch with the people they think he's too far aloof, he's distant. It doesn't work.[2]

Ex-President of a Conglomerate

I don't know of any situation in the corporate world where an executive is completely free and sure of his job from moment to moment. . . . The danger starts as soon as you become a district manager. You have men working for you and you have a boss above. You're caught in a squeeze. The squeeze progresses from station to station. I'll tell you what a squeeze is. You have the guys working for you that are shooting for your job. The guy you're working for is scared stiff you're gonna shove him out of his job. . . . There's always the insecurity. You bungle a job. You're fearful of losing a big customer. You're fearful so many things will appear on your record, stand against you. You're always fearful of the big mistake. You've got to be careful when you go to corporation parties. Your wife, your children have to behave properly. You've got to

> fit in the mold. You've got to be on guard. When I was president of this big corporation . . . [the] corporation specified who you could socialize with, and on what level. . . . The executive is a lonely animal in the jungle who doesn't have a friend.[3]

Not everyone experiences business organizations as these three people have. Nonetheless, their descriptions of organizational life touch on many of the problematic ethical issues business organizations create: alienated workers doing repetitive work, feelings of oppression created by the exercise of authority, heavy responsibilities heaped on the shoulders of managers, power tactics employed by managers anxious to advance their career ambitions, and pressures placed on subordinates and superiors as they both try to get their jobs done. Other ethical issues can be added to the list: health problems created by unsafe working conditions, conflicts of interest created by an employee's allegiance to other causes, absence of due process for nonunionized employees, and invasion of privacy by management's legitimate concern to know what's going on in the organization they manage. The list could go on.

This chapter explores these and other ethical problems raised by worklife in business organizations. The chapter is divided into three main parts. The first part begins by describing a traditional model of the organization: the organization as a "rational" structure. The following sections then discuss the employee's duties to the employer as defined by this traditional model, and the employer's duties to the employee, again as defined by this model. The second main part of the chapter turns to describing what some say is a more realistic view of the organization: the organization as a "political" structure. The sections in this part of the chapter discuss the two main kinds of ethical issues implied by this "political" view of the firm: employee rights and organizational politics. The third main part of the chapter discusses a more recent view of the organization: the organization as a network of personal relationships. The discussion of this third, still emerging view is, of necessity, briefer than the discussions of the other views which have a much longer history of development.

8.1 The Rational Organization

rational model of a business organization A view of the organization that sees it as a structure of formal (explicitly defined and openly employed) relationships designed to achieve some technical or economic goal with maximum efficiency.

The more traditional, **"rational" model of a business organization** defines the organization as a structure of formal (explicitly defined and openly employed) relationships designed to achieve some technical or economic goal with maximum efficiency.[4] E. H. Schein provides a compact definition of an organization from this perspective:

> An organization is the rational coordination of the activities of a number of people for the achievement of some common explicit purpose or goal, through a division of labor and function and through a hierarchy of authority and responsibility.[5]

formal hierarchies of authority The positions and relationships identified in the organizational chart that represents the various official positions and lines of authority in the organization.

If an organization is looked at in this way, then the most fundamental elements of the organization are the **formal hierarchies of authority** identified in the organizational chart that represents the various official positions and lines of authority in the organization. Figure 8.1 provides a simplified example.

Figure 8.1

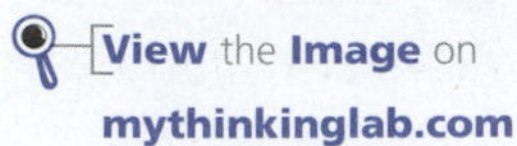

View the **Image** on **mythinkinglab.com**

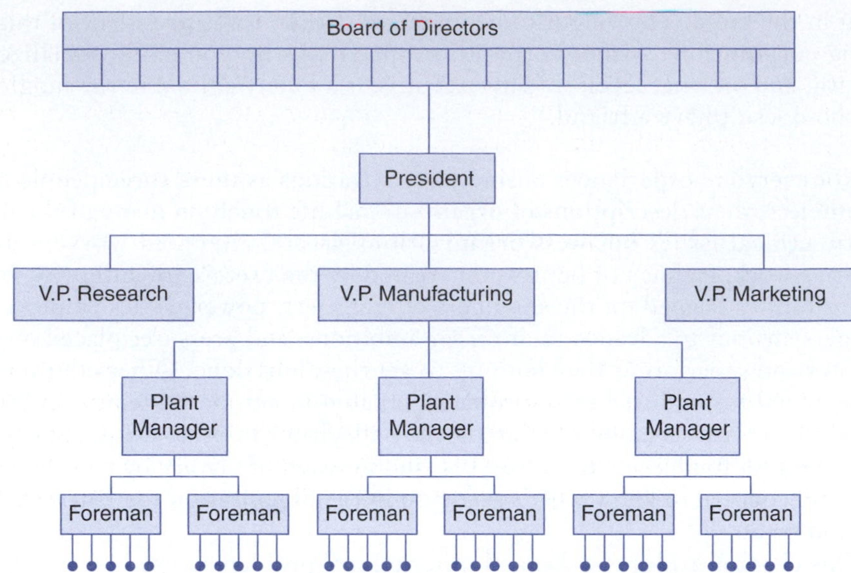

operating layer Those employees and their immediate supervisors who directly produce the goods and services that constitute the essential outputs of the organization.

middle managers Managers who direct the units below them and are in turn directed by those above them in ascending formal lines of authority.

top management The board of directors, the chief executive officer, and the CEO's staff.

At the bottom of the organization is the "**operating layer**": those employees and their immediate supervisors who directly produce the goods and services that constitute the essential outputs of the organization. The Ford spot-welder quoted at the beginning of this chapter was located at this level. Above the operating layer of laborers are ascending levels of "**middle managers**" who direct the units below them and who are in turn directed by those above them in ascending formal lines of authority. The plant manager quoted earlier worked within these middle levels of the organization. At the apex of the pyramid is **top management**: the board of directors, the Chief Executive Officer (CEO), and other company officers such as the President, Chief Financial Officer (CFO), Chief Technology Officer (CTO), Chief Human Resources Officer (CHRO), and various Vice Presidents. The ex-president quoted earlier inhabited these upper levels of the organization.

The rational model of the organization supposes that most information is collected from the operating layers of the organization, rises through the various formal management levels, each of which aggregates the information, until it reaches top management levels. On the basis of this information, the top managers make general policy decisions and issue general commands, which are then passed downward through the formal hierarchy, where they are amplified at each managerial level until they reach the operating layer as detailed work instructions. These decisions of the top managers are assumed to be aimed at a more or less known economic goal, such as efficiency, productivity, profits, maximum return on investment, and so on. The goal is defined by those at the top of the hierarchy of authority, who are assumed to have a legitimate right to make this decision.

What is the glue that holds together the organization's many layers of employees and managers and that fixes these people onto the organization's goals and formal hierarchy? Contracts. The model conceives of the employee as an agent who freely and knowingly agrees to accept the organization's formal authority and to pursue its goals in exchange for a fair wage and reasonable working conditions. These contractual agreements—some explicit and some left implicit—cement each employee into the organization by defining each employee's duties and scope of authority within the organization. By virtue of these contractual agreements, the employee has a moral responsibility to obey the employer in the course of pursuing the organization's goals, and the employer in turn has a moral responsibility to provide the employee with the wage and working conditions it agreed to provide. As we have already discussed at some length in previous chapters, when two persons knowingly and freely agree to exchange goods or services with each other, each party to the agreement acquires an ethical obligation to fulfill the terms of the contract. Utilitarian theory provides additional support for the view that the employee has an obligation to loyally pursue the goals of the firm: Businesses will function most efficiently and productively if employees single-mindedly pursue the firm's goals. If each employee were free to use the resources of the firm to pursue personal ends, chaos would ensue and everyone's utility would decline.

The basic ethical responsibilities that emerge from these "rational" aspects of the organization focus on two reciprocal moral obligations: (1) the obligations of the employee to the employer such as to obey organizational superiors, loyally pursue the organization's goals, and avoid any activities that might threaten those goals; and (2) the obligations of the employer to the employee such as to provide the employee with a just wage and just working conditions. We will examine these two reciprocal obligations in turn.

Quick Review 8.1

The Rational Model of a Business Organization

- Formal hierarchies identified in the organizational chart are the firm's fundamental realities.
- Organizations seek to coordinate the activities of members so as to achieve their goals with maximum efficiency.
- Information rises from the bottom of the organization to the top.
- Contracts obligate the employee to loyally pursue the organization's goals and the employer to provide a just wage and just working conditions.

The Employee's Obligations to the Employer

In the rational view of the firm, the employee's main ethical duty is to work toward the goals of the firm and avoid any activities that might harm those goals. To be unethical, basically, is to deviate from these goals to serve one's own interests in ways that, if illegal, can be a form of "white-collar crime."[6]

As administrator of the company's finances, for example, the financial manager is entrusted with its funds and has the responsibility of managing those funds in a way that will minimize risk while ensuring a suitable rate of return for the company's shareholders. Financial managers have this contractual duty to the firm and its investors because they have contracted to provide the firm with their best judgment and to exercise their authority only in the pursuit of the goals of the firm and not for their own personal benefit. Financial managers fail in their contractual duty to the firm when they misappropriate funds, when they waste or squander funds, when they are negligent or fraudulent in the preparation of financial statements, when they issue false or misleading reports, and so on.

These traditional views of the employee's duties to the firm have made their way into the "**law of agency**"—that is, the part of law that specifies the legal duties of "agents" (e.g., employees) toward their "principals" (e.g., their employers).[7] The "restatement" of the law of agency, for example, states in Section 385 that "an agent is subject to a duty to his principal to act solely for the benefit of the principal in all matters connected with his agency"; and Section 394 prohibits the agent from acting "for persons whose interests conflict with those of the principal in matters in which the agent is employed."[8] In short, the employee must pursue the goals of the firm and must do nothing that conflicts with those goals while working for the firm.

law of agency That part of the law that specifies the legal duties of "agents" (e.g., employees) toward their "principals" (e.g., employers).

There are several ways in which the employee might fail to live up to the duty to pursue the goals of the firm: The employee might act on a "conflict of interest," the employee might steal from the firm, or the employee might use the position as leverage to force illicit benefits out of others through extortion or commercial bribery. We turn now to examine the ethical issues raised by these tactics.

conflict of interest Occurs when employee has an interest that provides an incentive to do his or her job in a way that serves that interest and not necessarily the interests of the employer he or she is obligated to serve.

Conflicts of Interest

Conflicts of interest in business arise when an employee or an officer of a company (1) is engaged in carrying out a certain task (or using his judgment) for his employer and (2) the employee has an interest that provides him with an incentive or motive to do the task (or use his judgment) in a way that serves that interest, and (3) the employee has an obligation to do the task (or use his judgment) in a way that serves the interests of his company free of any incentive to serve another interest. More simply, an employee has a conflict of interest when he has an interest that provides an incentive to do his job in a way that serves that interest and not necessarily the interests of the employer he is obligated to serve. Suppose, for example, that Mary is the employee of a large company and she has the job of choosing the supplier from which her employer will buy raw materials. Suppose she also owns a small firm that makes the kind of raw materials her employer needs. Then, her interest in having her own firm make money gives her an incentive to choose her own firm to supply the raw materials even if it does not offer the best terms to her employer.

Quick Review 8.2

Necessary Conditions for a Conflict of Interest to Arise

- Employee or officer is engaged in carrying out a certain task for his or her employer.
- Employee has an interest that gives him or her an incentive to do the task in a way that serves that interest.
- The employee has an obligation to do the task in a way that serves the interests of his or her employer free of any incentive to serve another interest.

It is important to notice that the mere *existence* of an interest that provides an incentive or motive that *could* influence an employee's actions on behalf of his or her employer is enough to give that employee a conflict of interest even if the employee does not allow the interest to influence him or her. That is, the mere existence of such an incentive or motive, even if it does not influence the employee's actions in any way, is enough to count as a conflict of interest. Suppose, for example, that John is trying to choose the supplier from which his employer will buy raw materials. And suppose that John honestly resolves to be completely objective when choosing suppliers, and honestly resolves that he will not choose the company he owns unless it offers the best terms to his employer. And suppose he actually is objective and ends up not choosing his own firm because it did not offer his employer the best terms. Nevertheless, John had a conflict of interest. He had a conflict of interest because he had an incentive or motive to choose his own firm, and the mere existence of that incentive or motive is a conflict of interest even if in the end it does not influence what he does for his employer, i.e., even if in the end he did not act on that incentive or motive.

Conflicts of interest do not have to be financial. Suppose, once again, that Mary's job is choosing a company to supply raw materials to her employer. And suppose Mary's son is a salesman for one of the firms that sells those raw materials. Since Mary has an interest in seeing her son succeed in his job, she has an incentive to give him her employer's business even if other firms offer better terms for the same raw materials. So Mary has a conflict of interest, but in this case she does not have a financial interest, but an interest in helping someone with whom she has a close relationship. Conflicts of interest that are based on financial relationships are sometimes called ***objective* conflicts of interest**, while conflicts of interest that are based on emotional ties or other kinds of relationships are sometimes called ***subjective* conflicts of interest**.

objective conflicts of interest Conflicts of interest that are based on financial relationships.

subjective conflicts of interest Conflicts of interest that are based on emotional ties or on relationships.

Conflicts of interest can be created when the employee of one company holds another job or consulting position in another firm with which the employee's own company deals or competes. An employee of one bank, for example, would have a conflict of interest if the employee took on a second job with a competing bank. At the very least, the employee's loyalties would be divided between serving the interests of each competing bank. Since the banks compete with each other, the employee could help one bank by giving that bank information about the other bank that hurts that other bank, yet as an employee of that other bank, he had an obligation to serve the interests of that other bank and failed to live up to that obligation. Similarly, a conflict of interest would be created if an accountant working for an insurance company also provides "independent" auditing services for some of the firms the insurance company insures. The accountant has an incentive to pass on to the insurance company (one employer) some of the private information gathered when auditing the books of those other firms (who were also employing her). Passing on the information will serve the interests of her own company, but as an independent auditor, the accountant also had an obligation to serve the interests of the companies that hired her to do their audits and she failed to live up to that obligation.

Conflicts of interest may be actual or potential.[9] A ***potential* conflict of interest** occurs when an employee has an interest that could influence what he does for his company if the employee were performing a certain task for his company *but he has not yet been given that task to perform*. An ***actual* conflict of interest** occurs when an employee has an interest that could influence what he does for his employer when the employee performs a certain task for that employer *and he has actually been given that task to perform*. For example, Alma has a merely *potential* conflict of interest if she owns stock in a construction company that submits a bid for construction work her employer needs to have done, but she has no part in choosing which construction company her employer will choose. But Alma's conflict becomes an *actual* conflict of interest if she actually has the job of choosing the company that will do the work for her employer. Notice that the difference between a potential and actual conflict of interest depends on the *task* the employee is supposed to perform, not on whether the interest does or does not influence the employee.

potential conflict of interest Occur when an employee has an interest that could influence what the employee does for the employer if the employee were to perform a certain task for the employer *but he or she has not yet been given that task to perform.*

actual conflict of interest Occurs when an employee has an interest that could influence the judgments the employee makes for the employer if the employee were to perform a certain task for the employer *and he or she has actually been given that task to perform.*

If we accept the view (outlined in Chapter 2) that agreements impose moral duties, then actual conflicts of interest are unethical because they are contrary to the implied agreement that a worker freely makes when taking a job with a firm. The personnel of a firm are hired to do their jobs in a way that serves the interests of the firm. By accepting a position within the firm, an employee agrees that his or her judgments and actions will not be encumbered by any interests that could lead him or her to serve those interests instead of the interests of the firm. To knowingly then encumber one's judgments or actions by taking on an interest that can influence those judgments or actions, violates the rights and duties created by the agreement and so is unethical. Conflicts of interest are also unethical on utilitarian grounds. If employees were allowed to have conflicts of interest, then employees in effect would be allowed to have incentives to serve their own interests at the expense of their employer's interests. This would (1) result in many instances when employers would be harmed by the actions of their employees and (2) undermine the trust employers need to be able to place on employees who work on their behalf and would thereby decrease the utility of the employer/employee relationship.

As we have seen, a conflict of interest can be present even when the interest involved does not actually influence the employee's actions but *could* do so. It is sometimes asked whether there are any general guidelines for determining when an employee's interests are significant enough to say that they *could* influence his or her job or judgment, i.e., significant enough to say that they constitute an incentive or motive even though the employee does not allow them to influence him. There are no general guidelines here since much depends on the employee's position in the firm, the nature of his job, how much he stands to gain from the transactions involved, and the impact the employees' actions will have on others inside and outside the firm. However, to eliminate the possibility of any employee interest that might provide a conflict of interest, many companies (a) specify the exact amount of stock, if any, that the company will allow employees to hold in firms with which the company does business or with which the company competes; (b) prohibit certain relationships with employees of competitors, buyers, or suppliers; and (c) require key officers to disclose all their outside financial interests.

Some ethicists have claimed that to allow even the *appearance* of a conflict of interest is wrong. An ***apparent* conflict of interest** exists when an employee has no actual conflict of interest, but other people looking at the employee's situation may come to believe (wrongly) that he or she has an actual conflict of interest. Suppose, for example, that I own a construction company that submits bids for a construction job my employer wants to have done. And suppose that I have nothing to do with choosing the construction company and have no influence whatsoever over the choice. Then, I have

apparent conflict of interest A situation in which an employee has no actual conflict of interest, but in which other people looking at the situation may come to believe (wrongly) that there is an actual conflict of interest.

no *actual* conflict of interest. But suppose, further, that my employer chooses my company without knowing it is my company. And suppose that other construction companies find out that my company was chosen. Then, those other companies may come to believe that I unfairly influenced my employer, and so they may come to believe that I had an actual conflict of interest and that because of this conflict, the choice of my construction company was unfair. So even the *appearance* of a conflict of interest can undermine people's trust in the fairness and impartiality of processes that people need to trust are fair and impartial (if those processes are going to be accepted and used by people). For this reason, it is often claimed that it is wrong to allow even the appearance of a conflict of interest.

There are three main ways in which employees can avoid conflicts of interest or can get rid of them when they arise. We said earlier that a conflict of interest exists when three conditions exist: an employee or officer of a company (1) is engaged in carrying out a certain task for his or her employer and (2) the employee has an interest that gives him or her an incentive to do the task in a way that serves that interest, and (3) the employee has an obligation to do the task in a way that serves the interests of his or her company free of any incentive to serve another interest. Conflicts of interest can be avoided by making sure that these three elements are not all present simultaneously; moreover, when a conflict of interest arises, it can be eliminated by eliminating one of these three elements. Suppose, for example, that I have a conflict of interest because I own one of the companies that submits bids for a construction contract and I am the one who chooses which company will get the contract. Then, I can eliminate this conflict of interest in one of three ways. (1) I can get out of performing the task that creates the conflict of interest, in this case the task of choosing who gets the contract. That is, I can ask my employer to "recuse" me from the task of choosing who gets the contract, or I can "recuse" myself. (2) I can eliminate the interest that might give me an incentive to serve that interest, in this case my ownership of one of the companies that is submitting bids. I can eliminate the interest, for example, by selling or otherwise getting rid of my ownership of this company. (3) I can eliminate or change my obligation to do the task in a way that serves the interests of my company free of any incentive to serve another interest. For example, I can leave my employer and then I no longer have an obligation to serve his interests. Or I can reveal the interest I have to my employer, i.e., reveal that I own one of the companies that is submitting bids. My employer might then let me continue in the task and let me continue to have this interest, perhaps because he or she can monitor my decisions to ensure the interest does not influence my judgment or perhaps because my employer just knows and trusts me. Since my employer has explicitly allowed me to do this task and to do it even though I have this incentive, I am no longer obligated to be free of any incentive to serve another interest while doing this task. Although I still have the obligation to serve my employer's interests, I no longer have the obligation to be free of the incentive that arises from owning one of the companies that is submitting a bid. My employer changed my obligation by allowing me to evaluate the bids even though I own one of the companies submitting bids. Since I still have the obligation to serve his interests, however, I must strive to be objective when evaluating the bids, and must do all I can to ensure I will not be influenced by the fact that I own one of the companies submitting bids.

Quick Review 8.3

A Conflict of Interest can be Eliminated or Avoided by

- "Recusing" (removing) oneself from the task in which the conflict of interest arises
- Eliminating the interest that creates the conflict of interest
- Eliminating or changing the obligation of serving the employer's interests and remaining free of any incentive to serve another interest while serving the employer.

Conflicts of interest can be created by a variety of different kinds of situations and activities. Two kinds of situations and activities demand further attention: commercial bribes and gifts.

commercial bribe
A consideration given or offered to an employee by a person outside the firm with the understanding that, when the employee transacts business for the firm, the employee will deal favorably with that person or that person's firm.

Commercial Bribes A **commercial bribe** is something of value that is given or offered to an employee by a person outside the employee's company who intends it to lead the employee to deal favorably with that person or the person's firm. The bribe may consist of money, tangible goods, the "kickback" of part of a payment, preferential treatment, or any other kind of benefit. Suppose Marco is a purchasing agent, for example. Then he is accepting a bribe when he accepts money from a supplier who gives it to him in order to receive favored treatment when Marco makes his purchasing decisions. However, if an employee *demands* a bribe from persons outside the firm, then that employee is engaged in ***commercial extortion***. For example, if Marco is a purchasing agent who buys only from vendors who agree to give him a kickback then Marco is engaged in extortion. Extorting or accepting a bribe obviously creates a conflict of interest that violates the employee's contractual agreement to use his or her unbiased judgment on behalf of the employer.

commercial extortion Occurs when an employee demands a consideration from persons outside the firm as a condition for dealing favorably with those persons when the employee transacts business for the firm.

Gifts Accepting gifts may or may not be ethical. The purchasing agent, for example, who accepts small gifts from a salesperson without asking for the gifts and without making such gifts a condition of doing business may be doing nothing unethical. If the agent does not give favored treatment to the giver of a gift and is not prejudiced against those who fail to give a "gift," no actual conflict of interest is created. A potential conflict of interest, however, may exist and accepting gifts may encourage a practice that could become an actual conflict of interest or that may be subtly affecting the independence of a person's judgment. Vincent Barry suggests that the following factors should be considered when evaluating the ethics of accepting a gift:[10]

1. What is the value of the gift? That is, is it substantial enough that it could influence one's decisions?
2. What is the purpose of the gift? That is, is the gift intended or accepted as a bribe?
3. What are the circumstances under which the gift was given? That is, was the gift given openly? Was it given to celebrate a special event (Christmas, a birthday, a store opening)?
4. What is the position of the recipient and of the giver of the gift? That is, is the recipient in a position to influence his own firm's dealings with the giver of the gift, and is the giver in a position to benefit from the actions of the recipient?
5. What is the accepted business practice in the area? That is, is the gift part of an open and well-known industry practice?
6. What is the company's policy? That is, does the company forbid acceptance of such gifts?
7. What is the law? That is, is the gift forbidden by a law, such as a law prohibiting gifts in sports recruiting?

Quick Review 8.4

The Ethics of Accepting Gifts Depends on

- The value of the gift
- The purpose of the gift
- The circumstances of the gift
- The job of the recipient.
- Accepted and public local practices
- Company policies on gifts
- Legal prohibitions on gifts.

Theft Part of the employee's agreement with the employer is that he or she will use the resources and goods of the firm in the pursuit of the firm's legitimate aims. For the employee to use company resources for his or her own benefit is a form of theft because to do so is to take or use property that belongs to another (the employer) without the consent of its rightful owner.

Employee theft is often petty, involving the theft of small tools, office supplies, or clothing. At the managerial level, petty theft sometimes occurs through the manipulation or padding of expense accounts, although the amounts involved are sometimes substantial. Other forms of managerial theft, sometimes referred to as *white-collar crime*, are embezzlement, larceny, fraud in the handling of trusts or receiverships, and forgery. The ethics of these forms of theft, however, are relatively clear.

Not always as clear are some particularly modern kinds of theft: thefts involving the theft of various kinds of information. For example, what is the ethics of hacking into a company's data bank when I do not do anything other than just look around? Or of copying a company's computer programs or its computerized data if doing so will not change the original? Unless authorized explicitly or through a company's formal or informal policies, all these activities are forms of theft because they all involve taking or using property that belongs to someone else without the consent of its owner. The fact that I did not damage, change, or carry away what I used for my own benefit is irrelevant to the simple fact that I used property without the owner's permission to do so. The main difference between the property that is taken in these examples and most other kinds of property, of course, is that the property that is taken in these examples consists of information. Information, like the information contained in a data bank or the programs owned by a company are not tangible property, and the employee who examines, uses, or copies such information or programs can leave the original information or programs unchanged (the company might never even realize what the employee did). Nevertheless, unauthorized examination, use, or copying of computer information or programs constitutes theft.

Theft of information is best understood by considering the nature of property, which we discussed in Chapter 3: Property consists of a bundle of exclusive rights that a specific person has with respect to a specific asset. "Exclusive" here means that the right belongs only to the owner and excludes all others except those authorized by the owner. The most important of these exclusive rights are: the right to use the asset; the right to decide whether and how others may use the asset; the right to sell, trade, or give away the asset; the right to any income or other benefits produced by the asset; and the right to modify or change the asset.[11] (These rights, like all rights, are limited by the rights of others, such as the right not to be harmed.) All of these rights can and do apply to any information, including digitized information, and computer programs that a company used its own resources to develop or that the company purchased with its own financial resources. Consequently, such information and programs are the property of the company, and only the company has the bundle of exclusive rights related to that property, including the right to its use or the benefits deriving from its use. To usurp any of the rights of the owner of a piece of property, including the rights pertaining to its use, is therefore theft, even when the property consists of information and even if in using the information I leave the original copy of the information unchanged.

Copying digitized information is sometimes defended on the grounds that "it doesn't hurt anyone." But as we saw in our discussion of moral rights in Chapter 2, when violations of rights are concerned, it is a mistake for a person to say that he or she did nothing wrong because "It didn't hurt anyone." A person's rights can be violated and the person can be wronged, we saw, even when the person is not injured or hurt in any way. (This, we saw, is one of the ways in which moral rights considerations differ from utilitarian considerations.) Using someone's property without his consent is a violation of the person's property rights, in particular the right to use or have others use his property only as he chooses. When a person's property rights are violated, that person has been wronged and the one who wronged him has engaged in wrongdoing, even if the violation of the property-owner's rights did not inflict any injuries on the property owner and even, in fact, if the property owner never finds out that his property rights were violated. Thus, when an employee uses the employer's property to benefit himself without the employer's consent, the employee is engaged in wrongdoing regardless of whether or not the employee changed or damaged the original property and regardless of whether the employer was hurt or injured in any way. The violation of the property right is wrong by itself and its wrongfulness does not require any additional infliction of harm.

Some information is referred to as a "trade secret." A trade secret (sometimes called "proprietary information") consists of nonpublic information that (a) concerns a company's own activities, technologies, future plans, policies, or records and that if known by competitors would materially affect the company's ability to compete commercially against those competitors; (b) is owned by the company (although it might not be patented or copyrighted) because it was developed by the company for its private use from resources it owns or was legitimately purchased for its own use from others; and (c) the company indicates through explicit directives, security measures, or contractual agreements with employees that it does not want anyone outside the company to have. For example, if a company, using its own engineering and laboratory resources, develops a secret process to manufacture computer drives that can carry more data than any other company's drives, and it takes explicit measures to ensure that process is not known to anyone else, then detailed information about that process is a trade secret. Similarly, lists of suppliers or customers, research results, formulas, computer programs, computer data, marketing and production or strategic plans, and any other information developed by a company or its employees for the company's own private use from its own resources can all constitute trade secrets. Because employees, especially managers and those involved in company research and development, have access to trade secrets that the company must entrust to them if it is to carry on its business, they often have the opportunity to use such secrets for their own personal benefit by dealing with competitors. Such unauthorized use of trade secrets by employees is unethical because it is using the property of an owner for a purpose not sanctioned by that owner, and because the employee has an implied (or even, in some cases, an explicit) contract not to use company resources for purposes not sanctioned by the company.[12] For example, a female engineering employee who is hired to oversee the development of a secret manufacturing process that gives her company a competitive edge over others acts wrongly if she decides to leave that company to work for a competitor that promises her a higher salary in exchange for setting up the same process she developed while working for her former employer.

But carrying away information that employees acquire while working for a company raises an important issue: how does such *information* differ from the *skills* one acquires while working for a company? The distinction is important because the skills that an employee acquires by working for a company can be and usually are considered part of his or her own person and to that extent are not the property of the employer, while proprietary information is. Unfortunately, it is not always easy to distinguish skills from proprietary information because many high-level skills consist, in part, of "know-how" that can be considered a kind of information. In such cases, it may be all but impossible to separate the skill from the information. Take, for example, Donald Wohlgemuth, a general manager who became dissatisfied with his salary and his working conditions while he oversaw a B. F. Goodrich secret technology for making spacesuits for the government.[13] Wohlgemuth subsequently negotiated a job with International Latex, a Goodrich competitor, at a much higher salary with greater responsibilities. At Latex, however, he was hired to manage a division that involved, among other things, the manufacture of spacesuits for the government. Goodrich managers objected to his working for a competitor where he might use the proprietary information that Goodrich had developed as it became experienced in making spacesuits. When they questioned the ethics of his decision, Wohlgemuth angrily (and perhaps thoughtlessly) replied that "loyalty and ethics have their price and International Latex has paid the price," a reply that Goodrich interpreted as a confession that Wohlgemuth was giving their trade secrets to Latex. The Ohio Court of Appeals ruled, however, that Goodrich could not keep Wohlgemuth from selling his *skills* to another competitor, although it imposed on Wohlgemuth an injunction restraining him from disclosing to Latex any of the *trade secrets* of B. F. Goodrich. However, the court did not explain how Wohlgemuth, Goodrich, or Latex were to distinguish between the "information" and the "skills" Wohlgemuth had acquired while working for Goodrich. In the end, Wohlgemuth continued doing what he had been doing with Latex and, from Goodrich's perspective, he continued making use of, and so stealing, the proprietary information they had worked years to develop.

Quick Review 8.5

Theft of Information

- Includes the theft of digitized programs, music, movies, e-books, etc., as well as trade secrets, company plans, and proprietary formulas or other data
- Is theft even if the original is not taken nor changed but only copied, examined, or used without the consent of the owner
- Violates the owner's right to have his property used as he chooses, even if the theft does not injure the owner
- The skills one acquires from a company are not information and so it is not theft to take them when leaving the company, although skills are often hard to distinguish from information.

HP's Secrets and Oracle's New Hire

On August 6, 2010, the Board of Directors of computer company Hewlett-Packard (HP) fired Mark Hurd, CEO of the company. Earlier Hurd had been accused of sexual harassment by Jodie Fisher—a former *Playboy* model hired to work at HP marketing events that Hurd had attended. Investigators found that Hurd did not violate the company's sexual harassment policies, but said he had falsified some expense account entries, apparently to conceal his relationship with Fisher, a relationship which Hurd, a married man, insisted was not sexual. The falsified entries violated HP's written business ethics standards, the Board said, so it had to fire him, although his contract required they give him about $30 million as a severance package. The size of the severance was in part due to the fact that when Hurd became CEO HP was in trouble and he not only managed to turn it around, but also increased company revenues by almost 50 percent, for which stockholders were extremely grateful. Although he said he did not prepare his own expense reports, Hurd admitted: "There were instances in which I did not live up to the standards and principles of trust, respect, and integrity that I have espoused at HP and which have guided me throughout my career."

About a month after leaving the company, Hurd announced he had been hired by Oracle as President with a salary of $950,000 a year, a bonus of $10 million, and stock options for 10 million shares of Oracle. Like HP, Oracle is also a computer company and so is a major direct competitor of HP. As HP's former CEO, Hurd knew HP's weaknesses and its future products, pricing, margins, customers, planned acquisitions, research discoveries, and company strategies including how it planned to compete against Oracle. Some news reports noted that Hurd's inside knowledge of "HP's strategy and markets and its enterprise customers" was certain to help Oracle. HP's Board agreed and sued Hurd, arguing he had signed a "confidentiality agreement" to keep all HP information secret, especially from competitors and that in his new position, he could not perform his duties for Oracle without necessarily using and relying on HP's trade secrets and confidential information. Defenders of Hurd argued that HP had so many lines of business the agreement would have effectively barred him from any employment in which he could use his executive skills, so it was unfair and invalid both legally and

Mark Hurd was former CEO of HP

Jodie Fisher initially said Hurd sexually harassed her

morally. The confidentiality agreement Hurd had signed while at HP read:

> This agreement concerns trade secrets, confidential business and technical information, and know-how not generally known to the public...which is acquired or produced by me in connection with my employment by HP...I agree to use such information only in the performance of HP duties...and to use all reasonable precautions to assure that such information is not disclosed to unauthorized persons or used in an unauthorized manner, both during and after my employment with HP....I agree that for a period of twelve months following the termination of my employment with HP... I will not provide services to a competitor in any role or position (as an employee, consultant, or otherwise).

Larry Ellison is CEO and founder of Oracle Corporation

At Oracle, Hurd replaced a former President, Charles Phillips, who had been fired after a woman, YaVaughnie Wilkins, said she was his mistress and announced on a series of large billboards posted along major roads in New York, San Francisco, and Atlanta: "You are my soulmate forever." Like Hurd, Phillips was also married although Phillips divorced shortly after the billboards appeared.

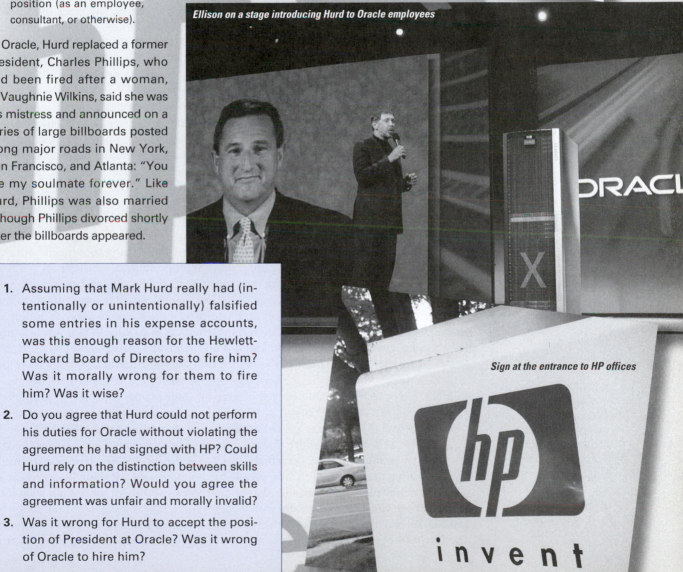

Ellison on a stage introducing Hurd to Oracle employees

Sign at the entrance to HP offices

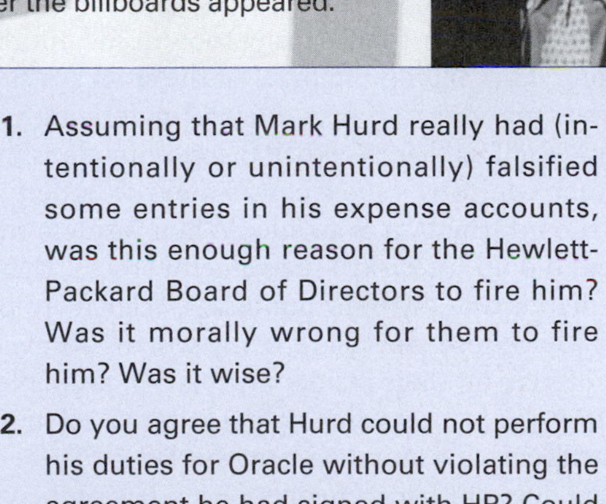

1. Assuming that Mark Hurd really had (intentionally or unintentionally) falsified some entries in his expense accounts, was this enough reason for the Hewlett-Packard Board of Directors to fire him? Was it morally wrong for them to fire him? Was it wise?
2. Do you agree that Hurd could not perform his duties for Oracle without violating the agreement he had signed with HP? Could Hurd rely on the distinction between skills and information? Would you agree the agreement was unfair and morally invalid?
3. Was it wrong for Hurd to accept the position of President at Oracle? Was it wrong of Oracle to hire him?

Some companies have tried to avoid the problem of having employees steal trade secrets—or acquired skills—by having employees sign contracts agreeing not to work for competitors for one or two years after leaving the company. However, courts have generally rejected the validity of such contracts. Other companies have dealt with these problems by agreeing to provide departing employees with continuing remuneration or future retirement benefits in exchange for their not revealing proprietary information, although this leaves the employee free to decide what part of what he or she learned while working for the company is information and what is part of his or her skill-set.

Before leaving the subject of stealing a company's trade secrets, it is worth recalling that a company's property rights over proprietary information are not unlimited. In particular, they are limited by the rights of other agents, such as the rights of employees to know the health risks associated with their jobs. A company's right to keep information secret is not absolute, but must be balanced against the legitimate rights of other parties.

insider trading The act of buying and selling a company's stock on the basis of "inside" information about the company.

Quick Review 8.6

The Ethics of Insider Trading

- Insider trading is said to be unethical because it is theft of information that gives the insider an unfair advantage.
- But it has been defended because (a) it ensures stock prices reflect the true value of the stock, (b) it harms no one, (c) having an advantage over others in the stock market is not wrong in itself and is common with experts.
- These defenses have been criticized because (a) the information the insider uses is not his or hers and so is stolen, (b) trading on inside information has harmful effects on the stock market and increases the costs of buying and selling stocks, (c) the advantage of the inside trader is not like the advantage of an expert because unlike the expert's, it is based on theft.

Insider Trading As a start, we can define ***insider trading*** as buying or selling a company's stock on the basis of "inside" information about the company. "Inside" or "insider" information about a company is proprietary information about a company that is not available to the general public outside the company, but whose availability to the general public would have a material or significant impact on the price of the company's stock. For example, George, the president of a defense company learns that the company is about to receive a multibillion-dollar contract from the government before anyone outside the company is aware of this. So George buys several shares of his company's stock, knowing that its value will rise when the news of the contract becomes public. His purchase of stock is considered to be insider trading. George might also tip off his father, who also hurries to buy some stock before the general public learns about the contract. His father's purchase is also considered to be insider trading.

Insider trading is illegal. During the past decade, a large number of stockbrokers, bankers, and managers have been prosecuted for insider trading. Insider trading is also unethical—not merely because it is illegal, but because, it is claimed, the person who trades on insider information in effect "steals" information and thereby gains an unfair advantage over members of the general public.[14] Several people, however, have argued that insider trading is socially beneficial and, on utilitarian grounds, should not be prohibited but encouraged.[15] We need to look at those arguments.

First, it is sometimes argued, insiders and their friends bring their inside information to the stock market and, by trading on it, bid up the price of the stock (or bid it down) so that its stock market price rises (or falls) to reflect the true underlying value of the stock. Experts on the stock market tell us that the stock market functions most efficiently when the market price of each company's stock equals the true underlying value of the stock as determined by the information available. When insiders trade stocks on their inside information and bid up (or down) the value of stocks, they in effect bring their information to the market and, by their purchases, "signal" to others the information they have about what those stocks are really worth. So insider traders perform the valuable service of making their inside information available to the stock market, thereby ensuring that the market value of stocks more accurately reflects their true underlying value and securing a more efficient market.

Second, it is argued, insider trading does not harm anyone. Defenders of the view that insider trading is wrong sometimes claim that the insider who has special "inside" information somehow harms those people who unwittingly sell their stocks to the insider, not realizing that the insider knows their stocks are worth more than what he or she is paying. But those who claim that insider trading is *not* wrong, point out that when people sell their stocks it is because they need or want the money at that moment. Regardless of whether they sell to the insider or some other party, they will get whatever the current market price of their stock is, i.e., the price before the insider enters the market. Later, of course, when the insider's information becomes available to everyone, they will regret selling because the value of the stock they sold will rise. Yet at the moment they wanted to sell their stock, they would not have received more for their stock from others than what the insider gave them, and they would have received the same if the insider had not entered the market. Moreover, the defenders of insider trading argue, when insiders begin buying up stock on the basis of their inside information, the price of the stock gradually begins to rise. This means that people who need to sell their stocks during that period of rising prices will get more for their stock than they would have received if the insider had not stepped in to raise the price. Therefore, not only does the insider not harm those who sell stocks to him or her right from the beginning, the insider also benefits those who sell stocks to him or her (or others) later.

Third, the defenders of insider trading argue, it is untrue that the insider trader has an unfair advantage over others who do not have access to inside information. The fact is that many of the people who buy and sell stocks on the stock market have more or better information than others. For example, some traders claim that they can analyze coming economic trends, future industry trends, probable new discoveries, and other occurrences and that they can use their analyses to generate information about the future (and so present) value of certain stocks not generally available to the public. There is clearly nothing wrong or unfair about their use of this information to buy or sell stocks. More generally, there is nothing basically unethical or unfair about having an information advantage over others in the stock market.

Those who claim that insider trading is unethical, however, point out that the defenders of insider trading ignore several important facts about insider trading. First, the information that the insider trader uses does not belong to him or her. The executives, managers, employees, and others who work inside a company and who are aware of inside events that will affect the price of the company's stock do not own the company. The resources they work with, including the information that the company makes available to them, are resources that belong collectively to the shareholders. Employees have an ethical (or "fiduciary") duty to refrain from using company information to benefit themselves or their friends. Just as all employees have an ethical duty to use company resources only for the benefit of the shareholder-owners, they also have an ethical duty to use company information only for the benefit of shareholder-owners. Therefore, an insider who takes confidential inside company information and uses it to enrich him or herself is in effect a thief stealing what is not his or hers.

Second, argue those who hold that insider trading is unethical, the information advantage of the insider really is unfair or unjust. Because the information of the insider is information that he or she stole, it is quite unlike the information advantage of stock experts or analysts. The information advantage of the insider is unfair because it is unjustly stolen from others—the company's collective owners—who made the investments that ultimately produced the information he or she stole. The insider's advantage ultimately comes from stealing the fruits of someone else's labor or resources. This is quite unlike the information advantage of the analyst who owns the information she uses because it was produced through her own labors or purchases.

Third, those who claim that insider trading is unethical argue that it is untrue that no one is harmed by insider trading. Both empirical and theoretical studies have shown that insider trading has two effects on the stock market that are harmful to everyone in the market and to society in general. First, insider trading tends to reduce the size of the market, and this harms everyone. Everyone knows that insiders have an advantage, so the more insider trading that people suspect is going on in the market, the more they will tend to leave the market and the smaller it will get. The reduced size of the market will have a number of harmful effects, including (a) a decline in the liquidity

ON THE EDGE

Insider Trading or What Are Friends For?

Noah Freeman and Donald Longueuil were tight friends. When Freeman married his girlfriend, Hannah in 2009, Longueuil was his best man. And when Longueuil became engaged to his girlfriend, Mackenzie, he asked Freeman to be his best man. They met shortly after Freeman graduated from Harvard University and Longueuil from Northeastern University. Both shared a passion for speed skating—Longueuil narrowly missed qualifying for the U.S. Olympic speed skating team. The two met when both joined the Bay State Speedskating Club in Boston. They remained close friends over the years, often skating in races together and taking ski trips together in Utah and New Hampshire. When a girlfriend of Freeman's broke up with him, he was distraught. He could not have made it through, he later said, without Longueuil's friendship. Sometimes, Freeman said, he felt so bad that he could not get out of bed, but Longueuil would come by his place and "get him going." Freeman later met his future wife Hannah, and Longueuil met Mackenzie. Hannah and Mackenzie were also friends who attended Princeton University and were both on Princeton's rowing team, so the two couples often did things together, frequently involving sports activities.

Both Longueuil and Freeman worked for hedge fund companies where their jobs were to grow the funds by investing the fund's money in stocks. When Freeman got a position with Empire Capital, a large hedge fund company, he helped Longueuil land a position in the same company. Later, both worked for SAC Capital, a $12 billion hedge fund, and were each earning over $1 million a year. They met and became friends with Samir "Sam" Barai who also worked with hedge funds. In 2008, Barai started his own hedge fund, Barai Capital Management, with the help of a close friend, Jason Pflaum. To help them research stocks, Longueuil, Freeman, Barai, and Pflaum worked with Primary Global Research (PGR), an "expert network" firm that charges hundreds of thousands of dollars to introduce big investors to "consultants" whom PGR pays to provide expert advice about specific industries or companies. Consultants are often managers of companies in the industry about which they provide advice. Freeman, Barai, and Pflaum were introduced to Winifred Jiau, an expert on technology companies to whom they spoke by phone. Her advice cost them $200,000, but she was able to provide them with information about Marvell Technology Group. She told them what Marvell Technology's revenues, gross margins, and earnings per share would be before the company publicly announced this information. She told them than Marvell's earnings would be higher than expected so the stock was sure to increase in value. Freeman called Longueuil and gave him this information. Barai's hedge fund bought several thousand shares of Marvell stock and made $820,000; Longueuil's fund did the same and made $1.1 million. Another consultant gave Pflaum information about the earnings of two other companies, Advanced Micro Devices and Fairchild Semiconductor. Still other PGR consultants provided information about Nvidia Corporation, Actel Corporation, Cypress Semiconductor, and others. But in 2010, the FBI approached Freeman and Pflaum, and said they would prosecute them for insider trading unless they provided evidence against their friends Longueuil and Barai. They agreed to testify. The four men are no longer friends. Don Longueuil and Mackenzie's wedding was cancelled. Primary Global Research denied knowing what its consultants told the former friends.

1. Were the actions of Longueuil, Freeman, Barai, and Pflaum morally wrong? Assuming they were wrong, then was Freeman and Pflaum's agreement with the FBI a betrayal? What would an ethic of care say about that agreement? Is insider trading something government should be spending its time prosecuting?
2. Was Primary Global Research (PGR) in any way morally responsible for what the friends did? Was Winifred Jiau?

of stocks because it is harder to find buyers and sellers for stock, (b) an increase in the volatility (variability) of stock prices because small variations will make relatively larger differences in the smaller market, (c) a decline in the market's ability to spread risk because there are fewer parties among whom to spread risks, (d) a decline in market efficiency due to the reduced number of buyers and sellers, and (e) a decline in the utility gains available to traders because of the decline in available trades.[16]

A second negative effect of insider trading is that it increases the costs of buying and selling stocks in the market (i.e., the transaction costs), and this is also harmful. Stocks in the New York stock market are always bought and sold through an intermediary called a *specialist*, who charges a small fee for purchasing the stocks of those who want to sell and for holding stocks for those who want to buy them later. When a specialist senses that insiders are coming to him, he will realize that the stock insiders are selling to him—and which the specialist is obligated to hold for others—will later turn out to be worth less than he paid for it (otherwise why would the insiders with their inside information have gotten rid of it?). Therefore, to cover himself from potential future losses, the specialist will start to raise the fee he charges for his services as an intermediary (by increasing the bid-ask spread). The more insiders there are, the more the specialist must raise his fees, and the more costly it becomes to trade that stock. Although in the extreme case the costs may rise so high that the market in a stock breaks down completely, in the less extreme case the rising costs will merely make the stock market just that much more inefficient. In either case, insider trading has a harmful effect on the market.[17]

There are, then, good reasons supporting the view that insider trading is unethical because it violates stockholders' rights, it is based on an unjust informational advantage, and it harms society's overall utility. In short, insider trading violates our moral standards of rights, justice, and utility. But the issue continues to be greatly debated and is still not completely settled.

The law on insider trading, however, is fairly settled, although its exact scope is unclear. The Securities and Exchange Commission (SEC) has prosecuted a large number of insider trading cases, and court decisions in these cases have tended to establish that insider trading is illegal. It has been determined that it consists of trading in a security while in possession of nonpublic information that can have a material effect on the price of the security and that was acquired, or was known to have been acquired, in violation of a person's duty to keep the information confidential.[18] As this definition indicates, it is not just company employees who can be guilty of insider trading, but anyone who knowingly buys or sells stock using information that they know was acquired by a person who had a duty to keep that information confidential. That is, anyone is guilty who trades in stock knowingly using stolen, private information that can affect the stock's price.

The Employer's Obligations to the Employee

The basic moral obligation that the employer has toward employees, according to the rational view of the firm, is to provide them with the compensation they have freely and knowingly agreed to receive in exchange for their services. There are two main ethical issues related to this obligation: the fairness of wages, a special problem in developing nations, and the fairness of employee working conditions.[19] Both wages and working conditions are aspects of the compensation employees receive from their services, and both are related to the question of whether the employee contracted to take a job freely and knowingly. If an employee was "forced" to accept a job with inadequate wages or inadequate working conditions, then the work contract would be unfair.

Wages From a worker's point of view, wages are the principal (perhaps the only) means for satisfying the basic economic needs of the worker and the worker's family. From the employer's point of view, wages are a cost of production that must be kept low lest the product be priced out of the market. Therefore, every employer faces the dilemma of setting fair wages: How can a fair balance be struck between the employer's interests in minimizing costs and the workers' interest in providing a decent living for themselves and their families?

There is no simple formula for determining a "fair wage." The fairness of wages depends in part on the public supports that society provides the worker (Social Security, Medicare, unemployment compensation, public education, welfare, etc.), nonwage benefits companies traditionally provide, the freedom of labor markets, the contribution and productivity of the worker, the needs of the worker and the worker's family, and the competitive position and earnings of the firm. Although there is no way to determine fair salaries with mathematical exactitude, however, we can at least identify a number of factors that should be taken into account in determining wages and salaries in most countries.[20]

1. *The going wage in the industry and the area.* Although labor markets in an industry or an area may be manipulated or distorted (e.g., by job shortages), they generally provide at least rough indicators of fair wages if they are competitive and if we assume competitive markets are just. In addition, the cost of living in the area must be taken into account if employees are to be provided with an income adequate to their families' needs. In developing nations, employers should ensure that wages enable employees to live reasonably and to provide for their families.
2. *The firm's capabilities.* In general, the higher the firm's profits, the more it can and should pay its workers; the smaller its profits, the less it can afford. Taking advantage of cheap labor in captive markets—such as those found in many isolated areas and in developing nations—when a company is perfectly capable of paying fair wages is exploitation.
3. *The job's nature including its risks, skill requirements, and demands.* Jobs that involve greater health and safety risks, require more training or experience, impose heavier physical or emotional burdens, or take greater effort should carry higher levels of compensation.
4. *Minimum wage laws.* The minimum wages required by law set a floor for wages. In most circumstances, wages that fall beneath this floor are unfair. Minimum wage laws should be respected even where government does not enforce those minimums.
5. *Relation to other salaries.* If the salary structure within an organization is to be fair, workers who do roughly similar work should receive roughly similar salaries.
6. *The fairness of wage negotiations.* Salaries and wages that result from "unfree" negotiations in which one side uses fraud, power, ignorance, deceit, or passion to get its way will rarely be fair. For example, when the management of a company uses the threat of relocation to force wage concessions out of a wholly dependent community, or when a union "blackmails" a failing company with a strike that is certain to send the firm into bankruptcy, the resulting wages have little likelihood of being fair.
7. *Local costs of living.* The goods and services that a family needs to meet their basic needs (food, housing, clothing, transportation, child care, and education) differ from one geographical region to another. Wages should be sufficient to enable a family of four to meet their basic needs (taking into account whether families in the region are traditionally one- or two-wage families), even if such wages would be above the minimum wage.

Quick Review 8.7

Fair Wages Depend on

- Wages in the industry and local area
- The firm's ability to pay
- The risks, skills, and demands of the job
- Minimum wage laws
- Fairness in comparison to other salaries in the firm
- Fairness of wage negotiations
- Local living costs (e.g., of a family of four).

These factors are difficult to weigh even in industrialized nations where employers have access to a great deal of labor market information and workers are protected by numerous laws that regulate wages. They are much more difficult to take into account in developing nations where wage regulations and protections are few and information is harder to obtain. Multinationals, of course, generally pay their workers in developing nations more than the prevailing local wage, i.e., more than local companies there pay their workers. Nevertheless, the wages companies from the developed world pay their workers in developing nations are often criticized as being too low. Three kinds of criticisms have been made about the wages paid in developing nations to workers that assemble apparel, shoes, or electronics for companies that market these goods in the United States (such as Nike, Adidas, Gap, Limited, etc.).

First, wages in developing nations are sometimes said to be too low relative to the wages of employees in industrialized nations where these companies are headquartered. For example, according to the U.S. Bureau of Labor Statistics, U.S. workers in the apparel industry were paid $15.29 an hour in 2007. The same year, according to the International Labor Organization (ILO), apparel workers in the Philippines received $ .82 an hour; in Bangladesh they received $.31 an hour; in Mexico, $2.75 an hour; in Thailand, $1.52 an hour; in Egypt, $1.02 an hour; in China, $1.59 an hour; in India, $1.00 an hour; and in Sri Lanka, $.38 an hour. These lower wages cannot be attributed to the "lower productivity" of workers in developing nations because the wage differences are disproportionate to the differences in productivity. According to the ILO, in an hour a U.S. worker produces about 3 times what a Philippino worker produces, but gets paid almost 20 times as much as the Philippino worker; a U.S. worker produces 5 times what a Bangladesh worker produces but gets paid 50 times as much; the U.S. worker produces 1.5 times what a Mexican worker does but gets 5 times as much; he produces 3 times what a Thai worker does but gets 10 times as much; he produces 4 times what a Chinese worker does but gets 10 times as much; and he produces 4 times what an Indian worker does but gets 16 times as much. These wage differences, many activists have argued, are unjust.

Quick Review 8.8

Some Say Wages in Developing Nations are too Low:

- Relative to wages of workers in developed nations, even taking productivity differences into account
- Relative to what companies in developed nations can afford given their overall profits, or relative to the profits they make from products assembled in developing nations
- Relative to what workers in developing nations need to live on.

Second, some critics argue that the wages companies in the industrialized world pay to workers in developing nations are too low relative to what those companies can afford or relative to what they make on the products assembled by workers in developing nations. Gap, for example, has been criticized because its profit margins provide enough for it to afford to pay workers in developing nations a bit more for their work. Gap has also been criticized because its suppliers pay workers in developing nations 28 cents to make a pair of pants that Gap sells for $40 dollars in the United States. Similarly, workers in El Salvador get paid about 24 cents to make an NBA jersey that the NBA sells for $140 in the United States. To critics, such wages are unfair because the large difference between the cost of making the product and the price at which it sells provides more than enough revenue for such companies to be able to afford to pay a few cents more in wages. Moreover, workers in developing countries have significantly greater need for a few cents more in wages than the companies have for a few cents more in profits.

Third, some critics have argued that wages in developing nations are too low relative to what a family needs to live. The term *living wage* is sometimes used to indicate what a wage earner would need to earn to support a family of four in a specific place. For example, according to a report by Labor Behind the Label, prevailing wages for apparel workers in Bangladesh were only 50 percent of what a family of four would need to live in Bangladesh; in Indonesia prevailing wages for apparel workers were 15 to 50 percent of a local living wage; in Lesotho their wages were 50 percent of a local living wage; in Sri Lanka their wages were 25 percent of a local living wage. To some critics, these shortfalls indicate that wages being paid to apparel workers in these nations are unjust because they ignore the needs of their workers.

However, a number of replies have been made to these criticisms. First, it is not clear that wages in one country (such as the United States) should be used as the basis for

Quick Review 8.9

Others Say Wages in Developing Nations are Fine:

- Wages should be set by markets, not by comparisons to other countries.
- Local factors are more important when setting wages than a company's profits.
- Costs of living are important, but wages should also consider the local average number of workers per household.

setting wages in other countries. Shouldn't local labor markets determine local wages? Second, it is also not clear that the retail price of a product in the United States should serve as the basis for setting the wages of workers who make the product in a developing country. Although a company's ability to afford a higher wage is one of several factors that should be considered when setting wages, this is not the same as saying that wages should be determined by the retail prices of the company's product. Other factors such as local labor markets, local cost of living, local industry wage levels, and so on, should also be considered. Third, while the local living costs and needs of workers and their families should influence wage levels, it is important to take into account the number of wage earners that is traditional in the households of workers of a given nation. If a developing nation, for example, traditionally has two or more wage earners per household, then wages that are only 50 percent of a living wage would not necessarily be unjust.

Working Conditions: Health and Safety Each year more than 4,000 workers are killed and 3,000,000 are seriously injured (killed or disabled) while on the job.[21] Ten percent of the job force suffers a job-related injury or illness each year, for a loss of over 31 million workdays annually. Delayed occupational diseases resulting from exposure to chemical and physical hazards kill off additional numbers. Annual costs of work-related deaths and injuries in the United States were $183 billion in 2008.[22]

Workplace hazards include not only the more obvious categories of mechanical injury, electrocution, and burns but also extreme heat and cold, noisy machinery, rock dust, textile fiber dust, chemical fumes, mercury, lead, beryllium, arsenic, corrosives, poisons, skin irritants, and radiation.[23] Many workplace hazards are not recognized until many years after they begin to inflict damage on workers. Asbestos, for example, takes about 20 years before the lung cancers appear that we now know it causes. Although inhaling asbestos fibers was long suspected of being a cause of lung diseases, it was not definitively discovered to be associated with cancer until 1964, long after tens of thousands of workers had been exposed to asbestos in shipyards and other construction projects.

In a similar way, until recently many workers were being exposed to manganese. We now know that manganese inhaled as a vapor or in airborne particles can cause cognitive disorders, tremors, weakness, inability to coordinate movements, and troubled breathing. Workers who have been exposed to manganese vapors on a daily basis include welders, miners, steel workers, some railroad workers, farm workers who have handled pesticides or fertilizers containing manganese, and plant workers involved in factory processes that use manganese. These workers face an uncertain future since many of them will become incapacitated and dependent on others for all their needs.

Occupational Safety and Health Administration (OSHA) Created by the U.S. Congress in 1970 "to assure as far as possible every working man and woman in the nation safe and healthful working conditions."

In 1970, the U.S. Congress passed the Occupational Safety and Health Act and created the **Occupational Safety and Health Administration** (OSHA) "to assure as far as possible every working man and woman in the nation safe and healthful working conditions."[24] Unfortunately, from the beginning, OSHA has been burdened with an inadequate number of field inspectors, and often inefficient forms of regulation. Nevertheless, the existence of OSHA has led many firms to create or improve their safety programs. One poll revealed that 36 percent of the firms surveyed had implemented safety programs as a result of OSHA, and 72 percent said that the existence of OSHA influenced them in their safety efforts.[25] This is reflected in occupational accident rates which have been declining in the United States. Between 1995 and 2009, the rate at which workers were being killed on the job declined dramatically from 18 deaths per 100,000 workers to 3.3 deaths per 100,000. In absolute numbers, the decline was from a total of 6,275 deaths due to occupational injuries in 1995, to a total of 4,340 deaths from occupational injuries in 2009.[26] The absolute number of seriously injured workers (i.e., workers who were disabled or who died), however, increased from 2 million in 1985 to 3.2 million in 2008.[27]

Risk is, of course, an unavoidable part of many occupations. A race-car driver, a circus performer, and a rodeo cowboy all accept certain hazards as part of their jobs.

If an employer (a) takes reasonably adequate measures both to inform him or herself and his or her workers about workplace risks and to eliminate workplace risks, and (b) fully compensates and insures workers for assuming risks that cannot be eliminated, and (c) workers freely and knowingly accept those remaining risks in exchange for the added compensation, then we may generally conclude that the employer has acted ethically.[28] The basic problem, however, is that in many hazardous occupations, these conditions do not obtain, particularly in less developed nations.

1. Wages will fail to provide a level of compensation proportional to the risks of a job when labor markets are not competitive or when markets do not register risks because the risks are not yet known. There are large areas in some developing nations, for example, where a single mining company has a monopoly on jobs. Or the health risks involved in mining or using a certain mineral, such as manganese, may not be known until many years afterward. In such cases, wages will not fully compensate for risks.
2. Workers might accept risks unknowingly because they do not have adequate access to information concerning those risks. Collecting information on the risks of handling certain chemicals, for example, can takes a great deal of time, effort, and money which may not be available in a developing nation. Determining the dangers of asbestos and manganese, for example, took many years of studies. Workers acting individually may find it too costly and time consuming to collect the information needed to assess the risks of the jobs they accept.
3. Workers might accept known risks out of desperation because they lack the mobility to enter other, less risky industries or because they lack information on the alternatives available to them. Low-income manganese miners or welders, for example, may know the hazards inherent in breathing manganese vapors. However, because they lack the resources needed to look elsewhere for a job or to move into a different kind of job, they may be forced to accept the one they have or starve.

Quick Review 8.10

Job Risks

- Are not justified when labor markets are uncompetitive and risks are unknown and uncompensated
- Are not justified when companies fail to collect information on risks and fail to inform workers of risk
- May not be justified when less-risky jobs are unavailable, or when workers lack information about less-risky alternatives.

When any of these three factors are present, the contract between employer and employee is no longer fair. The employer has a duty, in such cases, to take steps to ensure that the worker is not being unfairly manipulated into accepting a risk unknowingly, unwillingly, or without due compensation. Assuming that the employer has eliminated all workplace health and safety hazards that violate local laws and has eliminated all other hazards that can be eliminated with a reasonable investment, then:

1. If any workplace health and safety risks cannot be eliminated at a reasonable cost, the employer has an obligation to fund studies of those risks, to clearly and explicitly inform workers of the risks, particularly those involving health and life, and an obligation to compensate workers for any injuries they sustain.
2. Employers should offer wages that reflect the risk–premiums prevalent in other similar but competitive labor markets, so that workers are adequately compensated for the risks their jobs involve.
3. To insure their workers against unknown hazards, the employer should provide them with suitable health insurance programs and suitable disability insurance.
4. Employers have an obligation (working singly or together with other firms, perhaps through industry associations) to collect information on the health hazards that accompany a given job and make all such information available to workers.

Quick Review 8.11

Establishing Fair Working Conditions Requires

- Eliminating risks when cost is reasonable, studying potential risks of a job, informing workers of known risks, compensating workers for injuries
- Providing compensation for job risks similar to risk-premiums paid in other jobs
- Providing adequate medical and disability benefits
- Working with other firms to collect information about job risks.

sweatshop A workplace that has numerous health and safety hazards and poor working conditions, as well as low wages.

Health and safety issues are particularly problematic in developing nations where worker health and safety laws sometimes set extremely low standards or where governments do not have the resources to enforce the standards that are in place. The term ***sweatshop*** is sometimes used to describe a workplace that has numerous health and safety hazards and poor working conditions, as well as low wages. Clearly, sweatshop conditions are unethical, particularly in nations like the United States where sweatshops are illegal and in violation of various occupational health and safety laws. (Yet, the U.S. Department of Labor estimates that perhaps half of the remaining sewing shops in the United States qualify as sweatshops.) The existence of sweatshops in developing nations, however, is complicated by an added factor: Many sweatshops in developing nations are not owned by the companies for which they produce their goods. Many companies in the United States and other industrialized nations now "outsource" their manufacturing to foreign factories. Nike, for example, pioneered the strategy of designing its athletic shoes in the United States and contracting with factories in Asia to make its shoes in accordance with its designs. While Nike determines the materials, design, quality, and quantity of shoes the factory will produce, the factory itself is owned and managed by someone other than Nike. Virtually all athletic shoe companies today have adopted Nike's strategy of having their shoes manufactured by foreign factories they do not own. Many of these foreign factories are sweatshops with a great many health and safety hazards (and low pay) that can take a heavy toll on their workers.

Quick Review 8.12

Employer Is Morally Responsible for Bad Working Conditions if Employer

- Can and should improve them
- Knows about them
- Is not prevented from changing them.

A key issue that arises when a factory in a developing nation with sweatshop conditions makes products for a U.S. company that does not own the foreign factory is this: what responsibility does the U.S. company have for the sweatshop conditions in the foreign factory? The answer depends on the concept of moral responsibility that we discussed in Chapter 1, where we argued that people are responsible for injuries they cause or fail to prevent when they could and should have done so, provided they knew what was happening and acted out of their own free will. All of these conditions can present difficulties for U.S. companies. Sometimes companies in the United States have little control over what goes on in foreign factories in general; sometimes they do not know what is going on in those foreign factories; and sometimes their actions are constrained by pressures from competitors and stockholders.

Another workplace safety issue that has grown in significance is workplace violence. An average of about 1.7 million workers are the victims of workplace assaults and violence each year in the United States, and about seven hundred of these result in death. Almost a fifth of all U.S. occupational deaths today are the result of assaults and other forms of violence in the workplace. Hoiocide was the third-leading category of fatal occupational injuries in the United States in 2009. According to the U.S. Bureau of Labor Statistics, out of a total of 4,340 fatal work injuries in 2009, some 788 deaths were due to workplace assaults and violence; 521 of these deaths were classified as homicides. The proportion of workplace deaths that are the result of homicides or other violent acts has been rising (from 12 percent of all occupational deaths in 1998, to 18 percent in 2009) and the U.S. Department of Justice has even labeled the U.S. workplace as one of the "most dangerous places" to be in the United States. Seventy percent of all workplace killings occur during robberies of taxicab drivers (the most dangerous occupation), during store robberies (especially stores selling liquor, jewelry, or gasoline), during home deliveries, during truck deliveries, and in restaurant disputes. The other thirty percent are inflicted by angry coworkers (13 percent), customers (7 percent), acquaintances, spouses or former spouses, and relatives. Nonfatal workplace assaults occur primarily in hospitals, nursing homes, and social service agencies.

Clearly, employers have the same obligation to deal with the issue of workplace violence as they have to deal with other health and safety issues in the workplace: Study the workplace in order to identify potential hazards, eliminate those hazards that can be eliminated at a reasonable cost, and educate themselves and their workers about any remaining workplace risks. Thus, employers should familiarize themselves with the issue of workplace violence and assess the potential risks for such violence in their own particular workplace. They should try to eliminate the risk of workplace violence by developing programs to deal with anger and violence among employees and by putting physical mechanisms in place to protect employees from violent customers and clients. And they should train supervisors and employees to recognize the warning signs of violence and to learn how to deal with violence when it emerges.

8.2 The Political Organization

To anyone who has ever worked within a large organization, the goal-directed and efficient structure that the rational model of the organization attributes to business firms will seem somewhat incomplete, if not altogether unreal. Although much of the behavior within organizations accords with the orderly picture drawn by the rational model, a great deal of organizational behavior is neither goal-directed, efficient, or even rational. Employees within organizations often find themselves embroiled in intrigues, ongoing battles for organization resources, feuding between cliques, arbitrary treatment by superiors, scrambles for career advancement, controversies over what the organization's "real" goals are or should be, and disagreements over strategies for pursuing goals. Such behaviors do not seem to fit within the orderly pattern of the rational pursuit of organizational goals.[29] To understand these behaviors and the ethical issues they raise, we must turn to a second model of the firm—one that focuses less on its rational aspects and more on its political features: the **political model of the organization**.[30]

political model of the organization A view of the organization as a system of competing power coalitions and formal and informal lines of influence and communication that radiate from these coalitions; main ethical issues are related to the moral constraints on the use of power in the organization.

The political analysis of the organization that we now sketch is a more recently developed view of organizations than the rational analysis. Unlike the rational model, the political model of the organization does not look merely at the formal lines of authority and communication within an organization, nor does it presume that all organizational behavior is rationally designed to achieve an objective and a given economic goal such as profitability or productivity. Instead, the political model of the organization sees the organization as a system of competing power coalitions and formal and informal lines of influence and communication that radiate from these coalitions.[31] In place of the neat hierarchy of the rational model, the political model postulates a messier and more complex network of clustered power relationships and criss-crossing communication channels (see Figure 8.2).

In the political model of the organization, individuals are seen as grouping together to form coalitions that then compete with each other for resources, benefits, and influence. Consequently, the "goals" of the organization are those established by the historically most powerful or dominant coalition.[32] Goals are not given by "rightful" authority, but are bargained for among more or less powerful coalitions. The fundamental organizational reality, according to this model, is not formal authority or contractual relationships, but power: the ability of the individual (or group of individuals) to modify the conduct of others in a desired way without having one's own conduct modified in undesired ways.[33] An example of an organizational coalition and the nonformal power it can exert even over formal authorities is provided by this account of life in a government organization:

> We had this boss come in from Internal Revenue [to run this OEO department]. He wanted to be very, very strict. He used to have meetings every Friday—about people comin' in late, people leavin' early, people abusin' lunch time.... Every Friday, everyone would sit there and listen to this man. And we'd all go out and

Figure 8.2

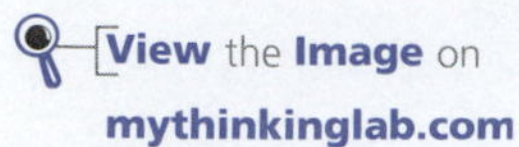

View the Image on mythinkinglab.com

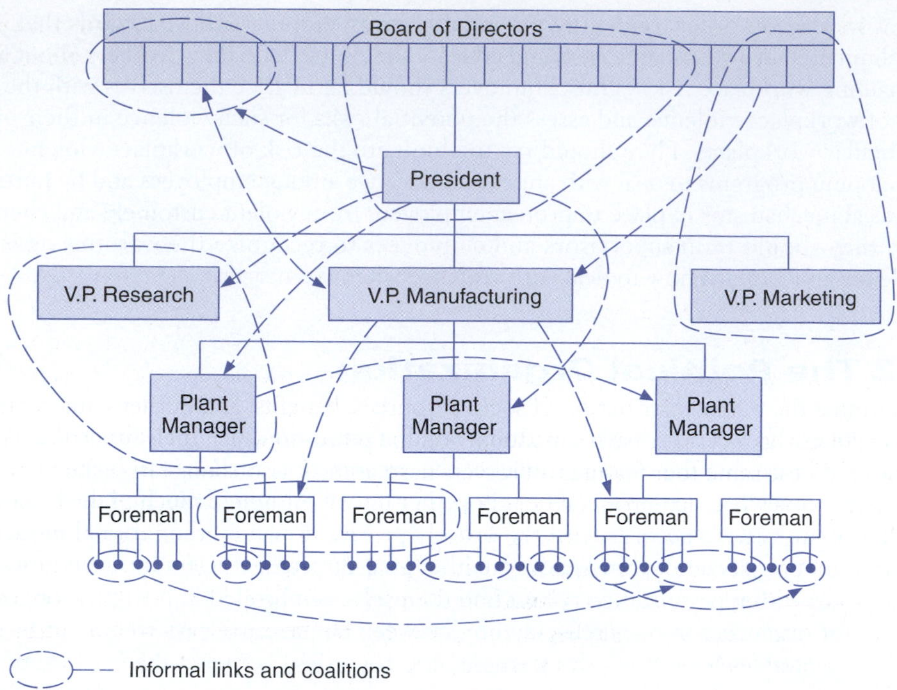

do the same thing again. Next Friday he'd have another meeting and he would tell us the same thing. (Laughs.) We'd all go out and do the same thing again. (Laughs.) He would try to talk to one and see what they'd say about the other. But we'd been working all together for quite awhile. You know how the game is played. Tomorrow you might need a favor. So nobody would say anything. If he'd want to find out what time someone came in, who's gonna tell 'em? He'd want to find out where someone was, we'd always say, "They're at the Xerox." Just anywhere. He couldn't get through.[34]

As this example shows, behavior within an organization may not be aimed at rational organizational goals such as efficiency or productivity, and both power and information may travel completely outside (even contrary to) formal lines of authority and communication. Nonetheless, formal managerial authority and formal communication networks provide rich sources of power. A worker was referring to the power of formal authority when he said, "I don't like the pressure.... If the foreman doesn't like you, he'll make you hold it.... Oh, yeah, the foreman's got somebody knuckling down on him, putting the screws to him." A manager was also referring to the power of formal authority when he said, "You have men working for you and you have a boss above. You're caught in a squeeze. The squeeze progresses from station to station." The formal authority and sanctions put in the hands of superiors are a basic source of the power they wield over subordinates.

If we focus on power as the basic organizational reality, then the main ethical problems we will see when we look at an organization are problems connected with the acquisition and exercise of power. The central ethical issues will focus not on the contractual obligations of employers and employees (as the rational model would focus them), but on the moral constraints to which the use of power within organizations must be subjected. The ethics of organizational behavior as seen from the perspective of the political model focus on this question: What are the moral limits, if any, to the exercise of power within organizations? In the sections that follow, we discuss two aspects of this question: (1) What, if any, are the moral limits to the power managers acquire and exercise over their subordinates? (2) What, if any, are the moral limits to the power employees acquire and exercise on each other?

Employee Rights

Observers of corporations have repeatedly pointed out that the power of modern corporate management is similar to that of a government.[35] This similarity is the basis of what we can call the "similarity argument" in support of employee rights. The similarity argument goes like this: Governments are defined in terms of four features: (1) a centralized decision-making body of officials who (2) have the power and recognized authority to enforce their decisions on subordinates (citizens); these officials (3) make decisions that determine the public distribution of social resources, benefits, and burdens among their subordinates, and (4) they have a monopoly on the power to which their subordinates are subject. These same four features, observers have argued, also characterize the managerial hierarchies that run large corporations: (a) Like a city, state, or federal government, the top managers of a corporation constitute a centralized decision-making body that has considerable power; (b) these managers wield power and legally recognized authority over their employees—a power that is based on their ability to fire, demote, or promote employees and an authority that is based on the law of agency that stands ready to recognize and enforce managerial decisions; (c) the decisions of managers determine the distribution of income, status, and freedom among the corporation's constituencies; and (d) through the law of agency and contract, through their access to government agencies, and through the economic leverage they possess, managers of large corporations effectively share in the monopoly on power that political governments possess.[36]

Quick Review 8.13

Similarity Argument

- Similarities between the power of management and government imply employees should have rights similar to citizens' rights.
- A company's management is a centralized decision-making body that exercises power, like a government.
- Managements wield power and authority over employees, like governments wield over citizens.
- Management has the power to distribute income, status, and freedom among the corporation's constituencies, like government does with respect to citizens.
- Management shares in the monopoly on power that government possesses.
- Since management's power over employees is so similar to government's power over citizens, employees should have rights that protect them from managers' power, just as citizens' rights protect them from government power.

These analogies between governments and managements, several observers have held, show that the power managers have over their employees is fully comparable to the power government officials have over their citizens. Consequently, if there are moral limits to the power government officials may legitimately exercise over citizens, then there are similar moral limits that should constrain the power of managers.[37] In particular, these authors argue, just as the power of government should respect the civil rights of citizens, so the power of managers must respect the moral rights of employees. What are these employee rights? The moral rights of employees would be similar to the civil rights of citizens: the right to privacy, the right to consent, the right to freedom of speech, and so on.[38]

The major objection to this similarity argument for employee rights is that there are a number of important differences between the power of corporate managers and the power of government officials, and these differences undercut the argument that the power of managers should be limited by employee rights comparable to the civil rights that limit the power of government. First, the power of government officials (in theory at least) is based on consent, whereas the power of corporate managers is (in theory again) based on ownership. Government officials rule because they have been elected or because they have been appointed by someone who has been elected; corporate managers *rule* (if that is the right word) because they own the firm for which workers freely choose to work or because they have been appointed by the owners of the firm. Consequently, because the power of government rests on the consent of the governed, that power can legitimately be limited when the governed choose to limit it. However, because the power of managers rests on ownership of the firm, they have the right to impose whatever conditions they choose to impose on employees, who freely and knowingly contracted to work on their firm's premises.[39] Second, the power of corporate managers, unlike that of most government officials, is effectively limited by unions: Most blue-collar and some white-collar workers belong to a union that provides them with a degree of countervailing power that limits the power of management. Accordingly, moral rights need not be invoked to protect the interests

Quick Review 8.14

Replies and Counter-replies to Similarity Argument:

- Power of government is based on consent and so is unlike the power of managers which is based on ownership of the company, but supporters of similarity argument respond that today power of managers does not come from owners.
- Unlike government, the power of management is limited by unions, but supporters of similarity argument respond that most workers today are not unionized.
- While it is hard for citizens to escape the power of a government, it is easy for employees to escape the power of managers by changing jobs, but supporters of similarity argument respond that changing jobs is not always so easy.

of employees.[40] Third, whereas a citizen can escape the power of a particular government only at great cost (by changing citizenship), an employee can escape the owner of a particular management with considerable ease (by changing jobs). Because of the relatively high costs of changing citizenship, citizens need civil rights that can insulate them from the inescapable power of government. They do not need similar employee rights to protect them from the power of a corporation whose influence is easily escaped.[41]

Advocates of employee rights have responded to these three objections in a number of ways: First, they claim, corporate assets are no longer controlled by private owners; they are now held by a dispersed and almost powerless group of stockholders. This kind of dispersed ownership implies that managers no longer function as agents of the firm's owners and, consequently, that their power no longer rests on property rights.[42] Second, although some workers are unionized, most today are not, and these nonunionized workers have moral rights that managers do not always respect.[43] Third, changing jobs is sometimes as difficult and traumatic as changing citizenship, especially for the employee who has acquired specialized skills that can be used only within a specific organization.[44]

There is, then, a continuing controversy over the adequacy of the general argument that, because managements are like governments, the same civil rights that protect citizens must also protect employees. Regardless of whether this general argument is accepted, a number of independent arguments have been advanced to show that employees have certain particular rights that managers should respect. We will look at these arguments in the next sections.[45]

The Right to Privacy As indicated in Chapter 6, the *right to privacy* can be defined as the right people have to determine what, to whom, and how much information about themselves shall be disclosed to others. The employee's right to privacy has become particularly vulnerable with the development of recent technologies, particularly computer technologies.[46] Employees who use telephones and computers can be legally monitored by their employer, who may wish to check how fast they are working, whether they are engaged in personal or business-related activities, or simply what they are doing. Polygraph or "lie detector" machines, although generally prohibited by federal law in most industries, are still allowed during internal investigations of suspected employee theft or economic loss and in a number of "exempt" industries. Computerized methods of obtaining, storing, retrieving, collating, and communicating information have made it possible for employers to collect and keep personal information about their employees, such as company medical records, credit histories, criminal and arrest histories, FBI information, and employment histories. Genetic testing, although not yet widely used by many companies, already allows employers to test an employee for about 50 genetic traits that indicate that the employee will be more likely than others to develop certain diseases (such as cystic fibrosis or sickle-cell anemia) or be affected by certain workplace toxins or occupational hazards. It is expected that, in the future, genetic tests of workers and job candidates will enable employers to screen out a wide range of workers whose genes indicate that they are likely to add to the company's medical insurance costs or add to the costs of installing workplace protections. Urine tests allow companies to screen out employees who take drugs, drink alcohol, or smoke tobacco at home. Written psychological tests, personality inventory tests, and honesty tests make it possible for an employer to uncover a wide range of personal characteristics and tendencies that most persons would rather keep private, such as their level of honesty or their sexual orientation. Not only have these innovations made a person's privacy more vulnerable, but they have come at a time when managers are particularly anxious to learn more about their employees. Advances in industrial psychology have demonstrated relationships between an employee's private home life or personality traits and on-the-job performance and productivity.

Sergeant Quon's Text Messages

Jeff Quon worked as a sergeant on the SWAT team of the Ontario, California Police Department. The Department provided him and all other officers with pagers that allowed text messaging with a monthly limit of 25,000 characters, above which the city of Ontario had to pay extra. The city issued a written "Communication Usage, Internet, and E-Mail Policy" which said "the use of these tools for personal benefit is a significant violation of City of Ontario Policy," but "some incidental and occasional personal use of the e-mail system, if limited to light personal communications" is permitted. In addition, the Policy continued, "The City of Ontario reserves the right to monitor and log all network activity including e-mail and Internet use, with or without notice; users should have no expectation of privacy or confidentiality when using these resources." The Policy reminded officers that all such "messages are also subject to 'access and disclosure' in the legal system and the media," i.e., they could be revealed if a court subpoenaed them during a trial or if reporters requested them under a freedom of information statute or a public records disclosure statute. Sergeant Quon signed an acknowledgement that he read and understood the policy. In addition, he attended a meeting where all officers were told that pager messages were considered emails under the policy "and could be audited." A few days later he received a memo reminding him of that policy.

When Quon went over the 25,000 character monthly limit on his pager for the first time, he was approached by a superior, Lieutenant Steve Duke. Lieutenant Duke reminded him that his messages "could be audited." However, the Lieutenant explicitly added, he would not "audit employees' text messages to see if the overage was due to work-related transmissions" so long as the employee "reimbursed the City for [the] overage." Only if Quon did not pay for the overage would it be necessary to "audit the transmission to see how many messages were work-related." Sergeant Quon paid the overage in full and when he went over the limit three or four more times, he also paid each overage in full and, as the Lieutenant had said, his messages were not examined. But when he went over the limit a fifth time, Lieutenant Duke did not ask Quon to pay for the overage but instead obtained a transcript of all his messages and read through them. He discovered that some messages were to or from Quon's wife, "while others were directed to or from his mistress" and some of these were sexually explicit. The Lieutenant showed these to his superior, Chief Scharf, and pointed out that the department's policy expressly prohibited "the use of inappropriate, derogatory, obscene, suggestive, defamatory, or harassing language" in messages.

1. What, ethically, should Chief Scharf do? What should Lieutenant Duke do?
2. Was Lieutenant Duke's assurance that he would not examine Sergeant Quon's messages so long as Quon paid for any overage an implicit agreement that he was entitled to rely on? Was it an implicit agreement that Duke was morally required to keep?
3. Did Lieutenant Duke or Chief Scharf violate Sergeant Quon's right to privacy? If they did, explain why; if they did not, then explain what additional events would have to happen for the incident to be a violation of the right to privacy and why those additions are necessary.
4. Since Quon worked for a city government, do you think the Fourth Amendment's right to freedom from government "unreasonable search and seizure" should apply?

Source: Erwin Chemerinsky, "Does the Fourth Amendment's Right to Privacy Protect Personal Communications over a Government-Issued Pager?' available online at *www.abanet.org/publiced/preview/Quon.pdf.*

As mentioned previously in Chapter 6, there are two types of privacy: psychological privacy, which is privacy regarding one's inner thoughts, plans, beliefs, values, feelings, and wants; and physical privacy, which is privacy with respect to one's physical activities, particularly those that reveal one's inner life and those that involve physical or personal functions that are culturally recognized as private.[47] Each of us has a significant interest in privacy, which justifies protecting privacy by surrounding it with the protection of a right. Privacy protects us: It lets us protect information about ourselves that could embarrass or shame us, it protects us from having others interfere in our lives merely because they disagree with our values, it lets us protect those we love from knowledge about ourselves that might hurt them, and, more generally, it protects our reputation. Privacy also empowers or enables us: It enables us to have intimacy, which lets us develop personal relationships of love, friendship, and trust; it enables us to maintain confidential relationships with professionals such as doctors, lawyers, and psychiatrists; it enables us to maintain private social roles that are distinct from our public roles; and it enables us to determine our self-identity by letting us control the way that society in general and selected individuals will look on us.

Hence, it is clear that employees, like others, have a significant interest in maintaining privacy over information about themselves, and so employees must be recognized as having a right to privacy. However, this right must be balanced against the rights and needs of others. In particular, employers sometimes have a legitimate right to inquire into the activities of employees or prospective employees. The employer is justified in wanting to know, for example, what a job candidate's past work experience has been and whether the candidate has performed satisfactorily on previous jobs. An employer may also be justified in wanting to identify the culprits when the firm finds itself the subject of pilferage or employee theft and of subjecting employees to on-the-job surveillance to discover the source of thefts. How are these rights to be balanced against the right to privacy? Three elements must be considered when collecting information that may threaten the employee's right to privacy: relevance, consent, and method.[48]

Quick Review 8.15

Employee Right to Privacy

- Is threatened by today's technologies
- Is justified because of the interest we have in the protective and enabling functions of privacy
- Requires that managers consider relevance, consent, and methods when collecting information about employees.

Relevance The employer must limit inquiry into the employee's affairs to those areas that are directly relevant to the issue at hand. Although employers have a right to know the person whom they are employing and to know how the employee is performing, employers are not justified in inquiring into any areas of the employee's life that do not directly and significantly affect the employee's performance. To investigate an employee's political beliefs or social life, for example, is wrong because it is an invasion of the employee's right to privacy. For the same reason, if a firm acquires information about an employee's personal life in the course of a legitimate investigation, it is wrong to record and keep the information, especially when such data would embarrass or otherwise injure the employee if it were leaked.

The dividing lines between justified and unjustified investigations are fairly clear with respect to lower-level employees: There is clearly little justification for investigating the marital problems, political activities, or emotional characteristics of clerical workers, sales workers, or factory laborers. The dividing line between what is and is not relevant, however, becomes less clear as one moves higher in the firm's management hierarchy. Executives are called on to represent their company before others, and the company's reputation can be significantly damaged by an executive's private activities or emotional instability. A chief executive officer's drinking problem or membership in a disreputable association, for example, will affect that officer's ability to represent the firm. When hiring for such positions, the firm may be justified in inquiring into a candidate's personal life or psychological history because these can be relevant to what the candidate is being hired to do.

Consent Employees must be given the opportunity to give or withhold their consent before the private aspects of their lives are investigated. Every person, as Kant argued, has the moral right to be treated only as they have consented to be treated. The firm, therefore, is justified in inquiring into the employee's life only if the employee has a clear understanding that the inquiry is being made and clearly consents to this as part of the job or can freely choose to refuse the job. The same principle holds when an employer undertakes some type of surveillance of employees for the purpose of, say, uncovering or preventing pilferage. Employees should be informed of such surveillance so they can ensure they will not inadvertently reveal their personal lives while under surveillance. Announcing such surveillance, moreover, may itself be sufficient to stop the pilferage.

Methods The employer must distinguish between methods of investigation that are both ordinary and reasonable, as well as methods that are neither. Ordinary methods include the supervisory activities that are normally used to oversee employees' work and that employees can be presumed to know about and to consent to as part of their explicit or implicit contract with the firm. Extraordinary methods include devices like hidden microphones, secret cameras, wiretaps, lie detector tests, personality inventory tests, and spies. Such extraordinary methods are unreasonable and unjustified unless the circumstances are extraordinary. Extraordinary methods of investigation might be justified if a firm is suffering heavy losses from employee theft that ordinary supervision has failed to stop. Extraordinary devices, however, are not justified merely because the employer hopes to be able to pick up some interesting information about employee loyalties. In general, the use of extraordinary devices is justified only when the following conditions have been met: (a) The firm has a problem that can be solved in no other manner than by employing such extraordinary means; (b) the problem is serious and the firm has well-founded grounds for thinking that the use of extraordinary means will identify the culprits or put an end to the problem; (c) the use of the extraordinary devices is not prolonged beyond the time needed to identify the wrongdoers or after it becomes clear that the devices will not work; (d) all information that is uncovered but not directly relevant to the purposes for which the investigation was conducted is disregarded and destroyed; and (e) the failure rate of any extraordinary devices employed (such as lie detectors, drug tests, or psychological tests) is taken into account, and all information derived from devices with a known failure rate is verified through independent methods that are not subject to the same failures.

> *Quick Review 8.16*
>
> **The Right to Freedom of Conscience**
>
> - Is justified by the interest we have in remaining true to our religious and moral convictions
> - Must be balanced against the legitimate rights of the firm, its stockholders, and fellow employees
> - Implies that whistleblowing to prevent a wrong that violates our moral convictions is *morally justified* when: (a) the wrong is clear, (b) other methods have failed, (c) it will prevent the wrong, and (d) the wrong is serious enough to justify the personal and other costs of whistleblowing
> - Whistleblowing is a *moral obligation* for a person when (a)–(d) hold, and, in addition, the person has a special duty to prevent the wrong or is the only person who will or can prevent the wrong, and the wrong involves an extremely serious harm to society's welfare, or extremely serious injustice, or extremely serious violation of rights.

The Right to Freedom of Conscience Employee sometimes discover that the corporation they work for is doing something that the employee believes is seriously and morally wrong. Indeed, individuals inside a corporation are usually the first to learn that the corporation is marketing unsafe products, polluting the environment, suppressing health information, or violating the law.

Responsible employees who find that their company is injuring society in some way will normally feel they have a moral obligation to get the company to stop its harmful activities and consequently, will bring the matter to the attention of their superiors. Unfortunately, if the internal management of the company refuses to do anything about the matter, the employee today has few other legal options available. If, after being rebuffed by the company, the employee has the temerity to take the matter to a government agency outside the firm or, worse, to disclose the company's activities to the public, the company has the legal right to punish the employee by firing. Furthermore, if the matter is serious enough, the company can reinforce this punishment by putting the matter on the employee's record and, in extreme cases, seeing to it that the employee is black-balled by other companies in the industry.[49]

Several authors have argued that this is in effect a violation of an individual's right to freedom of conscience.[50] It is a violation of the right to freedom of conscience because the individual is forced to cooperate with an activity that violates the individual's personal moral beliefs. What is the basis of this right? The right to freedom of conscience derives from the interest that individuals have in being able to adhere to their religious or moral convictions.[51] Individuals who have religious or moral convictions commonly see them as absolutely binding and can transgress them only at great psychological cost. The right to freedom of conscience protects this interest by requiring that individuals not be forced to cooperate in activities that they conscientiously believe are wrong.

These arguments, however, have had only a small impact on the law, which still by and large supports the employee's duty of maintaining loyalty and confidentiality toward the employer's business.[52] A few laws have been passed, however, that afford some protection to the employee who is concerned that his or her company is violating the law or is engaged in immoral activities. These laws protect the practice of what is called **whistleblowing**.[53] We will look at those laws shortly, but first we will discuss what whistleblowing itself is.

whistleblowing An attempt by a member or former member of an organization to disclose wrongdoing in or by the organization.

Whistleblowing **Whistleblowing** is an attempt by a member or former member of an organization to disclose wrongdoing in or by the organization including violations of the law, fraud, health or safety violations, bribery, or a potential or actual injury to the public. Mr. Mackowiak, for example, was hired as a welding inspector by University Nuclear Systems, Inc. (UNSI), a firm responsible for installing the heating, ventilating, and air-conditioning system at a nuclear power plant owned by the Washington Public Power Supply system. Mackowiak was supposed to inspect the work of UNSI employees and make sure it conformed to federal quality and safety standards—a task that was mandated by federal regulations requiring builders of nuclear power plants to give their inspectors the authority and organizational freedom they needed to fulfill their role as independent observers of the construction process. However, some UNSI employees refused to give Mackowiak access to areas in which work was being done in a manner that violated federal specifications. Mackowiak went to his superiors and told them that he believed the company was violating federal regulations, but he was illegally being prevented from inspecting the areas where the violations were taking place. When he was unable to get them to respond to his concerns, Mackowiak *blew the whistle* on the company. He met with officials of the Nuclear Regulatory Commission (NRC) at his home and disclosed to them his concerns about the safety and quality control of the work of UNSI. The NRC took his allegations seriously and conducted a full investigation of UNSI that verified the problems and forced the company to correct them. However, UNSI discovered that it was Mackowiak who had talked to the federal agents and early the following year the company fired him because, the company said, he had a "mistrustful attitude toward management," although his "inspection qualifications/expertise is excellent and he is a good inspector."[54]

Whistleblowing can be internal or external. If the wrongdoing is reported only to higher-ups within the organization, as Mackowiak initially did, it is internal whistleblowing. When the wrongdoing is reported to external individuals or bodies such as government agencies, newspapers, or public interest groups, the whistleblowing is said to be external. When Mackowiak reported his concerns to the Nuclear Regulatory Commission, for example, his act became external whistleblowing.

As Mackowiak's experience shows, blowing the whistle is often a brave act of conscience that can carry heavy personal costs. A study of whistleblowers found that the average whistleblower is a 47-year-old family man who has been a conscientious employee for 7 years and who has strong belief in universal moral principles.[55] The same study reported that 100 percent of the whistleblowers surveyed who worked for private businesses were fired by their employers; 20 percent could still not find work at the time of the survey; 25 percent had suffered increased financial burdens on their family; 17 percent lost their homes; 54 percent had been harassed by their peers at work; 15 percent viewed their subsequent divorce as a result of their whistleblowing; 80 percent suffered physical deterioration; 86 percent reported emotional stress, including feelings of depression, powerlessness, isolation, and anxiety; and 10 percent reported having attempted suicide. Nevertheless, most of the whistleblowers surveyed had few regrets and would do it again. Typical of the comments they made to the survey team were the following: "This has turned out to be the most frightening thing I have ever done. But it has also been the most satisfying. I think I did the right thing, and I have caused some changes to be made in the plant," "Do what is right. Lost income can be replaced. Lost self-esteem is more difficult to retrieve," and "Finding honesty within myself was more powerful than I expected."

It is sometimes argued that external whistleblowing is always wrong because employees have a contractual duty to be loyal to their employer and to keep all aspects of the business confidential. When an employee accepts a job, the argument goes, the employee implicitly agrees to keep all aspects of the business confidential and to single-mindedly pursue the best interests of the employer. The whistleblower violates this agreement and thereby violates the rights of the employer.

Although part of what this argument asserts is true, the conclusion is false. It is true that an employee enters an agreement to act on behalf of the employer in all matters pertaining to the business and that the employee also implicitly or explicitly agrees to keep trade secrets and other proprietary information secret. However, this agreement is not unqualified, and it does not impose on the employee unlimited obligations toward the employer. As we saw in an earlier discussion, agreements and contracts are void if they require a person to do something immoral. Consequently, if an employee has a moral obligation to prevent other people from being harmed and the only way to prevent the harm is by blowing the whistle on one's employer, an employment agreement cannot require the employee to remain silent. In such a situation, the employment agreement would be void because it would require immorally failing to do what the employee is morally obligated to do. Thus, external whistleblowing is justified if it is necessary to prevent a wrong that one has a moral duty to prevent, or if it will yield a benefit that one has a moral right or duty to provide.

It is also false, as it is sometimes argued, that external whistleblowing is always morally justified on the grounds that all persons, including employees, have a right to freedom of speech. When employees disclose what is going on in a firm to external parties, the argument holds, they are merely exercising their right to freedom of speech and their act is, therefore, morally justified. However, this argument ignores the fact that the right to freedom of speech, like all other rights, is limited by the rights of other persons. In particular, an employee's right to freedom of speech is limited by the rights of the employer and other parties. Because of the employment contract, the employer has a right to have employees keep proprietary matters secret and to have the employee pursue the employer's best interests, provided the employee is not thereby forced to do anything immoral. Moreover, other parties—such as stockholders or fellow employees—who can be injured by external whistleblowing also have a right not to be subjected to such injuries needlessly or without a proportionately serious reason. Thus, external whistleblowing can be justified only if other means—such as internal whistleblowing—of preventing a wrong have been tried, but have failed and only if the harm that is to be prevented is much more serious than the harm that will result to other parties.

External whistleblowing is morally justified if

1. there is clear, substantiated, and reasonably comprehensive evidence that the organization is engaged in some activity that is seriously wronging or will seriously wrong other parties;
2. reasonably serious attempts to prevent the wrong through internal whistleblowing have been tried and have failed;
3. it is reasonably certain that external whistleblowing will prevent the wrong; and
4. the wrong is serious enough to justify the injuries that external whistleblowing will probably inflict on oneself, one's family, and other parties.

To say that external whistleblowing is *justified* is not the same as saying that it is *obligatory*. Although it may be morally permissible for a person to blow the whistle on a company, this does not mean that the person also has a moral duty or moral obligation to do so.[56] Under what conditions is it not only permissible but obligatory for a person to engage in external whistleblowing? Whistleblowing is merely a means to an end—the end of correcting or preventing a wrong—therefore, a person has an obligation to take this means only to the extent that there is an obligation to achieve the end. Clearly, a person has a moral obligation to engage in whistleblowing only when there is a moral obligation to prevent the wrong that whistleblowing will prevent. When does a person have an obligation to prevent a wrong? Assuming that above conditions 1 to 4 are met, so that whistleblowing is at least permissible, a person has an obligation to blow the whistle when (a) that specific person has a moral duty to prevent the wrong, either because it is part of the person's specific professional responsibilities (e.g., as an accountant, environmental officer, professional engineer, lawyer, etc.) or because no one else can or will prevent the wrong in which the company is involved; and (b) the wrong involves serious harm to society's overall welfare, serious injustice against a person or group, or serious violation of the basic moral rights of one or more people. For example, when a company is involved in activities that can result in substantial health injuries to many people who have a right to be protected from such injuries, and no one else in the company is willing to bring these activities to a halt, then I have an obligation to prevent the wrong even if this means resorting to whistleblowing.

In many companies conscientious employees have to resort to external whistleblowing because the company has not provided a way for them to voice their concerns internally, or because they fear reprisals if they do so.[57] To overcome these problems, many companies have set up "ethics hotlines"—toll-free telephone numbers—that employees can use to report legal or ethical violations anonymously to upper management or to an "ethics officer" who is empowered to investigate the allegations.[58]

The U.S. Congress has now passed several laws that protect whistleblowers from retaliation. For example, the "Whistleblower Protection Act" prohibits retaliation against *government employees* who report violations of a law or management actions that create substantial dangers to public health or safety. The Sarbanes-Oxley Act protects *employees of publicly traded companies* who report wrongdoing to public authorities. And the False Claims Act not only prohibits retaliation against whistleblowers who report fraud company against the government, but rewards them by giving them between 15 and 30 percent of what the government recovers. In spite of these laws, however, many whistleblowers still pay heavy costs when they blow the whistle on their employer. Some managers ignore these laws thinking the company will shield them from legal sanctions, and fellow employees often ostracize a whistleblower because they feel he or she "snitched" or "ratted" on their company.

Workers' Right to Participate in Decisions that Affect Them A democratic political tradition has long held that government should be subject to the consent of the governed because individuals have a right to liberty, and this right implies that they have a right to participate in the political decisions that affect them. Within a democracy, therefore, political decision making usually has two characteristics: (1) Decisions that affect the group are made by a majority of its members, and (2) decisions are made after full, free, and open discussion.[59] Either all the members of the group participate in these decision-making processes or they do so through elected representatives.

A number of authors have proposed that these ideals of democracy should be embodied in business organizations.[60] Some have argued that enabling the individual employee within the organization to participate in the decision-making processes of the organization is an "ethical imperative."[61] As a first step toward such democracy, some have suggested that although decisions affecting workers should not be made by workers, they should, nonetheless, be made only after full, free, and open discussion with workers. This would mean open communication between workers and their supervisors and the establishment of an environment that encourages consultation with workers. Employees would be allowed to freely express criticism, receive accurate information about decisions that will affect them, make suggestions, and protest decisions.

A second step toward "organizational democracy" would give individual employees not only the right to consultation, but also the right to make decisions about their own immediate work activities. These decisions might include matters such as working hours, rest periods, organization of work tasks, and scope of responsibility of workers and supervisors.

A third step toward extending the ideals of democracy into the workplace would allow workers to participate in the major policy decisions that affect the general operations of the firm. Many European firms, for example, particularly in Germany, have adopted the concept of *codetermination*.[62] German law requires that firms in the basic industries (coal, iron, and steel) and firms with more than 2,000 employees have a board of directors elected in part by stockholders and in part (usually one less than half) by employees. In most German companies, "work councils" composed of workers are kept informed and consulted about major issues that will affect them such as plant shutdown or relocation, mergers with other firms, or introduction of fundamentally new labor methods. The board of directors elect a "director of human resources" who is part of top management and who serves as a representative of the workers on the management team. Relations between management and labor are generally harmonious and cooperative and decisions are usually based on consensus. Productivity is high and most decisions take a long-term and inclusive approach to issues.

Full organizational democracy has not been particularly popular in the United States. Part of the reason, perhaps, is that employees have not shown a great deal of interest in participating in the firm's broader policy decisions. A more important reason, however, is that U.S. ideology distinguishes sharply between the power exercised in political organizations and the power exercised within economic organizations: Power in political organizations, it is assumed, should be democratic, whereas power in economic organizations should be left in the private hands of managers and owners.[63] Whether this ideological distinction is valid is something the reader must decide.

Some management thinkers have urged managers to bring democratic processes into business organizations in the guise of *participative management*. They have argued that bringing democratic leadership styles into business organizations will increase worker satisfaction and productivity. So on utilitarian grounds more democracy should be integrated into the organization. One of the earliest such views was that of Douglas McGregor who described two "theories" managers can have about

Quick Review 8.17

The Right to Participate

- Is based on the right to freely decide how I will lead my life and to participate in decisions that affect my life
- Can mean open discussion, or consultation, or full participation in policy decisions
- Supports the kind of participative management advocated by McGregor's "Theory Y," Miles' "human relations" and "human resources" models, and Likert's System 3 "consultative" and System 4 "participative" systems of organization
- McGregor, Miles, and Likert supported their views with the utilitarian argument that adopting their theories made organizations more productive.

employees.[64] In one theory, "Theory X," managers assume that employees are naturally lazy and need to be rewarded, punished, and controlled to get them to work toward organizational objectives. Managers who subscribe to Theory X tend to be more authoritarian, controlling, and so less democratic. In the other theory, "Theory Y," managers assume that employees want and can develop the capacity to accept responsibility and can be trusted to find the best means for achieving these goals on their own. Theory Y, McGregor held, is a more accurate description of modern workers, and so managers should use a participative and democratic style of management if they want to create a more effective and productive organization.

A later view, espoused by Raymond Miles, largely agreed with McGregor, but went a step beyond him by distinguishing not two but three mental "models" of employees managers can hold.[65] They could hold a "traditional" model like McGregor's Theory X, or a "human relations" model like Mile's Theory Y. But a third more enlightened model of workers is a "human resources" model, which assumes that workers want to contribute to meaningful goals that they help establish democratically, and can exercise more self-direction than most managers believe they can. Miles proposed that if managers take a "human resources" view of workers, worker satisfaction and organizational effectiveness will increase. Yet another view, developed by Rensis Likert, went one more step beyond Miles's theory to posit not three, but four "systems of organization" that could serve as the basis for running a company: System 1, the "exploitive authoritative"; System 2, the "benevolent authoritative"; System 3, the "consultative"; and System 4, the "participative."[66] Likert argued that System 4, which incorporates the highest levels of democratic employee participation and self-direction, would yield the highest levels of organizational effectiveness and productivity.

participative management
A management style that emphasizes inclusion of employees in evaluation and decision-making processes.

If democratic **participative management** styles like those advocated in different ways by McGregor, Miles, and Likert make organizations more effective and productive, then on utilitarian grounds, managers should bring these elements of democracy into organizations. However, the research on whether a more democratic participative management style leads to greater worker satisfaction and a more effective and productive organization has not come to firm conclusions. In some companies (e.g., Semco, a Brazilian company)[67] participative management has been spectacularly successful, enabling entire plants to be turned from unproductive "disasters" into highly efficient "dynamos."[68] In other companies, participative management has not had substantial positive effects on performance or productivity although it usually has positive effects on employee job satisfaction.[69] Moreover, critics of the participative approach to management have argued both that people are different and do not all want to participate in management decision-making and that organizations and organizational tasks are different and are not all suited to participatory decision-making. If this is correct, then the utilitarian argument in favor of democracy as "participative management" at most shows that managers should use participative management and its democratic processes, but only with the right people and in the right organizational contexts.[70] Organizational democracy might not be for everyone! Nevertheless, many authors have argued, given the large place that business organizations are now occupy in our daily lives, democracy will touch only the peripheral areas of our lives if it is restricted to political organizations.[71]

The Right to Due Process versus Employment at Will When a General Motors' internal investigation uncovered what it considered sufficient evidence of a secret employee scheme to defraud the company, without consulting the employees the investigative team felt were involved, GM quickly doled out what one journalist called "an almost ruthless brand of corporate justice" in his description of the subsequent firings at GM's Tarrytown, New York, offices. Only a few days before their paid Christmas holidays were to begin, and with no previous warning, GM officials called 25 salaried employees into a series of three offices where they were fired in the first office, then stripped of their company cars and other benefits in the second office, and finally, in the third office, were given the cab fare they needed to get home. One employee who had worked for the company for more than 20 years later indicated that he "recalls watching in disbelief as a GM functionary with a map and a ruler measured off the distance to his home and handed him $15." Within a matter of hours the GM officials fired virtually the entire staff that had formerly supervised all Chevrolet dealers in New York City.[72]

Until recently, U.S. labor law has given a prominent position to the principle of **employment at will**, the doctrine that employers "may dismiss their employees at will... for good cause, for no cause, or even for causes morally wrong, without being thereby guilty of legal wrong."[73] The doctrine of employment at will has been defended on several grounds, each of which appeals to ethical considerations. One argument in support of the doctrine is the property rights argument. This argument is based on the claim that because she owns the company, the employer has the right to decide who will work in the company and who will not. Just as the owner of a house has the right to decide who can come into her house to live with her and can base her decision on whatever criteria she wants, so also the owner of a business has the right to decide who will work with her in her business and can base her decision on whatever criteria she wants. Private property rights, as we have seen, include the right to decide how one's property can be used and who can use one's property. In this view, then, the employee has no right to object to or to contest the employer's decisions because as a nonowner, the employee has no right to determine how the business will be run while the employer has the right to hire or fire at will.

employment at will The doctrine that, unless employees are protected by an explicit contract (such as union employees), employers "may dismiss their employees at will... for good cause, for no cause, or even for causes morally wrong, without being thereby guilty of legal wrong."

A second argument in defense of the doctrine of employment at will is based on the idea of freedom of contract. This argument claims that every person has a right to freely enter into what ever agreements he or she chooses to enter. Recall from earlier chapters, we mentioned that Locke argued that everyone has the right to liberty and that Kant argued that everyone has a right to be treated as a free rational being. Both Locke's and Kant's views can be taken to imply that every person ought to be given the freedom to do whatever they choose, provided they do not violate the rights of others. In particular, everyone ought to have the freedom to make whatever agreements they want to make with others. Just as the employee ought to be left free to choose whether to work or quit working for an employer, so the employer ought to be left free to choose whether or not to agree to hire or fire a worker. The employer, then, has the right to hire or dismiss an employee at will "for good cause, for no cause, or even for causes morally wrong."

Quick Review 8.18

Arguments Supporting Employment at Will

- The employer owns the company and ownership gives him or her the right to decide whether and how long an employee will work in his or her company.
- Everyone has the right to do what they choose (provided they do not violate the rights of others) and so has the right to make whatever agreements they choose, including the agreement with employees to hire and fire them at will.
- Businesses will operate most efficiently if employers have the freedom to hire or fire employees as they see fit.

A third argument in support of employment at will is a utilitarian argument that business people often make. The argument is, simply, that businesses will operate most efficiently if employers have the freedom to hire or fire employees as they see fit without having to explain their actions. The employer is in the best position to know whether the business needs the services of a particular worker. If employers could not fire workers unless they could come up with good reasons for firing them, then many times they might have to keep workers who were not needed because it was difficult to provide a clear justification for firing them that everyone would find acceptable. Indeed, in many countries that do not allow employers to hire and fire at will, business people complain that it is difficult to fire workers no matter how poorly they are performing. To avoid such inefficiencies, it is best to let employers hire or fire employees at will.

The doctrine of employment at will has come under considerable attack.[74] First, opponents argue, employees often are not free to accept or reject employment without suffering considerable harm because they may have no other job available. Moreover, even when they are able to find alternative employment, workers pay the heavy costs involved in engaging in a job search and of struggling to live without an income while they are searching. Consequently, one of the fundamental assumptions on which employment at will is based—that employees "freely" accept employment and are "free" to find employment elsewhere—does not always hold. Second, critics of employment at will claim, employees generally make a conscientious effort to contribute to the firm, but do so with the understanding that the firm will treat them fairly in return. Workers surely would not freely choose to work for a firm if they believed the firm would treat them unfairly. Therefore, there is a tacit agreement that the firm makes to treat workers fairly, and workers, therefore, have a quasi-contractual right to fair treatment which excludes being fired "for no cause or even for causes morally wrong." Third, it is argued, workers have a right to be treated with respect as free and equal persons. Part of this right is the right to nonarbitrary treatment and the right not to be forced to suffer harm unfairly or on the basis of false accusations. Because firings, reductions in pay, demotions, and reprisals harm employees—particularly when they have no other job alternatives—these violate the employee's right when they are arbitrary or based on false accusations. Employees, therefore, may not be fired arbitrarily as the doctrine of employment at will would allow. Finally, while it may be true that ownership gives the owner the right to decide how his or her property will be used, this right, like all rights, has to be balanced against, and is limited by, the rights of others. Even the owner of a house, for example, has no right to treat the occupants unfairly, and if the owner has led the occupants to believe they can rely on him for shelter, the owner has no right to arbitrarily toss them out. For all these reasons, a recent trend has developed away from the doctrine of employment at will, and the doctrine has gradually been replaced by the view that the employer's right to fire, demote, or penalize is limited by the employee's right to "due process."[75]

right to due process The right to a fair decision-making process when decision makers impose sanctions on employees.

For many people, the right to due process is the most critical right employees have. In employment, ***the right to due process*** refers to the right to a fair process of decision-making when decision makers impose sanctions on employees. The right to due process is based on the idea that every human being has a right to be treated fairly and that this right includes the right to a fair and impartial application of rules, as well as the right to be allowed to explain oneself and to know that one is being sanctioned for true and legitimate reasons.

An ideal system of due process would be one in which individuals were given clear antecedent notice of the rules they were to follow, which gave a fair and impartial hearing to those who are believed to have violated the rules, which administered all rules consistently and without favoritism or discrimination, which was designed to ascertain the truth as objectively as possible, and which did not hold people responsible for matters over which they had no control.

It is obvious why the right to due process is seen by many people as the most critical right of employees: If this right is not respected, employees stand little chance of seeing their other rights respected. Due process ensures that individuals are not treated arbitrarily, capriciously, or maliciously by their superiors in the administration of the firm's rules, and it sets a moral limit on the exercise of the superior's power.[76] If the right to due process were not operative in the firm, then even if the rules of the firm protected the employee's other rights, these protections might be enforced sporadically and arbitrarily.

The most important area in which due process plays a role is in the hearing of grievances. By carefully spelling out a fair procedure for hearing and processing employee grievances, a firm can ensure that due process becomes an institutionalized reality. Trotta and Gudenberg identify the following as the essential components of a fair and effective grievance procedure:

1. Three to five steps of appeal depending on the size of the organization. Three steps usually suffice.
2. A written account of the grievance when it goes past the first level. This facilitates communication and defines the issues.
3. Alternate routes of appeal so that the employee can bypass his or her supervisor if he or she desires. The personnel department may be the most logical alternate route.
4. A time limit for each step of the appeal so that the employee has some idea of when to expect an answer.
5. Permission for the employee to have one or two co-workers accompany him or her at each interview or hearing if he chooses. This helps overcome fear of reprisal.

Quick Review 8.19

The Right to Due Process

- Is justified because without it all other employee rights are at risk
- Requires that individuals be notified of the rules they must follow, that they be given a fair and impartial hearing when accused of violating the rules, that rules be applied consistently, that processes through which sanctions are decided be designed to determine the truth objectively and that people not be held responsible for what they could not avoid
- Is institutionalized through fair grievance procedures.

The Right to Work Article 23.1 of the United Nations' "Universal Declaration of Human Rights" states: "Everyone has the right to work, to free choice of employment, to just and favorable conditions of work and to protection against unemployment." The **right to work**, as the Universal Declaration of Human Rights understands the concept, is the moral right to earn one's living by working. It is not, as some state laws use the phrase, the right to refuse to join a union without losing one's job. At one time, workers in some companies had to join the company union or leave the company. Today twenty-two states have laws that prohibit being forced to join a union in this way and these laws are generally called "right to work laws." But the Universal Declaration of Human Rights means something very different by the "right to work." As the United Nations says in Article 6 of another fundamental document, the "International Covenant on Economic, Social, and Cultural Rights," the right to work implies "the right of everyone to the opportunity to gain his living by work which he freely chooses or accepts." The assumption here is that "to gain his living by work" is such a fundamental value for a person that it should be surrounded with the protections afforded by having the status of a right.

right to work The right to earn one's living by working.

Why would anyone claim that for a person "to gain his living by work" is a fundamental value worthy of being granted the status of a right? For many people work is only a necessary evil: it is an activity characterized by drudgery, exhaustion, tediousness, and difficulty, and nothing more than a necessary means to the money we need to survive. In this common view of work it has only an instrumental value, something we have a duty to do, and the question is: why would anyone claim we have a "right" to something we would rather avoid? The answer is that even in this very narrow understanding of work, it is still something of tremendous importance precisely because it is a means to our survival. So important is its instrumental value as a means to survival that it should be protected and guaranteed by having the status of a right.

But there is a broader understanding of work that views it as having intrinsic value. First, work is the basic economic contribution that each person makes to his or her society. The work you and I do for our employer ultimately produces something that provides a benefit to society and that constitutes our main economic contribution to society. Through work we feel useful and our recognition of work as a contribution to society is demonstrated by the kind of negative effects that a lack of work has on us. Several studies have shown that when people are unemployed, they become depressed, feel ashamed and anxious, feel self-doubt, and report that they feel "worthless," or "useless."[77] So deep are these feelings that even after a person finds work, he will continue to feel stigmatized by his period of unemployment and this stigma will often accompany him throughout his life. These psychological responses to unemployment are the natural reaction to the belief that through work we make a contribution to society that we no longer make when we are unemployed and so we feel shame and feel worthless and useless. Such shame and feelings of being useless may not be appropriate in view of the fact that it is possible for us to make other, non-economic contributions to society. But they are, nevertheless, indicative of the fact that at very deep levels we recognize that our work, however menial or lowly, has value.

Quick Review 8.20

The Right to Work

- It is justified because of the interest we have in the instrumental and intrinsic value of work.
- Work has a critical instrumental value because it is a means to our survival.
- Work has an intrinsic value because (a) it is our basic economic contribution to society and helps us feel worthwhile and useful, (b) it lets us develop our potential and identity as a particular human being, (c) it lets us develop our character and virtues, and (d) it is a source of self-esteem and self-respect.
- The right to work is threatened by unemployment which in the United States has many causes including: recessions, use of new technologies, outsourcing of jobs to low-wage countries, free trade agreements, and our shift from a manufacturing to a service economy.
- Company layoffs also threaten the right to work and have many causes including: decline in demand, changes in consumer demand, product obsolescence, the pursuit of cheaper workers, mismanagement, and the need to consolidate operations.

Second, work enables us to develop our potential as the particular human being we are. In work we exercise and develop the particular talents, abilities, and skills that come to characterize part of who we are. The person who teaches develops the skills and attitudes toward learning that characterize a teacher and he or she comes to identify him or herself as a teacher; the waiter acquires the skills and abilities needed to serve diners and gradually comes to think of him or herself as a waiter. Through work we become much of who we are insofar as our work to a large extent determines what we become. Of course, we do not define ourself only in terms of our work, since we can also become a good friend, a skier, a guitar player, a Buddhist, a father, or any of the thousands of other roles our society makes available to us. Nevertheless, the work we do is one of the major components of who we become.

Through work we also develop our character. We learn to apply ourselves, to persevere and be diligent, to be industrious and productive, to be trustworthy and reliable, to be self-disciplined, responsible, and creative. As we move from one kind of work to another, we learn new skills and new ways of thinking and solving problems. We learn to get along with different kinds of people, to cooperate with them, to develop new friendships, and to feel a sense of belonging.

Finally, work is a fundamental source of self-esteem and self-respect. Work creates value which is why it is paid for. The work that we do ultimately produces something that has enough value that someone will pay to buy it. Our ability to work with others in the production of value is a source of the esteem and respect we feel for ourselves.

The reason why we can be said to have a right to work, then, is clear. Work is a means to our survival, it is our main economic contribution to society, it becomes part of our self-identity, it allows the development of our character, and it is a source of our self-esteem and self-respect. Because work is of such critical value, it is worth protecting with the status of a right even if we often find it tedious, arduous, and difficult.

But although we can argue that everyone has a right to work, the reality is that workers are often out of a job. In early 2010, for example, more than 10 percent of the U.S. population was unemployed, a total of more than 15 million men and women. Among U.S. teenagers, the unemployment rate was about 26 percent; among blacks it was 16 percent; and among Hispanics it was 12 percent. Similarly high unemployment was widespread, and even worse, around the world. In 2010, Portugal's unemployment rate was 11 percent; Ireland's rate was 14 percent; Spain's rate was 20 percent; Bosnia and Herzegovina's rate was 42 percent; South Africa's rate was 25 percent; Mongolia's rate was 12 percent; Latvia's rate was 20 percent; Estonia's rate was 20 percent; and the Dominican Republic's rate was 14 percent. Such high unemployment rates had not been seen since the early 1980s. Although the high number of unemployed U.S. and foreign workers in 2010 was largely due to a prolonged and particularly severe global recession, unemployment is a persistent feature of all modern economies.[78]

Setting aside the effects of recession, a number of factors, at least in the United States, have contributed to the unemployment that threatens the right to work. First, improvements in technology have made workers more productive, and this in turn has made it possible for U.S. companies to manufacture more goods with fewer workers. A second important, but more controversial, factor has been the transfer of many U.S. jobs to foreign, particularly developing, countries.[79] There are a number of reasons for this "outsourcing" of jobs. First, wages tend to be much lower in developing countries: U.S. steelworkers earn $23 an hour including benefits, whereas Latin American workers earn $2 an hour. This makes it cheaper to manufacture goods overseas than in the United States. Second, free trade agreements, such as the World Trade Organization (WTO) agreements, the North American Free Trade Agreement (NAFTA), and others, have made it easier for U.S. companies to relocate their operations to developing countries such as Mexico and China. A third factor is the shift of the United States (and other industrialized countries) from an agricultural economy to a manufacturing economy and then to a service economy. In the early twentieth century, the United States transitioned from an agricultural economy—one in which most workers are engaged in agriculture—to a **manufacturing economy** in which most are engaged in manufacturing such as making automobiles, televisions, and steel. Then, in the late twentieth century, the U.S. transitioned from a manufacturing into a **service economy**—one in which most workers are in service industries such as the banking, restaurant, legal, educational, software design, fashion design, and medical industries. Developing nations such as China, India, and Mexico are only now transitioning from an agricultural economy to a manufacturing economy, and in the process are taking over many of the manufacturing jobs that were formerly located in the United States, but which the United States spun off as it transitioned out of manufacturing into services.[80]

manufacturing economy An economy in which a large portion of employees are engaged in work that is aimed at producing manufactured products, such as the auto or steel industries.

service economy An economy in which most employees are engaged in so-called service industries where work consists largely of providing services to others, such as the banking, restaurant, legal, educational, software design, fashion design, and medical industries.

A company's decision to lay off some of its workers can also be a threat to the right to work. Businesses lay off workers for several other reasons. Manufacturers may lay off workers or close all together because of changes in consumer demand for their products. A company's products can become obsolete (e.g., facilities manufacturing kerosene lamps); demand can shift away from a certain product design before the plant has time to retool (e.g., a gas shortage can quickly shift demand away from large U.S. cars to the smaller cars being manufactured abroad); consumers can devote smaller parts of their budgets to manufactured or agricultural goods (e.g., in 1910 Americans spent 60 percent of their income on food and clothing; today they spend only 18 percent). And manufacturers can lay off workers because of a managerial decision to consolidate operations in a few large facilities (e.g., a small, profitable steel operation may be closed down after a merger and its operations shifted to another plant that is more efficient and has higher profit margins), or a decision to put short-term profits ahead of long-term investment (e.g., a team of managers might delay buying new equipment to show higher earnings on their quarterly report).

Whatever the cause—displacement of jobs to other nations, changes in domestic demand, rising productivity, mismanagement, or a company's pursuit of cheaper workers—layoffs and plant closings are threats to the right to work and impose high costs on workers and their communities. Workers' life savings are exhausted. Many lose their homes to foreclosure, are forced to accept menial jobs with drastically lower salaries and status, lose their pension rights, and suffer acute mental distress resulting in feelings of worthlessness and self-doubt, psychosomatic illnesses, alcoholism, family quarrels, child and spouse abuse, divorce, and suicide. Communities are harmed because closed plants mean declining tax revenues, loss of business from unemployed workers, and increased revenues that must be spent to provide social services for the unemployed. In some cases, entire towns have been reduced to ghost towns when the plant on which most of the local labor force depended left.[81]

Plant closings are unavoidable in a market economy such as ours for many of the reasons we have already seen. However, much can be done to protect the right to work by helping workers who are out of a job find new jobs, or by ensuring that workers do not lose their jobs. Some studies suggest that other nations do much more to protect workers from losing their jobs than the United States does. In a major study of industrialized nations, for example, a team of scholars led by Peter J. Kuhn found there are two approaches governments take to deal with layoffs.[82] Governments in some countries take a "palliative approach" that provides help to workers only *after* a layoff has occurred, when government may step forward to provide "retraining, mobility assistance, and income support." These countries include the United States, Canada, Great Britain, Australia, and Denmark. Governments in other countries, however, not only use these palliative measures but in addition also take a "preventative approach" that tries to prevent layoffs *before* they happen by requiring, for example, "extensive consultation and bargaining" between workers, business, and government in order to find a way to avoid the plant closure. If a company cannot avoid closing one of its plants, then these countries require the company to transfer employees to other plants within the company and to provide outplacement services for employees who cannot transfer so no one is laid off. If some layoffs are still unavoidable, then these countries try to prevent unemployment by requiring long advance notice periods during which workers can search for another job. These countries include the Netherlands, Japan, France, Germany, and Belgium. The experience of this second group of countries shows that much more can be done to help workers than what the United States and other nations do for them.

Countries such as Sweden, Germany, and Great Britain all require longer advance notice of impending plant closures than the United States does.[97] In Germany, France, Sweden, and the Netherlands, workers have a right to participate (e.g., through their unions) in closure decisions, perhaps even by being given the opportunity to purchase the plant and operate it themselves. It is significant that all of these countries have tended to have lower unemployment rates than the United States.

Quick Review 8.21

Protecting the Right to Work

- The United States and other countries protect the right to work with "palliative" policies that help workers find new jobs after they have lost their jobs; other countries in addition use "preventative" policies that try to ensure workers do not lose their jobs to begin with.
- Companies that have to lay off workers can respect their employees' right to work by providing advance notice, severance pay, health benefits, early retirement, job transfers, job retraining, the possibility of employee purchase, and avoiding a sudden reduction of their local tax contributions.

But even when shutdowns are necessary, the moral rights of workers involved should continue to be respected. Among the rights that must be respected are the workers' right to be informed about impending shutdowns that will affect them. Moreover, utilitarian principles imply that the harm caused by layoffs should be minimized. And if workers have a right to work, then firms should do what they can to enable their laid off workers to prepare themselves to find future jobs. Firms can do this by offering retraining programs, job transfers, and relocation. Finally, considerations of justice imply that workers and communities that have made substantial contributions to a plant during its operating life should be repaid by company assurances that it will not unjustly abandon worker pension plans or worker health plans. These ethical considerations are nicely folded together in the suggestions that William Diehl, a former senior vice president in the steel industry, makes concerning eight steps that companies can take to minimize the harmful effects of layoffs, plant closings and involuntary job losses:[83]

1. *Advance Notice* If the company can notify workers of a closing date 12 to 18 months in advance, they would have time to prepare for it.…[A few] day's notice of closing is totally unjust and unacceptable.
2. *Severance Pay* A commonly suggested formula is for each worker to receive severance pay equal to 1 week's earnings for every year of service.…
3. *Health Benefits* Worker's health benefits should be covered by the company for at least 1 additional year after the employee is dismissed.
4. *Early Retirement* Workers who are within 3 years of normal retirement should be retired on full pension, with years of service computed as if they had worked until age 65.

5. *Transfer* In the case of a multiplant corporation, all workers at the facility should have the opportunity to transfer to an equally paying job at another plant, with full moving expenses covered by the employer.
6. *Job Retraining* Company-sponsored training programs should be established to train and place workers in other jobs in the local community. These programs should also include family counseling for all employees.
7. *Employee Purchase* Workers and the local community should be given the opportunity to purchase the plant and operate it under an Employee Stock Ownership Plan (ESOP) ... [whenever] viable....
8. *Phasing Out of Local Taxes* Companies should phase out their local taxes over a 5-year period. This may involve a voluntary contribution to the local taxing authority if the plant and equipment are disposed of in a way that will severely reduce property taxes.

The Right to Organize Just as owners have the right to freely associate with each other to establish and run a business, so do workers have the **right to organize** which is the right to associate with each other to establish and run a union. The same rights of free association that justify the formation and existence of corporations also underlie the right of workers to form the worker organizations we call *unions*.[84]

right to organize The right of workers to associate with each other to establish and run a union.

The worker's right to organize into a union derives, also derives from the right of all people to be treated as free and equal persons. Corporate employers, especially during periods of high unemployment or in regions where only one or a few firms are located, have much more power in negotiations with individual employees than the employee does. Unions have therefore traditionally been justified as a means for balancing the power of the corporation and the power of the worker so that the worker, in solidarity with other workers, can achieve an equal footing when negotiating with the corporation.[85] Thus, unions achieve an equality between worker and employer that the isolated worker could not secure, and they thereby secure the worker's right to be treated as a free and equal person in job negotiations.

Not only do all workers have a right to form unions, but their unions also have a right to strike.[86] The right of unions to call a strike derives from the right of each worker to quit working so long as doing so violates no prior agreements or the rights of others. Union strikes are therefore morally justified so long as the strike does not violate a prior legitimately negotiated agreement not to strike (which the company might have negotiated with the union) and so long as the strike does not violate the legitimate moral rights of others (such as citizens, whose right to protection and security might be violated by strikes of public workers such as firefighters or police). Companies, then, have an obligation to respect the rights of workers both to form unions and to strike, and this right extends to the workers of all nations.

Despite the well-accepted view that unions and union strikes are morally legitimate, there has been a good deal of dissatisfaction toward them in the United States. Although unions represented 35 percent of the workforce in 1947, by the early 1990s, they represented only 16 percent.[87] By 2004, unions represented only about 14 percent of the labor force and by 2010, representation had declined to 12 percent. From an earlier record of winning 75 percent of all elections to unionize, unions must now be satisfied with winning only about 45 percent of worker votes.[88] There are a variety of factors responsible for this decline in union membership, including an increase in white-collar and female workers, the shift from manufacturing to service industries, and a decline in public confidence in unions. One of the major causes is rising opposition to unions on the part of managers and a disturbing increase in the use of illegal tactics to defeat union organizing campaigns.[89] This is unfortunate and shortsighted

Quick Review 8.22

The Right to Organize

- This derives from the same right owners have to join together to form a company, i.e., from the right to freely associate with others to establish and run an organization as well as the right to be treated as an equal in negotiations with organizations.
- Unions have a right to strike that derives from every worker's right to quit working so long as doing so does not violate other's rights.
- Union membership declined from 35 percent of workers in 1947 to 14 percent in 2010.
- Many developing countries do not protect the right to organize, but U.S. companies can often allow their workers there to unionize anyway.

because the decline in the effectiveness of unions has been accompanied by a consequent increase in the appeal to legislatures and the courts to establish rigid legal protections against the abuses that unions were originally established to secure. As the effectiveness of workers' rights to unionize and strike continues to shrink, we can count on a proliferation of laws to secure the rights that worker organizations can no longer accomplish.

Workers in many developing nations have much more restricted rights to organize into unions than U.S. workers. In fact, many U.S. companies move to developing nations such as Mexico, Central America, Indonesia, Thailand, China, India, and other Asian nations because weak unions there lead to weak wage demands and low worker protections, all of which adds up to lower costs. The key ethical issue for companies that operate in countries with weak union rights is this: What obligation does a company have to respect the right to unionize for workers in its factories when these rights are either not recognized by the local government or are only weakly enforced by local government? This question is especially difficult to answer when a company contracts with a foreign company in a developing nation. As we noted earlier, U.S. apparel and shoe companies such as Nike, Adidas, Reebok, the Gap, Limited, Dress Barn, Lane Bryant, Wal-Mart, Tommy Hilfiger, Calvin Klein, Levi Strauss, Abercrombie & Fitch, Talbots, Brooks Brothers, and many others do not make their own products, but have them made in factories owned by foreigners in developing nations. What responsibility, if any, does a company have for the respect or lack of respect that such foreign factories show toward their workers? As we suggested earlier, questions about the responsibility of one company for the way a hired factory treats its workers depend on whether the company (1) can and should do something to change the way the factory is treating its workers, (2) knows about the way the factory is treating its workers, and (3) is not prevented from acting or pressured by external or uncontrollable forces.

Organizational Politics

The discussion so far has focused primarily on formal power relationships within organizations—that is, the ethical issues raised by the power that the formal structure of the organization allows managers to exercise over their subordinates. These power relations are sanctioned and overt: They are spelled out in the firm's "organizational chart," inscribed in the contracts and job descriptions that define the employee's duties to the firm, recognized by the law (of agency), openly employed by superiors, and largely accepted as legitimate by subordinates.

The ethical constraints on the use of this formal power that we reviewed have also been approached from a largely formal perspective. The rights to privacy, due process, freedom of conscience, and consent can all be formalized within the organization (by formulating and enforcing rules, codes, and procedures) just as the power relationships they constrain are formalized.

However, as we have already seen, organizations also contain informal pockets and channels of power: sources of power that do not appear on organizational charts and uses of power that are covert and perhaps not recognized as legitimate. We turn now to look at this underbelly of the organization: organizational politics.

organizational politics The processes in which individuals or groups within an organization use nonformally sanctioned power tactics to advance their own aims.

Political Tactics in Organizations There is no settled definition of ***organizational politics***. For our purposes, however, we can adopt the following definition: the processes in which individuals or groups within an organization use nonformally sanctioned power tactics to advance their own aims; we call such tactics *political tactics*.[90] A word of caution is necessary, lest the reader interpret *their own aims* to mean "aims in conflict with the best interests of the organization." Although the aims of a coalition in a firm may conflict with the best interests of the firm, such conflict is neither inevitable nor even, perhaps, frequent. Two factors tend to suppress such conflicts: (1) The careers of individuals often depend on the health of their organizations, and (2) long-time association with an organization tends to generate bonds of loyalty to the organization. Often, therefore, what one person perceives as a conflict between a certain group's aims and the best interests of the organization is in fact a conflict between the beliefs of that person and the beliefs of the group concerning what the "best interests" of the organization are. The group may genuinely believe that X is in the best interests of both the organization and itself, whereas the person may genuinely believe instead that Y, which conflicts with X, is what is in the best interests of the organization.

Because organizational politics aim at advancing the interests of one individual or group (such as acquiring promotions, salary or budget increases, status, or even more power) by exerting nonformally sanctioned power over other individuals or groups, political individuals tend to be covert about their underlying intents or methods.[91] Virginia E. Schein, for example, gave this illustration of a department head intent on strengthening her position in an organization:

> The head of a research unit requests permission to review another research group's proposal in case she can add information to improve the project. Her covert intent is to maintain her current power, which will be endangered if the other research group carries out the project. Using her informational power base, her covert means are to introduce irrelevant information and pose further questions. If she sufficiently confuses the issues, she can discredit the research group and prevent the project from being carried out. She covers these covert intents and means with the overt ones of improving the project and reviewing its content.[92]

The fact that political tactics are usually covert means that they can easily become deceptive or manipulative. This is evident if we examine some examples of the kinds of tactics used in organizational politics. In a recent study of managerial personnel, respondents were asked to describe the political tactics they had experienced most frequently in the organizations in which they had worked.[93] The following kinds of tactics were reported:

> *Blaming or attacking others* Minimizing one's association with plans or results that are failing or have failed and blaming one's rivals for the failure or "denigrating their accomplishments as unimportant, poorly timed, self-serving, or lucky."
>
> *Controlling information* Withholding information detrimental to one's aims or distorting information "to create an impression by selective disclosure, innuendo," or overwhelming the subject with "objective" data (graphs, formulas, tables, summations) designed to create an impression of rationality or logic and to obscure important details harmful to one's interests.
>
> *Developing a base of support for one's ideas* Getting others to understand and support one's ideas before a meeting is called.
>
> *Image building* Creating the appearance of being thoughtful, honest, sensitive, on the inside of important activities, well-liked, and confident.
>
> *Ingratiation* Praising superiors or those with power and making them feel that one admires them or developing good rapport with them.

Associating with the influential Trying to get one's superiors or those with power to feel that one is a friend.

Forming power coalitions and developing strong allies Forming or joining groups that are already formed and that can help one in pursuing one's interests.

Creating obligations Making others feel obligated to oneself by performing services or favors for them.

Some researchers have argued that the basic source of power is the creation of dependency: A acquires power over B by making B dependent on A for something. Some authors identify the following two categories of political tactics as encompassing the main kinds of tactics by which such dependencies can be created:[94]

Getting control over scarce resources desired by others Controlling employees, buildings, access to influential persons, equipment, and useful information.

Establishing favorable relationships Getting others to feel obligated to oneself, making others think one is a friend, building a reputation as an expert, and encouraging others to believe that one has power and that they are dependent on that power.

Organizational politics can have a significant impact on the lives of their targets. They are often used by individual managers and coalitions in internal struggles to get control of a corporation, and individuals caught up in such struggles can have their careers destroyed. For example, when the dynamic CEO of Bendix Corporation, Bill Agee, began transforming Bendix from a stodgy manufacturing company into a diversified high tech firm, he angered managers whose organizations and budgets he cut. Many secretly complained to William Panny, the company's President, who was known to disagree with Agee's plans for Bendix, and who was rumored to be Agee's successor. That year Agee hired Mary Cunningham, a recent graduate of Harvard Business School, to be his executive assistant. Friends said she was "brilliant," "sophisticated," and "a financial genius." Cunningham used her considerable financial skills to identify and analyze acquisitions that were in line with Agee's new vision for the company, and Agee followed her advice, which was always on target. The next year Agee promoted her to Vice President for Strategic Planning. The promotion upset managers who felt she had not been there long enough to deserve it. They told Panny that Agee now listened only to Cunningham and was inaccessible to others. When Cunningham later prepared a three-volume analysis of the company's auto division, Panny and other managers harshly criticized it, saying it was useless and contained nothing they did not already know. Behind her back they derisively referred to her and her staff as "Snow White and the Seven Dwarfs." They began spreading rumors that Agee had promoted her only because the two had a romantic relationship. When Agee learned that Panny was about to ask the company's Board of Directors to "investigate their relationship," Agee fired him. Then the Directors began receiving anonymous letters with malicious innuendos about Agee and Cunningham. Agee called a special meeting of 600 corporate staff. In a brief talk he said "I know it has been buzzing around that Mary Cunningham's rise in this company ... has something to do with a personal relationship we have." But those rumors, he asserted, are completely false: He had no romantic involvement with Cunningham and had promoted her solely on her merits. But after his talk someone leaked it to the local newspaper, which ran a front page story the next morning on the "romantic rumors." By evening the story was national news. Cunningham was forced to resign and Agee's standing in the company was significantly weakened. A director later confided to Cunningham that she had been used to get at Agee.[95]

The Ethics of Political Tactics Obviously, political behavior in an organization can easily become abusive. As the incident at Bendix illustrates, political tactics can be used to advance private interests at the expense of organizational and group interests, they can be manipulative and deceptive, and they can seriously injure those who have little or no power or political expertise. However, political tactics can also be put to the service of organizational and social goals, they may sometimes be necessary to protect the powerless, and they are sometimes the only defense a person has against the manipulative and deceptive tactics of others. The dilemma for the individual in an organization is knowing where the line lies that separates morally legitimate political tactics from those that are unethical.

Very few authors have discussed this dilemma.[96] This is unfortunate because although few organizations are totally pervaded by political behavior, it is also the case that no organization is completely free of politics. We are all political animals even if our political campaigns are largely confined to the office. Here we only start to analyze the many complex ethical issues raised by the political maneuvering that inevitably goes on within organizations. The issues can best be approached by addressing four questions that can focus our attention on the morally relevant features of using political tactics: (1) The utilitarian question: Are the goals one intends to achieve by the use of the tactics socially beneficial or socially harmful? (2) The rights question: Do the political tactics used as means to these goals treat others in a manner consistent with their moral rights? (3) The justice question: Will the political tactics lead to an equitable distribution of benefits and burdens?[97] (4) The caring question: What impact will the political tactics have on the web of relationships within the organization?

The Utility of Goals Utilitarian principles require that managers pursue those goals that will produce the greatest social benefits and the least social harm. If we assume that business organizations generally perform a socially beneficial function and that activities that harm the organization will probably diminish these social benefits, then utilitarianism implies that the individual manager should avoid harming the organization and should work to ensure that the organization carries out its beneficial social functions as efficiently as possible. For example, the basic function of most businesses is to produce goods and services for consumers. Insofar as a business organization is serving this function in a socially beneficial and nonharmful way, the employee should avoid harming the business and should strive to ensure that the business carries on its productive function with a minimum of waste.

Two kinds of political tactics directly contradict this norm and are, therefore, typically judged unethical: political tactics that involve the pursuit of personal goals at the expense of the organization's productive goals, and political tactics that knowingly involve inefficiency and waste. Suppose, for example, that the head of a research unit secretly withholds critical information from other research units in the same company so that his or her own unit will look better than the others. As a result, his or her career ambitions are advanced and his or her unit gets a larger budget allocation the following year. Was his or her tactic of withholding information to gain an edge on others morally legitimate? No. The tactic was clearly inconsistent with the efficient pursuit of the company's productive functions.

Of course, businesses do not always have socially beneficial and nonharmful goals. Pollution, planned obsolescence, price-fixing, and the manufacture of hazardous products are some obvious organizational goals that utilitarianism would condemn. To the extent that a business pursues such goals, the employee has a duty not to cooperate (unless, perhaps, threatened with personal losses of such magnitude that the employee is in effect coerced to comply). Utilitarian principles imply that to voluntarily pursue goals that are socially harmful or to voluntarily cooperate in such a pursuit is immoral, regardless of what kinds of political tactics one uses.

Unfortunately, organizational goals are not always clear because there may be no consensus over what the organization's goals actually are. This is especially the case, for example, when a company is in the process of undergoing a change in management or a change in organization and more or less widespread bargaining erupts over what the new goals should be. This was the situation at Bendix when Panny and other managers disagreed with the direction in which Agee was taking the company. When organizational goals are in the process of being redefined in this way, the various coalitions and individuals within the organization will usually attempt to use political tactics to install the goals that each wants, either through a unilateral exercise of power (e.g., a new management may try to get rid of all the old staff and hire its own team) or through political compromise (e.g., the new management may try to persuade the old staff to accept new goals). In such fluid situations, the individual has no choice but to examine the goals being proposed by the various coalitions and make a conscientious attempt to determine which goals are the most socially beneficial in the long run. Whereas the use of political tactics to install illegitimate organizational goals would be unethical, political tactics may be used to ensure the installation of morally legitimate goals, provided that the tactics meet the following two criteria.

Moral Rights and Political Means Some political tactics are obviously deceptive, as when a person creates the impression of an expertise that the person does not in fact have. Other tactics are manipulative. For example, it is manipulative to feign love to extract favors from a person. Deception and manipulation are both attempts to get people to do (or believe) something that they would not do (or believe) if they knew what was going on. These sorts of political tactics are unethical to the extent that they fail to respect a person's right to be treated not merely as a means, but also as an end; that is, they fail to respect a person's right to be treated only as they freely and knowingly consented to be treated. Such moral disrespect is exhibited in many of those political tactics that take advantage of our emotional dependencies and vulnerabilities, both of which provide others with the cheapest and most reliable levers for acquiring power over us. For example, a skilled administrator can become adept at pretending friendship and concern and adept at getting others to look on the administrator with affection, respect, loyalty, indebtedness, trust, gratitude, and so on. The administrator can then exploit these feelings to get subordinates to do things that they ordinarily would not do, especially if they knew the deception involved and knew the covert motives on which the administrator acted. A skillful administrator might also learn to take advantage of particular individuals' personal vulnerabilities, such as vanity, generosity, sense of responsibility, susceptibility to flattery, gullibility, naivete, or any of the other traits that can lead people to unwittingly put themselves at the mercy of others. By covertly taking advantage of these vulnerabilities, the manager can get employees to serve the manager's aims, although they would not do so if they knew the covert motives on which the manager acted. Or, as happened at Bendix, managers can use ridicule, false rumors, or deceptive innuendo to undermine another person's position.

However, are deceptive and manipulative political tactics always wrong? What if I am forced to work in an organization in which others insist on using deceptive and manipulative tactics against me? Must I remain defenseless? Not necessarily. If the members of an organization know that certain kinds of covert political tactics are in common use within an organization, and if they nonetheless freely choose to remain within the organization and become skillful in using and defending themselves against these tactics, then one can presume that these organizational members have tacitly consented to having those kinds of covert political tactics used against themselves. They have freely agreed to play an organizational game, as it were, in which everyone knows that fooling the other players and maneuvering them out of winning positions is all part of the game. Dealing with them on the basis of this tacit consent would not violate their right to be treated as they have freely and knowingly chosen to be treated.

However, the use of deceptive or manipulative political tactics is clearly unethical when they are used against persons who (a) do not know or do not expect that these kinds of tactics will be used against themselves, (b) are not free to leave the organization in which these tactics are being used, or (c) are not skilled at defending themselves against these tactics. Using a deceptive or manipulative tactic in any of these instances violates the moral respect due to persons, especially if the tactic injures people by maneuvering them into unknowingly acting against their own best interests.

Quick Review 8.23

Approaches to the Ethics of Political Tactics

- Utilitarian: Are the tactics used intended to advance socially beneficial or harmful goals?
- Rights: Do the tactics employed treat others in a way that is consistent with their moral rights?
- Justice: Will the tactics lead to an equitable distribution of benefits and burdens?
- Caring: What impact will the tactics have on relationships within the organization?

The Justice of the Results Political tactics can create injustices by distorting the equality of treatment that justice demands. An individual who controls an organization's budget or information system, for example, may covertly administer that system unjustly by showing favoritism to those persons or groups who can advance the individual's career. Such political tactics blatantly violate the basic principle of distributive justice discussed earlier: Individuals who are similar in all relevant respects should be treated similarly, and individuals who are dissimilar in relevant respects should be treated dissimilarly in proportion to their dissimilarity.

Political tactics can also create injustices among those employees who have few or no political skills. Those without political skills are easily maneuvered into accepting a smaller share of the organization's benefits than their abilities or needs may merit in comparison to others. Benefits are then no longer distributed to these people on the basis of their relevant characteristics—an injustice is committed against them.

Not only can political tactics leave others better or worse off than they deserve, but politics can also be used to gain unjust advantages for oneself. An engineer who is competing with another engineer for promotion to department head, for example, may cultivate and flatter his or her superiors while using innuendo to discredit his or her rival. As a result, he or she may get the promotion, although the other engineer was more qualified. Using political tactics in this way to acquire advantages on the basis of nonrelevant characteristics is also unjust.

The Impact on Caring In addition to these inequities, the prolonged prevalence of political tactics within an organization can have long-term and debilitating effects on the quality of the personal relationships that pervade the organization. Several researchers have found that the use of power in organizations tends to routinize the dehumanized treatment of less powerful individuals. David Kipnis, for example, found that individuals who exercise power find themselves increasingly tempted to (a) increase their attempts to influence the behavior of the less powerful, (b) devalue the worth of the performance of the less powerful, (c) attribute the cause of the less powerful's efforts to power controlled by themselves rather than to the less powerful's motivations to do well, (d) view the less powerful as objects of manipulation, and (e) express a preference for the maintenance of psychological distance from the less powerful.[98] Power, in short, corrupts.

Chris Argyris and others have maintained that those who are controlled by the powerful "tend to feel frustration, conflict, and feelings of failure"; that they "adapt" by leaving the organization, trying to climb the organization's ladder, retreating to aggression, daydreaming, regression, or simple apathy; and that the organization becomes characterized by competition, rivalry, and hostility.[99] Therefore, in deciding whether to use political tactics, one should seriously consider the long-range consequences that the exercise of power implied by these tactics can have on oneself and one's relationships with those in the organization.

8.3 The Caring Organization

So far we have looked at organizations as having two aspects. First, we have considered organizations as hierarchical collections of individuals who are connected to each other and to the organization by contractual agreements and formally defined hierarchies of authority. We have called this aspect of the organization the *rational* organization. Overlying the rational organization's formal lines of authority is a second system, which we have called the *political* organization: the network of power relationships, coalitions, and informal lines of communication through which individuals seek to achieve their goals and what they see as the goals of the organization.

It is possible to conceive of organizations as consisting of yet a third, quite different kind of system. Recent thinkers have suggested that organizations can and should be thought of as networks of relationships in which "connected selves" form webs of ongoing personal relationships with other "connected selves." In this model of the organization, the focus of employees is not on the pursuit of power, profit or personal goals, but on the caring interpersonal relationships that exist among the individuals within the organization and those external individuals with whom the organization interacts. We encounter this aspect of the organization when we become mutual friends with the people with whom we work, come to care for them, look out for their well-being, and seek to deepen and preserve these caring relationships. Employers, too, may grow close to their employees, deepening their relationships with employees and coming to seek ways of caring for the particular needs of these particular individuals and of developing their potential. When a fire destroyed the main plant of Malden Mills, for example, the CEO, Aaron Feuerstein, refused to lay off the idled workers, but continued to pay them from his own pocket although they were not working, saying that they were "part of the enterprise, not a cost center to be cut. They've been with me for a long time. We've been good to each other, and there's a deep realization of that." The members of an organization may befriend even their clients and customers, truly caring for them and genuinely seeking the well-being of those particular clients with whom they deal. Such caring for the well-being of clients can be most evident in organizations of professionals that provide services for their clients, such as hospitals, schools, law firms, and consulting firms that have ongoing relationships with the people they serve.

This aspect of organizational life is not adequately described by the contractual relationships that underlie the "rational" model of the organization, nor by the power relationships that underlie the "political" model. Perhaps, this aspect of the organization is best described as ***the caring model of the organization***, because its dominant realities are those that are emphasized by an ethic of care: interpersonal relationships. Jeanne M. Liedtka described the caring organization as an organization, or part of an organization, in which caring is

a. focused entirely on persons, not "quality," "profits," or any of the other kinds of ideas that much of today's "care-talk" seems to revolve around;
b. undertaken as an end in and of itself, and not merely a means toward achieving quality, profits, etc.;
c. essentially personal, in that it ultimately involves particular individuals engrossed, at a subjective level, in caring for other particular individuals;
d. growth-enhancing for the cared-for, in that it moves them towards the use and development of their full capacities, within the context of their self-defined needs and aspirations.[100]

caring model of the organization A view of the organization in which the dominant moral concepts are those that arise from an ethic of care.

Quick Review 8.24

Characteristics of the Caring Model of the Organization

- Caring is focused entirely on persons, not on "profit" or "quality."
- Caring is undertaken as an end in itself not as a means to productivity.
- Caring is essentially personal.
- Caring is growth-enhancing for the cared-for.

It has been argued that business organizations in which such caring relationships flourish will exhibit better economic performance than the organization that restricts itself to the contractual and power relationships of the rational and political organization.[101] In the caring organization, trust flourishes because "one needs to be trusting if one sees oneself as interdependent and connected."[102] Because trust flourishes in the caring organization, the organization does not have to invest resources in monitoring its employees and trying to make sure that they do not violate their contractual agreements. Thus, caring lowers the costs of running an organization and reduces the "costs of disciplinary actions, theft, absenteeism, poor morale and motivation."[103] In the genuinely caring organization, of course, caring is not motivated by the desire to reduce such costs, but is pursued for its own sake, as item (b) above indicates.

It has also been argued that business organizations in which caring flourishes develop a concern for serving the customer and creating customer value that in turn enables such organizations to achieve a competitive advantage over other organizations. In such a business organization, the focus is not on producing differentiated or low-cost products for growing markets, but on creating value for particular customers and remaining tuned to their evolving needs. Such a focus on knowing and serving the customer, it is argued, enables the company to continually adapt to the rapid changes that characterize most markets today. Moreover, the caring that gives rise to a focus on the customer can also inspire and motivate employees to excel in a way that contractual and power relations do not. Bartlett and Ghoshal, for example, argued:

> But...contractually based relationships do not inspire the extraordinary effort and sustained commitment required to deliver consistently superior performance. For that, companies need employees who care, who have a strong emotional link with the organization.[104]

There may be few, perhaps even no, organizations that perfectly embody the caring organization, but some well-known firms come close. W. L. Gore & Associates, Inc., for example, the extremely successful company that invented and now manufactures the well-known GORE-TEX line of fabrics, is an organization that has no managers, no titles, no hierarchy.[105] Instead, every employee is trusted to such an extent that he or she is left free to decide what job each will voluntarily commit to do according to where each feels he or she can make the best contribution. Leaders emerge when employees are willing to follow them because they are convinced the leader has a worthwhile idea or project. Every employee has one or more "sponsors" who work closely as coaches to help the employee develop to full potential and who serve as the employee's "advocates" when a "compensation team" (consisting of fellow employees) reviews the contribution the employee has made to decide what compensation the employee should receive the following year. Company units are kept small (under 200 people) so that everyone can get to know everyone else and so that all communications are open, direct, and person to person. In such an unstructured and unmanaged organization, all work done within the organization must ultimately rely on the relationships that employees form with each other. Over time, employees come to care for each other and for the customers for whom they are trying to create value.

Although organizations like W. L. Gore are rare, still most organizations, to a greater or lesser extent, have aspects of the caring organization. In some organizations, such as W. L. Gore, the caring organization dominates the rational and political aspects of the organization. In most others, however, the contractual and political aspects are more prominent. Yet in many, there are at least some employees and managers who respond to the demands of caring by nurturing the relationships they have with each other and by attending to the concrete and particular needs of fellow employees and of their customers.

In the contractual model, the key ethical issues arise from the potential for violations of the contractual relation. In the political model, the key ethical issues arise from the potential for the misuse of power. The key ethical issues from the perspective of the caring organization are the potential for caring too much and the potential for not caring enough.

Quick Review 8.25

Problems of the Caring Organization

- Caring too much for others which can lead to "burnout" when the needs of others are given too much weight compared to the needs of the self.
- Not caring enough for others because fatigue, self-interest, or disinterest leads us to ignore their needs, or because the organization systematically drives out caring with layoffs, bureaucracy, managerial styles that see employees as disposable, or rewards that encourage competitiveness and discourage caring.

The Moral Problem of Caring Too Much The needs of those for whom we care can demand a response from us that can overwhelm us, leading eventually to "burnout."[106] Here the conflict is between the needs of others and the needs of the self. Several writers have argued that the ethic of care requires achievement of a mature balance between caring for the needs of others and caring for one's own needs.[107] Others have argued that "burnout" occurs not because people are overwhelmed by the needs of others, but because organizations place bureaucratic burdens on caregivers and limit their autonomy and influence in decision making.[108] In addition to conflicts between the needs of the self and the needs of others, the demands of caring can lead to a different kind of conflict: The needs of those for whom we care can demand a response that conflicts with what we may feel we owe others. This is the problem of balancing partiality toward those for whom we care with the impartial demands of other moral considerations, such as the impartial demands of fairness or of moral rights.[109] For example, a person may be torn between caring for a friend who is violating company policy and fairness toward the company that requires that such violations be reported. Which demand should be satisfied: the demands of caring partiality or the demands of impartial morality?

The Moral Problem of Not Caring Enough More pressing, however, are failures to live up to the demands of caring. This may happen on a personal basis or an organizational level. We may personally see a fellow employee or customer in need, but fatigue, self-interest, or simply disinterest may lead us to ignore that need. On a broader organizational level, the entire organization may systematically drive out caring through indiscriminate layoffs, the creation of large impersonalized bureaucracies, the use of managerial styles that see employees as disposable costs, or the use of reward systems that discourage caring and reward competitiveness.

How should these kinds of moral issues be resolved? Unfortunately, at this time the answers are not clear. Research and thinking on the caring organization and caring in organizations is so recent that no clear consensus has emerged on how issues such as these should be resolved. We have come here to the very edges of current thinking in ethics.

Questions for Review and Discussion

Study and Review on **mythinkinglab.com**

1. Define the following concepts: the rational model of the organization, employee's obligations to the firm, law of agency, conflict of interest, actual/potential conflicts of interest, commercial bribe, commercial extortion, morality of accepting gifts, insider information, theft, fair wage, OSHA, the political model of the organization, power, government-management analogy, right to privacy, physical/psychological privacy, relevance, consent, extraordinary methods, right to freedom of conscience, whistle blowing, right to participate, right to due process, organizational politics, political tactics, the caring organization.
2. Relate the theory of the employee's obligations to the firm in this chapter to the discussion on contractual rights and duties in Chapter 2. Are there any inconsistencies between them? Relate the six criteria for just wages in this chapter to the various standards of justice developed in Chapter 2. Are the six criteria consistent with the various standards? Do the standards of justice imply or suggest any other criteria that should be used in setting just wages? Relate the discussions of employee rights in this chapter to the discussion of moral rights developed in Chapter 2. Are these two discussions consistent? Does your review of the discussion of moral rights suggest to you that there are other important employee rights that are not discussed in this chapter; if so, what are they?
3. Compare and contrast the rational model of the organization with the political model and the caring model. Would you agree with the following statement: "The rational model of the organization assumes that the corporation is based on consent, while the political model assumes it is based on power, and the caring model assumes the corporation is based on interpersonal relationships"? Which of the two models do you think provides the more adequate view of organizations you are familiar with, such as the university or college you attend or companies you have worked for? Explain your answers.
4. In view of the contractual agreement that every employee makes to be loyal to the employer, do you think whistleblowing is ever morally justified? Explain your answer.
5. Do you agree or disagree with the claim that corporate managements are so similar to governments that employees should be recognized as having the same "civil rights" as citizens have? Explain the reasons for your answer.
6. Evaluate the desirability of the "caring model of the organization." Should managers or employees deliberately try to make organizations more like the caring model?

Web Resources

Readers interested in researching the topic of ethical issues related to employees and organizational life might want to start with the Occupational Safety and Health Association Web page (*http://www.osha.gov*); the National Institute for Occupational Safety and Health (*http://www.cdc.gov/niosh*); the topics of labor and employment law at HG.org (*http://www.hg.org/employ.html*); and at the 'Lectric Law Library (*http://www.lectlaw.com/temp.html*). Information on unions is provided by the American Federation of Labor–Congress of Industrial Organizations (*http://www.aflcio.org*). The Campaign for Labor Rights provides information on labor issues (*http://www.campaignforlaborrights.org/*). Information on sweatshops around the world can be found at several web sites including *http://www.greenamerica.org/programs/sweatshops*, *http://www.globalex change.org/campaigns/sweatshops*, *http://usas.org*, *http://www.behindthelabel.org*, and *http://www.maquilasolidarity.org*.

CASES

Explore the Concept on mythinkinglab.com

Death at Massey Energy Company

It happened around 3:00 PM on Monday, April 5, in the Upper Big Branch coal mine at Montcoal, West Virginia, one of several mines owned by the Massey Energy Company. The morning shift of miners was still in the process of changing places with the afternoon shift. Members of each group were being shuttled in and out of the entrance in transport vehicles called "mantrips." Nine of the morning shift miners had just come out of one of the mantrips, and were walking out of the mine when they suddenly felt a blast of air blow past them, so strong it almost pushed them over. They all knew what it meant. Turning around, several hurried back into the mine, and shortly came upon seven of their fellow miners dead, next to the mantrip that had just brought them up from below. Two others were alive but injured. A deadly explosion had ripped through the underground coal mine, killing or trapping an unknown number of the miners inside. At the time of the explosion, a total of 61 miners were working underground.[1] Stanley Stewart, one of the miners, later described what it had been like:

> On April 5th, I was sitting on a mantrip at about 3 PM with several other miners approximately 300 feet underground. We were getting ready to head to the section when I felt a breeze coming from inside the mine. The intensity picked up quickly and I realized that something bad was happening so I left the mantrip and started making my way toward the outside. Before I could get out the air velocity increased to what I felt was "hurricane strength" and I felt my feet wanting to leave the ground. The air was full of dust debris and I couldn't see. Although I didn't have far to go I panicked, afraid that I might not make it out to safety.[2]

Fortunately, Stewart made it out safely. Other miners who tried to go down into the cavern to help, were stopped by the smoke and toxic fumes billowing through the mine. Many of the miners who had been underground somehow found their way up to the surface. Although smoky air limited visibility to about two feet, around 6:00 PM the first rescue team entered the mine, each rescuer equipped with an oxygen tank and mask. Because the supply of air in the tanks was limited, each team could search only a small part of the massive labyrinth of passageways before being forced to come out and be relieved by another team. Their progress was slow since the overwhelming force of the blast had littered the floor of the mine with tangled debris. The blast had twisted rail lines "like pretzels" and it had exploded machinery and hurled their parts over the floor of the mine. Huge boulders and rocks had been thrown everywhere. The first team found a dead miner, and the teams that followed them throughout the evening continued to find more bodies.

By 2:00 AM, the bodies found by the rescue teams brought the death toll to 25. Although four miners were still unaccounted for, the rescue effort was forced to stop at 2:30 AM. The levels of methane, an explosive gas, and carbon monoxide, a toxic gas, were increasing inside the mine, making it too dangerous for the rescuers to continue. Workers would have to drill holes to ventilate the mine and rid it of the dangerous gases before rescuers could enter again. The drilling got underway around 4:00 PM on Tuesday afternoon. Families of the missing miners hoped that the miners had managed to make their way into one of the mine's "refuge chambers," small emergency rooms equipped with food, water, and enough oxygen to last about 90 hours. There were two refuge chambers in the area of the explosion.[3]

By Wednesday morning, the drillers had broken through into the mine and started pumping out the methane, but it was not until the next day, Thursday morning, that rescue teams were allowed to enter the mine again. They were forced to stop four hours later because air samples showed the mine was still saturated with methane. Another team tried to enter the mine on Friday morning, but was again forced to come out when rising smoke levels indicated fires were still burning somewhere inside the mine. Nevertheless, the second team had reached one of the refuge chambers. It was empty. Meanwhile, workers had been pumping nitrogen into the mine through the drill holes hoping to neutralize the explosive gas and dust. That afternoon, when rescuers were once again cleared to enter the mine they headed for the second refuge chamber. No one was in the chamber; instead, the rescuers found the lifeless bodies of the four missing men lying in the tunnels. Altogether, 29 miners were killed in the worst mining disaster in forty years. The question on everybody's mind was what had caused the deadly explosion inside the Upper Big Branch Mine.

From the first day after the explosion, newspapers had been reporting that Massey Energy mines in general, and the Upper Big Branch Mine in particular, had been cited thousands of times for safety violations by the U.S. Mine Safety and Health Administration (MSHA), an agency of the federal government charged with overseeing employee safety in the mining industry. In fact, the Upper Big Branch

Mine had been cited more than 50 times for safety violations during the previous month alone, and many of Massey Energy's other coal mines had equally poor safety records.[4]

Massey Energy Company was founded in 1920 in Richmond, Virginia as a coal brokering business. The company acquired its first coal mine in 1945. In 1981, the company was acquired by Fluor Corporation, and with its backing, the mining business rapidly grew. In 1992, Don Blankenship, who had joined the company in 1982, was appointed Chairman and CEO of Massey. In 2000, he oversaw Massey's transformation into an independent company when it split off from Fluor Corporation's non coal-related businesses. Over the next several years, the company continued to grow and by 2010, it was annually producing about 40 million tons of low-sulfur bituminous coal in 42 underground mines and 14 surface mines scattered throughout West Virginia, Kentucky, and Virginia. Massey processed and distributed the coal through 22 processing and shipping centers. The company had 5,851 employees, and in 2009 it had net profits of $104 million on total revenues of $2.7 billion.[5]

Under the leadership of CEO Don Blankenship, the company's operations had aroused considerable controversy, much of it related to their impact on the environment. In 1984, when Blankenship was president of Rawl, a subsidiary of Massey Energy Company, he was faced with the problem of disposing of the millions of gallons of coal slurry the mines were producing. Coal slurry is a watery mud that runs off as coal is washed to remove its impurities. The slurry carries with it several toxic substances commonly found in coal, such as arsenic, lead, and cadmium. Blankenship came up with the idea of disposing of the slurry by piping it deep into abandoned coal mines. But there were cracks running through the walls and floors of the mines, and apparently the toxics in the slurry leaked through the cracks and ended up contaminating the underground aquifer that fed the wells from which the surrounding communities drew their drinking water. The company was forced to pay $3.5 million in fines for the environmental disaster it had created. Then, in 2000 the dam of a small lake filled with coal slurry collapsed, sending 250 million gallons of toxic slurry flooding through Kentucky's rivers, leaving behind over 100 miles of contaminated waterways and destroying the drinking water sources of surrounding towns. That same year, two of its other coal mines had to pay fines for contaminating West Virginia's waterways. In 2006, the company paid additional fines of $1.4 million to settle five environmental lawsuits and 14 environmental enforcement actions. In 2008, the company paid another $20 million to settle a government lawsuit charging the company with 4,000 violations of the Clean Water Act.[6]

But in 2010, most of the criticisms leveled against Massey Energy Company focused on the company's lack of attention to employee safety. In the days following the Upper Big Branch Mine explosion, in fact, Massey was repeatedly accused of having the worst safety record in the industry. The average number of worker injuries in U.S. mines is 4.03 injuries per 200,000 miners. Yet, ten of Massey Energy's underground coal mines, including the Upper Big Branch coal mine, had accident injury rates ranging between 4.49 and 9.78 injuries per 200,000 workers. Not only did these mines have more injuries than the national average, but at least four had more than twice the national average.[7] Rick Melberth, director of OMB Watch, a regulatory watchdog group, pointed out that Massey and its Upper Big Branch mine were unusually lax in the area of worker safety. "There are huge mines out there that produce a lot more coal, have a lot more hours worked and can operate without violations," he said.[8]

This was not the first time that Massey Energy's safety problems were accused of having led to the loss of lives. In January 2006, a fire had erupted in a Massey coal mine in Logan County, West Virginia and two miners were killed. A state investigation concluded that the deadly fire was due to several safety violations that the company had failed to correct. One was a failure to fix a conveyor belt that caught fire, another was allowing the accumulation of combustible materials that had fed the fire, another was the absence of carbon monoxide monitors that could have alerted the miners to the fire, another was the absence of required fire extinguishers, and another was improper ventilation controls. A few months before the 2006 fire, CEO Blankenship had written a memo suggesting managers should concentrate on producing coal and not waste time responding to requests to fix things: "If any of you have been asked by your group presidents, your supervisors, engineers, or anyone else to do anything other than run coal . . . you need to ignore them and run coal. This memo is necessary only because we seem not to understand that the coal pays the bills." In 2009, the company paid $4.2 million in criminal and civil penalties to settle federal charges that the company had willfully violated federal safety standards and that those violations were responsible for the two miners' deaths.[9]

Safety violations had plagued the Upper Big Branch Mine for some time. A year before the 2010 explosion, the mine had been cited eight times for "substantial" violations related to its methane monitors. Regulations required that the mine have methane monitors to warn of any dangerous buildup of methane gas. Methane gas is an odorless gas that gathers in the seams of coal deposits, and it is common for the gas to leak out and accumulate in coal mines, creating a deadly risk since methane is highly flammable and explosive. The mine's operator was supposed to calibrate the methane monitors in the tunnels at least once a month to ensure they were in working order and capable of accurately sensing when the gas had reached dangerous levels. But twice, federal inspectors had found that Massey was calibrating its methane monitors only once every three months creating a risk that the monitors might not be able to properly detect dangerous levels of methane. Federal regulators also found that the company was not ventilating the mine properly. Ventilation prevents accumulations of methane gas, as well as of coal dust which, like methane, is combustible and can add to an explosion. The inspectors had forced the company to temporarily stop work in some sections of the mine until the ventilation problems had been corrected. While it was not clear exactly what had ignited the explosion of April 5, it was almost certain that it was caused by accumulations of methane and coal dust.

Those were not the only safety issues at the mine. The month before the explosion, the U.S. Mine Safety and Health Administration (MSHA) had cited the Upper Big Branch mine for a total of 50 safety violations, 12 of which were related to problems with ventilation of the mine that should have prevented the accumulation of methane gas and coal dust.[10] Since the start of the year inspectors, had issued 68 citations for violations they termed "high negligence" and three of "reckless" disregard. In addition to poor ventilation of coal dust and methane gas, the mine had also been cited for failure to maintain proper escape ways, failure to control dust, inadequate protection from roof falls, and for allowing combustible materials to accumulate in the mine. Since 2005, MSHA had cited the mine for a total of 1,342 safety violations, and levied $7.6 million in proposed fines against Massey Energy. The company, however, had contested 422 of those violations.[11] Challenging MSHA citations allowed the company to delay paying the fines for years. Of the more than $7.6 million in fines that had been pending since 2005 against Massey Energy, the company had only paid $2.3 million by 2010.

At the center of the storm of criticism that engulfed the company after the mine explosion was CEO Blankenship who had been paid $11.8 million in salary, bonuses, and other benefits in 2008. The families of several miners accused him of putting profits ahead of safety. Born in 1950, Blankenship grew up in Stopover, Kentucky, a poor village made up mostly of shacks and trailer homes. His mother divorced his father shortly after he was born, and Blankenship ended up being raised by his mother. A childhood friend of his said "He was a very competitive kid—he didn't like to fail... He was always trying to figure out what he could get away with." In high school, Blankenship played baseball and was elected president of his class. When he graduated, he enrolled in Marshall University in Huntington, where he majored in accounting and managed to graduate within three years. Afterwards, he worked as an accountant for the Keebler Company, married and had two children. Then, in 1982, the Massey Energy Company contacted Blankenship and offered him a job in one of its subsidiaries, named Rawl. He accepted the offer and two years later, he was named president of Rawl. Blankenship continued his rise up the company's ranks until, in 1992, he was named CEO and chair of the entire company.

Families of the dead miners accused Blankenship of "always cutting corners on safety, pushing for more coal."[12] Blankenship vehemently denied this:

> From the day I became a member of Massey's leadership team 20 years ago, I have made safety my number one priority... The result has been a 90 percent reduction in our lost time accident rate, which has been better—often dramatically better—than the industry average for 17 of the last 19 years. So let me state for the record—Massey does not place profits over safety. We never have, and we never will.[13]

While Blankenship acknowledged that Massey had received a large number of safety citations, this was not unusual, he said, for a coal company:

> Violations are unfortunately a normal part of the mining process... There are violations at every coal mine in America, and Upper Big Branch was a mine that had violations... I think the fact that MSHA, the state, and our fire bosses and the best engineers that you can find were all in and around this mine, and all believed it to be safe in the circumstances it was in, speaks for itself as far as any suspicion that the mine was improperly operated.[14]

And, in a startling move, Blankenship also suggested that MSHA itself might have been responsible for the deaths of the 29 miners:

> Against the advice of our own experts, MSHA required several changes since September 2009 that made the ventilation plan significantly more complex. This change in ventilation significantly reduced the volume of fresh air to the face of the longwall mining operation during this period.... We opposed the changes because our own engineers believed they made the mine less safe, not because they were more costly or because they interfered with production.[15]

During congressional hearings, however, survivors of the explosion and relatives of those who had died testified that conditions in the mine were not always up to standards, and that the miners felt too threatened to raise objections. One survivor, Stanley Stewart, testified:

> My name is Stanley Stewart. Most people know me as "Goose." I have worked in coal mines for

34 years and at the Upper Big Branch mine for 15 of those years. I worked at the Upper Big Branch mine until the day of the accident and was 300 feet underground the day the explosion occurred.... The area of the mine we were working was liberating [releasing] a lot of methane. Mine management never fully addressed the air problem when it would be shut down by inspectors. They would fix it just good enough to get us to load coal again, but then it would be back to business as usual.... My experience in the mines showed me that the ventilation system they had didn't work. And with so much methane being liberated, and no air moving it gave me the feeling that area was a ticking time bomb. I was told prior to the April 5th explosion, that they had experienced at least 2 fireballs [small flare-ups of methane] on the drum of the shearer. This leads me to believe the methane was indeed building in that area, showing lack of air and ventilation problems.... No one felt they could go to management and express their fears or the lack of air on our sections. We knew that we'd be marked men and the management would look for ways to fire us. Maybe not that day, or that week, but somewhere down the line, we'd disappear. We'd seen it happen and I told my wife, I felt like I was working for the Gestapo at times.[16]

A relative of one of the dead miners said:

My name is Alice Peters and I am the mother-in-law of Edward Dean Jones. Dean was killed in the explosion on April 5th at the Upper Big Branch mine. Dean was married to my daughter, Gina, and they have one son, Kyle. Kyle suffers from cystic fibrosis and has medical problems that require constant medical care.... Dean told me many times that he had concerns about the ventilation at the Upper Big Branch mine. He often told me and his wife that he was afraid to go to work because the conditions at the mine were so bad. He also told me that, at least 7 times, he was told by Massey supervisors that, if he shut down production because of the ventilation problems (bad air), he would lose his job. They knew about his son and that Dean needed to keep his job to make sure his son could get the medical care he needed.[17]

The relative of another of the miners who had been killed testified:

My name is Leo Long. I had a grandson that was killed in the Upper Big Branch mine at Massey. You know, he stayed with me for years and years. I put him through school, he graduated, went to work. I seen him every day, every night. After he got married, he moved right beside of me and I'd see him when he'd come in of an evening from work from the mines.... And he told me something [about]... the methane. He said that the company had a way to bridge [the wiring of the methane monitors on] the continuous miner [a machine that continuously digs for coal] to keep it working [even] if the methane got so [high], when the methane gets so high, it [the monitor] is supposed to shut everything down. But Massey had a way to keep the continuous miner working, bringing coal out. Money come before the men did. You was only a number.[18]

But while many people blamed the company for the deaths of the miners, some critics also faulted MSHA, the federal agency that was supposed to protect miners. For one thing, the agency was understaffed and its inspectors were overworked. In addition, a government audit of the agency released the week before the mine explosion said that more than half of the agency's inspectors failed to attend required training courses and the agency neither kept track of their attendance nor did it sanction them.

Critics also pointed out that regulations passed in 2007 hampered MSHA's ability to sanction mining companies. Mining companies, Massey Energy in particular, regularly challenged the citations of MSHA inspectors, a process that required MSHA to submit the challenge to a panel of judges called the Federal Mine Safety and Health Review Commission (MSHRC). But because MSHRC did not have enough judges to review the challenges in a timely fashion, years often passed before companies were forced to address the citations.[19]

Although MSHA had the authority to close down a mine if the mine had a substantial number of citations, it had not been able to close the Upper Big Branch mine.[20] On December 6, 2007, MSHA had sent a letter to Rick Hodge, superintendent of the Upper Big Branch mine, stating that the mine had accumulated so many violations that it would be closed down if it received any more "Significant and Substantial" violations. The letter read:

In accordance with Section 104(e) of the Federal Mine Safety and Health Act of 1977 and 30CFR Part 104, the Mine Safety and Health Administration has conducted a pattern of violation (POV) screening of compliance records for the Upper Big Branch Mine... for the 24 months ending September 30, 2007. A POV screening is used to determine if Section 104(e) is applicable to a particular mine. If implemented, Section 104(e) requires all subsequent

> violations designated as Significant and Substantial be issued as closure orders with all persons withdrawn from the affected area, except those necessary to correct the violation. An operator can be removed from Section 104(e) sanctions only after an inspection of the entire operation results in no Significant and Substantial violations. This letter is your notification that a potential pattern of violation exists at the Upper Big Branch Mine.[21]

After receiving the letter, however, officials of Massey Energy challenged several of the citations on which it was based, and corrected enough of the significant and substantial violations it had received during the previous 24 months, to allow its total violations to fall below the level needed to force its closure. Consequently, although MSHA had frequently closed down sections of the mine when it demanded the company remedy a particular ventilation problem, it never forced the entire mine to shut down in order to force it to make significant changes.

In October 2009, MSHA had again reviewed the citations the Upper Big Branch mine had received. But, regulators later discovered, the computer program that processed the review had an error within it. According to Secretary of Labor Hilda L. Solis, "Had the error in the computer program been corrected, the mine could have been placed into potential pattern of violation status in October of 2009." But the error was not corrected until after the 29 miners were killed in the explosion.[22]

Cecil Roberts, President of the United Mine Workers of America (UMWA), the largest miners' union in the United States, focused the union's criticisms on Massey and connected its lack of union representation with its poor record of mine safety. A union, he felt, would have fought for better enforcement of safety regulations to protect the miners. But CEO Blankenship was aggressively anti-union. In 1996, he had convinced the company to leave the collective bargaining agreements with the UMWA that all the other major coal companies had accepted. That same year Blankenship had to testify in a federal lawsuit during which he said that "No [coal] operator in their right mind would go union."[23] At his urging, the company gradually phased out and closed down any mines that had earlier been unionized. By 2009, only 76 out of the company's 5,851 workers were still unionized. The company had fought particularly hard to make sure that the Upper Big Branch mine was not unionized. When the UMWA mounted a drive to unionize the workers at the mine, the company threatened to close the mine if its workers unionized, and in 1997 they narrowly voted down the union. During the congressional hearings on the mine disaster, several miners testified on the difference a union might have made:

> My name is Gary Quarles. I am the father of Gary Wayne Quarles who was killed as a result of the explosion at the Upper Big Branch mine on April 5, 2010. Gary Wayne was my only son and my best friend..... I also am a coal miner.... I worked in union mines for 23 years and have worked in non-union mines the rest of the time... Safety inspections were much different in the union mines I've worked at versus the non-union Massey mines. When an MSHA inspector comes onto a Massey mine property, the code words go out "we've got a man on the property." Those words are radioed from the guard gates and relayed to all working operations in the mine.... When the word goes out, all effort is made to correct any deficiencies or direct the inspector's attention away from any deficiencies.... When I worked at union mines, workers at the mine would accompany the MSHA inspectors during their inspections.... When the MSHA inspector comes to a Massey mine, the only people accompanying him are Massey company people. No coal miner at the mine can point out areas of concern to the MSHA inspector.... The Upper Big Branch mine was clearly not safe and as a result 29 miners died, including my son. Someone needs to be held responsible for these deaths.[24]

Other miners pointed out that in unionized mines, miners do not have to enter areas that are unsafe:

> My name is Eddie Cook. I'm Adam Morgan's uncle. Adam was 21 [when] the explosion took him away from us. I worked at Cleveland Cliffs Pinnacle mine [which is] union.... As a union person, we have the right to refuse to do work we think is unsafe. Non-union mines, you don't have that. You don't have the right to refuse. If you refuse, they tell you to "get your bucket and go home," you know. "If you don't want to work here, we've got people out on the street wanting your jobs. And if you don't like the way we run it, you can go home."[25]

Stanley Stewart made a similar point:

> I worked close to 20 years in the union and 15 years non-union so I've been on both sides of the fence long enough to know the difference in how miners feel in both types of working

> environments. In the union if you had safety concerns you had the right to refuse to work in unsafe conditions without fear of your job. You felt at ease and comforted by your rights. Working at a non-union mine you do not feel that comfort. You know you have to operate with a lack of air or in unsafe conditions.[26]

On June 15, 2010, investigative teams exploring the mine discovered a large crack in the floor of the mine. Speaking for his company, Blankenship said that the crack may have allowed methane to leak into the tunnel before the explosion on April 5, which would then have been an unforeseeable and unpreventable event. Blankenship also released a letter that MSHA had written to the company on July 15, 2004, in which MSHA noted that the mine had been subject to several methane "outbursts." He claimed that the memo showed that the mine should have had a ventilation system that provided more air than normal to compensate for the periodic increases of methane, yet, he also claimed, MSHA had mandated a ventilation system that provided less air than normal.[27] On July 22, 2010, investigators announced that an examination of data from the mine's primary ventilation exhaust fan had found that on the day of the accident a sudden and large surge of methane gas had occurred within the mine. The mysterious release of gas was so large, experts said, that it could have rapidly filled a large part of the mine's interior.[28] Investigators also found near the bodies of some of the miners who had been killed, a portable handheld methane monitor that showed methane levels in the area had gone from zero to 5 percent in 3 minutes. Methane gas is not explosive until it reaches concentrations of 5 percent to 15 percent.[29] It was unclear whether there was any connection between the crack in the mine's floor and the surge of methane gas, and between either of these and the explosion on April 5.

On Friday, December 3, 2010, Massey Energy Company announced that at the end of the year, Blankenship would step down from his position as CEO and Chair of the company. It was not clear whether the company's board of directors had asked him to resign or he had decided to do so on his own. In a statement Blankenship said only, "After almost three decades at Massey, it's time for me to move on."

Questions

1. In your judgment, and given only the facts described in the case above, should the management of Massey Energy Company be held morally responsible for the deaths of the 29 miners? Explain your answer.
2. Suppose nothing more is learned about the explosion other than what is described in the case above. Do you think Don Blankenship should be held morally responsible for the deaths of the 29 miners?
3. Given only the facts described in the case above, should the MSHA be held morally responsible (at least in part) for the deaths of the 29 miners?
4. The miners seem to have had some idea of the risks of working in the Upper Big Branch Mine. Should they be held at least partially responsible for their own deaths?
5. In light of the differences between mines without unions like the Massey mines, and other mines that had unions, do you think all mines should be forced to have a union?
6. Miners in the Upper Big Branch mine were paid about $60,000 a year (in some cases less, and in other cases more, depending on seniority and several other factors) for work that required no more than a high school education. The average salary for all jobs in the United States is about $43,000. In light of the chapter's discussion of job risks, would you say that the company was handling job risk in an ethically appropriate manner?
7. List all the ethical obligations that you believe the management of Massey Energy Company did NOT fulfill. Explain the ethical basis of each of the obligations on your list.

Notes

1. Michael A. Fuoco, "A Timeline of Events at the Upper Big Branch Mine," *Pittsburgh Post-Gazette*, April 7, 2010.
2. *The Upper Big Branch Mine Tragedy*, Field Hearing Before the Committee on Education and Labor, U.S. House Of Representatives, One Hundred Eleventh Congress, Second Session; Hearing Held In Beckley, WV, May 24, 2010, Serial No. 111–65, (Washington, DC: U.S. Government Printing Office, 2010), p. 34
3. Michelle James, "A Timeline Look at the Upper Big Branch Mine Disaster," *The Register Herald*, April 11, 2010.
4. Phil Mattera, "Massey Energy," *Crocodyl, Collaborative Research on Corporations*, April 12, 2010, accessed January 17, 2011 at *http://www.crocodyl.org/wiki/massey_energy*.
5. Phil Mattera, "Massey Energy," April 12, 2010.
6. Ibid.
7. *National Public Radio* (NPR), April 12, 2010, "Massey Energy's Other High-Injury Mines, accessed at *http://www.npr.org/templates/story/story.php?storyId=125864564*.
8. Peter Overby, "Documents Reveal Extensive Violations at Mine," *National Public Radio*, April 9, 2010, accessed January 20, 2011 at *http://www.npr.org/templates/story/story.php?storyId=125788709&ps=rs*.
9. Christopher Maag, "Unacceptable Risk: The Real Price of Coal Mining," *Popular Mechanics*, August 23, 2010.
10. Steven Mufson, Jerry Markon, and Ed O'Keefe, "West Virginia Mine Has Been Cited for Myriad Safety Violations," *The Washington Post* April 7, 2010.

11. Steven Mufson, "Massey Energy Has Litany of Critics, Violations," *The Washington Post*, April 6, 2010.
12. Jeff Goodell, "The Dark Lord of Coal Country," *Rolling Stone*, November 29, 2010.
13. Don L. Blankenship, Chair and CEO, Massey Energy, Testimony before the Subcommittee on Labor, Health and Human Services and Education and Related Agencies, Committee on Appropriations, United States Senate, May 20, 2010.
14. Ian Urbina and Michael Cooper, "Deaths at West Virginia Mine Raise Issues About Safety," *The New York Times*, April 6, 2010.
15. Don L. Blankenship, Chair and CEO, Massey Energy, Testimony before the Subcommittee on Labor, Health and Human Services and Education and Related Agencies, Committee on Appropriations, United States Senate, May 20, 2010.
16. *The Upper Big Branch Mine Tragedy*, Field Hearing. May 24, 2010, pp. 34–35.
17. Ibid., p. 28.
18. Ibid., p. 66.
19. Ed O'Keefe, "U.S. Mine Safety and Health Administration Faces Training and Oversight Problems," *The Washington Post*, April 7, 2010.
20. Mufson, Markon, and O'Keefe, "West Virginia Mine Has Been Cited for Myriad Safety Violations."
21. Letter accessed January 25, 2011 at *http://www.msha.gov/MEDIA/PRESS/2007/POV12072007/Performance Coal Company.pdf*.
22. Statement of U.S. Secretary of Labor Hilda L. Solis on Upper Big Branch Mine and pattern of violation status, January 18, 2011, accessed January 30, 2011 at *http://www.msha.gov/Media/PRESS/2010/NR100413.asp*.
23. *Charleston Gazette*, April 20, 1996.
24. *The Upper Big Branch Mine Tragedy*, Field Hearing. May 24, 2010, p. 23.
25. Ibid., p. 27.
26. Ibid., p. 36.
27. CNN Wire Staff, "Crack Found in Floor of West Virginia Mine Where 29 Men Died," *CNN*, June 15, 2010.
28. CNN Wire Staff, "Investigators: W.V. Mine Filled Suddenly with Methane," *CNN*, July 22, 2010.
29. Tim Huber, "MSHA: Methane Monitor Showing Explosive Level Found at UBB," *The Register-Herald*, August 27, 2010.

CASES

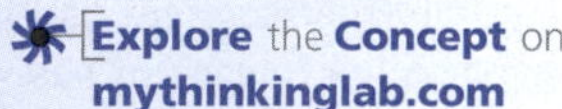

Who Should Pay?[1]

The stakes were high for Gene Elliot, whose on-the-job injuries were estimated to be serious enough to merit at least a $2.4 million settlement. But who should pay for his injuries: Turner Construction or B&C Steel? Or should Elliot be forced to pay for at least part of his injuries because of his own carelessness?

Gene Elliot worked for Mabey Bridge and Shore, a small business that rented temporary steel pedestrian foot bridges to other companies. The temporary bridges had to be put together by the renter, and Elliot's job was to go to the site where the steel bridge was going to be installed, show the renter how to bolt the bridge sections together and how to install the bridge over a river or waterway, and inspect the bridge to make sure it was done properly and according to Mabey Bridge's high standards. Elliot was a devoted hard worker who strove to do everything possible to ensure that a bridge installation was successful and according to Mabey Bridge's standards.

Turner Construction was a general contractor hired to build Invesco Field at the Mile High Stadium in Denver, Colorado. Part of the job involved installing a temporary pedestrian bridge over the Platte River near the stadium. Turner Construction subcontracted (hired) B&C Steel to build and install the bridge, which Turner Construction would pay for. B&C Steel was a small company that specialized in putting together and installing steel structures like those Mabey Bridge rented out. B&C Steel would pick up the bridge, put it together, and install it for Turner Construction.

Turner Construction rented the long steel bridge from Mabey Bridge. Mabey Bridge agreed that the rental included the services of Gene Elliot, who would be loaned to Turner Construction to instruct and inspect the bridge assembly and installation. B&C Steel's workers picked up the bridge sections from Mabey Bridge's warehouse and drove them to the river, but did not unload the bridge sections where they had to be assembled. B&C Steel then had to move the sections to the correct site, but did not plan for the fence, guardrails, and trolley tracks that were in the way and later had to work around these obstructions. B&C Steel began bolting the bridge sections together. When Elliot inspected the job, he found the bridge had been bolted together upside down. Elliot made B&C Steel do the job over, while he climbed up and down and over the bridge, continuously checking and making sure that all the bolts were tight and all the pieces were in the right place so that the installation would be a success. When the bridge was finished, B&C Steel workers used a truck to move the long steel structure to the edge of the river. Unfortunately, B&C Steel had not adequately checked the route and their truck hit a low-hanging power line, which sparked and started a fire. The fire department arrived and put out the fire. Afterwards, the installation job continued.

B&C Steel workers set up a crane on the other side of the river near a retaining wall, and a strong nylon strap was strung from the crane, over the water, and tied to one end of the bridge, which was set on rollers. The B&C Steel crane would lift and pull the bridge over the river to its side, while workers on the other side of the river pushed on their end of the bridge. The work began, and as the pulling crane held the bridge suspended in the air about a quarter of the way over the river, Elliot noticed that the retaining wall which was supporting the crane on the other side of the river was beginning to collapse, causing the crane to begin to tip sideways. The B&C Steel crane operator on the other side began to untie the strap holding the bridge. Concerned that once the strap was cut the bridge would fall into the river and the installation would end in failure, Elliot ran up on the bridge and gave the standard emergency OSHA all-stop signal that all construction workers know means not to move anything. But the bridge, still attached to the crane, somehow moved, and Elliot fell, sustaining numerous pelvic injuries and a severed urethra (the tube that carries urine). The cause of the movement was never established.

Elliot sued Turner Construction and B&C Steel for negligence resulting in economic losses of $28,000, non-economic injuries of $1,200,000, and permanent impairment of $1,200,000. These figures were established by a qualified expert in the field of worker injuries and were not seriously contested.

Turner Construction, however, denied its responsibility. It claimed that Turner was Elliot's temporary employer and workers' compensation law required employers to pay only the economic losses, here only $28,000, suffered by their employees. Turner Construction pointed to the law, which stated: "Any company leasing or contracting out any part of the work to any lessee or subcontractor, shall be construed to be an employer and shall be liable to pay [only] compensation for injury resulting therefrom to said lessees and subcontractors and their employees." Turner Construction claimed that Mabey Bridge was a subcontractor to Turner to the extent that it provided the services of Elliot to Turner, so Turner should be construed to be Elliot's temporary employer. Moreover, Colorado's workers' compensation law, which was designed to ensure that employers always paid for worker injuries "grants an injured employee compensation from the employer without regard to negligence and, in return, the responsible employer is granted immunity from common law negligence liability."

B&C Steel claimed that it, too, was not responsible, because according to the law a company is not responsible for negligence when an injury is not "reasonably foreseeable" to the company. B&C Steel contended that a reasonable person could not have anticipated that placing the crane near to the retaining wall and subsequently attempting to remove the nylon strap holding up the bridge might end by prompting someone to get on the bridge in an attempt to save it from falling into the river. On the other hand, B&C Steel claimed, since "Elliot chose to remove himself from a secure and safe position and placed himself in one that he understood was potentially unsafe," Elliot was himself responsible for his injuries.

Elliot claimed that he was not really Turner Construction's employee, since he was working for Mabey Bridge. He also argued that B&C Steel had shown a pattern of negligence from the time that the bridge was received until the time that it was installed. B&C Steel and its employees, he said, were unprepared for the project and negligently failed to adequately plan for it, as shown by the sequence of events leading up to his injury. B&C Steel, therefore, did not exercise the degree of care that a reasonably careful person should have exercised in similar circumstances and so was liable to him for his injuries. He himself was not responsible, Elliot said, because a good, devoted employee would try his best to ensure that the bridge installation did not end in failure, and he would have been perfectly safe if the standard OSHA all-stop signal had been followed by B&C Steel employees, as he had a right to expect it to be.

Questions

1. In your judgment, and from an ethical point of view, should Turner Construction and/or B&C Steel pay for all or part of the $2,428,000 (if part, indicate which part)? Explain your view.
2. In your judgement, and from an ethical point of view, should Elliot be held wholly or partially responsible for his injuries and left to shoulder all or part of the $2,428,000 cost of his injuries (if part, indicate which part)? Explain.
3. In your judgement, is the Colorado worker's compensation law to which Turner Construction appealed fair? Explain your view.

Note

1. This case is based entirely on *Eugene Elliot v. Turner Construction Company and B&C Steel*, United States Court of Appeals, Tenth Circuit, August 24, 2004, case no. 03-1209.

Notes

Chapter 1

1. P. Roy Vagelos, "Social Benefits of a Successful Biomedical Research Company: Merck," *Proceedings of the American Philosophical Society*, December 2001, v. 145, n. 4, p. 577. Additional materials on Merck's history of dealing with river blindness can be found on its website at *http://www.merck.com/corporate-responsibility/access/access-developing-emerging/mectizan-donation-riverblindness/home.html* and at *http://www.mectizan.org*.
2. P. Roy Vagelos and Louis Galambos, *The Moral Corporation: Merck Experiences*, (Cambridge University Press: New York, 2006), p. 2.
3. *Wall Street Journal*, "Merck to Donate Drug for River Blindness," October 22, 1987, p. 42.
4. David Bollier, "Merck & Company" (Stanford, CA: The Business Enterprise Trust, 1991), p. 5.
5. Ibid., p. 16; see also, Vagelos and Galambos, *The Moral Corporation: Merck Experiences*.
6. To see Merck's reports of its performance in the area of social responsibility, see its website at *http://www.merck.com/corporate-responsibility*.
7. Thomas J. Peters and Robert H. Waterman, Jr., for example, made this point in their popular book *In Search of Excellence* (New York: Harper and Row, 1982).
8. "Ethic," *Webster's Third New International Dictionary*, Unabridged (Springfield, MA: Merriam-Webster Inc., 1986), p. 780. Similar definitions can be found in any recent dictionary.
9. Kermit Vandivier, "Why Should My Conscience Bother Me?" in Robert Heilbroner, ed., *In the Name of Profit* (Garden City, NY: Doubleday & Co., Inc., 1972), p. 6; another version of this article is Kermit Vandivier, "The Aircraft Brake Scandal," *Harpers Magazine*, vol. 244, April 1972, pp. 43–52.
10. Vandivier, "Why Should My Conscience Bother Me?" pp. 5 and 6.
11. U.S. Congress, *Air Force A-7D Brake Problem: Hearing before the Subcommittee on Economy in Government of the Joint Economic Committee, 91st Congress, 1st session*, August 13, 1969, p. 2.
12. Vandivier, "Why Should My Conscience Bother Me?," p. 4.
13. U.S. Congress, *Air Force A-7D Brake Problem*, pp. 5 and 6.
14. E. Turiel, *The Development of Social Knowledge: Morality and Convention*, (Cambridge: Cambridge University Press, 1983); E. Turiel, M. Killen, and C. Helwig, "Morality: Its Structure, Functions, and Vagaries," in J. Kagan and S. Lamb, eds., *The Emergence of Morality in Young Children*, (Chicago: University of Chicago Press, 1987); J. Dunn and P. Munn, "Development of Justification in Disputes with Mother and Sibling," *Developmental Psychology*, vol. 23 (1987), pp. 791–798; J. Smetana, "Preschool Children's Conceptions of Transgressions: Effects of Varying Moral and Conventional Domain-Related Attributes," *Developmental Psychology*, vol. 21 (1985), pp. 18–29; J. Smetana, "Toddler's Social Interactions in the Context of Moral and Conventional Transgressions in the Home," *Developmental Psychology*, vol. 25 (1989), pp. 499–508; J. Smetana and J. Braeges, "The Development of Toddlers' Moral and Conventional Judgments, *Merrill-Palmer Quarterly*, vol. 36 (1990), pp. 329–346; L. Nucci, "Children's Conceptions of Morality, Social Conventions, and Religious Prescription," in C. Harding, ed., *Moral Dilemmas: Philosophical and Psychological Reconsiderations of the Development of Moral Reasoning*, (Chicago: Precedent Press, 1986).
15. Smetana and Braeges (1990), Ibid.; Dunn and Munn (1987), Ibid.; Smetana (1989), Ibid.
16. M. Hollos, P. Leis, and E. Tureil, "Social Reasoning in Ijo Children and Adolescents in Nigerian Communities," *Journal of Cross-Cultural Psychology*, vol. 17 (1986), pp. 352–374; L. Nucci, E. Turiel, and G. Encarnacion-Gawrych, "Children's Social Interactions and Social Concepts: Analyses of Morality and Convention in the Virgin Islands," *Journal of Cross-Cultural Psychology*, vol. 14 (1983), pp. 469–487; M. Song, J. Smetana, and S. Kim, "Korean Children's Conceptions of Moral and Conventional Transgressions," *Developmental Psychology*, vol. 23 (1987), pp. 577–582.
17. H. L. A. Hart, *The Concept of Law* (London: Oxford University Press, 1961), pp. 84–85. See also Charles Fried, *An Anatomy of Values* (Cambridge, MA: Harvard University Press, 1970), pp. 91–142.
18. The point is made in Thomas E. Hill, "Reasonable Self-Interest," *Social Philosophy and Policy*, vol. 14, no. 1 (1997).
19. The classic source of this observation is Immanual Kant, see his *Groundwork of the Metaphysics of Morals*, [1785], translated by Mary Gregor, (Cambridge, UK: Cambridge University Press, 1997). More recently, the idea that moral norms must be universal has been fundamental to the work of several philosophers including: Richard M. Hare, *The Language of Morals*, (Oxford University Press, 1952), and *Freedom and Reason*, (Oxford University Press, 1963); Marcus G. Singer, *Generalization in Ethics*, (Eyre and Spottiswoode, 1963); Alan Gewirth, "Categorical Consistency in Ethics," *Philosophical Quarterly*, (1967); Philip Pettit, "Non-Consequentialism and Universalizability," *The Philosophical Quarterly*, vol. 50 (2000), pp. 175–190; Jurgen Habermas, *Moral Consciousness and Communicative Action*, translated by Christian Lenhardt and Shierry Weber Nicholsen, (Cambridge, MA: The MIT Press, 1990).
20. See, for example, Rachels, *Elements of Moral Philosophy*, pp. 9–10.
21. Baier, *Moral Point of View* (New York: Random House, 1965), p. 107.
22. The point is made in Peter Singer, *Practical Ethics*, 2nd ed. (New York: Cambridge University Press, 1993), pp. 10–11.
23. Richard B. Brandt, *A Theory of the Good and the Right* (New York: Oxford University Press, 1979), pp. 166–169.

24. Jack Anderson, "Enron Blame Game Missing Real Target," *Laredo Morning Times*, March 26, 2002, p. 4A [incorrectly printed date on page is March 25]; and Jack Anderson, "The Country's Corporations Can't Be Jailed," *Laredo Morning Times*, June 23, 2002, p. 2D. (Both archived at *http://www.lmtonline.com/news/archive*).
25. For the first view, see Peter A. French, *Collective and Corporate Responsibility* (New York: Columbia University Press, 1984); Kenneth E. Goodpaster and John B. Matthews, Jr., "Can a Corporation Have a Conscience?"*Harvard Business Review*, 1982, v. 60, pp. 132–141; Thomas Donaldson, "Moral Agency and Corporations," *Philosophy in Context*, 1980, v. 10, pp. 51–70; David T. Ozar, "The Moral Responsibility of Corporations," in *Ethical Issues in Business*, Thomas Donaldson and Patricia Werhane, eds. (Englewood Cliffs, NJ: Prentice-Hall, 1979), pp. 294–300. For the second, see John Ladd, "Morality and the Ideal of Rationality in Formal Organizations," *The Monist*, 1970, v. 54, n. 4, pp. 488–516, and "Corporate Mythology and Individual Responsibility," *The International Journal of Applied Philosophy*, Spring 1984, v. 2, n. 1, pp. 1–21; Patricia H. Werhane, "Formal Organizations, Economic Freedom and Moral Agency," *Journal of Value Inquiry*, 1980, v. 14, pp. 43–50. The author's own views are more fully developed in Manuel Velasquez, "Why Corporations Are Not Morally Responsible for Anything They Do," *Business & Professional Ethics Journal*, Spring 1983, v. 2, n. 3, pp. 1–18, and "Debunking Corporate Moral Responsibility," *Business Ethics Quarterly*, October 2003, v. 13, n. 4, also similar to the author's views are those in Michael Keeley, "Organizations as Non-Persons,"*Journal of Value Inquiry*, 1981, v. 15, pp. 149–155.
26. See, for example, the decision of the Supreme Court of the state of Wisconsin, *Milwaukee Toy Co. vs. Industrial Comm'n of Wis.*, 203 Wis. 493, 234 N.W. 748 (1931), where the court said that the corporate fiction could be set aside when "applying the corporate fiction would accomplish some fraudulent purpose, operate as a constructive fraud, or defeat some strong equitable claim."
27. Angelo Capuano, "The Realist's Guide to Piercing the Corporate Veil: Lessons from Hong Kong and Singapore," *Australian Journal of Corporate Law*, vol. 23 (2009), pp. 1–38.
28. See, for example, the long discussion of these issues in LaRue Tone Hosmer, *The Ethics of Management*, 3rd ed. (Homewood, IL: McGraw-Hill/Irwin, 1995), pp. 34–55.
29. For these and other criticisms, see Alan H. Goldman, "Business Ethics: Profits, Utilities, and Moral Rights," *Philosophy and Public Affairs*, Spring 1980, v. 9, n. 3, pp. 260–286.
30. See Alex C. Michales, *A Pragmatic Approach to Business Ethics* (Thousand Oaks, CA: Sage Publications, 1995), p. 45.
31. Kati Cornell Smith, "Worldcon Gets 5; Testimony Wins Stoolie Sullivan Easy Jail Time," *New York Post*, August 12, 2005.
32. John Lehmann, "Two Former WorldCom Execs Admit They Cooked the Books," *New York Post*, October 11, 2002.
33. See Phillip I. Blumberg, "Corporate Responsibility and the Employee's Duty of Loyalty and Obedience: A Preliminary Inquiry," in *The Corporate Dilemma: Traditional Values Versus Contemporary Problems*, Dow Votaw and S. Prakash Sethi, eds. (Englewood Cliffs, NJ: Prentice Hall, 1973), pp. 82–113.
34. Quoted in Blumberg, "Corporate Responsibility," p. 86.
35. Richard Wachman, "Greek Deal Puts Goldman Sachs in the Firing Line–Again," *The Observer*, February 28, 2010.
36. See John Finnis, *Natural Law and Natural Rights* (Oxford: Clarendon Press, 1980), pp. 295–350; John Rawls, *A Theory of Justice* (Cambridge, MA: Harvard University Press, 1971), pp. 108–114; Alan Donagan, *The Theory of Morality* (Chicago: University of Chicago Press, 1977), pp. 108–111.
37. For a similar version of this argument, see Alex C. Michalos, *A Pragmatic Approach to Business Ethics*, pp. 54–57.
38. These are some of the more well-known companies cited over several years in the annual list of "100 Best Corporate Citizens" issued by *Corporate Responsibility Magazine*. See *Corporate Responsibility Magazine*, March, 2010.
39. Much of this research is summarized and reviewed in Manuel Velasquez, "Why Ethics Matters," *Business Ethics Quarterly*, vol. 6, no. 2, (1996), pp. 201–222.
40. John M. Darley, "Morality in the Law: The Psychological Foundations of Citizens' Desires to Punish Transgressions," *Annual Review of Law and Social Science*, vol. 5 (2009), pp. 1–23; see also, D. T. Miller, "Disrespect and the Experience of Injustice," *Annual Review of Psychology*, vo. 52 (2001), pp. 527–553.
41. In addition to Velasquez, "Why Ethics Matters," which reviews the literature and research in this area, consult Blair H. Sheppard, Roy J. Lewicki, and John W. Minton, *Organizational Justice* (New York: Lexington Books, 1992), pp. 101–103. On the higher wages workers demand to work for a firm they see as socially responsible in comparison to one they see as socially irresponsible, see R. H. Frank, "Can Socially Responsible Firms Survive in a Competitive Environment?" in D. M. Messick and A. E. Tenbrunsel, eds., *Research on Negotiations in Organizations* (Greenwich, CT: JAI Press, 1997).
42. J. Brockner, T. Tyler, and R. Schneider, "The higher they are, the harder they fall: The effect of prior commitment and procedural injustice on subsequent commitment to social institutions," paper presented at the annual academy of management meeting, Miami Beach, FL (August 1991).
43. R. Folger and M. A. Konovsky, "Effects of Procedural and Distributive Justice on Reactions to Pay Raise Decisions," *Academy of Management Journal*, 1989, v. 32, pp. 115–130; S. Alexander and M. Ruderman, "The Role of Procedural and Distributive Justice in Organizational Behavior," *Social Justice Research*, 1987, v. 1, pp. 177–198; see also T. R. Tyler, "Justice and Leadership Endorsement," in R. R. Lau and D. O. Sears, eds., *Political Cognition* (Hillsdale, NJ: Erlbaum, 1986), pp. 257–278.
44. T. R. Tyler and E. A. Lind, "A Relational Model of Authority in Groups," in M. Zanna, ed., *Advances in Experimental Social Psychology*, vol. 25 (New York: Academic Press, 1992); J. Greenberg, "Cultivating an Image of Justice: Looking Fair on the Job," *Academy of Management Executive*, 1988, v. 2, pp. 155–158; D. W. Organ, *Organizational Citizenship Behavior: The Good Soldier Syndrome* (Lexington, MA: Lexington Books, 1988).
45. Jean B. McGuire, Alison Sundgren, and Thomas Schneewels, "Corporate Social Responsibility and Firm Financial Performance,"*Academy of Management Journal*, December 1988, p. 869.
46. For a review of these studies and a new study that found no correlation one way or another, see Kenneth E. Alpperle, Archie B. Carroll, and John D. Hatfield, "An Empirical

Examination of the Relationship Between Corporate Social Responsibility and Profitability," *Academy of Management Journal*, June 1985, pp. 460–461.

47. "Responsible Investing in a Changing World," *Business Ethics*, November/December, 1995, p. 48.
48. Milton Friedman, "The Social Responsibility of Business is to Increase its Profits," *The New York Times Magazine*, September 13, 1970.
49. R. Edward Freeman and David L. Reed, "Stockholders and Stakeholders: A New Perspective on Corporate Governance," p. 91, *California Management Review*, vol. 25, no. 3, (Spring, 1983), pp. 88–106.
50. Robert Phillips, *Shareholder Theory and Organizational Ethics*, (San Francisco, CA: Berrett-Koelher Publishers, Inc., 2003).
51. Archie Carroll, "Corporate Social Responsibility: Evolution of a Definitional Construct," *Business & Society*, (1999), vol. 38, no. 3, September 1999, pp. 26–295; quote from p. 283.
52. Shaohua Chen and Martin Ravallion, "The Developing World is Poorer than We Thought, But No Less Successful in the Fight against Poverty," Policy Research Working Paper 4703, World Bank, Development Research Group, September 2009. Accessed May 29, 2010 at *http://go.worldbank.org/HAG6SG9G30*.
53. Branko Milanovic, "Global Inequality Recalculated," Policy Research Working Paper 5061, World Bank, Development Research Group: Poverty and Inequality Team, August 2008. Accessed May 29, 2010 at *http://go.worldbank.org/HR1M8IEX50*.
54. Business ethics in the international arena is a topic that is still not well developed in the literature on business ethics. See my discussion of the problems with current approaches in Manuel Velasquez, "International Business Ethics," *Business Ethics Quarterly*, October 1995, v. 5, n. 4, pp. 865–882; and "International Business, Morality, and the Common Good," *Business Ethics Quarterly*, January 1992, v. 2., n. 1, pp. 27–40.
55. The importance of singling out issues of development is a point made by Thomas Donaldson in *The Ethics of International Business*, pp. 102–103.
56. Arnold Berleant, "Multinationals and the Problem of Ethical Consistency," *Journal of Business Ethics*, August 1982, v. 3, pp. 185–195.
57. Norman Bowie, "Business Ethics and Cultural Relativism," in Alan R. Malachowski, *Business Ethics: International and Environmental Business Ethics*, (New York: Routledge, 2001), pp. 135–146.
58. James Rachels, "Can Ethics Provide Answers?," in *Can Ethics Provide Answers? and Other Essays in Moral Philosophy* (Rowman and Littlefield, 1997), pp. 33–39.
59. The arguments for and against ethical relativism are surveyed in Manuel Velasquez, "Ethical Relativism and the International Business Manager," *Studies in Economic Ethics and Philosophy* (Berlin: Springer-Verlag, 1997); an outstanding book-length argument against ethical relativism is John W. Cook, *Morality and Cultural Differences* (New York: Oxford University Press, 1999).
60. Thomas Donaldson and Thomas Dunfee, *Ties that Bind: A Social Contracts Approach to Business Ethics*, (Cambridge, MA: Harvard University Press, 1999).
61. See Donald R. C. Reed, *Following Kohlberg: Liberalism and the Practice of Democratic Community* (Notre Dame, IN: University of Notre Dame Press, 1997), which provides a useful summary and critical analysis of Kohlberg's theory, how that theory developed over the years, and the kinds of criticisms to which it has been subjected. Another useful critical summary from a group of researchers who are basically sympathetic to Kohlberg is James Rest et al., *Postconventional Moral Thinking: A Neo-Kohlbergian Approach* (Mahwah, NJ: Lawrence Erlbaum Associates, Publishers, 1999).
62. This summary is based on Lawrence Kohlberg, "Moral Stages and Moralization: The Cognitive-Developmental Approach," in Thomas Lickona, ed., *Moral Development and Behavior: Theory, Research, and Social Issues* (New York: Holt, Rinehart and Winston, 1976), pp. 31–53.
63. See Reed, *Following Kohlberg*, for a comprehensive overview of the criticisms that have been lodged against Kohlberg's theory and research.
64. See Carol Gilligan, *In a Different Voice: Psychological Theory and Women's Development* (Cambridge, MA: Harvard University Press, 1982).
65. For reviews of the literature surrounding Kohlberg and the Gilligan critique, see Norman Sprinthall and Richard Sprinthall, *Educational Psychology*, 4th ed. (New York: Random House, 1987), pp. 157–177; and Nancy Eisenberg, Richard Fabes, and Cindy Shea, "Gender Differences in Empathy and Prosocial Moral Reasoning: Empirical Investigations," in Mary M. Brabeck, *Who Cares? Theory, Research, and Educational Implications of the Ethic of Care* (New York: Praeger, 1989).
66. Among the studies that have failed to find significant gender differences in moral reasoning are Robbin Derry, "Moral Reasoning in Work Related Conflicts," in *Research in Corporate Social Performance and Policy*, vol. 9, William Frederick, ed. (Greenwich, CT: JAI, 1987), pp. 25–49; Freedman, Robinson, and Freedman, "Sex Differences in Moral Judgment? A Test of Gilligan's Theory," *Psychology of Women Quarterly*, 1987, v. 37.
67. William Damon, "Self-Understanding and Moral Development from Childhood to Adolescence" in W. M. Kurtines & J. L. Gewirtz (eds.), *Morality, Moral Behavior, and Moral Development*, pp. 109–127, (New York: Wiley, 1984), p. 116.
68. Anne Colby and William Damon, *Some Do Care: Contemporary Lives of Moral Commitment*, (New York: The Free Press, 1992), p. 300; see also, Anne Colby and William Damon, "The Uniting of Self and Morality in the Development of Extraordinary Moral Commitment, in G. G. Noam and T. E. Wren (eds), *The Moral Self*, pp. 149–174, (Cambridge, MA: MIT Press, 1994).
69. Augusto Blasi, "The Moral Personality: Reflections for Social Science and Eduction, in W. M. M. W. Berkowitz and F. Oser, (eds.), *Moral Education: Theory and Application*, pp. 433–444, (Hillsdale, NJ: Lawrence Erbaum Associates, 1985), p. 438.
70. Augusto Blasi, "Emotions and Moral Motivation," *Journal for the Theory of Social Behavior*, v. 29, (1999), pp. 1–19; quote is from p. 11.
71. Nancy Eisenberg, "Emotion, Regulation, and Moral Development," *Annual Reviews of Psychology*, vol. 51 (2000), pp. 665–697.
72. Joshua Greene and Jonathan Haidt, "How (and Where) Does Moral Judgment Work?," *Trends in Cognitive Science*, vo. 6, no. 12, pp. 517–523; see also Antonio Damasio, *Descartes' Error: Emotion, Reason, and the Human Brain*, (New York: Penguin, 2005).
73. Antonio Damasio, *op. cit.*, p. 8.

74. This passage is an updated and paraphrased version of a similar passage in Edward J. Stevens, *Making Moral Decisions* (New York: Paulist Press, 1969), pp. 123–125.
75. For a fuller discussion of this approach, see Stephen Toulmin, Richard Rieke, and Allan Janik, *An Introduction to Reasoning* (New York: Macmillan Inc., 1979), pp. 309–337.
76. See Richard M. Hare, *Freedom and Reason* (New York: Oxford University Press, 1965), pp. 30–50, 86–111.
77. The difficulties are discussed in John R. Searle, *Speech Acts* (New York: Cambridge University Press, 1969), pp. 182–188.
78. An excellent and compact account of these features may be found in Lawrence Habermehl, "The Susceptibility of Moral Claims to Reasoned Assessment," in *Morality in the Modern World*, Lawrence Habermehl, ed. (Belmont, CA: Dickenson Publishing Co., Inc., 1976), pp. 18–32.
79. See Marcus G. Singer, *Generalization in Ethics* (New York: Alfred A. Knopf, Inc., 1961), p. 5; Hare, *Freedom and Reason*, p. 15.
80. James Rest, *Moral Development: Advances in Research and Theory*, (New York: Praeger, 1986).
81. T. M. Jones, "Ethical Decision Making by Individuals in Organizations: An Issue-Contingent Model," *Academy of Management Review*, vol. 16 (1991), pp. 366–395.
82. Albert Bandura, G. V. Caprara, and L. Zsolnai, "Corporate Transgressions Through Moral Disengagement," *Journal of Human Values*, vol. 6 (2000), pp. 57–63; see also, Albert Bandura, "Moral Disengagement in the Perpetration of Inhumanities," *Personality and Social Psychology Review*, vol. 3 (1999), no. 3, pp. 193–209; Albert Bandura, "Selective Moral Disengagement in the Exercise of Moral Agency," *Journal of Moral Education*, vol. 31 (2002), no. 2, pp. 101–119.
83. David Messick and Michael Bazerman, "Ethical Leadership and the Psychology of Decision Making," *Sloan Management Review*, vol. 37 (1996), pp. 9–22.
84. Jeff Donn and Seth Borenstein, "AP Investigation: Blowout Preventers Known to Fail," *ABC News*, May 8, 2010, accessed May 8, 2010 at *http://abcnews.go.com/Business/wireStory?id=10591505.*
85. Richard Mauer and Anna M. Tinsley, "Gulf Oil Spill: BP Has a Long Record of Legal, Ethical Violations," *The Miami Herald*, May 8, 2010, accessed May 8, 2010 at *http://www.miamiherald.com/2010/05/08/1620292/gulf-oil-spill-bp-has-a-long-record.html.*
86. Don Moore, Philip Tetlock, Lloyd Tanlu, and Max Bazerman, "Conflicts of Interest and the Case of Auditor Independence: Moral Seduction and Strategic Issue Cycling," *Academy of Management Review*, vol. 31 (2006), no. 1, pp. 10–29.
87. B. Victor and J. B. Cullen, "The Organizational Bases of Ethical Work Climates," *Administrative Science Quarterly*, vol. 33 (1988), pp. 101–125; L. Trevino, K. Butterfield, and D. McCabe, "The Ethical Context in Organizatins: Influences on Employee Attitudes and Behaviors," *Business Ethics Quarterly*, vol. 8 (1998), no. 3, pp. 447–476.
88. Ibid., p. 17.
89. Aristotle, *Nichomachean Ethics*, Bk. 7, chapters 1–10.
90. Richard Holton, "How is Strength of Will Possible?" in S. Stroud and C. Tappolet, eds., *Weakness of Will and Practical Rationality*, (Oxford: Oxford University Press, 2003), pp. 39–67.
91. Stanley Milgram, "Behavioral Study of Obedience," *Journal of Abnormal and Social Psychology*, vol. 67 (1963).
92. A person can also be morally responsible for good acts. But because we are concerned with determining when a person is excused from doing wrong, we discuss moral responsibility only as it relates to wrongdoing and to being excused therefrom.
93. "Job Safety Becomes a Murder Issue," *Business Week*, August 6, 1984; "3 Executives Convicted of Murder for Unsafe Workplace Conditions," *The New York Times*, June 15, 1985; "Working Them to Death," *Time*, July 15, 1985; "Murder Case a Corporate Landmark," part I, *Los Angeles Times*, September 15, 1985; "Trial Makes History," part II, *Los Angeles Times*, September 16, 1985. Their conviction was later overturned.
94. This agreement goes back to Aristotle, *Nicomachean Ethics*, Martin Ostwald, trans. (New York: The Bobbs-Merrill Company, 1962), bk. III, ch. 1. Recent discussions of moral responsibility have questioned this agreement, but this recent discussion raises issues that are too complex to examine here. Readers interested in the issue may want to consult the essays collected in John Martin Fischer and Mark Ravizza, eds., *Perspectives on Moral Responsibility* (Ithaca, NY: Cornell University Press, 1993), especially the editors' "Introduction" and their essay "Responsibility for Consequences." The theory of moral responsibility I adopt draws heavily from John Martin Fischer and Mark Ravizza, *Responsibility and Control: A Theory of Moral Responsibility* (New York: Cambridge University Press, 1998), particularly my characterization of acting "of one's own free will," which is intended to be eqivalent to their notion of "acting from one's own reasons-responsive mechanism" (see pp. 28–91).
95. Jim Jubak, "They Are the First," *Environmental Action*, February 1983; Jeff Coplon, "Left in the Dust," *Voice*, March 1, 1983; George Miller, "The Asbestos Cover-Up," *Congressional Record*, May 17, 1979.
96. See the discussion of this in Hare, *Freedom and Reason*, pp. 50–60.
97. "Overdriven Execs: Some Middle Managers Cut Corners to Achieve High Corporate Goals," *Wall Street Journal*, November 8, 1979.
98. Alan Donagan, *The Theory of Morality* (Chicago: University of Chicago Press, 1977), pp. 154–157, 206–207.
99. Singer, *Practical Ethics*, p. 152.
100. See W. L. LaCroix, *Principles for Ethics in Business* (Washington, DC: University Press of America, 1976), pp. 106–107; Thomas M. Garrett, *Business Ethics*, 2nd ed. (Englewood Cliffs, NJ: Prentice Hall, 1986), pp. 12–13; Henry J. Wirtenberger, S. J., *Morality and Business* (Chicago: Loyola University Press, 1962), pp. 109–114; Herbert Jone, *Moral Theology*, Urban Adelman, trans. (Westminster, MD: The Newman Press, 1961), p. 236.
101. Peter A. French, "Corporate Moral Agency," in Tom L. Beauchamp and Norman E. Bowie, eds. *Ethical Theory and Business* (Englewood Cliffs, NJ: Prentice Hall, 1979), pp. 175–186; see also Christopher D. Stone, *Where the Law Ends* (New York: Harper & Row, Publishers, Inc., 1975), pp. 58–69, for the legal basis of this view.
102. See Manuel Velasquez,"Debunking Corporate Moral Responsibility," *Business Ethics Quarterly*, October 2003, v. 13, n. 4, pp. 531–562, and "Why Corporations Are Not Morally Responsible for Anything They Do," *Business & Professional Ethics Journal*, Spring 1983, v. 2, n. 3, pp. 1–18; see also the two commentaries on this article appearing in the same journal by Kenneth E. Goodpaster, 2, n. 4, pp. 100–103; and Thomas A. Klein, v. 3, n. 2, pp. 70–71.

103. David Sylvester, "National Semi May Lose Defense Jobs," *San Jose Mercury News*, May 31, 1984.

Chapter 2

1. Investor Responsibility Research Center, Inc., *U.S. Corporate Activity in South Africa, 1986*, Analysis B, January 28, 1986.
2. Timothy Smith, "South Africa: The Churches vs. the Corporations," *Business and Society Review*, 1971, pp. 54, 55, 56.
3. *Texaco Proxy Statement*, 1977, item 3.
4. The details of this well-known case are derived from the findings of fact stated by the court in *Grimshaw vs. Ford Motor Co.*, App., 174 Cal. Rptr. 348. Grimshaw was a young teenager when he was traumatically seared over much of his body and face in a Pinto fire that resulted from a rear-end collision in San Bernardino, California. Details of the cost-benefit study are based on Ralph Drayton, "One Manufacturer's Approach to Automobile Safety Standards," *CTLA News*, February 1968, v. VIII, n. 2, p. 11; and Mark Dowie, "Pinto Madness," *Mother Jones*, September/October 1977, p. 28. A book-length treatment of the case is Lee P. Strobel, *Reckless Homicide? Ford's Pinto Trial* (South Bend, IN: And Books, 1980).
5. Thomas A. Klein, *Social Costs and Benefits of Business* (Englewood Cliffs, NJ: Prentice-Hall, 1977).
6. Among the more well-known utilitarian moralists are Peter Singer, *Practical Ethics*, 2nd ed. (London: Cambridge University Press, 1993); and Richard B. Brandt, *A Theory of the Good and the Right* (New York: Oxford University Press, 1979).
7. Jeremy Bentham, *The Principles of Morals and Legislation* (Oxford, 1789); Henry Sidgwick, *Outlines of the History of Ethics*, 5th ed. (London, 1902) traces the history of utilitarian thought to Bentham's predecessors.
8. Henry Sidgwick, *Methods of Ethics*, 7th ed. (Chicago: University of Chicago Press, 1962), p. 413.
9. John Stuart Mill, *Utilitarianism* in John Stuart Mill, *Utilitarianism, Liberty, and Representative Government*, (London: J. M. Dent & Sons, Ltd., 1910), p. 16.
10. Richard Brandt, *Ethical Theory* (Englewood Cliffs, NJ: Prentice-Hall, 1959), p. 386; see also Dan W. Brock, "Utilitarianism," in Tom Regan and Donald Van DeVeer, eds., *And Justice for All* (Totowa, NJ: Rowman and Littlefield, 1982), pp. 217–240.
11. For example, William Stanley Javons, *Theory of Political Economy* (1871); Alfred Marshall, *Principles of Economics* (1890); Cecil Arthur Pigou, *Wealth and Welfare* (1912); for a contemporary defense of utilitarianism in economics, see J. A. Mirrlees, "The Economic Uses of Utilitarianism," in Sen and Williams, eds., *Utilitarianism and Beyond*, pp. 63–84.
12. See Paul Samuelson, *Foundations of Economic Analysis* (Cambridge, MA: Harvard University Press, 1947). A system is "Pareto optimal" if no one in the system can be made better off without making some other person worse off; an "indifference curve" indicates the quantities of one good a person would willingly trade for greater or lesser quantities of another good.
13. E. J. Mishan, *Economics for Social Decisions: Elements of Cost-Benefit Analysis* (New York: Praeger Publishers, Inc., 1973), pp. 14–17. See also E. J. Mishan, ed., *Cost-Benefit Analysis*, 3rd ed. (London: Cambridge University Press, 1982).
14. For example, Wesley C. Mitchell, "Bentham's Felicific Calculus," in *The Backward Art of Spending Money and Other Essays* (New York: Augustus M. Kelley, Inc., 1950), pp. 177–202; but see the replies to these measurement objections in Paul Weirch, "Interpersonal Utility in Principles of Social Choice," *Erkenntnis*, November 1984, v. 21, pp. 295–318.
15. For a discussion of this problem, see Michael D. Bayles, "The Price of Life," *Ethics*, October 1978, v. 89, n. 1, pp. 20–34; Jonathan Glover, *Causing Death and Saving Lives* (New York: Penguin Books, 1977); Peter S. Albin, "Economic Values and the Value of Human Life," in Sidney Hook, ed., *Human Values and Economic Policy* (New York: New York University Press, 1967).
16. G. E. Moore, *Principia Ethica*, 5th ed. (Cambridge: Cambridge University Press, 1956), p. 149.
17. Alastair MacIntyre, "Utilitarianism and Cost-Benefit Analysis: An Essay on the Relevance of Moral Philosophy to Bureaucratic Theory," in Kenneth Syre, ed., *Values in the Electric Power Industry* (Notre Dame, IN: University of Notre Dame Press, 1977).
18. For example, Mark Sagoff, "Some Problems with Environmental Ethics," and Steven Kelman, "Cost-Benefit Analysis: An Ethical Critique," both in Christine Pierce and Donald VanDeVeer, eds., *People, Penguins, and Plastic Trees*, 2nd ed. (Belmont, CA: Wadsworth, 1995).
19. Raymond A. Bauer and Dan H. Fenn, Jr., *The Corporate Social Audit* (New York: Sage Publications, Inc., 1972), pp. 3–14; John J. Corson and George A. Steiner, *Measuring Business's Social Performance: The Corporate Social Audit* (New York: Committee for Economic Development, 1974), p. 41; Thomas C. Taylor, "The Illusions of Social Accounting," *CPA Journal*, January 1976, v. 46, pp. 24–28; Manuel A. Tipgos, "A Case Against the Social Audit," *Management Accounting*, August 1976, pp. 23–26.
20. Tom L. Beauchamp, "Utilitarianism and Cost-Benefit Analysis: A Reply to MacIntyre," in Beauchamp and Bowie, eds., *Ethical Theory*, pp. 276–282; and Herman B. Leonard and Richard J. Zeckhauser, "Cost-Benefit Analysis Defended," *QQ-Report from the Center for Philosophy and Public Policy*, Summer 1983, v. 3, n. 3, pp. 6–9.
21. See Amitai Etzioni and Edward W. Lehman, "Dangers in 'Valid' Social Measurements," *Annals of the American Academy of Political and Social Sciences*, September 1967, v. 373, p. 6; also William K. Frankena, *Ethics*, 2nd ed. (Englewood Cliffs, NJ: Prentice-Hall, 1973), pp. 80–83.
22. See Kenneth Arrow, *Social Choice and Individual Values*, 2nd ed. (New York: John Wiley & Sons, Inc., 1951), p. 87; and Norman E. Bowie, *Towards a New Theory of Distributive Justice* (Amherst, MA: The University of Massachusetts Press, 1971), pp. 86–87.
23. Steven Edwards, "In Defense of Environmental Economics," and William Baster, "People or Penguins," both in Christine Pierce and Donald VanDeVeer, eds., *People, Penguins, and Plastic Trees*, 2nd ed. (Belmont, CA: Wadsworth, 1995). See also the techniques enumerated in Mishan, *Economics for Social Decisions*.
24. E. Bruce Frederickson, "Noneconomic Criteria and the Decision Process," *Decision Sciences*, January 1971, v. 2, n. 1, pp. 25–52.
25. Bowie, *Towards a New Theory of Distributive Justice*, pp. 20–24.

26. See J. O. Ormson, "The Interpretation of the Philosophy of J. S. Mill," *Philosophical Quarterly*, 1953, v. 3, pp. 33–40; D. W. Haslett, *Equal Consideration: A Theory of Moral Justification* (Newark, DE: University of Delaware Press, 1987).
27. David Lyons, *Forms and Limits of Utilitarianism* (Oxford: Oxford University Press, 1965). Some ethicians hold, however, that act utilitarianism and rule utilitarianism are not really equivalent; see Thomas M. Lennon, "Rules and Relevance: The Act Utilitarianism–Rule Utilitarianism Equivalence Issue," *Idealistic Studies: An International Philosophical Journal*, May 1984, v. 14, pp. 148–158.
28. China.org.cn, "Disney in Child Labor Storm," accessed May 18, 2010 at *http://www.china.org.cn/china/news/2009-05/17/content_17787852.htm*.
29. U.S. State Department, *Country Reports on Human Rights Practices for 2002* (February 2003).
30. See Peter DeSimone, "2004 Company Report—C1, Walt Disney Human Rights in China," February 9, 2004, © 2004 by the Investor Responsibility Research Center; and Carolyn Mathiasen, "2004 Background Report—C1 Human Rights in China," February 9, 2004, © 2004 Investor Responsibility Research Center (both at *http://www.irrc.org*).
31. Timesonline, "Disney Toys Made in 'Sweatshops,'" *Sunday Times*, December 23, 2007, accessed May 19, 2010 at *http://www.timesonline.co.uk/tol/news/world/asia/article3087300.ece*.
32. David Barboza, "U.S. Group Accuses Chinese Toy Factories of Labor Abuses," *The New York Times*, August 22, 2007; David Barboza, "In Chinese Factories, Lost Fingers and Low Pay," *The New York Times*, January 5, 2008.
33. National Labor Committee, "Toys of Misery Made In Abusive Chinese Sweatshops,"
34. H. J. McCloskey, "Rights," *The Philosophical Quarterly*, 1965, v. 15, pp. 115–127; several book-length discussions of rights are available, including Alan R. White, *Rights* (Oxford: Clarendon Press, 1984); Samuel Stoljar, *An Analysis of Rights* (New York: St. Martin's Press, 1984); and Henry Shue, *Basic Rights* (Princeton, NJ: Princeton University Press, 1981); for a review of the literature on rights, see Jeremy Waldron, "Rights," in Robert E. Goodin and Philip Pettit, eds., *A Companion to Contemporary Political Philosophy* (Oxford: Blackwell, 1995); an outstanding historical account of the evolution of the concept of a right is Richard Tuck, *Natural Rights Theories, Their Origin and Development* (New York: Cambridge University Press, 1979).
35. For a more technical, but now widely accepted classification of legal rights, see Wesley Hohfeld, *Fundamental Legal Conceptions* (New Haven, CT: Yale University Press, 1919, rpt. 1964), pp. 457–484.
36. There are different ways of characterizing the relation between rights and duties, not all of them equally sound. For example, some authors claim that a person is granted rights only if the person accepts certain duties toward the community that grants those rights. Other authors claim that all my rights can be defined wholly in terms of the duties of others. Both of these claims are probably mistaken, but neither claim is being advanced in this paragraph. The view of this paragraph is that moral rights of the kind identified in the previous paragraph always can be defined at least in part in terms of duties others have toward the bearer of the right. To have a moral right of this kind always implies that others have certain moral duties toward me; but it does not follow that if others have those duties, then I have the corresponding right. Thus, the claim is that the imposition of certain correlative moral duties on others is a necessary, but not sufficient condition for one's possession of a moral right.
37. See Richard Wasserstrom, "Rights, Human Rights, and Racial Discrimination," *The Journal of Philosophy*, October 29, 1964, v. 61, pp. 628–641.
38. Ibid., p. 62.
39. Feinberg, *Social Philosophy*, pp. 59–61.
40. Ibid.
41. See, for example, Milton Friedman, *Capitalism and Freedom* (Chicago, IL: The University of Chicago Press, 1962), pp. 22–36; Friedrich Hayek, *The Road to Serfdom* (Chicago, IL: The University of Chicago Press, 1944), pp. 25–26.
42. Peter Singer, "Rights and the Market," in John Arthur and William Shaw, eds., *Justice and Economic Distribution* (Englewood Cliffs, NJ: Prentice-Hall, 1978), pp. 207–221.
43. H. L. A. Hart, "Are There Any Natural Rights," *Philosophical Review*, April 1955, v. 64, p. 185.
44. J. R. Searle, *Speech Acts* (Cambridge: The University Press, 1969), pp. 57–62.
45. Thomas M. Garrett, *Business Ethics*, 2nd ed. (Englewood Cliffs, NJ: Prentice-Hall, 1986), pp. 88–91.
46. Ibid., p. 75. See also John Rawls, *A Theory of Justice* (Cambridge, MA: Harvard University Press, The Belknap Press, 1971), pp. 342–350.
47. For a Kantian approach to business ethics see Norman E. Bowie, *Business Ethics: A Kantian Perspective*, (London: Blackwell Publishers, 1999); a fine and balanced explanation of Kant's moral theory is Roger J. Sullivan, *Immanuel Kant's Moral Theory* (New York: Cambridge University Press, 1989); Onora O'Neill has recently articulated a refreshingly clear interpretation of Kant in a series of essays collected in Onora O'Neill, *Constructions of Reason: Explorations of Kant's Practical Philosophy* (Cambridge: Cambridge University Press, 1989); for an accessible overview of Kant's philosophy, see Paul Guyer, ed., *The Cambridge Companion to Kant* (New York: Cambridge University Press, 1992).
48. Immanuel Kant, *Groundwork of the Metaphysics of Morals*, H. J. Paton, trans. (New York: Harper & Row, Publishers, Inc., 1964), p. 70.
49. Ibid., p. 91.
50. Ibid., p. 96.
51. See Feldman, *Introductory Ethics* (Englewood Cliffs, NJ: Prentice-Hall, 1978), pp. 119–128; and Rawls, *A Theory of Justice*, pp. 179–180.
52. Kant, *Groundwork*, p. 105. On the equivalence of the two versions of the categorical imperative, see Sullivan, *Immanuel Kant's Moral Theory*, pp. 193–194.
53. Page 93 in Gregory Vlastos, "Justice and Equality," p. 48 in Richard Brandt, ed., *Social Justice* (Englewood Cliffs, NJ: Prentice Hall, 1964), pp. 31–72. See, for example, A. K. Bierman, *Life and Morals: An Introduction to Ethics* (New York: Harcourt Brace Jovanovich, Inc., 1980), pp. 300–301; Charles Fried, *Right and Wrong* (Cambridge, MA: Harvard University Press, 1978), p. 129; Dworkin, *Taking Rights Seriously*, p. 198; Thomas E. Hill, Jr., "Servility and Self-Respect," *The Monist*, January 1973, v. 57, n. 21, pp. 87–104; Feinberg, *Social Philosophy*.
54. See John Stuart Mill, *On Liberty* [1860], chapter II.
55. For a similar argument based on Kant's first formulation of the categorical imperative, see Marcus Singer, *Generalization in Ethics* (New York: Alfred A. Knopf, Inc., 1961),

pp. 267–274; for one based on Kant's second formulation, see Alan Donagan, *The Theory of Morality* (Chicago, IL: The University of Chicago Press, 1977), p. 85; also see I. Kant, *Metaphysical Elements of Justice* (New York: Bobbs-Merrill Co., Inc., 1965), pp. 91–99.

56. See Alan Gewirth, *Reason and Morality* (Chicago, IL: The University of Chicago Press, 1978), who argues for these rights (p. 256) on the basis of a principle that, although different from Kant's first formulation in some important respects, is nonetheless very much like it: "Every agent must claim that he has rights to freedom and well-being for the reason that he is a prospective purposive agent ... it follows, by the principle of universalizability, that all prospective purposive agents have rights to freedom and well-being" (p. 133); Donagan, *The Theory of Morality*, pp. 81–90, argues for these on the basis of Kant's second formulation.
57. See Singer, *Generalization in Ethics*, pp. 255–257, for a discussion of how Kant's first formulation provides a basis for the obligation to keep one's promises and for truthfulness in the making of promises; see Donagan, *Theory of Morality*, pp. 90–94, for a discussion of the same subject in terms of the second formulation.
58. See Jonathan Harrison, "Kant's Examples of the First Formulation of the Categorical Imperative," in Robert Paul Wolff, ed., *Kant, A Collection of Critical Essays* (Garden City, NY: Doubleday & Co., Inc., 1967), pp. 228–245; see also in the same work the reply by J. Kemp and the counterreply by J. Harrison, both of which focus on the meaning of "is willing."
59. Fred Feldman, *Introductory Ethics*, pp. 123–128; Robert Paul Wolff, *The Autonomy of Reason* (New York: Harper Torch Books, 1973), p. 175.
60. For example, J. B. Mabbott, *The State and the Citizen* (London: Arrow, 1958), pp. 57–58.
61. Feldman, *Introductory Ethics*, pp. 116–117.
62. For example, Richard M. Hare, *Freedom and Reason* (New York: Oxford University Press, 1965), who uses Kant's first formulation (p. 34), defends himself against the example of the "fanatic" in this way.
63. Robert Nozick, *Anarchy, State, and Utopia* (New York: Basic Books, Inc., Publishers, 1974), p. ix.
64. Ibid., pp. 30–31.
65. Ibid., p. 160; see also pp. 160–162.
66. Kant, *The Metaphysical Elements of Justice*, p. 93.
67. U.S. Congress, Senate, *Brown Lung: Hearing Before a Subcommittee of the Committee on Appropriations, 95th Congress, 1st Session*. 9 December 1977, pp. 3, 52, 53, 54, 59, and 60.
68. John Rawls, "Justice as Fairness," *The Philosophical Review*, 1958, v. 67, pp. 164–194; R. M. Hare, "Justice and Equality," in Arthur and Shaw, eds., *Justice and Economic Distribution*, p. 119.
69. Rawls, *A Theory of Justice*, pp. 3–4.
70. See, for example, Rawls, *A Theory of Justice*, p. 542, and Joel Feinberg, "Rawls and Intuitionism," pp. 114–116 in Norman Daniels, ed., *Reading Rawls* (New York: Basic Books, Inc., Publishers, n.d.), pp. 108–124; and T. M. Scanlon, "Rawls' Theory of Justice," pp. 185–191, ibid.
71. See, for example, Vlastos, "Justice and Equality."
72. Rawls, *A Theory of Justice*, pp. 126–130.
73. William K. Frankena, "The Concept of Social Justice," in Brandt, ed., *Social Justice*, pp. 1–29; C. Perelman, *The Idea of Justice and the Problem of Argument* (New York: Humanities Press, Inc., 1963), p. 16.
74. Feinberg, *Social Philosophy*, pp. 100–102; Perelman, *Idea of Justice*, p. 16.
75. Christopher Ake, "Justice as Equality," *Philosophy and Public Affairs*, Fall 1975, v. 5, n. 1, pp. 69–89.
76. Kai Nielsen, "Class and Justice," in Arthur and Shaw, eds., *Justice and Economic Distribution*, pp. 225–245; see also Gregory Vlastos, *Justice and Equality*. Vlastos interprets "equality" in a much different sense than I do here.
77. Morton Deutsch, "Egalitarianism in the Laboratory and at Work," in Melvin J. Lerner and Riel Vermunt, eds., *Social Justice in Human Relations*, vol. 1 (New York: Plenum Publishing Corporation, 1991); Morton Deutsch, "Equity, Equality, and Need: What Determines Which Value Will Be Used as the Basis of Distributive Justice?" *Journal of Social Issues*, 1975, v. 31, pp. 221–279.
78. K. Leung and M. H. Bond, "How Chinese and Americans Reward Task-Related Contributions: A Preliminary Study," *Psychologia*, 1982, v. 25, pp. 32–39; K. Leung and M. H. Bond, "The Impact of Cultural Collectism on Reward Allocation," *Journal of Personality and Social Psychology*, 1984, v. 47, pp. 793–804; Kwok Leung and Saburo Iwawaki, "Cultural Collectivism and Distributive Behavior," *Journal of Cross-Cultural Psychology*, March 1988, v. 19, n. 1, pp. 35–49.
79. Bernard Williams, "The Idea of Equality," in Laslett and Runciman, eds., *Philosophy and Society*, 2nd series (London: Blackwell, 1962), pp. 110–131.
80. Feinberg, *Social Philosophy*, pp. 109–111.
81. The evidence does not seem, however, to support this view. See Lane Kenworthy, *In Search of National Economic Success* (Thousand Oaks, CA: Sage Publications, 1995), who shows that societies with greater degrees of equality seem to be more productive than others; see Morton Deutsch, "Egalitarianism in the Laboratory and at Work," ibid., for evidence that even in small work groups equality does not seem to result in lowered productivity.
82. See Bowie, *A New Theory of Distributive Justice*, pp. 60–64.
83. See D. D. Raphael, "Equality and Equity," *Philosophy*, 1946, v. 21, pp. 118–132. See also, Bowie, *A New Theory of Distributive Justice*, pp. 64–65.
84. See Manuel Velasquez, "Why Ethics Matters," *Business Ethics Quarterly*, April 1996, v. 6, n. 2, p. 211.
85. Ibid.
86. See K. Leung and M. H. Bond, "How Chinese and Americans Reward Task-Related Contributions," and K. Leung and S. Iwawaki, "Cultural Collectivism and Distributive Behavior."
87. See Francis X. Sutton, Seymour E. Harris, Carl Kaysen, and James Tobin, *The American Business Creed* (Cambridge, MA: Harvard University Press, 1956), pp. 276–278; the classic source is Max Weber, *The Protestant Ethic and the Spirit of Capitalism*, Talcott Parsons, trans. (London: 1930); see also, Perry Miller, *The New England Mind: From Colony to Province* (Cambridge, MA: Harvard University Press, 1953), pp. 40–52.
88. See A. Whitner Griswold, "Three Puritans on Prosperity," *The New England Quarterly*, September 1934, v. 7, pp. 475–488; see also Daniel T. Rodgers, *The Work Ethic in Industrial America* (Chicago, IL: The University of Chicago Press, 1978).
89. John A. Ryan, *Distributive Justice*, 3rd ed. (New York: The Macmillan Co., 1941), pp. 182–183; Nicholas Rescher, *Distributive Justice* (New York: The Bobbs-Merrill Co., Inc., 1966), pp. 77–78.

90. Rescher, *Distributive Justice*, pp. 78–79; Ryan, *Distributive Justice*, pp. 183–185.
91. Rescher, *Distributive Justice*, pp. 80–81; Ryan, *Distributive Justice*, pp. 186–187.
92. Karl Marx, *Critique of the Gotha Program* (London: Lawrence and Wishart, Ltd., 1938), pp. 14 and 107; Louis Blanc, *L'Organization du Travail* (Paris, 1850), cited in D. O. Wagner, *Social Reformers* (New York: The Macmillan Co., 1946), p. 218; Nikolai Lenin, "Marxism on the State," pp. 76–77; on the question of whether Marx had a theory of distributive justice, see Ziyad I. Husami, "Marx on Distributive Justice," in Marshall Cohen, Thomas Nagel, and Thomas Scanlon, eds., *Marx, Justice, and History* (Princeton, NJ: Princeton University Press, 1980), pp. 42–79.
93. Marx, *Critique of the Gotha Program*; see also John McMurtry, *The Structure of Marx's World View* (Princeton, NJ: Princeton University Press, 1978), ch. I.
94. Bowie, *A New Theory of Distributive Justice*, pp. 92–93. See also Norman Daniels, "Meritocracy," in Arthur and Shaw, eds., *Justice and Economic Distribution*, pp. 167–178. For an interesting examination of international data that suggest that equality does not undermine work incentive, see Kenworthy, *In Search of National Economic Success*, pp. 48–49.
95. Bowie, ibid., pp. 96–98.
96. Robert Nozick, *Anarchy, State, and Utopia*, p. 160.
97. Rawls, *A Theory of Justice*, pp. 65–75.
98. Ibid., pp. 577–587.
99. Ibid., pp. 298–303.
100. Ibid., p. 61.
101. Ibid., pp. 108–114 and 342–350.
102. Ibid., pp. 75–83 and 274–284.
103. Ibid., pp. 83–90.
104. Ibid., pp. 17–22.
105. Ibid., pp. 136–142.
106. Ibid., pp. 46–53.
107. The core of the argument is at Rawls, *A Theory of Justice*, pp. 175–183, but parts may also be found at pp. 205–209, 325–332, 333–350, 541–548.
108. See the articles collected in *Reading Rawls*, Daniels, ed.; see also Brian Barry, *The Liberal Theory of Justice* (Oxford: Clarendon Press, 1973); Robert Paul Wolff, *Understanding Rawls* (Princeton, NJ: Princeton University Press, 1977).
109. Rawls, *A Theory of Justice*, pp. 105–108.
110. Ibid., p. 276.
111. On the relation between justice and due process, see David Resnick, "Due Process and Procedural Justice," in J. Roland Pennock and John W. Chapman, eds., *Due Process* (New York: New York University Press, 1977), pp. 302–310.
112. On the relation between justice and consistency in the application of rules, see Perelman, *The Idea of Justice*, pp. 36–45; proportionality in punishment is discussed in John Kleinig, *Punishment and Desert* (The Hague: Martinus Nijoff, 1973), pp. 110–133; and C. W. K. Mundle, "Punishment and Desert," *Philosophical Quarterly*, 1954, v. IV, pp. 216–228.
113. Henry J. Wirtenberger, *Morality and Business* (Chicago, IL: Loyola University Press, 1962), pp. 109–119; see also Herbert Jone, *Moral Theology*, Urban Adelman, trans. (Westminster, MD: The Newman Press, 1961), pp. 225–247.
114. This account of the Malden Mills incident is based on stories in *Parade Magazine*, September 8, 1996; *The Boston Globe*, December 5, 1995, December 13, 1995, January 12, 1996, and January 16, 1996; *Sun* (Lowell, MA), December 17, 1995 and November 5, 1995; *The New York Times*, July 24, 1994, December 16, 1995, July 14, 1996; and Penelope Washbourn, "'When All Is Moral Chaos, This Is the Time for You to Be a Mensche': Reflections on Malden Mills for the Teaching of Business Ethics," unpublished paper presented at The Society for Business Ethics Annual Meeting, August 10, 1996, Quebec City, Quebec.
115. See, for example, Cottingham, "Ethics and Impartiality," *Philosophical Studies*, 1983, v. 43, pp. 90–91.
116. See William Godwin, in K. Codell Carter, ed., *Enquiry Concerning Political Justice* (Oxford: Clarendon House, 1971), p. 71; and Peter Singer, *Practical Ethics*, 2nd ed. (Cambridge: Cambridge University Press, 1993), pp. 10–12, 21.
117. See Lawrence Blum, *Moral Perception and Particularity* (Cambridge: Cambridge University Press, 1994); Lawrence Blum, *Friendship, Altruism, and Morality* (London: Routledge & Kegan Paul, 1980); John Kekes, "Morality and Impartiality," *American Philosophical Quarterly*, October 1981, v. 18.
118. N. Lyons, "Two Perspectives: On Self, Relationships and Morality," *Harvard Educational Review*, 1983, v. 53, n. 2, p. 136.
119. Lawrence A. Blum, *Moral Perception and Particularity* Cambridge: Cambridge University Press, 1994), p. 12; Robin S. Dillon, "Care and Respect," in Eve Browning Cole and Susan Coultrap-McQuin, eds., *Explorations in Feminist Ethics: Theory and Practice* (Bloomington and Indianapolis, IN: Indiana University Press, 1992), pp. 69–81; see also Mary C. Raugust, "Feminist Ethics and Workplace Values" in Eve Browning Cole and Susan Coultrap-McQuin, ed., ibid., p. 127.
120. Nell Noddings, *Starting at Home: Caring and Social Policy*, (Berkeley: University Of California Press, 2002).
121. See the essays collected in Shlomo Avineri and Avner de-Shalit, eds., *Individualism and Communitarianism* (Oxford: Oxford University Press, 1992).
122. Michael Sandel, *Liberalism and the Limits of Justice* (Cambridge: Cambridge University Press, 1982) p. 150.
123. See Sandel, *Liberalism*, p. 179; MacIntyre, *After Virtue* (Notre Dame, IN: University of Notre Dame Press), pp. 204–205.
124. Nell Noddings, *Caring* (Berkeley, CA: University of California Press, 1984), distinguishes between caring for and caring about on pp. 21–22; she refers to what I have called "caring after" as "institutional" caring on pp. 25–26.
125. See Sara Ruddick, *Maternal Thinking* (New York: Ballantine Books, 1989).
126. Lawrence Walker, "Sex Differences in the Development of Moral Reasoning: A Critical Review," and Catherine G. Greeno and Eleanor E. Maccoby, "How Different is the 'Different Voice'?" both in Mary Jeanne Larrabee, ed., *An Ethic of Care: Feminist and Interdisciplinary Perspectives* (New York: Routledge, 1993); for some evidence of some differences between men and women in how they deal with moral dilemmas, see T. White, "Business Ethics and Carol Gilligan's 'Two Voices,'" *Business Ethics Quarterly*, 1992, v. 2, n. 1, pp. 51–59. White provides some highly provocative suggestions about the implications of an ethic of care to business ethics.
127. See Joan C. Tronto, "Beyond Gender Difference to a Theory of Care," in ibid.; and Debra Shogan, *Care and Moral Motivation* (Toronto: The Ontario Institute for Studies in Education Press, 1988).

128. See Alan Gewirth, "Ethical Universalism and Particularism," *Journal of Philosophy*, June 1988, v. 85; John Cottingham, "Partiality, Favoritism, and Morality," *Philosophical Quarterly*, 1986, v. 36, n. 144.
129. This balancing of caring for self versus caring for others is a central theme in Carol Gilligan, *In a Different Voice: Psychological Theory and Women's Development* (Cambridge, MA: Harvard University Press, 1982).
130. Ivan F. Boesky in Jeffrey Madrick, ed., *Merger Mania* (New York: Holt, Rinehart and Winston, 1985), p. v.
131. Tim Metz and Michael W. Miller, "Boesky's Rise and Fall Illustrate a Compulsion to Profit by Getting Inside Track on Market," *The Wall Street Journal*, November 17, 1986, p. 28.
132. Ibid.
133. Peter Carlson, "High and Mighty Crooked: Enron is Merely the Latest Chapter in the History of American Scams," *The Washington Post*, February 10, 2002, p. F01.
134. S. Prakash Sethi and Paul Steidlmeier, *Up Against the Corporate Wall: Cases in Business and Society* (Upper Saddle River, NJ: Prentice-Hall, 1997), p. 47.
135. Alasdair MacIntyre, *After Virtue* (Notre Dame, IN: University of Notre Dame Press, 1981), p. 204.
136. See Edmund L. Pincoffs, *Quandaries and Virtues* (Lawrence, KS: University Press of Kansas, 1986). All quotes in the following paragraphs are from this work.
137. Gilbert Harmon, "Moral Philosophy Meets Social Psychology: Virtue Ethics and the Fundamental Attribution Error," *Proceedings of the Aristotelian Society*, New Series, vol. 99 (1999), pp. 315–331; see also, John Doris, *Lack of Character: Personality and Moral Behavior*, (Cambridge, U.K.: Cambridge University Press, 2002); P. Railton, "Made in the Shade: Moral Compatibilism and the Aims of Moral theory," *Canadian Journal of Philosophy*, Supplementary Vol. 21 (1997).
138. J. M. Darley and C. D. Batson, "From Jerusalem to Jerico: A Study of Situational and Dispositional Variables in Helping Behavior," *Journal of Personality and Social Psychology*, Vol. 27 (1973).
139. Craig Haney, Curtis Banks and Philip Zimbardo, "Interpersonal Dynamics in a Simulated Prison," *Interpersonal Journal of Criminology and Penology*, vol. 1 (1973), pp. 69–97. Additional articles and materials on Zimbardo's prison experiment may be found at *http://www.prisonexp.org/psychology/42.*
140. Philip Zimbardo, *The Lucifer Effect: Understanding How Good People Turn Evil*, (New York: Random House, 2007)
141. Daniel Lapsley and Darcia Narvaez, "A Social-Cognitive Approach to the Moral Personality," in D. K. Lapsley and D. Narvaez, eds., *Moral Development, Self and Identity*, pp. 189–212, (Mahwah, NJ: Erlbaum, 2004)
142. L. E. Bolton and A. H. Reed, "Sticky Priors: The Perseverance of Identity Effects on Judgment," *Journal of Marketing Research*, vol. 41 (2004), no. 4, pp. 397–441.
143. A. Blasi, "Moral Character: A Psychological Approach," in D. K. Lapsley & F. C. Power eds., *Character Psychology and Character Education*, 67–100, (Notre Dame: University of Notre Dame Press, 2005); A. Blasi, "Moral Functioning: Moral Understanding and Personality," in D. K. Lapsley & D. Narvaez, eds., *Moral Development, Self, and Identity*, pp. 335–348, (Mahwah, N.J.: Lawrence Erlbaum, 2004); K. Aquino & A . Reed, "The Self-Importance of Moral Identity," *Journal of Personality and Social Psychology*, vol. 83, no. 6, pp. 1423–1440.
144. G. R. Weaver, "Virtue in Organizations: Moral Identity as a Foundation for Moral Agency," *Organization Studies*, vol. 27 (2006), no. 3, pp. 341–368.
145. Scott Reynolds, "A Neurocognitive Model of the Ethical Decision-Making Process: Implications for Study and Practice," *The Journal of Applied Psychology*, vol. 91 (2006), no. 4, pp. 737–748. For a review of the large literature on "two system" models of reasoning, see: Jonathan St. B. T. Evans, "Dual-Processing Accounts of Reasoning, Judgment, and Social Cognition," *Annual Review of Psychology*, vol. 59 (2008), pp. 255–278; J. A. Bargh and T. L. Chartrand, "The Unbearable Automaticity of Being," *American Psychologist*, vol. 54 (1999), pp. 462–4-79; J. A. Bargh and E. L. Williams, "The Automaticity of Social Life," *Current Directions in Psychological Science*, vol. 15 (2006), pp. 1–4.
146. Eleanor Rosch, "Natural Categories," *Cognitive Psychology*, vol. 4 (1973), pp. 328–350; Eleanor Rosch, "Prototype Classification and Logical Classification: The Two Systems," pp. 73–86 in E. K. Scholnick, ed., *New Trends in Conceptual Representation: Challenges to Piaget's Theory?*, (Hillsdale: Lawrence Erlbaum Associates, Publishers, 1983); Eleanor Rosch, "Principles of Categorization," pp. 27–48 in E. Rosch and B. B. Lloyd, eds., *Cognition and Categorization*, (Hillsdale: Lawrence Erlbaum Associates, Publishers, 1978); G. Lakoff, *Women, Fire and Dangerous Things: What Categories Reveal About the Mind*, (Chicago: Chicago University Press, 1987); U. Hahn and M. Ramscar, *Similarity and Categorization*, (New York: Oxford University Press, 2001); Darcia Narvaez & Tonia Bock, "Moral Schemas and Tacit Judgment or How the Defining Issues Test is Supported by Cognitive Science," *Journal of Moral Education*, vol. 31 (2002), no. 3, pp. 297–314.
147. Albert R. Jonsen and Stephen Toulmin, *The Abuse of Casuistry: A History of Moral Reasoning*, (Berkeley, CA: University of California Press, 1988).
148. F. Schauer, "Precedent," *Stanford Law Review*, vo. 39 (1987), pp. 571–605.
149. Agnar Aamodt and Enric Plaza, "Case-Based Reasoning: Foundational Issues, Methodological Variations, and System Approaches," *Artificial Intelligence Communications*, vol. 7 (1994), no. 1, 39–52.
150. The term *intuition* is used by many psychologists to include not only the kind of unmediated knowledge we are talking about here, but to also include any kind of unconsciously acquired knowledge including the knowledge acquired through the use of prototypes. We are using here the term *intuition* in a narrow sense that excludes the kind of knowledge we acquire through the use of prototypes.
151. Jonathan Haidt, "The Emotional Dog and Its Rational Tail: A Social Intuitionist Approach to Moral Judgment," *Psychological Review*, vol. 108 (2001), pp. 814–834.
152. Fiery Cushman, Liane Young, and Marc Hauser, "The Role of Conscious Reasoning and Intuition in Moral Judgment," *Psychological Science*, vol. 17 (2006), no. 12, pp. 1082–1089.
153. See James Rachaels and Peter Singer.

Chapter 3

1. See World Bank, *Globalization, Growth and Poverty* (New York: Oxford University Press, 2002), accessed June 20, 2004 at *http://www.econ.worldbank.org/prr/globalization/text-2857.*

2. Vivian S. Toy, "The End of the Line; As the Swingline Factory in Queens Closes, Veteran Workers Wonder What's Next for them,"*The New York Times*, January 17, 1999.
3. Judy Temes, "Giant Sucking Sound Heard in Queens Factory: Moving to Mexico Would Let Swingline Cut wages by 85%; 450 would Lose Jobs," *Crain's New York Business*, May 26, 1997.
4. Tom Robbins, "Swingline Takes Jobs to Mexico," *Daily News (New York)*, July 6, 1997; Joel Millman, "Fortune Brands Seeks Savings in Mexico," *The Globe and Mail (Canada)*, August 7, 2000.
5. Elizabeth Becker, "U.S. Corn Subsidies Said to Damage Mexico," *The New York times*, August 27, 2003.
6. Jim Toedtman and Letta Taylor, "Jobs Move Again: Factory Work Shifted to Mexico after NAFTA Now Goes to Asia," *Newsday*, December 28, 2003.
7. Associated Press Financial Wire, March 14, 2007.
8. Donald G. McNeil, Jr., "Indian Company Offers to Supply AIDS Drugs at Low Cost in Africa," *New York Times*, February 7, 2001.
9. AVERT, "AIDS, Drug Prices and Generic Drugs," accessed June 10 at *http://www.avert.org/generic.htm*.
10. Joseph A. DiMasi, Ronald W. Hansen, Henry G. Grabowski, "The Price of Innovation: New Estimates of Drug Developent Costs,"*Journal of Health Economics*, vol. 22 (2003), pp. 151–185.
11. Robert Weissman, "A Long Strange TRIPS: the Pharmaceutical Industry Drive to Harmonize Global Intellectual Property Rules and the Remaining WTO Legal Alternatives Available to Third World Countries," *University of Pennsylvania Journal of International Economic Law*, vol. 17 (1996), no. 4, pp. 1069–1125.
12. Ibid.
13. Associated Press, March 22, 2007.
14. Nicholas Zamiska, "Abbott Escalates Thai Patent Rift: Firm Pulls Plans to Offer New Drugs In Spat with Regime," *Wall Street Journal*, March 14, 2007.
15. Robert L. Heilbroner, *The Economic Problem*, 3rd ed. (Englewood Cliffs, NJ: Prentice-Hall, 1972), pp. 14–28; see also Paul A. Samuelson, *Economics*, 9th ed. (New York: McGraw-Hill Book Company, 1973), pp. 17–18.
16. See Charles E. Lindblom, *Politics and Markets* (New York: Basic Books Inc., Publishers, 1977), Chapters 2, 3, 5, and 6 for a discussion contrasting these two abstractions and for a subtle criticism of their adequacy.
17. See Martin Schnitzer, *Comparative Economic Systems*, 8th ed. (Cincinnati, OH: South-Western College Publishing, 2000), pp. 113ff.
18. Ibid., pp. 21ff.
19. See "Economic Systems," *The New Encyclopedia Britannica*, v. 17 (Chicago, IL: Encyclopedia Britannica, Inc., 1993), p. 913.
20. Joseph Schumpeter, *A History of Economic Analysis* (New York: Oxford University Press, 1954), pp. 370–372 and 397–399. For a treatment of 20th-century controversies, see Otis Graham, *Toward a Planned Society: From Roosevelt to Nixon* (New York: Oxford University Press, 1976).
21. Milton Friedman, *Capitalism and Freedom* (Chicago, IL: The University of Chicago Press, 1962), p. 14; see also John Chamberlain, *The Roots of Capitalism* (New York: D. Van Nostrand Company, 1959), pp. 7–42.
22. For a useful introduction to the notion of an ideology and an introduction to key ideologies, see Andrew Heywood, *Political Ideologies: An Introduction*, 3rd ed. (New York: MacMillan, 2003).
23. George C. Lodge, *Perestroika for America: Restructuring Business-Government Relations for World Competitiveness* (Boston, MA: Harvard Business School Press, 1990), pp. 15, 16, 17.
24. The literature on Locke is extensive; see Richard I. Aaron, *John Locke*, 3rd ed. (London: Oxford University Press, 1971), pp. 352–376 for bibliographic materials.
25. John Locke, *Two Treatises of Civil Government*, (London: George Routledge and Sons, 1887), pp. 192, 193, and 194.
26. Ibid., p. 240.
27. Ibid., pp. 204.
28. Ibid., p. 256.
29. Ibid., p. 258.
30. C. B. Macpherson, however, argues that Locke was attempting to establish the morality and rationality of a capitalist system; see his *The Political Theory of Possessive Individualism: Hobbes to Locke* (Oxford: The Clarendon Press, 1962).
31. Friedrich A. Hayek, *The Road to Serfdom* (Chicago, IL: University of Chicago Press, 1944); Murray N. Rothbard, *For a New Liberty* (New York: Collier Books, 1978); Gottfried Dietz, *In Defense of Property* (Baltimore, MD: The Johns Hopkins Press, 1971); Eric Mack, "Liberty and Justice," in John Arthur and William Shaw, eds.,*Justice and Economic Distribution* (Englewood Cliffs, NJ: Prentice-Hall, 1978), pp. 183–193; John Hospers, *Libertarianism* (Los Angeles, CA: Nash, 1971); T. R. Machan, *Human Rights and Human Liberties* (Chicago, IL: Nelson-Hall, 1975).
32. Nicholas Zamiska, *op. cit.*
33. Nicholas Zamiska, "Thai Move to Trim Drug Costs Highlights Growing Patent Rift," *Wall Street Journal*, January 30, 2007.
34. The Ministry of Public Health and the National Health Security Office, Thailand, "Facts and Evidences on the Ten Burning Issues Related to the Government Use of Patents on Three Patented Essential Drugs in Thailand: Document to Support Strengthening of Social Wisdom on the Issue of Drug Patent," February 2007.
35. Cynthia M. Ho, "Unveiling Competing Patent Perspectives," *Houston Law Review*, vol. 3 (2009), pp. 1047–1114.
36. Locke, *Two Treatises*, p. 311; for a fuller treatment of Locke's views on the law of nature, see John Locke, W. von Leyden, ed., *Essays on the Law of Nature* (Oxford: The Clarendon Press, 1954).
37. William K. Frankena, *Ethics*, 2nd ed. (Englewood Cliffs, NJ: Prentice-Hall, 1973), pp. 102–105.
38. Robert Nozick, *Anarchy, State, and Utopia* (New York: Basic Books, Inc., 1974).
39. For versions of this argument, see Lindblom, *Politics and Markets*, pp. 45–51.
40. Arthur M. Okun, *Equality and Efficiency* (Washington, DC: The Brookings Institution, 1975), pp. 1–4.
41. U.S. Census Bureau, Current Population Reports, P60-236, *Income, Poverty, and Health Insurance Coverage in the United States: 2008*, (Washington, DC: U.S. Government Printing Office, 2009), Table 4, "People and Families in Poverty by Selected Characteristics: 2007 and 2008," and Table A-3, "Selected Measures of Household Income Dispersion: 1967–2008."
42. U.S. Census Bureau, 2008 American Community Survey 1-Year Estimates, Table B19081, "Mean Household Income of Quintiles–Universe: Households," September 2009.

43. Mark Nord, Margaret Andrews, and Steven Carlson, "Household Food Security in the United States, 2008," United States Department of Agriculture, Food and Nutrition Service, 2009. Economic Research Report No. 83 (ERS-83), November 2009.
44. U.S. Census Bureau, Current Population Reports, P60-236, *Income, Poverty, and Health Insurance Coverage in the United States: 2008*, Table 7, "People without Health Insurance Coverage by Selected Characteritistics: 2007–2008."
45. National Coalition for the Homeless, "How Many People Experience Homelessness?" (Washington, DC: National Coalition for the Homeless, July 2009).
46. Edward N. Wolff, "Recent Trends in Household Wealth in the United States: Rising Debt and the Middle-Class Squeeze—An Update to 2007," Working Paper, Levy Economics Institute of Bard College, Annandale-on-Hudson, NY, March 2010, Table 2 and Table 4; accessed June 4, 2010 at *http://www.levyinstitute.org/pubs/wp_589.pdf.*
47. See Patricia Werhane, *Adam Smith and His Legacy for Modern Capitalism* (New York: Oxford University Press, 1991); S. Hollander, *The Economics of Adam Smith* (Toronto: University of Toronto Press, 1973).
48. Adam Smith, *An Inquiry into the Nature and Causes of the Wealth of Nations* [1776] (New York: The Modern Library, n.d.), p. 423.
49. Ibid., p. 55.
50. Ibid., p. 14.
51. Ibid., pp. 55–58.
52. Ibid., p. 651.
53. Friedrich A. Hayek, "The Price System as a Mechanism for Using Knowledge," and Ludwig von Mises, "Economic Calculation in Socialism," both in Morris Bornstein, ed., *Comparative Economic Systems: Models and Cases* (Homewood, IL: Richard D. Irwin, Inc., 1965), pp. 39–50 and 79–85.
54. Thomas Aquinas, *Summa Theologica*, II–II, q. 66, a. 2.
55. For example, David Hume, Essay XLI, *An Inquiry Concerning the Principles of Morals*, part II, pp. 423–429, in *Essays, Literary, Moral, and Political*, by David Hume, Esq. (New York: Ward, Lock, & Co., Warwick House, no date).
56. These criticisms can be found in any standard economic textbook, but see especially Frank J. B. Stilwell, *Normative Economics* (Elmsford, NY: Pergamon Press, 1975).
57. But see Werhane, *Adam Smith and His Legacy*, who argues that Smith did not hold that individuals are motivated only by self-interest. Instead, she argues, Smith's views in *The Wealth of Nations* must be supplemented with his views on "sympathy," "approbation," "propriety," "virtue," and "sentiment," which are spelled out in his earlier treatise, *Theory of the Moral Sentiments.*
58. See, for example, J. Philip Wogaman, *The Great Economic Debate: An Ethical Analysis* (Philadelphia, PA: The Westminster Press, 1977), pp. 61 and 85.
59. See Vaclav Holesovsky, *Economic Systems, Analysis, and Comparison* (New York: McGraw-Hill Book Company, 1977), Chs. 9 and 10.
60. Oskar Lange, "On the Economic Theory of Socialism," in Bornstein, ed., *Comparative Economic Systems*, pp. 86–94.
61. The standard work on Keynes is Alvin H. Hansen, *A Guide to Keynes* (New York: McGraw-Hill Book Company, 1953).
62. John Maynard Keynes, *The General Theory of Employment, Interest, and Money* (London: Macmillan & Co., Ltd., 1936). For an accessible summary of Keynes's views, see his article "The General Theory of Employment," *Quarterly Journal of Economics*, September 1937, v. 51, pp. 209–223.
63. For an overview of the so-called "Post Keynesian School," see the collection of papers in J. Pheby, ed., *New Directions in Post Keynesian Economics* (Aldershot, UK: Edward Elgar, 1989), and M. C. Sawyer, *Post Keynesian Economics, Schools of Thought in Economics Series 2* (Aldershot, UK: Edward Elgar, 1988).
64. See Sheila C. Dow, "The Post-Keynesian School," in Douglas Mair and Anne G. Miller, eds., *A Modern Guide to Economic Thought* (Aldershot, UK: Edward Elgar, 1991).
65. John Hicks, *The Crisis in Keynesian Economics* (Oxford: Basil Blackwell, 1974), p. 25.
66. Charles Darwin, *The Origin of Species by Means of Natural Selection* (New York: D. Appleton and Company, 1883), p. 63.
67. Herbert Spencer, *Social Statics, Abridged and Revised* (New York: D. Appleton and Company, 1893), pp. 204–205; for an account of Spencerism in America, see Richard Hofstadter, *Social Darwinism in American Thought* (Boston, MA: Beacon Press, 1955).
68. Adam Smith, *The Wealth of Nations*, p. 424.
69. David Ricardo, *On the Principles of Political Economy and Taxation*, (Georgetown, DC: Joseph Milligan, 1819), pp. 115–116.
70. J. Michael finger and Philip Schuler, eds., *Poor People's Knowledge: Promoting Intellectual Property in Developing Countries*, (Washington, DC: The World Bank, 2004), p. 4.
71. For these and other illustrations cited by Marx, see his *Capital*, vol. I, Samuel Moore and Edward Aveling, trans. (Chicago, IL: Charles H. Kerr & Company, 1906), pp. 268–282.
72. Karl Marx, "Estranged Labor," in Dirk Struik, ed., *The Economic and Philosophic Manuscripts of 1844*, Martin Milligan, trans. (New York: International Publishers, 1964), pp. 106–119.
73. Ibid., pp. 110–111.
74. Ibid., pp. 108–109.
75. Ibid., p. 116.
76. Karl Marx and Friedrich Engels, *Manifesto of the Communist Party* (New York: International Publishers, 1948), p. 9.
77. "Estranged Labor," p. 150.
78. Ibid, p. 150.
79. Marx and Engels, pp. 37–38.
80. Marx and Engels, p. 48.
81. Marx and Engels, p. 49.
82. Ibid.
83. The classic expression of this distinction is Karl Marx, *A Contribution to the Critique of Political Economy*, N. I. Stone, ed. (New York: The International Library Publishing Co., 1904), pp. 11–13.
84. Marx and Engels, *Manifesto*; see also Karl Marx, *The German Ideology*, (Amherst, NY: Prometheus Books, 1998 [1845]), Part I: Feuerbach, section C. "The Real Basis of Ideology."
85. Karl Marx, *The German Ideology*, (Amherst, NY: Prometheus Books, 1998 [1845]).
86. See McMurtry, *Structure of Marx's World-View*, pp. 72–89.
87. Marx, *Capital*, vol. I, pp. 681–89.
88. Marx, *Capital*, vol. II, pp. 86–87.
89. Marx, *Capital*, vol. I, pp. 689 ff.
90. Marx and Engels, *Manifesto*, p. 30.
91. Karl Marx, *The German Ideology*.

92. Irving Kristol, "A Capitalist Conception of Justice," in Richard T. DeGeorge and Joseph A. Pickler, eds., *Ethics, Free Enterprise and Public Policy* (New York: Oxford University Press, 1978), p. 65; see also H. B. Acton, *The Morals of Markets* (London: Longman Group Limited, 1971), pp. 68–72.
93. John Bates Clark, *The Distribution of Wealth* (New York: The Macmillan Co., 1899), pp. 7–9, 106–107; for a critique of this argument, see Okun, *Equality and Efficiency*, pp. 40–47.
94. Milton Friedman, *Capitalism and Freedom*, pp. 168–172.
95. See, for example, the arguments in John Rawls, *Political Liberalism* (New York: Columbia University Press, 1993), pp. 37–43; and *A Theory of Justice* (Boston, MA: Harvard University Press, 1971).
96. See *Work in America: Report of the Special Task Force to the Secretary of Health, Education and Welfare* (Cambridge, MA: MIT Press, 1973).
97. See Thomas E. Weisskopf, "Sources of Cyclical Downturns and Inflation" and Arthur MacEwan, "World Capitalism and the Crisis of the 1970s," in Richard C. Edwards, Michael Reich, and Thomas E. Weisskopf, eds., *The Capitalist System*, 2nd ed. (Englewood Cliffs, NJ: Prentice-Hall, 1978), pp. 441–461.
98. Herbert Marcuse, *One Dimensional Man* (Boston, MA: Beacon Press, 1964), pp. 225–246.
99. Frank Ackerman and Andrew Zimbalist, "Capitalism and Inequality in the United States," in Edwards, Reich, Weisskopf, eds., *The Capitalist System*, pp. 297–307; and Michael Reich, "The Economics of Racism," ibid., pp. 381–388.
100. See Robert Hunter Wade, "Winners and Losers: The Global Distribution of Income Is Becoming More Unequal; That Should Be a Matter of Greater Concern than It Is," *The Economist*, April 28, 2001, pp. 79–81; "The Rising Inequality of World Income Distribution," *Finance and Development*, December 2001, v. 38, n. 4; and "Globalization, Poverty and Income Distribution: Does the Liberal Argument Hold?" accessed June 20, 2004 at *http://www.brookings.edu/gs/research/projects/glig/worldshort inequalityjune02.pdf.*
101. See, for example, Richard Rorty, "For a More Banal Politics," *Harper's*, May 1992, v. 284, pp. 16–21.
102. See Lodge, ibid.
103. See, for example, Paul Samuelson, *Economics*, 9th ed. (New York: McGraw-Hill Book Company, 1973), p. 845.
104. See "List of Countries by Income Equality," Wikipedia, accessed June 20, 2010 at *http://en.wikipedia.org/wiki/List_of_countries_by_income_equality#cite_note-3* ; see also U.S. Central Intelligence Agency, "Guide to Country Comparisons," *The World Factbook*, 2010, accessed June 20, 2010 at *https://www.cia.gov/library/publications/the-world-factbook/rankorder/rankorderguide.html.*
105. Paul Steidlmeier, "The Moral Legitimacy of Intellectual Property Claims: American Business and Developing Country Perspectives,"*The Journal of Business Ethics*, December 1993, pp. 161–162.
106. More exactly, the U.S. Copyright Term Extension Act (CTEA) of 1998 says that a copyright held by the individual author lasts for the life of the author plus 70 years, whereas if a business owns a copyright it lasts for 95 years from the year of first publication or 120 years from the year of its creation, whichever is shorter.
107. More exactly, patents on manufactured articles and processes expire after 20 years, whereas design patents expire after 14 years. Patents are granted only when the invention is novel, useful, and nonobvious.
108. See Francis Fukuyama, *The End of History and The Last Man* (New York: The Free Press, 1992).

Chapter 4

1. Grant Gross, "LG Display Executive Pleads Guilty in LCD Price-fixing Case," *PCWorld*, April 28, 2009.
2. Department of Justice, "President of Iowa Ready-mix Concrete Company Pleads Guilty to Price-fixing and Bid Rigging," press release dated May 24, 2010, accessed June 15, 2010 at *http://www.justice.gov/atr/public/press_releases/2010/258984.htm.*
3. Department of Justice, "Former Qantas Airline Executive Agrees to Plead Guilty to Participating in Price-Fixing Conspiracy on Air Cargo Shipments," Press Release, May 8, 2008, accessed June 10, 2010 at *http://washingtondc.fbi.gov/dojpressrel/pressrel08/wf050808.htm.*
4. Department of Justice, "Former Executive Indicted for His Role in Color Display Tube Price-Fixing Conspiracy," Press Release, March 30, 2010, accessed June 9, 2010 at *http://www.justice.gov/atr/public/press_releases/2010/257277.htm.*
5. Sharen D. Knight, ed., *Concerned Investors Guide*, NYSE Volume 1983 (Arlington, VA: Resource Publishing Group, Inc., 1983), pp. 24–25.
6. Ralph Nader and Mark J. Green, "Crime in the Suites," *New Republic*, April 29, 1972, pp. 17–21.
7. Vikas Anand, Blake E. Ashforth, and Mahendra Joshi, "Business as Usual: The Acceptance and Perpetuation of Corruption in Organizations," *Academy of Management Executive*, vol. 19 (2005), no. 4.
8. The elementary account that follows can be found in any standard economics textbook, for instance, Paul A. Samuelson, *Economics*, 11th ed. (New York: McGraw-Hill Book Company, 1980), pp. 52–62.
9. Daniel B. Suits, "Agriculture," in Walter Adams, ed., *The Structure of American Industry*, 5th ed. (New York: Macmillan Inc., 1977), pp. 1–39.
10. The reader may recall that one of the major criticisms leveled at the capitalist conception of justice is that it says people should be paid the exact value of the things they contribute, yet it gives no criterion for determining the "value" of a thing. Because different people place different values on things, this indeterminacy seems to make the capitalist conception of justice hopelessly vague: A price that is "just" in terms of the value one person places on a thing may be "unjust" in terms of the value another person places on that same thing. However, the values given to things by perfectly competitive markets are just from every participant's point of view because at the point of equilibrium all participants (both buyers and sellers) place the same value on commodities and prices converge on this uniquely just value.
11. See Robert Dorfman, *Prices and Markets*, 2nd ed. (Englewood Cliffs, NJ: Prentice-Hall, 1972), pp. 170–226.
12. Russell G. Warren, *Antitrust in Theory and Practice* (Columbus, OH: Grid, Inc., 1975), pp. 58–59.
13. Milton Friedman, *Capitalism and Freedom* (Chicago, IL: The University of Chicago Press, 1962), p. 14.
14. Warren, *Antitrust*, pp. 76–77.

15. It has been argued, however, that a company in which caring flourishes will have a competitive economic advantage over a company in which such caring does not obtain. See Jeanne M. Liedtka, "Feminist Morality and Competitive Reality: A Role for an Ethic of Care?" *Business Ethics Quarterly*, April 1996, v. 6, n. 2, pp. 179–200.
16. Again, any standard economics textbook can be consulted for these elementary ideas, for example, H. Robert Heller, *The Economic System* (New York: Macmillan Inc., 1972), p. 109.
17. Dean Takahashi, "Why Vista Might Be the Last of Its Kind," *Seattle Times*, December 4, 2006.
18. C. W. DeMarco, "Knee Deep in Technique: The Ethics of Monopoly Capital," *Journal of Business Ethics*, 2001, v. 31, pp. 151–164.
19. For an excellent and elementary review of both the theory and empirical evidence on monopoly profits, see Thomas Karier, *Beyond Competition: The Economics of Mergers and Monopoly Power* (New York: M. E. Sharpe, Inc., 1993).
20. See George J. Stigler, "Monopoly and Oligopoly by Merger," *The American Economic Review*, v. 40 (Proceedings of the American Economic Association, 1950), pp. 23–34; for a more recent review of the literature on oligopolies, see Karier, *Beyond Competition*.
21. Warren, *Antitrust*, p. 271.
22. The numerous studies confirming this relationship are surveyed in Douglas F. Greer, *Industrial Organization and Public Policy*, 2nd ed. (New York: Macmillan, Inc., 1984), pp. 407–414; Greer also critically evaluates the few studies that seem to show no such relationship.
23. Greer, *Industrial Organization*, pp. 416–417.
24. Anne Szustek, "Hitachi Will Plead Guilty in LCD Price-Fixing Case," *Finding Dulcinea*, March 11, 2009, accessed June 28, 2010 at *http://www.findingdulcinea.com/news/business/2009/march/Hitachi-Agrees-to-Plead-Guilty-In-LCD-Price-Fising-Case.html*; and Kevin Cho, "LG Display, Sharp Shares Fall on Price-Fixing Fine," *Bloomberg*, November 13, 2008.
25. Almarin Phillips, *Market Structure, Organization, and Performance* (Cambridge, MA: Harvard University Press, 1962), pp. 138–160.
26. Warren, *Antitrust*, pp. 233–235.
27. Newman S. Peery, Jr., *Business, Government, & Society: Managing Competitiveness, Ethics, and Social Issues* (Englewood Cliffs, NJ: Prentice-Hall, 1995), pp. 400–401.
28. *Eastman Kodak Company, Petitioner, v. Image Technical Services, Inc., et. al.*, Supreme Court of the United States, (90-1029), 504 U.S. 451 (1992).
29. Malcom Burns, "Predatory Pricing and the Acquisition Costs of Competitors," *Journal of Political Economy*, vol. 94 (1986), p. 266.
30. Quoted in Leslie D. Manns, "Dominance in the Oil Industry: Standard Oil from 1865 to 1911," p. 11, in David I. Rosenbaum, ed., *Market Dominance: How Firms Gain, Hold, or Lose It and the Impact on Economic Performance*, (Westport, Connecticut: Praeger, 1998), pp. 11–37.
31. Walter Adams and James W. Brock, "Tobacco: Predation and Persistent Market Power," in David I. Rosenbaum, op. cit., pp. 39–53.
32. Siri Schubert and T. Christian Miller, "At Siemens, Bribery Was Just a Line Item," *The New York Times*, December 21, 2008.
33. Neil H. Jacoby, Peter Nehemkis, and Richard Fells, *Bribery and Extortion in World Business* (New York: Macmillan Inc., 1977), p. 183.
34. Donald Cressey, *Other People's Money: A Study in the Social Psychology of Embezzlement*, (Montclair, NJ: Patterson Smith, 1973).
35. Jeffrey Sonnenfeld and Paul R. Lawrence, "Why Do Companies Succumb to Price-Fixing?" *Harvard Business Review*, July–August 1978, v. 56, n. 4, pp. 145–157.
36. Ibid., p. 75.
37. Jesse W. Markham, "The Nature and Significance of Price Leadership," *The American Economic Review*, 1951, v. 41, pp. 891–905.
38. United States v. Topco Assocs., Inc., 405 U.S. 596, 610 (1972).
39. See J. M. Clarm, "Toward a Concept of Workable Competition," *American Economic Review*, 1940, v. 30, pp. 241–256.
40. John Kenneth Galbraith, *American Capitalism: The Concept of Countervailing Power*, rev. ed. (Cambridge, MA: The Riverside Press, 1956), pp. 112–113.
41. Robert H. Bork, *The Antitrust Paradox: A Policy at War with Itself* (New York: Basic Books, 1978), pp. 20–58, 405.
42. Richard Posner, "The Chicago School of Antitrust Analysis," *University of Pennsylvania Law Review*, 1979, v. 925.
43. See the summary of the research on the claim that size and efficiency are correlated in Douglas F. Greer, *Business, Government, and Society*, 3rd ed. (New York: Macmillan Publishing Company, 1993), pp. 175–178.
44. J. Fred Weston, "Big Corporations: The Arguments For and Against Breaking Them Up," *Business and Its Changing Environment*, proceedings of a conference held by the Graduate School of Management at UCLA, July 24–August 3, 1977, pp. 232–233; see also John M. Blair, *Economic Concentration: Structure, Behavior, and Public Policy* (New York: Harcourt Brace Jovanovich, 1972).
45. J. A. Schumpeter, *Capitalism, Socialism, and Democracy* (New York: Harper, 1943), pp. 79ff.
46. L. Von Mises, *Planned Chaos* (New York: Foundations for Economic Education, 1947).

Chapter 5

1. Energy Information Administration, "United States of America Country Analysis Brief, 2004," accessed June 22, 2004 at *http://www.eia.doe.gov/emeu/cabs/usa.html.*
2. United Nations Environment Programme, *Global Environment Outlook, GEO4: Summary for Decision Makers*, (Valletta, Malta: Progress Press Company Limited, 2007), excerpts from pp. 8–12.
3. William G. Pollard, "The Uniqueness of the Earth," in Ian G. Barbour, ed., *Earth Might Be Fair* (Englewood Cliffs, NJ: Prentice-Hall, 1972), pp. 95–96.
4. Mihalis Lazaridis and Ian Colbeck, eds., *Human Exposure to Pollutants via Dermal Absorption and Inhalation*, (New York: Springer, 2010); for an older overview of the health effects of air pollution, see World Resources Institute, *World Resources 1998–1999: Environmental Changes and Human Health* (New York: Basic Books, 1998).
5. C . See D. S. Arndt, M. O. Baringer, and M. R. Johnson, eds., State of the Climate in 2009, *Bull. Amer. Medeor Soc.*, v. 91, (2010), no. 6, pp. S1–S224.
6. See Arndt, Baringer, and Johnson, eds., State of the Climate in 2009; see also the EPA website on global warming at *http://www.epa.gov/globalwarming/index.html.*

7. Reports of the IPCC are available at *http://www.ipcc.ch*; excerpts are also available at *http://www.epa.gov/globalwarming/publications/reference/ipcc/index.html.*
8. Paul R. Epstein, "Is Global Warming Harmful to Health?" *Scientific American*, August 2000, v. 283, n. 2, pp. 50–57.
9. Lester R. Brown, ed., *State of the World, 2000* (New York: W. W. Norton & Company, 2000), p. 200; see, more generally, World Meteorological Organization, *Scientific Assessment of Ozone Depletion: 1994*, WMO Global Ozone Research and Monitoring Project—Report No. 37, Geneva, 1995; the executive summary of the WMO report is available at *http://www.al.noaa.gov/WWWHD/pubdocs/Assessment94/executive-summary.html#A.*
10. U.S. Environmental Protection Agency, "Ozone Science Fact Sheet," 1997, available at *http://www.epa.gov/ozone/science/sc_fact.html.*
11. United States Environmental Protection Agency, "What You Should Know about Refrigerants When Purchasing or Repairing a Residential A/C System or Heat Pump," April 26, 2000, available at *http://www.epa.gov/ozone/title6/phaseout/22phaseout.html.*
12. U.S. Environmental Protection Agency, "Environmental Effects of Acid Rain," April 1999, available at *http://www.epa.gov/acidrain/effects/envben.html.*
13. See B. J. Mason, *Acid Rain: Its Causes and Effects on Inland Waters* (Oxford: Clarendon Press, 1992).
14. Environmental Protection Agency, *National Air Quality and Emissions Trends Report, 1998* (EPA 454/R-00–003), March 2000, p. 81.
15. Quoted in Huey D. Johnson, ed., *No Deposit—No Return* (Reading, MA: Addison-Wesley Publishing Co., Inc., 1970), pp. 166–167.
16. "Bad Air's Damage to Lungs Is Long-lasting, Study Says," *San Jose Mercury News*, March 29, 1991, p. 1f; see also Philip E. Graves, Ronald J. Krumm, and Daniel M. Violette, "Issues in Health Benefit Measurement," in George S. Tolley, Philip E. Graves, and Alan S. Cohen, eds., *Environment Policy*, vol. II (Cambridge, MA: Harper & Row, Publishers, Inc., 1982).
17. U.S. Environmental Protection Agency, *Our Nation's Air: Status and Trends Through 2008*, Contract No. EP-D-05-004, Work Assignment No. 5-07, Office of Air Quality Planning and Standards, Research Triangle Park, North Carolina, EPA-454/R-09-002, February 2010.
18. Lester Lave and Eugene Seskind, *Air Pollution and Human Health* (Baltimore, MD: Johns Hopkins University Press, 1977).
19. Ibid., pp. 723–733.
20. Freeman, *Air and Water Pollution Control*, p. 69.
21. Office of Management and Budget, "Informing Regulatory Decisions: 2003 Report to Congress on the Costs and Benefits of Federal Regulations," p. 9, accessed June 23, 2004 at *http://www.whitehouse.gov/omb/inforeg/2003_cost-ben_final_rpt.pdf.*
22. United States Environmental Protection Agency, "Water Quality Conditions in the United States: A Profile from the 1998 National Water Quality Inventory Report to Congress," July 2000, summary of the *National Water Quality Inventory: 1998 Report to Congress*, available at *http://www.epa.gov/305b/98report/98summary.html.*
23. See U.S. Environmental Protection Agency, *National Air Pollutant Emission Trends, 1900–1998*, EPA-454/R-00-002.
24. Council on Environmental Quality, *Environmental Trends*, p. 31.
25. X. M. Mackenthun, *The Practice of Water Pollution* (Washington, DC: U.S. Government Printing Office, 1969), Ch. 8.
26. Wagner, *Environment*, pp. 102–107.
27. J. H. Ryther, "Nitrogen, Phosphorus, and Eutrophication in the Coastal Marine Environment," *Science*, 1971, v. 171, n. 3975, pp. 1008–1013.
28. L. J. Carter, "Chemical Plants Leave Unexpected Legacy for Two Virginia Rivers," *Science*, 1977, v. 198, pp. 1015–1020; J. Holmes, "Mercury Is Heavier Than You Think," *Esquire*, May 1971; T. Aaronson, "Mercury in the Environment," *Environment*, May 1971.
29. F. S. Sterrett and C. A. Boss, "Careless Kepone," *Environment*, 1977, v. 19, pp. 30–37.
30. L. Friberg, *Cadmium in the Environment* (Cleveland, OH: C.R.C. Press, 1971).
31. See Presson S. Shane, "Case Study-Silver Bay: Reserve Mining Company," in Thomas Donaldson and Patricia H. Werhane, eds.,*Ethical Issues in Business* (Englewood Cliffs, NJ: Prentice-Hall, 1979), pp. 358–361.
32. Infoplease, "Oil Spills and Disasters," accessed July 25, 2010 at *http://www.infoplease.com/ipa/A0001451.html;* see also Joshua E. Keating, "The World's Ongoing Ecological Disasters," *Foreign Policy*, July 16, 2010, accessed March 30, 2010 at *http://www.foreignpolicy.com/articles/2010/07/16/the_world_s_worst_ongoing_disasters.*
33. D. Burnham, "Radioactive Material Found in Oceans," *New York Times*, May 31, 1976, p. 13.
34. Council on Environmental Quality, *Environmental Trends*, p. 47.
35. Ibid.
36. World Health Organization, *Progress on Sanitation and Drinking Water: 2010 Update*, (Geneva, Switzerland: World Health Organization, 2010), pp. 7 and 18.
37. United Nations World Water Assessment Programme, *The United Nations World Water Development Report 3: Water in a Changing World*, (Paris: The United Nations Educational, Scientific and Cultural Organization, 2009).
38. Freeman, *Air and Water Pollution Control*, p. 159.
39. For these and other reports on communities affected by leaked or buried toxic substances, see the website blog "Contaminated Nation" at *http://contaminatednation.blogspot.com/.*
40. U.S. Environmental Protection Agency Office of Solid Waste, *Coal Combustion Waste Damage Case Assessments*, July 9, 2007; accessed July 26, 2010 at *www.publicintegrity.org/assets/pdf/CoalAsh-Doc1.pdf*; see also, Kristen Lombardi, "Coal Ash: The Hidden Story: How Industry and the EPA Failed to Stop a Growing Environmental Disaster," February 19, 2009, at The Center for Public Integrity website accessed July 27 at *http://www.publicintegrity.org/articles/entry/1144/.*
41. Shaila Dewan, "Hundreds of Coal Ash Dumps Lack Regulation," *The New York times*, January 6, 2009.
42. Paul Keith Conkin, *The State of the Earth: Environmental Challenges on the Road to 2100*, (Lexington, KY: University Press of Kentucky, 2006) p. 107.
43. Council on Environmental Quality, *Environmental Trends*, p. 139.
44. Ibid., p. 140.
45. Ibid.
46. Scott M. Kaufman, Nora Goldstein, Karsten Millrath, and Nickolas J. Themelis, "State of Garbage in America," *BioCycle*, January 2004, v. 45, n. 1, pp. 31–42.

47. See U.S. Environmental Protection Agency, "National Priorities List," accessed June 25, 2004 at *http://www.epa.gov/superfund/sites/query/queryhtm/nplfin.htm.*
48. See U.S. Environmental Protection Agency, "Industrial Waste Management," accessed June 25, 2004 at *http://www.epa.gov/industrialwaste.*
49. Council on Environmental Quality, *Environmental Trends*, p. 139.
50. Ibid.
51. Ibid.
52. Council on Environmental Quality, *Environmental Quality 1983* (Washington, DC: U.S. Government Printing Office, 1984), p. 62.
53. See U.S. Nuclear Regulatory Commission, "NRC Statement on Risk Assessment and the Reactor Safety Study Report in Light of the Risk Assessment Review Group Report," January 18, 1979.
54. U.S. Nuclear Regulatory Commission, "Final Generic Environmental Statement on the Use of Plutonium Recycle in Mixed Oxide Fuel in Light Water Cooled Reactors," NUREG-0002, vol. 1, August 1976.
55. See Theodore B. Taylor and Mason Willrich, *Nuclear Theft: Risks and Safeguards* (Cambridge, MA: Ballinger Publishing Co., 1974).
56. Thomas O'Toole, "Glass, Salt Challenged as Radioactive Waste Disposal Methods," *The Washington Post*, December 24, 1978.
57. U.S. General Accounting Office, GAO Report to Congress B-164052, "Cleaning Up the Remains of Nuclear Facilities—A Multibillion Dollar Problem," EMD-77-46 (Washington, DC: U.S. Government Printing Office, 1977).
58. Sam H. Schurr et. al., *Energy in America's Future* (Baltimore, MD: The Johns Hopkins University Press, 1979), p. 35.
59. Ellen Winchester, "Nuclear Wastes," *Sierra*, July/August 1979.
60. Charles Officer and Jake Page, *Earth and You: Tales of the Environment* (Portsmouth, NH: Peter E. Randall Publisher, 2000); see also Harry Goodwin and J.M. Goodwin, "List of Mammals which have Become Extinct since 1600: An Extension and Updating of the List Drawn Up by the Late James Fisher in 1968," International Union for Conservation of Nature, Morges, Switzerland, 1973, accessed online on July 26, 2010 at *http://data.iucn.org/dbtw-wpd/commande/downpdf.aspx?id=8547&url=http://www.iucn.org/dbtw-wpd/edocs/OP-008.pdf.*
61. C. S. Wong, "Atmospheric Input of Carbon Dioxide from Burning Wood," *Science*, 1978, v. 200, pp. 197–200.
62. G. M. Woodwell, "The Carbon Dioxide Question," *Scientific American*, 1978, v. 238, pp. 34–43.
63. International Union for Conservation of Nature, "Table 1: Numbers of threatened species by major groups of organisms (1996–2010)," *IUCN Red List of Threatened Species. Version 2010.2.*, Summary Statistics, accessed July 28 2010 at *http://www.iucnredlist.org/about/summary-statistics.*
64. Boris Worm et. al., "Rebuilding Global Fisheries," *Science*, July 31, 2009, vol. 325, no. 5940, pp. 578–585.
65. Mindy Selman and Suzie Greenhalgh, *Eutrophication: Sources and Drivers of Nutrient Pollution*, WRI Policy Note, Water Quality: Eutrophication and Hypoxia, no. 2, (Washington, DC: World Resources Institute, June 2009), 8 pp.
66. An exponential rate of depletion is assumed in the Club of Rome report; Donella H. Meadows, Dennis L. Meadows, Jergen Randers, and William W. Behrens, III, *The Limits to Growth* (New York: Universe Books, 1972).
67. U.S. Congress Office of Technology Assessment, *World Petroleum Availability: 1980–2000* (Washington, DC: U.S. Government Printing Office, 1980).
68. M. K. Hubbert, "U.S. Energy Resources: A Review as of 1972," Document No. 93–40 (92–72) (Washington, DC: U.S. Government Printing Office, 1974).
69. Ibid.
70. See the very readable and excellent overview of this issue in Tim Appenzeller, "The End of Cheap Oil?" *National Geographic*, June 2004, pp. 80–109.
71. See Colin Cambell, "The End of Cheap Oil?" *Scientific American*, March 1998; Jean H. Laherrère, "Future Sources of Crude Oil Supply and Quality Considerations," DRI/McGraw-Hill/French Petroleum Institute, June 1997; L. F. Ivanhoe, "Get Ready for Another Oil Shock!" *The Futurist*, Jan–Feb., 1997; the estimates of David Greene are in Appenzeller, "The End of Cheap Oil?" p. 90.
72. Davis, *The Seventh Year*, p. 128.
73. Ibid., pp. 131–132.
74. Paul R. Portney, ed., *Current Issues in Natural Resource Policy* (Washington, DC: Resources for the Future, 1982), pp. 80–81.
75. Robert B. Gordon, Tjalling C. Koopmans, William D. Nordhaus, and Brian J. Skinner, *Toward a New Iron Age?* (Cambridge, MA: Harvard University Press, 1987).
76. Ibid., p. 153.
77. U.S. Geological Survey, *Mineral Commodity Summaries*, February 2000, p. 23.
78. David Cohen, "Earth's Natural Wealth: An Audit," *New Scientist*, issue 2605, (May 23, 2007), pp. 34–41.
79. The term is Garrit Hardin's; see his "The Tragedy of the Commons," *Science*, December 13, 1968, v. 162, n. 3859, pp. 1243–1248.
80. Richard M. Stephenson, *Living with Tomorrow* (New York: John Wiley & Sons, Inc., 1981), pp. 205–208.
81. Ibid., p. 204.
82. United Nations Population Fund, Stan Bernstein and William F. Ryan, eds., *State of the World Population 2003* (New York: United Nations Population Fund, 2003), p. 74.
83. Carl J. George and Daniel McKinely, *Urban Ecology: In Search of an Asphalt Rose* (New York: McGraw-Hill Book Company, 1974).
84. L. Gari, "Arabic Treatises on Environmental Pollution Up to the End of the Thirteenth Century," *Environment and History*, vol. 8 (2002), no. 1, pp. 475–488.
85. The quote by Aristotle is from his *Politics*, Bk. 1, Ch. 8; the quote by Aquinas is from his *Summa Contra Gentiles*, Bk. 3, Part 2, Ch. 112; and the quote from the Old Testament is from *Genesis* 1:28.
86. Barry Commoner, *The Closing Circle* (New York: Alfred A. Knopf, Inc., 1971), Ch. 2.
87. See Kenneth E. F. Watt, *Understanding the Environment* (Boston, MA: Allyn & Bacon, Inc., 1982).
88. Matthew Edel, *Economics and the Environment* (Englewood Cliffs, NJ: Prentice-Hall, 1973); for the term *spaceship earth*, see Kenneth Boulding, "The Economics of the Coming Spaceship Earth," in Henry Jarret, ed., *Environmental Quality in a Growing Economy* (Baltimore, MD: Johns Hopkins Press for Resources for the Future, 1966).
89. George Perkins *Man and Nature*, [1864] (Cambridge, MA: Harvard University Press, 1965), p. 76.

90. For discussions favoring this view as well as criticisms, see the essays collected in Donald Scherer and Thomas Attig, eds.,*Ethics and the Environment* (Englewood Cliffs, NJ: Prentice-Hall, 1983).
91. Quoted in Bill Devall, *Simple in Means, Rich in Ends, Practicing Deep Ecology* (Salt Lake City, UT: Peregrine Smith Books, 1988), pp. 14–15.
92. Routley, R. and Routley, V., 1980. "Human Chauvinism and Environmental Ethics" in Mannison, D., McRobbie, M. A., and Routley, R. (eds.) *Environmental Philosophy*, Canberra: Australian National University, Research School of Social Sciences, pp. 96–189.
93. Ted Gup, "Owl vs. Man," *Time*, June 25, 1990, pp. 56–62; Catherine Caufield, "A Reporter at Large: The Ancient Forest," *New Yorker*, May 14, 1990, pp. 46–84.
94. Devall, *Simple in Means, Rich in Ends*, p. 138.
95. Peter Singer, *Animal Liberation* (New York: Random House, Inc., 1975).
96. Tom Regan, *The Case for Animal Rights* (Berkeley, CA: University of California Press, 1983); in a similar vein, Joel Feinberg argues that animals have interests and consequently have rights in "The Rights of Animals and Unborn Generations," in William T. Blackstone, ed., *Philosophy and Environmental Crisis* (Athens, GA: University of Georgia Press, 1974).
97. See William Aiken, "Ethical Issues in Agriculture," in Tom Regan, ed., *Earthbound: New Introductory Essays in Environmental Ethics* (New York: Random House, Inc., 1984), pp. 247–288.
98. People for the Ethical Treatment of Animals, "Companies that Do Test on Animals" accessed July 28 at *http://search.caringconsumer.com/*.
99. Kenneth Goodpaster, "On Being Morally Considerable," *Journal of Philosophy*, 1978, v. 75, pp. 308–325; see also Paul Taylor, "The Ethics of Respect for Nature," *Environmental Ethics*, 1981, v. 3, pp. 197–218; Robin Attfield, "The Good of Trees," *The Journal of Value Inquiry*, 1981, v. 15, pp. 35–54; and Christopher D. Stone, *Should Trees Have Standing? Toward Legal Rights for Natural Objects* (Boston, MA: Houghton Mifflin, 1978).
100. Aldo Leopold, "The Land Ethic," in *A Sand County Almanac* (New York: Oxford University Press, 1949), pp. 201–226; see also J. Baird Callicott, "Animal Liberation: A Triangular Affair," *Environmental Ethics*, Winter 1980, v. 2, n. 4, pp. 311–338; John Rodman, "The Liberation of Nature?" *Inquiry*, 1977, v. 20, pp. 83–131; K. Goodpaster argues that the "biosphere" as a whole has moral value in "On Being Morally Considerable"; Holmes Rolston, III, holds a similar position in "Is There an Ecological Ethic," *Ethics*, 1975, v. 85, pp. 93–109; for a variety of views on this issue, see Bryan G. Norton, ed., *The Preservation of Species* (Princeton, NJ: Princeton University Press, 1986).
101. Albert Schweitzer, *Out of My Life and Thought*, trans. A. B. Lemke (New York: Holt, 1990), p. 130.
102. Ibid., p. 131.
103. Paul Taylor, *Respect for Nature* (Princeton, NJ: Princeton University Press, 1986), p. 80.
104. Ibid., pp. 121–122.
105. W. K. Frankena, "Ethics and the Environment," in K. E. Goodpaster and K. M. Sayre, eds., *Ethics and Problems of the 21st Century* (Notre Dame, IN: University of Notre Dame Press, 1979), pp. 3–20.
106. For other criticisms of these arguments, see Edward Johnson, "Treating the Dirt: Environmental Ethics and Moral Theory," in Tom Regan, ed., *Earthbound: New Introductory Essays in Environmental Ethics* (New York: Random House, 1984), pp. 336–365; see also the discussion between Goodpaster and Hunt in W. Murray Hunt, "Are Mere Things Morally Considerable?" *Environmental Ethics*, 1980, v. 2, pp. 59–65; and Kenneth Goodpaster, "On Stopping at Everything: A Reply to W. M. Hunt," *Environmental Ethics*, 1980, v. 2, pp. 281–284.
107. See, for example, R. G. Frey, *Interests and Rights: The Case Against Animals* (Oxford: Clarendon Press, 1980), and Martin Benjamin, "Ethics and Animal Consciousness," in Manuel Velasquez and Cynthia Rostankowski, eds., *Ethics: Theory and Practice* (Englewood Cliffs, NJ: Prentice-Hall, 1985).
108. For useful treatments of the ethics of environmental issues, see Dale Jamison, ed., *A Companion to Environmental Ethics* (New York: Blackwell Publishers, 2000); and Robin Attfield, *The Ethics of Environmental Concern* (New York: Columbia University Press, 1983).
109. William T. Blackstone, "Ethics and Ecology," in William T. Blackstone, ed., *Philosophy and Environmental Crisis* (Athens, GA: University of Georgia Press, 1974); see also his later article, "On Rights and Responsibilities Pertaining to Toxic Substances and Trade Secrecy," *The Southern Journal of Philosophy*, 1978, v. 16, pp. 589–603.
110. Ibid., p. 31; see also William T. Blackstone, "Equality and Human Rights," *Monist*, 1968, v. 52, n. 4; and William T. Blackstone, "Human Rights and Human Dignity," in Laszlo and Grotesky, eds., *Human Dignity*.
111. Quoted in Keith Davis and William C. Frederick, *Business and Society* (New York: McGraw-Hill Book Company, 1984), pp. 403–404.
112. Alon Rosenthal, George M. Gray, and John D. Graham, "Legislating Acceptable Cancer Risk from Exposure to Toxic Chemicals," *Ecology Law Quarterly*, vol. 19 (1992), no. 2, pp. 269–362.
113. Robert H. Haveman and Greg Christiansen, *Jobs and the Environment* (Scarsdale, NY: Work in America Institute, Inc., 1979), p. 4.
114. Richard Kazis and Richard L. Grossman, "Job Blackmail: It's Not Jobs or Environment," p. 260, in Mark Green, ed., *The Big Business Reader* (New York: The Pilgrim Press, 1983), pp. 259–269.
115. See U.S. Department of Labor, *Mass Layoffs in 1987–1990*, Bureau of Labor Statistics Bulletins 2395, 2375, 2310; see also E. B. Goodstein, "Jobs or the Environment? No Tradeoff,"*Challenge*, January–February 1995, pp. 41–45.
116. For an analysis of the impact of this executive order, see the essays collected in V. Kerry Smith, ed., *Environmental Policy Under Reagan's Executive Order* (Chapel Hill, NC: The University of North Carolina Press, 1984).
117. There are a number of texts describing this approach. An elementary text is Tom Tietenberg, *Environmental and Natural Resource Economics* (Glenview, IL: Scott, Foresman & Company, 1984); a more compact treatment is Edwin S. Mills, *The Economics of Environmental Quality* (New York: W. W. Norton & Co., Inc., 1978), Ch. 3; for several viewpoints, consult Robert Dorfman and Nancy Dorman, eds.,*Economics of the Environment* (New York: W. W. Norton & Co., Inc., 1977).

118. For a still useful review of the literature on external costs, see E. J. Mishan, "The Postwar Literature on Externalities: An Interpretative Essay," *Journal of Economic Literature*, March 1971, v. 9, n. 1, pp. 1–28.
119. Not only is much of the electrical power industry still monopolized, but in the short run, at least, demand is relatively inelastic. Over the long run, demand may have the more elastic characteristics we assume in the example.
120. See E. J. Mishan, *Economics for Social Decisions* (New York: Praeger Publishers, Inc., 1973), pp. 85ff.; also E. J. Mishan, *Cost-Benefit Analysis*, 3rd ed. (London: Allen & Unwin, 1982).
121. S. Prakesh Sethi, *Up Against the Corporate Wall* (Englewood Cliffs, NJ: Prentice-Hall, 1977), p. 21.
122. See Mishan, "The Postwar Literature on Externalities," p. 24.
123. William J. Baumal and Wallace E. Oates, *Economics, Environmental Policy, and the Quality of Life* (Englewood Cliffs, NJ: Prentice-Hall, 1979), p. 177.
124. Ibid., pp. 180–182.
125. Ibid., pp. 182–184.
126. Mishan, "The Postwar Literature on Externalities," p. 24.
127. Mills, *Economics of Environmental Quality*, pp. 111–112.
128. Ibid., pp. 83–91.
129. For a number of cases that apply these techniques, see Yusuf J. Ahmad, Partha Dasgupta, and Karl-Goran Maler, eds., *Environmental Decision-Making* (London: Hodder and Stoughton, 1984).
130. Thomas A. Klein, *Social Costs and Benefits of Business* (Englewood Cliffs, NJ: Prentice-Hall, 1977), p. 118.
131. Ibid., p. 119; the literature on social accounting for business firms was once vast; see U.S. Department of Commerce, *Corporate Social Reporting in the United States and Western Europe* (Washington, DC: U.S. Government Printing Office, 1979); Committee on Social Measurement, *The Measurement of Corporate Social Performance* (New York: American Institute of Certified Public Accountants, Inc., 1977).
132. See Boyd Collier, *Measurement of Environmental Deterioration* (Austin, TX: Bureau of Business Research, The University of Texas at Austin, 1971).
133. See Michael D. Boyles, "The Price of Life," *Ethics*, October 1978, v. 89, n. 1, pp. 20–34; for other problems with using cost-benefit analysis in environmental areas, see Mark Sagoff, "Ethics and Economics in Environmental Law," in Regan, ed., *Earthbound*, pp. 147–178, and Rosemarie Tong, *Ethics in Policy Analysis* (Englewood Cliffs, NJ: Prentice-Hall, 1986), pp. 14–29.
134. Much of the material in this and the following paragraphs is based on the superb analysis in Robert E. Goodwin, "No Moral Nukes," *Ethics*, April 1980, v. 90, n. 3, pp. 417–449.
135. Committee on Social Measurement, *The Measurement of Corporate Social Performance* (New York: American Institute of Certified Public Accountants, Inc., 1977).
136. U.S. General Accounting Office, *The Nation's Nuclear Waste* (Washington, DC: U.S. Government Printing Office, 1979), p. 12. For a criticism of this kind of policy analysis, see Tong,*Ethics in Policy Analysis*, pp. 39–54.
137. Murray Bookchin, *Defending the Earth: A Dialogue Between Murray Bookchin and Dave Foreman*, Steve Chase, ed. (Boston: South End Press, 1991), p. 58.
138. Karen J. Warren, "The Power and Promise of Ecological Feminism," *Environmental Ethics*, Summer 1990, v. 12, p. 126.
139. Val Plumwood, "Current Trends in Ecofeminism," *The Ecologist*, January/February 1992, v. 22, n. 1, p. 10.
140. Nell Noddings, *Caring, A Feminine Approach to Ethics and Moral Education* (Berkeley, CA: University of California Press, 1984), p. 14.
141. Karen J. Warren, "The Power and the Promise of Ecological Feminism," in Christine Pierce and Donald VanDeVeer, eds., *People, Penguins, and Plastic Trees, Basic Issues in Environmental Ethics*, 2nd ed. (Belmont, CA: Wadsworth, 1995), pp. 218 and 223.
142. Martin Golding, "Obligations to Future Generations," *Monist*, 1972, v. 56, n. 1, pp. 85–99; Richard T. DeGeorge, "The Environment, Rights, and Future Generations," in K. E. Goodpaster and K. M. Sayre, eds., *Ethics and Problems of the 21st Century*, pp. 93–105.
143. DeGeorge, "The Environment, Rights, and Future Generations," pp. 97–98.
144. Ibid.
145. Martin Golding, "Obligations to Future Generations," *Monist*, 1972, v. 56, n. 1, Gregory Kavka argues, however, that full knowledge of the needs of future people is not required to accord them moral standing in "The Futurity Problem," in Ernest Partridge, *Responsibilities to Future Generations* (New York: Prometheus Books, 1981), pp. 109–122; see also Annette Baier, "For the Sake of Future Generations," in Regan, ed., *Earthbound*, pp. 214–246.
146. John Rawls, *A Theory of Justice* (Cambridge, MA: Harvard University Press, 1971), p. 289.
147. Ibid., pp. 285 and 288.
148. Among authors who favor Rawls in their treatment of our obligations to future generations are R. and V. Routley, "Nuclear Energy and Obligations to the Future," *Inquiry*, 1978, v. 21, pp. 133–179; K. S. Shrader-Frechette, *Nuclear Power and Public Policy* (Dordecht, Boston, and London: Reidel, 1980); F. Patrick Hubbard, "Justice, Limits to Growth, and an Equilibrium State," *Philosophy and Public Affairs*, 1978, v. 7, pp. 326–345; Victor D. Lippit and Koichi Hamada, "Efficiency and Equity in Intergenerational Distribution," in Dennis Clark Pirages, ed., *The Sustainable Society* (New York and London: Praeger Publishers, Inc., 1977), pp. 285–299. Each of these authors, however, introduces modifications to Rawls's position.
149. Attfield adopts this "Lockean principle" from G. Kavka, "The Futurity Problem."
150. Attfield, *The Ethics of Environmental Concern*, pp. 107–110.
151. J. Brenton Stearns, "Ecology and the Indefinite Unborn," *Monist*, October 1972, v. 56, n. 4, pp. 612–625; Jan Narveson, "Utilitarianism and New Generations," *Mind*, 1967, v. 76, pp. 62–67.
152. Robert Scott, Jr., "Environmental Ethics and Obligations to Future Generations," in R. I. Sikora and Brian Barry, eds., *Obligations to Future Generations* (Philadelphia, PA: Temple University Press, 1978), pp. 74–90; but see Kavka, "The Futurity Problem," who argues against discounting.
153. Joan Robinson, *Economic Philosophy* (London: Penguin Books, 1966), p. 115.
154. William G. Shepherd and Clair Wilcox, *Public Policies Toward Business*, 6th ed. (Homewood, IL: Richard D. Irwin, Inc., 1979), pp. 524–525.
155. Susan Murcott, Sustainable Development: A Meta-Review of Definitions, Principles, Criteria Indicators, Conceptual Frameworks and Information Systems. Annual

Conference of the American Association for the Advancement of Science. IIASA Symposium on "Sustainability Indicators." Seattle, Wa. Feb 13–18, 1997; Barbar Becker, "Sustainability Assessment: A Review of Values, Concepts, and Methodological Approaches," *Agricultural Issues*, vol. 10, (Washington, D.C.: Secretariat of the Consultative Group on International Agricultural Research, The World Bank, February 1997).

156. World Commission on Environment and Development, *Our Common Future*, (London: Oxford University Press, 1987).
157. Herman E. Daly, "Sustainable Growth: An Impossibility Theorem," in Herman E. Daly and Kenneth N. Townsend, eds., *Valuing the Earth: Economics, Ecology, Ethics*, (Boston, MA: The MIT Press, 1993), pp. 267–274.
158. E. F. Schumacher, *Small Is Beautiful* (London: Blond and Briggs, Ltd., 1973).
159. Herman E. Daly, ed., *Toward a Steady-State Economy* (San Francisco, CA: W. H. Freeman & Company, Publishers, 1974), p. 152.
160. See, for example, Wilfred Beckerman, *In Defense of Economic Growth* (London: Jonathan Cape, 1974); Rudolph Klein, "The Trouble with Zero Economic Growth," *New York Review of Books*, April 1974; Julian L. Simon, *The Ultimate Resource* (Princeton, NJ: Princeton University Press, 1981).
161. E. J. Mishan, *The Economic Growth Debate: An Assessment* (London: George Allen & Unwin Ltd., 1977).
162. See Heilbroner, *An Inquiry into the Human Prospect, Updated for the 1980s*.
163. Several of these scenarios are reviewed in James Just and Lester Lave, "Review of Scenarios of Future U.S. Energy Use," *Annual Review of Energy*, 1979, v. 4, pp. 501–536; and in Hughes, *World Futures*.
164. Meadows, Meadows, Randers, and Behrens, *The Limits to Growth* (New York: Universe Books, 1974).
165. Meadows et al. revised their models but came up with very similar results in D. H. Meadows, D. L. Meadows, and J. Randers, *Beyond the Limits: Confronting Global Collapse, Envisioning a Sustainable Future* (Post Mills, VT: Chelsea Green, 1992); for other examples, see the many much more recent and depressing papers collected at *http://www.dieoff. org/index.html*.
166. Ibid., p. 132.
167. H. S. D. Cole, Christopher Freeman, Marie Jahoda, and K. L. R. Pavitt, eds., *Models of Doom: A Critique of the Limits to Growth* (New York: Universe Books, 1973); William Nordhaus, "World Dynamics: Measurement Without Data," *Economic Journal*, December 1973, v. 83, pp. 1156–1183; Herman Kahn, William Brown, and Leon Martel, *The Next 200 Years* (New York: William Morrow & Company, Inc., 1976); Charles Maurice and Charles W. Smithson, *The Doomsday Myth* (Stanford, CA: Hoover Institution Press, 1984); and Piers Blaikie, "The Use of Natural Resources in Developing and Developed Countries," in R. J. Johnston and P. J. Taylor, *A World in Crisis* (Cambridge, MA: Basil Blackwell, 1989), pp. 125–150.
168. In a later study, the Club of Rome moderated its predictions but confirmed the essentials; see D. H. Meadows et al., *Beyond The Limits*; see also the papers collected at *http://www.dieoff.org/index.html*.
169. Heilbroner, *The Human Prospect*.
170. On the link between environmental resource use and the uneven distribution of world wealth, see Willy Brandt, *North-South: A Program for Survival* (Cambridge, MA: MIT Press, 1980).

Chapter 6

1. National Highway Traffic Safety Administration, *Fatality Analysis Reporting System Encyclopedia (FARS)*, accessed January 19, 2011 at *http://www-fars.nhtsa.dot.gov*; and Centers for Disease Control and Prevention. *Web-based Injury Statistics Query and Reporting System (WISQARS)*, accessed January 19, 2011 at *http://www.cdc.gov/injury/wisqars/index.html*; National Highway Traffic Safety Administration, Traffic Safety Facts Research Note, "Highlights of 2009 Motor Vehicle Crashes," (DOT HS 811 363), accessed January 30, 2011 at *http://www-nrd.nhtsa.dot.gov/Pubs/811363.pdf*.
2. Jiaquan Xu, Kenneth D. Kochanek, Sherry L. Murphy, Betzaida Tejada-Vera, *National Vital Statistics Reports*, vol. 58 (2010), no. 19, pp. 18–19 and Firearm and Injury Center at Penn, *Firearm Injury in the U.S.* (2009 version), accessed January 21, 2011 at *www.uphs.upenn.edu/ficap/resourcebook/pdf/monograph.pdf*.
3. Centers for Disease Control and Prevention, "Tobacco Use Targeting the Nation's Leading Killer: At A Glance, 2010," accessed August 12, 2010 at *http://www.cdc.gov/chronicdisease/resources/publications/aag/osh.htm*.
4. Centers for Disease Control and Prevention, "Unintentional Drug Poisonings in the United States," July 2010, accessed January 15, 2011 at *http://www.cdc.gov/HomeandRecreationalSafety/Poisoning/brief_full_page.htm*.
5. Centers for Disease Control and Prevention, "Playground Injuries: Fact Sheet," accessed January 15, 2011 at *http://www.cdc.gov/HomeandRecreationalSafety/Playground-Injuries/playgroundinjuries-factsheet.htm*.
6. U.S. Consumer Product Safety Commission. *2009 Annual Report of ATV Deaths and Injuries*. December 2010.
7. Denise Chow, "What Were the Worst Product Recalls in History?" *Life's Little Mysteries* (Website), May 27, 2010, accessed August 13, 2010 at *http://www.lifeslittlemysteries.com/what-were-the-worst-product-recalls-in-history—0681/*.
8. U.S. Consumer Product Safety Commission, *2011 Performance Budget Request, Saving Lives and Keeping Families Safe*, Submitted to the Congress February 2010, p. 9.
9. The facts summarized in this paragraph are drawn from Penny Addis, "The Life History Complaint Case of Martha and George Rose: 'Honoring the Warranty,'" in Laura Nader, ed., *No Access to Law* (New York: Academic Press, Inc., 1980), pp. 171–189.
10. Quoted in Ed Pope, "PacBell's Sales Quotas," *San Jose Mercury News*, April 24, 1986, p. 1C; see also "PacBell Accused of Sales Abuse," *San Jose Mercury News*, April 24, 1986, p. 1A; "PacBell Offers Refund for Unwanted Services," *San Jose Mercury News*, May 17, 1986, p. 1A.
11. Larry D. Hatfield, "PUC Fines Pac Bell Millions for Sales Tactics," *San Francisco Examiner*, Thursday, December 23, 1999; Thomas Long, Mindy Spatt, "Debate on Phone Company Sales Practices CON, Wakeup Call Over Deceit," *San Francisco Chronicle*, January 20, 2000; information on the Guardian lawsuit is from the complaint entitled *The Guardian Corporation et. al. v. AT&T Services, Inc.*, United States District Court, Southern District of California, Case no. 10 CV 1846 WQH CAB, September 3, 2010.
12. Several of these criticisms are surveyed in Stephen A. Greyser, "Advertising: Attacks and Counters," *Harvard Business Review*, March 10, 1972, v. 50, pp. 22–28.
13. U.S. Consumer Product Safety Commission's National Electronic Injury Surveillance System, *NEISS Data*

Highlights–2009, accessed August 21, 2010 at *http://www.cpsc.gov/neiss/2009highlights.pdf.*
14. Based on figures provided by the National Center for Statistics and Analysis, *2002 Annual Assessment of Motor Vehicle Crashes*, accessed July 23, 2004 at *http://www-nrd.nhtsa.dot.gov/2002annual_assessment/long_term_trends.htm.*
15. National Highway Traffic Safety Administration, Traffic Safety Facts Research Note, "Highlights of 2009 Motor Vehicle Crashes," (DOT HS 811 363), accessed January 30, 2011 at *http://www-nrd.nhtsa.dot.gov/Pubs/811363.pdf*, and Naumann, Rebecca B., Dellinger, Ann M., Zaloshnja, Eduard, Lawrence, Bruce A. and Miller, Ted R. "Incidence and Total Lifetime Costs of Motor Vehicle–Related Fatal and Nonfatal Injury by Road User Type, United States, 2005," *Traffic Injury Prevention*, vol. 11 (2010), no. 4, 353–360.
16. Paul A. Samuelson and William D. Nordhaus, *Macroeconomics*, 13th ed. (New York: McGraw-Hill Book Company, 1989), p. 41.
17. See Robert N. Mayer, *The Consumer Movement: Guardians of the Marketplace* (Boston, MA: Twayne Publishers, 1989), p. 67; and Peter Asch, *Consumer Safety Regulation* (New York: Oxford University Press, 1988), p. 50.
18. For an overview of the research on irrationality in decision making, see Max Bazerman, *Judgment in Managerial Decision Making*, 3rd ed. (New York: John Wiley & Sons, Inc., 1994), pp. 12–76.
19. Asch, *Consumer Safety Regulation*, pp. 74, 76.
20. Ibid.
21. For references to these studies, see Asch, *Consumer Safety Regulation*, pp. 70–73.
22. See Thomas Garrett and Richard J. Klonoski, *Business Ethics*, 2nd ed. (Englewood Cliffs, NJ: Prentice-Hall, 1986), p. 88.
23. Immanual Kant, *Groundwork of the Metaphysic of Morals*, H. J. Paton, ed. (New York: Harper & Row Publishers, Inc., 1964), pp. 90, 97; see also, Alan Donagan, *The Theory of Morality* (Chicago, IL: The University of Chicago Press, 1977), p. 92.
24. John Rawls, *A Theory of Justice* (Cambridge, MA: Harvard University Press, Belknap Press, 1971), pp. 344–350.
25. *Crocker v. Winthrop Laboratories, Division of Sterling Drug, Inc.*, 514 Southwestern 2d 429 (1974).
26. See Donagan, *Theory of Morality*, p. 91.
27. Frederick D. Sturdivant, *Business and Society*, 3rd ed. (Homewood, IL: Richard D. Irwin, Inc., 1985), p. 392.
28. Ibid., p. 393.
29. The U.S. Consumer Products Safety Commission's notices of dangerous consumer products and recalls are accessible on the Commission's website at *http://www.cpsc.gov.*
30. A somewhat dated but still incisive discussion of this issue is found in Vance Packard, *The Wastemakers* (New York: David McKay Co., Inc., 1960).
31. Quoted in address by S. E. Upton (vice president of Whirlpool Corporation) to the American Marketing Association in Cleveland, OH, December 11, 1969.
32. National Commission on Product Safety, Final Report, quoted in William W. Lowrance, *Of Acceptable Risk* (Los Altos, CA: William Kaufmann, Inc., 1976), p. 80.
33. See Louis Stern, "Consumer Protection via Increased Information," *Journal of Marketing*, April 1967, v. 31, n. 2.
34. Lawrence E. Hicks, *Coping with Packaging Laws* (New York: AMACOM, 1972), p. 17.
35. See the discussions in Richard Posner, *Economic Analysis of Law*, 2nd ed. (Boston, MA: Little, Brown and Company, 1977), p. 83; and R. Posner, "Strict Liability: A Comment," *Journal of Legal Studies*, January 1973, v. 2, n. 1, p. 21.
36. See, for example, the many cases cited in George J. Alexander, *Honesty and Competition* (Syracuse, NY: Syracuse University Press, 1967).
37. *Henningsen v. Bloomfield Motors, Inc.*, 32 New Jersey 358, 161 Atlantic 2d 69 (1960).
38. See Friedrich Kessler and Malcolm Pitman Sharp, *Contracts* (Boston, MA: Little, Brown and Company, 1953), pp. 1–9.
39. *Codling v. Paglia*, 32 New York 2d 330, 298 Northeastern 2d 622, 345 New York Supplement 2d 461 (1973).
40. Edgar H. Schein, "The Problem of Moral Education for the Business Manager," *Industrial Management Review*, 1966, v. 8, pp. 3–11.
41. See W. D. Ross, *The Right and the Good* (Oxford: The Clarendon Press, 1930), Ch. 2.
42. Donagan, *Theory of Morality*, p. 83.
43. Rawls, *Theory of Justice*, pp. 114–117, 333–342.
44. Discussions of the requirements of due care may be found in a variety of texts, all of which, however, approach the issues from the point of view of legal liability: Irwin Gray, *Product Liability: A Management Response* (New York: AMACOM, 1975), Ch. 6; Eugene R. Carrubba, *Assuring Product Integrity* (Lexington, MA: Lexington Books, 1975); Frank Nixon, *Managing to Achieve Quality and Reliability* (New York: McGraw-Hill Book Co., 1971).
45. See, for example, Michael D. Smith, "The Morality of Strict Liability in Tort," *Business and Professional Ethics*, December 1979, v. 3, n. 1, pp. 3–5; for a review of the rich legal literature on this topic, see Richard A. Posner, "Strict Liability: A Comment," *The Journal of Legal Studies*, January 1973, v. 2, n. 1, pp. 205–221.
46. George P. Fletcher, "Fairness and Utility in Tort Theory," *Harvard Law Review*, January 1972, v. 85, n. 3, pp. 537–573.
47. Posner, *Economic Analysis of Law*, pp. 139–142.
48. See "Unsafe Products: The Great Debate Over Blame and Punishment," *Business Week*, April 30, 1984; Stuart Taylor, "Product Liability: The New Morass," *The New York Times*, March 10, 1985; "The Product Liability Debate," *Newsweek*, September 10, 1984.
49. "Sorting Out the Liability Debate," *Newsweek*, May 12, 1986.
50. Ernest F. Hollings, "No Need for Federal Product-Liability Law," *Christian Science Monitor*, September 20, 1984; see also Harvey Rosenfield, "The Plan to Wrong Consumer Rights," *San Jose Mercury News*, October 3, 1984.
51. Irvin Molotsky, "Drive to Limit Product Liability Awards Grows as Consumer Groups Object," *The New York Times*, March 6, 1986.
52. Television Advertising Bureau, Ad Revenue Track, "Historical Cross-Media Ad Expenditures," accessed on August 10, 2010 at *http://www.tvb.org/rcentral/adrevenuetrack/cross-media/2006_2008.asp.*
53. Ibid.
54. Raymond A. Bauer and Stephen A. Greyser, *Advertising in America: The Consumer View* (Cambridge, MA: Harvard University Press, 1968), p. 394.
55. Walter Weir, *Truth in Advertising and Other Heresies* (New York: McGraw-Hill Book Company, 1963), p. 154.
56. See also J. Robert Moskin, ed., *The Case for Advertising* (New York: American Association of Advertising Agencies, 1973), passim.
57. See "Ads Infinitum," *Dollars & Sense*, May/June 1984. For an ethical analysis of the information content of advertising,

see Alan Goldman, "Ethical Issues in Advertising," pp. 242–249 in Tom Regan, ed., *New Introductory Essays in Business Ethics* (New York: Random House, Inc., 1984), pp. 235–270; the view that advertising is justified by the "indirect" information it provides is advanced in Phillip Nelson, "Advertising and Ethics," in Richard T. DeGeorge and Joseph A. Pichler, eds., *Ethics, Free Enterprise, and Public Policy* (New York: Oxford University Press, 1978), pp. 187–198.

58. See Stephen A. Greyser, "Irritation in Advertising," *Journal of Advertising Research*, February 1973, v. 13, n. 3, pp. 7–20.
59. See Michael Schudson, *Advertising, the Uneasy Persuasion* (New York: Basic Books, Inc., Publishers, 1984), p. 210; David M. Potter, *People of Plenty* (Chicago, IL: The University of Chicago Press, 1954), p. 188; International Commission for the Study of Communication Problems, *Many Voices, One World* (London: Kogan Page, 1980), p. 110.
60. Mary Gardiner Jones, "The Cultural and Social Impact of Advertising on American Society," in David Aaker and George S. Day, eds., *Consumerism*, 2nd ed. (New York: The Free Press, 1974), p. 431.
61. Stephen A. Greyser, "Advertising: Attacks and Counters," *Harvard Business Review*, March 10, 1972, v. 50, pp. 22–28.
62. For an overview of the economic literature on this issue, see Mark S. Albion and Paul W. Farris, *The Advertising Controversy, Evidence on the Economic Effects of Advertising* (Boston, MA: Auburn House Publishing Company, 1981), pp. 69–86, 153–70; for an informal discussion of the issue, see Jules Backman, "Is Advertising Wasteful?" *Journal of Marketing*, January 1968, pp. 2–8.
63. Phillip Nelson, "The Economic Value of Advertising," in Yale Brozen, *Advertising and Society* (New York: New York University Press, 1974), pp. 43–66.
64. Richard Caves, *American Industry: Structure, Conduct, Performance* (Englewood Cliffs, NJ: Prentice-Hall, Inc., 1972), p. 101.
65. David M. Blank, "Some Comments on the Role of Advertising in the American Economy—A Plea for Reevaluation," in L. George Smith, ed., *Reflections on Progress in Marketing* (Chicago, IL: American Marketing Association, 1964), p. 151.
66. See the discussion in Thomas M. Garrett, *An Introduction to Some Ethical Problems of Modern American Advertising* (Rome, GA: The Gregorian University Press, 1961), pp. 125–130.
67. Ibid., p. 177.
68. See E. F. Schumacher, *Small Is Beautiful* (London: Blond and Briggs, Ltd., 1973); and Herman E. Daly, ed., *Toward a Steady-State Economy* (San Francisco, CA: W. H. Freeman, 1979), "Introduction."
69. Nicholas H. Kaldor, "The Economic Aspects of Advertising," *The Review of Economic Studies*, 1950–51, v. 18, pp. 1–27; see also William S. Comanor and Thomas Wilson, *Advertising and Market Power* (Cambridge, MA: Harvard University Press, 1975).
70. See L. G. Telser, "Some Aspects of the Economics of Advertising," *Journal of Business*, April 1968, pp. 166–173.
71. See John Kenneth Galbraith, *The Affluent Society* (Boston, MA: Houghton Mifflin Company, 1958).
72. John Kenneth Galbraith, *The New Industrial State* (New York: New American Library, 1967), p. 211.
73. Ibid., p. 215.
74. See the discussion of manipulation in advertising in Tom L. Beauchamp, "Manipulative Advertising," *Business & Professional Ethics Journal*, Spring/Summer 1984, v. 3, n. 3 & 4, pp. 1–22; see also in the same volume the critical response of R. M. Hare, "Commentary," pp. 23–28.
75. See George Katova, *The Mass Consumption Society* (New York: McGraw-Hill Book Company, 1964), pp. 54–61.
76. F. A. von Hayek, "The Non Sequitur of the 'Dependence Effect,'" *Southern Economic Journal*, April 1961.
77. Vance Packard, "Subliminal Messages: They Work; Are They Ethical?" *San Francisco Examiner*, August 11, 1985; see also W. B. Key, *Media Sexploitation* (Englewood Cliffs, NJ: Prentice-Hall, 1976).
78. "Ads Aimed at Kids Get Tough NAD Review," *Advertising Age*, June 17, 1985.
79. Cynthia Kooi, "War Toy Invasion Grows Despite Boycott," *Advertising Age*, March 1986, v. 3.
80. Howard LaFranchi, "Boom in War Toys Linked to TV," *Christian Science Monitor*, January 1986, v. 7. LaFranchi notes that the average child watches 800 ads for war toys and 250 war-toy television segments in a year, or the equivalent of 22 days in the classroom. See also Glenn Collins, "Debate on Toys and TV Violence," *The New York Times*, December 12, 1985.
81. See the discussion of manipulation in advertising in Tom L. Beauchamp, "Manipulative Advertising," *Business & Professional Ethics Journal*, Spring/Summer 1984, v. 3, n. 3 & 4, pp. 1–22; and in the same volume the critical response of R. M. Hare, "Commentary," pp. 23–28; see also Alan Goldman, "Ethical Issues in Advertising," pp. 253–260; and Robert L. Arrington, "Advertising and Behavior Control," pp. 3–12, in *Journal of Business Ethics*, February 1982, v. 1, n. 1.
82. A critical discussion of several definitions of deception in advertising is found in Thomas L. Carson, Richard E. Wokutch, and James E. Cox, "An Ethical Analysis of Deception in Advertising," *Journal of Business Ethics*, 1985, v. 4, pp. 93–104.
83. Greg Hadfield and Mark Skipworth, "Firms Keep 'Dirty Data' on Sex Lives of Staff," *Sunday Times* (London), July 25, 1993; quoted in John Weckert and Douglas Adeney, *Computer and Information Ethics* (Westport, CT: Greenwood Press, 1997), p. 75.
84. Jeffrey Rothfeder, *Privacy for Sale* (New York: Simon & Schuster, 1992).
85. Richard A. Spinello, *Case Studies in Information and Computer Ethics* (Upper Saddle River, NJ: Prentice-Hall, 1997), pp. 108–109.
86. See Charles Fried, *An Anatomy of Values: Problems of Personal and Social Choice* (Cambridge, MA: Harvard University Press, 1970), p. 141.
87. See Garrett, *Business Ethics*, pp. 47–49, who distinguishes these two types of privacy (as well as a third kind, "social" privacy).
88. The analyses in this paragraph and the following are drawn from Fried, *Anatomy of Values*, pp. 137–152; Richard A. Wasserstrom, "Privacy," in Richard A. Wasserstrom, ed., *Today's Moral Problems*, 2nd ed. (New York: Macmillan, Inc., 1979); Jeffrey H. Reiman, "Privacy, Intimacy and Personhood," *Philosophy and Public Affairs*, 1976, v. 6, n. 1, pp. 26–44; and James Rachels, "Why Privacy Is Important," *Philosophy and Public Affairs*, 1975, v. 4, n. 4, pp. 295–333.

Chapter 7

1. *Fisher v. the University of Texas.*
2. *Grutter v. Bollinger*, 539 U.S. (2003) Docket Number: 02-241; this case and documents related to the case are available at *http://www.umich.edu/~urel/admissions/legal/grutter.*

3. Feb 18 2003 Brief *amici curiae* of 3M and other Leading Businesses accessed August 1, 2004 at *http://www.umich.edu/~urel/admissions/legal/gratz/amici.html.*
4. *Grutter v. Bollinger*, 539 U.S. (2003) Docket Number: 02-241.
5. ABC, *Prime-Time Live*, October 7, 1993.
6. For example: Joanna Lahey, "Age, Women and Hiring: An Experimental Study," (2005) NBER Working Paper #11435, National Bureau of Economic Research, Cambridge, MA; For a review of these so-called "audit studies," see Devah Pager, "The Use of Field Experiments for Studies of Employment Discrimination: Contributions, Critiques, and Directions for the Future," *The Annals of the American Academy of Political and Social Science*, (2007), vol. 609, no. 1, pp. 104–133; for a briefer and more informal review of audit studies see the entry, "Audits for Discrimination," by John Yinger, in W. Darity, ed., *International Encyclopedia of the Social Sciences*, 2nd ed., (Macmillan Reference USA, 2007).
7. Devah Pager, *Marked: Race, Crime, and Finding Work in an Era of Mass Incarceration*, (Chicago: University of Chicago Press, 2007); James Heckman and Peter Siegelman, "The Urban Institute Audit Studies: Their Methods and Findings," pp. 187–258 in Michael Fix and Raymond J. Strucyk, eds., *Clear and Convincing Evidence: Measurement in America* (Washington, DC: Urban Institute Press, 1993); Devah Pager, "The Mark of a Criminal Record," *American Journal of Sociology*, March 2003, v. 108, n. 5, pp. 937–975; Marianne Bertrand and Sendhil Mullainathan, "Are Emily and Greg More Employable than Lakisha and Jamal? A Field Experiment on Labor Market Discrimination," American Economic Review, vol. 94 (2004), no. 4, 991–1013; John Yinger, "Measuring Racial Discrimination with Fair Housing Audits: Caught in the Act," *The American Economic Review*, vol. 76 (2001), no. 5, pp. 881–893; Jan Ondrich, Stephen Ross, and John Yinger, "Now You See It, Now You Don't: Why Do Real Estate Agents Withhold Houses from Black Customers?" *Review of Economics and Statistics*, vol. 85 (2003), no. 4, pp. 854–873.
8. This morally charged meaning is now perhaps the dominant meaning given to the term *discrimination* and is found in any relatively recent dictionary; see, for example, *Webster's New Collegiate Dictionary* (Springfield, MA: G. & C. Merriam Company, 1974), p. 326, where a main meaning attributed to the term *discriminate* is "to make a difference in treatment or favor on a basis other than individual merit," and where a meaning attributed to *discrimination* is "prejudiced or prejudicial outlook, action, or treatment."
9. Joe R. Feagin and Clairece Booker Feagin, *Discrimination American Style*, 2nd ed. (Malabar, FL: Robert E. Krieger Publishing Company, 1986), pp. 23–33.
10. U.S. Congress, Senate, Subcommittee on Labor of the Committee on Labor and Public Welfare, *Compilation of Selected Labor Laws Pertaining to Labor Relations*, Part II, 93rd Congress, 2nd Session, September 6, 1974, p. 610.
11. U.S. Equal Employment Opportunity Commission, *Affirmative Action and Equal Employment: A Guidebook for Employers*, II (Washington, DC: Government Printing Office, 1974), p. D-28.
12. The necessity of basing analyses of discrimination on statistical grounds and the uselessness of attempting an individual case-by-case procedure are discussed by Lester Thurow in "A Theory of Groups and Economic Redistribution," *Philosophy and Public Affairs*, Fall 1979, v. 9, n. 1, pp. 25–41.
13. Walter B. Connolly, Jr., *A Practical Guide to Equal Employment Opportunity*, 2 vols. (New York: Law Journal Press, 1975), vol. 1, pp. 231–42; for a discussion of the relevance of statistics, see Tom Beauchamp, "The Justification of Reverse Discrimination," in W. T. Blackstone and R. Heslep, *Social Justice and Preferential Treatment* (Athens, GA: The University of Georgia Press, 1977), pp. 84–110.
14. U.S. Census Bureau, Table A-1, "Households by Total Money Income, Race, and Hispanic Origin of Householder: 1967 to 2008," *Income, Poverty, and Health Insurance Coverage in the United States: 2008*, Current Population Reports, P60-236(RV) issued September, 2009.
15. William J. Carrington and Kenneth R. Troske, *Gender Segregation in Small Firms* (Washington, DC: Center for Economic Studies of the U.S. Census Bureau, October 1992) [CES Report No. 92–13]; a short version of this report is available from the U.S. Census Bureau as a Statistical Brief entitled "Two Different Worlds: Men and Women From 9 to 5" (SB/94–24), issued February, 1995.
16. Jessica Semega, "Men's and Women's Earnings by State: 2008 American Community Survey," U.S. Census Bureau, American Community Survey Reports, ACSBR/08-3, issued September, 2009.
17. Barbara Reskin and Irene Padavic, *Women and Men at Work* (Thousand Oaks, CA: Pine Forge Press, 1994), p. 106.
18. Judy Goldberg Dey and Catherine Hill, *Behind the Pay Gap*, (Washington, DC: the American Association of University Women Educational Foundation, 2007).
19. Robert Pear, "Women's Pay Lags Further Behind Men's," *The New York Times*, January 16, 1984, p. 1; see also, "Gender Gap/Dollar Gap," *Los Angeles Times*, January 25, 1984.
20. Poverty level figures are from the U.S. Census Bureau at *http://www.census.gov/hhes/www/poverty/data/threshld/*; College costs are from the National Center for Education Statistics, U.S. Department of Education Institute of Education Sciences at *http://nces.ed.gov/fastfacts/display.asp?id=76.*
21. This relationship has been demonstrated by several studies. See, for example, Stephanie Boraas and William M. Rodgers III, "How Does Gender Play a Role in the Earnings Gap? An Update." *Monthly Labor Review*, March 2003, pp. 9–15.
22. Barbara Reskin and Irene Padavic, *Women and Men At Work* (Thousand Oaks, CA: Pine Forge Press, 1994), pp. 82–84 and U.S. Department of Labor, Office of Federal Contract Compliance Programs, Glass Ceiling Commission, *Good for Business: Making Full Use of the Nation's Human Capital* (Washington, DC: Government Printing Office, 1995), pp. 11–12.
23. See Bradley R. Schiller, *The Economics of Poverty & Discrimination*, 6th ed. (Englewood Cliffs, NJ: Prentice-Hall, 1995), pp. 193–194, and U.S. General Accounting Office, "Women's Earnings: Work Patterns Partially Explain Difference Between Men's and Women's Earnings," GAO-04-35, October 2003, p. 2.
24. Reskin and Padavic, *Women and Men at Work*, pp. 39–43; see also U.S. General Accounting Office, "Women's Earnings," p. 2.
25. Jacob Mincer and Solomon W. Polachek, "Family Investments in Human Capital: Earnings of Women," *Journal of Political Economy*, March/April, 1982, Part II, v. 82, pp. s76–s108; see also Reskin and Padavic, *Women and Men at Work*, pp. 39–43.
26. See Mary Corcoran, Greg J. Duncan, and Martha S. Hill, "The Economic Fortunes of Women and Children," in Micheline R. Malson, Elisabeth Mudimbe-Boyi, Jean F. O'Barr,

and Mary Wyer, eds., *Black Women in America* (Chicago, IL: The University of Chicago Press, 1988), pp. 97–113; Mary Corcoran, "A Longitudinal Approach to White Women's Wages," *Journal of Human Resources*, Fall 1983, v. 18, n. 4, pp. 497–520; and Paula England, "The Failure of Human Capital Theory to Explain Occupational Sex Segregation," *Journal of Human Resources*, Summer 1982, v. 17, n. 3, pp. 358–370.

27. "Study Blames Barriers, Not Choices, For Sex Segregation," *San Jose Mercury News*, December 20, 1985, p. 21E.
28. Randall K. Filer, "Sexual Differences in Earnings: The Role of Individual Personalities and Tastes," *The Journal of Human Resources*, Winter 1983, v. 18, n. 1.
29. Mary Corcoran and Greg J. Duncan, "Work History, Labor Force Attachment, and Earnings Differences Between the Races and Sexes,"*The Journal of Human Resources*, Winter 1979, v. 19, n. 1, pp. 3–20; see also Gerald Jaynes and Robin Williams, eds., *A Common Destiny: Blacks and American Society* (Washington, DC: National Academy Press, 1989), pp. 319–323.
30. Goldberg Dey and Catherine Hill, Ibid., pp. 17–18.
31. The data in this paragraph are drawn from William B. Johnston and Arnold E. Packer, *Workforce 2000: Work and Workers for the Twenty-first Century* (Indianapolis, IN: Hudson Institute, 1987).
32. All of the studies in this paragraph are cited in Clint Bolick and Susan Nestleroth, *Opportunity 2000* (Indianapolis, IN: Hudson Institute, 1988), pp. 21–22.
33. Ibid., p. 67.
34. U.S. Census Bureau, Current Population Reports, Educational Attainment in the United States: 2007, Series P20-550.
35. Ibid.
36. Gary Orfield, Daniel Losen, Johanna Wald, Christopher Swanson, *Losing Our Future: How Minority Youth are Being Left Behind by the Graduation Rate Crisis*, (Cambridge, MA: The Civil Rights Project at Harvard University, 2004).
37. Dick Lilly, "City Staff Survey Finds Harassment," *Seattle Times*, October 8, 1991, p. B3; "Female Execs See Marketing as Fastest Track," *Sales & Marketing Management*, August 1993, p. 10; "Survey Finds Most Women Rabbis Have Been Sexually Harassed on Job," *United Press International*, August 28, 1993; "Female Jail Guards Fight Against Harassment by Male Colleagues," *Houston Chronicle*, October 17, 1993, p. A5.
38. Reported in Terry Halbert and Elaine Inguilli, eds., *Law and Ethics in the Business Environment* (St. Paul, MN: West Publishing Co., 1990), p. 298.
39. Eliza G. C. Collins and Timothy B. Blodgett, "Sexual Harassment . . . Some See It . . . Some Won't," *Harvard Business Review*, March/April 1981, v. 59, n. 2.
40. *Charlotte Lynn Rawlins Yates and Cheryl Jenkins Mathis v. Avco Corporation*, 814 F. 2d 630 (1987), U.S. Court of Appeals, Sixth Circuit.
41. Gretchen Voss, "Women Harassing Men," *Marie Claire*, accessed August 21, 2010 at *http://www.marieclaire.com/sex-love/relationship-issues/articles/women-harassing-men-1*.
42. Thomas Jefferson, *Declaration of Independence*.
43. *Dred Scott v. Sanford*, 60 U.S (19 How) (1857) at 407 and 421. See Don E. Fehrenbacher, *The Dred Scott Case* (New York: Oxford University Press, 1978).
44. *Bradwell v. Illinois*, 83 U.S. (16 Wall) (1873). See Leo Kanowitz, *Women and the Law* (Albuquerque, NM: University of New Mexico Press, 1969), p. 36.
45. Norman Daniels, "Merit and Meritocracy," *Philosophy and Public Affairs*, Spring 1978, v. 7, n. 3, pp. 208–209.
46. For economic analyses of the costs and benefits associated with discrimination, see Gary S. Becker, *The Economics of Discrimination*, 2nd ed. (Chicago, IL: The University of Chicago Press, 1971); Janice Fanning Madden, *The Economics of Sex Discrimination* (Lexington, MA: D.C. Heath and Company, 1973). For a critical review of this literature, see Annette M. LaMond, "Economic Theories of Employment Discrimination," in Phyllis A. Wallace and Annette M. LaMond, eds., *Women, Minorities, and Employment Discrimination* (Lexington, MA: D.C. Heath and Company, 1977), pp. 1–11.
47. Ibid., p. 214.
48. See the discussion of this view in Sharon Bishop Hill, "Self-Determination and Autonomy," in Richard Waserstrom, eds., *Today's Moral Problems*, 2nd ed. (New York: Macmillan, Inc., 1979), pp. 118–133.
49. On this issue, see Janet S. Chafetz, *Masculine, Feminine, or Human?: An Overview of the Sociology of Sex Roles* (Itasca, IL: Peacock, 1974); and Joyce Trebilcot, "Sex Roles: The Argument from Nature," *Ethics*, April 1975, v. 85, n. 3, pp. 249–255.
50. See, for example, Thomas Nagel, "Equal Treatment and Compensatory Discrimination," *Philosophy and Public Affairs*, 1973, v. 2, p. 360; and Ronald Dworkin, *Taking Rights Seriously* (Cambridge, MA: Harvard University Press, 1977), pp. 232–237.
51. Susan Haack, "On the Moral Relevance of Sex," *Philosophy*, 1974, v. 49, pp. 90–95; Jon J. Durkin, "The Potential of Women," in Bette Ann Stead, ed., *Women in Management* (Englewood Cliffs, NJ: Prentice-Hall, 1978), pp. 42–46.
52. Richard Wasserstrom, "Rights, Human Rights, and Racial Discrimination," *The Journal of Philosophy*, October 29, 1964, v. 61, pp. 628–641.
53. Richard Wasserstrom, "Racism, Sexism, and Preferential Treatment: An Approach to the Topics," *UCLA Law Review*, 1977, v. 24, pp. 581–622.
54. This is, for example, the underlying view in John C. Livingston, *Fair Game?* (San Francisco: W. H. Freeman and Company, 1979), pp. 74–76.
55. Richard M. Hare, *Freedom and Reason* (New York: Oxford University Press, 1963), pp. 217–219.
56. John Rawls, *A Theory of Justice* (Cambridge, MA: Harvard University Press, Belknap Press, 1971), pp. 83–90.
57. Feagin and Feagin, *Discrimination American Style*, pp. 43–77.
58. Charles Perelman, *The Idea of Justice and the Problem of Argument* (London: Routledge and Kegan Paul, 1963).
59. Equal Employment Opportunity Commission, Title 29 Code of Federal Regulations, Section 1604.11, Sexual Harassment.
60. *Rabidue v. Osceola Refining Company*, 805 F. 2d 611 (1986), U.S. Court of Appeals, Sixth Circuit, Circuit Judge Keith, Dissenting in Part, quoted in Terry Halbert and Elaine Inguilli, eds., *Law and Ethics in the Business Environment* (St. Paul, MN: West Publishing Co., 1990), p. 301.
61. This was, for example, the position of the majority opinion in *Rabidue v. Osceola Refining Company*.
62. Gretchen Morgenson, "Watch That Leer, Stifle That Joke," *Forbes*, May 15, 1989, p. 72.
63. Barbara Lindemann Schlei and Paul Grossman, *Employment Discrimination Law*, 1979 Supplement (Washington, DC: The Bureau of National Affairs, Inc., 1979), pp. 109–120.
64. John Lawrie, "Subtle Discrimination Pervades Corporate America," *Personnel Journal*, January 1990, pp. 53–55.

65. See *Smith v. Liberty Mutual Insurance Company*, 395 F. Supp., 1098 (1975), and *Sommers v. Budget Marketing Inc.*, 667 F. 2d 748 (1982).
66. Terence Roth, "Many Firms Fire AIDS Victims, Citing Health Risk to Co-Workers," *Wall Street Journal*, August 12, 1985; Dorothy Townsend, "AIDS Patient Sues Kodak Over Firing, Claims Bias," *Los Angeles Times*, April 2, 1986; Jim Dickey, "Firing Over AIDS Test Claimed," *San Jose Mercury News*, October 11, 1985, p. 1B.
67. Centers for Disease Control and Prevention. Cases of HIV infection and AIDS in the United States, by race/ethnicity, 1998–2002. HIV/AIDS Surveillance Supplemental Report, 10 (No.1), Tables 8 and 9, accessed August 10, 2004 at *http://www.cdc.gov/hiv/stats/hasrlink.htm.*
68. Robert N. Webner, "Budding Movement Is Seeking to Stop Fat Discrimination," *Wall Street Journal*, October 8, 1979, p. 33.
69. See Richard D. Mohr, "Gay Rights," in Patricia H. Werhane, A. R. Gini, and David Ozar, eds., *Philosophical Issues in Human Rights* (New York: Random House, Inc., 1986), pp. 337–341; David Margolick, "Court Blocks Job Denials for Obesity," *The New York Times*, May 8, 1985, p. 18; Cris Oppenheimer, "A Hostile Marketplace Shuts Out Older Workers," *San Jose Mercury News*, December 9, 1985.
70. Margaret Beale Spencer, "CNN Pilot Demonstration," dated "4-28-10" accessed August 20, 2010 at *http://i2.cdn.turner.com/cnn/2010/images/05/13/expanded_results_methods_cnn.pdf.*
71. Walter B. Connolly, *A Practical Guide to Equal Employment Opportunity*, 2 vols. (New York: New York Law Journal Press, 1975), v. 1, pp. 359–373.
72. *United Steelworkers of America v. Weber*, 99 S. Ct. 2721 (1979).
73. Rogene A. Buchholz, *Business Environment and Public Policy* (Englewood Cliffs, NJ: Prentice-Hall, 1982), pp. 287–288.
74. Quoted in "High Court Dumps Quotas in Labor Case," *Washington Times*, June 13, 1984, p. 1.
75. "A Right Turn on Race?" *Newsweek*, June 25, 1984, pp. 29–31; Stuart Taylor, "Reagan Attack on Quotas in Jobs Goes to High Court," *The New York Times*, August 6, 1985, p. 17.
76. Aaron Epstein, "Layoffs Can't Favor Minority Workers," *San Jose Mercury News*, May 20, 1986, p. 1a.
77. See, for example, "The New Politics of Race" and "A Crisis of Shattered Dreams," in *Newsweek*, May 6, 1991, pp. 22–26, 28–31.
78. See, for example, Barry R. Gross, *Discrimination in Reverse: Is Turnabout Fair Play*?; for a contrasting view, see also Alan H. Goldman, *Justice and Reverse Discrimination* (Princeton, NJ: Princeton University Press, 1979).
79. See, for example, the articles collected in Barry R. Gross, ed., *Reverse Discrimination* (Buffalo, NY: Prometheus Books, 1977).
80. Theodore V. Purcell and Gerald F. Cavanagh, *Blacks in the Industrial World* (New York: The Free Press, 1972), p. 164.
81. See Bernard Boxill, *Blacks and Social Justice* (Totowa, NJ: Rowman & Allanheld, 1984), pp. 147–172; see also the essays collected in Marshall Cohen, Thomas Nagel, and Thomas Scanlon, eds., *Equality and Preferential Treatment* (Princeton, NJ: Princeton University Press, 1977); and William T. Blackstone and Robert D. Heslep, eds., *Social Justice & Preferential Treatment* (Athens, GA: The University of Georgia Press, 1977).
82. George Sher, "Reverse Discrimination, the Future, and the Past," in *Ethics*, October 1979, v. 90, pp. 81–87; and George Sher, "Preferential Hiring," in *Just Business*, Tom Regan, ed. (New York: Random House, Inc., 1984), pp. 32–59. An excellent discussion of affirmative action programs is Robert K. Fullinwider, *The Reverse Discrimination Controversy* (Totowa, NJ: Rowman and Littlefield, 1980).
83. Paul W. Taylor, "Reverse Discrimination and Compensatory Justice," *Analysis*, 1973, v. 33, pp. 177–182; see also Anne C. Minas, "How Reverse Discrimination Compensates Women," *Ethics*, October 1977, v. 88, n. 1, pp. 74–79.
84. Bernard Boxhill, "The Morality of Reparations," *Social Theory and Practice*, 1972, v. 2, n. 1, pp. 113–122.
85. Alan H. Goldman, "Limits to the Justification of Reverse Discrimination," *Social Theory and Practice*, 1975, v. 3, n. 3, pp. 289–306.
86. See Karst and Horowitz, "Affirmative Action and Equal Protection," *Virginia Law Review*, 1974, v. 60.
87. There are innumerable discussions of this objection to the compensation justification; see, for example, the series Michael Bayles, "Reparations to Wronged Groups," *Analysis*, 1973, v. 33, n. 6; L. J. Cowan, "Inverse Discrimination," *Analysis*, 1972, v. 33, n. 10; Roger Shiner, "Individuals, Groups, and Inverse Discrimination," *Analysis*, June 1973, v. 33; Paul Taylor, "Reverse Discrimination and Compensatory Justice," *Analysis*, June 1973, v. 33; James W. Nickel, "Should Reparations Be to Individuals or Groups?" *Analysis*, April 1974, v. 34, n. 9, pp. 154–160; Alan Goldman, "Reparations to Individuals or Groups?" *Analysis*, April 1975, v. 35, n. 5, pp. 168–70.
88. Judith Jarvis Thomson, "Preferential Hiring," *Philosophy and Public Affairs*, Summer 1973, v. 2, n. 4, p. 381; for a similar claim with respect to Blacks, see Graham Hughes, "Reparation for Blacks?"*New York University Law Review*, 1968, v. 43, pp. 1072–1073.
89. Martin H. Redish, "Preferential Law School Admissions and the Equal Protection Clause: An Analysis of the Competing Arguments,"*University of California at Los Angeles Review*, 1974, p. 389; see also Bernard R. Boxill, "The Morality of Preferential Hiring," *Philosophy and Public Affairs*, Spring 1978, v. 7, n. 3, pp. 246–268.
90. Robert Simon, "Preferential Hiring: A Reply to Judith Jarvis Thomson," *Philosophy and Public Affairs*, Spring 1974, v. 3, n. 3, pp. 312–320; Gertrude Ezorsky, "It's Mine," *Philosophy and Public Affairs*, Spring 1974, v. 3, n. 3, pp. 321–330; Robert K. Fullinwider, "Preferential Hiring and Compensation," *Social Theory and Practice*, Spring 1975, v. 3, n. 3, pp. 307–320.
91. For examples of utilitarian arguments, see Thomas Nagel, "Equal Treatment and Compensatory Discrimination," *Philosophy and Public Affairs*, Spring 1973, v. 2, n. 4, pp. 348–363; James W. Nickel, "Preferential Policies in Hiring and Admissions," *Columbia Law Review*, v. 1975, 75, pp. 534–558; Ronald Dworkin, "The De Funis Case: The Right to Go to Law School," *New York Review of Books*, February 5, 1976, v. 23, n. 1, pp. 29–33.
92. Owen M. Fiss, "Groups and the Equal Protection Clause," *Philosophy and Public Affairs*, Winter 1976, v. 5, n. 2, pp. 150–151.
93. James W. Nickel, "Classification of Race in Compensatory Programs," *Ethics*, 1974, v. 84, n. 2, pp. 146–150.
94. Virginia Black, "The Erosion of Legal Principles in the Creation of Legal Policies," *Ethics*, 1974, v. 84, n. 3; William T. Blackstone, "Reverse Discrimination and Compensatory

Justice," in Blackstone and Heslep, eds.,*Social Justice and Preferential Treatment* (Athens, GA: University of Georgia Press, 1977).

95. Robert K. Fullinwider, "On Preferential Hiring," in Mary Vetterling-Braggin, Frederick A. Elliston, and Jane English, eds.,*Feminism and Philosophy* (Totowa, NJ: Littlefield, Adams and Company, 1978), pp. 210–224.
96. See Nickel, "Preferential Policies."
97. Nagel, "Equal Treatment and Compensatory Discrimination."
98. Lawrence Crocker, "Preferential Treatment," in *Feminism and Philosophy*, Vetterling-Braggin et al., eds., pp. 190–204.
99. George Sher, "Justifying Reverse Discrimination in Employment," *Philosophy and Public Affairs*, Winter 1975, v. 4, n. 2, pp. 159–170.
100. Carl and Callahan, "Negroes and the Law," *Journal of Legal Education*, 1965, v. 17, p. 254.
101. Kaplan, "Equal Justice in an Unequal World," *N.W.U. Law Review*, 1966, v. 61, p. 365.
102. Theodore V. Purcell and Gerald F. Cavanagh, *Blacks in the Industrial World* (New York: The Free Press, 1972), pp. 30–44. See also the articles on alternative feminist futures collected in Carol Gould, ed., *Beyond Domination* (Totowa, NJ: Rowman and Allenheld, 1983).
103. Carl Cohen, "Race and the Constitution," *The Nation*, February 8, 1975; Lisa H. Newton, "Reverse Discrimination as Unjustified," *Ethics*, 1973, v. 83, pp. 308–312.
104. Ronald Dworkin, "Why Bakke Has No Case."
105. Ibid.
106. For example, Glenn C. Loury, "Performing Without a Net," in Curry, ed., *Affirmative Action Debate.*
107. Shelby Steele, *The Content of Our Character: A New Vision of Race in America* (New York: St. Martin's Press, 1990), pp. 112–118.
108. Sonia L. Nazario, "Many Minorities Feel Torn by Experience of Affirmative Action," *Wall Street Journal*, June 27, 1989, pp. A1, A7.
109. Ibid.
110. Roper Center for Public Opinion, Question ID: USGALLUP.950317.R31; see also M.C. Taylor, "Impact of Affirmative Action on Beneficiary Groups: Evidence from the 1990 General social Survey," *Basic and Applied social Psychology*, vol. 15 (1994), pp. 143–178.
111. Sidney Hook, "Discrimination Against the Qualified?" *The New York Times*, 1971.
112. See Nickel, "Preferential Policies," p. 546.
113. For example, Gross, *Discrimination in Reverse*, p. 108; for a reply to Gross, see Boxill, "The Morality of Preferential Hiring."
114. Theodore V. Purcell, "A Practical Way to Use Ethics in Management Decisions," paper for the Drew-Allied Chemical Workshop, June 26–27, 1980; and Nickel, "Preferential Policies."
115. Felice N. Schwartz, "Management Women and the New Facts of Life," *Harvard Business Review*, January–February, 1989, pp. 65–76.
116. Bolick and Nestleroth, *Opportunity 2000*, pp. 28–50.
117. Ibid., pp. 65–94; see also, Beverly Geber, "Managing Diversity," *Training*, pp. 23–30.
118. Quoted in Investor Responsibility Research Center, "Equal Employment Opportunity, 1990 Analysis E" (Washington, DC: Investor Responsibility Research Center, Inc., 1990.), pp. 3–4.

Chapter 8

1. Studs Terkel, *Working: People Talk About What They Do All Day and How They Feel About What They Do* (New York: Pantheon Books, Inc., 1979), pp. 159, 160, 161.
2. Ibid., pp. 178, 179.
3. Ibid., pp. 405, 406.
4. See James D. Thompson, *Organizations in Action* (New York: McGraw-Hill Book Company, 1967), pp. 4–6; see also John Ladd, "Morality and the Ideal of Rationality in Formal Organizations," *Monist*, 1970, v. 54.
5. E. H. Schein, *Organizational Psychology* (Englewood Cliffs, NJ: Prentice-Hall, 1965), p. 8.
6. The classic analysis of white-collar crime is Edwin H. Sutherland, *White Collar Crime* (New York: Holt, Rinehart and Winston, Inc., 1949); see also Marshall B. Clinard, Peter C. Veager, Jeanne Brissette, David Petrashek, and Elizabeth Harries, *Illegal Corporate Behavior* (Washington, DC: U.S. Government Printing Office, 1979).
7. See Philip I. Blumberg, "Corporate Responsibility and the Employee's Duty of Loyalty and Obedience: A Preliminary Inquiry," in Dow Votaw and S. Prakash Sethi, eds., *The Corporate Dilemma* (Englewood Cliffs, NJ: Prentice-Hall, 1973), pp. 82–113.
8. Quoted in Ibid., pp. 87 and 88.
9. Thomas M. Garrett and Richard J. Klonoski, *Business Ethics*, 2nd ed. (Englewood Cliffs, NJ: Prentice-Hall, 1986), p. 55.
10. Vincent Barry, *Moral Issues in Business* (Belmont, CA: Wadsworth Publishing Company, Inc., 1986), pp. 237–238.
11. See Lawrence C. Becker, *Property Rights* (London: Routledge & Kegan Paul, 1977), p. 19.
12. For more extended discussion of the ethics of trade secrets, see DeGeorge, *Business Ethics*, pp. 292–298.
13. This case is recounted in Michael S. Baram, "Trade Secrets: What Price Loyalty?" *Harvard Business Review*, November/December 1968.
14. See, for example, Patricia H. Werhane, "The Ethics of Insider Trading," *Journal of Business Ethics*, November 1989, v. 8, n. 11, pp. 841–845.
15. See Robert W. McGee, "Applying Ethics to Insider Trading," *Journal of Business Ethics*, vol. 77 (2008), no. 2, pp. 205–217; Bill Shaw, "Should Insider Trading Be Outside the Law?" *Business and Society Review*, Summer 1988, pp. 34–37; and Tibor R. Machan, "What Is Morally Right with Insider Trading?" *Public Affairs Quarterly*, vol. 10 (April 1996), pp. 135–142; the classic defense of insider trading along the lines sketched later is Henry G. Manne, *Insider Trading and the Stock Market* (New York: The Free Press, 1966) and "In Defense of Insider Trading," *Harvard Business Review*, November/December 1966, v. 113, pp. 113–122. A defense of insider trading that also provides a useful bibliography of Manne's work is Robert W. McGee, "Insider Trading: An Economic and Philosophical Analysis," *The Mid-Atlantic Journal of Business*, November 1988, v. 25, n. 1, pp. 35–48.
16. See H. Mendelson, "Random Competitive Exchange: Price Distributions and Gains from Trade," *Journal of Economic Theory*, December 1985, pp. 254–280.
17. See L. R. Glosten and P. R. Milgrom, "Bid, Ask, and Transaction Prices in a Specialist Market with Heterogeneously Informed Traders," *Journal of Financial Economics*, March 1985, pp. 71–100; T. Copeland and D. Galai, "Information Effects on the Bid-Ask Spread," *Journal of Finance*, December 1983, pp. 1457–1469; G. J. Bentson and R. Hagerman, "Determinants of Bid-Ask Spreads in the Over-the-Counter

Market," *Journal of Financial Economics*, January–February 1974, pp. 353–364; P. Venkatesh and R. Chiang, "Information Asymmetry and the Dealer's Bid-Ask Spread: A Case Study of Earnings and Dividend Announcements," *Journal of Finance*, December 1986, pp. 1089–1102.

18. Gary L. Tidwell and Abdul Aziz, "Insider Trading: How Well Do You Understand the Current Status of the Law?" *California Management Review*, Summer 1988, v. 30, n. 4, pp. 115–123.
19. The following analysis of wages and working conditions draws from Garrett, *Business Ethics*, pp. 53–62.
20. See Garrett, *Business Ethics*, pp. 38–40; and Barry, *Moral Issues in Business*, pp. 174–175.
21. *Statistical Abstract of the United States, 2010*, Table No. 641, "Workers Killed or Disabled on the Job: 1970 to 2001."
22. National Safety Council, "Summary from Injury Facts, 2010 Edition," accessed August 18, 2010 at *http://www.nsc.org/news_resources/injury_and_death_statistics/Pages/InjuryDeathStatistics.aspx*.
23. William W. Lowrance, *Of Acceptable Risk* (Los Altos, CA: William Kaufmann, Inc., 1976), p. 147.
24. Occupational Safety and Health Act of 1970, Public Law, 91-596.
25. Peter J. Sheridan, "1970–1976: America in Transition—Which Way Will the Pendulum Swing?" *Occupational Hazards*, September 1975, p. 97.
26. Numbers for 2009 are from the U.S. Department of Labor, Bureau of Labor Statistics, Table A-1. "Fatal Occupational Injuries by Industry and Event or Exposure, All United States, 2009," Census of Fatal Occupational Injuries–Current and Revised Data, accessed August 20, 2010 at *http://stats.bls.gov/iif/oshcfoi1.htm#charts*, and numbers for other years are from U.S. Department of Labor, "Worker Fatalities in Charts to 2009," Bureau of Labor Statistics, Census of Fatal Occupational Injuries Charts, 1992–2009 at *http://stats.bls.gov/iif/oshcfoi1.htm#charts*.
27. *Statistical Abstract of the United States, 2010*, Table No. 641, "Workers Killed or Disabled on the Job: 1970 to 2007," accessed August 17, 2010 at *http://www.census.gov/compendia/statab/cats/labor_force_employment_earnings/injuries_and_fatalities.html*; figures for 2008 are from National Safety Council, "Summary from Injury Facts, 2010 Edition," accessed August 18, 2010 at *http://www.nsc.org/news_resource/injury_and_death_statistics/Pages/InjuryDeathStatistics.aspx*.
28. See Russell F. Settle and Burton A. Weisbrod, "Occupational Safety and Health and the Public Interest," in Burton Weisbrod, Joel F. Handler, and Neil K. Komesar, eds., *Public Interest Law* (Berkeley, CA: University of California Press, 1978), pp. 285–312.
29. For a compact contrast of rational and political behaviors, see Robert Miles, *Macro Organizational Behavior* (Santa Monica, CA: Good Year Publishing, 1980), pp. 156–161. A fuller and more historical discussion of the "rational" and "political" approaches to organization is Henry Mintzberg, *Power In and Around Organizations* (Englewood Cliffs, NJ: Prentice-Hall, 1983), pp. 8–21.
30. For some analyses of the firm based on the "political" model, see Mintzberg, *Power In and Around Organizations*; Samuel B. Bacharach and Edward J. Lawler, *Power and Politics in Organizations* (San Francisco, CA: Jossey-Bass, Inc., Publishers, 1980); James G. March, "The Business Firm as a Political Coalition," *Journal of Politics*, 1962, v. 24, pp. 662–668; Tom Burns, "Micropolitics: Mechanisms of Institutional Change," *Administrative Science Quarterly*, VI, 1962, pp. 255–281; Michael L. Tushman, "A Political Approach to Organizations: A Review and Rationale," *Academy of Management Review*, April 1977, pp. 206–216; Jeffrey Pfeffer, "The Micropolitics of Organizations," in Marshall W. Meyer et al., eds., *Environments and Organizations* (San Francisco, CA: Jossey-Bass, Inc., Publishers, 1978), pp. 29–50.
31. See R. M. Cyert and J. G. March, *A Behavioral Theory of the Firm* (Englewood Cliffs, NJ: Prentice-Hall, 1963); H. Kaufman, "Organization Theory and Political Theory," *The American Political Science Review*, 1964, v. 58, n. 1, pp. 5–14.
32. Walter R. Nord, "Dreams of Humanization and the Realities of Power," *Academy of Management Review*, July 1978, pp. 674–679.
33. On the primacy of power in organizations, see Abraham Zaleznik, "Power and Politics in Organizational Life," *Harvard Business Review*, May–June 1970, pp. 47–60. The definition of *power* in the text is derived from Virginia E. Schein, "Individual Power and Political Behaviors in Organizations: An Inadequately Explored Reality," *Academy of Management Review*, January 1977, pp. 64–72. Definitions of power are, of course, controversial.
34. Terkel, *Working*, p. 349. Many more examples of political behaviors can be found in Samuel A. Culbert and John J. McDonough, *The Invisible War* (New York: John Wiley & Sons, Inc., 1980).
35. For example, Richard Eells, *The Government of Corporations* (New York: The Free Press of Glencoe, 1962); and Arthur Selwyn Miller, *The Modern Corporate State* (Westport, CT: Greenwood Press, 1976).
36. See Earl Latham, "The Body Politic of the Corporation," in Edward S. Mason, ed., *The Corporation in Modern Society* (Cambridge, MA: Harvard University Press, 1960).
37. See, for example, David W. Ewing, *Freedom Inside the Organization* (New York: McGraw-Hill Book Company, 1977), pp. 3–24; Garrett, *Business Ethics*, pp. 27–30.
38. David W. Ewing, "Civil Liberties in the Corporation," *New York State Bar Journal*, April 1978, pp. 188–229.
39. This ownership and contract argument is the basis of traditional legal views on the employee's duty to obey and be loyal to his employer. See Blumberg, "Corporate Responsibility," pp. 82–113.
40. Donald L. Martin, "Is an Employee Bill of Rights Needed?" in M. Bruce Johnson, ed., *The Attack on Corporate America* (New York: McGraw-Hill Book Company, 1978).
41. Ibid.
42. The classic exposition of this view is Adolf Berle and Gardner Means, *The Modern Corporation and Private Property* (New York: Macmillan, 1932).
43. Jack Stierber, "Protection Against Unfair Dismissal," in Alan F. Westin and Stephen Salisbury, eds., *Individual Rights in the Corporation* (New York: Pantheon Books, Inc., 1980).
44. David W. Ewing, *Freedom Inside the Organization* (New York: McGraw-Hill Book Company, 1977), pp. 36–41.
45. Several of these arguments are summarized in Patricia H. Werhane, *Persons, Rights, and Corporations* (Englewood Cliffs, NJ: Prentice-Hall, 1985), pp. 108–122.
46. See John Hoerr, "Privacy in the Workplace," *Business Week*, March 28, 1988, pp. 61–65, 68; Susan Dentzer, "Can You Pass the Job Test?" *Newsweek*, May 5, 1986; Sandra N. Hurd, "Genetic Testing: Your Genes and Your Job," *Employee Responsibilities and Rights Journal*, 1990, v. 3, n. 4, pp. 239–252; U.S.

Congress, Office of Technology Assessment, *Genetic Monitoring and Screening in the Workplace*, OTA-BA-455 (Washington, DC: U.S. Government Printing Office, October 1990); Arthur R. Miller, *The Assault on Privacy: Computers, Data Banks and Dossiers* (Ann Arbor, MI: University of Michigan Press, 1971).

47. See Garrett, *Business Ethics*, pp. 47–49, who distinguishes these two types of privacy (as well as a third kind, "social" privacy).
48. The remarks that follow are based in part on Garrett, *Business Ethics*, pp. 49–53; for a more stringent view, which concludes that polygraphs, for example, should not be used at all by employers, see George G. Brenkert, "Privacy, Polygraphs, and Work," *Business and Professional Ethics Journal*, Fall 1981, v. 1, n. 1, pp. 19–35.
49. For examples, see Alan F. Westin, *Whistle Blowing, Loyalty and Dissent in the Corporation* (New York: McGraw-Hill Book Company, 1981); and Frederick Elliston, John Keenan, Paula Lockhart, and Jane van Schaick, *Whistleblowing, Managing Dissent in the Workplace* (New York: Praeger Publishers, Inc., 1985).
50. For example, Ewing, *Freedom Inside the Organization*, pp. 115–127.
51. See John Rawls, *A Theory of Justice* (Cambridge, MA: Harvard University Press, 1971), pp. 205–211.
52. See Blumberg, "Corporate Responsibility."
53. For example, Ralph Nader, Peter J. Petkas, and Kate Blackwell, *Whistle Blowing* (New York: Grossman Publishers, 1972); and Charles Peters and Taylor Branch, *Blowing the Whistle: Dissent in the Public Interest* (New York: Praeger Publishers, Inc., 1972); for a comprehensive study of whistleblowing, see Frederick Elliston, John Keenan, Paula Lockhart, and Jane van Schaick, *Whistleblowing Research, Methodological and Moral Issues* (New York: Praeger Publishers, Inc., 1985).
54. *Mackowiak v. University Nuclear Systems, Inc.*, 753 F. 2d 1159 (9th Cir. 1984).
55. C. H. Farnsworth, "Survey of Whistleblowers Finds Retaliation but Few Regrets," *The New York Times*, February 21, 1988.
56. Richard T. DeGeorge, *Business Ethics*, 3rd ed. (New York: Macmillan Publishing Company, 1990), p. 211; see also Richard DeGeorge, "Whistleblowing: Permitted, Prohibited, Required," in F. A. Elliston, ed., *Conflicting Loyalties in the Workplace* (Notre Dame, IN: University of Notre Dame Press, 1985). My discussion draws heavily on DeGeorge.
57. See Rowe and Baker, "Are You Hearing Enough Employee Concerns?" *Harvard Business Review*, May–June 1984.
58. For a description of these and other effective corporate ethics programs, see Manuel G. Velasquez, "Corporate Ethics: Losing It, Having It, Getting It," pp. 228–244, in Peter Madsen and Jay M. Shafritz, eds., *Essentials of Business Ethics* (New York: Meridian Books, 1990).
59. Robert G. Olson, *Ethics* (New York: Random House, Inc., 1978), pp. 83–84.
60. Martin Carnoy and Derek Shearer, *Economic Democracy, the Challenge of the 1980s* (White Plains, NY: M. E. Sharpe, Inc., 1980); Warren G. Bennis and Philip E. Slater, *The Temporary Society* (New York: Harper & Row, Publishers, Inc., 1968); Vincent P. Mainelli, "Democracy in the Workplace," *America*, January 15, 1977, pp. 28–30; see also the essays in Ichak Adizes and Elizabeth Mann Borgese, eds., *Self-Management: New Dimensions to Democracy* (Santa Barbara, CA: Clio Books, 1975).
61. Marshall Sashkin, "Participative Management Is an Ethical Imperative," *Organizational Dynamics*, 1984, v. 12, n. 4, pp. 4–22.
62. David P. Baron, *Business and Its Environment*, 3rd ed. (Upper Saddle River, NJ: Prentice-Hall, Inc., 2000) p. 472.
63. See Robert A. Dahl, *After the Revolution? Authority in a Good Society* (New Haven, CT: Yale University Press, 1970), pp. 117–118.
64. Douglas McGregor, *The Human Side of Enterprise* (New York: McGraw-Hill, 1960).
65. Raymond E. Miles, *Theories of Management: Implications for Organizational Behavior and Development* (New York: McGraw-Hill, 1975), p. 35.
66. Rensis Likert, "From Production- and Employee-Centeredness to Systems 1–4," *Journal of Management*, 1979, v. 5, pp. 147–56.
67. See David Vanderburg, "The Story of Semco: The Company that Humanized Work," *Bulletin of Science Technology and Society*, vol. 24 (October 2004), no. 5, pp. 430–434; Gary Hamel and Bill Breen, "Building an Innovation Democracy: W. L. Gore: Management Innovation in Action," in Gary Hamel, *The Future of Management*, (Boston: Harvard Business School Press, 2007); see also William F. Dowling, "At General Motors: System 4 Builds Performance and Profits," *Organizational Dynamics*, 1975, v. 3, n. 3, pp. 26–30.
68. For studies that have measured positive outcomes from participative management, see Soonhee Kim, "Participative Management and Job Satisfaction: Lessons for Management Leadership," *Public Administration Review*, vol. 62 (March/April 2002), no. 2, pp. 231–241.
69. For a 2010 assessment of research on participation in decision-making, see John W. Budd, Paul J. Gollan, and Adrian Wilkinson, "New Approaches to Employee Voice and Participation in Organizations," Human Relations, vol. 63 (March 2010) no. 3, pp. 303–310.
70. J. L. Kerr, "The Limits Of Organizational Democracy." *Academy of Management Executive*, vol. 18 (2004), no. 3, pp. 81–95.
71. R. L. Daft, (2004). "Theory Z: Opening the Corporate Door for Participative Management," *Academy of Management Executive* vol. 18 (2004) no. 4, pp. 117–121; Does Participative Leadership Enhance Work Performance by Inducing Empowerment or Trust? The differential effects on managerial and non-managerial subordinates," *Journal of Organizational Behavior*, vo. 31 (January 2010) no. 1, pp. 122–143; see also C. Pateman, "A Contribution to the Political Theory of Organizational Democracy," *Administration and Society*, v. 7 (1975), pp. 5–26.
72. Greg Conderacci, "Motorgate: How a Floating Corpse Led to a Fraud Inquiry and Ousters by GM," *Wall Street Journal*, April 24, 1982, pp. 1, 16.
73. Quoted in Lawrence E. Blades, "Employment at Will versus Individual Freedom," *Columbia Law Review*, 1967, v. 67, p. 1405.
74. See, for example, Patricia H. Werhane, *Persons, Rights, and Corporations*, pp. 81–93; Richard DeGeorge, *Business Ethics*, pp. 204–207.
75. Robert Ellis Smith, *Workrights* (New York: E. P. Dutton, 1983), pp. 209–215.
76. See T. M. Scanlon, "Due Process," in J. Roland Pennock and John W. Chapman, eds., *Due Process* (New York: New York University Press, 1977), pp. 93–125.
77. Esme E. Deprez, "Study Shows Psychological Impact of Unemployment," *Businessweek*, September 3, 2009; Margaret W. Linn, Richard Sandifer, and Shayna Stein, "Effects of Unemployment on Mental and Physical Health,"

American Journal of Public Health, vol. 75 (May 1985), no. 5, pp. 502–506; Arthur H. Goldsmith, Jonathan R. Veum, and William Darity, Jr., "Unemployment, Joblessness, Psychological Well-Being and Self-Esteem: Theory and Evidence," *Journal of SocioEconomics*, vol. 26 (1997), no. 2, pp. 133–158.

78. These international labor statistics (and many other international statistics) can be found at the *Wikipedia* article on "Lists of Countries and Territories at *http://en.wikipedia.org/wiki/Lists_of_countries_and_territories;* at the United Nations *Monthly Bulletin of Statistics Online*, at *http://unstats.un.org/unsd/mbs*, and for a select group of countries including the United States at the Bureau of Labor Statistics, International Labor Comparisons at *http://stats.bls.gov/fls/home.htm#laborforce*.
79. Josh Bivens, "Shifting Blame for Manufacturing Job Loss," Economic Policy Institute Briefing Paper.
80. Robert H. McGuckin, "Can Manufacturing Survive in Advanced Countries?" *Executive Action*, no. 93, March 2004, published by the Conference Board, accessed August 17, 2004, at *http://www.conference-board.org/pdf_free/EAReports/A-0093-04-EA.pdf*.
81. Don Stillman, "The Devastating Impact of Plant Relocations," in *The Big Business Reader*, Mark Green, ed. (New York: The Pilgrim Press, 1983), pp. 137–148.
82. See Peter J. Kuhn, ed., *Losing Work, Moving On: International Perspectives on Worker Displacement* (Kalamazoo, MI: W. E. Upjohn Institute for Employment Research, 2003).
83. William E. Diehl, *Plant Closings* (New York: Division for Mission in North America, Lutheran Church in America, 1985), pp. 14–16. For a discussion of the ethical issues involved in plant closings, see Judith Lichtenberg, "Workers, Owners, and Factory Closings," *Philosophy and Public Policy*, January 1985.
84. Richard DeGeorge, *Business Ethics*, p. 192.
85. J. K. Galbraith, *American Capitalism: The Concept of Countervailing Power* (Boston, MA: Houghton Mifflin, 1952).
86. Douglas Fraser, "Strikes: Friend or Foe of American Business and the Economy?" *Los Angeles Times*, November 3, 1985.
87. John Wright, ed., *The Universal Almanac* (Kansas City, MO: Andrews McMeel Publishing, 1996), p. 260.
88. "Beyond Unions," *Business Week*, July 8, 1985.
89. Ibid.
90. This definition is from Bronston T. Mayes and Robert W. Allen, "Toward a Definition of Organizational Politics," *Academy of Management Review*, October 1977, pp. 672–678; for a popular overview of the issues raised by organizational politics, see "Playing Office Politics," *Newsweek*, September 16, 1985, pp. 54–59.
91. Miles, *Macro Organizational Behavior*, pp. 161–164.
92. Schein, "Individual Power and Political Behaviors," p. 67.
93. Robert W. Allen, Dan L. Madison, Lyman W. Porter, Patricia A. Renwick, and Bronston T. Mayes, "Organizational Politics,"*California Management Review*, Fall 1979, v. 22, n. 1, pp. 77–83.
94. These are culled from the pages of John P. Kotter, *Power in Management* (New York: American Management Association, 1979), a book that argues that "skillfully executed power-oriented behavior" is the mark of the "successful manager."
95. This account of the Agee-Cunningham incident is based on the following sources: Peter W. Bernstein, "Upheaval at Bendix,"*Fortune*, November 3, pp 52 ff., S. Freedberg, G. Storch, and C. Teegartin, "Two At the Top," *The Detroit News*, October 5, 1980; Gail Sheehy, "Cunningham Encounters the Mildew of Envy," *Detroit Free Press*, Gail Sheehy, "Cunningham's Idealism Gets Lost in Corporate Jungle," *Detroit Free Press*, October 14, 1980, p. 3B.
96. See John R. S. Wilson, "In One Another's Power," *Ethics*, July 1978, v. 88, n. 4, pp. 299–315; L. Blum, "Deceiving, Hurting, and Using," in A. Montefiore, ed., *Philosophy and Personal Relations* (London: Routledge and Kegan Paul, 1973).
97. Gerald F. Cavanagh, Dennis J. Moberg, and Manuel Velasquez, "The Ethics of Organizational Politics," *Academy of Management Review*, July 1980; Manuel Velasquez, Dennis J. Moberg, and Gerald F. Cavanagh, "Organizational Statesmanship and Dirty Politics: Ethical Guidelines for the Organizational Politician," *Organizational Dynamics*, Autumn 1983, pp. 65–80.
98. David Kipnis, "Does Power Corrupt?" *Journal of Personality and Social Psychology*, 1972, v. 24, n. 1, p. 33.
99. Chris Argyris, *Personality and Organization* (New York: Harper & Brothers, 1957), pp. 232–237.
100. Jeanne M. Liedtka, "Feminist Morality and Competitive Reality: A Role for an Ethic of Care?" *Business Ethics Quarterly*, April 1996, v. 6, n. 2, p. 185.Jeanne M. Liedtka, "Feminist Morality and Competitive Reality: A Role for an Ethic of Care?"*Business Ethics Quarterly*, April 1996, v. 6, n. 2, p. 185.
101. Thomas I. White, "Business Ethics" and Carol Gilligan's "Two Voices," *Business Ethics Quarterly*, January 1992, v. 2, n. 1.
102. John Dobson and Judith White, "Toward the Feminine Firm: An Extension to Thomas White," *Business Ethics Quarterly*, July 1995, v. 5, n. 3, p. 466.
103. Ibid.
104. C. Bartlett and S. Ghoshal, "Changing the Role of Top Management: Beyond Strategy to Purpose," *Harvard Business Review*, November/December 1994, p. 81.
105. There are several case studies of W. L. Gore & Associates. See, for example, Frank Shipper and Charles C. Manz, "W. L. Gore & Associates, Inc.—1993," in Alex Miller and Gregory G. Dess, *Strategic Management*, 2nd ed. (New York: McGraw-Hill, 1996).
106. See Nell Noddings, *Caring*, pp. 73ff.
107. For example, Carol Gilligan, *In a Different Voice: Psychological Theory and Women's Development* (Cambridge, MA: Harvard University Press, 1982), Chs. 3 and 4.
108. R. Scott, A. Aiken, D. Mechanic, and S. Moravcsik, "Organizational Aspects of Caring," *Milbank Quarterly*, 1995, v. 73, n. 1, pp. 77–95.
109. An overview of the literature on this topic can be found in Marilyn Friedman, *What Are Friends For?* (Ithaca, NY: Cornell University Press, 1993), Ch. 3, entitled "The Social Self and the Partiality Debates."

Photo Credits

Page 1: JLImages/Alamy; pp. 2–3: Getty Images; p. 42 (left) Reuters/Corbis, (right) Scott J. Ferrell/Congressional Quarterly/Alamy; p. 43 (top) Gregory Heisler/AFP/Newscom, (center) Tim Sloan/AFP/Newscom, (bottom) James Nielsen/AFP/Newscom; pp. 72–73: Brand New Images/Lifesize/Getty Images; pp. 80–81: background, Peter Essick/Aurora Photos/Corbis; p. 80 (bottom right) Peter Essick/Aurora Photos/Corbis, (left) Scott J. Ferrell/Congressional Quarterly/Alamy; p. 81 (top) ALEX HOFFORD/epa/Corbis, (center) Kristian Buus/Alamy, (bottom) Peter Essick/Aurora Photos/Alamy; pp. 150–151: EIGHTFISH/Alamy; p. 178: (right) Robert Harding, (left) Peter Langer/DanitaDelimont.com/Newscom; p. 179: (top) Roger L. Wollenberg/UPI/Newscom, (center) Rahat Dar/epa/Corbis, (bottom) Philippe Lissac/Godong/Corbis; p. 196: Andrew Gombert/epa/Corbis; p. 212 (top) Patti Sapone/Star Ledger/Corbis, (bottom) John Connell/Corbis; p. 213 (top) Volker Steger/Photo Researchers, Inc. center Terry Vine/Stone/Getty Images, bottom John Connell/Corbis; p. 241: Michael Dwyer/Alamy; pp. 242–243: Mario Tama/Getty Images; p. 254: (first) Gregory Kramer/Shutterstock, (second) ARENA Creative/Shutterstock, (third) Veronika Vasilyuk/Shutterstock, (fourth) Stefan Redel/Shutterstock, (fifth) Comstock/Thinkstock Images, (sixth) Amy Nichole Harris/Shutterstock; p. 264–265: (background) Lou Linwei/Alamy; p. 264 (bottom) Andrew Wong/Reuters/Corbis, (top) Lou Linwei/Alamy; p. 265 (top and center) Lou Linwei/Alamy; p. 265 (bottom) Claro Cortes IV CC/LA/REUTERS; pp. 302–303 Lou-Foto/Alamy; pp. 316–317: (background) Advertising Archive/Courtesy Everett Collection; p. 316 (top) Handout/MCT/Newscom, (bottom) Bubbles Photolibrary/Alamy; p. 317: (top) John Powell/Bubbles Photolibrary/Alamy, (center) Advertising Archive/Courtesy Everett Collection, (bottom) Ezio Petersen/Newscom; p. 345: James Brittain View Pictures Ltd/Alamy; pp. 346–347: Ariel Skelley/Blend Images/Alamy; pp. 376–377 (background) Alex Wong/Getty Images News/Getty Images; p. 376 (bottom) Pat Canova/Alamy, (top) Alex Wong/Getty Images News/Getty Images; p. 377 (top) Alex Wong/Getty Images News/Getty Images, (center) Stephen Morton/Getty Images News/Getty Images, (bottom) KeDavies/Corbis Premium RF/Alamy; pp. 398–399: FOTOG/Tetra Images/Alamy; pp. 410–411: MTP/Alamy; p. 410 (bottom left) Mandek Ngan/AFP/Getty Images/Newscom, (bottom right) Byron Purvis/AdMedia/Newscom; p. 411 (top) Dean Treml/AFP/Newscom, (center) Robert Galbraith/REUTERS, (bottom) MTP/Alamy

Text Credits

Page 5: *There was a potential downside for me, personally*. Excerpt from P. Roy Vagelos and Louis Galambos. The Moral Corporation: Merck Experiences, p. 2 Copyright 2006 Cambridge University Press. Reprinted with permission.

Page 9: *I just can't believe this is really happening*. Adapted from Kermit Vandivier "Why should my conscience bother me?" In Robert Heilbroner IN THE NAME OF PROFIT. Copyright 1972 Doubleday, a division of Random House Inc. Used with permission.

Page 10: *My job paid well, it was pleasant and challenging*. Adapted from Kermit Vandivier "Why should my conscience bother me?" In Robert Heilbroner IN THE NAME OF PROFIT. Copyright 1972 Doubleday, a division of Random House Inc. Used with permission.

Page 19: *A second kind of argument. Adapted from Alex C. Michaels.* A Pragmatic Approach to Business Ethics. Copyright © 1995 Sage Publications, Inc.

Page 23: *In a free enterprise, private-property system*. Adapted from Milton Friedman, "The social responsibility of business is to increase its profits" New York Times Magazine, September 13, 1970.

Page 34: *The fact that different societies. James Rachels*. "Can ethics provide answers?" In Can Ethics Provide Answers and Other Essays in Moral Philosophy, pp. 33–39 Copyright © 1997 Rowman and Littlefield. Reprinted with permission.

Page 63: *On the Edge: Gun Manufacturers and Responsibility*. Adapted from Chris McGann, "Families of 2 Sniper Victims Sue Arms Dealer, Manufacturer" Seattle Post-Intelligence, January 17, 2003, p. 1A.

Page 68: *I was a rock star*. Aaron Beam, "Auditor's Get an Insider's View of Corporate Fraud" University of Texas News, April 12, 2010. Copyright © 2010 Reprinted by permission of Aaron Beam.

Page 69: *I just didn't have the courage*. Aaron Beam, "Auditor's Get an Insider's View of Corporate Fraud" University of Texas News, April 12, 2010. Copyright © 2010 Reprinted by permission of Aaron Beam.

Page 70: *There are a lot of sociopaths heading major corporations*. Reprinted by permission of Aaron Beam.

Page 74: *Nonwhites in South Africa are rightless persons*. Excerpt from Timothy Smith. "South Africa: The churches vs. the corporations" BUSINESS AND SOCIETY REVIEW, Copyright 1971 Reprinted by permission of John Wiley & Sons, Inc.

Page 75: *Texaco believes*. Courtesy of Texaco, Inc.

Page 80: *Should countries dump their waste into poor countries?* Adapted from "Let Them Eat Pollution" The Economist, February 8, 1992.

Page 91: *Principles*. Peter DeSimone "2004 Company Report-C1, Walt Disney Human rights in China" February 9, 2004. © 2004 by the Investor Responsibility Research Center; and Carolyn Mathiasen, "2004 Background Report. C1 Human Rights in China," February 9, 2004 © 2004 Investor Responsibility Research Center, *www.irrc.org*.

Page 92: *On the Edge: Working for Eli Lily and Company*. Adapted from Laurie P. cohen. "Stuck for Money" Wall Street Journal, November 14, 1996, p. 1.

Page 113: *From each according to what he chooses*. Excerpt from Robert Nozick. ANARCHY, STATE AND UTOPIA Copyright © 1977 Robert Nozick. Reprinted by permission of Basic Books, a member of the Perseus Books Group.

Page 127: *He was driven by work*. S. Prakash Sethi et al Up Against the Corporate Wall: Cases in Business and Society. (Englewood Cliffs, NJ: Prentice-Hall) Copyright © 1997 S. Prakash Sethi. Reprinted with permission of the author.

Page 130: *The virtues are to be understood*. Alasdair McIntyre. After Virtue, 3/e. Copyright © University of Notre Dame Press. Reprinted with permission.

Page 140: *Julie and Mark are brother and sister*. Jonathan Haidt. "The Emotional Dog and the Rational Tail: A Social Intuitionist Approach to Moral Judgment" Psychological Review, 108, 814–834. Copyright © American Psychological Association. Adapted with permission.

Page 140: *The action principle*. James S. Adelman, Gordon D.A. Brown, Jose F. Quesada. "Contextual diversity, not word frequency, determines word-naming and lexical decision times" Psychological Science, 12, 1082–1089. Copyright © 2006 Sage Publications, Inc. Reprinted with permission.

Page 143: *We will....* Courtesy of Triodos Bank.

Page 143: *Our results placed the company in the best*. Courtesy of Triodos Bank.

Page 143: *Roche received the Public Eye Award*. Courtesy of Triodos Bank.

Page 143: *Up to 90% of all transplanted organs in China*. Courtesy of Triodos Bank.

Page 144: *Dr. Schwan and that CellCept*. Minutes from the 92nd General Meeting of Roche Holding, Ltd, March 2, 2010.

Page 147: *An extensive, multimillion dollar socioeconomic development program*. Background: The Yadana Project and The Activist Lawsuits 12/2/2003. Unocal.

Page 157: *A state of perfect freedom*. Excerpt from John Locke. Two Treatises of Government (rev) Peter Laslett (ed.) p. 309 Copyright © 1963 Cambridge University Press. Reprinted with permission.

Page 158: *Every man has a property in his own person*. Excerpt from John Locke. Two Treatises of Government (rev.) Peter Laslett (ed.) Copyright © 1963 Cambridge University Press. Reprinted with permission.

Page 161: *Table 3.1 Distribution of Income and Wealth Among Americans, 2007*. Adapted from Edward N. Wolff. "Recent trends in household wealth in the United States: Rising debt and the middle-class squeeze—An update to 2007" working paper 589 in Jerome Levy Economics Institute Series, March 2010.

Page 173: *England may be so circumscribed that to produce*. David Ricardo. On the Principles of Political Economy and Taxation, 1871, ed. Piero Sraffa Copyright 1951 Reprinted with permission of Liberty Fund, Inc.

Page 178: *You sweat. You walk until your feet hurt. You have blisters*. Reprinted by permission of Human Rights Watch. Copyright © 2010. all rights reserved.

Page 177: *In what, then, consists the alienation of labor?* Economic and philosophic manuscripts of 1844 by MARX, KARL, Copyright 1964 Reproduced with permission of INTERNATIONAL PUBLISHERS COMPANY (NY) in the format Textbook and Other Book via Copyright Clearance Center.

Page 177: *Labor, to be sure*. Economic and philosophic manuscripts of 1844 by MARX KARL. Copyright 1964 Reproduced with permission of INTERNATIONAL PUBLISHERS COMPANY (NY) in the formats Text and Other Book via Copyright Clearance Center.

Page 180: *You are horrified*. Economic and philosophic manuscripts of 1944 by MARX KARL Copyright 1964 Reproduced with permission of INTERNATIONAL PUBLISHERS COMPANY (NY) in the formats Text and Other Book via Copyright Clearance Center.

Page 180: *It has been objected*. Economic and philosophic manuscripts of 1844 by MARX KARL Copyright 1964 Reproduced with permission of INTERNATIONAL PUBLISHERS COMPANY (NY) in the formats Texts and Other Book via Copyright Clearance Center.

Page 192: *It was clear to us*. Steven Ratner. "The auto bailout: How we did it" FORTUNE, October 21, 2009 Copyright © 2009 Time, Inc. Used under license.

Page 193: *There are only two economic systems in the world*. Excerpt from Michael R. Winther. "Five principles that are violated by the bailouts" Mackinac Center for Public Policy, March 13, 2009. Copyright © 2009 Reprinted with permission of the author.

Page 194: *Accolade vs. Sega*. SPINELLO, RICHARD, A. CASE STUDIES IN INFORMATION AND COMPUTER ETHICS, 1st Edition, © 1997, pp. 142–145. Reprinted by permission of Pearson Education, Inc., Upper Saddle River, NJ.

Page 198: *A South Korean executive*. Excerpted from Grant Gross, "LG display executive pleads guilty in LCD price fixing case" PC WORLD, April 28, 2009 Copyright © 2009. Reprinted with permission of PC world Communications, Inc.

Page 217: *Table 4.2 dominant brands and companies in oligopoly markets, 2010*. Based on Robert S. Lazich, Market Share Reporter, 2001 (Detroit, MI: Gale Research, 2001).

Page 224: *I think we are particularly vulnerable*. Jeffrey Sonnenfeld and Paul R. Lawreence. "Why do companies succumb to price-fixing?" Harvard Business Review, July/August, 1978, 56(4), 145–157 Copyright © 1978 Reprinted by permission.

Page 235: *for the first few years*. Excerpt from Mark Whitacre. "My Life as a corporate Mole for the FBI" FORTUNE September 4, 1995. Copyright © 1995 Time, Inc. Under license. Reprinted with permission.

Page 235: *When we started selling*. Excerpt from Mark Whitacre. "My Life as a corporate Mole for the FBI" FORTUNE September 4, 1995. Copyright © 1995 Time, Inc. Under license. Reprinted with permission.

Page 235: *It was during my first year*. Excerpt from Mark Whitacre. "My Life as a corporate Mole for the FBI" FORTUNE September 4, 1995. Copyright © 1995 Time, Inc. Under license. Reprinted with permission.

Page 244: *We now have evidence*. United Nations Environment Programme (UNEP).

Page 245: *My own view is that*. BARBOUR, EARTH MIGHT BE A FAIR REFLECTION ON ETHICS, RELIGION, AND ECOLOGY, 1st Edition, © 1972, pp. 95–96. Reprinted by permission of Pearson Education, Inc., Upper Saddle River, NJ.

Page 267: *The Deep Ecology Platform*. Arne Ness and George Sessions, "The Deep Ecology Platform" *www.deepecology.org/platform.htm*.

Page 269: *The man who has become a thinking being*. Excerpt from Albert Schweitzer OUT OF MY LIFE AND THOUGHTS (trans.) A.B. Lemke Copyright © 1990 Reprinted by permission of Henry Holt & Company.

Page 271: *Surveys conducted along the lower Columbia river*. Excerpt from Keith Davis and William C. Frederick BUSINESS AND SOCIETY. Copyright © 1984 Reprinted by permission of McGraw-Hill Companies.

Page 282: *We must look into the cultural forms*. Excerpt from Murray Bookchin and Dave Foreman DEFENDING THE EARTH: A Dialogue Between Murray Bookchin and Dave Foreman, Steve Chase (ed.) Copyright © 1991 Reprinted by permission.

Page 285: *Ask what is reasonable*. Reprinted by permission of the publisher from THEORY OF JUSTICE by John Rawls, p. 289, Cambridge, Mass.: The Belknap Press of Harvard University Press, Copyright © 1971, 1999 by the President and Fellows of Harvard College.

Page 310: *During your first year of ownership*. Quoted in address by S.e. Upton (vice president or Whirpool corporation) to the American marketing Association in Cleveland, OH, December 11, 1969.

Page 324: *Advertising death to kids?* Adapted from Meg Riordan, "Tobacco Industry Continues to Market to Kids" Campaign for Tobacco-Free Kids.

Page 331: *The Midland Bank has approval to hold details*. Adapted from Greg Hadfield and Mark Shipworth. "Firms keep dirty data on sex lives of staff, Sunday Times, London, June 25, 1993.

Page 341: *I lost my job*. *http://www.consumeraffairs.com/debt_counsel/credit_solutions.html*.

Page 341: *I used Credit Solutions*. *http://www.consumeraffairs.com/debt_counsel/credit_solutions.html*.

Page 341: *When I was in college*. *http://www.consumeraffairs.com/debt_counsel/credit_solutions.html*.

Page 381: *But it is absurd to suppose that the young blacks*. Judith Jarvis Thompson, "Preferential hiring" Philosophy and Public Affairs, vol. 2, No. 4, p. 381 Copyright © 1973. Reprinted by permission of John Wiley & Sons, Inc.

Page 381: *It might also be argued that*. Excerpt from Martin H. Redish. Preferential law school admissions and the equal protection clause: An analysis of the competing arguments. UCLA LAW REVIEW Copyright © 1974. Reprinted with permission.

Page 401: *An organization is*. E.H. Schein, Organizational Psychology, p. 8. Copyright © 1965 Pearson Education, Inc. Reprinted with permission.

Page 407: *The value of a gift*. Based on Vincent Barry. Moral Issues in Business, 1986 (Belmont, CA: Wadsworth).

Page 425: *On the Edge: Sergant Quon's Text messages*. Adapted from Erwin Chemerinsky, "Does the 4th Amendment's Right to Privacy Protect Personal Communications over a Government-Issued Pager?" available online at *www.abnet.org/publiced/preview/Quon.pdf*.

Page 441: *The head of a research unit*. The Academy of Management Review by ACADEMY OF MANAGEMENT REVIEW. Copyright 1977. Reproduced with permission of ACADEMY OF MANAGEMENT REVIEW (NY) in the formats Text and Other Book via Copyright Clearance Center.

Page 442: *Getting control over*. John P. Kotter. Power in Management. Copyright © 1979 American Management Association. Used with permission.

Page 447: *The caring organization*. Jeanne M. Liedtka "Feminist Morality and competitive Reality: A role for an Ethic of Care?" Business Ethics quarterly, vol. 6, No. 2 (April 1996), p. 185. Copyright © 1996. Used with permission.

Page 447: *But...contractually based relationships*. C. Bartlett and S. Ghosal. "Changing the role of top management: Beyond strategy to purpose" Harvard Business Review, N/D, 1994, p. 81. Copyright © 1984. Used with permission of Harvard Business Review.

Page 452: *Violations are, unfortunately, a normal part of the mining process*. Excerpt from Ian Urbina and Michael Cooper, "Death at West Virginia Mine Raises Issues About Safety" NEW YORK TIMES, April 6, 2010. Copyright © 2010 The New York Times Company. Reprinted with permission. All rights reserved.

Index